ATLANTIC STUDIES

BROOKLYN COLLEGE STUDIES ON SOCIETY IN CHANGE
No. 33

War and Society in East Central Europe
Vol. XIV

The Crucial Decade:
East Central European Society
and National Defense, 1859–1870

Béla K. Király, Editor

Social Science Monographs
Brooklyn College Press
Distributed by Columbia University Press
1984

EAST EUROPEAN MONOGRAPHS, NO. CLI

Copyright © 1984 by Atlantic Research and Publications
Library of Congress Card Catalog Number 83-50183
ISBN 0-88033-043-0
Printed in the United States of America

Table of Contents

Acknowledgments
  Béla K. Király — xi

Preface
  Béla K. Király — xiii

BOOK ONE: ESSAYS — 1

I. *Introduction* — 3

  A Crucial Time and Place for the History of Biology — 5
    Mordecai L. Gabriel

II. *Areawide Generalizations* — 13

  The Effects of the Franco-Sardinian-Austrian War, the Austro-Prussian War, and the Polish Insurrection on Romanian Political Development — 15
    Barbara Jelavich

  The Effects of the Unification of Romania on East Central Europe — 28
    Stephen Fischer-Galati

  The Effects of the January Insurrection on East Central Europe — 33
    Norman Davies

III. *The January Insurrection* — 39

  The Polish Theory of Partisan Warfare in the European Context — 41
    Emanuel Halicz

  The January Insurrection and the Theory of Partisan Warfare — 54
    Leonard Ratajczyk

  The Tactics of the Polish Troops in the 1863–64 Insurrection — 67
    Eligiusz Kozłowski

The Strategy and Tactics of the Tsarist Army during the
January Insurrection   81
   Leonard Ratajczyk

The Logistics of the Insurgent Troops in the January
Insurrection   92
   Lesław Dudek

The Social Structure of the Insurrection Army, 1863–64   108
   Eligiusz Kozłowski

The Urban Population in the January Insurrection   119
   Ryszard Bender

The Influence of Environmental Features on the Course of
the Fighting in the Polish January Insurection   134
   Tadeusz Mencel

Foreign Policy during the January Insurrection   148
   Jerzy Zdrada

The January Insurrection and the Emancipation of the
Peasants in the Polish-Russian Provinces   169
   Andreas Moritsch

The Birth of a Nation: The January Insurrection and the
Belorussian National Movement   185
   John T. Stanley

The Scandinavian Countries and the January Insurrection   203
   Emanuel Halicz

The Polish Insurrection of 1863 and the Czechs   221
   Joseph F. Zacek

The January Insurrection in Poland, 1863–1864, in the
Light of British Consular Reports   227
   Norman Davies

The Consequences of the January Insurrection   246
   Zygmunt Mańkowski

New Editions of Sources on the Polish Insurrection of 1863   259
   Stefan Kieniewicz

IV. *Wars and Revolutionary Movements in the Balkans, 1850–70*   267

Balkan Revolutionary Organizations in the 1860s and the
Peasantry   269
   Dimitrije Djordjević

The Bulgarian National Liberation Movement and the

Wars in Europe in the Fifties and Sixties of the Nineteenth Century Simeon Damianov	284
Serbia and the Wars of 1859 and 1866 Dragan R. Živojinović	296
The Evolution of the Greek Army (1828–68) Dimitris Michalopoulos	317
The Crimean War and Greek Society Dimitris Michalopoulos	331
War and Insurrection as Means to Greek Unification in the Mid-Nineteenth Century Evangelos Kofos	338
Greek Domestic Policies and the Irredentism of the 1860s: The 1866–69 Cretan Revolution Constantin Svolopoulos	352
V. *The Army and the Unification of Romania*	361
The Impact of the Crimean War on the Government and Armed Forces of Romania Ilie Ceauşescu	363
Army and Society: Cuza's Military Reforms Ilie Ceauşescu	376
The Role of the Army in the Modernization of the East Central European States: The Romanian Example Constantin Căzănişteanu	383
Foundations of the Independence Army: The Romanian Military in the Unification Era Gerald J. Bobango	388
The Military and the Establishment of the Romanian National State: Reciprocal Influences, 1856–62 Mihail E. Ionescu	397
Cuza, Florescu, and Army Reform, 1859–66 Radu R. Florescu	402
Romania's Foreign Military Relations, 1859–66 Florin Constantiniu	415
Romanian Military Collaboration with East Central European Struggles for Emancipation and National Unity, 1859–66 Ioan Talpeş	421

CONTENTS

VI. *Habsburg Neo-Absolutism against Hungarians: Secret Police Actions and Dragonnades* — 427

    The War Without Arms: The Secret Service of the Habsburg Monarchy, 1849–65 — 429
      Tibor Frank

    Habsburg Dragonnades in Hungary, 1861–62 — 444
      Éva Somogyi

VII. *Hungarians under Foreign Flags against Habsburg Absolutism* — 455

    Military Organizations of the Hungarian Exiles, 1859–67 — 457
      Lajos Lukács

    The Hungarian National Directorate and the 1859 War — 469
      Thomas Kabdebo

    Hungarian Armed Units in Italy, 1848–67 — 483
      Paolo Santarcangeli

    Defeat at Solferino: The Nationality Question and the Habsburg Army in the War of 1859 — 496
      István Deák

VIII. *The Compromise of 1867 and the Reestablishment of the Hungarian* Honvédség — 517

    The Military Compromise of 1868 and Hungary — 519
      Gunther E. Rothenberg

    The Founding of the *Honvédség* and the Hungarian Ministry of Defense, 1867–70 — 533
      Zoltán Szász

    Gyula Andrássy and the Founding of the *Honvédség* — 540
      János Décsy

BOOK TWO: SOURCES — 551

József Pawłikowski: *Can the Poles Attain Their Independence?* — 553
    Edited by Emanuel Halicz

Introduction — 555
    Emanuel Halicz

Can the Poles Attain Their Independence? — 583
    József Pawłikowski

CONTENTS

Appendix 1
John Bull in the Kingdom of Poland: The Estate of Janów in the Period of Peasant Emancipation, 1861–64 — 623

Appendix 2
Arrest of a Young Scottish Adventurer at Częstochowa, 1864: The Prospect of Siberia — 627

Appendix 3
Appeal of Generals György Klapka and Mór Perczel to the Hungarian Legionnaires, Genoa, May 20, 1859 — 629

Contributors — 631

List of Books Published in Brooklyn College Studies on Society in Change — 634

Acknowledgments

Brooklyn College Program on Society in Change conducts research, organizes conferences and publishes scholarly books. The Program has been encouraged and supported by Dr. Robert L. Hess, the President of Brooklyn College. The National Endowment for the Humanities awarded the Program a research grant for the years of 1978–1981, which was renewed for another three-year term (1981–1984). Without these substantial and much appreciated supports, the Program could not realize its goals, indeed could not exist. Additional financial contributions helped us in completing the research, holding conferences and covering the costs of preparation of the manuscript for publication. Among those institutions that aided our work are the Joint Committee on Eastern Europe of the American Council of Learned Societies and the Social Science Research Council; the International Research and Exchanges Board; the Center for Byzantine and Modern Greek Studies, Queens College CUNY; and the Institute on East Central Europe, Columbia University.

The copy editing was done by Mrs. Barbara Metzger and the preparation of the manuscript for publication by Mrs. Dorothy Meyerson and Mr. Jonathan A. Chanis, both on the staff of Brooklyn College Program on Society in Change. The maps were done by Mrs. Ida Etelka Romann.

Translations of various essays were made by Dr. Márió Fenyő, Professor Thomas M. Barker, and the editor. To all these institutions and personalities, I wish to express my most sincere appreciation and thanks.

Highland Lakes, New Jersey
August 20, 1983

Béla K. Király
Professor Emeritus
Editor-in-Chief

Preface

This volume is the fourteenth to appear in a series which, it is hoped, when completed, will offer a comprehensive survey of the many aspects of war and society in East Central Europe between the mid-eighteenth century and the end of the First World War.

The chapters of this and future volumes are selected from papers presented at a series of international, interdisciplinary scholarly conferences sponsored by the Program on Society in Change, Brooklyn College, and occasionally by other institutions of higher learning. They deal with peoples whose homelands lie between the Germans to the west, the Russians to the east and north, and the Black, Adriatic, and Mediterranean Seas to the south. They constitute a particular civilization, an integral part of Europe, yet substantially distinct from west and east. Within the area there are intriguing variations in language, religion, and government; so, too, are there differences in concepts of national defense, in the characters of the armed forces, and in ways of waging war. Study of such a complex subject demands an interdisciplinary approach. The scholars involved therefore come from several disciplines and from universities and other scholarly institutions in the United States, Canada, and Western Europe, as well as in those East Central European states whose society and armed forces are the subject of our study.

Investigations focus on comparative surveys of military behavior and organization in these various nations and ethnic groups in an attempt to see what is peculiar to them, what has been socially and culturally determined, and what is attributable to circumstance. An effort is made to define different patterns of military behavior, including decision-making processes, attitudes and actions of diverse social classes, and the restraints or lack of them shown in war. We endeavor to present considerable material on the effects of social, economic, political, and technological changes and of changes in the sciences applied to warfare and in international relationships on the development of doctrines of national defense and practices in military organization, command, strategy, and tactics. We also present data on the social origins and mobility of the officers' corps and the rank and file, on the differences between the officers' corps of the various services, and above all on the civil-military relationship and on the origins of the East Central European brand of militarism. The studies will, it is hoped, result in a better understanding of the societies, governments, and politics of East Central Europe.

The methodology takes into account that in the last three decades the study of war and national defense systems has moved away from the narrow concern with battles, campaigns, and leaders and come to concern itself with the evolution of the entire society. In fact, the interdependence of changes in society and changes in warfare and the proposition that military institutions closely reflect the character of the society of which they are part have come to be accepted by historians, political scientists, sociologists, philosophers, and other students of war and national defense. Recognition of this fact constitutes one of the keystones of our approach to the subject.

Works in Western languages adequately cover the diplomatic, political, intellectual, social, and economic histories of these peoples and this area. In contrast, few substantial studies of their national defense systems have yet appeared in Western languages. Similarly, though some substantial, comprehensive accounts of the nonmilitary aspects of the history of the whole region have been published in the West, nothing has yet appeared in any Western language about the national defense systems of the area as a whole. Nor has there been any study of the mutual effects of the concepts and practices of national defense in East Central Europe. This comprehensive study on war and society in East Central Europe is a pioneering work.

The nineteenth century is crucial for all these nations because it is the era of nation building. Many of these peoples formed nation-states during the period, a development in which their armed forces played critical roles. Even in the case of the Poles, whose state was partitioned in the eighteenth century and was not to be reestablished until the twentieth, insurrectionary armies played a vital part in consolidating national consciousness. The era the present volume deals with, as the title indicates, was a "crucial decade" in the evolution of East Central European societies and their armed forces. During this single decade, the Romanian army contributed much to the unification of the Romanian principalities. The Polish January Insurrection fundamentally changed Polish hopes and expectations in the short term, while in the long term it taught them that, despite their defeat, armed struggle remained the precondition for national liberation. The Hungarians, taking advantage of the favorable international and the internal circumstances of Austria, put an end to the corrupt Habsburg neoabsolutism and reestablished domestic self-government. These were the fundamental components of the "crucial decade." Beyond the ethnic regions of the Romanians, Hungarians, and the Poles, however, restlessness and conflict occurred also in other areas of East Central Europe. Serbs, Bulgarians, Greeks, and, for that matter, all the not yet liberated peoples of the Balkans were in ferment that foreshadowed the wars of liberation to come during the next decade and thereafter. The "crucial decade" of 1859–70 was rich in spectacular changes in various fields of human endeavor in the Western world—some eloquently exposed in the introduction by Professor Gabriel. The decade was also rich in phenomena of East Central European social change and change in the structure of the armed forces. They resembled changes in the West, yet they were different. That is what these essays reveal.

Highland Lakes, New Jersey
August 20, 1983

Béla K. Király

Book One:
Essays

I. Introduction

A Crucial Time and Place for the History of Biology*

Mordecai L. Gabriel

I am very happy to welcome you to Brooklyn College. This is the tenth Brooklyn College Conference on Society in Change and, like previous meetings, it is an international gathering. Professor Király, the Director of the Brooklyn College Program on Society in Change, and his colleagues are to be congratulated on assembling so distinguished an array of panelists from institutions of higher learning in Austria, Bulgaria, Canada, Denmark, the Federal Republic of Germany, Greece, Hungary, Italy, Poland, Romania, the United Kingdom, the United States of America, and Yugoslavia. If I may be permitted a few words of comment, as someone whose own discipline is rather removed from yours, I would like to express the reaction of a biologist to your theme. When I looked at the program of today's conference, "The Crucial Decade in East Central Europe," I could not help being struck by the fact that the period 1856–1870 and, in part, the locale were also a crucial time and place for the history of biology.

One of the most far-reaching influences upon the changes our society will face in the next few decades is unquestionably the current biological revolution: the consequences of our acquisition of the means of controlling and modifying the heredity of man, animals, plants, and microorganisms through what is called genetic engineering. I shall take as a paradigm of the power inherent in the new technology the recent development of techniques for synthesizing the genes that direct the formation of human insulin and for introducing these genes into bacteria that can then be grown and harvested to yield the human hormone.[1] I have chosen this example (though any number of others might serve) because it was precisely in the period and in the region to which this conference is devoted, while the political and military events that you are studying were taking place, that, removed from the turmoil, a number of individuals, in some instances unknown to each other, were making the fundamental discoveries that led to today's biological revolution.

The essential insights that eventually made possible this practical outcome were the following:

1. The particulate nature of inheritance—the fact that a hereditary trait is determined by a discrete and separable entity rather than by "blending" (Mendel, 1866).[2]

2. The chemical identity of the genetic material as a unique molecular species, largely located in the nucleus of the cell (Miescher, 1869).[3]

3. The capacity of carbon atoms to form chains and the representation of organic molecules by structural formulas depicting the spatial arrangement of their constituent atoms (Kekulé, 1858).[4]

4. The refutation of the doctrine of spontaneous generation and the development of sterile techniques, which inaugurated modern microbiology (Pasteur, 1861).[5]

5. The recognition that enzymatic action (such as fermentation) is a chemical process and that intracellular enzymes are definite chemical compounds, which paved the way for their isolation and purification (Traube, 1858).[6]

This clustering of dates underlines the fact that the third quarter of the nineteenth century was an extraordinarily fertile one in the history of biology.

If, as Popper has maintained, observation and experiment must be preceded and stimulated by theory,[7] a fundamental reason for this extraordinary efflorescence must be sought in the theoretical concepts which led to the formulation of a host of concrete problems susceptible to experimental attack.

The first of these seminal ideas was the cell theory, which postulated a common architecture for all organisms but at the same time posed the problem of accounting for their diversity of form and function. The second was the growing acceptance of the belief that the living organism could be understood in chemical and physical terms. The groundwork for this view had been laid in the eighteenth century, in the materialism of La Mettrie's *L'Homme machine* (1748) and the demonstration by Lavoisier and Laplace (1780)[8] that respiration and "animal heat" could be understood as a form of combustion.

By the nineteenth century a science of physiology was developing, utilizing the techniques of chemical analysis, physical measurements, and microscopic observation to study living functions as physico-chemical processes. The new synthesis and its emphasis on the chemical basis of life were promulgated by a number of influential teachers. One of them, Carl Ludwig, wrote in his *Lehrbuch der Physiologie des Menschen*:

It is the task of physiology to determine what functions are assumed in the animal organism by each of the more or less complex molecules. This task will have been completed when one knows the arrangement of the elements within the complex molecule, the amount of its latent heat, and the manner in which each individual molecule expresses its relationship to all the others present in the animal organism under given conditions.[9]

This theoretical outlook led to the logical extension of the cell theory to the physiology of the whole organism. Originally conceived as a mechanical building block, the cell came to be perceived as a unit of function as well.

Probably the most influential proponent of the new cell physiology was Rudolf Virchow (1821–1902), founder of the *Archiv für pathologische Anatomie* and for many years professor of pathology at the University of Berlin. His views, which guided two generations of researchers throughout Europe, are epitomized in an essay, "Cellularpathologie," published in his *Archiv* in 1855. The following excerpts from this essay are illustrative of Virchow's thesis:

. . . these tiny elements, the cells, are the actual loci of life and hence also of disease—the true bearers of vital function in plants and animals on whose existence life depends, and whose fine structure determines the vital expression of living things. Life, therefore, does not reside in the fluids as such, but only in their cellular parts. . . .

. . . What the individual is on a large scale, the cell is on a small scale—perhaps to an even greater degree. The cell is the locus to which the action of mechanical matter is bound, and only within its limits can that power of action justifying the name of life be maintained. *But within this locus it is mechanical matter that is active—active according to physical and chemical laws.* In order to comprehend the essentially cellular phenomena of life we must understand the composition, the mechanical characteristics, and the functional changes of cell substance. . . . I can only say that the cells are the vital elements from which the tissues, organs, systems and the whole individual are composed. Beyond them there is nothing but change. . . . I formulate the doctrine of pathological generation, and of neoplasia in the cellular pathological sense, in simple terms: *omnis cellula e cellula.* . . . All diseases are in the last analysis reducible to disturbances, either active or passive, of large or small groups of living units, whose functional capacity is altered in accordance with the state of their molecular composition and is thus dependent on physical and chemical changes of their contents.[10]

One of the early fruits of Virchow's emphasis on cellular investigation was the discovery of the pancreatic islet cells. In 1867 Paul Langerhans, a medical student working in Virchow's laboratory in Berlin, began an investgiation of the microscopic anatomy of the pancreas. His inaugural dissertation, published in 1869,[11] contained the first description of the cell islands that bear his name and that subsequently were shown to be the site of insulin synthesis. Twenty years later the role of the pancreas in diabetes was demonstrated by von Mering and Minkowski. Insulin was not discovered until the twentieth century (by Banting and Best in 1922).

Among Virchow's students were three towering figures of nineteenth-century biology: Wilhelm His, Ernst Haeckel, and Felix Hoppe-Seyler. We thus trace a direct intellectual lineage to Friedrich Miescher, the discoverer of nucleic acid: Friedrich's father Johann and his mother's brother Wilhelm His were both professors at the University of Basel.

It was on His's advice that Friedrich embarked on the study of histochemistry.[12] He went to the laboratory of Hoppe-Seyler at Tübingen in 1868 and began a study of the chemistry of lymphatic cells, a problem which accorded with Hoppe-Seyler's interests. Miescher soon turned from lymph cells, which were hard to come by, to pus cells, which he could obtain in abundance by washing discarded bandages salvaged from the Tübingen surgical clinic. (Infection of surgical wounds was so common at that time as to be regarded as a normal part of the healing process; Lister's introduction of antiseptic techniques dates fom 1867[13] and had not yet been widely adopted.) Within a few months, Miescher had succeeded in isolating nuclei from these cells and in detecting in the free nuclei a distinctive phosphorus-containing component. The same substance turned out to be a constituent of the nuclei of a variety of cell types. He named the new compound nuclein; today it is called DNA.[14] Miescher's manuscript reporting this discovery was completed in 1869; it was not published until 1871.

What was the role of nuclein? In his 1869 manuscript Miescher went no farther than to call attention to the existence of nucleins in a variety of cell types and to a possible connection between phosphorus and cell multiplication:

> I cannot help thinking that here lies the most essential physiological role of phosphorus in the organism. I have in mind specifically the well-known remarkable fact that in plants phosphorus is principally or almost exclusively accumulated at the growing points; surely the appearance of nuclei is restricted to the growing parts, i.e., to the cells in the course of multiplication. . . .[15]

Nuclein, Miescher went on to suggest, might possibly be a precursor of lecithin. To venture beyond this would have been rash speculation.

The role of the nucleus itself was still being debated, some opinion holding that it was a storage reserve for the cytoplasm. Ernst Haeckel argued for the implication of the nucleus in heredity:

> . . . the internal nucleus provides for the transmission of hereditary traits, the external plasma on the other hand for conformation, accommodation or adaptation to the conditions of the external world.
>
> Arguing especially in favor of this conception is the important role which the nucleus generally plays in the reproduction of cells. Almost always, cell division is preceded by division of the cell nucleus and both nuclei thus generated act as independent attraction centers about which the substance of the plasma gathers. The plasma on the other hand is of greater significance for the nutrition of the cell. A more passive role seems to be allotted to it in the multiplication of cells and its chief role appears to lie in the bringing of nutritive material to the nucleus and in mediating the communication between the cell and the external world. If we accordingly regard the plasma especially as the nutritive, the nucleus on the other hand as the reproductive constituents of the cell . . . we may justifiably regard the nucleus of the cell as the principal organ of heredity, the plasma as the principal organ of adaptation. . . .[16]

A number of leading biologists, among them Hertwig and Kölliker, regarded it as probable that nuclein was the physical basis of inheritance. Miescher himself was rather cool to such speculations, which he thought chemically simplistic.[17]

Gregor Mendel's first paper on heredity was published in the same year as Haeckel's *Generelle Morphologie* but was largely ignored. Mendel showed that inheritance was particulate in the sense that traits could persist in a latent state in a hybrid and reappear unchanged in their progeny. (A number of other particulate theories of inheritance were current in the latter half of the nineteenth century, notably Darwin's theory of pangenesis and Nägeli's *Ideoplasma* theory.) Mendel, who was fully aware of the union of pollen and egg cells in plant fertilization, pointed out that his results could be explained by random combination of pollen and egg cells if the various kinds of egg and pollen cells were formed on the average in equal numbers. His principal concern, however, was not with the physical nature of the carriers of heredity, but with the statistical distribution of traits, dealt with mathematically as symbols. A number of reasons have been proposed for the failure of biologists to appreciate Mendel's work in his lifetime. One, clearly, was its publication in a Moravian journal of miniscule circulation: the *Verhandlungen des Naturforschenden Vereines in Brünn* had a subscription and exchange list of 120.[18] No less important, however, was the fact that Mendel's formal treatment was out of keeping with the contemporary preoccupation with reductionist cell physiology.

Evidence identifying the cell nucleus as the basis for inheritance accumulated overwhelmingly during the next quarter-century, but the nature of heredity itself remained obscure through inattention to Mendel's work. Once his papers were rediscovered in 1900, the striking correspondence between Mendelian phenomena and the behavior of nuclei in the maturation of gametes and fertilization became clear, and the gap between cytology and genetics was soon closed.[19]

I will not attempt to summarize the twentieth-century advances that culminated in the discipline of molecular genetics. My purpose has been to show how separate, apparently unrelated lines of investigation converged into this synthesis that brought us to today's understanding of the chemistry of the gene and its role in the physiology of plants and animals and the acquisition of the power to recombine and transplant segments of DNA.

The enterprise of the historian is not only to chronicle events, but to understand them, bringing to bear upon the past the wisdom of hindsight. It is characteristic of the history of science that its major advances are made not by directed search so much as by what is almost a stochastic process that Popper has likened to a "natural selection of hypotheses" leading eventually to a confluence of ideas. As he puts it: "Assuming . . . upward direction of time, we should have to represent the tree of knowledge as springing from countless roots which grow up into the air rather than down, and which ultimately, high up, tend to unite into one common stem."[20] Tracing backward the history of ideas, like tracing any genealogy, is a selective process. This brief case history necessarily has followed only a few of the roots to the neglect of many others.

But the origin of genetic engineering in what the organizers of your conference have called the "crucial decade" is a relatively simple historical thread to trace compared with the complex web of causal connections you have undertaken to study. It therefore behooves me not to delay your deliberations further. Once again, we are pleased to have you at Brooklyn College, and we wish you a successful and productive conference.

Notes

*This essay is the opening address of the tenth Brooklyn College Conference on Society in Change ("War and Society in East Central Europe in the Era of Nation-States, 1856–1870"), held on May 3–5, 1982. Mordecai L. Gabriel is Professor of Biology and Acting Vice-President for Academic Affairs at Brooklyn College, City University of New York.

1. D. V. Goeddel, et al., "Expression in *Escherichia coli* of Chemically Synthesized Genes for Human Insulin," *Proceedings of the National Academy of Sciences (U.S.A.)* 76 (1979): 106–10.
2. Gregor Mendel, "Versüchen über Pflanzen-hybriden," *Verhandlungen des Naturforschenden Vereines in Brünn* 4 (1866): 3–47.
3. Friedrich Miescher, "Über die chemische Zusammensetzung der Eiterzellen," *Hoppe-Seyler's medizinisch-chemischen Untersuchungen* 4 (1871): 441–60. An abridged translation of this paper appears in M. L. Gabriel and S. Fogel, *Great Experiments in Biology* (Englewood Cliffs, N.J.: Prentice-Hall, 1956), pp. 233–39.
4. August Kekulé, "Uber die Constitution und die Metamorphosen der chemischen Verbindungen und über die chemische Natur des Kohlenstoffs," *Liebig's Annalen der Chemie und Pharmacie* 106 (1858): 129–59.
5. Louis Pasteur, "Mémoire sur les corpuscules organisés qui existent dans l'atmosphère: Examen de la doctrine des générations spontanées," *Annales des Sciences Naturelles (Zoologie)* 16 (1861): 5–98.
6. Moritz Traube, who held no academic appointment, worked at the time in an attic laboratory in his home in Ratibor, Silesia. His remarkably prescient paper, in which he also suggested that ferments were closely related to proteins, was published. See "Zur Theorie der Gährungs- und Verwesungserscheinungen, wie der Fermentwirkungen überhaupt," *Annalen der Physik* 103 (1858): 331–44.
7. Karl R. Popper, "Herbert Spencer Lecture: Evolution and the Tree of Knowledge," in *Objective Knowledge* (Oxford: Oxford University Press, 1972), pp. 256–84.
8. Antoine-Laurent Lavoisier and P. Laplace, *Mémoire sur la chaleur*, Mémoires de l'Académie des Sciences (Paris, 1780).
9. Joseph S. Fruton, *Molecules and Life* (New York: Wiley-Interscience, 1972), p. 180.
10. Rudolf Virchow, *Disease, Life, and Man*, trans. L. J. Rather (Stanford: Stanford University Press, 1958), p. 82.
11. Paul Langerhans, "Beiträge zur mikroskopischen Anatomie der Bauchspeicheldrüse, trans. H. Morrison, *Bulletin of the Institute of the History of Medicine* 5 (1937): 259–84.
12. For this and other biographical details on Miescher, see Franklin H. Portugal and Jack S. Cohen, *A Century of DNA* (Cambridge: MIT Press, 1977).
13. Lord Joseph Lister, "On the Antiseptic Principle in the Practice of Surgery," *The Lancet*, 1867, vol. 2, p. 353, and "Illustrations of the Antiseptic System of Treatment in Surgery," *The Lancet*, 1867, vol. 2, p. 668.
14. More correctly, Miescher's nuclein was a DNA complex called nucleohistone.
15. Miescher, "Über die chemische Zusammensetzung der Eiterzellen."
16. Haeckel, *Generelle Morphologie der Organismen* (Berlin, 1866), 2: 287–88.
17. Fruton, *Molecules and Life*, pp. 198–200.
18. L. C. Dunn, "Mendel: His Work and His Place in History," *Proceedings of the American Philosophical Society* 109 (1965): 189–98.

19. Walter S. Sutton, "The Chromosomes in Heredity," *Biological Bulletin* 4 (1902): 231–51.
20. Popper, *Objective Knowledge*, p. 262.

II. Areawide Generalizations

The Effects of the Franco-Sardinian-Austrian War, the Austro-Prussian War, and the Polish Insurrection on Romanian Political Development

Barbara Jelavich

Between 1859 and 1866, two major steps in the formation of the modern Romanian national state were taken: the double election of Alexandru Cuza in January and February 1859 and the accession of a foreign prince, Charles I, in 1866. Both of these actions were possible largely because of the international situation created by the three events with which this conference principally deals: the Franco-Sardinian-Austrian War of 1859, the Polish Insurrection of 1863, and the Austro-Prussian War of 1866. The two wars, in particular, provided an environment conducive to the advancement of Romanian national interests. Both wars commenced at a time when the great powers were debating how to meet Romanian actions. In 1859, the ambassadors in Paris were discussing the implications of the double election. The outbreak of the conflict in Italy prevented concerted action by the European governments. In June 1866, a similar conference of ambassadors in Paris was considering the problems connected with the assumption of power by Charles I when the war between Prussia and the Habsburg Empire commenced. Once more European attention was distracted and a favorable atmosphere provided for the acceptance of a major political change in Bucharest. The Polish Insurrection, occurring between the two events, produced an alteration in the diplomatic alignments which was eventually to prove to the Romanian advantage. The interrelationship between the three events and the significance of international treaty obligations for the Romanian national movement will be the focus of this paper.

At the Congress of Paris in 1856, the victorious allies—Great Britain, France, the Ottoman Empire, and Piedmont-Sardinia, supported by the Habsburg Monarchy—insisted on the abandonment by Russia of its protectorate over the Danubian Principalities. The provinces henceforth were to fall under the guardianship of the powers collectively. In theory, these governments now acquired the right to determine Romanian political institutions; thereafter any changes would require their approval. This situation was both to aid and to impede Romanian national development.

After 1856 the Romanian national leaders continued to seek the fulfillment of the program adopted after the failure of the revolution of 1848: the union of the Principalities and the accession of a foreign prince. In the accomplishment of these aims they could expect the opposition of the Ottoman Empire, usually backed by Britain, a supporter of Ottoman territorial integrity, and by other states whose interests might be injured by the formation of a united Romanian state, in particular Russia and the Habsburg Empire. Both of these latter governments controlled large Romanian populations, concentrated in Habsburg Transylvania and Russian Bessarabia. The Ottoman position, however, was fundamentally affected by its military weakness. Obviously, Ottoman desires could not be secured unless that government had the legal right to send an army into the Principalities in a time of crisis. Although the Ottoman Empire remained the suzerain power, after 1856 it could not occupy the provinces without the permission of the guarantors, whose approval of such an action was, except under highly unusual circumstances, extremely doubtful. A joint occupation by the neighboring states was usually not a feasible alternative because of the bad relations between Russia and the Habsburg Monarchy after the Crimean War.

Even with the virtual elimination of the possibility of an Ottoman military intervention, the Romanian statesmen faced formidable obstacles. With insufficient armed forces of their own and with their fate closely bound to the European treaty structure, they had to remain constantly alert to changes in the general European diplomatic balance. They had no completely reliable supporter among the other states. Even their closest friend, the France of Napoleon III, was more interested in events in Italy and Poland. Prussia and Piedmont, although advocates of national unification movements, were deeply involved in their own affairs. Britain, because of its desire to uphold Ottoman territorial integrity, and the Habsburg Monarchy, because of its fear of the effect of a national movement on its Romanian citizens, could be expected to remain opponents of Romanian advancement. Although Russian concerns were in many respects similar to those of Britain and Austria, that government in the years immediately following the Crimean War was for a short period linked with France in the diplomatic arena, a situation which was to be of immense aid to the accomplishment of the first stage of Romanian national unification.

Without the assurance of firm support from any other power and without an army, the Romanian leadership was forced to adopt the policy of the fait accompli. No attempt at a violent or revolutionary solution was made after 1848. The success of this policy was first demonstrated at the time of the double election of Alexandru Cuza.[1] After 1856 the guarantor powers took up their assigned task of endowing the Principalities with suitable political institutions. Although two sets of elections were held in Moldavia and Wallachia for assemblies whose purpose was to determine Romanian opinion, the powers ignored the clearly expressed desire for union. The compromise agreement, signed by the guarantors in August 1858, called for the maintenance of two separate provinces but with parallel institutions and with a central commission composed of representatives of both Principalities. The double election of Cuza five months later violated both the letter and the spirit of this agreement. The powers had decided upon separation—not union.

The guarantors all recognized that the August convention had been broken, but they could not agree on what should or could be done about it. As could be expected, the alignments remained as before. The Habsburg Empire, the Ottoman Empire, and, at first, Britain opposed this personal unification of the provinces. The Ottoman officials took the strongest stand. They wished the powers to insist on a reversal of the election. If the Principalities refused to comply, then the Ottoman government asked to be permitted to send in an armed force. Should, however, the guarantors allow this violation of a treaty to stand, then they wanted an alteration in the Treaty of Paris which would strengthen its right of armed intervention. In opposition, France, Russia, Prussia, and Piedmont supported the recognition of the election. These powers desired the personal union to be accepted for the reign of Cuza only. Their stand was based at least partly on their recognition of the extreme difficulty of implementing any other decision. Russia, in particular, strongly opposed the sanctioning of an Ottoman intervention. Since there was general agreement that treaties had indeed been violated, a conference of the guarantors had to be summoned.

At two meetings, held in Paris on April 7 and April 13, the Romanian problem was discussed in detail. The Habsburg and Ottoman representatives sought the annulment of the double election. The other powers, now joined by Britain, introduced a counterproposal which recognized the election of Cuza but as an exception. The British change of front was caused by that government's recognition of the difficulties of enforcing an annulment. The British position was, in addition, that the Porte should receive some compensation. At this point in the negotiations the outbreak of the war in Italy, involving three of the participants, effectively halted further progress. That crisis had been developing rapidly during the period of negotiations over Cuza's position. On March 9 the Piedmontese reserves were called up, on April 7 the Habsburg army was mobilized, and on April 23 the Austrian ultimatum was delivered. After the Austrian invasion of April 29 and the French entrance in support of Piedmont, European attention remained concentrated on that battlefield. Nevertheless, negotiations over the Romanian question continued.

Although the delay in the final decision had an unsettling effect on the Principalities, it did allow Cuza time to consolidate his position. He exercised his powers as prince in both provinces and convened the central commission. Deeply aware of Romanian military vulnerability, he made the strengthening of his armed forces a priority. As an initial step he assembled the militias of the two provinces at a joint camp at Floreşti. A strong partisan of close relations with France, he naturally supported the French-Piedmontese side. He was also perfectly willing to consider joining in the conflict if he could obtain money, arms, and advisers from Paris. On April 25 he wrote to his representative in Paris, Vasile Alecsandri:

> As a Romanian, I feel the need to raise my country in the eyes of the nations and in its own esteem; as prince, I am convinced of the necessity of acting vigorously and I have decided, for the happiness and *the independence* of my people, to gain all the advantage possible from the events which are about to take place. The time has come to awake from that torpor which made of us an easy prize and an object of cupidity for our powerful neighbors. We have decided to throw ourselves into the arena and to support to the limits of our power the policy of France, which is that of our prosperity and our greatness.[2]

The armistice of Villafranca in July, which resulted in an unsatisfactory partial unification of Italy, was a blow to the hopes of the nationalists throughout Europe. The continuation of the Italian struggle, which culminated in the proclamation of the Kingdom of Italy in March 1861, nevertheless kept this question the main preoccupation of European diplomacy.

Meanwhile, discussions continued among the guarantors over the fate of Cuza. The war in Italy had made even more obvious the difficulties of enforcing an annulment of the election. Despite the pressure of the majority of the powers, the Porte remained adamant. Only after the defeat of Austria and the armistice of Villafranca was progress achieved. Finally, in a single meeting held on September 6, the powers agreed to recognize the double election but only as an exception. In the future, princes were to be elected according to the provisions of the August convention. There were once again to be two princes and two assemblies. In return, the Ottoman government received some weak compensation; the formula governing its future ability to intervene militarily in the Principalities was altered, but it still needed the unanimous approval of the powers to act.

Despite these limitations, Cuza's position, at least as far as the guarantors were concerned, was now secure. The war in Italy had divided and distracted them. The defeat of the Habsburg Monarchy, the main supporter of the Ottoman position, was, of course, a major gain. In the next months the events in Italy leading to the unification under the leadership of Piedmont, in particular the expedition of Garibaldi to Sicily in May 1860, proved similarly advantageous. Not only did the Romanian nationalists applaud the victories of another Latin people, but Cuza, against assisted by outside events, was able to take another step forward, and in 1861 he united the administrations and assemblies of the provinces. Again the powers gave their consent because of the impracticability of opposition.

In contrast to the war in Italy, the Polish Insurrection of 1863 corresponded with no great advance in Romanian political development.[3] Nevertheless, the event had important repercussions both on internal politics and on the foreign relations of the state. The revolt came at a most inopportune moment for Cuza. The newly united Principalities needed first to face their grave domestic problems. An Eastern crisis could endanger their recent advances. Nevertheless, the Cuza government could not ignore a neighboring national movement. Close touch had been maintained not only with Italian revolutionary leaders, but also with the Hungarians and the Poles. Similarly, assistance was given to the Serbs and the Bulgarians. All of these actions involved endangering Romanian relations with a guarantor power. Support for the Italians and Hungarians caused a reaction in Vienna, aid to the Serbs and Bulgarians angered Constantinople, assistance to a Polish movement was bound to cause a violent reaction in St. Petersburg. The fact that these national movements had different primary targets complicated the Romanian position. Not all could be opposed at the same time. In addition, although the Habsburg Monarchy and the Porte had previously tried to block the Romanian moves, Russia, in alliance with France, had offered at least limited support. There were obvious disadvantages in alienating an apparent friend.

In the past, with their attention directed to achieving their own goals, the neighboring national leaders had all sought support in Bucharest because of the vital strategic location of the Romanian lands between Russia, the Habsburg Monarchy, and the other regions of the Ottoman Empire. The provinces were an ideal site for organization and for the stockpiling of arms. Already by 1863 Cuza had been forced to deal with two major incidents in this connection. In December 1860, the powers had intervened to attempt to halt the unloading of arms at Galaţi destined for Hungarian depots in the Principalities. In November 1862, the British, in particular, had protested the passage of a shipment of Russian arms across Romania to Serbia, where they could obviously be used against the Ottoman suzerain power.

The outbreak of the Polish Insurrection in January had the potential of presenting even greater complications, in particular with Russia. The main connection between the Romanian leadership and the Polish national movement was through the conservative emigration, with its headquarters in Paris. The first relations came in the 1830s when Romanian students in Paris were brought in touch with the Polish activities. At that time the Polish leader, Prince Adam Czartoryski, became interested in using the Principalities as an advance base for operations against Russia.[4] Since the provinces were then under firm Russian control, which caused great resentment in Romanian nationalist circles, Polish representatives were able to win sympathizers. There was also a limited degree of cooperation in 1848, when Polish and Romanian resentment was directed in particular against Russia. A major obstacle to future close cooperation, however, was provided by the differing views of the Ottoman Empire and its future held by the two revolutionary leaderships. Being primarily anti-Russian, the Poles shared with the Hungarians a favorable attitude toward the Porte, which had given them shelter after their unsuccessful insurrection of 1830 and had often offered their leaders in the emigration important posts in the Ottoman administration. The Polish program for the Ottoman Empire was its reorganization on a federal basis, not its partition into national states. Other problems also arose in the Polish-Romanian relationship. Once involved in Romanian affairs, the Polish representatives were drawn into the factional quarrels and the personal rivalries of the time; they thus gained enemies as well as friends. Moreover, the Polish national leadership, like the Italian, felt few qualms about sacrificing the Principalities for the achievement of its own goals. At the time of the Crimean War, Czartoryski had supported a plan by which the Ottoman Empire would give Austria the Principalities, which would then be united with Transylvania as a Romanian unit but under Habsburg control. In return, Vienna would agree to the establishment of an independent Poland and surrender Galicia to it.[5]

Although there was much initial enthusiasm in the Principalities when the 1863 revolt commenced, the negative aspects soon became apparent. Polish influence was strong. Money was collected, and the press supported the Polish cause. Iași in particular became a center of activity. There the Polish representative, Dr. Theofil Glück, was Cuza's personal physician. The revolutionary leaders wished to organize a legion in Moldavia which would then cross the frontier into Podolia. They hoped to use previously stockpiled Hungarian arms. Such activities, which would be observed and reported on by the representatives of the powers, were, of course, extremely dangerous. The possibility that the Russians would occupy Moldavia, as they had on many previous occasions, aroused much apprehension.

The situation caused particular embarrassment for Cuza. Not only did he fear a Russian reaction, but he was not certain of the political affiliations of the Poles within the country. In the past some Polish groups had worked with his opponents in Romanian political life. Moreover, the Polish suggestion of a possible trade with Vienna of the Principalities for Galicia was widely known. The neutral position now taken was thus the one best fitted to the circumstances.

The major incident involving this policy occurred in July 1863. Already in May, reports had been received that Colonel Zygmunt Miłkowski was organizing a group of volunteers in Tulcea. In July this band, numbering around two hundred, crossed into Romanian territory at Cahul and started to march toward Iași. Cuza immediately assigned Colonel Ioan Călinescu to stop this unauthorized action. When Miłkowski refused to lay down his arms, fighting commenced on July 3. The battle lasted for five hours; eighteen Romanians were killed and forty-five wounded; the Polish force had eighteen dead and thirty-one wounded. After their surrender, the Polish prisoners were placed under a very lenient detention, and many were allowed to escape.

Despite the dangers inherent in the situation, Cuza certainly would have adopted a more positive attitude had he been sure of the support of France. Certainly, in the past Napoleon III had given strong vocal encouragement to the Polish national movement. He had also actually gone to war to aid the Italians. Seeking guidance, Cuza in November appealed to Napoleon for direction. In a letter whose words were reminiscent of those he had used in 1859, Cuza wrote:

> It is without surprise that I have seen several organs of the French press, anticipating events, enumerate the considerable advantages that the

United Principalities, chosen as a base of operation, could procure for a French army. I have ascertained with satisfaction that this eventuality would be greeted with general delight throughout the entire country. . . . Sire, Romania, its resources, its army, its prince, are at the orders of Your Imperial Majesty. Romania, which would rise as one to repel a Russian or Austrian occupation, is at the orders of Your Imperial Majesty.[6]

By this time, however, it was clear that France would not act. Cuza received a noncommittal reply in December.[7] The Polish Insurrection, which could not have succeeded without outside intervention, was crushed by the spring of 1864.

Despite the generally unfavorable immediate effect of the insurrection on Romanian affairs, its long-range diplomatic consequences were generally positive.[8] Once it commenced, both France and Britain gave at least verbal encouragement to the rebels and delivered protests to St. Petersburg. The Habsburg officials were also delighted with this embarrassment to a government with which they had been on bad terms since the Crimean War. Faced by this opposition, Russia cooperated more closely with Prussia, a state which had a similar interest in crushing any Polish national manifestations. The French actions, while bringing no real benefit to the Poles, decisively affected the previous Franco-Russian entente. Henceforth, the Russian government abandoned the attempt to cooperate closely with Paris and sought a strengthening of its ties with Berlin. At the same time, the Russian attitude toward Romania became increasingly critical. The Polish episode was just one of many issues which divided the governments. The Russian foreign minister, Alexander M. Gorchakov, was now convinced that the Principalities had become a revolutionary center "doubly dangerous because of its geographic position."[9] The consequences of the growing Russian opposition and of the Russian-Prussian tie were to become apparent in the next crisis in Romanian political life.

In February 1866, Cuza was overthrown in a coup d'état. According to the treaties, separate elections should now have been held in the two Principalities for assemblies to select new princes. Instead, the provisional government established in Bucharest continued to administer the country on the former basis. The assembly remained in session and voted for Philip of Flanders, the second son of King Leopold of Belgium, as the next prince. The aim was to accomplish the other great goal of the national movement: the accession of a foreign prince. When Philip refused the nomination, the search for another candidate began.

Meanwhile, the powers had to decide how to deal with yet another Romanian violation of the treaties.[10] The will of the guaranteeing powers had again been defied. The Ottoman government at once called for the convoking of a conference to discuss the infraction of the agreements and to agree upon measures to remedy the situation. The strongest backer of the Ottoman protests was Russia; in a sharp shift from its position in 1859, it now pushed the Porte to act. The Russian stand was backed by the argument that the separation of the Principalities corresponded to the real wishes of the population. The best hope for a Russian success in securing the acceptance of this position lay in possible separatist agitation in Moldavia. Although such a demonstration did indeed occur in Iași in April, its limited extent and easy suppression showed how weak the separatist camp really was.[11] It should be noted also that the political status of the Principalities was endangered not only by Russia and the Ottoman Empire at this time, but also by France. In the spring of 1866 the French government was engaged in negotiations for a possible cession of the Principalities to the Habsburg Monarchy in return for that government's release of Venetia to Italy. The discussion failed when Vienna refused to accept such a proposition.

A conference of ambassadors met in Paris between March 10 and April 3. In these sessions the Ottoman government again took the strongest stand. The Russian opposition had to be muted, since that government had to consider the reaction of the other Balkan Orthodox people. The suppression of a national movement here, in contrast to Catholic Poland, could not be openly supported. Instead, the Russian representative at the conference, Baron Andreas Budberg, was instructed to argue that the terms of the convention must be upheld and that separation was the true wish of the Romanians. In the sessions he therefore supported the view that each Principality should elect an assembly to nominate a new native prince. In the first discussions the ambassadors were concerned primarily about whether separate elections should be held in Wallachia and Moldavia. No government seriously considered the possibility of a foreign prince; a suitable candidate who would accept the position was not believed to be available. Again in these meetings, the French government was the principal supporter of the Romanian national interests. Its representatives argued that the Principalities should make their own decisions, the guarantors intervening only if there were flagrant further violations of the treaties. This position was supported by Britain, again because the British statesmen could see no possibility of dividing the provinces except by force. In April the conference adjourned without reaching a decision.

Meanwhile, contrary to the expectations of the powers, the provisional government had found a candidate in Charles of Hohenzollern-Sigmaringen.[12] The prince was a member of the Catholic branch of the

Prussian ruling dynasty, but he had close connections with France and was generally believed to be the choice of Napoleon III. On April 16 a plebiscite was held in the Principalities which overwhelmingly confirmed the nomination of the provisional government. The entire question, however, caused great misgivings in the Prussian government. King William was not enthusiastic. Otto von Bismarck, in contrast, urged the prince to accept the position. After reaching a favorable decision in the first week in May, Charles had to make complicated plans for reaching his new country. Relations between Vienna and Berlin were deteriorating rapidly. The prince was a Prussian officer, and the armies were being mobilized. He therefore had to pass through Habsburg territory in disguise, arriving in Bucharest on May 22.

With these new events, the conference in Paris was summoned into session again on April 24 at the Russians' request. The representatives knew about the plebiscite concerning Charles's nomination. They all accepted the principle that the next Romanian prince should be a native, but they continued to disagree on the issue of union. In a session held on May 2 they agreed that the election of Charles violated the August convention and that the choice of a new ruler would have to be made by a specially elected assembly. Not even France declared for a foreign prince. The conference continued to debate the question during May. Charles, of course, had meanwhile accepted the position and assumed power. Although the guarantors all protested the action, they continued to be unable to come to an understanding on the vital question of exactly how Charles could be compelled to leave. France, Britain, Prussia, and Italy all opposed the use of force. In other words, despite the fact that the powers were united in their opposition to this new fait accompli, they were deeply divided over what should be done about it. It was obvious that the prince could not be deposed and the union dissolved without military action. Given the situation of the time, only an Ottoman army could carry through an occupation, and the majority of the powers remained firmly opposed to an Ottoman intervention.

At this moment, as in 1859, the attention of the powers was diverted by a far greater European crisis. The spring of 1866 was dominated not by general concern over events in Bucharest, but by the confrontation between Prussia and Austria over supremacy in the German lands. The negotiations in progress involved not only the principal antagonists, but also France and Italy. In April Bismarck concluded an offensive and defensive alliance with Italy. In June the Habsburg Monarchy made a treaty with France in which it promised to give Venetia to Italy in return for French neutrality in the coming war. Since the Prussian-Italian agreement contained similar stipulations concerning this province, the danger that the Principalities might be used in an exchange now passed.

The Austro-Prussian War was concluded with unexpected speed. The preliminary peace of Nikolsburg, signed on July 26, gave Prussia domination in northern Germany. In the next months the powers were primarily concerned with the reorganization in the German lands, which resulted in the establishment of the North German Confederation in 1867. The second humiliating defeat of the Habsburg Monarchy, the discomfort of France with the events, and the political reorganization in Central Europe were ultimately to have a beneficial effect on the Romanian situation.

When war broke out, the conference sessions of course came to an end. Once more the Romanian political leaders were given time to consolidate their position. The Prussian victory was of major significance for Charles personally. He was a Prussian prince; he had accepted the Romanian throne with the approval of Bismarck. Victorious Prussia would obviously not support efforts to remove him; the defeated Habsburg Monarchy could do little to oppose him. Moreover, the Russian attitude was now modified. The previous strong opposition of that government to Romanian national advancement had been caused at least in part by the fear that the Principalities were a revolutionary center, closely linked to France, that would encourage movements considered dangerous by St. Petersburg. Now, in close alignment with Prussia, the Russian government found many of its former fears subsiding. Conservative Prussia would not be likely to stand sponsor to movements which might threaten Russia. The two countries had a common interest in maintaining the partition of Poland. Moreover, Bismarck strongly recommended to the Romanian representatives that they cultivate good relations with Russia, and they took this advice. It was also apparent that Prussia would not compete for influence in Bucharest, but would instead, at least for the moment, support the Russian position. In addition, the Russian government, like the British, now had to recognize that changes could not be made without an Ottoman military intervention, an action which would damage the Russian reputation among the other Balkan Orthodox nationalities. Thus, finally, since no practical alternative existed, Russia, along with the other guarantors, accepted Charles as the hereditary ruler of Romania. No further attempts were made to dissolve the union. A foreign prince, it was hoped, would provide the political stability which had previously been lacking in the government of the Principalities.

Although it cannot be maintained that European recognition of the double election of Cuza and the accession to power of Charles would not have occurred without the two wars and the Polish Insurrection, these events certainly contributed to the accomplishment of Romanian national objectives. They distracted the guarantor powers and hindered them from forming a common front. With the exception of France, no great power after 1856 consistently supported the formation of a Romanian national state under a foreign prince. In fact, the guarantors usually favored the division of the provinces and native princes, a solution expressed in the convention of August 1858. Despite their general agreement on Romanian affairs, the powers were unable to adopt a unified policy toward actions that violated international agreements. To at least some extent their indecision was caused by their preoccupation with the events connected with the Italian, Polish, and German national movements and their division on how the crises which arose in their connection should be met. No government wanted a revival of the Eastern Question or a conflict in the Near East at a time when great changes were taking place in the center of Europe, an attitude which made it possible for the Romanian policy of the fait accompli to succeed. Thus the Romanian statesmen were exceedingly fortunate that international events favored their national interests.

Notes

1. The diplomatic aspects of the double election are discussed in T. W. Riker, *The Making of Romania* (Oxford: Oxford University Press, 1931); the Russian position is given in Barbara Jelavich, *Russia and the Romanian National Cause, 1858, 1859,* Slavic and East European Series (Bloomington: Indiana University Press, 1959; Archon reprint, 1974). Cuza's reign is the subject of Gerald J. Bobango, *The Emergence of the Romanian National State* (Boulder: East European Quarterly, 1979).
2. Cuza to Alecsandri, Bucharest, April 13/25, 1859, R. V. Bossy, *Agenția diplomatică a României în Paris și legăturile politice franco-române sub Cuza-Vodă* (Bucharest: Cultura Națională, 1931), pp. 165–67.
3. On the Polish Insurrection, see Bobango, *Emergence,* pp. 133–42; Gheorghe Duzinchievici, *Cuza Vodă și revoluția polona din 1863* (Bucharest: Carteă Românească, 1935); and P. P. Panaitescu, "Unirea principatelor romîne: Cuza Vodă și Polonii," *Romanoslavica* 5 (1962): 71–84.
4. On Polish-Romanian relations in this period, see Robert Allen Berry, "Czartoryski and the Balkan Policies of the Hôtel Lambert, 1832–1847" (Ph.D. diss., Indiana University, 1974), pp. 100–39, and Dan Berindei, "Relations roumano-polonais pendant la quatrième décennie du XIXe siècle: Précisions et contributions," *Revue des études sud-est européennes* 20 (1982): 129–44.

5. M. Kukiel, *Czartoryski and European Unity, 1770–1861* (Princeton: Princeton University Press, 1955), p. 278.
6. Cuza to Napoleon III, November 11, 1863, Bossy, *Agenţia diplomatică*, pp. 294–96.
7. Napoleon III to Cuza, December 20, 1863, ibid., p. 309.
8. On the diplomatic repercussions, see also Emanuel Halicz, "Some of the International Significance of the Polish Question in the Years 1840–1860," in *Polish National Liberation Struggles and the Genesis of the Modern Nation: Collected Papers* (Odense: Odense University Press, 1982), pp. 164–75.
9. Gorchakov to Novikov, March 9/21, 1864, G. Hilke, "Russlands Haltung zur rumänische Frage, 1864–1866," *Wissenschaftliche Zeitschrift der Martin-Luther-Universität Halle-Wittenberg* 14 (1965): 197, 198.
10. On the diplomatic background, see "England, Russia, and the Roumanian Revolution of 1866," in W. E. Mosse, *The Rise and Fall of the Crimean System, 1855–1871* (London: Macmillan, 1963); E. E. Chertan, "Velikie derzhavy i gosudarstvennyi perevorot 1866 g. v Rumynii," in *Voprosy istorii i istoriografii Iugo-Vostochnoi Evropy* (Kishinev: Izdatel'stvo 'Shtiintsa', 1977); and Gr. Chiriţa, "România in 1866: Coordinate ale politicii interne şi internationale," *Revista de istorie* 31 (1978): 2197–220.
11. Barbara Jelavich, "Russia and Moldavian Separatism: The Demonstration of April, 1866," in *Russland-Deutschland-Amerika: Festschrift für Fritz T. Epstein*, ed. Alexander Fischer, Günther Moltmann, and Klaus Schwabe (Wiesbaden: Fritz Steiner, 1978).
12. Although there is no satisfactory biography of Charles, the events of his nomination and assumption of power are described on a day-to-day basis in *Aus dem Leben König Karls von Rumänien*, vol. 1 (Stuttgart: J. G. Gotta'schen Buchhandlung, 1894), pp. 3–151, and Démètre A. Sturdza, *Charles Ier, Roi de Roumanie: Chronique-actes-documents*, vol. 1 (Bucharest: Charles Göbl, 1899), pp. 1–340.

The Effects of the Unification of Romania on East Central Europe

Stephen Fischer-Galati

The old adage "When France sneezes Europe catches a cold" must be refuted with equal energy as the belief that whenever one or another nation of East Central Europe sneezes Vienna, Constantinople, and St. Petersburg shudder. In fact, we all know that immunities to colds and sniffles were developed, through perhaps an overdose of "blood and iron," in Prussia and that this treatment, modified to conform to more old-fashioned home remedies, worked remarkably well in the capitals of the eastern empires.

This awareness is even recorded in the works of historians who have abided by the old Romanian dictum of "making a stallion out of a mosquito" when discussing the impact of revolts, revolutions, coups, and other political events of East Central Europe on neighboring countries, on various nationalities, on the historic evolution of Europe as a whole. We are all familiar with the often fragile hypotheses and proofs proffered with respect to such events as the first Serbian uprising, the Greek War of Independence, the revolt of Tudor Vladimirescu, the Bohemian Revolution of 1848, the Bulgarian massacres, and the various Polish misadventures—to mention but a few. This is not to say that those events were inconsequential, but merely to suggest that their importance has often been grossly exaggerated, if not misrepresented outright. It is interesting, therefore, that the union of the Romanian principalities in 1859 has not elicited extravagant claims with respect to its effects on the course of the history of the Habsburg, Ottoman, and Russian Empires. In fact, the low-key treatment of that truly important event is somewhat surprising; it may be ascribable to its having been overshadowed by the more momentous and decisive Franco-Sardinian-Austrian conflict of that very year. There may, however, be other reasons for the relative neglect of the union of 1859, such as recognition that all claims that might be made for its external significance could be—and have been—made for earlier or later events related to the dual election of Alexandru Ioan Cuza and the acknowledgment thereof by the reluctant Austrian and Ottoman leaders in 1859. What effect could be expressly assigned to the union?

One would unquestionably be its effect on the Romanians of the Habsburg Monarchy. Another would be the corollary impact on the anti-Romanian forces in the Monarchy, such as Hungarians, Saxons, and even the Habsburg establishment itself, not to mention the impact on anti-Habsburg forces of other than Romanian nationality. A third would be its effect on the Ottoman Empire and a fourth its effect on Balkan peoples aspiring to independence, such as Serbians and Bulgarians. Last but not least would be its impact on the Romanian population east of the Dniestr. An evaluation of these effects can provide at least interim answers to relevant questions.

Predictably, Romanian historiography on the impact of the union of the principalities on the Habsburg Empire stresses the positive response of fellow Romanians and the negative one by Vienna, Budapest, and others identified with the interests of the ruling classes. In its most exaggerated forms, emphasis is placed on the writings of the Transylvanian Romanian unionist Alexandru Papiu-Ilarian. However, even though he stated, among other things, that "when Cuza was elected prince, enthusiasm of the Romanians in Transylvania was perhaps greater than in the principalities . . ." and addressed Cuza as the executor of the historic legacy of Michael the Brave,[1] it seems fair to say that even he had serious reservations about the potential impact of the union on the Romanian unionist movement in Transylvania. The principal of these were related to the fragility of Cuza's mandate in the United Principalities themselves and to the compromises he would have to make with the "antidemocratic" Wallachian and Moldavian aristocracies to secure his position. The repeated admonitions to Cuza against abandoning democratic principles for the sake of political expediency express the concerns and suspicions of the Romanian leaders in Transylvania. In fact, they also express the unionists' awareness that the fall of the Bach regime and the ensuing reforms could substantially weaken their own cause unless the United Principalities were to adopt more liberal policies than the Habsburgs in the wake of the collapse of the absolute government.

Other Romanian leaders in the Habsburg Empire were more circumspect than Papiu-Ilarian, although accounts of the union and favorable nationalist comment abounded in the Empire's Romanian press. It is noteworthy, however, that the Romanian leaders failed to make any direct connection between the union and Cuza's subsequent attempts to secure recognition for his election by the reluctant Austrian government, on the one hand, and the fall of Bach and the subsequent reformist measures in the Empire, on the other. In this they expressed the realistic perception that the Franco-Sardinian-Austrian War was the determining factor and that Cuza was the beneficiary, rather than the cause, of Austrian acquiescence to the dual election. For that matter, all Habsburg policies after 1859 with respect to Romanians—whether in the Empire itself or outside it—were for some time only marginally related to the history of the Romanian principalities.

This is not to say that Vienna did not remain intrinsically opposed to and potentially fearful of the long-range effects of the union. Indeed, Vienna's fears, as they were expressed by Austria's ambassador to Constantinople, Antoine von Prokesch-Osten, in 1857, that "such a country . . . would be ruinous for Austria, a formidable instrument of aggression against us in the hands of Russia, a thorn in the flesh of Turkey"[2] were not allayed by the dual election or by its recognition by Vienna in August 1859. These considerations were, however, of secondary importance for decision making in Vienna in 1859 and in the years immediately thereafter.

Nor can it be said that the union had any profound impact on the attitudes of pro- or anti-Habsburg forces and nationalities in the Empire other than the Romanians. The historical clichés that the Hungarian aristocracy, the conservative Saxon patriciate, and other "reactionary" groups expressed either contempt for or fear of the union or, for that matter, took it as an example for their own struggle for national independence may be accurate but must be taken *cum grano salis* in the context of either "reaction" or "stimulation" in 1859 and the entire Cuza era. In sum, as far as the effect of the union of 1859 on the Habsburg Empire is concerned, it seems safe to say that it was, if not altogether negligible, certainly subordinated to that of other international and internal events that were basically unrelated to the union.

In one respect, however, the union stimulated action by anti-Habsburg forces of nationalities other than the Romanian, to wit, by post-1849 Hungarian émigrés seeking to exploit the problems of the Empire during the Franco-Sardinian-Austrian War. General György Klapka's attempts, on behalf of the Hungarian Revolutionary Committee, to secure the military cooperation of Serbia and the United Principalities in that war were indeed an integral part of Hungarian émigré strategy, as well as of Franco-Sardinian military planning. It is doubtful, however, whether Cuza's response to Klapka's overtures was more than one based on expediency—one designed to facilitate recognition by Vienna of the union. It is also doubtful that Klapka truly entertained hopes of meaningful Romanian support for the attainment of Hungarian goals. In fact, mutual suspicions clouded the issue of cooperation, which, after all, never came to fruition.

Strategic, tactical, and tentative responses also characterized reaction to the union in southeastern Europe and in Constantinople.

Romanian historiography has pointed to positive responses to the union by Bulgarian political activists in the principalities and also by Belgrade. Such responses are indeed recorded, but their historic significance has been played down even by exponents of maximalist interpretations of the impact of the union on Balkan independence movements. The struggling Bulgarians could at best envisage long-range benefits for their cause. The Serbians exercised great caution, for Michael Obrenović's own schemes transcended the scope of Cuza's and precluded endorsements of or commitments to political movements and actions elsewhere in East Central Europe that could in any way have jeopardized his own goals for Serbia and for his dynasty. This is not to say that Serbia did not recognize the significance of the union and its consequences for Constantinople, Vienna, and, eventually, even Belgrade, but simply to point out that the union was not necessarily a prototype or a prerequisite for Serbian independence from the Porte.

As for the Porte itself, its reaction to the dual election seems to have changed considerably from that originally expressed at the Vienna Conference of 1856 by the Grand Vizier—"The union of the principalities of Moldavia and Wallachia into a unitary state . . . would mean the dismemberment of the Empire." By 1859 Constantinople, while still unenthusiastic about the turn of events in the principalities, was realistic enough to recognize that the union was likely to diminish Russian influence in the principalities and, by extension, also the acutely perceived threat of continuing Russian interference in the affairs of the Ottoman Empire through the creation or exploitation of national and social unrest.

The only unanswered question regarding the impact of the union on East Central Europe thus remains that of the reaction of the Romanians of Bessarabia. Categorical but unsubstantiated statements and allusions stressing the enthusiasm of the Romanian inhabitants of the Russian-occupied territory east of the Dniestr are in all likelihood reliable. What is unknown, however, is the correspondence between Russia's overt support of the union and its actions and policies in Bessarabia proper. Such knowledge would allow accurate assessment of the policy of St. Petersburg in the late 1850s and early 1860s, not only toward Romania, but also toward other actual or incipient political movements designed to weaken the Ottoman and Habsburg Empires.

The impact of the union of the principalities on East Central Europe must thus be considered in relation not only to the specific Romanian events of 1859, but to the totality of East Central and general European events of that important year. It was clearly a major event in the history of Romania; it was, however, less important a one in the history of East Central Europe and Europe as a whole. Thus, it was primarily an essential link in the chain of events which eventually led to the unification of Greater Romania and the dissolution of the imperial structure of East Central Europe. Because it was not a link forged by the proverbial "blood and iron" so dear to nationalists and to some historians, however, the significance of its impact has been less heralded—and perhaps rightly so—than that of more glamorous revolutionary and military actions that have been used to legitimize the attainment of the avowed historic goals of the peoples, nations, and nationalities of East Central Europe.

Notes

1. Quoted in Thad Weed Riker, *The Making of Roumania: A Study of an International Problem, 1856–1866* (London: Oxford University Press, 1931), p. 215.
2. Quoted in Gerald J. Bobango, *The Emergence of the Romanian National State* (Boulder, Colorado: East European Quarterly, 1979), p. 75.

The Effects of the January Insurrection on East Central Europe

Norman Davies

At first sight, it may appear that the January Insurrection of 1863–64 had little effect on the affairs of East Central Europe. Although for the Poles it was clearly an event of prime importance, heralding the era of so-called positivism and fixing attitudes predominant for the rest of the nineteenth century, its impact on the European scene as a whole cannot be compared to that of the earthquake of 1848 or, indeed, to the shock waves of the Crimean War. Despite nearly two years of guerrilla warfare, the Polish insurgents failed not only to drive the Russians from Poland—which few can have seriously expected—but also to exact any significant political concessions or to make any progress in the direction of Polish autonomy. Indeed, in their failure, they provoked a wave of repression without parallel until the era of Hitler and Stalin and the Nazi-Soviet Pact of 1939–41. They failed to unite the Kingdom of Poland with the former Polish provinces in the western Russian guberniyas in Lithuania, Belorussia, and the Ukraine or with the Polish provinces of Austria and Prussia. Although, in the sphere of social policy, they did more than their predecessors of 1830 and 1831, they failed to rouse the mass of the peasantry or to involve all social classes in a united demonstration against Russian rule. Above all, they failed to win the active support of the sympathetic Western powers. Many fine words were spoken about Poland in 1863–64, and several stiff diplomatic protests were lodged: but, as in 1794, in 1831, in 1905, in 1939, and in 1944, the Poles were left by their Western sympathizers to be crushed in solitude. The diplomacy of the episode was particularly vacuous. Neither the moral indignation of Palmerston's foreign secretary Lord John Russell nor the threats and feints of the emperor of the French nor the enthusiasm of public opinion in Jacksonian America succeeded in deflecting the tsar from his chosen policy. The Russians, armed with the tacit approval of Prussia, were able to discipline their incorrigible Polish subjects without serious interference. Indeed, it is astonishing to think how many diplomatic historians have devoted books, theses, and learned articles to a subject which can only end with the conclusion that diplomacy achieved virtually nothing.

However, the total picture is not so simple. Just as the success or failure of the January Insurrection can hardly be judged exclusively in political and military terms, so its effects can hardly be confined to the immediate issues of the Russo-Polish conflict.

First, on the question of the feasibility of limited wars, the January Insurrection undoubtedly affected the calculations of all European statesmen of the day, not least of Otto von Bismarck in the most crucial phase of his career. It proved that a firm understanding between the two major powers of East Central Europe—Prussia and Russia—would permit either of them to conduct a local war with impunity. In 1863, Bismarck stood on the verge of the three limited campaigns which were to raise the Prussian army to a position of absolute supremacy in Europe, and in February he sent General Alvensleben to St. Petersburg to sign a military convention. Having thus protected Russia's rear in its war in Poland, he could reasonably expect repayment in the near future. Russian neutrality, and security on the eastern frontier of Poland, formed the essential precondition for Prussia's masterly victories in the West—in 1864 against Denmark, in 1866 against Austria, and in 1870 against France. What is more, since in the years after the January Insurrection the Russian army was fully absorbed in holding down and punishing the Polish provinces, Russia's neutrality in Prussia's wars was entirely predictable. The common fear of a recurrence of a Polish rebellion drove Prussia and Russia together and thereby improved the political context in which Bismarck's wars were prosecuted. It is a bitter reflection for Poles to contemplate, but it seems that the January Insurrection made a distinct contribution to Bismarck's finest hour and the creation of the German Empire. At the end of his career, Bismarck was to warn his successors that the foundation stone of German foreign policy must be to keep the peace with the Russian "barbarians." That Wilhelmian Germany ignored this advice, and led the empires of Eastern Europe onto a course which in 1914–18 ended in their mutual destruction, may in part be attributable to the fact that they were all too young and ambitious to remember the lessons of 1863.

Second, the January Insurrection influenced contemporary arguments on the theory of warfare and, in particular, on the efficiency of guerrilla warfare. The subject was not new, of course—the word "guerrilla" itself attesting to the problems of Napoleon's professional armies facing fierce civilian resistance during the Peninsular War in Spain—but in the early 1860s Europe was still reeling from the incredible success of Garibaldi's expedition to Sicily, where a few hundred amateur enthusiasts had defeated the army of the Bourbons and overturned their kingdom. The January Insurrection served to redress the balance. The Polish insurgents were no less enthusiastic than Garibaldi's Thousand and far more numerous, but they did not succeed in driving the Russian army from Poland. In this case, the cautious Russian strategy of containment produced the desired effect. By holding the towns with heavy garrisons and denying the insurgents free access to the frontier zones, the Russian army was able to confine the partisan bands to the woods and the open countryside, where they could do least damage. Although military observers were amazed by the persistence and performance under fire of the ill-equipped insurgents, they were bound to conclude that a well-trained professional army, given time, discipline, and a consistent policy, was more than equal to the challenge. This conclusion undoubtedly strengthened the case of conservative political elements in the ruling empires that sought to repress internal opposition by force.

Third, therefore, the January Insurrection affected the internal policies of the ruling empires. It gave the final proof, if proof were needed in the age of Kossuth and Garibaldi, that the forces of nationalism could not simply be ignored. Fifteen years after 1848, fifty years after the Napoleonic wars, and nearly one hundred years after the First Partition, the Poles of East Central Europe were feeling and acting more like a united nation than ever before. A clear response was needed. The tsarist government chose the path of repression—and not only in its policy toward Poland. The whole of Russia, and in particular those so-called Russian liberals who felt cheated by Alexander II's retreat from so-called liberalism, were ready to blame the Poles for their own misfortune. Bismarck followed the Russian example. Preoccupied with his machinations in Western Europe and, before long, with the problems of absorbing western Germany into his Prussian master's new empire, he could not afford to give his troublesome Poles any free rein in the East. The *Kulturkampf* launched in 1872, which in Bavaria and the Rhineland was limited in the main to a campaign against the Roman Catholic Church, in Pomerania, Posnania, and Silesia threw the whole weight of the German state behind an assault on Polish nationality and all manifestations of Polish culture. Not surprisingly, Austria took the opposite tack. Crushed and humiliated by the Prussian army at Königgrätz in 1866, the ramshackle empire of the Habsburgs possessed neither the wish nor the means to emulate the repressive policies of Berlin and St. Petersburg. Vienna chose the path of conciliation. In 1867, in the immediate aftermath of Königgrätz and as part of the *Ausgleich* which brought the Dual Monarchy of Austria-Hungary into being, negotiations were undertaken with a view to granting autonomy to Galicia and thereby handing this largely Polish province of Austria over to the emperor-king's loyal Polish subjects. The die was cast. The ruling empires had chosen their styles of government for the remainder of their existence and, in a sense, the manner of their ultimate demise fifty years later. The tsar, the autocrat of all the Russias, had gambled all on the one throw of forcing his "little souls" to love and obey him and was headed for bloody revolution. The kaiser, at the head of his "façade democracy," had placed his faith in the German army and the German economy and their ability to outmatch all rivals; he had committed his country to phrenetic ambition, competition, and, eventually, international retribution. The emperor-king had no real means to prevent his realm from starting down the slope of gentle disintegration. All three empires were doomed; Russia had chosen to die in shrieks and convulsions, Germany in an apoplexy of impotent rage, and Austria-Hungary with a shrug and a smile, to the strains of a waltz.

Last, the January Insurrection inevitably influenced attitudes toward the vital issue of reform in the ensuing decades. The tsarist ukase of March 1864 emancipating the serfs of Poland on preferential terms provides the clearest example of the age-old ploy of buying political loyalty by making social or economic concessions. It gave considerable credence to the fallacy that social change or economic prosperity can somehow absolve an unpopular regime from the responsibility for fundamental political reform. What is more, by enjoying a measure of success in the short term, it converted the fallacy into an argument for inaction. In the long term, however, the results were there for all to see. Polish society in Russia, despite its relative prosperity, was steadily alienated by the tsar's refusal to initiate political reforms. Indeed, as in Prussia, the policy of repression must be held responsible for the growth of national consciousness in all classes and for the growing determination to overturn established authority at the first opportunity. In Galicia, the most backward province of the region, in contrast, where social and economic conditions remained appallingly primitive, revolutionary tendencies were much less marked. Political reform in the guise of provincial autonomy earned the Habsburgs the gratitude and loyalty of their Galician subjects right to the end.

In conclusion, the effects of the January Insurrection were not so meager as they first appear. In its defeat, the January Insurrection could not fail to strengthen the forces of conservatism and autocracy, which were to reassert themselves, especially in postemancipation Russia and in Bismarckian Germany, in the ensuing period. Equally, however, by raising the standard of civil rights and of national self-determination it added to the complex of problems which the ruling empires were incapable of solving. In this way, the January Insurrection not only gave a new lease of life to the Polish cause, but also made a marked contribution to that East Central Europe of independent nation-states which was destined to come into its own at the end of the First World War.

Poland, it is said, is a phoenix which repeatedly rises from the ashes of its own destruction. The period of the January Insurrection was certainly an era of destruction, but the ashes undoubtedly concealed the seeds of regeneration.

III. The January Insurrection

The Polish Theory of Partisan Warfare in the European Context

Emanuel Halicz

The Polish theory of partisan warfare is in my estimation the essential problem of military theory in nineteenth-century Poland. Under Polish conditions, in a partitioned and subjugated country which had never reconciled itself to the loss of statehood, the problem of regaining freedom and independence was naturally uppermost. Because of the lack of statehood and of an army, a war for national independence could only begin as a national partisan war, free from any preconceived patterns and rules. This became especially true after the defeat of the November Insurrection, when the remnants of the government and the Polish army were annihilated. Despite its importance, however, the problem of partisan warfare was underestimated, even by Polish historians, up to the Second World War. Only after the war, because of the role played by resistance and partisan movements in the fight against Nazism and the rise of partisan warfare in Asia and Latin America, did this problem become of more general interest to historians. Among Polish historians, both in Poland and in the emigration, research on guerrilla warfare began in the late 1940s. The pioneer in this field was Marian Kukiel,[1] who focused on nineteenth-century Polish publications on the subject and the role these played in the development of European military thought. Many books and pamphlets were rescued from obscurity to be republished in scholarly editions, and Polish libraries and archives were thoroughly searched for new material. Thanks to this effort, an overall view of the subject was reached that has been of great importance for our knowledge of military theory in general and our understanding of the whole period of the national liberation struggle in Poland.[2]

I

The general conception of a Polish national war widely accepted before 1863 can be traced as far back as the insurrection of 1794. The military principles of the nineteenth-century uprisings and Polish theories of partisan and mass struggle were based essentially on ideas worked out in the eighteenth century. Their source lay in the ideas of the revolutionary struggle in France, and their main testing ground was the Kościuszko uprising. Tadeusz Kościuszko's idea was to launch against Russia and Prussia not only regular troops, but a mass levy from every stratum of the Polish people. In a letter to General Franciszek Sapieha dated May 12, 1794, Kościuszko set out the assumptions underlying the 1794 uprising as follows:

> Our war has its own specific character which only now can be fully understood. Its success is based largely on the widespread arousal of enthusiasm and on the general arming of the inhabitants of all our lands. In addition, it is necessary to arouse love for the country among those who, until now, did not even know that they had a Fatherland. To produce at once one hundred thousand front-line troops is difficult in our conditions, but to produce a mass three times one hundred thousand will be easy if only the landowners and clergy are willing and succeed in arousing the people. I know that the military, attached to the normal method of conducting a war, and particularly those from a foreign service will find constant difficulties in using such forces, but one must be able to depart from the ordinary rules of the times.

The source of these assumptions, then, was the conviction, almost to the point of dogma, that with the mobilization of the mass of the population an uprising could be based solely on the country's own resources without needing to seek the support or generosity of others. Kościuszko also saw that making the peasants free landowners could be a means to winning national independence, had faith in the possibility of raising an army numerically superior to the invading forces, and considered the scythe and the pike likely to be dangerous weapons in the hands of the Polish peasantry.

These innovative assumptions were accompanied by a search for new methods in the field of operations and tactics. A protracted offensive war waged at various points in the country was to constitute the basic form of struggle for the national army, at least during the first phase of armed action. This was Kościuszko's formula for achieving independence and freedom in 1794.

In 1800 Kościuszko produced the memorable pamphlet *Can the Poles Recover Their Independence?* (in fact written by his secretary, Józef Pawlikowski), his ideological and historical testament.[3] On the basis of experience at home and abroad, the writer came to the conclusion that a nation that desired independence must have faith in its own strength, and "if it is unable to maintain its own existence through its own efforts, but only through foreign support or generosity, it can safely be said that it will never achieve happiness, virtue, or fame." The way to win freedom was to free the peasants, since only then, against the four-hundred-fifty-thousand-strong armies of the occupying powers, would it be possible to field a Polish army of over a million—an army conscious of its goals, imbued with the determination to achieve freedom, and armed with scythes: "There is no weapon that can turn back the scythe, and there is no army in all Europe that could not be defeated by it."

Schooled as he was in the ideas of Jean-Jacques Rousseau and Marie Jean Antoine Condorcet on the immense perfectibility of human nature once man is set free, Kościuszko, as Kukiel emphasizes, was firmly established in his convictions by the practical results of the American and French revolutions. The influence of the ideas of Jacques Antoine-Hippolite Guibert is much in evidence, especially his notion of the modern state made up of free citizens imbued with love for the Fatherland and ready to sacrifice themselves for it. All this was the more emphatically confirmed by his own inspiring experience at Racławice.

The author recommended protracted fighting in various parts of the occupied country, a war carried on aggressively, in the manner of a guerrilla action. According to Kościuszko, the insurrection should start in many places at once. It should exploit the element of surprise but avoid pitched battles against superior forces, thus protracting the war and spreading the flame of popular revolution into the enemy's own country. Similar concepts of a national revolution can be observed in the insurrection of 1863. As Kukiel points out, this was no accident.

According to the writer, the basic problems of warfare, organization and leadership, would be solved during the course of the fighting itself, although supreme authority would be concentrated in the hands of a national commander with dictatorial power like Kościuszko in 1794. A congress modeled after the American one would be established to deal with legislative matters and would therefore constitute a kind of limitation on the power of the dictator.

This book contains observations and generalizations based on the experiences of the Swiss struggles for liberation in the Middle Ages, of the Dutch in the sixteenth century, and, in particular, of the United States and the revolutionary French at the end of the eighteenth century. It also refers to Polish experiences, some going back as far as the "war of harassment" under Stefan Czarniecki and others still fresh in the memories of the partisan fighters of the years of the Confederation of Bar; but most numerous are the examples drawn from the insurrection of 1794. In support of his thesis the writer also cites several military authorities of the century—Jean-Charles Folard, Maurice de Saxe, Henry Lloyd, and Raymond Montecuccoli—stating in addition that the scythe has proven more efficient than the bayonet.

It is not too difficult to understand why this work, all but forgotten during the Napoleonic era, later enjoyed such special esteem. It was reprinted twice in Warsaw during the November Insurrection, and, as the Austrian consul in Warsaw, Oechsner, reported to Metternich on January 15, 1831, it caused quite a stir. It was a most welcome propaganda weapon, and foreign theoreticians of national liberation struggles also consulted it. Until recently, a rather one-sided viewpoint prevailed which located Polish military thought almost completely within the framework of Western European theories. Introductory comparative research has shown the lack of foundation for this conclusion. It is true that Mazzini influenced the theories of Karol Bogumil Stolzman and Ludwik Tadeusz Bystrzonowski, but it is also true that the works of Kościuszko were a source of inspiration for Carlo Bianco di Saint Jorioz, Mazzini's intellectual mentor. In 1831 Bianco entered into close collaboration with Mazzini, whose 1833 work *Della guerra d'insurrezione conveniente all'Italia*[4] was based entirely on Bianco's *Della guerra nazionale insurrezione per bande applicata all'Italia*.[5] In this form Bianco's ideas, and some of Kościuszko's as well, were widely diffused and inspired many European revolutionary movements. Bianco accepted many of the propositions of Kościuszko's work, especially the optimistic calculations regarding the possibilities for mustering and arming insurrectionary forces (he concluded that the Italians were in position to muster two million men against an Austrian army of three hundred thousand), the idea that partisan warfare was the only possible form of insurrectionary warfare, and the idea that a basic condition for success was connecting the uprising with freedom, unity, and the peasants' struggle for land, and introduced them into his treatise; this constituted the fundamental framework for Mazzini's work.

Both Kościuszko and Bianco emphasized the fundamental differences between revolutionary and regular warfare. Also noticeable are their identical formulations and similar lines of reasoning. Perhaps, as Kukiel has suggested, the identity of the problems evoked similar trains of thought and related formulations. At the same time, there are fundamental differences between the two works. Bianco glorified the Spanish guerrilla war and the fighting of the Italian bandits who carried on a life-and-death underground struggle and resorted to terror against their opponents. He advocated total warfare in which the whole population took part, either voluntarily or under pressure. In such a war, all methods were allowed, and any weapon was useful—knives, sticks, pitchforks, axes, stones, and even catapults and bows and arrows. The revolution had to begin from chaos. The problem of organization during the first stage of the struggle did not much concern him. This war of attrition was to last until the enemy had been liquidated. As far as the strategy of this future popular war was concerned, the conception of guerrilla warfare was regarded as a sort of panacea. Assessing the role of social factors, Mazzini outlined a broad program of democratic reforms, but the socioeconomic demands of the peasantry were not sufficiently taken into account. Still, there were many similarities between the plans outlined by the Italian theoreticians and the propositions advanced thirty years previously in the Kościuszko pamphlet.

The Poles joined in the European discussion on the principles of partisan warfare initiated largely by the Italian revolutionaries at the beginning of the 1830s. The fundamental principles of partisan struggle —faith in one's own strength, the ease of waging a war for liberation using the means available in the country—were the issues that occupied those who were not for one moment reconciled to the loss of their own independent state. Poland tried to reduce the difficulties in which it found itself after the collapse of the November Insurrection—the lack of an army, of free territory, of an administration, of supplies—by overestimating the mobilizing power of a partisan war linked with land distribution to the peasantry at the moment the struggle began. The peasant masses, inspired by the will to fight and armed with scythes, stones, and sticks and only a few firearms, were to constitute, according to the theoreticians, an adequate counterforce to the armies of the occupying powers, numbering half a million and armed with rifles.

The Polish Carbonari and later the members of "Young Poland" were entirely under the spell of Mazzini's theories. The influence of the "Young Europe" ideology of Stolzman was widely acknowledged, but only recently has it become evident that the basic ideas set out in Stolzman's *Partisan Warfare*[6] are a travesty and even a more or less literal translation of many key passages of Mazzini's work. Generally speaking, they relate to basic methods of conducting partisan warfare, an assessment of the European situation, and the glorification of past partisan wars. A comparison of the arguments of Bianco and Mazzini with those of Stolzman leads to the conclusion that in relation to the methods of conducting partisan warfare, Stolzman attempted to transplant the Italian ideas in Polish soil, taking into account Polish national characteristics as well as natural factors. Stolzman also adopted much of the sociopolitical program advanced by Mazzini, which can be reduced to some rather vague aspirations in the direction of progress. Mazzini was decidedly opposed to the introduction of terror in relation to the propertied classes. National unity was the most important question, and social demands played only a secondary role. Two fundamental issues emerged at the head of his program: the need for unity and the creation of a republic.

Stolzman's formulations regarding the brotherhood of people were identical to those of "Young Europe." His reflections on the subject of the Slavs living under the Austrian monarchy were similar to the views of Mazzini, who saw them as potential allies in the struggle against the Habsburgs. His basic creed—insurrection on the basis of one's own resources and the possibility of mustering four million armed men (what optimism!)—brought him close to Kościuszko's ideas. Universality, aggressiveness, and resourcefulness were the chief attributes which should characterize the uprising. They were not, however, adequate weapons for the struggle against Poland's three oppressors. What would be decisive was the partisan weapon that had ensured the victory of the Albanians under George Skanderbeg, of the Serbs under George Karadjordjević and Miloš Obrenović over the Turks, America over Britain, and Russia, Germany, and Spain over the forces of Napoleon. (Stolzman overlooked the fact that in the cases of Russia, Germany, and Spain, partisan fighting was an auxiliary factor, the main role in the victory over Napoleon falling to the regular army.)

The problem of partisan warfare was taken up simultaneously with Stolzman by a well-known politician and writer on social issues. Henryk Kamieński differed from Stolzman in developing further the system of national warfare, as well as in the particular role he attributed to the settlement of the peasant question.[7] The revolutionary character of the armed insurrection, closely linked with persistent efforts to liquidate labor service and the granting of landownership to the peasantry, came almost to constitute the ideology and theory of successful struggle for national liberation. For him, the social revolution was not a secondary issue, but the most important weapon in the hands of the insurrection—the chief means of restoring to the nation the strength inherent in its people and inciting the masses to action. Without granting land to the peasantry, there could be no uprising. The people's war he proclaimed could only constitute the military complement to social unrest if it flowed from it and was based on it. The solution of the peasant question and partisan warfare constituted a single entity in the form of a people's war for independence, "the highest expression of the national uprising and the only way in the whole world to utilize all the nation's forces without exception to defend the soil of the Fatherland."

Kamieński paid more attention than did Stolzman to the revolutionary method by which the struggle was to be waged, to the necessity for instilling in the insurgents consciousness of the goals for which they were fighting. "Infecting our villagers with a people's war," he proclaimed, "is a more important military event than obtaining, by some miraculous means, several hundred thousand weapons, cannon, etc." Kamieński wanted Poland to achieve independence through social revolution, through the implementation of a program granting land to the peasantry and without bloodshed. Nevertheless, as a realist he reckoned with the possibility of resistance from some of the gentry and proposed the use of terror against them on the model of the French Revolution of 1793. Nor did he exclude the possibility that the peasant would throw himself on the manor instead of taking part in the uprising. The cure for such difficulties was to be "evangelism"—propaganda and educational work among all social classes, in particular among the peasantry.

Characteristically, Kamieński's view of the outbreak of the uprising itself was a negation of the romantic view of the struggle. The outbreak of war, in his opinion, should be not just the result of a conspiracy or an attack on this or that enemy installation, but an event intimately associated with the peak of the revolutionary movement of the masses, especially the peasantry. It was this that would be decisive for its force and dynamics. He divided the uprising into four phases. In the first two, the fighting would be done by partisan detachments which, as they liberated individual regions, would join to form larger units. In the next two phases, these units would join to form armies. It was impossible to believe, he argued, that the enemy could be defeated without concentrating the forces of the uprising—without a confrontation of army with army. In his opinion, a final settlement was to be sought in pitched battle, as in the French Revolution.

Kamieński's notion of a people's war was both original and mature. It was distinguished from other Polish theoretical works by its tendency to assign the uprising a revolutionary form, to equate it with social revolution, and to link the problem of partisan warfare with the struggle for national and social liberation. This doctrine was branded idealistic by Ludwik Mierosławski[8] and rejected by the central board of the Polish Democratic Society. In their opinion, social revolution—i.e., the granting of land to the peasants—should come by decree of a national government.

II

It is impossible to speak of only one approach to the problem of the Polish theory of partisan warfare. There were many military viewpoints; between 1832 and 1870, 147 works were written on struggles for national liberation, many of them on partisan warfare. The results were impressive for the richness of their ideas and approaches. Especially important and representative, and the most original and creative, were, however, the ideas of Kościuszko and Kamieński. Practically everyone referred to them, even those who did their utmost to be original and who did not agree with many of the suggestions they advanced. These included Ludwik Mierosławski, a great military writer who was a decided advocate of regular warfare.

After the November Insurrection, the principle of a regular war waged by the army of the rebel nation was advocated less frequently, and the idea of a revolutionary war, a partisan or people's struggle which would harass the enemy's forces, was advanced more frequently as the method most appropriate for the Poles. The discussion was initiated by Wojciech Chrzanowski,[9] who argued that partisan warfare could be waged with great success not only in mountainous country, but wherever the inhabitants had the courage to defend themselves and were not prepared to accept servitude. "In our present situation," wrote Józef Bem, "we can count only on a national uprising, a partisan war, because when the hour strikes for the uprising we shall have neither a large nor a properly organized national army."[10] Both Józef Wysocki[11] and Ludwik Bystrzonowski perceived the superiority of precisely this kind of army in the conditions in which Poland found itself after 1831.

The terminology of the theoretical literature displays considerable laxity and imprecision—in fact, chaos. Writers frequently use a variety of concepts to describe one and the same form of struggle. Many concepts, such as partisan fighting, partisan warfare, and small-scale or guerrilla warfare, are used interchangeably. Kościuszko, for example, makes no distinction between a "small war" and a "partisan war," and when he says "small-scale warfare" he actually means "partisan war." The units Kościuszko wanted to create were intended to carry out independent and offensive operations designed to lead to a further stage in the struggle for the liberation of the country.

For Kościuszko, a small war was the same as a partisan war and therefore had to fulfill strategic tasks. Others, including Ignacy Prądzyński, saw it as fulfilling narrow tactical functions. A similar point of view was advanced by W. Valentini, Karl Decker, and Miere de Corvey. Karol Borkowski distinguished two kinds of partisan struggle: partisan fighting (or small-scale warfare), which assisted the regular forces, and insurgent partisan fighting or partisan warfare—i.e., national and revolutionary wars of liberation.[12] Kamieński introduced into the literature the concept of the people's war, which was not to be subordinated to any military rules and regulations and was to be waged by the whole people fighting for national and social emancipation by all available means.

The emergence of the concept of partisan warfare introduced a distinction between it and partisan fighting, frequently referred to as small-scale warfare. Partisan fighting does not include fundamental military objectives; its task is secondary. In contrast, partisan warfare has strategic significance. Polish theorists of partisan and people's wars assumed that the fighting, whether initiated by the activity of dispersed partisan units or by the culmination of a mass movement, would in time give birth to a regular army, because only a regular army was capable of leading the nation to final victory. Stolzman saw the need to create corps in the second stage of an uprising as the great armed forces of the uprising. Kamieński saw the victorious stage of the people's war in the moment when a regular Polish army stood against the armies of the invading states, and for Bem the force that would bear the main burden of the struggle was to be mobile columns made up of émigrés and transformed into a regular army.

The theorists of Polish insurgent struggles created the conception of the nation under arms, undoubtedly drawing on the model of the French Revolution (especially the period of the Jacobin dictatorship), the Spanish experience of 1808–13, and the experience of the Italians in the 1820s. In doing so they overestimated Poland's forces and underestimated the strength of the enemy. The idea of the moral mobilization of the nation was dominant; the numerical calculations were wrong. Kościuszko, for example, in estimating the possible armed forces that Poland and the partitioning powers could field, became convinced that Poland would be able to raise 1.2 million soldiers and the invaders only four hundred fifty thousand. He was followed by the theorists of the Polish Democratic Society, Stolzman, Bem, Kamieński, and Mierosławski, who put the ratio in favor of the Polish side even higher. This mistake was continually repeated, although the experience of the uprisings was that numerically the armies of the partitioning states were twice or even three and more times as strong as the insurgents. In 1794 there were scarcely seventy thousand regular troops fighting continuously, and in the November Insurrection there were no more; the uprising in Great Poland involved no more than twenty thousand, and in the January Insurrection there were never more than thirty-five thousand insurgents in the field.

The calculations concerning the relative strengths of the opponents failed to take into account the fundamental difference between a hastily improvised army, short of trained commanders, poorly armed, and without organized backing, and the trained, well-armed, regimented armies of the partitioning powers. As far as arms are concerned, all of the Polish theorists, from Kościuszko to Kamieński, extolled the superiority of the scythe and the pike over firearms. Some cited the theories of Folard, Montecuccoli, and Aleksandr Suvorov in this connection, while others were entranced by the examples of Racławice and Szczekociny and, later, Miłosław and Wrzesnia. Though Kościuszko, while advocating the scythe, at the same time appreciated the role of firearms and cannon, these theorists proceeded as if he were an adherent of the view, propounded by Guibert, Stolzman, and Bem, that "the enemy could be beaten with whatever was at hand" and that "for a brave man a stone, a stick, a knife, an axe, or a scythe can suffice to defeat the enemy." They recognized, of course, that in the first stage of an uprising it was impossible to arm the peasants with firearms. "The myth of the scythe," which lasted down to the January Insurrection, stemmed not from any underestimation of military technology, but from the objective situation in which the country found itself. To supply a national army with enough modern arms, particularly at the moment of outbreak of an uprising, was an impossibility.

Perceiving the class and national conflicts in the societies of the partitioning states and seeing them as favorable to the Polish cause, the Polish theorists were inclined to view Polish society as a monolith despite its deep stratification, assuming that subjection liquidated class conflicts. Further, they underestimated the solidarity of the powers that formed the Holy Alliance, although they were aware of the anti-Polish attitude of Prussia and Austria in 1794 and 1830–31 and of the agreements concluded between them on the subject of Poland. Poland's geopolitical position was another factor operating against the Polish national liberation movement. Although serious conflicts existed between the partitioning states and the Western European powers, none of the Western powers was inclined to seek redress for Poland with armed force. There were indeed sometimes words of encouragement, particularly from France, but none of the powers came to the aid of Poland in its struggle.

Polish theory on partisan warfare was not created in a sociopolitical vacuum. Theorists most frequently sought inspiration in the struggle waged in their country, but they also looked to the various forms of struggle abroad—from the American Revolutionary War and the revolutionary struggle in France to examples drawn from the Wars of the Vendée, the Spanish guerrillas, the 1812–13 War, and the Italian war of liberation. Bystrzonowski based his conclusions on, among other things, the experiences derived from the struggles of the Balkan nations, the Algerians, and the people of Afghanistan. The foreign theorists most frequently cited were Karl Clausewitz, Gerhard Scharnhorst, August Wilhelm Anton Gneisenau, Willisen, and Mazzini. It is true that the Polish theorists, especially those of the emigration, assimilated French and even Austrian military ideas about liberation struggles, but Polish military writings, especially the work of Bystrzonowski, Chrzanowski, and Prądzyński, were known in the West and in Russia, translated into foreign languages, and utilized by writers in various countries. The military views of Mierosławski were also highly regarded, especially in France, Germany, and Italy, and were quoted by Marx and Engels. The theories of Bem reached France and Hungary, while Kamieński's influence extended far beyond the borders of Poland. Detailed analytical studies are needed to trace the spread of these ideas. Only a few issues have been raised here, but they would appear to be of considerable interest.

III

The theory of partisan warfare lay at the foundation of all the nineteenth-century Polish insurrectionary upheavals, especially the January Insurrection. The experience of this uprising confirmed the correctness of many of the recommendations of Stolzman, Kamieński, and Bem. The Poles' struggle enriched our experience regarding methods and means of conducting a war of liberation and especially regarding ways of basing partisan fighting on reserves of the local population, planning the course of the fighting, and linking partisan action with fighting by regular formations.

This experience was of interest not only to Russian or Prussian military circles. A Swiss observer, an officer of the general staff, Colonel Franz L. von Erlach, evaluated highly the struggle of the Poles:

> The present Polish war has great significance for any thinking Swiss soldier who observes it carefully, not only from the point of view of the state, but above all as a universal people's war, a partisan war. As a universal people's war it is a model of internal enthusiasm, sacrifice, noble-mindedness, unheard-of perseverance, and absolute courage which it would be difficult to surpass. Furthermore, it is an example for us of the consistent, powerful cooperation of a popular authority based on these virtues, which maintains itself in the face of enemy armed superiority over the insurgent detachments. . . . The nature of the Polish partisan war can serve us as a splendid example which can be applied and very successfully carried out in many parts of Switzerland.[13]

During the difficult days of the Nazi occupation, the Polish resistance movement went back to the recommendations set out in the pamphlet *Can the Poles Recover Their Independence?* The French resistance movement, searching for instruction materials for the partisans of the

Maquis, made use of Kamieński's *The People's War* and the pamphlet *L'insurrection est un art*, based on his views. (This pamphlet also appeared in Polish under the title *Powstanie jest sztuka*.) The Poles' achievements in the field of partisan warfare were of interest to the highest German authorities, and in 1940 a research unit of the German general staff produced a document entitled *Die polnische Methoden bei der Vorbereitung und Durchführung des Aufstandes gegen die Russen im Jahre 1863* (Polish Methods in Preparing and Carrying Out the Insurrection against the Russians in 1863). This was based on literature relating to the January Insurrection, mainly Polish works by such persons as Józef Piłsudski, Walery Przyborowski, and Julius Verdy du Vernois, a Prussian observer during the insurrection. The aim of the document was to utilize the Polish experiences in the Germans' struggle against the Polish resistance movement.

IV

Instead of a conclusion, I would like to make some suggestions for further investigation of the problem of Polish partisan warfare. It seems to me that it would be a good idea to continue our studies in the following directions:

1. Enlarging the scope of our studies, both in breadth and in depth. This would mean, among other things, a more thorough study of the theoretical works of less well-known writers (e.g., Borkowski).

2. Undertaking archival studies in Poland and abroad. It seems to me that we should pay more attention to the collections of the Polish Library in Paris. A closer look at the Czartoryski Library in Cracow might also be fruitful. Similarly, as far as I am aware, no one has investigated the potential material in the Russian and Prussian archives. Of prime importance here would be the Saltykov-Shchedrin Library in Leningrad and the Lenin Library in Moscow.

3. Examining in more detail the relationship between Polish and European theories of partisan warfare. Beyond the interdependence of Polish and Italian thinking on this subject through the 1830s, what about theories originating in other European countries in the nineteenth century?

4. Determining the extent to which Polish theoretical thinking was put into practice, both in the 1863 Insurrection and during the Second World War.

5. Refining our terminology. We often use interchangeably and without precision such terms as national war, people's war, guerrilla, partisan war, partisan fighting, and small-scale war (*Kleinkrieg*). It is time to give more precise definitions to these closely related but different phenomena.

6. Reprinting books, pamphlets, and leaflets on the concept of partisan war written in nineteenth-century Europe. As far as Kościuszko's

pamphlet is concerned, would it not be a good idea to have it translated into English, thus rendering it accessible to American and British readers? It is worth mentioning that it has already been translated into Russian and Japanese.

Notes

1. M. Kukiel, "Problèmes des guerres d'insurrection au XIXe siècle," *Antemurale* 2 (1955); idem, "Military Aspects of the Polish Insurrection of 1863–64," *Antemurale* 2 (1955).
2. E. Halicz, *Partisan Warfare in Nineteenth-Century Poland: The Development of a Concept* (Odense, 1975).
3. (J. Pawlikowski), *Czy Polacy wybić się mogą na niepodległość?* (Paris, 1800). See English translation on pp. 584–620.
4. G. Mazzini, *Della guerra d'insurrezione conveniente all'Italia*, vol. 2 (Imola, 1907).
5. C. Bianco, Comte di Saint Jorioz, *Della guerra nazionale d'insurrezione per bande applicata all'Italia* (Marseilles, 1830).
6. K. B. Stolzman, *Partyzantka, czyli wojna dla ludów powstających najwłaściwsza* (Warsaw, 1960).
7. H. Kamieński, *Katechizm demokratyczny czyli opowiadanie słowa ludowego przez Filareta Prawdowskiego* (Paris, 1845); idem, *Wojna Ludowa, przez X.Y.Z.* (Bendlikon, 1866).
8. L. Mierosławski, *Instrukcja powstańcza* (Warsaw, 1862).
9. W. Chrzanowski, *O wojnie partyzanckiej* (Paris, 1835).
10. J. Bem, *O powstaniu narodowym w Polsce* (Warsaw, 1956).
11. J. Wysocki, *Kurs sztuki wojskowej*, vol. 1 (Paris, 1842).
12. K. Borkowski, *Pamiętnik historyczny o wyprawie partyzanckiej do Polski* (Leipzig, 1863).
13. F. L. von Erlach, *Die Kriegsführung der Polen in Jahre 1863* (Darmstadt-Leipzig, 1866).

The January Insurrection and the Theory of Partisan Warfare

Leonard Ratajczyk

As far as its military character was concerned, the January Insurrection, in principle, was planned as a people's partisan war. This is clear from the Polish theoretical output of 1800–62, which I have discussed in vol. 4 of this series.[1] It is also confirmed by such contemporary witnesses of events as the Swiss colonel Franz L. von Erlach[2] and the German Marxist theoretician Friedrich Engels. Engels wrote to Karl Marx on February 17, 1863, with admiration of Polish heroism during the first days of the struggle, "It ought not be forgotten that the young Polish émigrés have their own military literature, in which every problem is discussed with particular consideration of Polish relations, and that the idea of partisan warfare in Poland, which is comprehensively elaborated, plays a very important role in it."[3]

After all, there was no other possibility. Where there is no regular army and the country is occupied by invaders, partisan warfare has been considered the most effective kind of fight for national independence. Successful partisan warfare can cause the insurgent forces to assume the form of a regular army that can go on to confront the army of the invaders. However, while this idea of partisan warfare had been elaborated long before the January Insurrection, its implementation faced difficulties of various kinds.

The Polish propertied classes (businessmen, bankers, landowners, and some of the intellectuals) who organized as the Whites during the patriotic demonstrations in the Kingdom of Poland in 1861 were in principle opposed to any armed uprising, their position depending as it did on good relations with all three invaders. Holding to their views, they negatively influenced the whole process of preparation for the insurrection. Meanwhile, part of the working masses (workers, craftsmen, peasants, and agricultural laborers), some of the intellectuals, and the young people who felt the slavery most keenly aimed at a struggle against the tsarist invaders. Progressive intellectuals, craftsmen, and

Warsaw workers organized as the Reds and set about the task of preparation and leadership of an insurrection. However, there was no consensus on the practical realization of the idea of partisan warfare among the Reds themselves. Their chief aim was to draw most of the society into the struggle. This was why enfranchisement of the peasants (that is, giving them the land they worked) was seen as necessary, in addition to seeking the cooperation of Russian revolutionaries.

I

Because of the need for secrecy, the plans for the insurrection called for close cooperation of the Reds with conspiratorial organizations within the tsarist army in the Kingdom of Poland. The working masses were to be drawn into the fight only at the moment of the outbreak. Thus precautions were maintained at the expense of the full participation of the nation.

The original plan had been worked out in the summer of 1862 by Captain Jarosław Dąbrowski, a graduate of the tsarist General Staff Academy and quartermaster of the Fourth Infantry Brigade. The plan assumed the capture of Warsaw, the fortress newly built there by the tsarist authorities after the failure of the November Insurrection, and Modlin Fortress (about forty kilometers north of Warsaw), which had the largest arsenal (over seventy-four thousand guns and eight hundred cannon), with the help of conspirators in the tsarist army whom Dąbrowski knew personally. The capture of Warsaw, the political center of the Kingdom of Poland, would solve the problem of armaments and make it easy to control the whole insurrection. With regard to the conditions for partisan warfare, however, it turned out to be very difficult. The Warsaw City Committee, influenced by the Whites, rejected the plan. At the same time, events made it impossible to execute it; the plot in the tsarist army was discovered, and Dąbrowski and several Russian officers who had taken part in it were arrested.

Aleksander Wielopolski, the leader of the civilian government of the Kingdom of Poland and an advocate of a spirit of conciliation, sought to block any further preparations for an insurrection by announcing a draft, or *branka* (the forced taking of recruits from their homes according to previously made-up lists), on December 6, 1862. The draft was aimed at some ten thousand young men involved in the conspiracy or sympathizing with it, and thus the most patriotic ones. These young people did not want to fall victim to the draft (compulsory service in the tsarist army then lasted for twelve years) and were determined to resist it. The society's sympathetic attitude toward them was insurance, as it were, of their success. Since Aleksandr Herzen and other leaders of the

Russian revolutionary democrats in exile had asked that the insurrection be postponed until the spring of 1863, expecting that the majority of Russian society would join it, Captain Zygmunt Padlewski, Dąbrowski's successor on the Warsaw City Committee, worked out a self-defense plan. Under this plan the young men subject to the *branka* would hide in the forest until spring, when they would begin the partisan war. The initiation of the *branka* in Warsaw on the night of January 14–15, 1863, leading to the flight to the neighboring woods of a large group of young men and the attendant concern for their welfare under winter conditions, forced an early start for the insurrection, before the support of the Western European countries could be obtained and before preparations for it were complete. Therefore the desperate decision to begin the insurrection met with no enthusiasm, and the Central National Committee of the Reds, calling itself the Provisional National Government, explained, on January 16, 1863, the need for that decision in an appeal to the people:

> The Central National Committee had made preparations to stop the draft but encountered unexpected difficulties. The French government, harassing us with the same zeal as the Russian gendarmes, had delayed the shipment to Poland of sufficient arms for immediate face-to-face combat with the enemy. Not discouraged by this fact, the Committee had devised other measures when the night *branka* took us by surprise.
>
> Poles! Are we to withdraw in the face of difficulties? Are we to send our brothers into dishonorable service of the enemy? No, on we go with boldness and faith in God and in the sacredness of our task. . . .
>
> The Central National Committee declares the whole country under martial law and orders all righteous sons of the Motherland to fight till the bitter end, even personally, against the draft, to liberate those already captured by the Russians, and to give shelter to the fugitives.[4]

At a Central National Committee meeting, Zygmunt Padlewski, in a historic speech, linked national independence with the need for solving the peasant problem and continued, "Allowing the Russians to levy means letting them solve the peasant problem (as the nobles' committee has already done) and at the same time breaking with the people. . . ." According to Padlewski, the young men who were to be rushed to the Caucasus by the tsarist authorities to slaughter and to put the Caucasians into chains "should be sacrificed to save the nation, to solve the peasant problem with a Polish nation, to create the foundations of a great people's war for the salvation of the whole nation." "As a soldier in the regular army," Padlewski said, "I understand all the difficulty of today's situation; I know that I can do no better than to die in the attempt to give the serfs what belongs to them. . . . We should declare enfranchisement, we should go to the land, arm ourselves, and attack the troops in the night; and, if there still be life in our bodies, we should go to the serf, give him back his due, and call him up to fight against the invaders."[5]

This was the program of the fight for independence on the part of the forces of the working masses. It created the basis for transforming the insurrection into the "great people's war" that had been dreamt of by Dąbrowski. Padlewski's plan suggested the simultaneous declaration of the insurrection and the enfranchisement of the peasants, who at that time constituted 75.5 percent of the population of the Kingdom of Poland. The creation of three partisan assembly areas was ordered. The aim was to capture, under Padlewski's leadership, Modlin Fortress and Płock for the seat of the National Government. In the eastern area, between the Vistula and the Bug, a partisan assembly under the command of Major Władysław Lewandowski was given the task of cutting off Warsaw from Russia. In the south, in the Swiętokrzyskie Mountains and their environs, the outbreak of the insurrection depended on Marian Langiewicz and Apolinary Kurowski of Kraków province. All the partisan units were to attack Warsaw after they had captured their own areas.

II

Because of unsatisfactory military preparations, the negative attitude of the majority of the rural nobles and rich townspeople toward the fight, and the failures in the first engagements, these aims were not achieved. Forty-five hundred poorly armed insurgents fought against 111,245 tsarist soldiers. On the first night, that of January 22–23, 1863, there were only nineteen attacks on garrisons and fourteen public gatherings of insurgents. Of these, only eight assaults were fully successful and seven further ones successful in part. In Płock province the most reactionary landowners gathered on January 25 and decided to "calm the insurrection by all means, send a letter of apology to the tsar, denounce Padlewski, Rolski, and Kokosiński, and send the Warsaw craftsmen to Prussia to stay until the tsar should forgive them."[6] Eventually, where thousands had been expected, hundreds appeared, where hundreds had been expected tens.

Though Padlewski's plan was not implemented, the tsar's army command, because of telegraphic communication breaks and alarming news, was surprised by the insurrection. It ordered troop concentration in the region at least up to battalion strength and defense of guberniyal and district cities.[7] This order created favorable conditions for the further development of the insurrection. The Central National Committee, correctly assessing the situation, on January 25 ordered the beginning of the insurrection in all districts with a view to their capture.[8] General Ludwik Mierosławski, the exiled hero of the "Springtime of Nations," was appointed leader of the insurrection. Mierosławski arrived in the Kingdom of Poland via Poznań in mid-February 1863. Here he faced the nobles' ill will toward him after two defeats of his partisan units, in Krzywosądz and Nowa Wieś, in Włocławek district. Being ill, he renounced the leadership and returned to Paris, leaving the military leadership of the insurrection to its fate. This was really an offense to his fighting countrymen.

The unfortunate performance of Mierosławski, his organizational inefficiency, and the fact that the members of the insurgent government scattered to join partisan units meant that the insurrection was deprived of military and political leadership. Ultimately, every commander was doomed to depend on his own initiative in the absence of any coordination by a higher authority of operations in a particular province. As Józef Piłsudski, a researcher of the military aspects of the January Insurrection and later marshal of Poland, put it,

> The insurrection is faced with the lack of leadership thought, not only in Warsaw, but also in centers of provincial authority; in consequence, military thought is left to its fate, scattered in as many directions as there are commanders, which causes disorganization within the Polish troops that weakens in the most serious way the already weakened aspect of any volunteer army, that is, its organizational unity, self-confidence, and faith in commanders and vice versa.[9]

In these circumstances, Padlewski, after his unsuccessful attack on Płock, turned to organizing partisan detachments in the area of Płock province. Antoni Jeziorański, military commander of Rawa district, formed a unit, joined Major Józef Śmiechowski, and captured Rawa on February 4. Then he went to the Świętokrzyskie woods to avoid facing larger contingents of the tsarist army. Walenty Lewandowski, who had been a volunteer in the Hungarian Revolution of 1848–49, came back to Poland from exile in 1862 and was appointed military commander of Podlasie and Lublin provinces. He organized the most vigorous actions of the January Night in Podlasie province, but he did not achieve the preplanned goals. Apolinary Kurowski, an experienced conspirator of 1846, was military commander of Kraków province, but, having failed in the attacks on Kielce and Jędrzejów, focused his activity on Olkusz district. Then, on February 17, weakened by his unsuccessful attack on Miechów, he joined Langiewicz. Marian Langiewicz, who had quarreled with Mierosławski, offered his services to the Reds and was appointed military commander of Sandomierz province and then also of Kraków. He began, somewhat inefficiently, the concentration of newly formed detachments in the neighborhood of Wąchock. Then, constantly pressed by the tsarist army, he began operations in the southwest. Prejudiced against partisan operations despite their possibilities, he aimed at concentration of all forces and combining of detachments such as Kurowski's, Jeziorański's, and Śmiechowski's, which of course drew much of the enemy's army against him.

After Padlewski's departure, there was for a time no one in the Provisional National Government who understood military matters. Then Eugeniusz Kaczkowski-Dębiński, an artillery captain with nine years of service in the French army, the Foreign Legion, and the Turkish army, an engineer on the Warsaw-Vienna Railway, and an organizer of the Conspiratorial War Department, came to work with the government staff. Perhaps it was on his own initiative that it was decided to give up the idea of constantly supporting the absentee Mierosławski's dictatorship and to take control of the insurrection. It was decided to appoint a commander for each of the three large areas and charge them with the task of forming of three insurgent armies. Wysocki was to be the commander of the left bank of the Vistula, Mierosławski of the right bank, and Padlewski of the north and the Płock and Augustów areas. This plan was interesting but not very practical, if only because of the absence from the battlefield of Mierosławski, who considered himself dictator, and the fact that his adversaries, Wysocki and Padlewski, would not fall into line with him. The plan was also crossed by events.

Despite, or perhaps because of, the fact that the initial period of the insurrection was characterized by brilliant military activities on the part of a few civilians, such as Kurowski and Czachowski, and a few lieutenants, captains, or majors who had knowledge and experience at the tactical unit level and were promoted to colonels and generals with a wide range of power, no detailed plan for the insurrection was developed, and initially not many successes on the battlefield were lasting ones. Everyone could be blamed for this—the members of the Provisional National Government, the soldiers who assumed higher offices, and those who passively watched the insurrection or actively fought against it. The opportunity to create some disarray in the tsarist army in the Kingdom of Poland and to inflame the people with enthusiasm for a general armed uprising had been lost.

III

Thanks to the European press, the insurrection was evoking increasing interest outside the Empire. By spring 1863, the Polish struggle for independence had already gained the support of Western Europeans. Soon afterward, the French, English, and Austrian governments undertook diplomatic interventions with regard to Russia. All this suggested the possibility of a European war in support of Poland. As would become apparent, this was only wishful thinking.

At the same time, the Polish propertied classes understood that if they were not to lose their influence and perhaps their fortunes and the prospect of control over the future independent Polish state, they would have to join the insurrection and control it. They did not believe in the effectiveness of partisan warfare and were afraid of a general arming of the peasants. Thus, they decided to take control over the insurrection, and pending the armed intervention of the Western European countries, turn the struggle against the tsarist army into a show of force. "The main thing is to exist and to fight as little as possible," General Zamoyski's wife wrote him in France on March 6, 1863. "I would like you, too, to send us this advice, since there are many who are not able to understand that there can be wars without battles. . . . If I have meant Władysław Cz. [Czartoryski] well, it is not a matter of battles, but the insurrection must continue to create the reason for diplomatic activities."[10] This was also the view of Prince Władysław Czartoryski, who lived in exile in France and was on good terms with Napoleon III.

The Whites' activity started with an attack on the leadership of the insurrection. The insurgent general Langiewicz, who had assembled over thirty-five hundred partisans in Kielce province, was induced to declare himself dictator. This meant that the Central National Committee was debarred from posts of authority and Mierosławski's dictatorship was suppressed. Langiewicz's dictatorship lasted only for nine days and caused the dispersal of the largest concentration of insurgent troops in the south of the Kingdom of Poland. When the Russians learned that the dictator of the insurrection commanded an insurgent unit near Kielce, they set off in pursuit of him, and this made Langiewicz leave the unit. His career as dictator ended with his arrest by the Austrians when he crossed the border with the intention of controlling the insurrection from Cracow, in the Austrian sector of partitioned Poland. After these failures, the Whites began a gradual takeover of the Provisional National Government.

This was the most propitious moment of the insurrection. By April, the struggle extended beyond the Kingdom of Poland to Lithuania, Belorussia, and the Ukraine. During the summer, the peasants poured in to join the insurgent units. The struggle came to naught, however, because it was converted into a show of force only. The insurgent government of Karol Majewski in Warsaw, operating on the Whites' behalf, approved of partisan operations only by small, dispersed units. Any mass levy by an insurgent unit was forbidden. When the leader of the armed forces in Kalisz and Mazowsze provinces, General Edmund Taczanowski, ordered an insurrection on August 15, the National Government sent its commissioner, Agaton Giller, to stop him.[11] Taczanowski's chief of staff, Colonel Franciszek Kopernicki, said later in his memoirs, "The general intended to call people in Kalisz and Mazowsze provinces to join the levy en masse; he asked the government for permission but was peremptorily forbidden to do so."[12] The commander of the Mazowsze province armed forces, Lieutenant Colonel Edmund Callier, wrote of the government's decision, "This fact confirmed me in the conviction that the National Government is as reluctant as can be to develop our insurrection and thus to defeat the Russians."[13] He then resigned his post.

The author of an anonymous pamphlet published in 1863 and entitled *Practical Remarks,* while not knowing the mechanism that had arrested the progress of the people's war, understood it and its harmfulness for the insurrection. He argued,

> Critically observing the present commanders' steps, it seems that they only roughly care about, if they have not generally given up the idea of, enlarging their units by a *branka,* supporting the partisan disturbances in the neighborhood, and calling upon the peasants and other classes of society to join the insurrection. Units composed only of intellectuals cannot capture the country; we must fill them up with a mass levy. Not being the owners of the administrative keys to the country, we can casually, irregularly give orders for a *branka* only in the more populous regions. Our task is to extract the greatest possible number of recruits from the country with the help of people stimulated by our example. We should make efforts at the possible enlargement of our territory wherever possible; we should avoid limiting it to the scanty area of a camp.[14]

Unfortunately, this is not what the Whites intended.

In consequence of the Whites' policy, the number of insurgents in the units was not more than some thirty thousand, despite the fact that the possibilities were much more promising. Volunteers from other countries—Russians, Frenchmen, Italians, and Hungarians—came to join the insurgent units. The insurrection was supported by Garibaldi, Mazzini, Herzen, Marx, Engels, and many other leaders of the masses in Europe.

The tsarist authorities reckoned with the possibility of a European war in support of Poland; this was why the army had been built up so intensively. At the same time, they aimed at negating the diplomatic intervention of the Western powers, and these efforts were not in vain. The tsarist army in the Kingdom of Poland was reinforced to one hundred ninety thousand and in the whole area of the insurrection, including Lithuania, Belorussia, and the Ukraine, to three hundred sixty thousand. All of the troops in the European part of Russia were combat-ready. In the meantime, Russia prevented the danger of a European war, at least in 1863, in the sphere of diplomacy by deceiving the Western governments with various promises.

The whole situation and the failures of some of the larger partisan units in August and September 1863 were discouraging to the Whites. Recognizing the growing discontent of people with the state of insurrection, Majewski's government resigned, and the Reds, who advocated armed struggle by the whole nation, took over. Their activity began, however, with an unsuccessful bomb threat against the tsarist deputy in the Kingdom of Poland, General Fedor Berg. Berg escaped uninjured and ordered a reign of terror in Warsaw. On September 30, the arrested members of the insurgent police—Janiszewski, Jagoszewski, Kosiński, Raczyński, and Zeller—were shot. The tsarist police traced some insurgent grenades to the Evans Factory, and on October 7, in the factory yard in the presence of the whole staff of the factory, Wilhelm Algier, the worker suspected of production of the grenades, was shot. In October and November, the gallows was set up in the city almost every day to hang workers suspected of conspiracy.

IV

The terror in Warsaw made it difficult for the Poles to control the insurrection, for it required exposing the members of the secret National Government to arrest every day. They had to gather at different places in the city. The necessity for the most active members of the insurgent government to leave Warsaw caused its disorganization. Into this crisis situation stepped the able partisan leader and organizer General Romuald Traugutt, returning to Warsaw from abroad, where he had been sent on a secret mission by the National Government. On October 17, he attended the usual secret meeting of the National Government and, after discussing the current difficulties and expressing his readiness to save the insurrection, announced that from then on the others were free to do as they wished, because this was the end of the National Government and he himself was assuming authority.

Traugutt, skeptical of the armed intervention of the Western European countries in defense of Poland, advocated a fight based entirely on its own forces. He decided to aim at sustaining the insurrection until spring and then switching to general partisan warfare.[15] His suggestions and orders caused a real revival of the vanishing armed movement in the Kingdom of Poland. Concentration of the partisan units (Bosak's and Kruk's) in the southern part of the Kingdom of Poland led to greater effectiveness of partisan operations, although they could have been better prepared and more efficiently executed. Even the little that had been done with regard to partisan raids, however, indicated the continuing strength of the insurgents and troubled the tsarist army considerably. The partisans attacked the divisional and regimental staffs in large garrisons, such as Lublin, Radom, and Kielce, appearing unexpectedly and keeping the tsarist soldiers in constant suspense. This elusive and unexpected enemy, with its surprise attacks, turned out to be more dangerous than the regular troops against which all their training had been directed. The inconspicuous partisan once again terrorized those who had become skeptical of his ability to fight. The meaning of the autumn partisan successes was the greater given tsarist authorities' aim of suppressing the insurrection in 1863.

A new form of national army was to be the basis of operations in the spring. A decree of December 15, 1863, ordered the formation of four insurgent corps from the existing units: one in Lublin and Podlasie provinces, commanded by General Michał Heidenreich-Kruk, a second in Sandomierz and Kraków provinces, commanded by General Józef Hauke-Bosak, a third in Augustów and Grodno provinces, commanded by Colonel Jan Koziełło-Skała, and a fourth in Płock and Mazowsze provinces, with no commander for the moment. In February 1864, the formation of another corps was ordered, to be commanded by Colonel Bolesław Dłuski-Jabłonowski and placed in Lithuania. In this way, Traugutt prepared for a shift from small, independently operating partisan units to a mass, uniformly organized insurgent army that could undertake large military operations and capture larger towns and tsarist garrisons.

The accomplishment of these measures encountered serious difficulties. The majority of the higher commanders made no effort to reorganize the insurgent forces. During the winter, only General Hauke-Bosak managed to form two divisions, with four regiments in each, five thousand partisans in all. One of these divisions was destroyed in February 1864 as a consequence of the inefficiency of the chief of staff of the Second Corps, Colonel Apolinary Kurowski, and of the Kraków division commander, Colonel Ludwik Zwierzdowski-Topór. The same happened to several other units. The rest were unable to wait for the mass effort Traugutt had planned for the spring. After the arrest of Traugutt and his associates on April 11, 1864, the few remaining insurgent troops were left to their own initiative.

The propertied classes' retreat from the insurrection, the lack of funds to buy and import arms and munitions from abroad, the inefficiency of many commanders and organizers, the intensification of the terror, the active operations of the tsarist army, and the tsarist Enfranchisement Act, intended to distract the peasants' attention, all caused the decay of the armed struggle in spring 1864. According to Kieniewicz, "The change in the peasants' attitude, along with the lack of help from outside, put an end to partisan warfare."[16]

V

Both the successes of the January Insurrection and its faults and errors confirmed the correctness of the theory of partisan warfare developed earlier. The military decline of the insurrection had been caused, among other things, by the fact that many insurgent leaders were unable to understand the value of partisan warfare and inconsistent in applying its principles. However, thanks to even the inconsistent use of the methods of partisan warfare, the January Insurrection, waged under the most difficult conditions and with the most unfavorable relationship of forces, was the longest of all the Polish national uprisings and covered the widest range of the society. It hastened the enfranchisement of the peasants in the Kingdom of Poland under the most favorable conditions, opening up broad possibilities for the development of progressive capitalist relations. It tested the possibilities and effectiveness of large partisan operations, partisan railway subversions, the principles of formation and operation of partisan units in woodless and suburban areas, etc. It established principles for the organization of an underground state in an occupied country.

The various methods and forms of the struggle for independence during the insurrection aroused the interest of even so quiet and secure a nation as the Swiss. Von Erlach reported to the Swiss authorities that the Polish methods might well be effective even in Switzerland.[17] The international meaning of the January Insurrection was much broader than this, however. The awakened international solidarity of the European peoples with the fighting Poles created general moral support for the idea of struggle "for your and our freedom," wherever it arose.

The experiences of the January Insurrection added up to quite a legacy for future generations of Poles. They were employed by the partisans of the 1905 revolution and of the Polish national uprisings of 1918–21 in Great Poland and Silesia, when the task was reorganizing the Polish state. The first partisan unit after the lost defensive war in 1939, commanded by Major Henryk Dobrzanski-Hubal, also recalled those experiences, and they were used by the Polish underground and partisan units during the Nazi occupation. Traditions of insurgent operations in Kielce, Lublin, and Podlasie provinces were conducive to the strong development of the partisan movement there during the years of the worst Nazi terror. "The year 1863 is the mine of experiences for us," wrote the organizers of the People's Guard and the People's Army in January 1944. Those experiences were also not forgotten by the Nazi authorities; Himmler enjoined his associates to study the patterns of conspiracy and partisan operations of the January Insurrection attentively in order to be better able to fight against Polish conspirators for independence.[18] It did not, however, help them much.

The repressions of the Nazis were answered by the Polish people with resistance that drew upon the rich experiences of the past, especially of the January Insurrection. Thus Polish society put into practice the principles of partisan warfare as the most effective form of struggle against armed force and violence. This is proof that the Polish nation, among the originators of the theory and practice of partisan warfare, is capable of applying its legacy in this sphere and that this legacy is not merely of historical value.

Notes

1. L. Ratajczyk, "The Evolution of Polish Theory on Partisan Warfare during the First Half of the Nineteenth Century," Béla K. Király, ed., *East Central European Society and War in the Era of Revolutions: 1775–1856* (New York, 1983).
2. F. L. von Erlach, *Partyzantka w Polsce w roku 1863* (Warsaw, 1960), p. 27.
3. *Marks i Engels o Polsce*, vol. 1 (Warsaw, 1960), p. 346.
4. *Dokumenty Komitetu Centralnego Narodowego i Rządu Narodowego 1862–1864* (Wrocław/Warsaw/Cracow, 1968), p. 36.
5. Józef Kowalski, *Rewolucyjna demokracja rosyjska a powstanie styczniowe* (Warsaw, 1955), p. 287.
6. Zbigniew Chądzyński, *Wspomnienia powstańca ż lat 1861–1863* (Warsaw, 1962), p. 83.
7. More detailed examination of the Russian troops' operations is given in my paper "Strategy and Tactics of the Tsarist Army during the January Insurrection," elsewhere in this volume.
8. *Dokumenty Komitetu Centralnego Narodowego*, pp. 41–42.
9. Józef Piłsudski, *Zarys historii militarnej powstania styczniowego* (Warsaw, 1929), p. 53.
10. Stefan Kieniewicz, *Sprawa włościańska w powstaniu styczniowym* (Wrocław, 1953), p. 306.
11. Józef Oxinski, *Wspomnienia z powstania polskiego 1863–1864* (Warsaw, 1965), p. 209.

12. Franciszek Kopernicki, *Pamiętnik z powstania styczniowego* (Warsaw, 1959), p. 39.
13. E. Callier, *Trzy ustępy z powstania polskiego 1863–1864* (Poznań, 1920), p. 97.
14. Library of the Academy of Sciences of the U.S.S.R., L'vov, Dzieduszyccy Collection VIII, "Practical Remarks," Warsaw, 1863, p. 13.
15. A more comprehensive treatment of Traugutt's aims and their realization is given in my book *Polska wojna partyzancka 1863–1864: Okres dyktatury Romualda Traugutta* (Warsaw, 1966), p. 395.
16. S. Kieniewicz, *Powstanie styczniowe* (Warsaw, 1972), p. 720.
17. Von Erlach, *Partyzantka w Polsce,* p. 150.
18. Emanuel Halicz, "Doświadczenia powstania styczniowego w ujęciu naczelnych władz hitlerowskich," *Wojskowy Przegląd Historyczny* 1965, no. 3, pp. 356–68.

The Tactics of the Polish Troops in the 1863–64 Insurrection

Eligiusz Kozłowski

It is difficult to identify any universally acceptable tactical pattern for the 1863–64 Insurrection. A variety of tactical solutions sprang from the lack of uniformity in the insurgent army and the different levels of military knowledge of the commanders and soldiers. Differences in equipment and weapons also had a significant influence on tactics. In the first stages of the insurrection, for example, there was a preponderance of side arms to firearms which forced the commanders to formulate new tactics. The terrain had to be taken into consideration also. In order to get a clearer picture of the tactics of the insurrection as a whole, the techniques used by individual commanders, their training, and the equipment of their regiments should be studied.

I

The insurgent army had at its disposal only infantry and cavalry; artillery units, which existed here and there and were attached to various regiments, played no significant role.[1] The insurgent army also contained medical, supply, and engineers' units.

The infantry units were organized into fusiliers and scythe bearers.[2] The former had at their disposal long military or hunters' firearms originating in Russia, Austria, Prussia, France, Belgium, or England; there were even a few American guns, mainly Colts, repeating guns with an elongated butt.[3] Some regiments were equipped with firearms of several kinds, which made training of the soldiers quite difficult.

The basic infantry unit was the battalion, which consisted of six companies: four of scythe bearers and two of fusiliers.[4] The scythe-bearer companies predominated at the beginning of the insurrection because of the shortage of firearms. When firearms began to flow into the country, the ratio began to change rapidly in favor of the fusiliers, and the scythe-bearer companies were gradually relegated to auxiliary functions. This somewhat derogatory treatment of the latter was criticized by the insurgent authorities because these units often consisted entirely of peasants and were therefore symbols of national unity in the struggle against the foreign oppressor.[5] Some units were equipped with rifles with a range of 1,200 m. The majority of firearms were smoothbore muskets with a maximum range of fewer than 600 m.[6]

An infantry battalion in attack deployed units equipped with firearms in a skirmish line that provided fire protection for the two to four scythe-bearer companies in front and at the flanks. In other words, men equipped with firearms escorted the scythe bearers close enough to charge the enemy while preventing him from firing on them more than once or twice.[7]

The infantry fought against charging cavalry in a rectangle. The scythe-bearer units formed two rows. Men in the first row held their scythes with one end against the ground and the other pointed at the enemy, thus forming a kind of palisade that effectively destroyed the riders and their horses. Men in the second row struck the attacker with their scythes. Units equipped with firearms were deployed in similar fashion, but of course they tried to break the cavalry charge with fire. The first row knelt to fire while the second fired from a standing position. These units were also prepared for hand-to-hand combat.[8]

The insurgent cavalry consisted predominantly of light horsemen equipped with side arms only. There were also mounted fusiliers, dragoons, and even a brigade of mounted national police.[9] The cavalry in general played a secondary role in the insurrection. Because cavalry was very expensive to maintain and required excellent horses and complex training, light cavalry units were small, sometimes only a squadron, and were used mainly for reconnaissance. Light cavalry was also used, however, for diversion and to cover the movements of major infantry units. A much more significant role was played by the heavy cavalry units, organized into squadrons, regiments, and brigades. Their mission was to undertake independent tasks such as charges intended to fend off enemy attacks or pursuits; they could defend their own flanks and attack those of the enemy.[10]

Infantry units were attached to cavalry units as auxiliary troops used to keep conquered areas garrisoned, to clear them of the remnants of enemy forces, or to tie down the enemy forces while the cavalry mounted a flank attack.[11] The cavalry's equipment consisted of pikes, sabers, pistols, and rifles. A cavalry attack was conducted with two lines. The first charged with side arms only; the second fired continuously while the first carried out its task. The grand total of cavalry never exceeded five thousand, and its military value was limited in comparison with the traditional Polish cavalry. Cavalry was more prone to panic than infantry and less disciplined.

The development of the two services was closely interrelated with the nature of the terrain on which they fought. For example, in densely wooded areas such as Lithuania and Belorussia, cavalry units were virtually absent. In contrast, in the Ukraine, where there were no major forests, cavalry predominated.[12] The activities of General B. Różycki's cavalry regiment are a case in point. The few infantry units in Różycki's group were transported in wagons so that they could keep up with the cavalry and cooperate with them. In the Kingdom of Poland, the cavalry had more important tasks to fulfill than in Lithuania or Belorussia, although its role was subordinate to that of the infantry.

A definite contrast existed between the Polish moderation vis-à-vis the enemy and the Russian lack of scruples. The Russians often resorted to the cruelest methods in an attempt to stamp out the insurrection. They burned villages whose inhabitants had aided the insurgents, executed anyone found carrying arms, killed the wounded, murdered prisoners, and employed torture and repression. They sought to destroy the morale of the army and the nation. The Poles avoided battles in densely populated areas so as not to expose the inhabitants to reprisals.[13]

II

The varied origins and degrees of training of the Polish officers were reflected in the effectiveness of their leadership and the tactics they employed. The officers corps consisted of former officers of the November Insurrection, the participants in the campaigns of 1848–49, Crimean War veterans, graduates of French, Russian, Austrian, Prussian, and even American schools (L. Zychliński), graduates of the Polish military school in Italy, and, finally, officers who were acquainted with military rules and regulations but had had no practical experience or proper training.[14] The majority of Polish officers who had served in foreign armies and those who had graduated from Polish military schools were trained to command platoons, companies, or, at best, battalions. Lacking higher military education, they were unable to act as commanders of larger and more complex army units.[15] Despite this, the insurrection produced several prominent military leaders endowed with natural talent, such as D. Czachowski, W. Wróblewski, and, among the professional officers, K. Kalita and Z. Chmieleński. They were able to rid themselves of the routines characteristic of the regular army and adjust to the conditions of insurrectionary combat.

The general doctrines of the insurrection were worked out by L. Mierosławski on the basis of his theory of conventional warfare. Mierosławski's opus, entitled *Insurrection*, was published in 1862. It was a true encyclopedia, including everything an insurgent leader had to know. K. Kukiel wrote of Mierosławski's work, "The war is presented here as a series of rules for all possible circumstances—real or irrational, true or false. And these rules or concepts were followed as closely as possible in the military activities of the insurrection; they were virtually learned by heart."[16] The tactical principles devised by Mierosławski for the initial phase of the struggle were extraordinarily simple. The first task was to conquer the towns controlled by enemy garrisons with the help of the local people, commanded by local leaders. Simultaneously, there was to be general conscription in territories free from enemy occupation and recruitment of volunteers in conquered towns or in areas which had natural defenses, where proper military training was to be started.[17] The tactics of Mierosławski advised aggressive action in the first phase, defense in the second. He emphasized the need for fortified camps. To neutralize the considerable effect of enemy fire, he proposed the use of "scythe-carts" (army vehicles propelled by the scythe bearers hiding in them) and rucksacks as protection. In fact, however, neither Mierosławski's tactical assumptions nor his inventions produced the desired effects. Some areas were indeed cleared of the enemy; in others, the military camps set up were destroyed by Russian counterattacks. The camps of A. Kurowski in Kraków province, M. Langiewicz in Sandomierz province, Z. Padlewski in the Płock area, and J. Matliński and Wl. Jablonowski in Podlasie are examples.

III

In the beginning, Polish military operations attained a certain success. The Russians were obliged to concentrate their forces by reducing their 180 garrisons to 42. However, the January Night exhausted the strength of the insurgents, and it was followed not by concentration and renewed activity, but by inertia.[18]

One failure was the attack on the town of Płock, where four hundred Russian soldiers were garrisoned. The Polish forces amounted to nearly a thousand men. The numerical superiority of the Poles was somewhat balanced by the Russians' superior armaments. The Poles were grouped in seven columns; one of them, operating inside the town, was to give the signal for the general attack by raiding the various posts of the enemy. The concept was excellent, but the execution left much to be desired. For lack of caution, many of the insurgents inside the town were arrested, and this frightened the townspeople. In spite of this, the Poles launched an attack with the six columns that remained outside. The advance of the columns lacked coordination, and several failed to reach their destinations on time;

consequently, the attack broke down. The Płock failure was due to the Polish leadership's lack of organizational and tactical skills.[19]

Not all the Polish operations were failures, however. For example, during the January Night a small Polish unit commanded by Figgetti carried out a successful raid in Jedlnia, in Sandomierz province, on an enemy engineers' company of two hundred eighty men garrisoned there. The attacking insurgents took advantage of the dark rainy night and managed to take the enemy completely by surprise. The main roads to the village were blocked, and the Russian command was liquidated. Subsequently, in complete silence the individual buildings which housed the unsuspecting enemy soldiers were taken one by one.[20]

Following the January 23 attacks, Polish local commanders took the initiative, with various results. Apolinary Kurowski, having been accidentally elevated to the position of military chief of Kraków province, organized the insurrectionary forces and planned their operations. At the beginning of February he commanded two thousand men. In a few minor skirmishes he cleared the enemy from the so-called frontier triangle, where the three parts of partitioned Poland met. After February 7 he gave up operational command and concentrated on organization and education. When his fortified camp at Ojców was threatened by the enemy, he decided to abandon it, but he persisted in the idea of striking at another important enemy stronghold, Miechów. The idea was a good one, but Kurowski was unable to work out a suitable tactic to realize it. One of the major mistakes was the lack of coordination between individual regiments. Furthermore, the troop movements were insufficiently covered, and the leadership broke down in battle. Kurowski lacked experience; he could not see the whole picture. His tactics were utterly primitive; for example, he directed a cavalry charge through the narrow streets of the town. The battle ended with a complete defeat of the Polish regiment on February 17, 1863. The same mistakes were repeated by Kurowski on February 21, 1864, at Opatów.[21]

Marian Langiewicz, Kurowski's neighbor in Sandomierz province, had been a professional officer in the Prussian artillery. After unsuccessful attacks on Bodzentyn and Szydłowiec, he tried to establish a fortified camp in Wąchock but, threatened by the enemy, instead began a several weeks' long mobile campaign that ended in defeat in the battle of Grochowiska. It is surprising that Langiewicz did not establish any cooperation with Kurowski before the collapse of the latter's unit. When Kurowski was overwhelmed by Russian troops, Langiewicz limited himself to minor attacks at Świętokrzyskie and Staszów[22] instead of throwing all his troops into the battle. Between the battle of

Małogoszcz on February 23 and the battle of Grochowiska on March 18, there were minor clashes at Pieskowa Skała, Skała, and Chrobrze, but the whole campaign was basically retreat and defense. Langiewicz excelled in maneuvers that prevented the enemy from surrounding him.[23] While he managed to save his troops after the defeat of Małagoszcz, the consecutive battles of Chrobrze and Grochowiska on March 17 and 18 caused a complete disintegration of his forces, and the provinces were lost.[24]

Another example of the disastrous effects of Polish inexperience is the case of Matliński's and Jabłonowski's camp in Podlasie, near Węgrów. At the beginning of February thirty-five hundred men were concentrated there, devoting their time to training and organization. The enemy's movements were not even being watched, and therefore the sudden arrival of enemy troops in the vicinity of Węgrów came as a surprise. Even the decision to defend Węgrów was a mistake, because the town, situated in a valley, was difficult to defend and no plans had been made for it. The battle of Węgrów was fought on February 3, after an encounter at Mokobody on February 2 in which an opportunity to defeat at least part of the Russian troops was wasted. If the Węgrów battle did not end in defeat, it was only because the Russians did not press their advantage and the young Polish soldiers, including the scythe bearers, put up fierce resistance that allowed the insurgents to retreat eastward in an orderly fashion. Ultimately, at Siemiatycze, on February 7, the Poles were dispersed.[25]

The experiences of these three large units show that, except for Langiewicz, the Polish leaders lacked tactical skill. They dreamt of conventional warfare, speculated about operational plans, and toyed with great strategies but were unable to carry out simple tactical tasks.[26] There were, however, individual commanders who instead of speculating about an attack on Warsaw or the Dniepr line strove to achieve tactical successes. They harassed the enemy materially and morally and at the same time built up the morale of their troops and of the nation as a whole. Perhaps they thought that the sum total of tactical victories would lead to strategic successes and create the foundations for warfare according to the principles prevailing at the time. This way of thinking was not necessarily a sure way to victory, for one might win battles and still lose the war.

IV

After the enemy had succeeded in defeating the three major and many minor Polish insurgent units, the insurrection switched to a defensive strategy reflecting the policies and hopes of the Whites, who wanted to maintain a show of force until the expected intervention of the Western Great Powers should materialize. Operations consisted of marches and countermarches, retreats and avoidance of combat. Very few encounters of this period bear the marks of a well-thought-out operation. This defensive posture was condemned in a government decree dated May 4, 1863, announcing a change to the offensive. However, the small insurgent detachments, deep in the woods, were out of touch with the central leadership and even with their closest neighbors and not infrequently were looking for "contacts" with the more active enemy.[27] Thus there were no offensive operations until the Traugutt dictatorship was established. As J. Piłsudski wrote, "the insurrection turned into a demonstration of power whose history is very interesting but which cannot really be referred to as war."[28] Yet the period had its advantages for the Polish cause. The operations helped nurture a number of first-class insurgent leaders capable of directing defensive combat, organizing retreats, and taking advantage of the possibilities of the terrain and of the enemy's mistakes. Even if the detachment of such a commander was defeated or dispersed, it returned to the battlefield in time, strengthened by reinforcements and ready to continue the struggle till the very end.

One of these emerging insurgent leaders was Dionizy Czachowski. For many weeks in the spring of 1863 he sparked the insurrection in Sandomierz and Kraków provinces. Constantly pursued by the enemy, he wandered from forest to forest, fought defensive battles, organized spectacular retreats, and often jumped at the enemy's throat singlehanded. With no professional training whatsoever, he displayed an extraordinary military genius. He had an excellent knowledge of the terrain, which allowed him to organize ambushes (at Stefanków on April 22, at Jeziorko on May 5, and at Białobrzegi on May 29). He also conducted successful battles in general retreat (at Rzeczniów on May 6, at Bobrza on June 10).[29] Whenever possible, he avoided battles in the open; if he had to fight one, he tried to be within easy reach of the nearest forest in case retreat should be necessary. Czachowski understood the importance of the reserve, which he would throw into the battle at its height, usually resorting to the use of side arms. The main role in Czachowski's military operations was assigned to the infantry, which had good tactical training and was characterized by the effective use of firearms. Czachowski was a master of quick marches across the back country he alone knew. In this way he led his pursuers astray and turned up where they least expected him.[30]

Ambushes were typical of insurgent warfare and often brought considerable gains. Another successful ambush was the battle of Żyrzyn on August 8, 1863, in which the Polish troops were commanded by General

Michał Heidenreich-Kruk.[31] In the majority of cases these ambushes were launched in or from wooded areas. The insurgent commanders would hide their reserves, often scythe bearers, in the woods, to emerge at a suitable moment to decide the outcome of the struggle.

A similarly renowned partisan commander was Zygmunt Chmieleński, a former officer in the Russian army who operated for several months in Sandomierz and Kraków provinces. Chmieleński effectively used varied tactics, among them rear defenses at crucial points. This was the case, among others, in the battles of Cierno and Mełchów. The battle of Cierno lasted for three days, during which Chmieleński's infantry displayed not only good training, but also perseverance in facing enemy fire and in mounting repeated cavalry charges on all four sides of the rectangle. The front moved through Wazyn in the direction of Czarnca. At Czarnca the enemy attacked him again and, after a brief exchange of fire, Chmieleński, aware of his troops' exhaustion and shortage of ammunition, ordered them to retreat to a safe place while he himself, with only eighty horsemen, confronted the advancing enemy and saved his main force, the infantry.[32] The battle of Mełchów was similarly fierce. Here the Poles launched counterattacks with side arms alone. This battle was a typical active defense. By employing such tactics as skillful deployment of troops and the use of reserves for counterattacks, they managed to retain the initiative throughout the battle; their leadership was effective and communication service worked well. The constant engagement of his troops and the continuing enemy pressure obliged Chmieleński to divide his forces into several smaller groups. After a few days the small units reunited at an appointed place. This served to confuse the enemy and make it difficult to track the individual insurgent groups.[33]

In the autumn of 1863 General Józef Hauke-Bosak's cavalry launched two successful raids. The first took place at the end of November. Hauke-Bosak's cavalry was deployed on the bank of the Krepianka, near Baltów, to create a protective cordon for the infantry there. Yet, when Hauke-Bosak learned that most of the enemy forces had left Opatów with the intention of "pacifying" the area, he executed a cavalry charge on the enemy at Opatów on November 25. Successfully completing the attack, the Polish cavalry moved west, still providing protective cover for the infantry. The enemy, surprised by the attack on Opatów, turned its attention to that town and undertook no action against the main Polish forces. Hauke-Bosak's raid safeguarded the redeployment of the Polish forces,[34] a typical function of the cavalry.

Another cavalry raid of three hundred fifty horsemen took place at the beginning of December. Its objective, apart from misleading the enemy, was to protect the infantry in its new position and to initiate insurgent activities in Kraków province. This cavalry squadron fought many minor skirmishes in various places, sometimes quite far apart. These operations gave the enemy the impression that the insurgent activities were being revived in all those places. To counter these insurgent activities the enemy carried out various operations, often in vain. At last the Russians confronted the Polish cavalry at Bodzechów on December 16 and defeated it. Despite the defeat, however, the mission of the squadron was realized: insurgent activities in both Kraków and Sandomierz provinces were revived. The enemy became confused because it was assumed that the uprising had died out in those areas.[35]

Elsewhere, successful defensive battles were fought by Polish insurgent troops. Between May 1 and May 5, General Antoni Jeziorański entered the Kingdom of Poland from Galicia with a regiment and fought two defensive battles in the Kobylanka forest near the border between Lublin province and Galicia. One may question Jeziorański's wisdom in taking up defense instead of trying to break through to the Kingdom, in view of the considerable military force he commanded, but he justified his decision in terms of the shortage of ammunition. Expecting the arrival of supplies at any moment, he entrenched himself in the forest marshes and fought off two attacks by a considerably larger Russian force. The Russians suffered heavy losses. Jeziorański's engineers excelled not only in preparing field fortifications, but also by fighting bravely in the battle.[36]

Another example of excellent preparation of defense positions was the three-day battle of Józef Trąmpczyński's regiment on June 27–29, 1863, at Drazdzewo, in Płock province, at Płaska Góra on the River Orzyc. Trąmpczyński, who had at his disposal a mere 240 men, including 100 riflemen, resisted enemy attack for three consecutive days despite fierce fighting. He constantly improved the field entrenchments and collected sufficient food and ammunition reserves. He selected a small unit and launched it as a diversion behind the ring of enemy troops which surrounded the Polish positions. The enemy outnumbered the Poles and had strong artillery. However, the artillery fire caused but little damage because of the well-built entrenchments, which were repaired and strengthened the minute the fire had stopped. Nor did the heavy all-night artillery attack on June 28–29 have any effect. The Russian commander, discouraged by his lack of success, launched his infantry across the marshes and bogs of the Orzyc to attack the Polish troops with side arms. Trąmpczyński discovered this stratagem in the nick of time, allowed the Russians to come close, and then smothered them with fire, forcing them to retreat with heavy losses.[37]

Another commander, Karol Krysiński, fighting in Podlasie, also displayed great tactical skill. His ability and the good tactical training of his soldiers were recognized by the Swiss colonel Franz von Erlach, who spent some time with Krysiński's regiment. At the beginning of November the regiment, nearly a thousand strong, was stationed in the southern part of Podlasie province. When the enemy discovered its position and tried to destroy it, Krysiński joined battle and forced the enemy to retreat on November 17. A day later, at the village of Kolano, W. Wróblewski's cavalry lured the enemy into ambush. The Polish infantry came out of hiding and nearly threw the enemy back, causing heavy losses. Wróblewski's cavalry, with its constant raids, diverted the enemy from the main Polish forces.[38]

The Polish leadership gained experience in battle and matured over time. The increasing skill of the leadership was demonstrated in the battle of Lubienie-Iłża on January 7, 1864. Here a regiment of the Sandomierz division under Kalita, which belonged to Hauke-Bosak's Second Corps, faced the enemy. The first phase of the battle took place in the Iłża forest in the vicinity of the village of Lubienie. The Poles prepared their position exceptionally scrupulously. They blocked all the roads in the vicinity and prepared a strong defensive position at the village. Two companies were left in the rear. As the enemy advanced along the road from Iłża, the Polish advance guard commenced the attack. Simultaneously Kalita launched his reserves at the enemy, forcing it to retreat, suffering great losses, from the crossfire of the two Polish units. The Poles pursued the enemy in the direction of Iłża. The enemy took up positions to the west of Iłża with the intention of counterattacking against the Poles' left flank. Kalita recognized the enemy's intentions and countered them, dispersing the Russians and forcing them to retreat.[39]

V

Polish tactics evolved and matured during the course of the insurrection, but this development was neither uniform nor simultaneous throughout the insurrectionary forces. The character of these tactics changed in every phase of the war.

In the first phase, the Poles fought offensive-defensive warfare. Several commanders recognized that a transition from insurgent activities to regular warfare was necessary, but such a transition was made difficult by the lack of a trained officers corps, the scarcity of arms, ammunitions, and other supplies, and the lack of a general framework of the organization of a regular army. There were no high-ranking officers qualified to organize a nationwide large-scale insurrection. No adequate plans had been drafted. None of those who were candidates for superior positions fulfilled the hopes of the insurgents that they would do the job properly.[40] The establishment of the general headquarters in the forests was also a mistake; it ought to have been established in Warsaw. Another obstacle to systematic operations was the individuality and independence of several insurgent leaders—a phenomenon not infrequent in revolutionary situations. Some of these commanders were reluctant to participate in a well-coordinated operation in which they might lose their individuality and freedom of action. Others were unwilling to participate in military operations that would provoke the Russians prior to the expected intervention of the Western Great Powers. The war at that stage was being fought not for victory but as a political demonstration,[41] and consequently battles planned in advance and conducted with determination to win were extremely rare. Even in the case of Jeziorański, who fought two successful defensive battles, his solely defensive mentality caused his ultimate defeat.

It was in December 1863 that the dictator Romuald Traugutt finally tried to introduce some fundamental changes in the organization of the army and its tactics and strategy. These changes included, among other things, the introduction of a uniform organizational pattern for the Polish army, with corps, divisions, and regiments. In addition, Traugutt banned the common practice of individuals' dismissing army units at will, thus putting an end to the prevailing system of "ownership" of insurgent units. He introduced an army command hierarchy and tried to solve the problems of soldiers' pay and uniforms.[42]

Traugutt also changed the tactics. He demanded greater aggressiveness of insurgent troops:

> Our troops have not attacked towns and villages even though in many of them the enemy troops were fewer than half a company. It is therefore advisable, after prior studies of the plans of these towns and the concentration of a few military units, to attack such towns if possible with the help of the inhabitants in order to disperse the Russian troops stationed there. In this way, we shall force Moscow to gather only in certain places, and consequently the movements of our own troops and the activity of civil defense will be much easier.[43]

These tactics were obviously a return to the original plans initiated by Mierosławski and later taken up, unfortunately without success, by Kurowski, Katliński, Langiewicz, and other commanders.[44] Despite the fact that Traugutt's efforts steered the uprising in the right direction, it was beginning to falter, and even Hauke-Bosak, the most outstanding of the Polish military leaders, could not manage to change its course.

Traugutt's last and most important achievement was the preparation in the spring of 1864 of the levy en masse. Up to this point the insurgents had included only two social groups, the middle and lesser nobility and the bourgeoisie and intelligentsia; the many millions of peasants were still excluded. The levy was intended to bring them into the insurrection. By the spring of 1864, however, the insurrection had already died out.[45]

Notes

1. J. Wyspianski, "1863 Artillerymen and Their Weapons" (in Polish), *Artillery Review* 13 (1935).
2. E. Kozłowski, *The Infantry in the 1863–64 Insurrection (Outline of Its Organization)* (in Polish), Studia i Materiały do Historii Wojskowośc, vol. 9, pt. 2 (Warsaw, 1963).
3. J. Podoski, "The Use of Side Arms in National Uprisings" (in Polish), in *Arms and Colors 1936: January Insurrection Exhibits in the Museum of the Polish Army,* vol. 3 (Warsaw, 1966).
4. Kozłowski, *Infantry,* pp. 263–66; idem, "The Polish Army in the Years 1832–64" (in Polish), in *An Outline of the History of the Polish Army up to the Year 1864,* vol. 2 (Warsaw, 1966), p. 488; St. Ploski, "The Tactics of Polish Insurgent Units" (in Polish), *Przegląd Historyczny* 34 (1937–38). During this period also appeared a number of infantry regulations manuals, published either abroad or in Poland by the National Government and differing mainly in their general layout.
5. Kozłowski, *Infantry,* p. 261; St. Ploski, "History of the Polish Infantry during the National Uprisings 1794–1863" (in Polish), in *The Book of Glory (Infantry)* (Warsaw, 1937); A. Sujkowski, "Emigration and the January Insurrection" (in Polish), in *Studies in the History of the Infantry, Commemorative Book 1830–1930* (Ostrów-Komorowo, 1930).
6. Kozłowski, *Infantry,* p. 260.
7. Ploski, "Tactics," pp. 493–94.
8. E. Kozłowski, *The Polish Military System in the Years 1832–1864* (in Polish) (Warsaw, 1966), pp. 490–92.
9. Small Cossack units—clothed in Cossack uniform and sometimes including authentic Cossack refugees from the Russian army—were attached to some regiments.
10. J. Grobicki, "Insurgent Cavalry in 1863" (in Polish), *Cavalry Review* 3 (1926); Ploski, "Tactics," p. 495. There also appeared, both in Poland and abroad, at least seven cavalry regulations manuals.
11. Ploski, "Tactics," p. 498; Kozłowski, *Polish Military System,* p. 494.
12. Kozłowski, *Polish Military System,* p. 494.
13. J. Piłsudski, *Zarys historii militarnej powstania styczniowego* (Warsaw, 1929); idem, *Pisma zbiorowe,* vol. 3 (Warsaw, 1937), pp. 131–32.

14. Br. Deskur, "From the Diary for My Grandsons" (in Polish), in *Materials for the History of the 1863–64 Insurrection* (L'vov, 1890), p. 148.
15. E. Kozłowski, *History of the Polish Army* (in Polish), vol. 2 (Warsaw, 1963), p. 262.
16. M. Kukiel, "Military Problems of the January Uprising," *Historical Files* (London) 3 (1963):99.
17. In this plan one may see a reflection of Mierosławski's operational tactics of 1846; see M. Kukiel, "The Conceptions of a National Insurrection before the 'Spring of Nations,'" *Historical Files* 2 (1948).
18. E. Kozłowski, "The January Insurrection 1863–64: Its Military Aspects, Experiences, and Lessons" (in Polish), *Military Thoughts* 1966, no. 1, pp. 74–75.
19. Ibid., pp. 78–79.
20. Ibid., p. 78.
21. E. Kozłowski, "From Węgrów to Opatów, February 3, 1863—February 21, 1864" (in Polish), in *Selected Battles of the January Insurrection* (Warsaw, 1962).
22. Kozłowski, "January Insurrection," p. 80.
23. Kukiel, "Military Problems," p. 105.
24. Kozłowski, "January Insurrection," p. 80.
25. Kozłowski, "From Węgrów to Opatów."
26. Great hopes were attached to the unit of General E. Taczanowski, in the western part of the Kingdom, as late as May 1863 (because of its victory in the battle of Pyzdry on April 29), but these hopes were dashed by its defeat at Ignacewo on May 8 (Kukiel, "Military Problems," p. 108).
27. Kozłowski, "January Insurrection," pp. 79, 87; Kukiel, "Military Problems," p. 109.
28. Piłsudski, *Zarys historii militarnej*, p. 129.
29. Ploski, "Tactics," p. 501.
30. Kozłowski, "From Węgrów to Opatów."
31. St. Długosz, *Czachowski* (Poznań, 1914); Piłsudski, *Zarys historii militarnej*, p. 135.
32. St. Zieliński, *Battles and Clashes 1863–64* (in Polish) (Rapperswil, 1913), pp. 179–80.
33. Zieliński, *Battles*, pp. 180–82.
34. E. Kozłowski, *General Józef Hauke-Bosak, 1834–1871* (Warsaw, 1973), p. 117; L. Ratajczyk, *Polska wojna partyzancka 1863–64: Okres dyktatury Romualda Traugutta* (Warsaw, 1966), p. 147.
35. Kozłowski, *Hauke-Bosak*, p. 23; Ratajczyk, *Polska wojna partyzancka*, p. 148.
36. Kozłowski, "From Węgrów to Opatów"; Piłsudski, *Zarys historii militarnej*, p. 135.
37. Piłsudski, *Zarys historii militarnej*, p. 135; Zieliński, *Battles*, pp. 237–38.
38. Ratajczyk, *Polska wojna partyzancka*, p. 170.
39. Kozłowski, "From Węgrów to Opatów"; Ratajczyk, *Polska wojna partyzancka*, p. 266.

40. Kozłowski, "January Insurrection," pp. 69–70; Piłsudski, *Zarys historii militarnej,* pp. 102, 138.
41. Piłsudski, *Zarys historii militarnej,* pp. 131, 136.
42. Kozłowski, *Hauke-Bosak,* p. 141; Ratajczyk, *Polska wojna partyzancka,* p. 247.
43. Ratajczyk, *Polska wojna partyzancka,* p. 105.
44. Kukiel, "Military Problems," p. 109; Piłsudski, *Zarys historii militarnej,* pp. 138–39.
45. Kozłowski, *Hauke-Bosak,* p. 146.

The Strategy and Tactics of the Tsarist Army during the January Insurrection

Leonard Ratajczyk

The strategy and tactics of the Russian army in the Kingdom of Poland in 1863–64 have so far been the subject of only a few limited critical analyses. The condition of the Russian army at the outbreak of the insurrection and the development of its strategy and tactics through 1863 were examined, quite one-sidedly and tendentiously, by the nineteenth-century Russian historian S. Gesket.[1] Later these matters were touched upon to some extent in lectures delivered by Józef Piłsudski, cofounder of the Polish Legions, in Cracow in 1912 and published in 1929.[2] Since the Second World War, Soviet historians have focused their attention mainly on the reorganization of the tsarist army[3] and upon the revolutionary movement within the army that cooperated with the insurrection.[4]

My own research on the methods employed by the Russian army during the January Insurrection was published, under the title "O metodach działania armii carskiej w powstaniu styczniowym," in the *Military Political Academy Bulletin* in 1959. This article is an updated and expanded version of that work.

Two basic periods in the Russians' development of methods of fighting against the insurgent troops can be distinguished. The first extends from the outbreak of the insurrection to the fall of 1863 and the second covers the period between then and the spring of 1864.

I

The January Insurrection found the Russian army in the middle of thorough army reforms. The experiences of the Crimean War had caused the tsar to reorganize the force which had secured for him domination over much of Asia and part of Europe.[5] The reforms initiated in 1862 included armament, organization, recruitment, the command of troops, training, and schooling. The creation of the first military districts was of practical significance for the preparations for the insurrection in the Kingdom of Poland. These districts were set up, in response to the revolutionary atmosphere in the Polish territory, in the summer of 1862. There were three of them at first: Warsaw, Vilna, and Kiev. By the end of 1862, Odessa had been added.[6] All the troops of a given military district fell under a military district commander. The governor-general was the commander of the frontier districts and possessed both military and civil authority. Because the governor of the Kingdom of Poland was the tsar's brother, Duke Constantine, this last change was not introduced there until his retirement in September 1863. The division was the largest tactical unit in the military district and usually drew from an area of one or more guberniyas.

The creation of the military districts was dictated not only by military needs, but also by political ones. Their task was to decentralize military leadership, to create the possibility of a better system of conscription and building up of the army in the event of war, and, also very important, to fight efficiently against the revolutionary movement in the Kingdom of Poland. The military district commanders were obliged to cooperate with the civilian authorities in cases in which the participation of the army was needed to preserve law and order.[7] They were thus permitted great freedom of action in the case of revolution or insurrection.

General aide-de-camp Ramsay was in command of the Warsaw Military District's troops from the end of 1862 to March 17, 1863. At the end of 1862 there were more than ninety thousand Russian soldiers, of whom about twenty-five thousand were based in Warsaw. In the district there were five infantry divisions, one cavalry division, ten Cossack regiments, six artillery brigades, one sapper engineers' brigade, and a number of separate units. The Third Infantry Division was in Warsaw, the Fourth Division in the western part of Warsaw guberniya, the Fifth Division in Lublin guberniya, the Sixth Division in Płock and Augustów guberniyas, and the Seventh Division in Radom and Płock guberniyas.[8] The Second Cavalry Division (six regiments), the Cossack regiments, and the artillery (152 infantry cannon and 24 cavalry cannon) were scattered all over the Kingdom of Poland. An infantry division consisted of four regiments, three battalions in each. A battalion consisted of four companies and a rifle company. Company strength was 200 men; a battalion had 1,000–1,100, a regiment 3,300–3,700. A cavalry regiment had 730–750 men, divided into four squadrons.[9]

The state of upheaval in the Kingdom of Poland in 1862 made the Warsaw authorities scatter their troops and thicken the network of garrisons. The presence of troops was also necessitated by the conscription system called *branka* (the forced taking of recruits from their homes according to previously drawn-up police lists).[10] For this reason the tsar's troops held more than 160 points at the outbreak of the insurrection.[11] The strongest garrisons, except for the one in Warsaw, were placed in the guberniyas' capitals and in the fortresses of Modlin, Dęblin, and Zamość. The thick network of Russian garrisons made the concentration and effective operation of the few small insurgent units very difficult.

However, the outbreak of the insurrection on January 22–23 was not what had been expected and threw the Russian troops into confusion. Warsaw Military District headquarters was cut off from its army by broken telegraph lines. Having received exaggerated information about assaults on garrisons, it had to take serious precautions in order to protect its troops and government offices. General Ramsay's Order no. 8 of January 23 dealt with immediate troop concentration and the creation of combat-ready independent detachments consisting of infantry, cavalry, and artillery.[12]

The military district had been divided into war departments, the chiefs of which were mostly commanders of divisions. Nine such departments had been created:[13] (1) Płock, with the Seventh Division units, including six administrative districts of Płock guberniya; (2) Lublin, with the Fifth Division units, including the area of Lublin guberniya; (3) Radom (with the headquarters of the Seventh Division and the majority of its units), including the area of Radom guberniya; (4) Kalisz, with the Fourth Division units, including the Kalisz, Konin, Łęczyca, and Sieradz administrative districts of Warsaw guberniya; (5) Warsaw, including Warsaw and the Warsaw and Stanisławów administrative districts; (6) Augustów, including the area of Augustów guberniya; (7) Warszawsko-Wiedeńska Railway, including the Wieluń, Piotrków, Łowicz, and Rawa administrative districts of Warsaw guberniya; (8) Warszawsko-Bydgoska Railway, including the Włocławek and Gostynin administrative districts of Warsaw guberniya; and (9) Warszawsko-Petersburska Railway, including the Warszawa-Łapy section.

As is apparent, the reorganization had been designed to decentralize command, which was of great importance in fighting against insurgent troops. It was also designed to concentrate the forces in order to protect the local authorities and lines of communication. The troops were gathered in about forty garrisons.[14] The strongest troop concentration was in Radom guberniya and the weakest in the western part of Warsaw guberniya. This would have been the best moment for action on the part of the insurgent troops, since it is during concentration that an army is least ready for combat. The insurgent troops did not take advantage of this fact, however, and the whole operation was carried out without difficulty.

On learning of the outbreak of the insurrection, the Ministry of War in St. Petersburg ordered recruitment for the units stationed in the Kingdom of Poland. All soldiers on leave were ordered back.[15] At the beginning of February, Russian troops held some reconnaissance missions. Reconnaissance units consisted of two or three infantry companies, cavalry, Cossacks, and occasionally a few cannon. The first contact with the insurgent troops brought the Russian army success. The majority of the units formed at the very beginning of the insurrection were defeated or dispersed by constant pursuit. It appeared to the tsar's army that the enemy was not as dangerous as it had at first seemed. In spite of this confidence in its advantage, the number of troops in Warsaw Military District was increased very quickly. According to the fighting-strength report of April 13, 1863, the Russian field army consisted of 92,591 soldiers, with 10,405 more in fortresses[16] and 2,336 in auxiliary units, a total of 105,332.[17] By the end of July this number had increased to 141,000[18] and by autumn to 170,000.[19] Simultaneously, the number of garrisons increased. The generally accepted estimate of the insurgent troops at the peak of the fighting, 30,000, seems inconsequential in comparison with these figures. For all their advantage, however, the Russians were for some time unable to put down the insurrection, and it was partisan warfare that was responsible for this. Not even their greatest efforts were sufficient to defeat the many small insurgent units.

At the beginning of the January Insurrection, the three main forms of combat action were search, clash, and close combat.[20] According to Gesket, the importance of search was twofold. It aimed, first, at close combat with the insurgent troops; furthermore, by "soothing the high feelings of the people," it indirectly counteracted the insurgents' propaganda. The success of the operation depended on cavalry reconnaissance and, more important, on the attitude of the people. Their help was highly valued by the Russian commanders and sought in many ways. Wooded areas and the limited number of cavalry units made reconnaissance difficult. In many cases, therefore, the Russians had to depend on natives' reports, and the peasants often deceived them and informed the insurgents.[21] Gesket claims that the concentration of the tsar's troops at the beginning of the insurrection unfavorably affected the search missions. He says that wherever vast areas were not under surveillance the troops had to cover long distances, often without result. Long marches made people tired and weakened their combat readiness. Again, the longer a search mission, the harder it was to carry out.

At the same time, to make the creation of new units difficult for the insurgents, search missions had to be carried out as often as possible. These missions, however, were often limited, and not only because of the troop concentrations. The Russian detachments stationed in district towns had the task of protecting the local authorities, escorting transport, and so forth. It was also necessary to leave some of the units intact. Therefore expeditionary detachments were sent out only from the largest garrisons, and this meant that it was impossible to develop sufficient advantage throughout the country for a successful struggle against the insurgents. The soldiers grew tired of continual night and day missions, and despite their efforts the majority of these missions did not lead to the smallest battle.

Clashes and close combat should have been organized in such a way as to surround the insurgent units and prevent their retreat. To achieve this it was necessary either to send in troops from different points so as to limit the enemy's ability to maneuver or to encircle at least one insurgent unit. The first method failed in the beginning because of the small number of garrisons. In general, the average clash went as follows: The Cossacks or dragoons would start the battle with close fire, and if they met with strong resistance from the insurgents they would retreat. With the arrival of the infantry the assault would be renewed. At dusk they would usually cease fire and go to the nearest village to sleep. This avoidance of inconvenience by the Russian commanders, partly explained by the danger of night combat or search missions in the woods, helped the insurgents and covered their retreat in some hard battles.[22] When the insurgents held a city or a village, after a few unsuccessful attacks the Russians would burn it down. By August 1863 in the Radom guberniya area, eight cities had been destroyed—Miechów, Wąchock, Małogoszcz, Bodzentyn, Suchednów, Janów, Ostrowiec, and part of Staszów.[23] As a result of military operations during the whole insurrection, eighty-five villages and sixteen cities out of four hundred fifty-three were destroyed.

In general, the tsarist army operations were characterized by ruthlessness. The only way of changing this was equal ruthlessness on the part of the insurgents. After the insurgent commander Colonel Dionizy Czachowski informed the Russian authorities that he would kill Russian prisoners in response to their killing Polish ones, only legal sentences were carried out in Sandomierz province. The insurgent National Government's efforts to have the insurgents acknowledged as belligerents, which would have affected the status of prisoners, had been rejected by the Russians. Under these circumstances, the insurgent troops were treated as gangs and captured insurgents as criminals.

The protection of garrisons against insurgent operations was the chief means of providing security for the Russian army. There were infantry companies and a number of Cossacks in each garrison. Communication was by dispatch rider. The duties of the military district commanders-in-chief were usually performed by commanders of regiments and battalions. Troops protected the military installation in the area of a garrison. The whole village was surrounded by pickets whose task it was to control movements into the settlement and alert the garrison. Apart from that, mounted patrols were sent out from time to time in all directions on so-called forays. The headquarters of the Russian units were even better protected; for example, Radom was surrounded night and day by troops.[24]

II

Despite the Russians' increasing advantage, by autumn insurgent armed resistance had not yet been suppressed. The possibility of armed interference in Europe made it impossible for the Russians to let the war in the Kingdom of Poland continue. To suppress the insurrection more quickly it was necessary to increase the efficiency of fighting, making it similar to General N. N. Muravev's policy in Lithuania. At the end of August, Emperor Alexander II informed his brother Grand Duke Constantine, the governor of the Kingdom of Poland, that suppressing the insurrection and restoring order in the Kingdom would require the ruthless dictatorship of the army.[25] Constantine left Warsaw in September, and Lieutenant General Count Fedor Berg was appointed in his place as governor and commander of the Warsaw Military District troops. Thus military and civil power were gathered in the hands of an old general and typical tsarist soldier. Berg immediately asked for military support. He pointed out that in order to suppress the insurrection it would be necessary for the army to "overrun the country."[26] Berg's request was granted, and the Eighth and Tenth Infantry Divisions and the dragoon brigade of the Third Cavalry Division were transferred to the Kingdom of Poland.[27] This was possible because of the suppression of the uprising in Russia and the developing insurrection in Lithuania.

The Russian authorities' activity was twofold. First, they tried to extort allegiance from the people and keep them from joining in the fighting. Second, they sought to employ the methods of fighting that would permit them to destroy the insurgent troops. People were forced to sign obsequious letters of thanks to the tsar. Overdue taxes were exacted ruthlessly. The commanders-in-chief had unlimited power; district commanders-in-chief made life-or-death decisions in their areas. Lawlessness and outrage were daily occurrences.

On October 11, 1863, Berg issued an order to military commanders-in-chief in the Kingdom of Poland[28] that identified their most important task as the quick suppression of the insurrection and the restoration of calm in the country, which the increasing number of troops would make possible. They were to be held personally responsible not only for the suppression of the "gangs" in their areas, but also for the prevention of the formation of any further such "gangs." Moreover, Berg's order pointed out that the members of these "gangs" were stationed in cities, villages, and manors and on the Russians' approach would hide in the woods or disguise themselves as peasants. To destroy insurgent detachments and prevent the formation of new ones, commanders-in-chief were obliged to send out units on two kinds of missions: to search for and destroy "the gangs of rebels" and to enforce the law—to stamp out any disorder. In connection with this, commanders-in-chief of military districts were ordered to assign the areas and the troops stationed in their neighborhood to section commanders, who were to send detachments into the countryside to fulfill their military and administrative duties.

The great advantage of the tsarist army over the insurgent troops led the Russians to the conclusion that the partisans would have to be pursued persistently in order to destroy their power. Because of the fact that the majority of the "gangs" were mounted, they had to be pursued by cavalry. Infantry was to follow, if possible, in wagons or be picked up along the way. Therefore the section commanders had to inform the leaders of the columns where the nearest tsarist units were. Small, partisan-like mounted detachments were sent to towns where there were no large "gangs" to destroy the small partisan units and capture their members.

The Russian units sent out for military and administrative purposes were obliged to search all villages, settlements, manors, and isolated farmsteads. Moving from one village to another, the columns had to make sure there were no insurgent troops or sympathizers where they were going. Column commanders were to check the censuses taken by parish chiefs, mayors, and village heads. The order called for particularly diligent search for weapons and ammunition dumps and other insurgent matériel.

The commanders-in-chief of military districts were ordered to guard the railroad tracks and telegraph lines. They had to provide protection for passing carts and mail coaches. The population of a given parish was held responsible for any damage. Every parish was to set up its own guard to cooperate with the tsarist authorities. The army was to force landowners to pay their taxes. Parish chiefs, mayors, and village administrators were to inform the commanders-in-chief about insurgent troop movements, supply depots, and so on.

Through this order, the supreme command of the tsarist army in the Kingdom of Poland tried to make the whole nation fight against the insurgents. At the same time, it also used its military force in a well-planned way. On December 10, 1863, *Dziennik Powszechny,* the government newspaper in Polish, reported that

> small mobile columns are moving in all directions with a military and administrative purpose. They are scouring the towns, villages, manors, and isolated farmsteads, gathering up the registration books and comparing them with the population. Those who are not registered are being arrested. At the same time, these units are searching for arms and ammunition depots and storage places for the food gathered under pressure by the gangs' commanders. They are guarding river crossings, railroad tracks, telegraph lines, and mail carriers. Their main administrative duty is to collect taxes. Besides, our forces are stationed in such a way that they cover most of the territory to protect its inhabitants from the cruelty of bands of robbers. . . .[29]

The protection of military rail transport varied with the insurgents' activities. At first, when they were simply dismantling the tracks, the Russian army guarded the tracks. When in summer 1863 the insurgents began to destroy railroad bridges and to launch full-scale attacks on consignments, the Russians strengthened their reconnaissance parties, and one or two coaches were pushed in front of the engine. Apart from this, military shipments were convoyed by troops.

In December 1863 and in January 1864, General Berg gave a number of orders aimed at ending the fighting against the insurgents. An order on December 27 set up military and police management.[30] Police power in the guberniyas and administrative districts was placed in the hands of commanders-in-chief. Civil governors and other provincial authorities were to be subject to the military commander-in-chief with regard to police matters. All the authorities in administrative districts were subordinated to their own local commanders-in-chief, who were given complete control and were able to do whatever they liked to restore the calm and security. The December 27 order called for the prosecution of local authorities and landowners who harbored dangerous and questionable persons. They were also to be brought to account for insufficient guarding of railways, bridges, telegraph lines, and so forth.

On January 5, 1864, a supplementary order was issued on the subject of commanders-in-chief of administrative districts and their relation to commanders.[31] It placed all local headquarters under the authority of administrative district commanders-in-chief. The local military police headquarters commander was to be the immediate subordinate of the military commander-in-chief of the administrative district. The border guard was also made subject to the frontier administrative district commander-in-chief, whose duty it was to control the activity of guard officers. The administrative district commander-in-chief had to inform the War Department chief and the general police superintendent about any disloyalty among border guard officers. The police were to report regularly on the political atmosphere of the district. When the administrative district commander-in-chief decided that joint action was necessary, he was to ask the commander of the unit stationed in the area for help. If his rank was higher than that of commander, he was given the right to use the field army on his own account. Having been informed of the presence of an insurgent unit in his district, the commander-in-chief would inform the commander of the troops, who would take steps to destroy it.

On January 20, 1864, Berg signed another order which specified the rights and duties of all the war and military commanders in the Kingdom of Poland.[32] It ordered the division of the district into smaller units to be governed by military commanders. Military department and district commanders-in-chief were given the right to remove anyone except the governor-general in the event of disloyalty. In this way, the army was given control over the country. Administrative districts or provinces were in effect ruled by the officers of the tsarist units disposed in them. This gave a strong impetus to the struggle against the insurgents.

In autumn 1863, the Russian garrison network had once again been increased, since the place of residence of each military section commander had to be guarded by the army. After this change, there were four to eight garrisons in each administrative district. In Radom guberniya there were administrative districts with an even greater number of sections; Miechów had eleven and Olkusz fifteen. The Russian army was able to reach any point in the Kingdom of Poland in three hours' time.[34] This enabled them to control every inch of terrain constantly and closely. Roundups of insurgent units were often possible. Particularly in the winter and spring of 1864, the activity of the Russian authorities and the army increased to such a point that the number of insurgent units very rapidly declined. After the isolated battles of May 1864, the insurrection burned out.

This general and, I think, incomplete outline of the tsarist army's efforts to deal with the insurgents shows that it was not a change in tactics that determined the failure of the insurrection. Rather, it was the constantly increasing number of Russian troops and the improvement of military and administrative methods, which cut off the insurgents from their social environment, deprived them of refuge, isolated them, and thus made it possible to destroy them. Furthermore, it was not only military measures that caused the overthrow of the insurrection. The coup de grace was the Enfranchisement Act of the spring of 1864, which completely diverted the attention of the Polish peasants (about 75 percent of the nation) and landowners from the insurrection. At the same time, the Western European countries stopped supporting the insurgents. It was under these circumstances that Poland's independence had to be postponed.

Notes

1. S. Gesket, *Vojennyja diejstvija v carstvie polskom v1863 g.* (Warsaw, 1894).
2. Józef Piłsudski, *Zarys historii militarnej powstania styczniowego* (Warsaw, 1929).
3. Peter Zajonchovskij, *Vojennyje reformy 1860–1870 godov v Rosii* (Moscow, 1952); A. Fiedorov, *Russkaja armija v 50–70 gg XIXv.* (Leningrad, 1959).
4. Włodzimierz Djakov and Ilia Miller, *Ruch rewolucyjny w armii rosyjskiej a powstanie styczniowe* (Wrocław/Warsaw/Cracow, 1967).
5. See Zajonchovskij, *Vojennyje reformy,* and Fiedorov, *Russkaja armija.*
6. Zajonchovskij, *Vojennyje reformy,* p. 88.
7. Ibid., p. 99.
8. Gesket, *Vojennyja diejstvija v carstvie polskom,* pp. 15, 17.
9. Ibid., p. 15, and list of military units.
10. Gesket's statement (p. 15) that the tsarist army was unprepared for combat because it was scattered all over the Kingdom of Poland is groundless. Piłsudski's view is more convincing: "Every revolution makes the government scatter its military units all over the country, because the various events, the various demonstrations of this or that part of society call for the participation of the army. The army is the last resort, and it is thrown in where it is needed. Thus, while usually concentrated, it comes to be widely dispersed" (J. Piłsudski, *Zarys historii militarnej,* p. 28).
11. Piłsudski, *Zarys historii militarnej,* p. 28.
12. Gesket, *Vojennyja diejstvija v carstvie polskom,* p. 22.
13. Ibid., maps at end of book.
14. Piłsudski, *Zarys historii militarnej,* p. 34. He also gives a more comprehensive analysis of the ways and reasons for concentration.
15. Vladimir Revunienkov, *Polskoje vosstanije 1863g. i jevropiejskaja diplomatija* (Leningrad, 1957), p. 221.
16. The fortresses of Modlin, Dęblin, Zamość, and Brześć played no role during the insurrection: the insurgent detachments were too weak to attack them. They served only as well-protected arsenals for the Russians. Warsaw Citadel was important because of its large prison, which securely confined quite a number of arrested persons.

17. Revunienkov, *Polskoje vosstanije,* p. 222.
18. Ibid., p. 297.
19. Ibid., p. 337.
20. Gesket, *Vojennyja diejstvija v carstvie polskom,* p. 368. I have given the description of these operations also according to Gesket. In principle, it agrees with the descriptions in the memoirs of the insurgents.
21. Ibid., p. 369.
22. The Swiss military observer Lieutenant Colonel F. von Erlach said of the Russian army that "its components lack independence, and it is outrageously heavy and awkward in its whole operation. . . . Independent movement of the individual soldier in the line is out of the question. He stands or approaches the designated place and shoots, and that is the end of his duties" (F. von Erlach, *Partyzantka w Polsce w roku 1863,* 2d ed. (Warsaw, 1960), p. 95. Insurgents' memoirs and the fact of the smashing of the insurgent units by the Russians seem to contradict this view. Furthermore, there were many commanders of various ranks, such as General Czengery, Major Bentkowski, or Dragoon Lieutenant Assiejev, who showed initiative and ingenuity with regard to methods of fighting against insurgent units.
23. These cities are mentioned in a letter to the chief of Radom War Department dated August 7, 1863, from Radom's governor, who considered their having been burned as a cause of stagnation in business (Provincial Record Office [WAP], Kielce, Radom Section, Office of the Chief of the War Department of Radom, 1861–66, vol. 7).
24. Anton Drążkiewicz, *Wspomnienia Czachowszczyka z 1863 r.* (L'vov, 1890), p. 32.
25. Revunienkov, *Polskoe vosstanije,* p. 335.
26. Ibid., p. 336.
27. Ibid., p. 337.
28. Prikazanije vojskam v carstvie polskom raspoloženym, g. Warszawa, no. 143, 11.X.1863, Provincial Record Office, Kielce, War Commander Files, folder II/4.
29. *Dziennik Powszechny,* December 10, 1863.
30. *Dziennik Powszechny,* December 29, 1863.
31. Instrukcja dla nacz. woj. w Królestwie Polskim, Provincial Record Office, Kielce, War Commander Files, folder II/4.
32. Ibid.
33. Zarządzenie generał-policmajstra dla woj. nacz. pow. w Królestwie Polskim z 25.X–6.XI.1864, Provincial Record Office, Kielce, War Commander Files, folder II/4.
34. A. Giller, *Historia powstania narodu polskiego w 1861–1864r.,* vol. 1, 2d ed. (Paris, 1897), p. 275.

The Logistics of the Insurgent Troops in the January Insurrection

Lesław Dudek

This essay is an attempt to outline the logistic principles and practices of the insurgent troops during the second part of the January Insurrection. This period began in late spring 1863, when the first stage of the insurrection had failed and the need for new strategic and tactical concepts was recognized. The idea of the establishment of large insurgent units concentrated in extensive rear areas not captured by the enemy had appeared in theoretical treatises of the 1830s, 1840s, and 1850s and in the plans prepared several months prior to the insurrection.[1]

I

The experience of the initial period of the insurrection proved that operations involving units as large as several thousand were impossible. New instructions were published by the National Government in May in which "insurgent warfare" was differentiated from the "partisan warfare" that accompanies conventional warfare waged by a regular army.[2] In deciding to switch to insurgent warfare, the National Government had to give up, for the time being at least, the original idea of liberating entire large areas from the enemy's influence. The new instructions emphasized that "insurgent warfare cannot have either a base [rear] or lines of operations; the entire territory is the theater of operation, and the cooperation and friendliness of people is its main strength." Furthermore, "insurgent units should be numerous and scattered all over the country rather than large," the maximum size being six hundred infantry and two hundred fifty cavalry.[3] Mobility was considered a must, even at the expense of supply columns, which were to be limited to a few carts loaded with a small supply of provisions and ammunition. It was recommended that units always camp in inaccessible places, with an escape route identified in advance, and that they take the enemy by surprise and avoid combat whenever the enemy was aware of them.

These principles of operations are reflected in the instructions with regard to logistics.

The system of supply established between May and the beginning of August was adapted to the new idea of insurgent warfare. Its principles were expounded in a series of regulations issued by the National Government.[4] The task of providing supplies to the insurgent units was delegated to the underground authorities of provinces, districts, regions, and parishes (communities).[5] The grass-roots official within the national insurgent administration was the "senior" (of a village) or "constable" (of a country town or city).[6] The network of insurgent authorities was quite dense, and this made it possible for the orders of the National Government to reach the people and supplies for the fighting units to be provided.

It was the mission of the provincial organizers of the armed forces, aided by an official in charge of military supply (or commissary), to collect stores of arms, ammunition, clothing, military equipment, harnesses, saddles, and carts for two infantry battalions and two cavalry squadrons, together with daily rations of food, fodder, and a certain number of horses for thirty days. It was also recommended that these stores be deployed at a few well-protected places in the province. On the written request of a military commander, provisions for the unit were issued by order of the provincial organizer. After each issue, the provincial organizer was obliged to restore the supplies to their initial status. Commanders were allowed to apply to lower-level officials of the civilian underground authorities or even directly to the people for food, fodder, and carts only. In such cases, the supplies came not from the provincial stores, but directly from their providers, and these latter were reimbursed by the underground district or provincial treasury.

Parish chiefs and their subordinates, the village "seniors," were instructed by the National Government to collect supplies for the provincial stores and to supply the district treasury with cash and carts.[7] This system relieved the unit commanders from time-consuming labor and from the complicated management of supply collection. Most important, it relieved them of the daily search for food.

The supply system included a territorial network of civil administration and actual supply of the combat units. The central organ of supply was the underground War Department of the National Government. It, of course, had no central magazines and was unable in itself to provide logistic services for the insurgent troops. Instead, its task was publication of instructions for the provision of those services—instructions regulating the inhabitants' obligations in transport, principles of encampment, health service, and supply of food and uniforms. Three of

the eight known members of the War Department after May 1863—
Mateusz Gralewski, Józef Galezowski, and Jan Kozieł-Poklewski—
has had considerable military training,[8] and it is believed that
they drafted the instructions on logistic services. A medical board of three persons functioned as the chief organ of medical service. It kept a register of the physicians sent to insurgent detachments, prepared professional directions, and delivered medical equipment.[9]

Provincial, district, regional, and parish organs of the supply system all had certain material reserves stored in magazines and a certain amount of money to supply insurgent troops. Subcommissaries or noncommissioned officers looked for clothing and food, issued cash receipts for food collected, and assisted in the collection or requisition of all kinds of goods.[10] Women grouped in so-called Fives prepared dressings for the wounded, produced clothing and underwear, collected gifts of supplies and cash, carried out welfare work, and took care of the families of insurgents killed in action or deported by the Russians and of fighting men. Such groups also existed in Galicia. The total number of people who were fully or partially engaged in the territorial logistic system in the Kingdom of Poland is estimated at several thousand.

Armed resistance also spread beyond the Kingdom into the so-called western guberniyas of the Russian empire: Białystok province, Lithuania, Belorussia, and even Podolia and Volhynia. In these latter provinces the insurrection was not as strong as in other areas. Although combat operations were carried out only in territories under Russian control, the insurrection was a universal Polish affair in which the Polish societies of the other two sectors of partitioned Poland also participated. The involvement of Poles in exile in Western Europe was quite significant. Activities in support of the insurrection were organized in Galicia by chief juries in Cracow and Lwów and a network of district cells. A branch of the National Government's War Department, concerned mainly with logistic matters, was established for a time in Cracow.[12] After March 1863, an underground board in the Prussian sector directed by Jan Dzialyński established a network of district boards throughout Great Poland.[13]

The National Government made efforts to introduce new principles of supply and organization of logistical services which were flexible enough to respond to the changes in combat operational principles. The vitality of these principles was substantiated indirectly by the fact that some of them were adopted eighty years later during the Nazi occupation of Poland.

II

The Treasury Department of the National Government managed the finances of the underground state. Initially, the principal source of revenues was the contributions of patriotic wealthy citizens of the Kingdom and of the western guberniyas. Citizens of the other two sectors of partitioned Poland and émigrés also made donations. During the years prior to the insurrection, social events—parties, dances, and other things—were organized, the entrance fees and proceeds of which were reserved for the needs of future armed resistance.[14]

From the beginning of April 1863 on, by a decree of the underground government, taxes were the main source of revenue. There was a 0.5 percent tax on real estate value and a 2–10 percent tax (a progressive tax) on the annual incomes of factory owners, merchants, professionals, clerks, teachers, and workshop owners. Simultaneously the National Government exempted citizens from the taxes assessed by the tsarist government, forbidding their collection.[15] The efficiency of the anonymous government tax collectors and the discipline of the majority of the society in paying their taxes were high. Indeed, even several tsarist officials paid taxes to the National Government.[16]

The Poles of Galicia and the Prussian sector contributed taxes and gifts, although there were some wealthy citizens who failed in these patriotic duties.[17] Other ways of raising funds were devised, the most spectacular being the requisition of 24 million złotys from the treasury of the Kingdom in June 1863. It is remarkable that this was done without violence; the National Government's order was simply obeyed without resistance by the clerks.[18] A heavily guarded store of two hundred thousand rubles was seized at Żyrzyn on August 8.[19] In the summer a government loan was floated, the bonds being purchased mainly by wealthy Polish exiles in France.

The Treasury Department obtained funds from lower-level institutions: the underground district treasuries delivered to it all their surplus funds. On the other hand, if district treasuries' expenses exceeded their incomes they could expect an allocation from the Treasury Department. All these were possible thanks to the extremely efficient insurgent postal system.

Stefan Kieniewicz's analysis of state finances,[20] though based on fragmentary data, suggests that about two-thirds of the income of the underground state was spent on weapons.

III

In the second stage of the insurrection, when the enemy had taken the initiative, the insurgents could not remain anywhere for long. Even in large woods or areas difficult of access, they could stay in the same place only for a few days. Consequently, the need arose to transport food from long distances.

Troops in forest camps were deployed in combat formations where possible for training and target practice, but the living conditions were poor, especially in cold and rainy weather. Insurgents slept on heaps of straw, blankets, and coats in drafty shelters.[21] However, the cohesion of troops was perfect.

Quarters in cities, villages, or settlements were more comfortable, but the quartering of the insurgents individually broke down organizational unity, made the assembly of units difficult and weakened their combat readiness, and exposed them to surprise attack by the enemy.[22] Frequently, soldiers were placed near a manor, some of them in buildings and some outdoors around a fire.[23]

A few hours' bivouac in a field or in the woods, often without a fire, offered minimal rest for men and horses, but this was often the situation when the soldiers were exhausted following a long march or an escape from close combat with the enemy.[24]

IV

The National Government's instructions on the insurgent soldiers' daily rations set them at a much higher level than in regular armies. The insurgent's daily ration included about 800 g of bread, 400 g of meat, 100 g of fat, 400 g of cereal (or peas), 13 g of salt, and a quarter of a liter of vodka.[25] Mealtimes were also established by regulation.[26] These orders could not always be realized. However, according to many reports, the commanders understood the importance of proper nourishment for their subordinates and, in various ways, according to the situation, tried to provide for their needs.

In camps, the cooks prepared meals in kettles. Cereal and thick pea soup with big pieces of meat in it was frequently the main dish. If there was no way of preparing hot meals, bread, fat, or sausage and vodka were delivered.[27] Sometimes the inhabitants of settlements and/or the landowners near whose manors the unit was deployed were ordered to feed the soldiers.[28] This alternative was often employed when the soldiers were quartered in settlements.

Periodically, there were supply difficulties; the hardships these occasioned are described in insurgents' memoirs. Their cause was not general lack of goods, but the necessity of movement in response to enemy activity. The insurgents were not always in a position to requisition or obtain food from the underground magazines. For such occasions, they carried food reserves with them. The commanders' anxiety to carry with them an "iron ration" of food and ammunition was understandable, but it called for a supply column that limited the maneuverability of the unit and obliged it to travel on roads.[29]

The fact that there is no evidence of any shortage of food among the insurgent troops is indirect proof of the efficiency of food supply.

V

The National Government issued on June 16, 1863, an order[30] specifying the following clothing for the insurgent soldier: jacket, trousers, coat, knee boots, smock (light linen tunic), pack, canteen, haversack, a pair of shirts, underpants, and foot cloths (which were wrapped around the feet in place of socks). Additional regulations on clothing were published by the National Government in a circular[31] which defined the cut, color, and even size of uniforms for officers, soldiers, and the members of the various branches. These regulations were never universally put into practice. The introduction they proposed of various trimmings and insignia of rank, similar to those of regular armies, was quite impractical for insurgent troops engaged in partisan warfare. Many commanders did, however, make efforts to standardize the clothing of their units. Recognizing that uniforms contributed to discipline and created a sense of unity, they established uniforms for individual units or even for whole provinces, especially after the summer of 1863,[32] although this practice never became universal. Uniforms tended to be made of thick woolen Polish homespun, which was warm and comfortable in the Polish climate, in camouflaging colors. In the Museum of the Polish Army there are some old-fashioned Polish overcoats (*czamara*) that give some idea of the insurgents' clothing. One is made of black wool, buttoned with hooks, another of deep-blue wool with a stand-up collar and six horn buttons.[33]

Von Erlach states that scythe bearers mostly dressed in Polish homespun and wore badges displaying the national eagle insignia. Riflemen dressed in hemp and flax doublets and Polish woolen four-cornered peaked caps. Both of the units visited by von Erlach had yellow facings.[34] General Hauke-Bosak's staff regulated the uniforms of the troops of Kraków and Sandomierz provinces in December 1864.[35]

Clothing was adapted to the weather in winter. It was based on what was commonly worn by peasants in the areas of combat operations so that supplies of cloth could be obtained locally. How well the insurgents were clothed depended on the efficiency of the local civilian authorities. Hauke-Bosak was able to provide relatively good clothing for his units at the turn of 1863–64.[36] On other occasions, the clothing delivered was unusable for combat purposes. Soldiers were plagued by the lack of underwear. Poorly clothed insurgents got sick; some of them fought barefooted.[37]

Foreign delivery of clothing was quite important. Units operating in southern and western parts of the Kingdom were better clothed than the rest because imported clothing could reach them. Cavalry units had better equipment because many noblemen volunteered for such units and brought their own.

VI

The shortage of firearms and ammunition was undoubtedly most painful and most frequent. This problem is emphasized in many memoirs and by many students of the insurrection. It is even reflected in one of the songs of the period, one of whose verses ends with the words: "Our people went to the woods without arms." Scythe-bearer detachments existed in almost every insurgent unit until the last days of the insurrection, even during the period of Traugutt's dictatorship. Hauke-Bosak wrote the underground authorities in western Galicia on January 1, 1864, "Above all, we need firearms and ammunition."[38] In almost every situation report, the lack of firearms and ammunition is a recurrent theme. The fact is that the predominance of firepower was on the enemy's side.[39]

The quality of domestic resources was poor. Rostworowski, a landowner and a rich man, joining the insurrection in June 1864, discussed the difficulties he faced in acquiring firearms:

> It was impossible to get a fowling piece; all of them were being used by the insurgents. . . . I was barely able to buy from hunters three quite old single-barreled guns. They were very long, with thick barrels, adapted from old rifles of over 200 meters' range. I ordered bayonets prepared for these three rifles. . . . We had gunpowder and percussion caps, although there were not many of them.[40]

In Leczyca district, the insurgents confiscated sporting firearms from the Schützenverein, a legal German shooting club.[41] The Samogitian insurgent inventory consisted mostly of fowling pieces owned by landowners and forest rangers.[42] Here the territorial supply system, based on the use of local resources, failed totally.

Apart from small amounts of firearms captured by the insurgents, the only source that could be relied on was foreign import. It was uncertain and hard to correlate in time and space with needs and transport facilities. Firearms from Belgium were sent in roundabout ways. The transaction was profitable for inspectors, customs officers, and railroad officers. Part of each shipment was usually lost in transit and part delivered to the Austro-Russian and Prusso-Russian borders to await transport. When a load reached the Kingdom at last, there still was the danger that the Russian troops would intercept it. Janczewski confessed to a jury that of seventy-six thousand rifles bought forty-four thousand had been seized before reaching the Kingdom and half of the remainder had been intercepted by the Russian authorities.[43] We may, of course, doubt the accuracy of Janczewski's calculations, but he does expose the scope of the problem and explain the shortage of firearms. Equally urgent was the lack of ammunition; according to Berg,[44] the attack on Żyrzyn was made possible only by the delivery at the last moment of fifteen thousand cartridges and percussion caps. Delivery of firearms and ammunition from Prussia and especially from Galicia, where the authorities were much more tolerant as regarded these transfers, influenced insurgent combat operations, causing marches of insurgent troops to meet expected deliveries.[45]

The variety of these sources of firearms meant that the types of firearms were varied. Disregarding fowling pieces, the insurgents were equipped with (1) Model 1841 Prussian Dreyse rifles, or needle guns, breech-loading rifles with a 13.7-millimeter bore that were capable of firing five rounds per minute, and also their 1849, 1854, 1857, 1860, and 1862 models (these rifles used special cartridges that were hard to obtain); (2) Austrian breech-loading matchlock rifles, Model 1849, with an 18.1-millimeter bore (which also used special ammunition); (3) Austrian muzzle-loading rifles, Models 1840 and 1842, with a 17.6-millimeter bore; (4) captured Russian muzzle-loading rifles, Model 1845, with an 18-millimeter bore; (5) Prussian muzzle-loading rifles, Model 1839, with an 18.5-millimeter bore; (6) Prussian muzzle-loading rifles, Model 1835, with a 16.3-millimeter bore; (7) Belgian muzzle-loading sporting rifles, with an 18-millimeter bore; (8) English-muzzle-loading rifles, Model 1853, with a 16-millimeter bore; and (8) modern Enfield rifles, Colt-type, with a 9-millimeter bore. Pistols and revolvers were imported from Belgium, Austria, Prussia, Russia, France, and England. The most popular revolvers were the American Colt Navy Model 1851 (a six-shooter with a 9-millimeter bore) and various versions of the Lafaucheux.[46]

Supplying ammunition to forces equipped with such a variety of weapons was quite difficult, and this difficulty was compounded by the constant need for maneuvers and the threat to communication lines between the insurgents and the magazines in Poland, in Galicia, and in the Prussian sector. One situation report speaks of the small amounts of cartridges and the fact that, like the bayonets, they did not fit.[47] This situation was undoubtedly frequent. Generally speaking, it can be said that providing the insurgents with firearms and ammunition was the weakest point of underground logistics.

VII

Supplying the insurgents with side arms, especially scythes, was of course much easier. Widely used in agricultural countries, scythes could be acquired from any local blacksmith. Sabers for cavalry and officers were hard to obtain, since in autumn 1861 the tsarist authorities had collected all weapons, including side arms. In Warsaw, the largest underground factory in the Kingdom produced only two hundred fifty sabers a year.[48] The need was satisfied with Austrian regular cavalry sabers in the 1845 and 1850 versions and Model 1861 officers' swords.[49] Insurgents were also equipped with sabers produced in some of the larger cities of Galicia. The best-known arms manufacturer was Ignacy Höfelmajer of Cracow.[50]

VIII

The insurgent medical service performed its duties under the most trying of circumstances. For one thing, the enemy controlled the places suitable for evacuation and hospitalization of the wounded. For another, the troops were in constant movement. Beyond this, the enemy often killed wounded insurgents not only on the battlefield, but also in houses and field hospitals. The medical service system administered by the underground authorities coped quite effectively with the first two factors, but it was helpless in the face of the third. The insurgent medical service consisted of two branches, the mobile units within fighting formations (doctors and army surgeons)[51] and the territorial underground provincial and district doctors who were responsible for nursing the wounded within the borders of their particular administrative units. A branch of the medical service consisting of paramedical personnel was aided by the parish chiefs, who were obliged to help the local women's committees. These committees were charged with collecting and treating the wounded on the battlefield, on the assumption that women would be less exposed to the enemy's cruelty than men.

The head of each underground organization was obliged to report to the district authorities on every clash which occurred in his area, giving the number of wounded and where they were taken. A copy of this report was also sent directly to the National Government. It was thus possible for the higher authorities to send additional medical personnel and supplies where they were needed, though often only with some delay. Local doctors and surgeons could be called to provide medical help for wounded partisans.[52] The wounded were hospitalized in two ways, depending on the attitude of the Russian commander of the particular area. If there was no danger that the wounded would be exterminated (e.g., in Zamość province, where General Khrushchev was kind to the wounded partisans), they were placed in town hospitals or in improvised first-aid stations. If there was such danger, they were placed individually or in small groups in places difficult to reach (in foresters' lodges, garrets, barns, and even wood distillers' kilns). Galician society came to the wounded insurgents' assistance, establishing, with the tolerance of the Austrian authorities, several large hospitals on the border. Besides, there were small hospitals in many border towns.[53]

Administering first aid during combat, in the open or in available houses, was extremely difficult.[54] If the enemy withdrew, doctors could comb the battlefield for wounded and then send them to territorial medical service centers or at least to a parish organization for further treatment. A few injured partisans might stay with their unit's supply column or, if their health worsened, be placed for safekeeping with the local underground authorities.[55] If the encounter was unfavorable for the insurgents and they had to withdraw, the lot of wounded partisans was tragic. Enemy soldiers usually killed insurgents left on the battlefield. At best, they stripped them and left them to their fate.[56] Some reports show that inhabitants of neighboring villages would hurry spontaneously if they heard shots to protect the injured partisans from enemy revenge. The National Government ordered commanders not to quarter and chiefs of territorial cells not to settle any magazines on hospital premises and to supply first aid and medical assistance to injured enemy soldiers and place them in national hospitals.[57]

Primitive living conditions made soldiers' hygiene difficult, especially in winter. One situation report reads, "Vermin and the lack of underwear were the painful calamity. In the evenings, even in severe cold, all of those partisans who were off duty stripped to the waist and shook the unwelcome guests out of their clothes over the fire, which gave off the particular crack of burning insects." Another participant in those events said that on leaving home for insurgent service he took large amounts of Persian insect powder (an anti-insect powder made of pyrethrum flowers [*Pyrethrum tanacetum*]).[58] The state of hygiene in woodland camps during the summer was better; "people washed much more frequently than I had expected," writes von Erlach.[59]

Dr. Władysław Jasiński reported having met wounded partisans and ill soldiers who had crossed into Galicia. He stated that the severe living conditions made tuberculars worse, but people with chronic gastritis and dyspepsia felt better and some of them even got rid of their ailments.

Infectious diseases such as dysentery, cholera, and typhus were very rare. Most frequent were rheumatism, foot problems, and colds. Beginning in the autumn Jasiński observed an increase in influenza and pneumonia and a few cases of diarrhea.[60]

The insurgents' state of health, then, could be considered satisfactory. Insurgents less hardened to difficult camp life left for home or for exile, perhaps representing a process of natural selection. Those in good health and the most hardened stayed with the insurgent units. Mortality was quite low.

IX

The insurgent troops did not have in any phase of the struggle the secure base of supply a regular army usually has. It was impossible, in spite of the plans drafted prior to the insurrection, to free an area large enough to develop supply institutions and reinforce the fighting elements from local resources. The concept of a logistic system was developed during the first three months of the insurrection and was based on the experiences of that period. It was gradually applied in the summer of 1863 and proved satisfactory, efficient, original, and well-adapted to Polish conditions. The system was based on an infrastructure that was utilized by both national and tsarist armed forces in various fields. Installations, structures, and institutions were used in different degrees by both belligerents, sometimes by the right of exclusion of one of them and sometimes, paradoxically, by way of a symbiosis.

The right of exclusion, for example, meant that barracks in large towns and fortresses could not be used by the insurgents. The same was the case with underground magazines; the tsarist army was unable to use them because it did not know where they were. A periodic right of exclusion meant, for example, that the Poles had to stay away from the roads on which superior Russian forces were marching. Since the Russian forces were six or seven times larger than those of the Poles in the Kingdom and even more than that in the western guberniyas, the exclusion of the Poles from various settings was incomparably more frequent than the exclusion of the Russians.

Both belligerents could use local supply, cattle for slaughter, cereals, fat, corn, fodder, manufactured goods, and mills, cereal factories, bakeries. Being concentrated in large garrisons, the Russian troops could not prevent the insurgents from using the products of the countryside, especially in remote areas. A National Government decree of May 10, 1863, prohibited any transactions with the Russians. Although that order made it difficult for tsarist troops to buy food and fodder, it did not put an end to it.

A postal service using coaches carried both letters and passengers. It was used by both tsarist officials and, in a conspiratorial way, of course, insurgent officials. The postal service gave priority to the National Government's officials and mail. This is an interesting example of the use of the same infrastructure by both belligerents, one of the phenomena which gave this war such an exceptional character. In any event, a war waged in an occupied country cannot be conducted in a conventional way.

Galicia and the Prussian sector, to some extent, were the base of supply for the insurgent troops. They helped them to collect goods of all kinds, to develop the medical service, and even to provide soldiers the sanctuary essential to a protracted insurrection.

X

The insurrection failed militarily. It did not achieve the aims set prior to its outbreak. Further, it was costly in terms of men killed and wounded and property destroyed.[61] The failure of the logistic system was one of the main causes of its defeat. The most serious shortcoming of that system was the lack of any overall logistic plan for the insurrection and of any advance preparation. As a consequence, no meaningful supply was provided for the insurgent troops during the first stage of the insurrection. Improvisation was therefore required, and improvements evolved slowly. Most important, the element of surprise essential to an insurrection could not be exploited. The organization of an effective logistic system took at least three months (May–August), and thus it was only some seven months after the outbreak of the insurrection that the supply system began to function properly.

It is, of course, impossible to determine precisely to what degree the errors in logistics influenced the outcome of the insurrection. Many other factors also affected the outcome and may have been more important. The shortage of firearms and ammunition was a fundamental problem of the insurrection and was never solved. A majority of scholars consider this one of the main reasons for the failure of the insurrection and, in particular, for the scope of that failure.

Notes

1. E. Halicz, "Problematyka wojskowa powstania styczniowego," in *Powstanie styczniowe 1863* (Warsaw, 1963), p. 140; *Towarzystwo Demokratyczne Polskie o sile zbrojnej narodowej,* ed. M. Anusiewicz (Warsaw, 1960); J. Moliński, *Przygotowania wojskowe do wybuchu powstania styczniowego (w okre-*

sie luty 1861-początek stycznia 1863), Studia i Materiały do Historii Wojskowości, vol. 8, pt. 2 (Warsaw, 1962), pp. 105, 121; S. Kieniewicz, *Powstanie styczniowe* (Warsaw, 1972), p. 329.
   2. *Powstanie pod względem wojennym: Instrukcja Rządu Narodowego,* ed. L. Ratajczyk (Warsaw, 1959), p. 3.
   3. Ibid., pp. 3–5.
   4. "Wypisy źródłowe do historii polskiej sztuki wojennej," in *Polska sztuka wojenna w okresie powstania styczniowego,* ed. E. Halicz, 14th fascicle (Warsaw, 1954), pp. 129–33, 66–71, 72–78; E. Elie, "Intendentura w 1863 roku," *Przegląd Intendencki* 8 (2)(1933): 28–30.
   5. In that period the Kingdom of Poland was divided by the National Government into eight provinces (within the five guberniyas) and thirty-nine districts (W. Trzebiński and A. Borkewicz, *Administrative Division of the Kingdom of Poland, 1815–1918* [Warsaw, 1956]). In the 1860s there were nearly seventeen hundred parishes (A. Stanecki, *Dioceses and Parishes in the Nineteenth and Twentieth Centuries* [Cracow], p. 1631).
   6. "Wypisy źródłowe do historii," p. 78.
   7. For additional information, see L. Dudek, *Służby kwatermistrzowskie w powstaniu styczniowym,* Studia i Materiały do Historii Wojskowości, vol. 14, pt. 2 (Warsaw, 1968), pp. 298–300.
   8. E. Maliszewski, *Organizacja powstania styczniowego* (Warsaw, 1905), p. 49.
   9. F. Białokur, *Materiały do opracowania służby zdrowia w powstaniu styczniowym 1863–1864* (Warsaw, 1927), pp. 6–7.
   10. "Wypisy źródłowe do historii," pp. 124, 128.
   11. Maliszewski, *Organizacja,* p. 65; J. K. Janowski, *Pamiętniki o powstaniu styczniowym,* 3 vols. (Łwów, 1923–31), 1: 312–15; W. Tokarz, *Kraków w początkach powstania styczniowego i wyprawa na Miechów,* 2 vols. (Cracow, 1915–16), 2: 10, 24.
   12. Janowski, *Pamiętniki,* 1: 307, 325; Tokarz, *Kraków,* 1: 33, 46, 147, 200–203, 212–13; 2: 23. See also L. Dudek, "System zaopatrywania w powstaniu 1863–64," in *Zaopatrywanie wojsk w dawnej Polsce* (Poznań, 1973), p. 408.
   13. S. Myśliborski-Wołowski, *Pomoc materialna społeczeństwa polskiego regencji bydgoskiej dla powstania styczniowego,* Studia i Materiały do Historii Wojskowości, vol. 20 (Warsaw, 1978), pp. 204–6.
   14. W. Karbowski, *Kampania z Dołęgi-Sierakowskiego na Żmudzi w 1863 roku,* Studia i Materiały do Historii Wojskowości, vol. 14, pt. 2 (Warsaw, 1968), p. 201.
   15. Kieniewicz, *Powstanie styczniowe,* p. 469.
   16. J. Piłsudski, "Rok 1863," in *Pisma zbiorowe,* vol. 6 (Warsaw, 1937), p. 164.
   17. Tokarz, *Kraków,* passim; Myśliborski-Wołowski, *Pomoc materialna,* pp. 207–13.
   18. Kieniewicz, *Powstanie styczniowe,* pp. 522–30. Unfortunately, five-sixths of the captured sum was pawn tickets, which were impossible to sell.
   19. Ibid., p. 566.

20. Ibid., pp. 570–76.
21. F. J. von Erlach, *Partyzantka w Polsce w 1863, w świetle własnych obserwacji zebranych na teatrze walki od marca do sierpnia 1863 roku*, trans. W. Tokarz (Warsaw, 1919), p. 134; J. N. Rostworowski, *Wspomnienia z lat 1863– 1864* (Cracow, 1900), p. 21; A. Filipowski, "Pamiętnik," in *Trzy pamiętniki z XIX wieku* (Cracow, 1978), p. 85.
22. K. Kalita, *Ze wspomnień krwawych walk* (Łwów, 1913, p. 81; A. Drążkiewicz, *Wspomnienia Czachowszczyka z 1863 r.* (Łwów, 1890), p. 94; Z. Krzywda, *Wspomnienia obozowe z r. 1863 i 1864* (Łwów, 1883), p. 22; S. Krzyżanowski, "Wspomnienia z czasów mojej młodości," in *Trzy pamiętniki z XIX wieku* (Cracow, 1978), p. 132.
23. Von Erlach, *Partyzantka*, pp. 136–37; Rostworowski, *Wspomnienia*, p. 13.
24. *Pamiętniki Junoszy oficera polskich żandarmów w powstaniu styczniowym*, ed. E. Halicz (Warsaw, 1960), pp. 66, 73–74; *Notatki osobiste Władysława Bentkowskiego z roku 1863*, ed. W. Tokarcz (Cracow, 1916), pp. 109–10; Drążkiewicz, *Wspomnienia*, pp. 23, 26, 97; *Imć pana rotmistrza Józefa Karpowicza postańca z roku 1863 wspomnienie*, ed. Jan Obst (Vilnius, 1928), p. 90; Krzyżanowski, *Wspomnienia*, p. 135.
25. "Wypisy źródłowe do historii," p. 128. In reducing these data to the metric system I used the charts in A. Gilewicz, *History of Poland*, vol. 2, pt. 4 (Warsaw, 1960).
26. "Wypisy źródłowe do historii," pp. 122, 123.
27. Von Erlach, *Partyzantka*, pp. 115–17, 125, 129, 133–34; Rostworowski, *Wspomnienia*, pp. 129, 132, 133, 135, 136, 146; S. Brykczyński, *Moje wspomnienia, Rok 1863*, 4th ed. (Warsaw, 1982), pp. 32, 59, 109–10; T. Wyszomirski, *Bitwa pod Węgrowem stoczona przez powstańców z wojskami carskimi 3.II.1863 w świetle relacji jej uczestnika Stanisława Krzemińskiego*, Studia i Materiały do Historii Wojskowści, vol. 8, pt. 2 (Warsaw, 1962), p. 338.
28. Brykczyński, *Moje wspomnienia*, pp. 20–21, 32, 35, 98–100; Rostworowski, *Wspomnienia*, pp. 13, 44; Kalita, *Ze wspomnień*, p. 73; Krzyżanowski, *Wspomnienia*, pp. 128–29, 134.
29. Krzywda, *Wspomnienia*, p. 19; Rostworowski, *Wspomnienia*, pp. 24–25, 66; von Erlach, *Partyzantka*, pp. 115–17; *Notatki osobiste Władysława Bentkowskiego*, pp. 19–20.
30. "Wypisy źródłowe do historii," p. 70.
31. Eile, "Intendentura," p. 49.
32. Brykczyński, *Moje wspomnienia*, pp. 98–100; *Pamiętniki Junoszy oficera*, p. 31; von Erlach, *Partyzantka*, pp. 97–98, 105–6; Rostworowski, *Wspomnienia*, pp. 16, 46; Drążkiewicz, *Wspomnienia*, p. 99.
33. W. Bigoszewska and M. Sloniewska, *Powstanie styczniowe w zbiorach Muzeum Wojska Polskiego* (Warsaw, 1966), pp. 75–77.
34. Von Erlach, *Partyzantka*, pp. 90–91, 99.
35. L. Ratajczyk, *Partyzantka generała Bosaka w powstaniu styczniowym*, Studia i Materiały do Historii Wojskowści, vol. 6, pt. 2 (Warsaw, 1960), p. 280.
36. Ibid., pp. 282–83; E. Kozłowski, *Działania wojenne oddziałów Bosaka w*

okresie powstania styczniowego, Studia i Materiały do Historii Sztuki Wojennej, vol. 3 (Warsaw, 1956), pp. 104–5.
37. Krzyżanowski, *Wspomnienia,* pp. 127, 135–36; Drążkiewicz, *Wspomnienia,* p. 10; *Józefa Karpowicza,* p. 89.
38. Ratajczyk, *Partyzantka generała Bosaka,* pp. 296, 298.
39. Krzyżanowski, *Wspomnienia,* pp. 128, 131, 146; Filipowski, "Pamiętnik," pp. 84–85; von Erlach, *Partyzantka,* pp. 90–92, 97–100; *Józefa Karpowicza,* p. 89; Brykczyński, *Moje wspomnienia,* p. 101.
40. Rostworowski, *Wspomnienia,* pp. 15–16.
41. H. Manikowski, *Powstanie styczniowe 1863–1864 w powiecie łęczyckim,* Studia i Materiały do Historii Wojskowości, vol. 8, pt. 2 (Warsaw, 1962), pp. 173–75.
42. Karbowski, *Kampania,* p. 201.
43. Z. Janczewski, K. Majewski, O. Awejde, and W. Daniłowski, *Zeznania śledcze w powstaniu styczniowym,* ed. S. Kieniewicz (Wrocław, 1956), pp. 56–57; see also S. Kobielski, "Broń powstańców z 1863 roku," in *Polska broń: Bron Palna* (Wrocław, 1974), pp. 144–51.
44. "Wypisy źródłowe do historii," p. 90.
45. Rostworowski, *Wspomnienia,* pp. 35, 37, 46, 76; *Józefa Karpowicza,* pp. 81, 99; for additional information on arms transfer, see Myśliborski-Wołowski, *Pomoc materialna,* passim.
46. Kobielski, "Broń powstańców," pp. 146–49; Bigoszewska and Słoniewska, *Powstanie styczniowe,* pp. 33, 35, 37, 38, 50, 53.
47. Rostworowski, *Wspomnienia,* p. 83.
48. J. Wojtasik, *Uzbrojenie a sztuka wojenna w polskich powstaniach narodowych lat 1794–1864,* Studia i Materiały do Historii Wojskowości, vol. 22 (Wrocław, 1979), p. 182.
49. Museum of the Polish Army Records Office in Warsaw, folder, "The January Insurrection 1863–1864, Characters." (Photograph.)
50. L. Lewicki, *Ignacy Höfelmajer rusznikarz i szabelnik krakowski,* Studia i Materiały do Dziejów Dawnego Uzbrojenia i Ubioru Wojskowego, vol. 2 (Cracow, 1964), p. 47 and fig. 11.
51. Von Erlach, *Partyzantka,* p. 118; *Notatki osobiste Władysława Bentkowskiego,* pp. 21–22; Archiwum Historii Medycyny, *Wiedenskie czasopisma lekarskie z 1863 o służbie zdrowia w powstaniu styczniowym, podał dr. M. Hanecki i inni* (Warsaw, 1963), p. 275.
52. Janowski, *Pamiętniki,* 1: 330; Janczewski et al., *Zeznania śledcze,* pp. 4, 168–69; "Wypisy źródłowe do historii," pp. 73–74, 78.
53. Von Erlach, *Partyzantka,* pp. 131–32; *Notatki osobiste Władysława Bentkowskiego,* pp. 21–22; Brykczyński, *Moje wspomnienia,* pp. 77–78; *Józefa Karpowicza,* pp. 38–40; "Relacja M. Fuska," in *Czterdziestą rocznicę powstania styczniowego 1863–1903* (Łwów, 1903), p. 117; Krzyżanowski, *Wspomnienia,* pp. 147–48; Archiwum Historii Medycyny, *Wiedeńskie czasopisma lekarskie,* passim. See also Z. Kosztyła, "Udział lekarzy w powstaniu styczniowym na Podlasiu," *Roczniki Akademii Medycznej w Bialymstoku* 8 (1962): 239, 242; Białokur, *Materiały,* pp. 10–11; S. Rudzki, *Zarys historii szpitalnictwa*

w Polsce (Warsaw, 1927), pp. 50–55.
54. Brykczyński, *Moje wspomnienia*, pp. 77, 178; *Notatki osobiste Władysława Bentkowskiego*, p. 148. See also Białokur, *Materiały*, p. 9; Archiwum Historii Medycyny, *Wiedeńskie czasopisma lekarskie*, p. 275.
55. Rostworowski, *Wspomnienia*, pp. 25, 50, 70.
56. Archiwum Historii Medycyny, *Wiedeńskie czasopisma lekarskie*, pp. 267, 272, 278.
57. Janowski, *Pamiętniki*, 1: 330; "Wypisy źródłowe do historii," p. 74.
58. Krzyżanowski, *Wspomnienia*, p. 135; Rostworowski, *Wspomnienia*, p. 16.
59. Von Erlach, *Partyzantka*, pp. 129–30.
60. Archiwum Historii Medycyny, *Wiedeńskie czasopisma lekarskie*, pp. 278–79.
61. Opinion concerning any other nonmilitary results of the insurrection is not an objective of this essay.

The Social Structure of the Insurrection Army, 1863-64

Eligiusz Kozłowski

The difference between the 1831 army and the insurgent troops of 1863 was the result of totally different objectives and conditioning. Until the defeat of the insurrection in 1831, the army of the Kingdom of Poland was a regular army. Its social structure, internal order, and interpersonal relationships were not only constitutional laws and internal regulations, but matters of written precedent.[1] The 1863 army was, above all, a volunteer army, and this to a large extent determined its social structure and led to a new social hierarchy in the Polish Kingdom. It was open to everyone who understood the need for armed force, recognized the risk involved, and saw the army as a realization of the objectives of the insurrection manifesto and the Enfranchisement Act. Thus, it had a double purpose which was lacking in the 1831 insurrection. If only in this, the roles of the 1863-64 and 1831 armies were different, and this predetermined different social structures.

A great many myths, designed for particular political purposes, have arisen around the social character and social structure of the 1863 Insurrection army. The historians who were, among others, responsible for the creation of these myths were A. Giller, W. Przyborowski, Bolesław Limanowski, and Józef Piłsudski. Giller was a representative of the petty bourgeoisie and espoused the idea of class reconciliation, offering a theory of the participation of the whole nation in the insurrection, with the peasants playing a secondary role. Przyborowski considered the minor and middle gentry the main force and assigned a rather insignificant role to the peasants;[2] the bourgeoisie was, according to him, incapable of leading the insurrection. Limanowski referred to the events of 1863 as an "armed movement" of "artisans and craftsmen," who alone were conscious of "national ties."[3] Piłsudski, who did not penetrate deeply enough into the social structure of the insurrection, although he was well acquainted with its military aspects, regarded officers, clerks, and students as the main proponents of armed struggle.

Translating this notion into class terminology, it is not hard to perceive that Piłsudski regarded the gentry and the bourgeoisie as the main driving force of the insurrection.[4]

Neither these four representatives of 1863 historiography nor any other scholar has clearly defined the character of the 1863 movement—whether it was the peasants, the gentry, the intelligentsia, or the middle classes that determined its course. Besides, the character of the insurrection was determined not solely by the numbers of representatives of various classes, but by the program they intended to implement on the basis of the Enfranchisement Act. From this point of view, the 1863 movement was certainly influenced by the gentry, the bourgeoisie, and the intelligentsia, for the social program set up by the January action could only be realized by these social groups. By supporting the Act the gentry held onto the basis of its existence, the estate, whereas the other two groups, connected with the agrarian problem more emotionally than in terms of real interest, seemed quite pleased with the decisions that were made.[5]

The opposite side, that is, the Russian authorities, tried to present the insurrection as solely gentry-inspired, supported by Rome and the Jesuits and lacking in any participation of other social groups, who were either indifferent or hostile to the political and social programs of the insurgents.[6] The reality, however, was different. From beginning to end, the 1863 Insurrection retained the character determined by the gentry, the middle classes, and the intelligentsia, with growing activity on the part of the peasants and increasing indifference on the part of wealthy landowners, the aristocracy, and the rich bourgeoisie, who were interested in it only with regard to preventing its further radicalization.

In the case of the peasants, the reasons for their involvement were different, but on the whole there was an increase in their number and percentage in various regiments. This phenomenon is especially noticeable at the point when the gentry, tired after several months of fruitless struggle and of bearing the material costs of the insurrection, began to withdraw from the ranks, causing the percentage of peasants in the insurgent army to increase even without any especially large influx of volunteers. Changes in peasants' attitudes are especially noticeable in Sandomierz and Kraków provinces, where the peasants' participation in the insurrection was initially very limited and their attitude indifferent or even hostile. The social clashes in these regions in 1861 are well known, and at the outbreak of the insurrection they were renewed. Cases of collaboration with the occupation forces were not uncommon, often taking the form of torture of the wounded insurgents. This movement was also directed against the estates that were the main material support of the insurgents. However, by the summer and autumn of 1863 the attitude of the peasants toward the insurrection was gradually changing; as their numbers in the regiments grew, the country cottage often became, side by side with the estate, an important source of provisions for the fighting. Memoirs from this period clearly indicate that there was a considerable percentage of peasants in the regiments, especially the scythe bearers, who were often under peasant command. One may, however, observe a different peasant attitude toward the insurrection in the northern territories of the Kingdom, which had been less involved in the antifeudal movement of 1861 and had not witnessed the 1846 "slaughter." In these regions there was also considerably greater insurgent activity among the gentry, especially in the densely populated Mazowsze, Podlasie, and Augustów areas.

Numerous recent papers dealing with the events of 1863 have concentrated on the problem of the social structure of the insurgent army, both at the level of the individual regiment and at that of the local and central authorities.[7] In my opinion, however, they do not give a full picture of the situation, although they certainly move us closer to it and should inspire further research. An undoubtedly fundamental paper on this problem is that of the Russian historian Vladimir M. Zaitsev based on materials from the files of courts of inquiry. Zaitsev included in his investigations the Kingdom of Poland, Lithuania, Belorussia, and the Ukraine. He also took into consideration the volunteers from the Austrian and Prussian partitions, as well as foreign volunteers.

A group of 9,497 persons arrested by the Russian authorities and permanently resident outside the Kingdom served as the basis for Zaitsev's calculations. The largest group among them was the peasants (2,948, 30.2 percent), followed by the gentry (2,521, 25.3 percent), town dwellers (2,156, 21.6 percent), clerks (456, 4.5 percent), clergy (166, 2.1 percent), and members of other professional groups (90, 1.2 percent). For 1,156 persons (15.1 percent) there is no clear indication of their social or professional status.

Of this group, 7,292 were natives of the Kingdom of Poland, while others came from either the Western provinces, the Empire, or the Prussian and Austrian partitions. In analyzing this group from the point of view of its social structure, one should bear in mind the general composition of the population of the Kingdom. Before the insurrection (in 1860) the population of the Kingdom was 4,840,500, with the peasants numbering 3,280,800, the gentry about 250,000, and town dwellers about 1,150,000. Men constituted a total of 2,340,000: 1,597,000 peasants, 570,000 burghers, and a little over 100,000 gentry.

Among the 7,292 natives of the Kingdom, the peasants amounted to

2,627 (36.2 percent), the gentry 2,062 (28.2 percent), and the burghers 1,888 (25.7 percent). Of the remainder, either their status has not been established (397, 5.4 percent) or they belonged to small professional groups (clerks, 98, 1.2 percent; clergy, 150, 2.0 percent; Jews, students, former soldiers, etc.). The peasants constitute the highest percentage, although the remaining two major social groups make up 53.9 percent, and if one could establish the social status of the small professional groups, which, in the nature of things, were derived from the gentry and the middle classes, the percentage of the latter two would increase. If we accept Zaitsev's data and convert them into numbers of men from the three major social strata, then the ratios of the arrested to the entire male population of these groups are as follows: gentry, 1 arrested for every 51 persons; burghers, 1 for every 302; peasants, 1 for every 608.

The number and percentage charts for the 1,488 persons from the Prussian and Austrian partitions are of special interest. Of the 747 Austrian subjects, 143 (19.1 percent) belonged to the gentry, 133 (17.7 percent) to the bourgeoisie, and 60 (8 percent) to the peasantry. For more than half of these persons social status has not been established. Prussian subjects numbered 478: 36 (7.5 percent) belonged to the gentry, 79 (16.6 percent) to the bourgeoisie, and 108 (22.4 percent) to the peasantry. Again, for more than half social status has not been established. One could postulate a stronger sense of patriotism among the peasants from Great Poland in comparison with the Galician peasants and a smaller involvement of the gentry in direct military activities, most likely springing from adherence to the "organic work" program and to the struggle with Germanization under Prussian partition.

Only 225 men came from the Lithuanian, Belorussian, and Ukrainian regions, of whom the gentry accounted for almost 50 percent (111). Peasants numbered 80, the majority from the Lithuanian and Belorussian territories, which were more prone to Polish influence and more densely populated by Poles and Lithuanians; the bourgeoisie was represented by only 30 men, but these territories were largely rural and dominated by Jews.

My own investigations of the social cross-section of the insurgents of 1863 are based mainly on my personal file comprising nearly 40,000 names. I subjected to analysis 8,453 persons, regardless of territorial origin, race, religious convictions, and language. The results of these investigations did not surprise me; in the first place were persons belonging to the gentry, irrespective of their material status, 1,941 (23 percent); they were followed by members of the intelligentsia, 1,486 (17.5 percent), burghers, 1,284 (15.3 percent), students, 841 (9.8 percent), former soldiers, 441 (5.2 percent), peasants, 431 (5.2 percent), clergy, 236 (2.7 percent), Jews, 80 (0.9 percent), and laborers, 72 (0.8 percent). The unidentified amounted to 1,641 (19.3 percent). Again, the percentage of gentry would increase considerably if the social status of the members of the intelligentsia and the students were established, as most people in these two groups belonged to the gentry. These results differ considerably from those of Zaitsev, especially with regard to the three fundamental social strata—gentry, bourgeoisie, and peasantry. The ratios of the arrested to the entire male population in the three major groups are also quite different: gentry, 1 repressed for every 60 persons; burghers, 1 for every 510; peasants, 1 for every 3,876.

More detailed analysis is possible at the level of the individual insurgent unit. The camp at Ojców, near Cracow, of Apolinari Kurowski was intended to serve as a kind of resource and manpower base for the entire insurrection. The historian W. Tokarz has already destroyed the myth of the genteel background of the volunteers from Cracow hastening to serve under Kurowski's command, a myth which surely originated after the death of Count Emanuel Moszyński and a few dozen gentry at the battle of Miechów on February 17, 1863. The first group of 27 volunteers from Cracow consisted of 15 craftsmen, 3 students whose social background is unknown, and 9 others who did not state their social status or profession and were probably jobless or only temporarily employed. We must remember, however, that the Galician conservatives, through their magazine *Time,* were busy conducting a campaign aimed at stopping the march past the cordon, and this was an injunction likely to be followed by the majority of the gentry and the rich bourgeoisie. One may suppose, therefore, that the majority of the people who did not state their social status were from craftsman-apprentice circles.

Another list of people belonging to Kurowski's camp mentions 318 names, of which as many as 183 are burghers, mostly craftsmen (masters, apprentices, and other laborers). One is struck by the exceptionally large proportion of shoemakers, tailors, masons, and carpenters. From the gentry there were only 16 volunteers, including 6 landowners and 3 leaseholders; the others were court officials, not necessarily gentry. There were only 3 peasants, referred to as freeholders; they may have been "peasant-burghers."[8] On this list there were 30 students from the Technical Institute in Cracow and 28 university students. The majority of the former derived from the bourgeoisie (21); of the latter, only 8 belonged to the bourgeoisie. Free professionals, such as doctors, lawyers, and officials, and domestic servants from town and country were very few. The preponderance of the burgher-craftsman element in this group of volunteers is therefore unquestionable. However, since Ku-

SOCIAL STRUCTURE OF THE ARMY

rowski's camp, at the peak of its development, numbered well over 2,000 persons, I established additionally the names of 276 of his soldiers, of whom 64 admitted to being students, 23 belonged to the gentry, and 92 were burgher-craftsmen, including as many as 42 apprentices. Only 21 persons gave their occupation as "farmer" (that is, "peasant"); clerks were represented by 16, former soldiers by 9 and domestic servants by 12. For 49 persons there is no information. Undoubtedly, burgher-craftsman and student elements prevailed in Kurowski's camp; other social and professional groups were not numerous, amounting to about 21 percent. One has to remember, however, that the gentry who sided with the Whites, opposed to the insurrection, entered the struggle only in March 1863, when Kurowski's camp no longer existed and the tiny corps of Marian Langiewicz in Sandomierz province was approaching its end at the battle of Grochowiska (March 18, 1863).

That in the first weeks of the insurrection the lower social classes played an important role is confirmed by a list of 451 prisoners from the Kingdom arrested by the Austrian authorities. Among them were 275 craftsmen and apprentices, 75 laborers and servants, 38 stewards and farmers (peasants), 23 private clerks, 11 students, and only 1 landowner.

I obtained equally interesting results from the investigation of a group of 1,747 men who were imprisoned by the Austrian authorities as Galician subjects and accused of having taken part or sought to take part in the insurrection. In this group as many as 1,482 represented the burgher-craftsman community, 1,127 of them young artisans (apprentices) or unemployed domestic servants, etc. Only 173 men were referred to in the files as students and 21 as squires (certainly squires' sons). Their sentences varied from seven days to several weeks or even months. The small proportion of gentry may be explained by the fact that it was relatively easy for them to buy their way out of prison.

In the final stages of the setting up of the Ojców camp, before the battle of Miechów (February 17, 1863), there arrived about 300 volunteers from the Dąbrowa coal-mining area. I have established that 68 of them were either laborers or miners. Over 80 percent of the volunteers from Kurowski's camp were between eighteen and thirty-five, but there were also thirteen-to-fifteen-year-olds and even 1831 veterans.

Of Langiewicz's 437 soldiers, as many as 218 came from burgher-craftsman backgrounds (50 percent); some of them represented the meanest occupations or were unemployed. For the latter, army service was a kind of social promotion and, what is more, guaranteed material gains, regardless of any patriotic involvement or wish to help in the realization of some vague social fancies. That there were only 33 peasants in this group may be explained by Langiewicz's policy toward the villagers (reprisals for activities directed against the insurrection and antigentry attitudes) and a general distrust on the part of the peasants of the Enfranchisement Act and the authorities that introduced it. Of the remaining 186 men, the gentry were represented by 34, 21 worked as servants on various estates, 47 were students, and 21 were clerks. For 63 persons social status has not been established.

Krzystof Dunin Wasowicz[9] tried to conduct similar investigations for M. Borelowski's regiment, but the difficulty here was that this commander made four journeys between Galicia and the Kingdom and one should, in fact, make separate calculations for each campaign. Since this was not possible, the author took into consideration the entire force at Borelowski's disposal (about 1,600 men) and for the 450 who were identified by name managed to establish the profession or social background of 280. The most numerous were students (67); they were followed by craftsmen (63), former army officers (36), members of the intelligentsia (28), foresters, farmers, and servants (25), squires (21), and court servants (11). Moreover, he identified 6 priests and clergymen, 11 peasants, and 9 men representing various lower occupations (waiters, shop stewards).

In my own investigations of the social (professional) composition of Borelowski's regiments, I established 687 names and divided them into a few major groups. However, the proportions did not change radically, and the burgher-craftsman element, together with the lowest occupations in the social hierarchy (domestic servants, shop stewards, etc.), still predominated (289). They were followed by students (109), members of the intelligentsia (42), clerks (37), laborers (12), and former soldiers (41). There were 43 representatives of the gentry and 41 men connected with the court. Only 21 peasants were identified, along with 7 Jews, 17 priests and clergymen, 3 sons of Orthodox priests, and 7 Ukrainians; 16 persons came from Lithuania. This preponderance of the burgher-craftsman element may have been triggered by the personality of the commander, who was himself a craftsman and may have attracted others belonging to his class. Borelowski was also a commander around whom there arose many legends of victorious battles.

The general picture of these three insurgent camps to some extent contradicts the conclusions arrived at on the basis of the analysis of the larger group of arrested persons. For example, for J. Wysocki's regiment, which took part in an attack on the Radziwiłł estate, in Russian Volhynia, I have established the social origins or professions of 570 men (out of 1,000): pupils and students (97), peasants (38), squires (109), burgher-craftsmen (240), clerks (60), former soldiers (37), domestic servants (32), members of the intelligentsia (17), and clergy, including seminarists (6). There were also 6 Ukrainians. As we move north, we find a less varied picture of the social structure of the insurrection. On the basis of Zaitsev's calculations, we see more participation by the gentry (on the whole, the poorest gentry) and the peasants. In Augustów province 48.2 percent of the arrested belonged to the gentry and 31.1 percent to the peasantry, whereas only 10 percent could be traced to the bourgeoisie. This was no doubt the result of the limited development of towns in this province, to a large extent populated by Jews, and of the patriotism of the Augustów gentry and peasants, as well as of the effectiveness of revolutionary propaganda. This preponderance of the gentry in the Augustów regiments is confirmed by the composition of Konstanty Ramotowski's regiment. Of the 173 soldiers identified, as many as 103 belonged to the gentry and 58 to the peasantry. The remainder represented a few other social and professional groups. In Ramotowski's regiment there were also 47 landowners and squires from Lithuania.

A totally different picture is found in the Ukraine. Having examined the court files on 625 persons, I found that 427 (68.3 percent) came from the gentry, 29 (4.7 percent) from the peasantry, 14 (2.2 percent) from the bourgeoisie, and 30 (4.8 percent) from the intelligentsia; 40 (6.4 percent) were students, 12 (1.9 percent) former soldiers, and 70 (11.2 percent) remained unidentified. The rest were individual representatives of the clergy, Jews, etc. These statistics are a faithful reflection of the whole system of internal relationships in this region, to a large extent inhabited by Orthodox Ukrainians hostile to the Poles, Roman Catholicism, and the insurrection. Hence, it was mainly the gentry who supported the idea of the insurrection and dominated in the ranks of the insurgents. The peasants participated only insofar as they were emotionally connected with the lord and the manor house; the Polish cause, of course, they did not understand. The relatively large percentage of students may be explained by the fact that the University of Kiev, as well as some secondary schools, had a high percentage of squires' sons. Also, the town intelligentsia (free professionals and, to some extent, officials) were Polish. The above data concern Kiev, Volhynia, and Podolia provinces.

Zaitsev had access to considerably richer data; he examined the files of 2,215 men, but his results are almost identical to mine. The gentry of the three provinces were represented by 1,179 (67 percent), the peasantry by 238 (10 percent), and the bourgeoisie by 89 (4 percent). A separate group is represented by 340 of the poorest Polish gentry, whom the tsarist authorities had leveled with the peasantry and the bourgeoisie by taking away their privileges. Part of this group became Russified and was even converted to Orthodoxy, remaining either indifferent or even hostile to the idea of the insurrection.

In Lithuania and Belorussia the gentry were also in the lead, although the peasants were in the second place. According to Zaitsev, in the six provinces there 7,907 men were arrested for their participation in the insurrection: 5,158 squires (65.4 percent), 1,813 peasants (23 percent), 452 burghers (5.8 percent), 262 clergymen (3.3 percent), 77 Jews (1 percent), and 56 officials (0.7 percent). A suitable illustration of the social structure of the insurgents in those provinces may be Świeciany district in Vilna province. Zaitsev established that there were 55 representatives of the gentry (73 percent), 10 peasants (13.3 percent), 3 burghers, and 7 clergymen, a total of 75 men. My findings concerning this district are slightly different, as the social origin or profession of 226 men was established. The gentry was represented by 102 (45.1 percent), the peasantry by 39 (17.2 percent), students by 16, clerks by 14, burghers by 6, teachers by 5, clergymen and churchwardens by 7, foresters and stewards by 4, laborers by 3, and officers by 2; there was 1 doctor. Yet, since a considerable percentage of the professional groups derived from the gentry, its participation was at least 15 percent greater. For 27 men there was no information concerning their profession or social status except that they came from Vilna province. If we compare these accounts with the ones from the Ukraine, we are struck by the high degree of peasant involvement, attributable to the different social, religious, and minority structures of these regions.

I have also analyzed a group of high-ranking insurgent army officers —all generals, colonels, and a certain number of majors—for their social and professional backgrounds. Of the 16 generals, only 2 had the title of Count (Józef Czapski and Józef Hauke-Bosak; Artur Goluchowski was permanently resident in Galicia and never saw the battlefield). Of 450 high-ranking officers, as many as 245 represented the gentry, although only 36 belonged to titled families; 74 were burgher-craftsmen and only 7 peasants. There were also 8 Jews and 23 foreigners. The social status or profession of the remainder has not been established.

It is also interesting to consider the previous army affiliations of these officers. Former Russian army officers are in the lead with 307; 27 were former Austrian army officers, 14 former Prussian army officers, and 16 had belonged to other armies, while 49 had begun their military careers in the army of the Kingdom of Poland, in the army of the 1831 Insurrection, in the Polish regiments of the "Springtime of Nations" movement, in the Crimean War, or in the Polish Military Academy in

Italy in 1861–62. A group of 37 officers had had no military training whatsoever.

It was a physical impossibility to examine the sociological and professional backgrounds of the entire file of 1863 Insurrection participants, for the simple reason that it consisted of 40,000 names. Would such an analysis provide the ultimate answer to the question that interests us? This question must remain unanswered. Therefore, I do not want to and cannot state definitely what the January Insurrection meant as a sociological phenomenon and, more precisely, as its armed expression— whether it was an instrument of the gentry or of the entire nation. One thing may certainly be said, however, and that is that it was not only the gentry who determined the social program of the insurrection and the social structure of the army. New social forces had appeared on the scene of the Polish nineteenth-century national uprisings, and these forces had put an end to the dominant political role of the gentry as the leading force in Polish insurrections.

Yet, if one were to attempt to assess the contribution of the various social strata to the insurrection, then undoubtedly one would have to admit that its nucleus was the town population, which was especially affected by tsarist conscription. The middle classes were self-conscious and determined to play, as they never had before, an active political role. This group consisted of petty industrialists, traders, craftsmen, clerks, and laborers. They were supported by a mass of minor gentry, often lacking any land and suffocating in the close atmosphere of town officialdom or even degraded to the role of town proletariat. It was these two social strata that gave birth to the Polish intelligentsia, which was as heavily involved in the preinsurrection activities as in the insurrection itself. Unfortunately, they lacked the will and the consistency to carry out the tasks posed by the insurrection in the social, military, and political spheres. Further, they were effectively torpedoed by the influential aristocratic circles, rich landowners and bourgeoisie, who, independently of their policy of conciliation with the invaders, were fearful of the increasing social tensions that threatened a transformation of the insurrection against the invaders into a social revolution directed also against the landowners. In assessing the peasants' participation in the insurrection one should probably admit that Przyborowski was right in putting them completely in the shade of the 1863 events. The memory of wrongs, both ancient and recent, turned out to be stronger than the illusion of national unity, especially among the huge masses of peasants burdened with villein service. More active participation by peasants may be observed only in regions where the bonds of serfdom had already been broken and where there was greater economic freedom, usually connected with higher levels of civilization and education. The myth of "national unity" was juxtaposed by Piłsudski with the concept of a "real civil war," which revealed itself, among other things, in the gentry's reluctance to join the insurrection, the indecision of the national leadership, the frequent political clashes within the leadership, the lack of a uniform political and military policy, and, finally, the absence of recognized authorities. According to Piłsudski, "the year 1863 is a turning point in our history; the old Poland is dying, the new is being born."[10]

Notes

1. E. Kozłowski, "Armia Królestwa Polskiego" in *Przemiany społeczne w Królestwie Polskim 1815–1864* (Wrocław, 1979).
2. S. Kozicki (Lubicz), *Sprawa włościańska w Polsce porozbiorowej* (Cracow, 1909); E. Kostołowski, *Studia nad kwestią włościańską w latach 1846–1864* (Łwów, 1938).
3. E. Przybyszewski, *Proletariat przemysłowy w polskim ruchu rewolucyjnym lat sześćdziesiątych* (Warsaw, 1961); W. Kula and J. Jedlicki, "Struktura społeczna Królestwa Polskiego w przededniu powstania styczniowego," in *Powstanie styczniowe 1863*, vol. 1 (Warsaw, 1964); S. Kieniewicz, "Społeczeństwo Królestwa Polskiego w powstaniu styczniowym," in *Powstanie styczniowe 1863*, vol. 1 (Warsaw, 1963).
4. J. Piłsudski, "Zarys historii militarnej powstania styczniowego," in *Pisma*, vol. 3 (Warsaw, 1937).
5. E. Przybyszewski, *Stowarzyszenie historyków-marksistów o powstaniu styczniowym* (Warsaw, 1961), pp. 25–34.
6. J. Kucharzewski, *Od białego do czerwonego caratu*, vol. 4: *Wyzwalanie Ludów* (Warsaw, 1931).
7. E. Halicz, "O składzie socjalnym oddziałów powstańczych w 1863–1864 r. w Płockiem," *Biuletyn Akademii Wojskowo-Politycznej*, no. 4 (1956).
8. P. Bańkowski, "Z dziejów powstania styczniowego w Kielecczyźnie," in *Pamiętnik Kielecki* (Kielce, 1947).
9. K. Dunin Wąsowicz, *Marcin Borelowski "Lelewel," blacharz-pułkownik powstania 1863 r.* (Warsaw, 1964).
10. J. Piłsudski, "Rok 1863: Na rubieży dwóch epok," *Insurrekcje*, no. 1 (1929), pp. 4–8.

The Urban Population in the January Insurrection

Ryszard Bender

The war for national independence was taken up anew by the Polish nation in the insurrection that erupted on the night of January 22–23, 1863. The armed struggle had been preceded by a movement[1] that had begun to involve the whole nation—all its social strata—a few years prior to the January Night. The movement manifested itself in two types of activities: patriotic and religious manifestations, on the one hand, and conspiracy intended to prepare the nation for the armed uprising, on the other. The urban population was active both in the movement and in the armed struggle.[2]

It is nearly impossible to assign a date to the beginning of the movement. It was undoubtedly precipitated by the events of 1855, which for the Poles of the Russian sector marked the end of one epoch and the beginning of another: the death of Tsar Nicholas I and the succession of Alexander II. Polish hopes set on the latter were soon shattered. In May 1856, when he arrived in Warsaw, he was enthusiastically greeted, but he said, "Whatever my father has done, he has done correctly." He stated that Poland must remain under the complete control of Russia. The young generation of Poles realized, however, that Russia in point of fact had lost the Crimean War and had begun to seek a rapprochement with Western Europe. Therefore, they thought it necessary to avail themselves of the opportunity this presented.[3]

In 1857, in place of the expected university, Warsaw acquired, with the tsar's assent, the Surgical-Medical Academy. Students promptly organized clandestine circles promoting the idea of independence.[4] The first of them was formed by Narcyz Jankowski, an arrival from Kijów.[5] After several political demonstrations organized by the Warsaw circles in the years 1858–59, a new form was developed that gave them the protective coloration of patriotically religious demonstrations. The Catholic church was at that time the only independent institution in Poland that the occupying powers had failed to subvert or subordinate.[6]

The first of these demonstrations was not a Catholic one, but this was an accident. On the death of the widow of General Józef Sowiński, the heroic defender of Warsaw killed in 1831 while defending the city against the Russians, appropriate agitation brought to her funeral—a Calvinist one—on June 11, 1860, several thousand inhabitants of Warsaw, mainly students, schoolboys, and craftsman youth. Several months later, on November 29, 1860, the thirtieth anniversary of the November Insurrection, a large crowd gathered at the shrine of the Virgin Mary near the Carmelites' church in Warsaw. The assembled were handed texts of patriotic and religious songs and effigies of Tadeusz Kościuszko and Jan Killiński (a shoemaker promoted to colonel by Kościuszko in the 1794 Insurrection). One of the leaders of the manifestation intoned the hymn of the Congress Kingdom. The hymn, composed in honor of Tsar Alexander I and beginning with the words "God, you have protected Poland," was now supplemented with the refrain "Fatherland, freedom, deign to return to us, Lord." From then on the hymn with the refrain was considered a revolutionary song by the Russian authorities, and its singing was banned. Also sung at the November demonstration was the national anthem "Poland has not yet perished."[7]

These events were aimed at encouraging Polish society to take courage and to resist the Russian suppression of patriotic demonstrations.[8] Subsequent demonstrations proved that Polish society had overcome its fear of opposing the prohibitions issued by the Russian authorities. Initially they took place exclusively in cities and primarily in Warsaw. In time they drew into the whirl of current events nearly the whole urban population and the peasantry from nearby villages.

The next demonstration was not just a local affair involving a single part of the city; the procession that departed from the Paulist Church on February 25, 1861, mobilized the whole population of Warsaw. It was led by Paradowski, a shoemaker, who carried the red-and-white Polish national flag. Singing "Holy is God," the procession entered the Old Town Market, where it was confronted by Russian soldiers and military police. Fighting broke out. The crowd was dispersed, and several dozen people were arrested. This incident brought about another huge demonstration two days later at Castle Square, aimed at forcing the Russians to free those arrested at the market. The demonstration of February 27, which also started out as a religious procession, came to a tragic end. The army was sent to scatter the crowds. Shots were fired, and five persons were killed: Brendel, a metalworker, Adamkiewicz, a tailoring apprentice, Arcichiewicz, a schoolboy, and two landowners, Karczewski and Rutkowski. Their bodies were recovered and taken to lie in state in the European Hotel. Anger and resentment were the prevailing feelings among the inhabitants of Warsaw. The tsar's governor general, Duke Mikhail Gorchakov, frightened by these incidents, ordered the army to withdraw to its barracks.[9]

In the face of these events, a meeting of a group of citizens was called under the chairmanship of the banker Leopold Kronenberg. A municipal delegation of fourteen eminent citizens—journalists, merchants, bankers, a Protestant minister, a rabbi, and two Catholic priests—was elected. The governor was asked for permission to present a petition to Tsar Alexander II to allow solemn burial of those killed and to place the security measures during the funeral in the hands of the delegation. Under the pressure of circumstances, Gorchakov agreed to these demands. Following Warsaw's example, other cities under Russian rule—Lublin, Radom, and Płock, among others—created municipal delegations. There, as in Warsaw, security guards were created; they were made up of so-called constables recruited among students, schoolboys, and craftsman youth to maintain law and order in the streets. Security guards maintained perfect order in Warsaw on March 2, 1861, during the funeral of the five killed, which attracted thousands of inhabitants of Warsaw as well as people from other cities and villages. In the funeral procession, holding hands in display of national cooperation, marched members of the gentry and peasantry, bankers, businessmen, and workers, priests and rabbis.[10]

The bloody incidents in Warsaw had repercussions throughout Polish territory. The whole nation felt united by the blood shed in Warsaw. The protest against the suppression of the Warsaw demonstrations took the form of widespread mourning. Requiem masses for the souls of the five dead were said in churches all over the country. They were attended by representatives of all social strata, but primarily by the urban population, particularly the lowest classes.[11] The Jewish population took part in Catholic masses or organized its own religious services for the five dead Poles.[12] Requiem masses were said in towns of all three sectors of partitioned Poland—Russian, Prussian, and Austrian—and were heavily attended by the peasantry. Services even took place in Moscow, held March 17, 1861, at the suggestion of the Poles, in the local French church.[13] During the masses, priests delivered sermons appropriate to the occasion, patriotic and religious in essence, which did not please the Russian authorities.[14] The Catholic church in Poland at that time took a thoroughly Polish national position.[15] The clergy came increasingly from the working classes. The Metropolitan of Warsaw Archbishop Antoni Melchior Fijałkowski gave his consent for priests to take part in demonstrations of a patriotic and religious nature, which in the future were to be inspired by the radical political group called the Reds. He even entreated them to "stand by the nation." Other bishops did the same and stood up for clergymen involved in such demonstrations. For example, the Podlasie Ordinary, Bishop Beniamin Szymański, officially approached the Russian authorities in defense of the Reverend Stanisław Brzóska, eventually to be the last participant in the January Insurrection, who was imprisoned in 1861 for a patriotic sermon delivered in the church of the town of Łúków.[16] Even the Apostolic See did not condemn the demonstrations, although it considered their organizers too radical.[17]

During the time when the requiem masses were being said in Warsaw, the people of all the Polish territories put on mourning attire, and this became a symbol of patriotism and an expression of protest. Mourning attire was worn most ostentatiously by the urban populace—craftsmen, students, and schoolboys. Mourning insignia were also worn by Polish clerks employed by the Russian administration. Even the gentry residing in cities wore mourning. Sometimes the mourning attire was only symbolic, just a black tie, a black ribbon, or a mourning band on a hat or a cap. Social pressure sometimes literally forced everyone to wear mourning.[18] Particularly in the cities, hardly anyone ventured out without mourning insignia.[19] From the spring of 1861 on, the whole Polish nation was plunged into mourning. This made the most striking impression in the cities, where the crowds filling the streets sometimes looked like funeral processions. Count Charles Forbes de Montalembert, observing all this, spoke of "a nation in mourning."[20]

The requiem masses said for those killed in Warsaw on February 27 and on April 8, during another patriotic and religious demonstration bloodily suppressed,[21] intensified the religious faith of the nation. From then on even purely political demonstrations began or ended with a religious element. Thus, for instance, in Lublin on April 2, 1861, a crowd of several thousand marched through the streets. The Russian authorities called out their soldiers. The demonstrators caterwauled against several detested civil servants—yelling and throwing cauldrons, pots, and other kitchen utensils—and then, kneeling in front of the picture of the Holy Virgin, sang religious songs before going home.[22] The army did not dare to use weapons against the singing crowd. Similar caterwauls were organized in other towns and cities, among them Radom, Płock, and Kalisz.[23]

In their turn, purely religious ceremonies, particularly processions, were turned into political demonstrations in the preinsurrection period. Processions were usually accompanied by the erection of crosses or figures of patron saints along the streets through which they passed, and these crosses and figures were now equipped with inscriptions or emblems referring to the bloody incidents in Warsaw on February 27 and April 8. The inscriptions read "To those killed in Warsaw," "To the subjugated nation," and "Tremble, enemies of the Cross," and the emblems might be a crown of thorns, manacles, the broken countenance of Christ, or the white eagle (the Polish national emblem).[24]

These large, powerful urban demonstrations, political in character and generally placed in a religious setting, constituted a novelty in the Polish war for independence and in the revolutionary movement in Europe. For the first time in the history of Poland they revealed the close connection between national, religious, and revolutionary slogans in the struggle for national independence.[25] The movement came to be called a moral revolution. It was considered in the country, and at times also in Europe, as superior to the French Revolution because it was free of bloodshed, based on the moral strength of the nation rather than on terror.[26]

The moral revolution initiated by the clandestine circles of the youth of Warsaw and supported by the Catholic and other clergy, including the Jews, gained the approval of the radicals who came to constitute the Reds. Conservative circles in Poland, which consisted of landowners and the wealthy bourgeoisie, fearing an insurrection, exploited the moral revolution to force administrative reforms and political concessions from the Russian authorities in Warsaw and St. Petersburg. They wanted the movement to come out into the open, in the belief that this would prevent it from leading to an insurrection. They hoped that reforms and concessions would make demonstrations unnecessary, and this argument was presented to the Russian authorities in St. Petersburg. The authorities did not immediately agree. The tsar's ukase of March 26, 1861, restored the state council of the Congress Kingdom and established local self-government in the form of provincial, district, and municipal councils.[27] At the same time, however, the tsar's authorities abolished all of the municipal delegations created after the Warsaw incidents of February 27. The Whites, including among others some members of the abolished municipal delegations, agitated for acceptance of the concessions introduced by the ukase. The Reds objected to the concessions, including the newly created municipal councils, and even more categorically to the functioning of those councils after the proclamation of martial law in the Congress Kingdom on October 14, 1861. The Central National Committee set up by the Reds instructed all councillors to cease participating in the councils on October 5, 1862.[28] The councillors in all the cities complied with this instruction, and by the end of 1862 the municipal councils had in fact ceased to exist; the tsar's authorities were unable to get the councillors to meet.

By that time control over national matters was already being exercised by the Central National Committee, which had emerged in June 1862 out of the former municipal delegation of Warsaw. The Central National Committee explicitly aimed at an insurrection, and before its eruption it was the supreme secret national authority. In time it generated various cells of the Polish secret underground state, which were subordinated to the Central National Committee in Warsaw and to its regional organs functioning in other cities. The Central National Committee created the secret National Organization, which integrated the majority of Polish society, preparing them for the war of independence, the outbreak of the insurrection.[29] The National Organization involved great masses of people in conspiratorial work in preparation for the armed uprising. Since the demonstrations impeded conspiracy, by the end of 1862 they had been almost completely abandoned.[30]

In conspiracy, the Polish secret underground state developed structures functioning side by side with those of the forces of the occupation, represented in Warsaw by the tsar's governor and the Russian administration, whose lower echelons included Poles. The Polish secret state was run by the Central National Committee, which was in hiding in Warsaw. Outside Warsaw, provincial leaders, residing in the provincial cities, were subordinated to it. Provincial commissars were emissaries between the Central National Committee and the provincial leaders. District leaders were subordinated to the provincial leaders and municipal leaders to the district ones. In cities and towns every block had its own secret agent subordinated to a precinct one who was in turn subordinated to the municipal leader. The conspirators preparing the insurrection were organized in tens, hundreds, and thousands; the heads of the latter, the so-called thousanders (*tysięcznicy*), were subordinated to the section (*wydziałowy*) leaders, who reported directly to the municipal leaders.[31] In every district of Warsaw and every small town there was a conspiratorial cell. Such cells existed also in every institution, workshop, church, and convent. Conspirators were also active in the Russian administration, the post offices, the railway, and the police. Secret national authorities were usually forewarned by the collaborating conspirators about planned arrests and searches. This hindered the spread of Russian repression. In contrast to the cities, the countryside, busy with farming, was less well organized.

A staunch opponent of the development of the secret underground state was Aleksander Wielopolski, who closely collaborated with Grand Duke Constantine, governor of Poland on the tsar's behalf,[32] and was by the tsar's nomination head of the civil government in the Congress Kingdom.[33] It was he who gave the Russian authorities the idea of introducing conscription into the Russian army (the so-called impressment) primarily of persons engaged in the conspiracy in order to avert or delay the outbreak of the expected insurrection.

The Central National Committee, at that time made up of Agaton Giller, Zygmunt Padlewski, Józef Kajetan Janowski, Jan Maykowski, and the Reverend Karol Mikoszewski, at the beginning of January 1863 decided to accept the impressment as sufficient reason for announcing the outbreak of the insurrection.[34] The impressment in Warsaw began on the night of January 14–15. Most of the conspirators who were proscribed managed to escape from Warsaw to the country, where conscription was to take place later, or headed for the forests, where insurgent units were being organized.[35] Some of them hid in the gentry's manors or peasants' houses, where they awaited the eruption of the uprising.[36]

Under the circumstances, the Central National Committee was transformed into the Provisional National Government, consisting of Oskar Awejde, Janowski, Mikoszewski, and Maykowski as secretary. This government issued a resolution about the outbreak of the insurrection throughout the Kingdom of Poland on the night of January 22–23, 1863.[37] General Ludwik Mierosławski was invited to come home from abroad and was appointed dictator and commander-in-chief of the insurrection. The Provisional National Government decided to leave Warsaw on the outbreak of the insurrection, fearing that the city would be cut off from the provinces. It left behind it in Warsaw the Executive Committee under the leadership of Stefan Bobrowski. On the afternoon of January 22, 1863, all the members of the Provisional National Government went by train to Kutno. There they intended to wait for the liberation of Płock by Zygmunt Padlewski, when the National Government was to come out into the open.[38] The liberation of Płock, however, never took place.

Other cities were not conquered, either, although on the night of January 22–23 and in the subsequent days there were twenty-four attacks on Russian garrisons, mainly in cities. Besides Płock, Biała Podlaska, Lubartów, Radzyń, Łuków, Kodeń, Szraż, Wysokie Mazowieckie, Tykocin, and Mężenin were attacked. In only a few of these towns did the insurgents briefly gain the upper hand. In all of them, after a few hours, in spite of the aid of the local citizens, they had to succumb to Russian power. None of the towns attacked was controlled for any considerable time.[39] Persistent fighting over some towns, e.g., Węgrów, lasted until the first days of February 1863 without success.[40] Marian Langiewicz planned attacks on eight towns situated around Radom, counting on partisan forces and on the support of the workers employed in metallurgical plants of some of these towns. On the night of January 22–23, Bodzentyn, Jedlnia, and Szydłowiec were attacked but not captured. Later Langiewicz took Wąchock for a short time and from it controlled the strategically important road from Warsaw to Cracow.[41] In Lublin province, Leon Frankowski called upon the students of the Polytechnical Institute in Puławy to join the insurrection, and they captured Kazimierz Dolny for a short period of time. Caught by the Russians after the battle of Słupcza, Frankowski was hanged in Lublin on April 16, 1863.[42] A doctor from Dubienka, Mikołaj Nieczaj, with a party of citizens from the town and neighboring towns and villages, liberated Hrubieszów from the Russians. Caught after the battle of Żalin on February 22, 1863, he was shot by the Russians in the district town of Krasnystaw; they ran over his grave with cannon to erase it from the face of the earth.[43]

In sum, the outcome of the January Night and the following days was more favorable for the insurgents than has so far been assumed in historical research. In many towns, Russian garrisons were gravely imperiled by the insurgents and often had to fight fierce battles. The insurgents gained experience in field battles as well as in street fights. They entered into cooperation with conspirators in the towns attacked. Often they acquired a good deal of firearms and ammunition from the enemy. In the first days of the insurrection, the urban population prevailed in partisan units. As a rule, they were young people who had managed to join the partisan troops before the impressment into the Russian army had begun. Later, as the insurrection was spreading, a great number of the gentry and the peasantry reinforced the insurgent units.

The spring and summer of 1863 brought an extension of the insurrection. Insurrectionary activities in the Russian sector were reinforced by Poles arriving from the Prussian and Austrian sectors.[44] From there also came firearms and ammunition purchased at times in Western Europe, among other countries in Belgium. The urban population of Galicia, the Duchy of Poznań, and Pomorze was very active in delivering supplies. While there were separate gentry and peasant insurgent units,[45] purely townsmen's units were nonexistent. The urban population usually fought in units consisting of representatives of various social groups.[46] Some of them were commanded by townsmen. Thus, for instance, one of the units was commanded by Marcin Borelowski (pseudonym Lelewel), a tinsmith and master well-driller who held the rank of colonel and was killed in the battle of Batorze on September 6, 1863.[47]

Almost the entire administration of the Polish underground state and the various executive organs of the National Government were in the hands of the urban population of Warsaw and other cities of the Russian sector during the insurrection. The secret national police was made up mostly of townsmen. Townsmen, and in particular the intelligentsia, were numerous in the structures of the insurgent National Government. The National Government, save for the periods of dictatorship, was a collegial body and made decisions by voting. These were carried out by executive and auxiliary organs of the government and by the local administration of the Polish underground state. Among the executive organs of the government were the state secretariat and, at various periods, departments of home affairs, foreign affairs, treasury, press, war, and police. The office of municipal leader was an important one, and subordinated to it were such departments as forwarding, post management, communication, and police. The functionaries of these institutions were recruited mostly from the urban population and occasionally from landowners or clerks from their estates. This was the case in Warsaw, in provincial cities, and in district towns—in sum, in the entire Kingdom of Poland. A similar situation obtained outside the Kingdom, in cooperating Lithuania and Belorussia. The autonomous insurgent committees operating there were made up of people brought up and educated in cities. Thus, for instance, the commander of the War Department in Lithuania, in Vilnius, the engineer Józef Kalinowski, formerly a Russian army captain, was a son of the headmaster of Collegium Nobilium in that city.[48]

Insurgent troops operating in the provinces, mainly in the woods, were in close contact with the Warsaw National Government and its agencies in Warsaw and other cities. Cities were visited by couriers from the insurgent units and delegated representatives of the national underground authorities to these units. Cities and towns served the insurgents as centers where they could obtain arms and ammunition purchased secretly from Russian soldiers or stolen from Russian magazines. For example, Kazimierz Wydrychiewicz secretly bought from the Russians in Lublin some fifteen thousand cartridges which he supplied to Michał Heidenreich-Kruk's troops.[49]

In the course of the insurrection, the capture of towns for several days or hours enabled the insurgent troops to obtain supplies not only of firearms, but also of other equipment. City garrisons and police were disarmed, treasuries taken over, and warehouses confiscated and their contents sold cheaply to the citizens, the proceeds going to support the insurgents. This was a regular procedure throughout the insurrection. For instance, on January 22–23, 1863, insurgents took 1,544 złoty 10 groszy from the treasury in Kraśnik.[50] In February 1863, insurgent detachments entered several towns in Zagłębie Dąbrowskie, among them Sosnowiec, where they took forty rifles, forty horses, a great many side arms, and 100 quintals of lead belonging to a Prussian firm in nearby Katowice (in Prussia).[51] In May 1863, the partisan unit of Władysław Konowicz disarmed Russian guards and seized salt warehouses in Magnuszew and Ryczywół; the salt was sold by the insurgents to the citizens of these and other towns.[52] The main warehouses in big cities such as Lublin, Kielce, or Radom, where Russian troops were concentrated, were not seized, because these cities were not attacked.[53] One result of the battle of Żyżyn on August 8, 1863, apart from the victory itself, was the seizing of the Russians' supply wagons and, above all, of 200,000 rubles.[54] The money thus acquired usually reached the cities, where it paid for the equipment necessary for the insurgent troops either secretly or, when the city had been temporarily captured, openly.

Therefore, the Russian army guarded even the smallest towns against contact with insurgent troops, and this is why so few towns were conquered and these usually only briefly. Large garrisons were stationed in towns also to prevent the urban population from cooperating with the insurgent units operating in the neighborhood. The Russians were not always successful in this. Sometimes, as a result of such cooperation, these towns as late as 1864 became battlefields of vital importance for the insurrection. Such was the battle fought by the insurgents against the Russian army on February 21, 1864, in Opatów. The Polish side assumed that street fights would be easier for them in the densely built-up area and that the Russians would not engage in heavy defense within the town because of its inflammable, chiefly wooden buildings. During the battle, however, these factors turned against the attacking Polish forces. Both made defense easier for the Russian army. Under the circumstances, even the help of the citizens did not tip the scales in the insurgents' favor. The Polish troops had to give up the attempt at taking the town. The battle of Opatów was fought, in fact, by only five infantry companies of insurgents commanded by Apolinary Kurowski and Ludwik Zwierzchowski against a much more numerous and better-armed enemy.[55]

It should be noted that, except for this battle and several others not mentioned here, most armed struggles were partisan actions rather than pitched battles. In the January Insurrection, as in the preceding Polish insurrections, various forms of partisan warfare or so-called small-scale warfare prevailed. In the nineteenth century, partisan warfare had a long tradition in Polish military thought. Many of the concepts of partisan warfare had arisen in Poland. This subject has been examined by, among others, Wojciech Chrzanowski and Wincenty Nieszokoć, Karol Bogumił Stolzman, and Henryk Kamieński,[56] but they deal only to a very limited extent with the relations between partisan warfare in the field and in the city.

From the outset, the 1863–64 Insurrection was intended by successive National Governments to be a partisan war, without excluding the possibility of a conventional large-scale war in the future. The brief presence in Poland of General Ludwik Mierosławski, a convinced advocate of conventional warfare, did not substantially change the situation.[57] Only the assumption of the dictatorship by Romuald Traugutt at the end of 1863 gradually changed the state of affairs. His decree of December 15, 1863,[58] introduced the organization typical of a regular army into the partisan detachments—forming a national army consisting of four corps from those detachments. However, the reorganization of the insurgent forces was never fully carried out. Therefore, at the end of the insurrection partisan warfare once again prevailed. It was very successful at times, for instance, in harassing the enemy's rear, but it made it difficult or impossible for the Polish side to capture the larger towns or cities and control small towns after seizing them, in spite of the citizens' cooperation.

In this situation, members of the urban population often joined the partisan detachments posted in the nearby woods. Less frequently, they took part in battles for the small towns in which they lived. At the time of the greatest intensity of insurgent warfare in the Kingdom of Poland there were around thirty thousand insurgents engaged in the fighting.[60] How many of these were recruited from the urban population has not yet been determined.

Of the urban population that remained in towns and did not join the insurgent detachments, the majority cooperated in various ways with the partisans and the insurrection. Cooperation with the insurgents was easiest for the inhabitants of small provincial towns, since insurgent troops often operated or camped in their vicinity. The insurgents did not approach the larger towns or cities, which usually had strong Russian garrisons. The civilian population of these cities, including Warsaw, often joined insurgent detachments or supplied them with firearms, equipment, and food. However, the population of cities was active mainly in the various institutions of the Polish underground state and influenced the development of the insurrection in this way. In Kielce, Lublin, and Podlasie provinces, toward the end of the insurrection, the insurgents got the most substantial help from the population of small towns. By secretly providing them with firearms and ammunition and at times with food delivered by the peasantry, these townsmen made it possible for small insurgent units to survive until the fall of 1864. It was in Podlasie that the Reverend Stanisław Brzóska, aided by the rural and urban population, was the last to give up the insurrectionary struggle.[61] Caught by the Russians on April 29, 1865, he was hanged by them in Sokołów on May 23.[62]

According to the files of the Russian local authorities, the city dwellers who joined insurgent units remained in them the longest, sometimes until the last moments of the insurrection. They were the last to leave the battlefield and fought to the bitter end, some of them up to the end of 1864, when the gentry and the peasantry of the neighborhood had already left for home without waiting for the total suppression of the insurrection.[63]

Notes

1. Stefan Kieniewicz, *Powstanie styczniowe* (Warsaw, 1972). The author divides his book into two parts: *Ruch* (Movement) and *Walka* (Armed Struggle).
2. Natalia Gąsiorowska, "Mieszczaństwo w powstaniu styczniowym," *Przegląd Historyczny* 34 (1937–38): 530–39.
3. Adam Szelągowski, "Dzieje Polski w czasach powstania styczniowego," in *Polska jej dzieje i kultura*, vol. 1 (Warsaw, 1930), pp. 300–303.
4. Walentyna Rudzka, "Młodzież Kongresówki w latach 1855–1861," *Przegląd Historyczny* 32 (1935): 210–12.
5. Georgii Frumienkov, "Kruzhok N. Jankovskogo," *Voprosy Istorii*, 1956, no. 1, pp. 113–16.
6. Julian Jastrzębczyk, *Krzyżowy charakter ruchu polskiego* (Łwów, 1864), p. 5.
7. *Zeznania śledcze o powstaniu styczniowym*, ed. S. Kieniewicz (Wrocław, 1956), pp. 131 and 201.
8. Ryszard Bender, *Chrześcijanie w polskich ruchach demokratycznych XIX stulecia* (Warsaw, 1975), pp. 123–24.
9. S. Kieniewicz, *Warszawa w powstaniu styczniowym* (Warsaw, 1954), pp. 60–63.
10. Ibid., pp. 65–69; Franciszka Ramotowska, *Rząd carski wobec manifestacji patriotycznych w Królestwie Polskim w latach 1860–1862* (Warsaw, 1971), pp. 51–63.
11. Walery Przyborowski, *Historia dwóch lat*, vol. 2 (Cracow, 1893), pp. 156–58.
12. R. Bender, "Ludność żydowska na Lubelszczyźnie w akcji przedpowstaniowej 1861–1862," *Biuletyn Żydowskiego Instytutu Historycznego*, no. 35 (1960), pp. 47–54.
13. Józef Kowalski, *Rewolucyjna demokracja rosyjska a powstanie styczniowe* (Warsaw, 1955), p. 38.
14. Wojewódzkie Archiwum Państwowe in Lublin (hereafter WAPL), Rząd

Gubernialny Lubelski, Wydział Administracyjny, vol. 1122, p. 15, pismo namiestnika Królestwa Polskiego do gubernatora lubelskiego z 20.IV.1861.
15. Mieczystais Żywczyński, "Kościół i duchowieństwo w powstaniu styczniowym," *Przegląd Historyczny* 34 (1937–38): 513.
16. R. Bender, "Sprawa ks. Stanisława Brzóski w 1861 r.," *Zeszyty Naukowe KUL* 5, no. 3 (1962): 59–63.
17. Józef Pelczar, *Pius IX a Polska* (Miejsce Piastowe, 1914), pp. 40–41.
18. WAPL, Gimnazjum Wojewódzkie Lubelskie, vol. 426, p. 29, pismo gubernatora lubelskiego do dyrektora gimnazjum z 15.IV.1861; R. Bender, "Młodzież szkolna Lublina w akcji przedpowstaniowej 1861–1863," *Przegląd Historyczno-Oświatowy* 5 (1962): 219–28.
19. Thadée Tyszkiewicz, *Ecrits sur la Pologne contemporaine (1862–1864)* (Brussels, 1864), p. 70.
20. Charles Forbes de Montalembert, *Une nation en deuil: La Pologne en 1861* (Paris, 1861).
21. Kieniewicz, *Warszawa w powstaniu*, pp. 83–86.
22. WAPL, Rząd Gubernialny Lubelski, akta tajne, vol. 15, p. 260, prezydent Lublina do gubernatora 2.IV.1861.
23. Maria Maj, "Udział młodzieży radomskiej w powstaniu styczniowym," *Rocznik Świętokrzyski* 2 (1971): 240–42. See also Witold Dąbkowski, *Powstanie styczniowe w Puszczy Kozienickiej* (Warsaw, 1974), pp. 52–56; R. Szwed, *Powstanie styczniowe w Zagłębiu Dąbrowskim* (Warsaw, 1978), pp. 27–30.
24. R. Bender, *Ludność miejska Lubelskiego w akcji przedpowstaniowej w latach 1861–1862* (Lublin, 1961), pp. 33–43.
25. Tadeusz Łepkowski, *Polska-narodziny nowoczesnego narodu 1764–1870* (Warsaw, 1967), p. 325.
26. R. Bender, "Rewolucja moralna 1861 r.," *Zeszyty Naukowe KUL* 4, no. 3 (1961): 83–92.
27. *Dziennik Praw Królestwa Polskiego*, vol. 57, pp. 333–39. See also Juliusz Struminski, "Rady miejskie i powiatowe w Królestwie Polskim," *Czasopismo Prawno-Historyczne* 4 (1952): 311–13; R. Bender, "Mieszczaństwo Lublina w wyborach samorządowych do Rady Miejskiej w 1861 r.," in *Dzieje burżuazji w Polsce*, ed. Ryszard Kołodziejczyk, vol. 2 (Wrocław, 1980), pp. 29–33.
28. *Dokumenty Komitetu Centralnego Narodowego i Rządu Narodowego 1862–1864* (Wrocław, 1968), p. 22.
29. F. Ramotowska, *Rząd Narodowy Polski w latach 1863–1864* (Warsaw, 1978), p. 8.
30. Agaton Giller, *Historia powstania narodu polskiego w 1861–1864 r.* (Paris, 1867), pp. 67–68.
31. Edward Maliszewski, *Organizacja powstania styczniowego* (Warsaw, 1922), pp. 34–36.
32. Irena Koberdowa, *Wielki książę Konstanty w Warszawie 1862–1863* (Warsaw, 1962).
33. Adam Skałkowski, *Aleksander Wielopolski w świetle archiwów rodzinnych*, vol. 3 (Poznań, 1947), pp. 22–23 and 150–53. See also Zbigniew Stan-

kiewicz, *Dzieje wielkości i upadku Aleksandra Wielopolskiego* (Warsaw, 1967), pp. 137-38.
34. *Zeznania śledcze o powstaniu styczniowym*, p. 35.
35. Kieniewicz, *Powstanie styczniowe*, pp. 353-54; *Raporty polityczne konsulów generalnych Francji w Warszawie 1860-1864*, ed. I. Koberdowa (Wrocław, 1965), p. 324.
36. S. Kieniewicz, *Sprawa włościańska w powstaniu styczniowym* (Wrocław, 1953), pp. 253-54. See also Emanuel Halicz, *Kwestia chłopska w Królestwie Polskim w dobie powstania styczniowego* (Warsaw, 1955), p. 235; R. Bender, *Reforma czynszowa w Ordynacji Zamoyskiej 1833-1864* (Lublin, 1969), pp. 206-10.
37. *Dokumenty KCN i Rządu Narodowego*, p. 40.
38. Ramotowska, *Rząd Narodowy*, p. 26; R. Bender, *Ksiądz Karol Mikoszewski (X. Syxtus) 1832-1886* (Warsaw, 1982), p. 63.
39. Kieniewicz, *Powstanie styczniowe*, pp. 369-72; J. Tomczyk, "Organizacja cywilno-wojskowa powstania styczniowego w Lubelskiem i na Podlasiu," *Rocznik Lubelski* 6 (1963): 36-48.
40. Eligiusz Kozłowski, *Od Węgrowa do Opatowa 3.II.1863-21.II.1864* (Warsaw, 1962), pp. 32-39.
41. Helena Rzadkowska, *Marian Langiewicz* (Warsaw, 1967), pp. 107-10.
42. WAPL, Rząd Gubernialny Lubelski, Wydział Administracyjny, vol. 1638, p. 131 and passim. See also Bender, *Ludność miejska Lubelskiego*, p. 101.
43. R. Bender, "Doktor Mikołaj Nieczaj," *Więź* 1967, no. 5, pp. 116-17.
44. *Galicja w Powstaniu styczniowym* (Wrocław, 1980). See also Zdisław Grot, *Rok 1863 w zaborze pruskim* (Poznań, 1963).
45. Kieniewicz, *Sprawa włościańska*, p. 332; Bender, *Reforma czynszowa w Ordynacji*, p. 210.
46. Tadeusz Mencel, "Walenty Lewandowski i początek powstania styczniowego na Podlasiu," and "Piąty oddział województwa lubelskiego Kajetana Cieszkowskiego-Ćwieka w powstaniu styczniowym," *Rocznik Lubelski* 6 (1963): 71-155.
47. Julian Sokulski, "Borelowski Marcin," in *Polski Słownik Biograficzny*, vol. 2 (Cracow, 1936), pp. 322-24.
48. R. Bender, *Powstaniec-zakonnik: O. Rafał Kalinowski* (Warsaw, 1977), pp. 52-56.
49. W. Przyborowski, *Dzieje 1863 r.*, vol. 4 (Cracow, 1897-1919), pp. 335-36.
50. WAPL, Rząd Gubernialny Lubelski, Wydział Administracyjny, vol. 1638, p. 15, pismo naczelnika powiatu zamojskiego z 24.I.1863. See also Tomczyk, "Organizacja," p. 44.
51. Szwed, *Powstanie styczniowe*, pp. 63-67.
52. Dąbkowski, *Powstanie styczniowe*, p. 147.
53. Leonard Ratajczyk, *Polska wojna partyzancka 1863-1864: Okres dyktatury Romualda Traugutta* (Warsaw, 1966), p. 254.
54. Nikolaj Pawliszczew, *Sedmicy polskogo miateża 1861-1864* (St. Petersburg, 1887), pp. 153-61. See also *Zeznania śledcze*, p. 263.

55. Kozłowski, *Od Węgrowa do Opatowa*, pp. 220–33; Ratajczyk, *Polska wojna partyzancka*, pp. 277–81.
56. E. Halicz, *Partisan Warfare in Nineteenth-Century Poland: The Development of a Concept* (Odense, 1975); P. Brock, *Polish Revolutionary Populism* (Toronto, 1977).
57. Marian Żychowski, *Ludwik Mierosławski 1814–1878* (Warsaw, 1963), pp. 537–56.
58. *Dokumenty KCN i Rządu Narodowego*, pp. 291–92.
59. Ratajczyk, *Polska wojna partyzancka*, p. 248.
60. M. Dubiecki, *Romuald Traugutt i jego dyktatura podczas powstania styczniowego* (Poznań, 1924), p. 15.
61. Krzysztof Groniowski, "Oddział księdza Brzóski," *Przegląd Historyczny*, 1959, no. 4, pp. 831–32.
62. Helena Maliszewska, "Brzóska Stanisław," in *Polski Słownik Biograficzny*, vol. 3 (Cracow, 1937), p. 70.
63. WAPL, Rząd Gubernialny Lubelski, Wydział Administracyjny, vols. 1123–24 and vols. 1637–40. See also WAPL, Naczelnik Wojenny Oddziału Zamoysko-Hrubieszowskiego, vol. 3.

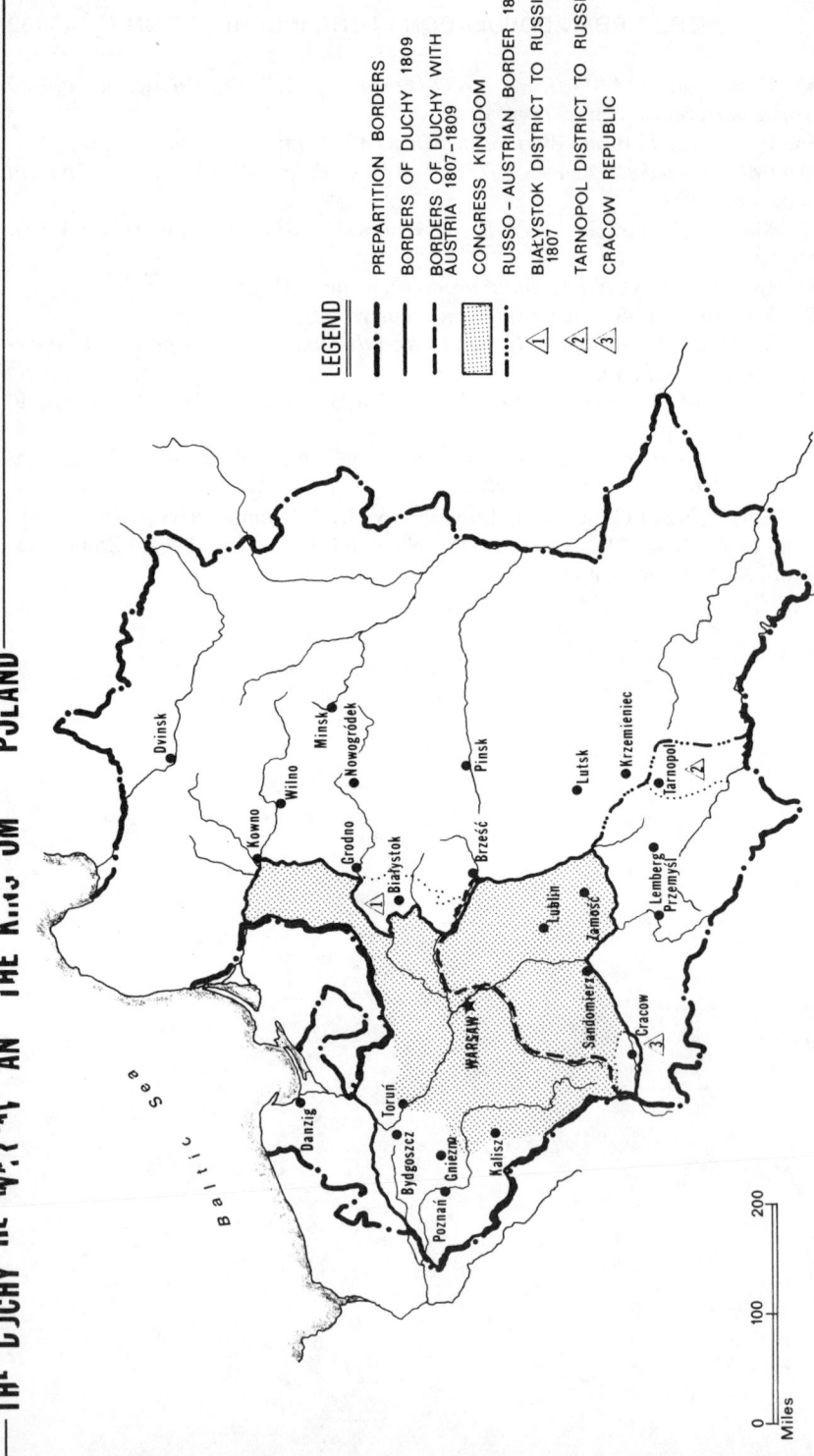

The Influence of Environmental Features on the Course of the Fighting in the Polish January Insurrection[1]

Tadeusz Mencel

On the January night that began the 1863 Insurrection in Poland, the aim of the leaders was to destroy Russian garrisons and capture numerous towns in the Congress Kingdom. The town of Płock was to become the seat of the National Government and the province of Płock the operational base of the insurgent army. These plans failed, and only the momentary disorientation of Russian forces and the order to concentrate smaller garrisons enabled the national organizations in many country towns with no Russian garrisons to gather volunteers, organize and train the first military detachments, and prepare uniforms, equipment, and weapons (swords, scythes, and pikes). In some towns the Polish insurgent authorities acted quite openly in those first days. However, fearing the arrival of Russian columns, they were soon forced to go underground, and the military detachments had to take to the woods.

From its beginnings, the January Insurrection had no chance of turning into a regular war, as there was no operational base and the Russian army, one hundred thousand strong, possessed a crushing superiority in numbers, equipment, and training over the insurgents, numbering fewer than twenty thousand men half-armed with scythes and pikes, hunting rifles, and several hundred carbines taken during attacks on Russian posts. Modern firearms—carbines, rifles, pistols—came from abroad only later and in insufficient quantity. At the start the insurrection was not supported by the whole of Polish society; in particular, the landed gentry, the rich townspeople, and, above all, the peasants stood apart from it. Thus it could not be a national war based on a mass levy. Under the circumstances, the insurrection became a guerrilla war in its very first weeks. It consisted in destroying and disarming small Russian columns under conditions favorable to the insurgents and cutting off transport and communication lines. Those tactics could not be used everywhere, as in many cases poorly armed and poorly trained insurgent units avoided engaging the stronger enemy.

Attempts at organizing an operational base were not, however, abandoned, and at the beginning of March 1863 plans were made to create a corps twenty thousand strong to expel the Russian garrisons from the Sandomierz and Kalisz provinces and to set up a national government in the town of Częstochowa. The dictatorship of Langiewicz thwarted these plans. At the end of March, Zygmunt Padlewski, operating in the province of Płock, proposed forcing the Russian troops out of their garrisons, pushing them in the direction of the Vistula, and confining them in the region of Modlin, which would have enabled the insurgents to secure operational grounds close to the Prussian border. No attempts were made to take the fortresses of Modlin and Brześć, which could have become important centers of opposition, and whose large stores of arms and munitions would have supplied tens of thousands of insurgents, who would thus have become regular army detachments. Because of the failure of these plans, the fortresses and towns of the Congress Kingdom remained bases for Russian troops.

The insurgents took to the woods. As early as January, would-be conscripts hid in the woods of Nieporęt and in the Kampinoska forest, where they found shelter in huts and around campfires during the blizzards of February 1863. In the forest camps, military drills were carried out; the insurgents were taught how to load and fire arms, how to form a firing line, and how to use scythes against the enemy. Under the conditions of guerrilla warfare, localities providing safe shelter were particularly important for the insurgents, especially in the beginning.

The configuration of the terrain, the water system, and the location of woods and forests were of great importance for guerrilla operations. The Kielecko-Sandomierska Upland, with its small mountain ranges, the highest of which were the Świętokrzyskie Mountains, cut by gullies and valleys and covered with thick woods, was one of the most suitable regions. Regular army detachments with their guns and supply columns could scarcely move in such an environment, but insurgent units found it comparatively easy. In the north the Świętokrzyskie Mountains were protected by the thick Iłża forest and the woods of Cisów, Opatów, and Ostrowiec. At the foot of these mountains, at Wąchock, General Langiewicz organized Polish units in safety, and it was only after two weeks that the Russians undertook to attack them.

In the northern part of Sandomierz province, the lowland at the confluence of the Pilica and Vistula Rivers comprised the solid mass of the Kozienicka forest and, along the Pilica, dense woods with many marshes. There were smaller concentrations of woods in the Krakowsko-Częstochowska Upland as well as along the Warta River at the Silesian border from Częstochowa to Kalisz province. In Kalisz province, at the curve of the Warta north of the town of Kalisz, there were some woods and marshes around little lakes and along streams, but this part of the province was only partially wooded.

The part of Mazowsze province on the left bank of the Vistula was similar in character. Only to the north of the Pilica were there large woods (the Lubochnia, between Rawa and Tomaszów) and the remnants of old forests (between Mszczonów and Skierniewice). The small Kampinoska forest was nearer Warsaw; longer strips of woods extended along the banks of the Vistula from Włocławek to Ciechocinek. Mazowsze province was relatively open county.

On the right bank of the Vistula—in the provinces of Płock and Łomża, bordering on the Lithuanian forests, the province of Podlasie, between the Bug and the Lower Wieprz River, and Lublin province, in the region of the Wieprz and Tyśmienica Rivers reaching the Austrian border on the Rivers Tanew and San—the terrain varied.

Płock province was the land bridge between the Congress Kingdom and Lithuania and Belorussia. The western part of the province, comprising both banks of the Wkra River, was, with the exception of a small strip of woods on the Vistula, rather open and traversed by numerous roads leading mostly to Warsaw. In the eastern part was Ponarwie, intersected by swampy tributaries of the Narew. Ponarwie comprised both extensive wooded areas and boggy meadows turning into inaccessible marshes out of which rose higher woodlands—the Zielona and Myszyniecka forests. Swampy streams—the Orzyc, the Omulew, the Pożoga, and the Szkwa—made road building difficult. Before the insurrection, the leaders of the conspiracy had planned to make the Myszyniecka forest (also called Kurpiowska) one of the two concentration points for insurgents (the other being Płock) because of its inaccessibility, its closeness to the Prussian border, and the patriotism of the local people, the Kurpie, many of whom hunted and poached and therefore possessed firearms. In the Prussian territory the Myszyniecka merged into the Pisz forest, a significant factor in the smuggling of arms from Prussia.

In the province of Augustów the swampy Ostrołęka and Łomża forests, the Czerwony wood, and the Wizna marsh were similar in character. In this region there were numerous poor-gentry villages whose patriotic inhabitants supported the insurgent units in the woods. At the confluence of the Narew and the Biebrza Rivers, the Biebrza marshes, which covered some hundreds of square kilometers, were difficult of access, and the Augustów forest, with its densely growing trees and its lack of roads, was excellent terrain for insurgent camps. In the extreme north of the Congress Kingdom, on the Niemen lowlands, there were large wooded areas with many marshes and lakes and a poor network of roads. Augustów province bordered in the west on eastern Prussia and in the east on the Russian guberniyas (called "provinces" by the insurgents) of Grodno, Vilna, and Kovno, where, from the spring of 1863 onward, there was animated insurgent activity involving the Polish, Lithuanian, and Belorussian inhabitants.

In the south, at the confluence of the Vistula and the Bug, within Mazowsze province, there were some woods in the vicinity of Radzymin, Nieporęt, and Minsk; at the confluence of the Bug and the Liwiec the woods were more extensive. To the south of the Wieprz many rivers with swampy banks made passage in some localities in Podlasie province difficult on account of the lack of roads. From Biała through Międzyrzec and Łuków to the Vistula at the estuary of the Wieprz there were woods, with intermittent cultivated fields, adjoining marshes, and small lakes on waterlogged or sandy lowlands. On the Vistula there were also wooded zones from the Wieprz to Warsaw. From Parczew, along the Tyśmienica and Krzna Rivers, to Chełm, in the Parczewsko-Włodawskie lake district, there were marshes partially covered with woods and interspersed with lakes. Between the Wieprz and the Vistula there were the Lubartów woods; to the south of Gołąb, along the Vistula, there were the woods of Urzędów, Janów, and Biłgoraj, joining the Solska forest at the border of Galicia along the Tanew River. Densely wooded borderlands, swampy streams, and wooded hills created transport difficulties for regular army detachments. Across that borderland passed insurgent units from Galicia, which, when attacked by Russian soldiers, dispersed, the majority of the volunteers retreating across the Austrian frontier. Arms and munitions were buried; secret stores and transfer stations for arms, munitions, uniforms, and underclothing were set up.

This brief survey shows that there were five areas of varying geographical suitability for guerrilla war. Woods and marshlands covered large areas and were good natural sites for insurgent camps. In the south, the Swiętokrzyskie Mountains were the best terrain, on the right side of the Vistula the Solska forest and the Parczewsko-Włodawskie lake district, where some bogs were inaccessible most of the year. In the north, the Myszyniecka forest and other forests and marshes extending farther northeast were separated from the south by the Warsaw-St. Petersburg railway line, opened in December 1862. In the very first days of the uprising the insurgents tried to cut off the communication with St. Petersburg by destroying telegraph poles, railway tracks, and even bridges. All the wooded and marshy areas had a scanty network of roads, were thinly populated, and, in particular, had no big towns.

The water network in those areas comprised mostly rivers and streams with swampy banks and many branches. The rivers in the Congress Kingdom were no serious obstacle for the insurgents. Only at the Galician border, between Niepołomice and Sandomierz, was there a major obstacle, the Vistula, and insurgents crossing the river met with attacks by Russian guards. Galician volunteers, unaccustomed to danger, suffered heavy losses in men and arms, and the survivors retreated into Galicia. It was not until January 1864, when the Vistula froze over, that small Polish units managed to cross into the Congress Kingdom. In other stretches of the river insurgent detachments, using many fords, repeatedly crossed in rafts, boats, and scows. Smaller rivers were no obstacle, as the insurgents most often used fords and, in order to impede the pursuit of the enemy, burned down bridges after having crossed them.

Insurgent units were organized in selected places in woods where camps had been established. At Piekło, also called Piekiełko (Hell or Little Hell), in Opoczno district, Dionizy Czachowski set up his own camp after having escaped from another camp at Grochowiska in March 1863. This area, intersected by deep gullies filled with dense woods and a thick undergrowth of juniper, brambles, and hazel, was impassable to regular detachments. As a result, the camp at Piekiełko served the insurgents well through almost the whole of the year 1863, and a major Russian raid reached it only in December. Czachowski used it until early November.

At the confluence of the Vistula and the Pilica, on a dry holm surrounded by swamps and woods, Władysław Kononowicz set up a camp for his detachment of six hundred men. There was only one path leading to the camp across the swamps, and it was permanently covered by water. In spite of this, the Russians discovered it, having bribed the local village administrator with 1,000 zlotys. Taken by surprise, the insurgents nevertheless managed to escape across the swamps, and on the holm the Russians found only burnt-down huts. The camp, however, ceased to exist.

As early as February 1863 a unit of fifty insurgents commanded by Rybiński set up a camp in Mława district, in the province of Płock, among the lakes in the marshes of the Skrwa River. The islet was protected by marshes on one side and by wire entanglements built by the insurgents on the other. A narrow path blocked with wagons was the only approach. The insurgents' long inactivity attracted the Russians on February 25; in the assault some insurgents escaped across the marshes, but the remainder beat off the attackers and only then retreated into the neighboring woods.

In the middle of May 1863, in the district of Ostrołęka, Ludwik Frycze and Polikarp Dąbrowski established a camp at Łączka, in a glade amongst vast marshes and swamps with only one small, narrow dike. The unit remained there organizing and training for a week, and, feeling safe, the commanders neglected to post sentries. The Russians availed themselves of this opportunity and on May 25 raided the camp. The insurgents suffered heavy casualties, and only a handful of them managed to retreat across the marshes.

Apparently equally difficult of access was the camp established in spring 1863 by Palemon Nowicki and Józef Trąmpczyński at Płaska Góra (Przasnysz district). The unit, two hundred fifty strong, was camping on a holm amidst large branches, overgrown with reeds, of the Orzyc River, accessible only by an underwater path. The importance of the camp was enhanced by its closeness to the Prussian border, across which arms could be smuggled. The holm was fortified by three lines of wire entanglements, and large food supplies were collected there. In June a Russian detachment of thirteen hundred men raided the holm. After their first attack had been beaten off, they broke the dike, drained off the water, and cut down the trees to permit the passage of their guns. They besieged the holm for several days, ultimately withdrawing because of the rumor (which later proved false) of approaching insurgent reinforcements. The Poles then retreated into the neighboring woods.

In Augustów province the insurgents found the best shelter in the Sztabin woods, where thick trees, high brush, and quagmires impeded the passage of regular army detachments. In May, in the vicinity of the village of Lipsko, on a hill called Kozi Rynek, which was surrounded by marshes, Konstanty Ramotowski-Wawer rested his unit, four hundred strong. In June they were attacked and, having suffered heavy casualties, had to retreat across the marshes. The fortified camp lost its importance.

In April 1863, a similar camp was established by Ludwik Narbutt in the province of Grodno, near Dubicze (Lida district), on a wooded holm amidst swamps. The holm was protected on one side by a lake and the river and on the other by a trackless forest. However, the camp was betrayed by a peasant who had joined the unit as a volunteer but later led the Russians to it. After hand-to-hand fighting on May 4, some insurgents managed to escape, but their casualties were heavy. Narbutt was killed and the unit dispersed.

Karol Krysiński set up a camp in the Parczew woods and marshes near the village of Lipniak (Włodawa district). The camp was situated on an islet amidst marshes, and communication with the outside world was possible only by way of wooden bridges and fords known to the local people. The camp was additionally protected by ditches, embankments, and wire entanglements, and, having a spring of fresh water, it was suitable for a rather long stay. The camp existed from spring of 1863 to the end of that year and was never discovered by the Russians. From it Krysiński made many raids upon Russian columns. There he trained new volunteers, mostly peasants, and dispatched mounted reconnoitering parties to distant places, in this way distracting the attention of the Russians from the site of the camp. In November 1863, Krysiński concentrated at Lipniak several units jointly numbering a thousand men and prepared the camp for winter by building new huts and barracks as well as ramparts and wire entanglements. In November, however, he attacked the Russian troops, and after several skirmishes his unit was defeated and dispersed, he himself crossing the border to Galicia.

On the marshlands of Jata (Łuków district), on a 150-meter-high plateau from which waters ran in all directions to nearby rivers, Father Stanisław Brzóska and his unit camped for some time. The plateau was wooded and marshy, but it had a fresh-water spring, and the few paths leading to it were known only to some of the local inhabitants. Jata was not discovered by the Russians until the very end of the insurrection and gave shelter to other insurgent units as well.

Camps in woods and marshes had good defensive positions, but in the event of Russian attack they offered hardly any escape route. Most frequently, since the enemy outnumbered them, the insurgents had to work their way across swamps, which resulted in heavy casualties and, in most cases, the routing of the unit. Czachowski's Piekiełko and Krysiński's Lipniak were examples of permanent camps that lasted for almost the whole of the year because the enemy's attention was distracted and the avenues of approach were well camouflaged.

There were many more small camps like these all over the country. "Woods are our fortresses," the insurgents used to say. Individual units usually had their own points of assembly and prearranged places for camps in the backwoods. These camps enabled the insurgents to organize and train in quiet. The conditions there were fairly good. The men lived in huts made of boards and brushwood and covered with bark or in barracks or, rather, dugouts. Wells were sunk and kitchens built; surgeons dressed wounds and treated contusions and illnesses, the most frequent of which was ague. Field hospitals of twenty to thirty beds, with equipment and medical staff, were organized in distant settlements in the woods.

Apart from natural conditions, the attitude of the local people was of great importance. They helped to find suitable sites for camps, to provide the insurgents with food, to inform them about enemy movements, to identify Russian spies, and to guide the insurgents across woods and marshes.

The initial fighting of the insurgent units, which were poorly or only partially equipped with firearms, resulted in dispersion or, more often, in defeat and rout. Only gradually, after having received consignments of firearms from abroad, were they able to take the offensive against the Russian columns. Fighting conditions and Russian atrocities—they killed off the wounded and shot the captives—made many partisan commanders avoid engagements, and attack by the enemy under unfavorable conditions most frequently resulted in defeat. Demoralized by constant flight from Russian troops, the insurgents scattered during battles, and the heroic examples of their officers were of no avail.

For this reason, in a decree issued May 4, the War Department of the National Government strongly condemned the passive tactics that had resulted in the Russian assumption of the initiative. As Russian detachments concentrated on pursuing the insurgents and forcing them into encounters, the Polish units were being demoralized and destroyed, and the spirit of the fight for independence was declining. "The tactics of guerrilla warfare," proclaimed the decree, "should first of all be aggressive." Polish units should constantly harass the enemy, cut his transport routes, and disorganize his means of communication and transport in order to transform passive resistance into "bold enterprise, merciless retaliation, and confidence in their own stength." This meant undertaking bold guerrilla action instead of mere shows of force. The decree emphasized particularly the necessity of confronting the small enemy units, the so-called flying columns, that were raiding the insurgent posts, plundering towns and villages, and taking revenge on their inhabitants.

Gradually experience was gained and some tactical principles of guerrilla warfare adopted—marches and countermarches, disbanding units temporarily in the event of danger and impossibility of defense, organizing services in forest camps, and establishing security and guard systems. Knowledge of the terrain and the ability to take advantage of its characteristics in order to set up camps and fight the enemy under the most advantageous conditions were basic elements of guerrilla tactics. Maintaining constant combat-readiness and discipline in the units was indispensable.

One of the most outstanding guerrilla commanders was Dionizy Czachowski, operating mostly in Sandomierz province, whose woods he knew so well that he could find his way across gullies and along forest paths even by night. During marches he could use thickets and streams to escape the Russians and then return to attack them in a more convenient situation. He camped most frequently in the woods of Iłża and Ostrowiec, where he organized rest for his guerrillas; owing to the strict discipline he maintained, his unit was distinguished by great efficiency and fighting readiness. His alertness to the enemy's approach was remarkable. Czachowski was capable of whipping soldiers in the midst of a meal to make them fight. He was cruel to peasants who served the enemy and hanged them ruthlessly, but at the same time he was popular in the villages and in the province of Sandomierz was called "king of peasants." His courage was an example to all. Czachowski avoided open spaces, where the Russians, armed with rifles with a range of a thousand paces, had the advantage over the insurgents, and took shelter in the woods. From the edge of the woods his riflemen kept up constant fire, while his scythe bearers flanked the enemy. During the struggle he did not supervise, but personally led his riflemen into the thick of the fight. In the course of his operations, from January till early November 1863, Czachowski fought over thirty battles and in many of them was victorious.

Sandomierz was also the scene of activity of Zygmunt Chmieleński, formerly an officer in the Russian army, who set an example of how to combat enemy troops heavily outnumbering the insurgents. In a fight at Cierno on September 22 he led his five hundred men out of a forest against fourteen hundred Russians. Forming part of his unit into a line, he kept the remaining men behind, using them during the attack to strengthen the front line and to send two more companies to charge the wings of the enemy force. Seeing themselves outnumbered, the Polish infantrymen formed a rectangle and backed out of the open field, thus diminishing their losses. Next, in order to get away from the enemy troops, Chmieleński put his infantrymen on wagons. Pursued by the Russians over the next three days, he led his unit without rest alongside roads running through wooded territory until he had left the enemy well behind and was able to stop in a dense forest. By then the men were so tired that all of them, including the pickets, instantly fell asleep. Luckily, the Russians did not try to enter the forest by night for fear of falling into a trap set by the insurgents. Later, surrounded by the enemy at Mełchów, Chmieleński divided his unit into twelve groups and gave each a route and an assembly point. Thanks to this they stole away between the Russian columns.

Karol Krysiński, operating in the provinces of Podlasie and Lublin, also possessed the knowledge of the terrain and the competence to camouflage his marches and stopping places. He was able to keep his unit of five hundred men, chiefly peasants, in constant combat-readiness. Franz von Erlach, a Swiss correspondent staying at his camp, wrote of Krysiński: "Everything—marching, resting, camping—was done with full alertness and as if another fight were imminent." Friendly local people frequently warned him of the approach of a Russian detachment.

When marching across the swamps, he sent ahead pontoniers to build bridges of tree trunks so that wagons loaded with arms and food could cross. After the unit had passed, the trunks were removed and all traces of the crossing obliterated. Food supplies were requisitioned at some distance from the stopping places. Thanks to Krysiński's abilities as an organizer and commander, his unit endured until November 1863 and fought over thirty skirmishes in which the Russians suffered heavy casualties.

Józef Jankowski-Szydłowski can be called a real "man of the woods." His "ceaseless toil" over the course of eleven months was very highly appreciated by the War Department of the National Government. Jankowski organized his unit in the Nieporęt woods (close to Warsaw), but later he was constantly on the move and fought in the provinces of Mazowsze, Podlasie, Lublin, and Sandomierz. Owing to the mobility of his unit he was able to avoid the enemy if they outnumbered the insurgents and occupied a better position. His unit was scattered several times but always reassembled in prearranged places. Finally, after over thirty skirmishes, he was defeated at Żelechów, having been flanked on three sides.

Józef Rucki operated from late April until early November, chiefly between Lublin and Chełm. He managed to avoid confronting the enemy for weeks, dodging over a well-known terrain and confusing the Russian pursuit so that frequently he was in their rear. He marched mostly by night, when the Russians, fearing an ambush, never entered the woods. "The night marches were the worst," complained one of the insurgents, as he described "stumbling over tree stumps and roots," but a brief rest in the woods soon restored their strength. The accounts of his unit show that in the marches through woods Rucki frequently employed wagons. In avoiding the Russians he was assisted by mounted gendarmerie as well as by hired scouts and guides who led the detachment along forest byways. Rucki's unit, comprising seventy cavalrymen, who operated as scouts, two hundred twenty riflemen, and seventy scythe bearers, fought only when the commander was certain of success. Rucki dismissed and reassembled his unit several times. Despite his tactics of avoiding battle, his unit was useful in repeatedly alarming the Russian columns and diverting them from the vicinity of the border so that new insurgent units could cross over from Galicia.

Józef Oxiński operated on the difficult terrain of Kalisz province, moving his unit through the woods from Uniejów to Piotrków. Since he was one commander who was eager to fight the enemy, he condemned shows of force and maintained that units that avoided fighting soon became demoralized and were eventually defeated without inflicting any losses on the enemy. To avoid being spotted by the Russians, he never stayed longer than forty-eight hours in a single camp in the woods and established new camps at intervals of twenty to thirty kilometers. His unit marched along field and forest paths, never taking public roads. To facilitate the passage through the woods he disbanded the cavalry unit and used wagons only when it was necessary to speed a retreat. Oxiński requisitioned food (an ox or a cow, a sack of cereal or peas) for payment for two days at a time while his unit was on the move, thus avoiding any requisition close to his camp. In the course of several months of fighting—from February to June 1863—he became, in his own words, a man of the woods, able to track down enemy detachments and to recognize the trails of Polish units. His favorite method of fighting was to organize an ambush in thick woods lining a road. On encountering the enemy, he occupied the edge of the wood in extended order and let the enemy approach to a distance of a hundred paces. Then two lines of his riflemen opened fire in turn. In May 1863 Oxiński's unit increased to fourteen hundred men and lost its mobility; it was routed at Przedborze on June 27, and Oxiński himself joined E. Taczanowski's unit as a volunteer.

Konstanty Ramotowski-Wawer was a guerrilla commander who chose to distract the enemy rather than fight him. From March to September he tried to avoid encounters with the Russians, and, having organized his unit in the province of Ostrołęka, he worked his way through Czerwony Bór (Red Forest) into the province of Augustów, burning behind him the bridges on the Narew, the Cisna, and the Pisna. Attacked by enemy forces, he managed to escape into the Sztabin woods, where he set up a camp at Kozi Rynek. Attacked again by the Russians in May and June, he fought several successful skirmishes, but, pursued by tne enemy, he went back to Łomża province in June. On the way to the assembly point in Czerwony Bór he crossed the Narew on rafts and retreated into the Ostrów woods, where his detachment increased to twenty-two hundred men. The Russians attacked them there and defeated them several times in July, finally routing them in early September 1863. The commander went abroad.

Father Antoni Mackiewicz's detachment in Kovno province in Lithuania had a special character, as it consisted almost entirely of peasants. It was an infantry unit; the partisans carried equipment and food in canvas bags on their backs, and this allowed quick breaking of camp and marches through trackless forests. Ammunition was carried in boxes resting on wooden poles. Partisans preserved silence; conversations were carried on in whispers. By skillful avoidance of the enemy the unit managed to survive until December, even though it fought twenty skirmishes, several of them successfully. With the approach of winter the commander disbanded his unit. While crossing the Niemen River, Mackiewicz was apprehended; he was hanged in Kaunas on December 28, 1863.

Adam Bitis, the commander of another peasant unit in Lithuania, also avoided fighting and set up ambushes, which supplied him with arms and ammunition.

Numerous defeats and routs of Polish detachments, disbanding and dividing them in late autumn 1863, resulted in the collapse of the guerrilla war (with the exception of General Hauke-Bosak's division). There remained only a few small units that fought until spring 1864.

Guerrilla warfare was strongly criticized from the very beginning. Langiewicz was of the opinion that the "constant loitering of partisan units" was a useless show of force rather than real fighting. Traugutt also maintained that, as there was no central military command, "everybody went where he pleased and did what he pleased; as one was losing a fight another might help him or not, as he wished." It was remarked that the methods necessary in guerrilla war, viz., avoiding battle and disbanding partisan units, were misused in a show of force. As a matter of fact, all commanders would dismiss their units after encounters with the enemy in order to escape pursuit. The dispersed insurgents would hide deep in the woods for several days and then reassemble at a prearranged place, where uniforms, underclothing, arms, and ammunition would be supplied them and the unit would be reorganized despite its losses.

On account of the Russian superiority in numbers and arms, fights in the open were exceptional, and insurgent units adjusted military tactics to their own capacities. Wherever the terrain allowed, commanders took positions at the edge of the woods, which screened the line of riflemen and, behind them, the scythe bearers and carabineers armed with Belgian rifles, if the unit possessed such weapons. Cavalry units aimed at provoking the enemy to attack at the edge of the wood and then protecting the flanks of the insurgent detachment. The enemy was allowed to approach the edge of the wood to the distance of a rifle shot. Then the insurgents discharged a volley, trying to break the enemy line, and if any soldiers came closer the riflemen or scythe bearers would scatter them. To prevent the partisans from using such tactics, the Russians tried to surround the Polish units and, as they outnumbered them greatly, were often successful in doing so. Forest ambushes were frequently used. The battle of Żyrzyn on August 8 was a typical ambush—on a forest road from Lublin to Dęblin, General Heidenreich-Kruk with twenty-five hundred men attacked a Russian unit of infantrymen and cossacks five hundred strong that had two cannon and was convoying the money mail. In the surprise attack the Russians suffered heavy casualties—about two hundred were killed or wounded and over a hundred fifty prisoners taken. The prisoners, however, were set free.

Guerrilla warfare during the January Insurrection proved that natural features—forests, mountains, and swamps—were important in protecting the partisans from the enemy. The capacity to use these natural features and constant combat-readiness were also necessary, however, along with the assistance of the local people, who warned the insurgents of the approaching enemy and helped them to move through the forest. Shows of force and the avoidance of fighting did not protect insurgent units from rout; once they had been surrounded, most of them perished. Guerrilla warfare was, therefore, the only possible mode of operation.

Notes

1. This paper was translated from the Polish original by Eleonora Horoszkiewicz. My investigations of this problem have been restricted mainly to the area of the Congress Kingdom, which was of essential importance for the military operations of the insurgents supported by the Polish inhabitants of Austrian and Prussian Poland. Military activities in Lithuania and Belorussia were merely an extension of those in the Congress Kingdom. While they bore witness, on the one hand, to the patriotism of the Polish population of those territories and, on the other, to the strong ties of Lithuanians and Belorussians with Poles, they were never of decisive importance. The paper is based on the general history of the insurrection presented in the monographs of W. Przyborowski, M. Berg, S. Zielińsi, J. Piłsudski, S. Kieniewicz, L. Ratajczyk, and E. Kozẇski. I have also used research papers dealing with military operations in individual regions of the Congress Kingdom (Podlasie, Lubelskie, Augustowskie, Zagłębie Dąbrowskie, Płockie, Krakowskie), as well as papers on the participation in the insurrection of the inhabitants of Prussia and Austrian Poland (where according to a proclamation of the Central National Committee dated February 7, 1863, there was to be no insurrection, the Poles living there being expected only to gather and pass on volunteers, arms, equipment, and funds).

Foreign Policy during the January Insurrection

Jerzy Zdrada

The policy of the European powers on the Polish question in the nineteenth century has been the subject of numerous studies and monographic essays, as have Polish activities in the arena of international politics. The most important problems of international relations—the significance of the Polish issue and the details of the activities of the Poles themselves—have already been examined and explained. Therefore, in the outline I am going to present, I would like to characterize, on the basis of research results, the aims, methods, and evolution of those Polish activities which contributed to the foreign policy of the January Insurrection.

I

After the defeat and the partition of Poland at the end of the eighteenth century, the people of Poland dreamed of recovering their independence through an uprising and by gaining help from the outside: peaceful political intervention by foreign governments, a European war in which a coalition of Western European countries would measure its strength against the invader, tsarist Russia, or help from the working classes in the form of a revolution that would destroy the old order in Central Europe. From the French Revolution to the January Insurrection, all of these avenues were pursued, separately or collectively, by the Poles in their struggle for independence.

Both in the years preceding the January Insurrection and during it, international activity was concentrated in the Hôtel Lambert, an émigré society headed by Prince Adam Jerzy Czartoryski, who was the accepted spokesman for the Polish question in Western Europe until the outbreak of the November Insurrection of 1830–31. Prince Adam set up a network of Polish political and propaganda institutions in all those countries in which activities in support of the Polish matter were possible and controlled them for thirty years. Either personally or with the help of his closest collaborators, he sought to inspire pro-Polish (or anti-Russian) policies in Paris, London, or Constantinople. In the years preceding the January Insurrection, Polish activity in the arena of international politics reached its peak during the Crimean War.

Its next stage began in Paris on July 15, 1860, when a so-called agency was established which, in September of that year, was transformed into a Bureau of Polish Affairs with Prince Władysław Czartoryski at its head. At the same time, the network of agents and political collaborators was renewed and expanded in England, Italy, Austria, Turkey, and the Balkans. Thus, practically speaking, the headquarters in Paris (the Bureau had its own departments and committees) acted as an unofficial Polish Ministry of Foreign Affairs and had, to some extent, its own diplomatic service. The activity of the Bureau followed three main lines: influencing the policies of the Western governments on the Polish question, exerting its influence on public opinion, and keeping in touch with home political centers. The point was that the activities of the Hôtel Lambert should be in agreement with the expectations and aspirations of the so-called Whites. With the increasing movement toward independence in the Russian sector of partitioned Poland, the mandate of the country strengthened the position of the Polish emigrant diplomats in exile as far as their contacts in Paris, London, and Vienna were concerned. Since the summer of 1860 the Hôtel Lambert had been receiving both money and orders from the active home patriots. It preserved its own autonomy, however, and had exclusive control over Polish activities abroad.

II

From the autumn of 1860 on, the events in the Kingdom of Poland that are often referred to as "the moral revolution" attracted the attention of political Europe. The movement toward independence began to manifest itself with growing strength. In February and April 1861 a great deal of blood was shed in the streets of Warsaw, hundreds of people being killed or injured; public opinion all over Europe was shaken by those tragic events. The Polish question was becoming more and more important in politics and diplomacy. The field for international activities of the emigrant politicians of the Hôtel Lambert gradually grew wider. Their most important aim was, first of all, to find a way out of the political blind alley into which the Polish question had been pushed by the Peace Congress of Paris in 1856. There were two tendencies of primary importance: the home patriots were encouraged (in accordance with the political aims of Napoleon III, who wished the anti-Russian blade of the Polish matter to grow dull) to fight for the restoration of the Kingdom's autonomy under the provisions of the Treaty of Vienna of 1815. This temporary aim was dictated by the significance of the Polish issue. On the other hand, a diplomatic and propaganda campaign to make London and Paris undertake political intervention on behalf of the Poles began in the arena of international politics. It was generally hoped that under international pressure the Russian government would give in and allow far-reaching concessions. Attempts to synchronize the policies of France and Austria toward the Polish question were made in consultation with Napoleon III, for it was hoped that the constitutional reforms in Austria would make it possible to turn Galicia into the center of a Polish political movement.

In the spring of 1861 Napoleon III had no intention of intervening on behalf of the Poles, since cooperation with Russia suited the power interests of France. Nevertheless, the Poles were advised in Paris to continue their "moral revolution," and the tactics that the Whites had adopted for their struggle for autonomous concessions were regarded as promising. In spite of the emperor's reserve, this attitude toward the problem encouraged the Poles to continue the national movement in the Russian sector. In 1861 neither Paris nor the Polish side was fully aware of the fact that the temporary policy, together with the internal dynamics of any national movement, could only stimulate further political struggle, giving St. Petersburg the alternative of either withdrawing from Polish territory or holding onto it either by its surrender or by force of arms. The Hôtel Lambert and the Whites in the Kingdom hoped that these extreme measures would not have to be taken if the Western powers intervened in St. Petersburg as had earlier been agreed.

This was the main aim of Polish foreign policy from the spring of 1861 on. Its methods and the range of difficulties can be observed, for example, in the political activities directed by the Hôtel Lambert in Britain. The events of 1861 in Warsaw had made an impression on the people of Britain. The aim of the Polish diplomats was to turn these pro-Polish sympathies into a tool by means of which pressure could be put on the British cabinet to undertake the expected political measures against Russia, in this way exerting an influence on Vienna's Polish policy. Finally, stimulating pro-Polish sympathies among the British public was to relax London's reserve toward the policy of Napoleon III. The Polish issue was to serve, as it were, as a plane of understanding and cooperation between France and Britain.

In presenting their aims and political aspirations in London, the Poles insisted on making it clear that since March 1861 the concessions made according to the spirit of the provisions of the Treaty of 1815 were no longer of primary importance; what mattered most was Poland's independence. Appealing to the Congress of Vienna was merely a matter of tactics, serving as a starting point which would make possible diplomatic intervention by the Western powers. The Whites presented an analogous program to the British consul in Warsaw.

It was obvious that Henry Palmerston and John Russell would not approve this maximum program. In their opinion, a Polish-Russian compromise based on substantial autonomy for the Kingdom of Poland would satisfy British interests. It was less than the Poles had hoped for but more than the Russians were ready to give way to. The attitude of the Foreign Office was therefore something to hold onto and build on, the more so as a fierce debate over the Polish issue had just broken out in Parliament. The British cabinet, however, declined to undertake any official diplomatic intervention, and the politicians of the Hôtel Lambert were honestly and straightforwardly told this. However, in the state of affairs in the Kingdom of Poland and abroad in those days, the statement of the British ministers and the fact that the Polish issue had been discussed in Parliament were equally important. The progress of events in the Polish territories brought to light new facts which eventually forced the political circles to change their opinion. This was the state of affairs after martial law had been imposed in the Kingdom of Poland in October 1861: the Poles had gained new arguments, and the British cabinet decided to send a warning to Russia, condemning the tsar's policy in the Polish territories in a diplomatic note. From the present point of view the note to some extent initiated Britain's diplomatic intervention in defense of the Polish nation. It was in fact the turning point in London's policy for which the Poles had been waiting, the more so as the Foreign Office began to associate the Polish issue with the Eastern one in its messages to St. Petersburg.

This policy of London objectively favored the Poles, for it exerted a strong influence on St. Petersburg during the negotiations with regard to the realization of Aleksander Wielopolski's program. The Hôtel Lambert took advantage of all the ways of influencing public opinion. Pro-Polish speeches were delivered in Parliament again in March-April 1862, and once more John Russell officially spoke against any diplomatic intervention in Polish affairs. The minimum program, however—the system of concessions gained by Wielopolski—was considered satisfactory for the moment. It was obvious that at that time British interests had nothing in common with Poland's endeavors to regain full independence.

The activities of the Hôtel Lambert in Paris also ended in a partial success. It was pointed out that only handing control of the Kingdom over to the Poles and making adequate administrative and school concessions in Lithuania would prevent an insurrection. Napoleon III, in reply, advised patience and proclaimed himself in favor of legal means; he refused to notice obvious provocations from the Russians and, finally, warned the Poles that France could not take any initiative as far as Polish affairs were concerned, whereas on the contrary Russia was ready to take decisive anti-Polish action.

The main current of Polish political and propaganda actions ran in Paris and London and even sometimes in Vienna. It was accompanied by actions in Italy, Rome, Stockholm, the Balkans, and Constantinople. In the years preceding the January Insurrection, it was clear that the character of these actions was merely subsidiary: the Poles were looking for allies who would be willing to cooperate with France and Britain not only politically, but also militarily. In Sweden, since 1861, the Finnish issue had been effectively used as a means of stimulating anti-Russian sympathies. In Italy the conflict between Turin and Vienna was taken advantage of, and it became possible to attempt to form a Polish military unit; it was this state of affairs, however, that determined the Polish failure, for in return for its recognition of the United Kingdom of Italy Russia demanded that the Polish military-political center be done away with. Rome played an important role in Polish policy. The Polish movement was religious as well as political and social, and so Russian repressions fell upon the church as well. Pius IX was at first very cautious and reserved, but the progress of events soon made it impossible to remain indifferent to the tsar's repressions, and criticizing Russia for its attitude toward the Catholic church in the Polish territories was immediately regarded as support for the Polish national movement. The situation enabled the Hôtel Lambert to exert a strong influence on official Roman circles. In the Balkans anti-Russian sentiments were aroused and fed. For thirty years the Poles had hoped that the Eastern question would become their most important ally. However, the Poles' situation on the Bosporus largely depended on French-Russian relations: with the relations between Paris and St. Petersburg growing closer, the actions of the Hôtel Lambert grew weaker. Nevertheless, some attempts were made to come to an agreement with Serbian and Romanian politicians, financial and political support was often given to the Circassians, who were resisting the Russians in the Caucasus, and plans for a revolt among the Don Cossacks were made in cooperation with Russian revolutionaries. At that time, the cooperation between the Polish and Russian revolutionary political movements was in the hands of the Reds, who controlled a few centers of democrats in exile and indirectly entered into collaboration with the revolutionary groups in the West of Europe (e.g., Garibaldi, Giuseppe Mazzini, Lajos Kossuth). In the summer of 1862 the Central National Committee, which was controlled by the Reds, wrote down a general program of actions of an international character and began to establish a network of foreign agencies. While it could not get at the governments, it did succeed in signing a formal agreement with the Russian revolutionaries, which, from the Poles' point of view, was very important. It was a kind of a treaty between the two underground states, Polish and Russian, which were joining forces to fight the tsar's tyranny. During the negotiations with Aleksandr Herzen and Mikhail Bakunin's group in London and with the leaders of Zemlya i Volya in St. Petersburg, the problem of borders was particularly difficult to settle. The Poles insisted that the Russians recognize their right to organize an insurrection in the whole of the territory that had been Poland before the partitions (including Lithuania, Belorussia, and the Ukraine), whereas the Russians demanded the Poles' acceptance of a formula according to which the inhabitants of those territories would have the right to self-determination, i.e., to declare for union either with Russia or with Poland. In the end a compromise was made that adopted the Polish point of view on the scope of the insurrection but established that when the insurrection and the revolution had ended, the people living in those territories were to be allowed to decide on their future fate. The aim of the Polish side was above all to achieve a full annulment of the partition.

Summing up Polish foreign policy at the end of 1862, it must be said that the Polish issue had reached a deadlock. After two years of persistent diplomatic efforts and propaganda, the Poles had failed to make the Western powers recognize the necessity of political intervention. All this foreshadowed the attitude of the world powers during the insurrection. Meanwhile, in the Russian sector the aspirations of the people and the policy of St. Petersburg were making the outbreak of an insurrection inevitable.

III

The insurrection in the Kingdom of Poland broke out on January 22, 1863. The Provisional National Government that directed the fighting, similarly to the earlier Central National Committee, had no clear ideas about foreign policy and diplomatic activities in relation to the Western governments. At that time the Reds were interested mainly in weapons supplies and in information and propaganda. As a result, the activities of the National Government's agents abroad came to little and produced no international effects on the insurrection. The hopes of assistance from European revolutionaries proved an illusion, and the appeals of Giuseppe Mazzini, Giuseppe Garibaldi, or Lajos Kossuth would not have been any real help. The hopes of a revolution in Russia were also disappointed.

Consequently, diplomatic and political activities were in fact in the hands of the Hôtel Lambert. Taken by surprise and lacking any precise information about the range, character, and leadership of the insurrection, they maintained a wait-and-see attitude. Considering the overwhelming military superiority of Russia, it was believed that the insurrection would inevitably be suppressed in a few weeks' time. The Hôtel Lambert, however, did not come out against the movement. Its reasons were both political and psychological: the outbreak of a military struggle for independence in the country obliged patriots to help the insurgents.

Aware of the international situation, which was unfavorable for the Polish question, the Hôtel Lambert group was in a very difficult position; on the one hand, everything possible should be done to make the Great Powers act in favor of the insurrection; on the other hand, continuation of the hostilities against the will of the Great Powers might only bring more victims and would not yield any benefits. Thus, the first thing to do was to inspire pro-Polish (that is, pro-insurrection) attitudes in the French and English press. Expansion of the Hôtel Lambert's international activities became possible only when France and Britain had become alarmed by the Alvensleben Convention, which established the rules of cooperation between Russia and Prussia in response to the insurrection. This meant that the Great Powers could no longer pretend that the insurrection was an internal affair of the Russian Empire. It is well known that in reacting to the Russo-Prussian convention Paris and London acted according to their own political interests and the Polish question was rather far from their minds. Napoleon III directed his intervention against Berlin and hoped he would gain the support of London and Vienna. It did not come to a joint action; nevertheless, at the end of February 1863 France and England addressed a note to Berlin in which they protested the Russo-Prussian convention. This fact indirectly struck St. Petersburg. Apart from that, the British Foreign Office sent a note to St. Petersburg on March 2, 1863, in which it pointed out the necessity of restoring to Poland the state consistent with the decisions of the Congress of Vienna in 1815. Thus the political actions which had been initiated inevitably led to the Polish question, and this enabled the diplomats in exile to take part in the game of the European cabinets.

The French anti-Prussian initiatives and the British note, which were known to the Polish diplomats, showed that the Great Powers held themselves aloof from the Polish question. However, no clear conclusion could yet be drawn. The insurrection was still going on, international tension was increasing, and the alliance between Paris and St. Petersburg was in fact nonexistent. It was common sense to initiate political and propaganda actions in Paris, London, and Vienna. To foster the emerging favorable circumstances, the hostilities in the lands of Poland had to last. What is more, the secret suggestions sent by the Poles of the entourage of Napoleon III had been the same since mid-February 1863.

Thus in the second half of February 1863 the hostilities in the "western guberniyas" caused radical changes in international relations and made the Polish question the most important issue in the policy of the Great Powers, and at the same time the new relations in Europe encouraged the Poles to continue the insurrection in the hope of diplomatic intervention by the Great Powers or even a European military conflict. Therefore, in mid-February 1863 the Hôtel Lambert for the first time instructed the Whites to support the insurrection, which until then had been directed by the Reds. The Whites conformed to these instructions. In this period the Hôtel Lambert acted quite independently of the country; there was no controlling center that could handle the foreign policy of the insurrection.

IV

Since the first weeks the foreign policy of the insurrection had been inclined toward cooperation with Napoleon III and the pursuit of direct help from France and Austria. Polish activities in London had since February 1863 been conducted by General Władysław Zamoyski, who brought forward pro-Polish debates in Parliament and inspired public opinion. Since mid-February he had undertaken some confidential activities in favor of Anglo-French cooperation. Zamoyski realized that it was in Britain's political and economic interest to have peaceful relations with Russia. Therefore, in talking to British politicians he mentioned only diplomatic actions on behalf of the restitution of the legal and political status of the Kingdom of Poland within the Russian Empire, according to the provisions of the Treaty of 1815. He had promoted this idea since 1861; in February 1863, thanks to him, it was raised in Parliament and backed by its members. The same attitude could be observed in various meetings held at that time. The result was that public opinion demanded that the cabinet break off diplomatic relations with Russia and accept Poland as a belligerent.

After the outbreak of the insurrection, Polish diplomacy had two major duties: to inform the country about the development of the situation abroad and to influence public opinion and, by means of it, indirectly to influence the governments of the Great Powers in favor of the Polish question. After a few weeks, when the diplomatic activities on behalf of the Polish question had been developed, the Hôtel Lambert started systematic actions aimed at persuading the political circles of Paris, London, and Vienna to give real assistance to the fighting country. The main aim of the Poles was to involve the Great Powers in the diplomatic action which had already been started. The idea was that a gradual deterioration, caused by the Polish question, of relations between Paris, London, and Vienna, on the one hand, and St. Petersburg and Berlin, on the other, would increase, in a way automatically, the danger of a military conflict, even against the will of the governments involved, and in the end would force them into hostilities.

This is why the Polish information sent to Paris and London said that fighting was widespread and that the Austrian government approved of the insurrection. The argument that Austria was potentially ready to act on behalf of Poland was aimed at encouraging Paris and London to take firm anti-Russian diplomatic measures. The anti-Russian attitude of Sweden, influenced by the Polish diplomatic activities in March and April 1863 and expressed by its readiness to take part in a coalition war against Russia, was to affect Napoleon III in a similar way.

In the first year of the insurrection, Polish foreign policy was based on the assumption that there was a real chance of getting help from Austria. Therefore, both the insurgent National Government in Warsaw and the diplomats from the Hôtel Lambert, although they differed greatly on several tactical points, tried to win over Vienna, to calm its fears, to show the concurrence of Polish and Austrian interests in a political weakening of Russia, and to point out the benefits to Vienna of the restoration of Poland as a secundogeniture of the Habsburg dynasty. They stressed the possibility of freedom of movement for Austria as far as territorial and political expansion in the Balkans was concerned. It was clear both to the National Government and to the Hôtel Lambert that it would be impossible to organize an anti-Russian coalition without Austria.

As I have said, Władysław Czartoryski transmitted French suggestions to the leaders in the country. He was the source of the information, advice, and evaluation of the international situation that Warsaw needed to make decisions about the tactics of the hostilities in the "western guberniyas." This was particularly important in the first months of the insurrection, which were decisive for its character and extent.

The talks between Władysław Czartoryski and Napoleon III and his collaborators in March 1863 were of great importance to the further development of the insurrection. As early as March 10, the Poles heard from the entourage of Napoleon III that the duration and spread of the insurrection were crucial conditions for its eventual success, since the course of events could be favorable to Poland. The Poles were informed that diplomatic efforts to initiate French-Austrian cooperation on the Polish question had been started. This news referred to the so-called mission of the Austrian ambassador to Paris Prince Richard Metternich, which failed because Vienna did not want to be fettered by an alliance with France if Britain did not join it. In fact the Hôtel Lambert was well informed about this, since Władysław Czartoryski had had several talks with Napoleon III, Prince Richard Metternich, British Ambassador Henry Richard Cowley, Edouard Drouyn de Lhuys, Alexandre Walewski, and other French diplomats.

The failure of Prince Metternich's mission settled the question of war in Europe: the fears and divergences of interests revealed by London, Paris, and Vienna ruled out the possibility of organizing an anti-Russian coalition. All other diplomatic steps were only political half-measures. Not everybody in the capitals of Western Europe realized what the failure of the French initiative to enter into an alliance with Austria really meant, and the Polish diplomats did not draw the right conclusions either. They continued to think that the course of international events would direct the policy of the Great Powers toward intervention in favor of the insurrection. This was of great significance to Polish foreign policy during the next eight months.

Although Napoleon III told Władysław Czartoryski on March 26, 1863, that a European war should not be expected, at the same time he informed him that there would be diplomatic intervention by the three Great Powers in favor of struggling Poland. The Poles were in a dilemma whether to advise the country to continue fighting when the emperor promised nothing except diplomatic action. It was obvious that intervention depended on further hostilities. At first, Paris was reluctant to encourage the insurrection in a clear way, but the necessity to continue it was stressed indirectly. The caution gradually disappeared, and on March 27 Alexandre Walewski, citing the emperor's opinion, declared that continuation of the insurrection might bring significant solutions, while putting an end to it might result in only minor concessions from St. Petersburg. Czartoryski was told that "the boundaries of future Poland will be drawn with the blood of the insurgents." Similar words of encouragement came from Cowley, who suggested that diplomatic measures should lead to the restitution of the Polish state or at least to the autonomy of all the lands of former Poland. Cowley pointed out to Czartoryski on March 28 that the probability of a war had not diminished. The same conclusions could be drawn from the evaluation of the situation presented to Czartoryski by Prince Metternich on his return from Vienna.

The Hôtel Lambert concluded that a diplomatic intervention would not relieve the international tension in a quick and peaceful way, and therefore a war in Europe was probable. This prospect defined the tasks of the foreign policy of the insurrection. Its doctrine was formulated by Władysław Czartoryski and his collaborators in the Hôtel Lambert in late March 1863 and presented (together with a precise characterization of the international situation) in the memorial of March 30, 1863, which was sent to the Whites in Warsaw and Cracow and then to the Provisional National Government.

Prince Czartoryski drew the attention of the Whites in the country to the fact that "the continuation of the Polish insurrection was indispensable, since only this might provide diplomatic negotiations with a basis strong enough to create something secure and durable or to prove the necessity of war." Hostilities were needed to influence the cabinets and public opinion in the West, and "a complete cessation of military activities would be an irreparable defeat—it was of the utmost necessity to continue them." What is more, the partisan war would maintain unrest in the "western guberniyas," and its military demonstrations would have their propaganda and political effect in the West; thus it would influence the course of diplomatic negotiations and keep the majority of the Polish forces ready for a military intervention against Russia. In this way "the doctrine of the insurrection—a military demonstration, fully dependent on the hope of foreign aid—" was formulated. The hostilities in the country were aimed at poisoning international relations and eventually causing the outbreak of a European war.

The further course of events proved to some extent that Czartoryski's evaluations and forecasts were sound; a real diplomatic agreement proved impossible, and by spring 1863 war appeared even more likely. However, the expectation of an automatic increase in conflict between the Western states and Russia was not fulfilled. War was not desired in the Western capitals, and Russia endeavored to avoid it without making any concessions to the intervening powers.

This was proved by the course and the consequences of the first intervention of the Great Powers in April 1863. The French and British notes of April 10 and the Austrian note of April 12 revealed to St. Petersburg a lack of unanimity of the intervening cabinets; the French note appeared the mildest, and only the British cabinet referred to Russia's international obligations. The Hôtel Lambert was aware of the weaknesses of the April notes. Nevertheless, the fact that they were exchanged was favorable to the question of the insurrection; it was the first joint action in favor of the Polish question. It was expected that the notes would be rejected by St. Petersburg. Then, it was hoped, a second act of intervention would take place, this time a military one. A politically skillful Russian answer which conformed to the real feelings in the government circles in London, Vienna, and Paris prevented this possibility. St. Petersburg rejected the intervention but gave the impression of being eager to continue diplomatic discussion of a solution of the Polish question in terms of the ideas of 1815.

V

In May 1863 Władysław Czartoryski had been formally appointed chief foreign agent by the National Government. The Bureau of Polish Affairs was changed into the Chief Agency, the open headquarters of the foreign policy of the insurrection. Czartoryski's position was significantly strengthened: he was the representative of the underground Polish state accepted by the nation. He was a Polish ambassador to Paris and London and was formally subordinate to the Foreign Department of the National Government, which functioned as a ministry. In fact, Czartoryski directed the foreign policy of the insurrection: the whole network of the Polish foreign service (which was based mainly on the people from the Hôtel Lambert) was subordinate to him. Because of the conditions of underground communication between Warsaw and Paris, the National Government gave him significant freedom of movement within a generally defined program.

The instructions of the National Government were to elucidate that "the Polish question was a question of law, justice, and order." These were the three principles of the foreign policy of the insurrection. The inalienable right to independence of the Polish nation was regarded as most important. The National Government asserted that independent Poland would guarantee "complete equality of civil and political rights irrespective of origin and religion" for all citizens and thus equality of rights for other nations. The question of the boundaries of independent Poland was a particularly delicate one. Taking Austria into consideration, the government did not want to stress the necessity of the restoration of Poland to its prepartition boundaries. At the same time, however, it avoided any declarations which might imply that the struggle concerned only the "western guberniyas." All arguments deriving from international law, history, and social, national, and religious relations were employed to prove two main theses: that the nation satisfied the necessary conditions for constituting an independent state and that independent Poland would be a guarantor of "order, peace, and justice" in Europe.

The Poles at first thought that the second stage of diplomatic intervention would bring results favorable to the Polish question. Pro-Polish attitudes were very strong, the conviction of the possibility of a coalition operation was widespread, and Napoleon III assured Czartoryski that talks concerning the restoration of Poland composed of the Kingdom of Poland and possibly Galicia were being held between Paris, London, and Vienna. The Polish diplomat declared, however, that this was a minimal program and pointed out the necessity of annexing Poznania to Poland.

However, as early as mid-May 1863 the Poles had the opportunity to recognize the actual international situation. This was offered by the talks held in London between Czartoryski, Władysław Zamoyski, and Henry Palmerston and John Russell on the preliminary conditions Russia should fulfill before further talks on the Polish question. The British proposed an armistice in the Kingdom of Poland; other military and political details remained unsettled. Czartoryski informed Palmerston that the National Government would accept the proposal of an armistice providing that the Great Powers clearly stated that Russia's rejection of them would be a *casus belli*. At the same time, he tried to convince the Foreign Office that, together with the armistice in all the lands to which the insurrection had spread, the Poles should be considered belligerents. The idea of depriving Russia of the international sanction to rule in the lands of Poland was also mentioned.

Palmerston and Russell rejected the Polish suggestions and insisted that the proposal of an armistice in the Kingdom of Poland be accepted. The tendency of the British to reduce demands toward Russia and even their willingness to withdraw from the intervention on behalf of the insurrection were visible. It was not concealed from the Poles that Britain did not want a war and had never fought for anybody else. At the same time, however, Palmerston said that the persistence and development of the insurrection might create an atmosphere favorable to the consideration of Poland as a belligerent. This was a kind of instruction for Czartoryski, who was seeking confirmation of the significance of further hostilities.

At the end of May 1863 Władysław Czartoryski obtained complete information about the conditions the three intervening Great Powers were to present in St. Petersburg. Napoleon III suggested calling a congress to resolve the Polish question; the British Foreign Office, accepting such a congress, stressed a one-year armistice in the Kingdom, the withdrawal of the army to its fortresses, the transfer of administration to the Poles, and, eventually, the restoration of Poland, composed of the Kingdom and Cracow, as a Habsburg secundogeniture. Vienna, for its part, worked out the so-called six points, a program of concessions in the Kingdom more modest than Aleksander Wielopolski's. What is more, Austrian diplomats insisted that London withdraw at least some of its claims concerning an armistice.

Czartoryski recognized the Austrian "six points" as a "cruel irony." It became the aim of Polish diplomacy to demolish the Austrian proposals and the British version of the armistice and thus to influence the outcome of talks between Paris, London, and Vienna. Activities were directed toward the British Foreign Office. Czartoryski tried to convince Palmerston on April 4 that the Austrian project was harmful to the Polish question and contrary to international law, since the status of the Kingdom of Poland, resulting from the Treaty of 1815, required far broader institutional solutions than those which were being introduced in Galicia by Austria. The Polish plan for an armistice was described by Czartoryski as a mere amnesty for the Poles that gave complete military freedom of movement to Russia.

Once again, Palmerston and Russell rejected his arguments. What is more, they reminded him that Britain had the right, but not the duty, to intervene. After these talks Czartoryski was aware that the Polish question had changed for the worse. The National Government immediately received information about the actual situation together with a full account of his secret political soundings.

Agreeing to the idea (but not the details) of an armistice, the Polish side formulated its own proposals: An armistice in the whole area involved in the insurrection should be a sine qua non of further talks. The Russian army was to withdraw to fortresses and bigger towns; all the arrested were to be set free; a free election to Parliament was to be organized and its work secured. An international committee accompanied by representatives of both sides was to be appointed to supervise the armistice, and a representative of the National Government was to have the right to take part in its talks on the conditions of the armistice. The Austrian "six points" were totally rejected. This attitude annoyed Paris and London.

After his talks with Palmerston on April 4, 1863, Czartoryski recognized that there was little chance that the Great Powers would help the Poles with the insurrection. The lack of unity as to the Great Powers' proposals was favorable from the Polish point of view, but when after the crisis in the French government at the beginning of August Paris abandoned all responsibility for maintaining the insurrection and refused to hear of recognizing the Poles as belligerents, it became clear that the situation was bad. Following the National Government's instructions, Czartoryski warned the Great Powers that the lack of assistance from their governments would cause the social radicalization of the insurrection and an alliance of the Poles with the forces of international revolution that would imperil the order of Europe. Writing to the National Government, however, Czartoryski stressed the need to maintain hostilities and to wait for more favorable international circumstances. The situation was in fact compulsory; no one at that time was able to make a decision to end the insurrection.

VI

From what has already been said, Austria's reluctance to intervene in the Polish question is clear. Austria was not sure of Napoleon III and was afraid to risk getting involved in a war against Russia. (At the same time, Austria's reserve restrained Britain.) If it took part in the intervention at all, it was only out of fear of political isolation. The Polish issue was "both a terror and a temptation," as Julian Klaczko vividly described it. Everybody was aware of this, both in the National Government and in the Hôtel Lambert. It was obvious, however, that without active support from Austria, which at that time was closely allied with France, it would be difficult to defeat Russia. Thus, one of the most essential aims of the foreign policy during the insurrection was to win Austria over to the Polish cause. In connection with this, in the summer of 1863 the National Government made a few important declarations and established a diplomatic agency in Vienna (previously the associates of the Hôtel Lambert had operated there in secret).

The Poles stressed the fact that there was a strict interdependence between the safety and stability of the Habsburg Monarchy and the restoration of an independent Poland. Efforts were made to convince Vienna that the insurrection was purely national, not revolutionary. It was pointed out that there was a political necessity to rebuild a strong, powerful Polish state with its eastern border on the Dźwina and the Dniepr, for only thus would its sovereignty and Europe's (and particularly Austria's) political interests be guaranteed; pushing Russia farther east and weakening Prussia by rebuilding the Polish state would allow Austria to retain its domination in Germany and expand into the Balkans. If the Poles failed, however, Russian Pan-Slavism would spread as far as Galicia or even the Slavic territories of the Kingdom of Hungary. It was declared that Galicia might remain outside the borders of independent Poland if it were given far-reaching autonomy.

The offers and declarations of the National Government, which had been calculated to make close Austro-French relations possible, could not counteract Vienna's deep-rooted conviction that an independent Polish state would strive to unite all the Polish territories, including Galicia, and that the success of the insurrection would stimulate national movements in the Habsburg Monarchy, thus acting objectively to Austria's disadvantage. Therefore the Polish declarations, which had been forced on the National Government in any case by the international situation, were ineffective. Besides, the efforts of Polish diplomacy (and French as well) missed their mark because the congress in Frankfurt in August 1863 inaugurated a new stage in Austria's policy toward German problems. Since this meant the end of Austro-French cooperation, it indirectly struck a blow against the Polish question. The situation changed after Vienna's German plans had failed. The National Government had been right in supposing that now Austria would strengthen its political alliance with France and Britain.

The attempts to win Vienna over to the Polish side were indirectly connected with the activity of the representatives of the National Government in Rome. The activity was in agreement with efforts of French diplomacy aimed at obtaining Pius IX's support for the French-Austrian alliance. Rome's support of the Polish question would be an important moral factor for the insurgents, but for the foreign policy of the insurrection it was of great instrumental value. We know that there was a conflict between Rome and St. Petersburg because of the tsar's attitude toward the Catholic church in the Russian sector. Although Rome did not approve of the insurrection, it also refused to condemn the Polish patriotic-religious movement, and after the spring of 1863 Pius IX was less reluctant to express his pro-Polish sympathies. The pope's caution was a consequence of the progress of the diplomatic intervention. The Poles' position in Rome was fairly good, and they had access to Pius IX and other notables of the Vatican. In the summer of 1863, when the stage had been set by considerable propaganda, the National Government, in its messages to Pius IX, often pointed to the fact that the Polish people were fighting for freedom and faith, both threatened by tsarist Russia. This approach proved effective, and Pius IX indirectly gave the insurrection his support, which led to a further deterioration of Rome's relations with St. Petersburg. The most significant aim had not been achieved, however: Pius IX did not take advantage of his influence to make Vienna help Poland, and he refused to recognize the agency of the National Government officially. He knew very well that the intervention of the world powers would be helpful to the cause of the insurrection.

The Russian reply to the notes written by the three world powers in August marked the beginning of the final stage of diplomatic discussions of the Polish question. Russia contested their right to mention the Polish affair, as everybody in St. Petersburg was convinced that a war would not break out before winter and the insurrection would have been suppressed by the spring of 1864.

It was hoped once more on the Polish side that the world powers would accept Gorchakov's challenge. The official *Le Moniteur* in Paris published the National Government's telegram to Czartoryski of April 15, 1863, in which the Russian interpretation of the Treaty of Vienna of 1815 was criticized and Czartoryski was reminded of the provisions of the treaty referring to all the Polish territories within the borders of 1772. The National Government pointed out that an insurrection was a fight to regain enduring national rights. It also stressed the fact that under the cover of diplomatic negotiations Russia was feverishly arming itself. The fact that the document had been published was considered proof of Napoleon III's support of the insurrection. It soon turned out that this assumption was incorrect. For the time being, however, it made it easier for the Polish diplomats to carry on with their activities, which were aimed at providing the fighting nation with not only verbal but real help.

New attempts were made in Paris and London to have the Poles acknowledged as belligerents, citing two precedents, the cases of the Greeks and the Belgians; the rejection of the offer of a truce by Turkey (in 1826) and Holland (in 1830), respectively, allowed the world powers to help the insurgents. In Paris Napoleon III and his ministers took evasive action and advised the Polish side to turn to London and Vienna for help. In the last week of September the Hôtel Lambert received a secret message from Vienna which said that there was a chance of French-Austrian cooperation if Napoleon III would specify the conditions of the action in favor of the Polish matter and offer adequate political guarantees, for instance, with regard to possible territorial compensations for the Habsburg Monarchy. In spite of all their skepticism, the Polish diplomats once more acted as confidential mediators, conveying the Austrian point of view to Napoleon III. Czartoryski, referring to the previous declarations of the National Government, promised that Poland would give up Galicia temporarily and give the throne to Archduke Rainer.

Napoleon III did not want to take the initiative, although Paris assured Vienna of French help in the event of a Russian attack. In these circumstances, Czartoryski made an attempt to overcome Vienna's indecision: he warned the Austrians that lack of help from the world powers would soon turn the Polish insurrection into the ignition of European revolution, which would threaten Austria above all. Further, if Russia were to win, Pan-Slavism would be a great danger for the monarchy. Therefore the restoration of an independent Poland was in Austria's interest, as it would act as a buffer protecting the monarchy from Russia and Prussia. A plan of adequate compensation for Galicia was put forward: in Prussia, in the Balkans (among others, Bosnia and Hercegovina), in the Danubian Principalities, and even in Italy. There was even a suggestion that the Polish crown be offered to Archduke Rainer. This was the most important and far-reaching Polish offer to Vienna, especially regarding the section referring to compensation. It seems fantastic today, but in those days and circumstances it did not seem unlikely to the Austrian politicians. They had been familiar with some of these ideas for months, having heard them from the closest associates of Napoleon III.

Simultaneously, political soundings were being taken in London, where the Polish note of September 20, 1863, concerning the problem of acknowledging the insurgents as belligerents found a favorable moment. In his answer to Aleksandr Gorchakov, Russell was thinking of a declaration of Russia's losing its right to the Kingdom of Poland, which the Poles had been suggesting to him since the spring. A declaration of this kind would be of great political significance, for it would imply that the Polish territories were de jure under Russian occupation. The Foreign Office proposed such a note to the governments of France and Austria. Napoleon III agreed, but Johann Bernhard von Rechberg, realizing that accepting this declaration would bring a threat of war, insisted that London undertake to give military help. London could not satisfy this condition, and it soon turned out that all this talk was only diplomatic claptrap.

Nevertheless, for a few weeks it seemed that Britain was on the verge of breaking off diplomatic relations with Russia. Therefore, soon afterwards Czartoryski came to London. The realities, however, did not meet Polish expectations: it was true that on October 8, Russell sent a note to Ambassador Napir threatening Russia with deprivation of the international sanctions according to which it ruled Poland, but almost immediately the note was annulled and replaced with another one that was practically meaningless from a political point of view. In these circumstances, Czartoryski's talks with Palmerston and Russell were no longer important. The Polish diplomat at last realized that the Poles could count on neither help nor friendship from the British cabinet. The Polish question in Britain met with rejection: London did not want a war and saw no point in prolonging diplomatic intervention. Finally, all hopes of a joint action of the three world powers were gone with the wind. Diplomatic intervention in favor of the Polish question ended in failure, and thus Polish foreign policy during the insurrection proved to be a failure, too. On November 5, 1863, this was confirmed by Napoleon III's speech.

VII

Polish diplomacy in the Balkans and in Turkey complemented the main directions of the foreign policy of the insurrection. The main goal of the Poles here was to put up a diversionary political and military action in the Black Sea region of the Balkans and the Caucasus to tie up some of the Russian forces and to provoke a new conflict in the east. All possible means were used to involve Turkey in this game. Arms and volunteers were smuggled into the Polish theater of insurrection operations, and the resistance of the Circassians against the Russian army was encouraged (a Polish military expedition to the Caucasus was organized, and Poles represented the interests of the Circassians in London and in Paris). Constantinople was encouraged to undertake a preventive war against Russia; it was cautioned that sooner or later Russia would seek retaliation for the defeat of 1856. Attempts were also made to induce the Romanian principalities into war with Russia, but Bucharest, though inclined to cooperate with the Poles, obviously linked any such decision with the standpoint of Napoleon III.

After spring 1863, the National Government sought allies against Prussia as well as against Russia. No contacts with Berlin were established: the Alvensleben Convention established Otto von Bismarck's anti-Polish attitude unambiguously. On the other hand, the Prussian prime minister twice attempted to entangle the Poles: in March 1863 with his idea of restoring the Polish state to a Prussian protectorate and in February-March 1864 with the mirage of mediation in St. Petersburg and insistence on an end to the insurrection. This time Bismarck also wooed the Poles with the idea of creating a petty buffer state on the Vistula. These offers were ignored as unacceptable from the Polish viewpoint. For their part, the Poles developed a serious propaganda action in the German countries.

In October 1863 there was a crisis among the insurrectionary authorities in Poland; Romuald Traugutt took command of the fighting, and this influenced Polish diplomatic activities. The failure of diplomatic intervention had shaken the existing conception of insurrection politics. A reorganization of foreign services was carried out with the effect that the political authority of Czartoryski and the Chief Agency in Paris was transferred to the insurrection authorities in Warsaw.

After the speech of Napoleon III it was clear that the Polish question had entered a state of diplomatic stagnation—until the spring, it was thought. Nevertheless, no opportunity was overlooked to raise the Polish issue in the press, in parliaments, and in political talks in Paris and in London. The so-called Danish crisis was observed with the hope that it might hasten a European military confrontation. Paris encouraged the continuation of the insurrection. The Hôtel Lambert's diplomats attempted to strengthen the pro-French orientation in London, but already in February 1864 Palmerston and Russell were persuading the Poles to abandon the insurrection.

Despite disappointments, the Hôtel Lambert and the National Government based their politics on the assumption of the good will of France. Indeed, at the beginning of the insurrection they had no choice. Napoleon III really was the Poles' last hope. However, at the end of 1863 Romuald Traugutt began to be critical of the emperor's policies and of Czartoryski's excessive dependence on initiatives originating in French governing circles. Disappointment with the Austrian policies was also growing. Traugutt backed the former National Government's Vienna declarations but made it clear that there would be no further concessions or commitments. Moreover, he made no secret of the fact that Poland, if disappointed by governments, would seek the support of peoples, above all of Austria's enemies. This was a kind of political pressure on Vienna, and Czartoryski, who entertained illusions of a Franco-Austrian alliance, warned against it.

In the winter of 1864 Traugutt decided to switch alliances. This had become especially important after the February 29, 1864, announcement of a state of siege in Galicia; Austria had sided with Russia. The National Government had tried up to that point to avoid provoking Vienna, hoping for help or at least neutrality from Austria. Now the Poles started to build up an anti-Austrian coalition of Italians, Hungarians, Croats, Serbs, and Czechs. They speculated that a war between Italy and Austria over Venetia would touch off a rebellion in Hungary and in the Slavic countries of Austria, which would bring France into the war. Such a development would create favorable conditions for the success of the Polish Insurrection. The hopes linked with the revolutionary movement turned out to be as deceptive as those based on help from governments. All agreements, contracts, and alliances remained on paper only as a sign of common interests and at the same time an indication of the weakness of the contracting parties, unable to realize their revolutionary plans.

In March 1864 the Polish politicians faced the dramatic question of whether to continue the insurrection or to stop it. The military resistance in Poland was dying out, resignation was increasing, and there was no hope of any international help. It was clear, nevertheless, that the failure of the insurrection would destroy the Polish question for decades and that struggle was required for the political survival of the nation. Struggle was the principal trump card of Polish foreign politics during the insurrection.

Soundings in Paris and London made it obvious to Czartoryski that there was no hope of any intervention. Finally, on April 18, Napoleon III stated that there was no chance even of negotiation with Russia for humanitarian conditions of surrender (e.g., amnesty). "We are alone and we shall remain alone," the head of Polish foreign affairs wrote bitterly to the National Government, appealing to it to stop the insurrection. He added: "The future will inevitably prove that the restoration of Poland is crucial and vital not only for the Western states, but also for every truth- and liberty-loving human being: now is not the time."

The January Insurrection and the Emancipation of the Peasants in the Polish-Russian Provinces*

Andreas Moritsch

In speaking here of the Polish-Russian provinces or guberniyas, I mean the areas that were directly annexed to the Russian Empire in the course of the Polish partitions of 1772–95: the three Lithuanian provinces of Vilna, Kovno, and Grodno, the three Belorussian guberniyas of Minsk, Vitebsk, and Mogilev, and the three provinces of the southwestern Ukraine, Volhynia, Podolia, and Kiev. In Russian the label *Zapadniy kray,* "Western District," referred in a wider sense to the whole area and above all to the six northwestern governments. Since German-language publications also tend to use the expression "Western District" (*Westgebiet*), I shall employ it here, without, however, wishing to imply any political meaning.

My themes are the abolition of serfdom and the ending of peasant obligations to landowners in the Western District. The latter measure was carried out in a radical fashion in response to the 1863 Insurrection. The Polish rebels' aim of restoring Poland's independence within its pre-1772 frontiers, politically unwise in several respects, made it much easier for St. Petersburg to crush the insurrection in the Western District. Two characteristics of the region facilitated the Russian response to the actions of the insurgents. The first was the ethnic situation. The upper strata of society, especially the landowning nobility, were Polish or Polonized with only a few exceptions—a fact particularly stressed by Russian and Polish publications. A large part of the urban population consisted of Jewish tradesmen and artisans. The mass of the people, the peasants, in contrast, were Orthodox Belorussians and Ukrainians and Catholic Lithuanians. The second feature was an agrarian system different from that of the rest of the empire. Whereas peasant agriculture and the rural way of life within the empire had been determined by the *obshchina* or commune, with its subdivided form of tenure (collective peasant holdings or *obshchinnoe zemlevladenie*), from the time Peter the Great introduced the head tax, hereditary tenure of individual, fiscally registered farms (*podvornoe zemlevladenie*) had predominated in the western guberniyas since Sigismund Augustus's reform providing for the standardization of rural lands. Only in eight of the twelve districts of Vitebsk and in Mogilev did collective tenure prevail.[1] This meant that in the Western District the conditions for modernizing peasant agriculture—in particular, a prior consolidation of scattered strips into farmsteads—were incomparably better than in the rest of the empire.

I stumbled upon the fact of a fundamentally different agrarian development in the Western District (and also in the Baltic provinces and Bessarabia) in the course of the research for my forthcoming work on agriculture and agrarian policy in Russia in the decades before the October Revolution.[2] It is quite clear from the statistical data that agriculture in the Western District had evolved much more rapidly than in other parts of the empire. Extensive farming of the kind that remained customary elsewhere—for example, the simple three-field pattern of the eastern regions, the alternate grazing and cropping sequence of the steppes, the slash-and-burn techniques of the northern forest region, and cattle raising mainly on pasture—had in the Western District already yielded to the managerially more intensive forms of the improved three-field system, the rotation of cereals and produce, and cattle raising in barns.[3] The proportion of noble-owned estates far exceeded the overall Russian average, and the land was exploited to a significantly greater extent by the proprietors themselves (demesnal farming), with broader employment of machinery and, however early the date, of mineral fertilizers.[4] The manorial style of farming—i.e., with unpaid peasant labor and equipment—typical of the adjacent eastern regions was the exception rather than the rule. The production of both estate owners and peasant farmers was already market-oriented.[5]

It is thus fair to say that capitalistic practices had taken firm hold of agriculture in the Western District. The "servile vestiges" (*krepostnicheskie ostatki*) and the "work-off system" (*otrabotochnaia sistema*) or socage that Lenin found to be characteristic of the Russian guberniyas, sharecropping, and other forms of peasant-landlord interdependence were by now more or less obsolete. One may interpret as a convincing piece of evidence for the economically better-grounded position of the nobility in the Western District the fact that its landed holdings had declined in the period 1862–1911 from 19.2 million *desiatini** to only 14.4 *desiatini,* that is, by one-fourth, while in all of European Russia—including the Western District—noble lands had decreased by half, from

87.2 million to 43.2 million *desiatini*.[6] Hence there can be no doubt that Polish estate owners were more successful than their Russian peers, and this notwithstanding the fact that the St. Petersburg government was anything but well disposed toward them. The 1863 decrees concerning the implementation of the peasant reform were unquestionably intended to harm the Polish nobles economically.

It is appropriate to ask why agrarian circumstances in the Western District were so unexpectedly favorable during the decade before the October Revolution. We cannot be satisfied with the argument frequently advanced in the older historiographic accounts to the effect that Polish and Baltic German nobles were simply more efficient and enterprising than sluggish, sybaritic Russian landowner types like Goncharov's Oblomov. The reasons in fact extend all the way from better climatic conditions, a more advantageous location in terms of transportation to domestic and foreign consumer markets, a greater division of labor between town and country, and a more developed infrastructure to the previously mentioned more sophisticated system of agriculture and the political neutrality of the Polish nobility, the result of which was a stronger inclination toward economic activity. Until now little attention has been paid by historians to another, truly fundamental reason: the way in which the peasants had escaped their servile bonds. The Russian government had sought to alienate the Belorussian, Lithuanian, and Ukrainian peasants from their rebellious masters and to punish the landowners for their participation in the January Insurrection by immediately depriving them of their manorial prerogatives. The complete dissolution of the ties that had subjugated the peasant to his lord—something the authorities did not dare to attempt in the case of the Russian landed nobility—had been meant to strike the Polish nobility as hard a blow as possible. However, the consequence of this tactic had been not an economic weakening of the big Polish proprietors, but rather the opposite: an enhanced tendency toward rationalized management of their estates.

In the comments that follow I shall briefly discuss the circumstances that led to the radical execution of the peasant reform in the Western District and thereafter substantiate my argument with regard to the positive economic effects of the government's actions.

The emancipation decree of February 19, 1861, with which the "Great Reform" was introduced, applied to forty-seven provinces of European Russia and thus encompassed all of the Western District. The three Baltic provinces, where the serfs had been set free between 1816 and 1819 without obtaining land, formed an exception. The Kingdom of Poland contrasted sharply with the Russian Empire in that the process of liberation in the former had taken place in three gradual stages. As early as 1807 the peasants had been accorded personal freedom. In 1846 their right to own the land they occupied and cultivated had been confirmed. Finally, in 1864, following the example of the Western District, peasant obligations toward estate owners were annulled. Thereby—in characteristic tsarist Russian fashion—use was made of the persons (particularly N. A. Milyutin) who had conceived the 1861 reform and had then been dismissed from state service in order to placate the aroused landowning nobility.

As indicated earlier, the economic and legal presuppositions for the peasant reform in the Western District were different from those in the rest of European Russia. Already during the first half of the nineteenth century more propitious marketing conditions for agricultural products had led to an extension of demesnal farming and to an initial modernization of management procedures.[7] Cultivation of crops for industrial use as well as of fodder and potatoes had increased, and processing plants had begun to arise on the estates. Although around the middle of the nineteenth century the bulk of the landowners' fields was tilled by peasants with their own equipment in fulfillment of the socage obligation—in other words, to work off the rental debt for the land they tilled themselves[8]—their lords had begun to realize that remunerated labor was more productive than the unwilling services of villeins. The tendency to expand estates resulted in both the confiscation of the plowman's holdings and increased demands for servile assistance. Peasant plots were repossessed, and the impoverishment of the rural population was accelerated. Social differentiation among the peasants was also promoted by the existence of individual family farms. More efficient cultivators who took agrarian innovations on the estates as their model and likewise began to produce for the marketplace managed to build up their acreage and/or their income mainly at the expense of ever more pauperized fellow villagers. It became possible for a new stratum of well-to-do peasants to emerge.

St. Petersburg, which had begun to combat the exactions of the Polish nobility after the November 1831 rising, reacted with the so-called Bibkov Inventory Rules. This legislation, greatly feared by the landlords, provided for strict reporting of the proportion of land farmed by the peasants on their own behalf and of the services supplied to landowners. The inventory rules went into effect in the southwestern region as early as 1847; in the northwestern region, the nobility was at first successful in fending them off. The 1838 reform of state-controlled peasants was also carried out more thoroughly in the Western District than in other parts of the empire.

When during the course of the Crimean War Russia's weakness became evident precisely in that sphere—the military—in which it had been thought strongest, the preconditions for a fundamental socioeconomic reformation of the empire existed for the first time. For the state to gain a truly effective hold on the tangible means of power (revenue and army recruits) it was necessary above all else to abolish serfdom. The ruling elites were fully aware of the fact that the Russian landowning nobility was still in no position—and surely not inclined—to dispense altogether with the gratuitous labor of servile peasants. Such a change presupposed an adequate economic infrastructure, and this was lacking. To be sure, in the Western District just the opposite was true. Already on the occasion of Tsar Alexander II's coronation the governor-general of Lithuania, Nazimov, had pointed out that "in the western provinces, especially those that border on Austria or Prussia and near the Baltic guberniyas, the idea of peasant emancipation is more firmly rooted in the heads of the landlords" than in the central parts of Russia.[9] The great caution, indeed, anxiety, with which the reformers approached their task was manifested in the words of the interior minister S. S. Lanskoii, who in 1857 expressed the view, regarding the tactics for effecting peasant reform, that "starting in the west, it would be possible, by careful prior calculation, to move eastward step by step, each one of which would be modest and well-pondered."[10]

Indeed, Nazimov had started to consult with the Lithuanian nobility in the previous year. In September 1857 the governor-general reported to the government that Lithuania's landowning nobility believed the peasants should be set free without receiving any land. Alexander II's reaction was to issue the Nazimov Rescript of November 20, which initiated a much broader discussion of peasant emancipation in provincial commissions throughout the whole of European Russia. The guidelines contained in the rescript indicated the contours of the forthcoming 1861 reform that was destined to free the peasantry with ownership of at least part of the soil they were tilling for their own sustenance.

The immensely complicated and detailed piece of legislation that was hammered out by drafting committees during the three following years included special arrangements for both the northwestern districts and the southwestern Ukraine.[11] The justification for these clauses was that individual farms existed in the areas in question, that the requisite equipment was at hand, and that the percentage of landless villagers was already high. Doubtless, the exceptional regulations were intended to hit Polish estate owners harder than their Russian counterparts. Noteworthy are the "local rules" (*mestnoe polozhenie*) for the provinces of Vilna, Kovno, Grodno, Minsk, and the four Livonian districts of

Vitebsk—i.e., the districts that lacked arable or grazing commons. In addition to general articles they contained a passage that guaranteed the peasants' rights to the lands they were cultivating. The many protests of the landowning nobility—Nazimov spoke of its imminent ruin[12]—were of no avail. Tsar Alexander II personally explained the true intent of the emancipation act: though the government's chief concern in drafting the reform laws had been to protect the interests of the estate owners, the peasants could not have been liberated without being granted land. Had they been deprived of it, both the landlords and the state would have suffered. The sovereign also referred to negative experiences in other countries, where the implementation of new regulations had almost always been accompanied by violence.[13]

The opposition of both the nobility and the peasants in the Western District to the Law of February 2, 1861, was revealed in the fact that the documents certifying judicial settlements (*ustavnaiia gramota*)—that is, the recording of deeds and the computation or determination of peasant obligations toward estate owners—were issued even more slowly than in the other provinces. It is unfortunate that the judicial agreements and the redemption contracts (*vyskupnie sdel'ki*) have still not been published for the whole of the empire. We thus have only an incomplete picture of the everyday realities of the emancipation and demanorialization of Russia's peasantry. However, the available, albeit skimpy data for Mogilev and the eight circuits of Vitebsk—in which the commons system prevailed and manumission was effected according to the Greater Russian "local rules"—demonstrate that the peasants had to yield as much as a quarter of the land they occupied to the estate owners.[14] In the rest of the northwestern district, land could be taken away from the peasants only if (1) their holdings were larger than was recorded in the inventories; (2) the seignior was left with less than a third of his original domain; or (3) the estate had fewer than twenty-one serfs. It thus becomes clear why the estate owners sought to delay the judicial agreements and to keep the peasants as long as possible in a state of "temporary obligation" (*vremenaiia obyazanost*).

There can be no question that the peasant reform, designed as early as 1851 to be more rigorous for the Western District, exacerbated the existing bad relations between the Polish nobility and the St. Petersburg government. Since the late fifties many landlords had been showing sympathy for the Polish national independence movement.[15] Among Russian revolutionaries and even in the case of certain Slavophiles such as Pogodin, efforts to resurrect an independent Polish state were either strongly supported or benevolently regarded. On March 15, 1861, Herzen published in his *Kolokol*—proscribed in Russia, yet much read up to the very apex of society—an article entitled "Vivat Polonia." Banned literature circulated widely in the Western District, and an underground rebel network had been created well before the 1863 Insurrection.[16] On September 19, 1862, an assembly of noblemen in Podolia approved the text of an appeal to Alexander II to unite the southwestern provinces of Podolia, Volhynia, and Kiev with the Kingdom of Poland.[17] The Minsk nobility expressed the same wish in November of that year.[18]

In the face of an incipient rebellion, the St. Petersburg government had to take action. On September 22, 1862, a "Western Commission" made up of the highest government officials was established. Its function was to design proposals and measures for incorporating the Western District into the empire and "restoring law and order in these provinces."[19] At the request of the Western Commission the Interior Ministry produced a "sketch of the general development of affairs in the Western District," the basic conclusions of which may be summarized as follows:[20] Only the villagers sided with the government; everybody else was hostile to it. It would be feasible to play off the peasants against the nobles and drive the latter into exile. There would then, of course, be the danger that the peasant rising would not be limited to specific demands or to the Western District and might result in the destruction "of the general principles of social order not only throughout the whole Western District, but also in the adjacent guberniyas and, ultimately, as the consequence of a contagious example, in the other parts of the empire as well."[21] The Western Commission therefore decided in favor of continuing to follow a zigzag course. For his part, Interior Minister Valuev opined that one might "cautiously encourage" the mutual misunderstanding of peasants and landlords.[22]

However, the rebels were counting on the peasants too. It had long been clear that the social question would play a decisive role in the coming insurrection and that only an uprising which involved a broad range of social strata would have any chance of success. Of particular interest in this regard is a letter of Herzen, dated September 8, 1862, to the Warsaw Central Committee. It reads in part: "the basic ideas that now animate Poland's rebellion are unequivocal recognition of the peasant's right to the land he tills and full acceptance of every nation's prerogative to decide its own destiny."[23] The letter states further that the principles of the Polish nationalist movement are entirely populist, that they in no way reflect noble conservatism, and that the goal is both to put an end to class differences and to distribute the land to the peasants.[24] On January 23, 1863, the National Central Committee Acting as the Provisional Government simultaneously proclaimed the rebellion and the complete dissolution of the bonds subjecting peasants to landlords. Article 1 of the decree read:

> Any and every landed holding to the usufruct of which the cultivator has been entitled by virtue of socage, rental payment, or any other obligation becomes as of this date . . . , along with the garden, dwelling, and farm buildings belonging thereto as well as associated rights and privileges, the exclusive hereditary property of the current tenant without any obligations, fees, socage, or rent whatsoever and under the sole condition of paying his due share of taxes and rendering appropriate services to the fatherland.[25]

Additional articles enjoined payment of compensation by the state to former owners in accordance with the value of their property, declared all enactments of the [foreign] occupying power null and void, and stated that detailed regulations for executing the decree would be published in later ordinances. A second decree promised that the state, drawing upon its own lands, would provide the landless rural population with farms of at least two and a half acres (3 morgs) in return for active participation in the struggle against the occupying forces.[26]

The insurgents' agrarian program also applied to the Western District. The St. Petersburg government was now in a very difficult position. It, too, saw that much depended on the attitude of the peasants. Bakunin, who applauded every rebellion, was asked whether a reunification of the Western District with Poland was feasible and replied as follows: "Declare Poland to be a peasant country, and then many of these races—perhaps all of them if Russia lags behind [you in this respect]—will follow you; . . . where freedom beckons to the nations, there they will go."[27] The government reacted relatively rapidly. On March 1, 1863, after the rising had spread to the Western District, it revised the local rules for the provinces of Vilna, Kovno, Grodno, Minsk, and the four Livonian districts of Vitebsk. On May 1, 1863— that is, after spring plowing, harrowing, and planting—all "temporally limited" obligations of peasants to landlords were cancelled. While peasants still did not achieve unrestricted ownership of the soil—they would first have to discharge their debt for it—they nevertheless acquired far-reaching rights of disposal over their holdings. Payment, reduced by 20 percent, was compulsory.

On April 9 revision committees set to work. Their task was to check the judicial settlements in order to ensure that the peasants received deeds for all of the land they occupied as well as that which had been taken from them since the establishment of the inventories. Officials of the local organs responsible for carrying out the reform were replaced almost entirely with Russians. It was characteristic of the government's way of doing things that, afraid that the floodtide of peasant demands might spill into the neighboring eastern districts, it initially restricted the revision process to the aforementioned Lithuanian and Belorussian districts and only on November 2, 1863, included the remainder of Belorussia. In April the Polish population of the southwestern Ukraine also joined the insurrection, and so, by an ordinance of July 30, 1863 (with the effective date of September 1), the regulations were extended to Kiev, Podolia, and Volhynia.[28]

Also typical of the hypocritical, exclusively power-politically oriented policies of St. Petersburg is the fact that the authorities entrusted the suppression of the rebellion and the implementation of the pro-peasant legislation in Lithuania and Belorussia to General M. M. Muravev, who was famous as an obdurate proponent of serfdom (*krespostnik*) and had earned the nickname of "Executioner" while governor-general of Vilna. Assuming his new post in May of 1863, he acted immediately and as ruthlessly as possible. He had 240 rebels publicly hanged and incited the peasants to flout their masters. In one of his first proclamations to the peasants he wrote: "You are no longer obliged in any way to serve your lords; you are completely independent of them; even if many landowners of Polish origin continue to demand socage and to burden you with duties in order to benefit themselves, it is merely a matter of abuses which we will stop by taking the strictest possible measures."[29]

We may now inquire about the response of the peasants in whom both sides had placed their hopes. Since the peasant uprisings of the Middle Ages it has again and again proved to be the case that the peasants saw as their enemy not the distant, divinely chosen, and therefore just ruler, but the omnipresent landlord, who controlled their lives down to the very last detail and often demanded exorbitant services of them without the justification of providing help when they needed it. Indeed, during the first days of the Polish rebellion there appeared to be a danger in many parts of the Kingdom that the events which had occurred in Galicia in 1846 might be repeated.[30] Only after the rebels had begun to carry out their agrarian program consistently did it seem for a while that the social and political goals of the insurrection could be coordinated. However, as the influence of the Whites upon the rebel leadership grew, the chance of a genuine upheaval—if in fact it had ever existed—slipped by. Most peasants probably supported the insurrection, but, in light of their mistrust of the landowners and because of the tsarist government's repressive actions, they thought it wise to play a waiting game.[31]

The situation in the Western District was different. The Orthodox Belorussian and Ukrainian peasants and the numerous Old Believers who had settled there as lessees were inveterate opponents of the insurgents' objectives. Even though rebel proclamations in Belorussian and Ukrainian[32] guaranteed freedom, equality, landed property for everybody, abolition of all dues, fair treatment for every nationality, and autonomous administration, the peasants saw in such promises only the subterfuge of the despicable landlords. Thus the government succeeded in defeating the rebellion in the Western District in only a few months. The efforts of the tsarist troops were supported by the peasants' plundering of numerous estates, especially in those places where resistance to St. Petersburg was strongest.[33] The hope that it might be possible, after the expulsion of the landlords, to partition tracts of noble lands among themselves was probably an important motive for the peasants. They refused all services to the seigniors, denounced them, and captured rebel detachments and turned the prisoners over to the authorities. Only in Catholic Lithuania did the insurrection enjoy much popular support.[34] Here priests like Brzóska and Mackiewicz stepped forward as leaders of the common folk, while the peasant decree of the Central Committee was punctiliously executed. Moreover, the border districts of the Union contained a relatively broad stratum of ennobled peasants who sympathized with the political aims of the insurrection.

The rebels' declared intention of reviving Poland within its 1772 borders proved disadvantageous to their movement in a number of respects. The non-Polish population of the affected territory feared that reunification would mean a renewal of the odious system of noble rule. For its part, the St. Petersburg government, both at home and abroad, was able to exploit skillfully the insurgents' exaggerated demands. After the national catastrophe of the Crimean War and in the midst of Alexander II's "liberal" reforms, Russian society was in ferment. As a consequence of the abrogation of its rights to servile labor, the landowning nobility felt "offended" and claimed that it was facing economic ruin. The liberals remained unsatisfied by the reforms, and there were signs of the first organized revolutionary groups. Under such circumstances the Polish rebellion in the Western District offered an opportunity for creating a far-reaching consensus between the government and the public. The conviction that Russian national honor was at stake made it possible for the struggle against the Polish rebels to be portrayed as a "holy" patriotic cause. Even the liberals chimed in, adding their voices to the enthusiastic nationalistic chorus. The liberal war minister, D. A. Milyutin, writing to his brother, N. A. Milyutin (destined to play a decisive role in the 1864 peasant reform in the Kingdom of Poland), trenchantly described the situation:

Our whole society is in an incomparably better humor than before; only the most obdurate nihilists still consider it their duty to demonstrate objectivity, indeed sympathy for the Poles; undeniably, the great majority of reasonable people are experiencing a surge of patriotism which gives the lie to all the stories spread in other countries by émigrés and malevolent tourists.[35]

As a result of diplomatic notes from France, Britain, and Austria (sanctioned by numerous other European states) on April 10 and 12, a danger also began to loom from abroad. Russian patriots closed ranks behind the government. Katkov's press did what it could to stoke the fires of Russian nationalism. Herzen and the revolutionary democrats still loyal continued to depict the Polish insurrection as a democratic movement, but their arguments fell increasingly on deaf ears. The number of subscribers to *Kolokol* fell by two-thirds in 1863. The chief of police could write in his report: "Thus we have succeeded in banishing the revolutionary cloud that was gathering over Russia and threatening to burst over our heads."[36]

Ever more frequent and vociferous were the demands that the Western District be purged of its Polish element. The former Slavophile but later Russocentric Pan-Slavist M. P. Pogodin, whose writings were a veritable barometer of the public mood, had proclaimed at the outbreak of the Crimean War in 1864: "Announce the independence of Poland, and Austria, Prussia, and all Germany will tremble."[37] As late as 1856 he was advocating full autonomy for a Poland still linked to Russia in the person of the tsar, albeit with a frontier that followed linguistic lines. In 1863 Pogodin, like many other Slavophiles, regretted his previous pro-Polish stance and in March of that year formulated demands that would be realized a few months later:

> I, too, admit that I am guilty; I long thought that the Poles would give up the idea of retaining their old conquests in Russia; . . . I now renounce this illusion . . . ; the Poles must be driven from the western provinces at all costs—ferreted out, sent on their way, led off, in the higher interest of the state; they must turn over money and forfeitable bonds to us; they must leave together with their priests, valuables, mourning clothes, and all movable goods; however, the immovable, real property, the land, is of our blood; it is Russian, and the Poles shall not have an inch of it![38]

With Russian public opinion behind him, Muravev pursued a brutal expulsion policy. It was all the easier to do this because it became clear in the course of the summer that the European powers were not going to exert themselves to the extent of intervening on the side of the Poles. Numerous properties belonging to the rebels were confiscated. (Only in

December of 1865 did the government bother to encumber the Poles' legal rights to dispose of their estates.) The ethnic and religious affiliations of noble landowners in the Western District were also quite different after 1863. To what extent this was a result of physical removal or of more or less voluntary assimilation is difficult to say. Whereas the nobility remained almost entirely Polish in Kovno and Vilna, its proportions occasionally fell by as much as 50 percent or more in the other provinces of the Western District.

Changes in the landholding and personal legal status of the peasants were fundamental. The revision commissions, which sat until 1865, altered most judicial settlements to benefit the plowman. Whereas peasants in other provinces lost roughly 18 percent of their arable land upon emancipation,[40] those of the Western District gained by one-quarter.[41] At the same time the redemption sums were greatly reduced, since they were adjusted to reflect the actual value of the land. Whereas the amount owed exceeded the value of the land in the non-chernozem region by 121 percent and in the chernozem districts by 56 percent, it was only about 8 percent more in the Western District.[42] A good illustration of the improved position of the cultivator is the example of thirty-five properties of the Radziwiłł family in Minsk. According to the judicial agreements the peasants of these estates were supposed to receive 26,873 *desiatini* of land and to pay an indemnity of 631,380 rubles. The review committees increased the peasants' holdings by 44,557 *desiatini* and lowered the debt to 263,017 rubles.[43]

In order to make certain that peasants on state domains (though they were generally better off than the ex-serfs) would not be at a disadvantage, further improvements were effected. According to a decree of May 16, 1867, the state peasants also had to pay compensation, but redemption was extended over a period of forty-nine years with the interest (*obrochnaia podat*) raised by only 10 percent. At the same time their holdings were augmented by about 25 percent. A ceiling of three rubles per *desiatina* was set in order to prevent Polish landlords from increasing rents. This rule remained in effect until 1876, when a special system was devised enabling renters either to purchase their holdings outright or to pay compensation for them. No less crucial for the future agrarian development of the Western District than the improved conditions of peasant tenure was the complete dissolution of the ties between serf and seignior. Redemption was obligatory. In return the peasants were given broad rights to dispose of their holdings, although they still did not attain full ownership. They also kept usufructary rights—particularly to pasturage—and access to wood on estate land.

What effects did the peasant reform in the Western District, carried out in so sweeping a manner, have upon agricultural development? I have suggested that both estates and peasant farms in the provinces in question were modernized at a much faster pace than in the rest of the Russian Empire. (This process was to serve as an example for Stolypin's agrarian reform in the post-1906 era.)[44] The previously discussed absence of subdivided, communal tenure (*obshchinnoe zemlevladenie*) was surely an important factor, but the basic reason was the fact of a radical divorce. Estates and peasant lands were separated in both a legal and a practical economic sense, i.e., by severance of the seignorial ties that had guaranteed peasant dependency.

The landlords were now forced to accelerate farming of their own properties by the employment of day laborers. More favorable market conditions facilitated this shift to self-management. While in the central Russian provinces communal peasants continued to till estate lands with their own sparse and primitive equipment, throughout the Western District a system of lucrative large-scale farming closely linked to processing plants sprang up. Another commonly encountered phenomenon was so-called capitalistic rental. Big estates were partitioned into farms (*fol'vark, ferma*) of about 400 *desiatini* and handed over to lessees.[45] Modernization of agronomy and stock breeding made rapid progress. In the southwest, as a result of the intensive cultivation of beets and wheat, a highly efficient sugar-refining and grain-milling industry developed.[46] In the northwest an increase in the production of potatoes, sugar, and flax encouraged the distilling activity of textile manufacturers and intensive cattle raising for dairying purposes. In Vitebsk between 1887 and 1900 the cultivated area was expanded by 27.7 percent and herds of steers and swine grew by 44.7 percent. In Vilna between 1887 and 1900 plowed acreage rose by 29.7 percent; fodder spread between 1881 and 1901 from a total of 5,100 to 42,200 *desiatini,* and by 1910 potatoes were being grown on 10 percent of the arable land.[47]

The modernization of estate farming set an example for the peasants. Since they were not bound by a rigid system of field utilization as were their communally organized Russian confrères and did not need to worry about losing their plots on the occasion of the next redistribution of collective land, the preconditions for individual farming and hence for management improvements were far more favorable. The existence of hereditary, individual tenure also permitted the development of a highly mobile market for the sale of farmsteads. As might be expected, there was a distinct tendency for land to pass into the hands of more efficient cultivators, and a large stratum of well-to-do peasants emerged, particularly in the northwest. In 1905 the proportion of peasants in the

Lithuanian provinces with more than 10 *desiatini* of property was 77 percent, and the average size of peasant farms was about 14.9 *desiatini*.[48] As modernization proceeded, villages spontaneously disintegrated, since it was more practical to dwell in isolated houses in the midst of one's own fields (*Einödhöfe, chutor*).[49] The peasants pressed ahead as fast as possible with highly productive stock raising through intensive use of barns. With the resultant supply of manure they were also able to raise soil yields. The enormous increase in population may be viewed as evidence of more auspicious economic circumstances. Whereas in the whole of European Russia the population shot up by 115.4 percent between 1858 and 1914, the expansion in Lithuania amounted to 149.7 percent. The opposite side of the coin, socially speaking, was the disproportionate growth of a rural proletariat. By the turn of the century the Western District was also the fountainhead for Russia's emigration.

In summary, the Russian government sought to punish the Polish nobility of the Western District for its involvement in the January Insurrection of 1863 by implementing an extreme version of agrarian reform. Its attempt to destroy the economic base of the Polish landlords backfired; radical peasant reform in fact encouraged the modernization of agriculture. The Western District witnessed the development of highly profitable estate farming and the rise of a stratum of affluent peasants. Conversely, in the central parts of the empire, where the 1861 reformers—fearing the Russian nobility's reaction—did not dare to disentangle small husbandmen from their seignorial counterparts and thus to foster individualization, the peasant question was destined to become the powder keg of future revolutions.[51]

Notes

* Translator's note: The peculiarly retrograde character of East Central Europe's agrarian social structure in the first half of the nineteenth century necessitates the use of a medley of English terms, i.e., words stemming from widely separated periods of Anglo-American history. Thus, a "proprietor," "landlord," or "estate owner" is the seignior or lord of a domain that contains both peasant plots and a demesne.

1. V. I. Picheta, *Agrarnaia reforma Sigizmunda-Avgusta v Litovsko-Russkom gosudarstva* (Moscow, 1958); Iu. M. Iurginis, "Vliianie agrarnoi reformi seredini XVI v. na proizvoditel'nie sili Litvi," in *Problemi agrarnoi istorii s drevneishikh vremen do XVIII v. vkliuchitel'no*, pt. 1 (Minsk, 1978), pp. 12–18.

2. A. Moritsch, "Landwirtschaft und Agrarpolitik im Russland vor der Revolution" (Habilitationsschrift, University of Vienna, 1981).

3. Ibid., pp. 294–312.
4. Ibid., p. 483, table 11, and p. 484, table 14.
5. Cf. I. D. Koval'chenko, "Agrarverhältnisse und Bauernbewegung in Russland am Ende des 19. und zu Beginn des 20. Jahrhunderts," in *Deutschland und Russland im Zeitalter des Kapitalismus 1861–1914* (Wiesbaden, 1977), pp. 24–25.
* Translator's note: One *desiatina*, or "tenth," an obsolete imperial Russian unit of surface measure, is equivalent to 1.09 hectares or 2.69 U.S. acres.
6. Moritsch, "Landwirtschaft," p. 484, table 16.
7. Cf. M. B. Fridman, *Otmena krepostnogo prava v Belorussii* (Minsk, 1958), pp. 13–22.
8. Ibid., pp. 17, 88.
9. Quoted by Fridman, *Otmena,* p. 68.
10. Ibid.
11. See *Mestnoe polozhenie o pozemel'nom ustroistve krest'ian, vodvorennikh na pomeshchikh zemliakh v guberniiakh Kievskoi, Podol'skoi i Volinskoi* (St. Petersburg, February 19, 1861) and the corresponding document for the guberniyas of Vilna, Grodno, Kovno, Minsk, and part of the guberniya of Vitebsk.
12. Fridman, *Otmena,* p. 104.
13. *Zhurnali Sekretnogo i Glavnogo komitetov po krest'ianskomu delu,* vol. 2, pp. 5–6.
14. Fridman, *Otmena,* p. 104.
15. Ibid., pp. 150–51.
16. N. N. Leshchenko, *Krest'ianskoe dvizheni na Ukraine v soiazi s provedeniem reformi 1861 goda (60e gody XIX st.)* (Kiev, 1959), pp. 377–79.
17. Ibid., p. 380.
18. H. Fleischhacker, *Russische Antworten auf die polnische Frage 1795–1917* (Munich-Berlin, 1941), p. 88.
19. Cited by Fridman, *Otmena,* pp. 152–53.
20. Ibid., p. 153.
21. Quoted by Fridman, *Otmena,* p. 153.
22. Ibid.
23. *Kolokol,* October 1.
24. Ibid.
25. *Wydawnictwo materialów do historii powstania 1863–1864,* vol. 1, pp. 33–34.
26. Ibid., p. 35.
27. Quoted by Fleischhacker, *Russische Antworten,* p. 89.
28. Leshchenko, *Krest'ianskoe dvizhenie,* pp. 414–16.
29. Milovidov, "Osvobozhdenie krest'ian Severo-Zapadnogo kraia" in *Vilenskii kalendar* (Vilna, 1902), p. 327.
30. J. J. Krulik, "Die Bauernreform vom Jahre 1864 im Königreich Polen" (Ph.D. diss., University of Vienna, 1926), p. 66.
31. I. I. Kostiusko, *Krest'ianskaia reforma 1864 goda v Tsarstve Polskom* (Moscow, 1962), p. 61.

32. Among other things, a "Golden Bull" (*zolota hramota*) was circulated in the southwestern Ukraine. It was supposed to produce the impression of that "wonderful act of deliverance" for which the peasants were waiting.
33. Leshchenko, *Krest'ianskoe dvizhenie*, pp. 408–9.
34. Krulik, "Die Bauernreform," p. 71.
35. Quoted by Fleischhacker, *Russische Antworten*, p. 95.
36. Ibid., pp. 100–101.
37. M. P. Pogodin, *Pol'skii vopros 1831–1867* (Moscow, 1867), p. 37.
38. Ibid., pp. 99–100.
39. N. P. Vakar, *Belorussia: The Making of a Nation, A Case Study* (Cambridge, Mass., 1956), pp. 73–74.
40. Fridman, *Otmena*, p. 169.
41. According to P. A. Zaiochkovskii (*Otmena krepostnogo prava v Rossii* [Moscow, 1968], p. 238), the extent of the increase in peasant-held land in the individual western guberniyas was as follows: Vilna 16 percent, Kovno 19 percent, Grodno 12 percent, Minsk 41 percent, Vitebsk 17 percent, Kiev 21 percent, Volhynia 15 percent, Podolia 18 percent. (Data for Mogilev are not given; since the *obshchina* form of tenure prevailed in this province, it may be assumed that there were hardly any changes vis-à-vis the pre-1861 era.)
42. A. E. Lositskii, *Vykupnaia operatsiia* (St. Petersburg, 1906), p. 16.
43. Fridman, *Otmena*, p. 165.
44. Moritsch, "Landwirtschaft," p. 301.
45. Ibid., p. 307.
46. *Entsiklopedicheskii slovar' Granat*, vol. 10, col. 327.
47. Ibid., cols. 164, 166; vol. 17, col. 158.
48. Moritsch, "Landwirtschaft," p. 301 and p. 484, table 14.
49. *Entsiklopedicheskii slovar' Granat*, vol. 24, col. 440–2.
50. Moritsch, "Landwirtschaft," p. 481, table 1.
51. For an exhaustively documented analysis of military operations during the 1863 Insurrection, see Janusz Wojtasik, "The Influence of Armament on the Art of War in the Polish National Risings in the 18th and 19th Century" [*sic*] in *Military Technique, Policy, and Strategy* (Warsaw, 1976), pp. 95–196, esp. pp. 162 ff. Wojtasik expressly recognizes the militarily damaging effects of peasant neutrality (p. 176) and emphasizes the guerrilla character of the fighting, which lasted a full fourteen months. Short of trained troops and weapons, the Poles could only have succeeded had the major European powers actively supported them.

The Birth of a Nation:
The January Insurrection and the Belorussian National Movement

John T. Stanley

Before the January Insurrection of 1863 a Belorussian nation did not exist. The other countries of East Central Europe had foreign relations with the Poles; Belorussia, in contrast, had been an integral part of the Polish Commonwealth until 1772, and its development was far more affected by Polish events than were those of the Czech nation or the Scandinavian countries. Poles and Belorussians were different peoples, but they had a common past and spoke mutually comprehensible tongues. Common social interests bound together the nobility (*szlachta*) of the Commonwealth despite their distinct Polish, Lithuanian, Ukrainian, or Belorussian origins. Over the centuries of shared statehood, the distinction between Belorussian and Pole blurred. The similarity of the two languages certainly contributed to this blurring, as did the creation by the Union of Brest (1596) of an Eastern-rite church subordinate to Rome. The attitude evinced in Mickiewicz's "Book of Polish Pilgrimage" was common among the Poles. "The Lithuanian and the Mazurian are brothers . . . [but] their name is one: Pole."[1]

There was no distinct Belorussian national consciousness. "Belorussian" could be used only to describe a geographical region, a peasant people, or a language. In the villages, however, Belorussian still survived as a means of oral communication,[2] even if the peasants merely described their nationality as *tuteishy*. Polonization was the price of education and social advancement for any Belorussian. The 1863 Insurrection provided the first opportunity for forging a distinct Belorussian consciousness. Mass support for the insurrection inevitably meant peasant support; within the historical boundaries of the Grand Duchy of Lithuania the peasantry was primarily Belorussian. Reinforced by the Grand Duchy's traditional separatism, the peasant question became the key issue of Belorussian nationalism in 1863. For the first time, political activists had to work with the knowledge that the local population was neither Polish nor Russian, but something distinct from, if related to, both.

The Belorussian lands had no distinct frontiers. The Poles considered them their eastern *kresy* and the Russians their northwestern *guberniyas*. In 1863 these lands were defined by the guberniyas of Grodno, Minsk, Vitebsk, Mogilev, and Vilna, a territory with a population of five and one-half million.[3] The class structure of this region was little different from that of other parts of the Russian Empire: noblemen, a large group by Western European standards but still constituting less than 1 percent of the population; townspeople, a group only a little more numerous than the nobility and largely dwelling in small towns; and a peasantry composing over 90 percent of the population.[4] In contrast to the rest of the Russian Empire, however, the northwestern guberniyas had a nobility that was generally Polish, a town population that was predominantly Jewish,[5] and a peasantry overwhelmingly Belorussian. Although St. Petersburg viewed the territory as the patrimony of Rus', it had been wrested from the Polish Commonwealth only in the late eighteenth century.

Placed on the outskirts of European civilization, Belorussia as a region was only beginning to develop economically in the mid-nineteenth century. The construction of the Warsaw-to-St. Petersburg railway line quickened the life of the territory, but the biggest industries were still breweries or distilleries. Cloth factories and sugar refineries were also present, but industry was in its most primitive state. The chief trade centers were the annual fairs; agriculture remained the mainstay of economic life.[6]

In 1863 no distinct administrative divisions separated the Belorussian lands from the rest of the empire. After the first partition of Poland in 1772, a separate Belorussian Government-General had been organized, but the new Russian rulers obviously did not look for support from the large Belorussian peasant population. Instead they sought to base their rule on the nobility, as they did elsewhere in the empire. Since the nobility in the region was Polish, a direct result of this policy was the continued Polonization of the area. The revolt of the Poles in 1830, however, changed the direction of Russian policy. In 1840, for example, the Lithuanian Statute was abolished, and Russian law was enforced in the territory. In the same year, Russian replaced Polish as the language of instruction in the *gymnasium* of Minsk. Finally, the use of the name "Belorussian" was abandoned, and the territory became known officially as the Northwestern Guberniyas.

While their economic and administrative structure did not distinguish the Northwestern Guberniyas from the rest of the empire, the language and customs of the peasantry did give the Belorussian lands their own identity. While the Poles looked upon Belorussian as a dialect of Polish with archaisms and Russicisms and Russians viewed it as simply a Russian dialect Polonized in its vocabulary, ethnographers such as Adam Kirkor began to study the customs of the Belorussian lands,[7] and such scholars as Teodor Narbutt and Jan Barszczewski demonstrated that Belorussian customs were quite different from those of either the Polish or the Russian peasantry. Together with the studies of Belorussian ethnography, archeology, and folklore came the first attempts to use the Belorussian language as a literary medium.[8]

The first anonymous works—a Belorussian parody of the *Aeneid* and a setting of *Taras on Parnassus* (which turned the home of the gods into a Belorussian village)—were little more than literary novelties.[9] However, an increasing number of authors began to use this peasant "dialect." An example of this phenomenon is Vintsenty Dunin-Martsinkevich's 1846 libretto for Stanisław Moniuszko's opera *Sialanka (The Peasant Girl)*, which used Polish for the noblemen but Belorussian for the peasants.[10] The Belorussian literature of the first decades, however, is little more than a genre of Polish literature. Aleksander Rypiński's *Białaruś (Belorussia)* displayed in its subtitle an attitude common to all of the literature produced in this period; it described the contents of the volume as "the poetry of the simple people of this, our Polish province."[11] Many of these literary figures produced poetry in both Polish and Belorussian—Adam Kirkor, Jan Barszczewski, Jan Czeczot, Syrakomla (pseudonym of Wincenty Kondratowicz), Artsem Veryha-Dareŭski, and even Vintsenty Dunin-Martsinkevich.[12] The latter published a number of poetry collections, and his one-act play *Pinskaia Shliakhta (The Pinsk Gentry)* is still performed on Belorussian stages.[13] Dunin-Martsinkevich is therefore considered the first professional Belorussian writer.[14] Pedagogical works were also produced: the first printed book in modern Belorussian was *Krótkie zebranie nauka chrześciańskiej,* which appeared in 1835.[15] Invariably, the works of this period simplify and idealize noble-peasant relations and are as much the result of sentimentalism as of the romanticism which was still the dominant literary style of the period.

The Belorussian literary movement was tied to Polish developments, and the Russian authorities viewed the fledgling literature as an attempt to Polonize the peasantry.[16] The first issue of the Polish journal *Bojan* was confiscated in 1839 because it included a folk song in Belorussian.[17] In 1859 the use of the Latin alphabet for Belorussian was outlawed, and consequently the entire edition of Dunin-Martsinkevich's translation of Adam Mickiewicz's epic poem *Pan Tadeusz* was seized and burned. In

1865 all Belorussian publications were forbidden. In 1852 a decree forbade stage performances "in the language of the common people."[18] When Pavel Mikhail Shpilevskii compiled a Belorussian grammar in 1846, the Russian Imperial Academy of Sciences refused to accept it as scientific: "dialects may not have grammatical categories of their own." Ksawery Niedźwlecki's grammar of 1854 received a similar rebuff. A large number of linguists, however, considered Belorussian as a separate East Slavic language. Whether they called it "Krivichian" (coined by Johann Christoph von Adelung) or "Baltic Russian" (Nikolai Ivanovich Nadezhdin's term), the scholarly recognition of Belorussian's linguistic differentiation from Russian and Polish solidified.[19] Conditions for the development of a Belorussian literature, however, could hardly have been more unfavorable. As a result, its development was fragmentary and slow.

The Russian government did not view the territory in national terms. Outside the Jews, it saw only Catholic and Orthodox. The Orthodox were considered to be loyal to the tsar; the Catholics (and the former Uniates) were potential rebels. In 1827, the government forbade the conversion of Uniates to Roman Catholicism; in 1839 the Uniate church was simply banned within the empire in an attempt to weaken the "Polish" character of the region. The Poles themselves were convinced that the region was as much a part of Polish culture as before 1772. When Aleksandr Herzen asked Władysław Mickiewicz in 1863 if the inhabitants of the region should not be asked whether they were Polish, the poet's son responded: "Ce n'est pas plus utile que de demander au habitants de Moscou et de Tver, s'ils sont Russes."[20]

By 1863 the separate ethnicity of the Belorussian people was acknowledged in much scholarly work, and a separate Belorussian literature had been born, if not fully developed. There was no political counterpart to this cultural development, however. Political movements within the historical boundaries of Lithuania were copies of those in the Congress Kingdom of Poland and exclusively Polish. Although there were both Whites (conservatives) and Reds (radicals) in the Belorussian territories, the Whites were far weaker in their organization and more limited in their aims than were the Reds. As early as March 1861 the Reds were organized in Hrodno (Grodno), and in the spring the patriotic manifestations and religious demonstrations spread to Vilnius (Wilno, Vilna), Kaunas (Kówno, Kovno), and Minsk.[21] No White organization existed, however, until the insurrection was already under way. Between the two groups were two areas of dispute which were of importance to the future of Belorussian nationalism: "Lithuanian" separatism and the peasant question.

Since the peasantry formed the greatest part of the population, it was the key to any proposed mass uprising. The Whites feared a peasant uprising and hoped to exclude the peasants from politics. The Reds, on the other hand, hoped to use the peasantry in any rebellion against tsarist authority. The great latifundia of the Polish nobility were in central and eastern Belorussia. At mid-century, landholders with more than five hundred serfs constituted less than 3.5 percent of the nobility but controlled 41.5 percent of the peasant population.[22] In western Belorussia, smaller landholdings prevailed, but this difference required an even more intense exploitation of peasant labor. In some parts of Minsk and Grodno guberniyas, 568 days of corvée were the norm for a family.[23] Consequently, peasant uprisings were quite common. The abolition of serfdom by Alexander II in 1861 did not quell peasant unrest. Indeed, the number of peasant disturbances actually increased.[24] This peasant dissatisfaction was an issue which the Reds hoped to build upon and use in a nationalist insurrection. The Whites, however, were actively involved in putting down any peasant rebellion. They were not interested in linking social and national issues. A. Fogmajster, a member of the Hrodno revolutionary organization and a landlord himself, proclaimed in a statement to the authorities after his capture: "No one wanted revolution."[25]

Konstantin Kalinowski (Kastus Kalinouski) (1838–64) was the most insistent in pressing the peasant question. A Pole by birth, he was raised on a small estate in the Hrodno region.[26] As a student he was in contact with revolutionary groups in both Moscow and St. Petersburg and adopted ideas similar to those of Aleksandr Herzen, Mikhail Bakunin, and Nikolai Ogarev.[27] Rejecting conspiratorial methods as useless, Kalinowski hoped for a full-scale peasant revolution, an uprising which could be channeled against the Russian government to become a powerful tool in the hands of the radicals. Peasant disturbances had always been limited by the poorly developed consciousness of the peasantry. Kalinowski hoped to enlarge that consciousness by demonstrating to the Belorussian peasantry that their problems were caused by tsarism and could be combatted and even defeated. "We can not only feed [others] with the peasants' bread, but also teach them the peasants' truth."[28]

Kalinowski therefore began to publish the first Belorussian newspaper, *Mużyckaja praúda* (*The Peasant Truth*). Other circulars had been distributed to the peasants—*Hutarka dvukh susedau* (*Tale of the Two Neighbors*), Wincenty Koratyński's *Hutarka staraha dzeda* (*The Old Man's Tale*), and *Hutarka belaruska* (*The Belorussian Tale*). While all these pamphlets were designed to show the Belorussian peasant the disadvantages of Russian rule and remind him of a more comfortable past under the Polish Commonwealth, any discussion of social reform was carefully avoided.[29] The Polish activists' pamphlets in Belorussian did force the local authorities to respond in kind with *Razskazy na belorusskom narechi* (*Tales in the Belorussian Dialect*).[30] Kalinowski's newspaper was quite different from these brochures and pamphlets, however. Written in the Latin script, *Mużyckaja praŭda* devoted each of the six numbers issued before the insurrection to a different problem plaguing the peasantry. "Six years have already passed since they began to speak of peasant freedoms. They speak and write much but do nothing. . . . From the Muscovites (*Moskale*) and the lords there is no reason to expect anything."[31] In each of the issues Kalinowski and his collaborators concentrated on a specific problem.[32] The first was devoted to criticizing the 1861 peasant reform, the second to exposing social injustice and denouncing corvée and land fees, the third to a demand for political freedoms for the peasantry, the fourth to criticism of the tsarist regime and its bureaucrats, the fifth to a denunciation of conscription and its twenty-five years of military service, and the sixth to protest against the oppression of the Uniate church.[33]

Kalinowski did not write all of the newspaper issues, of course. He did provide the motivation behind the newspaper, however. Walerian Wróblewski, another Polish radical and a future general in the Paris Commune of 1871, is generally considered to have been the author of the third issue, for instance. Feliks Rożański also is known to have contributed to the newspaper.[34]

Publishing a newspaper in the Belorussian language, however, was not enough. Most of the peasants were illiterate, and there was no legal method of distribution. Kalinowski and his band therefore took to the road—traveling from village to village, reading the newspaper to the gathered peasants, discussing the issues it raised, hoping to develop a progressive consciousness. Kalinowski's organization in Hrodno included at least two peasants—Matvei Tsiakhna and Kazimir Stankevich—as well as estate employees and ex-students. In Minsk guberniya, Feliks Kliukoŭski traveled between the villages of Slutsk and Pinsk districts, living in the peasants' huts, and used Belorussian to prepare the way for revolution. Kamilla Dunin-Martsinkevich, the daughter of the poet, also was a member of the Minsk group trying to organize a school for peasant children. The leader of the Minsk organization was Vikenty Klimavich, educated but of peasant origin. In the Belorussian regions of Vilna guberniya, Zygmunt Mineiko directed the revolutionary organization. Mineiko also was from a traditional village although educated as an engineer.[35] After the outbreak of the January Insurrection, revolutionaries continued to use *Mużyckaja praŭda* as a method of spreading the news about the National Central Committee's peasant program.³⁶

The work of propagandizing went slowly and was not equally effective everywhere in Belorussia. In Hrodno guberniya, where Kalinowski himself knew the peasants and their villages, the Reds met their greatest response; in Vitebsk and Mogilev guberniyas there was little success.³⁷ Having grown up among the local peasantry and having been indoctrinated in the peasants' importance by both Polish and Russian revolutionaries, Kalinowski came to idealize this social group and called them his "brothers" in the columns of *Mużyckaja praúda*. At the center of the peasant question was the issue of land. The Polish revolutionaries had learned much from the 1830 Insurrection, in which peasant involvement had been minimal. They understood that landownership was most important to the peasant and hoped to harness this issue to encourage peasant participation in the national struggle. The Reds were inspired by Tadeusz Kościuszko's victory at Racławice (1794) as well as by the writings of Herzen and Bakunin.³⁸ The peasants' armed revolt was to bring about not only freedom from the Muscovites, but also their own liberation, in a classless society in which each peasant would own the land he worked. The White leader Jakub Gieysztor labeled Kalinowski a "peasantophile" (*chłopoman*), and it is in this sense that this Red may be termed a "revolutionary democrat."³⁹

At the end of July 1862 the Provincial Lithuanian Committee was organized and in contact with the Central National Committee in Warsaw.⁴⁰ Nester du Laurens was the Central National Committee's representative in Vilnius, and he soon found himself at odds with the local radicals. Du Laurens saw the Lithuanian Committee as subordinate to Warsaw, and he sought to base its underground activities among the ethnic Poles. Kalinowski, however, believed that "noble participation in the insurrection is not only unnecessary, but even harmful."⁴¹ He reminded his peasant audience that the lords "fear our freedom."⁴² For those nobles who did not join the insurrection, Kalinowski sought only the worst: "Let the nobility who do not come with us perish. Then the peasant axe should not stop even at the cradle of a noble's child."⁴³ Ludwik Zwierzdowski, the partisan commander in Orsha district, gave the order to "hang landlords who most oppress the peasants [in order] to encourage peasants to join the band."⁴⁴

At the beginning of the January Insurrection, the newly formed Provisional Provincial Government in Lithuania issued a manifesto emancipating the serfs and promising them the land they worked. An additional decree of February 1, 1863, offered 3 morgs (2.13 hectares) of land to any landless peasant who served in the army as a volunteer.

Promises of compensation were also made to the landlords, however. In general, the new Polish authorities' agrarian program was extremely moderate.[45] In circulating the Warsaw government's *Insurrectional Instructions*, however, Kalinowski inserted his own eighth point: "The most notable oppressors of the peasants, as an example to the common people, will be punished with death. . . . ."[46] Given the nationality of the landlords in Belorussia, this instruction could only be aimed at fellow Poles. Kalinowski clearly saw the insurrection as an opportunity not only to alleviate national oppression, but also to eliminate social exploitation. He considered cooperation with the Polish national liberation movement the most effective method of combatting Russian authority, but he differed in his goals and methods from most of the Reds and all of the Whites.

The 1863 Insurrection in Lithuania lasted only a few months (from January through June) before developing into a series of guerrilla skirmishes limited to a few regions of Hrodno and Vilna guberniyas.[47] The terrorist tactics of Mikhail Muravev quickly destroyed the landlords' organization in Lithuania, leaving only scattered bands of Reds. Faced with the possibility of a peasant rebellion stirred up by the Reds, most Polish landlords proclaimed their support for St. Petersburg.[48] It is important to note that the very regions in which Kalinowski and his followers had propagandized most effectively were the areas in which the insurrection survived the longest—eastern Hrodno and northern Kaunas.[49] When Muravev organized peasant brigades (*straż wiejskie*), Kalinowski, then commissar in Hrodno, saw the need for counteraction and therefore published the seventh, and last, issue of *Mużyckaja praúda* in June 1863. Kalinowski repeated the Central National Committee's agrarian policy, promising the peasant ownership of his own land, the free choice of religion, and social equality. He also distributed a "Proclamation from the Polish Government over the Whole Lithuanian and Belorussian Country to the People of the Lithuanian and Belorussian Land," dated June 11/23.[50] Kalinowski's increasingly radical manifestos had little effect, however, in the face of Russian terrorism and a general lack of peasant support.[51] By September 1863 he was the sole remaining member of the Lithuanian committee on Belorussian soil. In October, he issued a manifesto denouncing the Roman Catholic consistory of Vilnius for acceding to Muravev's demands for a denunciation of the rebellion. The insurrection was winding down, however, despite Kalinowski's best efforts. The last battle of the partisans in Hrodno guberniya took place on October 7, in Vilna guberniya on October 20. Kalinowski himself was arrested on the night of January 29, 1864, and hanged in March.[52] In a statement to the authorities while in prison, he blamed the failure of the insurrection on the social antagonism between peasant and lord.[53]

If the peasant question divided Reds from Whites, the question of Lithuanian subordination to Warsaw was another contentious issue. Lithuanian separatism had a long history, extending back to the Union of Lublin (1569). The Grand Duchy of Lithuania had entered into this union with the Kingdom of Poland as an equal. Although its ruling elite was Polonized over the centuries, the interests of Poles and Lithuanians were never precisely the same. Poles living within the former boundaries of the Grand Duchy did not see themselves as merely inhabitants of another Polish province, looking to Warsaw for guidance and leadership. The Provincial Lithuanian Committee had insisted on its own authority within the Grand Duchy's former frontiers, arguing that the Białystok organization should be subordinated to Vilnius. Moreover, it saw itself as equal in its authority on Lithuanian territory to the Central National Committee in Warsaw. Throughout the insurrection, as the Provincial Lithuanian Committee became first the Provisional Provincial Government in Lithuania, then the Governing Division of the Province of Lithuania, and finally the Executive Division in Lithuania, such disputes continued to erupt between the revolutionary governments in Warsaw and Vilnius. Such separatist disputes were obviously not proofs of a Belorussian or Lithuanian nationalism. All involved in these quarrels were Poles, by both birth and culture, seeking to reestablish a Poland within the boundaries of 1772.[54] Indeed, the Belorussian national movement of this period has been described as "Polish provincial patriotism, more a Belorussian particularity of a general Polish movement than a conscious Belorussian nationalism."[55] But the difference in outlook between the two groups permitted the Belorussian renaissance of the mid-nineteenth century and was the basis for the future development of separate and differing nationalisms.

Polish scholars and litterateurs had nourished the seeds of a Belorussian literature, using the spoken language for the first time as a literary medium. In 1863 Polish revolutionaries also molded the vocabulary and principles of Belorussian political nationalism. In Kalinowski's newspaper, revolutionary ideas had been expressed in the peasant's native language, in a form comprehensible to the Belorussians. The principles of *Mużyckaja praúda* became the foundation for the political development of Belorussian nationalism.

There were a number of causes for the political differences between Warsaw and Vilnius. The Central National Committee was not familiar with the Lithuanian situation and had called the insurrection before the Lithuanian organization was prepared. More importantly, however,

Warsaw viewed the insurrection as a Polish national one, naturally involving all social classes but aiming at political independence. Social change was merely a means to that political end. In writing to Aleksandr Herzen, the Central National Committee in Warsaw characterized his Russian movement as social (*zemskoe*) and theirs as national.[56] The Lithuanian committee knew that a purely Polish uprising had no special appeal for the Belorussian peasantry, who identified Polishness with their lords. Indeed, in Vitebsk and Mogilev guberniyas the Polish insurrection was met with a peasant insurrection against it.[57]

In his social goals, Kalinowski went beyond his fellow Lithuanian Reds. He sought peasant liberation as a goal of equal importance to the independence of Poland. Poland's independence was significant because it would lead to a true peasant emancipation. Kalinowski's means and ends were the precise reverse of those of the Warsaw Committee.

Kalinowski was familiar with Bakunin's conception of a Slavic federation in which the Belorussians would be represented. Through Mikola Kostomarev, he was also familiar with the reconstituted Cyril and Methodius Society formed by the Ukrainian nationalists.[58] Acknowledging Kalinowski's desire for a Slavic federation, however, does not mean the 1863 Insurrection in the Belorussian territories was an "indivisible part of the all-Russian revolution."[59] Kalinowski had contacts with numerous Russian revolutionaries and particularly with Zemlia i Volia, but he wished Belorussia to be part of a reconstituted and federal Polish Commonwealth the dissolution of which had ruined the peasantry.[60] He deeply believed that the basic traditions of the former Commonwealth were democratic while those of Russia were fundamentally autocratic. He therefore considered that the Belorussian cause could be satisfied only within the bounds of the larger, Polish national cause. He idealized the Polish Commonwealth as a state based on equality and social justice, which he contrasted to the peasants' oppression within the Russian Empire. Naturally, he was sympathetic to the efforts of Russians to carry out revolution; their activities would weaken the imperial government's hold on Belorussia. He did not see the future of Belorussia as safe under the "Muscovites," however. Kalinowski and all the Polish Reds were influenced by the examples of Herzen, Ogarev, and Bakunin. This influence, however, must be considered within the context of the Polish revolutionary tradition.[61]

In *Mużyckaja praúda* the word "Belorussian" does not appear. Kalinowski addressed his Belorussian audience using the word *mużyk* (peasant). Only after his arrest in January 1864 did he begin to call his readers "Belorussians." In the letters collected under the title *Z pad szubienicy* (*From Under the Gallows*), Kalinowski reminded his readers that it was only from the Poles—a "brother nation"—that aid could be expected. However, he said, the Belorussians must fight for their own freedom, not expect it from others—a slap which he almost certainly aimed at the Whites. "When you see . . . your brothers struggling for truth, do not remain behind, but, seizing whatever you can . . . go and fight with your people for human and national rights, for your faith, for your native land."[62] Kalinowski urged the creation of Belorussian schools and finally called the Belorussians a nation (*naród*). Russia was the enemy: "As long as [the Muscovites] are among us, there will be no truth, wealth, or any kind of science. . . . You will live happily when there are no Muscovites over you."[63] He therefore tied this Belorussian nation to Poland, reminding his followers that the "Poles' cause is our cause."[64] But his own attitudes toward the Polish landlords during the insurrection revealed that the Belorussian and Polish nations would not always have the same interests or pursue the same goals. Both Poles and Russians had used the local language as a means of propaganda without any recognition of a separate Belorussian nationality. Kalinowski's last writings represent the first consciousness of a distinctly political nationalism.[65]

The Polish revolutionaries could not outflank the Russian government over the peasant question. In 1863 Alexander II made concessions to the peasants of the Northwestern Guberniyas and put his changes into force. Kalinowski attempted to counterattack the imperial government's action by repeating the Central National Committee's slogans. The Polish emancipation decrees never received much attention, however. Despite a warning attached to the decree of February 1, 1863, that "whoever will not obey this manifesto, be he landlord, peasant, official, or any other, will be prosecuted according to Polish military law," there was no real method of enforcing it against Polish landlords, who were supposed to be one of the foundations of the insurrectionary regime.[66] Even adherents to the insurrection ignored the decree when it went against their own interests. Given the brevity of effective Polish rule in the area, the Polish emancipation had little impact. The Poles themselves were divided over its form. When Alexander II had asked the local nobility to submit their own plans for reform before the imperial emancipation proclamation, the Polish nobility of the Belorussian lands had sought to liberate the serfs without land. Most of the Polish revolutionaries hoped to use Polish noble support; the goal of the insurrection was Polish national independence, not an agrarian revolution.[67] Any definite effort to enforce the Warsaw government's emancipation decree could only serve to divide the Polish cause against itself. The Russian government, however, viewed the Orthodox peasants as loyal and the Polish nobility as traitorous. Their strategy was to pit Orthodox peasant against Catholic lord. The March 1863 manifesto was successful in achieving this end.

While making concessions to the Belorussian peasantry, however, St. Petersburg hoped to stamp out Belorussian nationalism, considering it an ally of Polish revolutionary thought. After the insurrection was defeated, Russian became the language of instruction in all schools. Belorussian publications were banned, to become legal once more only in 1889. No periodicals in Belorussian were permitted before 1906.[68]

If St. Petersburg sought to obliterate all differences between Russians and Belorussians by force, there were Russians who had been awakened to the existence of an East Slavic brother and were interested in studying this peasant nation. Both Ivan Aksakov and Mikhail Katkov welcomed the discovery of "these new 'blood brothers.'" The incidents of Belorussian peasant resistance to the Polish insurrectionaries led Russian nationalists to believe that a new weapon against the Poles had been found. Russians thus came to dominate Belorussian studies.[69] Before 1864 Poles had dominated this field; afterwards, Russian scholars made the greatest number of contributions.

Belorussian nationalism followed a familiar path from ethnic study to literary movement and from cultural patriotism to political nationalism. The study and use of the Belorussian languge and literature were nurtured within a Polish milieu for the first few decades of its existence. Tsarist oppression of both Polish and Belorussian national movements united the two peoples in their strategy. Belorussian political culture thus arose within the Polish political tradition. The 1863 Insurrection therefore may be viewed as the beginning of Belorussian political nationalism. Against tsarism, serfdom, national oppression, and social inequality—this minimum program provided by the January Insurrection satisfied all those involved in the Belorussian national movement. Dunin-Martsinkevich's literary works had separated the national and social questions; Kalinowski's activity served to unite them.

The social conflict in the Belorussian lands between Polish nobility and Belorussian peasantry quickly became apparent once liberal principles became political imperatives. If 1863 represents the starting point of Belorussian politics, it also represents the last moment when the Commonwealth of 1772 would remain the goal for both Belorussian and Pole, regardless of political viewpoint. Ultimately, the conservative Russian authorities could more easily satisfy the Belorussian peasant's desire for more secure tenure of the land. Satisfaction of this urge, however, did not halt the development of Belorussian nationalism.

Placed within the frontiers of the Russian Empire, that "prison of nationalities," Belorussian nationalism was legally suppressed, but it could not be stifled. Indeed, Kalinowski's execution provided the nascent movement with its first martyr. The peasants remembered this period of insurrection in their folklore as well. In "A Song for God's Hour" (*Pieshn na bozhy chas*), 1863 is remembered as a moment when the peasants "felt equal to the lords,/And took up their scythes in freedom's cause."[70] The imperial government was forced to alter its original 1861 emancipation to the benefit of the peasantry. In *From Under the Gallows,* Kalinowski reminded the Belorussians: "Who knows how long we would still labor under serfdom if it were not for the Polish Insurrection?"[71]

The effect of the insurrection can also be seen in the life and work of Frantishak Bahushevich, one of Belorussia's most important nineteenth-century writers. A teacher in the village school at Dotsiski, Lida district, he joined the insurrection and was wounded in a skirmish near Suwałki. This experience cemented Bahushevich's hostility to the Russians. Despite his close contacts with the Polish literati, however, he looked forward to an independent Belorussian nation, not the recreation of the Commonwealth.[72] It was Bahushevich's work which spanned Belorussian literature in the second half of the nineteenth century, linking Belorussian nationalists in the 1890s with the events of 1863.

The January Insurrection of 1863 provided few solid answers for the new Belorussian national movement, but it did pose the fundamental questions for the Belorussian activists. What was the relationship of the Belorussians to their neighbors, the Poles and the Russians? How were the peasants to be brought into the struggle for national existence? What political organization was the new nation to develop? The 1863 Insurrection had demonstrated that there was a Belorussian nation. Belorussian nationalists had much left to achieve, but the first "seeds" of the Belorussian nation were planted in 1863.[73]

Notes

1. Adam Mickiewicz, "Księga pielgrzymstwa polskiego," *Dzieła poetyckie* (Warsaw, 1938), p. 250.
2. Examples of Belorussian oral poetry from the 1860s are "Schod," "Hutarka Daniły sa Shchiapanam," and "Razmova pana z chłopam" (Arnold B. McMillin, *The Vocabulary of the Byelorussian Literary Language in the Nineteenth Century* [London, 1973], pp. 39–40).
3. "Naselnystva," *Belaruskaia Savetskaia Entsyklapedyia,* vol. 12 (Minsk, 1975), p. 55.
4. Marceli Kosman, *Historia Białorusi* (Wrocław, 1979), p. 224. In 1856,

townspeople were 8 percent of the regional population. Mahileŭ (30,734 inhabitants) was the largest town; Minsk (30,149), Vitebsk (27,868), Hrodno (26,187), and Brest (20,665) were the chief remaining ones (Ia. Karneichyk, *Belaruskaia natsyia* [Minsk, 1969], p. 55). Despite Mahileŭ's marginally greater size, Minsk was considered more important commercially. Shpilevski called Minsk the "capital of Belorussia" (ibid., p. 50).

5. Half the population of Minsk was Jewish in the mid-nineteenth century; 70 percent of the craftsmen in Hrodno in 1857 were Jews. In the smaller towns, the numbers were even greater; in Poniewież 89 percent of the inhabitants were Jewish. In Vilna guberniya 64 percent of the townspeople were Jews (Dawid Fajnhauz, "Ludność żydowska na Litwie i Białorusi a Powstanie styczniowe," *Żydowski Instytut Historii Biuletyn* 10, no. 37 [1961]: 9–10). Although many Jews understood Polish, it was difficult to involve the Jewish population in the January Insurrection. "The Jews created a closed society" (Benedykt Dybowski, "Pamięci Jozefata Ohryzki," *Biblioteka Warszawska* 5 [1907]: 215–16). Only in a few cases did the insurrectionists actively seek Jewish support, however. Roman Rogiński, upon occupying Biała Podlaska, called new elections with the participation of peasants and Jews. Władysław Simanowicz, leader of the insurrection in Slonim district, propagated egalitarian ideas among the Jews and Tartars (Fajnhauz, "Ludność żydowska," p. 33). Such cases were isolated reminders that not even the Reds had a specific program for the involvement of the large Jewish population, despite the proclamations of equality.

6. Samuel Agurskii, *Ocherki po istorii revoliutsionnogo dvizheniia v Belorussii (1863–1917)* (Minsk, 1928), p. 10; Karneichyk, *Belaruskaia natsyia*, pp. 48–50. More extensive treatment of Belorussian economic development in this period is given in M. F. Bolbas, *Razvitie promyshlennosti v Belorussii (1795–1861)* (Minsk, 1966), and V. V. Chepko, *Sel'skoe khoziaistvo Belorussii v pervoi polovine XIX v.* (Minsk, 1966).

7. Paul N. Wexler, *Purism and Language: A Study in Modern Ukrainian and Belorussian Nationalism (1840–1967)* (Bloomington, 1974), pp. 206–7, 210; Z. Ia. Tal'virskaia, "Nekotorye voprosy obshchestvennogo dvizheniia v Litve i Belorussii v kontse 50-kh—nachale 60-kh godov i podpol'naia literatura," in *Revoliutsionnaia Rossiia i revoliutsionnaia Pol'sha (vtoraia polovina XIX v.)* (Moscow, 1967), pp. 12–13.

8. Nicholas P. Vakar, *Belorussia: The Making of a Nation* (Cambridge, 1956), p. 77.

9. Kosman, *Historia*, p. 218; McMillin, *Vocabulary*, pp. 34–35.

10. Wexler, *Purism*, p. 220.

11. Aleksander Rypiński, *Białoruś: Kilka słów o poezii prostego ludu tej naszej polskiej prowincii, o jego muzijce, śpiewie, tancach, etc.* (Paris, 1840), as quoted in Peter Scheibert, "Der weissrussische politische Gedanke bis 1919," *Jomsburg* 2 (1938): 335–36.

12. Tal'virskaia, "Nekotorye voprosy," pp. 16–22; Wexler, *Purism*, p. 220.

13. Arnold B. McMillin, *A History of Byelorussian Literature* (Giessen, Germany, 1977), p. 97; Kosman, *Historia*, p. 220; Tal'virskaia, "Nekotorye vo-

prosy," pp. 25–27. The poet's works are collected in V. I. Dunin-Martsinkevich, *Zbor tvoraŭ* (Minsk, 1958).
14. McMillin, *History,* p. 95.
15. McMillin, *Vocabulary,* p. 38.
16. The Poles themselves reinforced this belief. In a Paris lecture, Aleksander Rypiński told his audience that Belorussia "will always be Polish, since the language itself is binding the people with Poland, not with Moscow" (Vakar, *Belorussia,* pp. 75–76).
17. McMillin, *History,* p. 77–78.
18. McMillin, *Vocabulary,* p. 38.
19. Vakar, *Belorussia,* pp. 77–78.
20. Ibid., p. 71.
21. Stefan Kieniewicz, *Powstanie styczniowe* (Warsaw, 1972), p. 175.
22. Kosman, *Historia,* pp. 225–26.
23. Ibid.
24. Ibid., p. 228.
25. S. M. Baikova, "Agrarnyi vopros v vosstanii 1863 g. v Belorussii," *Ezhegodnik po agrarnoi istorii vostochnoi Evropy 1963 g.* (Vilnius, 1965), pp. 46–47.
26. The standard biographies of Kalinowski are Wiktor Kordowicz, *Konstanty Kalinowski* (Warsaw, 1955), and Anatolii F. Smirnov, *Kastus Kalinovskii* (Moscow, 1959). Neither is completely satisfactory. In English there is Leo Horosko, "Kastus Kalinouski," *Journal of Byelorussian Studies* 1 (1965): 30–35.
27. Henadz Kiseleŭ, "K kharakteristike revoliutsionnogo mirovozzreniia K. S. Kalinovskogo ('Svedeniia' V. F. Ratcha kak istoricheskii ostochnik)," in *Slavianskoe istochnikovedenie* (Moscow, 1965), pp. 38, 44–45.
28. "Niechaj się wszyscy dowiedzą że my możemy nie tylko karmić swoim chlebem, ale i uczyc swojej chłopskiej prawdy," *Mużyckaja praŭda,* no. 1 (reprinted in *Prasa tajna z lat 1861–1864* 1 [Wrocław, 1966]: 320–21 and in English translation in Belaruski instytut navuki i mastastva, *Zapisy* 14 [1976]: 93–131).
29. In "The Old Man's Tale" it is said, "The time will soon come when the Poles will fight the Russians and restore freedom to Belorussia" (Vakar, *Belorussia,* pp. 80–81). Also see Ivan N. Lushchitskii, "Russkaia revoliutsionnaia demokratiia i peredovaia obshchestvenno-politicheskaia mysl' v Belorussii v period vosstaniia 1863 g.," in Minsk, Universitet, *Nauchnye trudy po filosofii* 1 (1956): 103.
30. Two editions of the "Tales in the Belorussian Dialect" were published, in 1863 and 1864 (McMillin, *Vocabulary,* p. 40).
31. *Mużyckaja praŭda,* no. 1; *Prasa,* pp. 320–21.
32. The individual issues are not dated. However, from the contents of each issue one can hazard a date with reasonable accuracy. The first issue was published in the first half of July 1862 and no. 2 in the second half of that month; nos. 3 and 4 are from August 1862 and nos. 5 and 6 were published in November and December 1862 (Lushchitskii, "Russkaia revoliutsionnaia," pp. 68–69).
33. Although it is uncertain that Kalinowski wrote the sixth issue, he did view the Uniate church as the national church of the Belorussians. Roman Catholi-

cism he considered a tool of the Polish nobility, and certainly its hierarchy was staffed from the *szlachta*. The Russian Orthodox church, tightly controlled by St. Petersburg, was seen as merely the tool of the Muscovites. Of course, there was no Belorussian Orthodox church at that time. Kalinowski himself was not religious and, like all Reds, was anticlerical. He believed the Uniate church could be used in fostering a Belorussian national spirit and should therefore be restored to its legal position and given back the churches surrendered to the Russian Orthodox church in 1839.

34. Tal'virskaia, "Nekotorye voprosy," pp. 65–77; McMillin, *History,* pp. 88–89.
35. Baikova, "Agrarnyi vopros," pp. 49–51.
36. Ibid., pp. 53–55.
37. Ibid., pp. 51, 58; D. Vasileŭski, "Sialianstva Vitsebskai i Mahileŭskai guberan' u paustan'ni 1863 hodu," *Polymia,* no. 6 (1928): 148–61.
38. Krzysztof Kąkolewski, "Konstanty Kalinowski i jego pisma w latach 1862–1864," *Z dziejów współpracy rewolucyjnej Polaków i Rosjan w drugiej połowie XIX wieku* (Wrocław, 1956), p. 203; Scheibert, "Der weissrussische politische Gedanke," p. 338.
39. Kisileŭ, "Kharakteristike," p. 40.
40. Anatolii F. Smirnov, "Manifestatsionnoe dvizhenie v Belorussii i Litve 1861 goda," in Akademiia nauk SSSR. Institut istorii, *Revoliutsionnaia situatsiia v Rosii v 1859–1861 gg.* (Moscow, 1960), pp. 462–66. Smirnov counts 227 manifestations in Belorussia and Lithuania from May to mid-December 1861 (p. 471). Kalinowski himself did not believe that the demonstrations of 1861 had prepared the peasantry for the insurrection.
41. Jakub Gieysztor, *Pamiętniki,* vol. 1 (Vilnius, 1913), p. 222.
42. Kąkolewski, "Kalinowski," pp. 200–201.
43. Ibid., p. 199.
44. Ibid., p. 205.
45. The Polish manifesto is reprinted in *Khrestomatiia po istorii Belorussii* (Minsk, 1977), p. 286.
46. Kieniewicz, *Powstanie styczniowe,* pp. 415–16.
47. The first military action on Lithuanian territory occurred as early as January 23, 1863, when Suraż in Białystok district was attacked. The uprising suffered its first defeat in the Belorussian lands shortly afterwards, at Siemiatyczy on February 7. The escaping Polish participants fled to the Polesian swamps, where they did not find any support in the Belorussian peasantry. Following yet another defeat—at Borky on February 26—the remaining insurrectionaries were captured and handed over to the Russian authorities by the local peasants themselves (ibid., p. 416).
48. St. Petersburg saw the danger to Russian rule if the Polish national cause were tied to the peasant question. Faced with the need to counteract the revolutionary decrees of January 22 and February 1, 1863, the tsarist regime responded with its own program on March 1. This decree represented a substantial change from the 1861 reforms, and it applied only to the guberniyas of Vilna, Kovno, Grodno, Minsk, and the northern districts of Vitebsk. In its

decree, the Russian government declared all remaining obligations between peasant and lord to cease as of May 1. Peasant payments for their newly acquired land would be reduced by 20 percent and this money would be paid to the treasury, which would finance the purchase of the land from the nobles (Baikova, "Agrarnyi vopros," p. 56).

49. Kieniewicz, *Powstanie styczniowe,* pp. 496–97, 541, 606–7. Baikova, "Agrarnyi vopros," p. 57, cites examples of peasant aid to the insurrectionists, but all are in Grodno guberniya.

50. Kalinowski as a civil administrator and organizer was highly praised even by Jakub Gieysztor and J. Grabiec (pseudonym of Józef Dąbrowski). Gieysztor remarked that Kalinowski "was very active, and certainly the organization was never so exactly carried out." Grabiec noted that in Grodno guberniya Kalinowski "introduced a civilian organization on a broad scale" (Kąkolewski, "Kalinowski," p. 215).

51. Claims of the participation of seventy-seven thousand peasants, often made in Soviet publications, are a great exaggeration. See Iu. I. Zhiugzhda, "Razvitie demokraticheskogo dviezheniia v Litve v 60-kh godakh XIX v. i vliianie na nego russkogo revoliutsionno-demokraticheskogo dvizhenia," *Istoricheskie zapiski* 45 (1954): 189, and Ivan N. Lushchitskii, *Narysy pa historyi hramadska-palitychna i filasofskai dumki u Belarusi u druhoi palavine XIX v.* (Minsk, 1958), p. 105. V. N. Pertsev, "Kastus' Kalinouski," *Polymia,* no. 10 (1945), p. 94, even insists that the insurrection be considered an "agrarian revolution." A. F. Smirnov, *Kastus Kalinovskii,* p. 42, takes the same position. It is a Soviet historian, however, who effectively demolishes these myths of the Stalinist era. See M. V. Misko, "Ob osveshchenii kharaktera vosstaniia 1863 g. v Litve i Belorussii v nekotorykh rabotakh sovetskikh avtorov," in Moscow. Universitet. Kafedra istorii iuzhnykh i zapadnykh slavian, *Slavianskaia istoriografiia* (Moscow, 1966), pp. 143–48.

52. "Donesenie shtabs-kapitana kn. Dolgorukovo o kazni K. Kalinovskogo," in *Khrestomatiia,* p. 291. Upon Kalinowski's arrest, the Executive Division had transferred leadership to Józef Kalinowski, but he too was arrested in March 1864. This act finished the Red organization in Lithuania.

53. Kieniewicz, *Powstanie styczniowe,* p. 699. In his statement to the Russian authorities while in prison, Kalinowski admitted that the "peasant . . . could not trust the lords, and looked at the Polish cause as landlords' plotting" (Kąkolewski, "Kalinowski," p. 214).

54. Misko, "Ob osveshchenii kharaktera vosstaniia," pp. 150–51, 157–58, 160.

55. Dmytro Doroshenko, *Belorusi i ikh natsional'ne vidrodzhennia* (Kiev, 1908), p. 50.

56. "Ot Tsentral'nogo Natsional'nogo Pol'skogo Komiteta v Varshave gg. izdateliam 'Kolokola,'" *Kolokol,* no. 146 (October 1, 1862), pp. 1–2.

57. In eastern Belorussia, the peasants had not been prepared for the insurrection as had those in Grodno and Minsk guberniyas and, mistaking it for an attempt to reverse the 1861 reforms, took up arms against the Polish nobility (Baikova, "Agrarnyi vopros," pp. 58–59).

58. Scheibert, "Der weissrussische politische Gedanke," p. 338.

59. Lushchitskii, "Russkaia revoliutsionnaia," pp. 64–65.
60. Misko, "Ob osveshchenii kharaktera vosstaniia," pp. 151–54.
61. Peter Brock, *Polish Revolutionary Populism* (Toronto, 1977).
62. McMillin, *History*, pp. 88–89.
63. Agaton Giller, *Historja powstania narodu polskiego w 1861–64*, vol. 1 (Paris, 1868), pp. 334–35.
64. Adam Stankevich, *Kastus Kalinoŭski: "Mużyckaja Praŭda" i ideja Nezależnosci Biełarusi* (Vilnius, 1933), p. 38. "Pismo ad Jaska Haspadara," formerly attributed to Kalinowski, is now considered to be the work of "members of Agaton Giller's nationalist circle" (McMillin, *Vocabulary*, pp. 38–39; also see Misko, "Ob osveshchenii kharaktera vosstaniia," pp. 153, 163).
65. It may seem strange that the first Belorussian nationalist was ethnically a Pole. One should remember, however, that the first Czech patriots were German-speaking and that Czech nationalism also had been nurtured in the provincial patriotism of the Bohemian nobility. Dobner, Voight, and Ungar were linguistically Germans, and neither Durych nor Pelc was hostile to the Bohemian Germans. All of Josef Dobrovsky's major works were written in either German or Latin. The Slovak national movement in the late eighteenth century also offers parallels for a student of Belorussian nationalism (Robert Auty, "Czech and Slovak Thought in the Second Half of the Eighteenth Century," in *Colloque sur le mouvement des idées dans les pays slaves pendant la seconde moitié du XVIIIe siècle, Uppsala, 1960* [Rome, 1962], pp. 137–38, 149–50). Adam Kirkor himself referred to the Czech example (Tal'virskaia, "Nekotorye voprosy," p. 16.
66. Baikova, "Agrarnyi vopros," p. 53.
67. Misko, "Ob osveshchenii kharaktera vosstaniia," pp. 162–63.
68. McMillin, *Vocabulary*, p. 40.
69. Vakar, *Belorussia*, p. 77.
70. McMillin, *History*, p. 88.
71. Kąkolewski, "Kalinowski," pp. 213–14.
72. McMillin, *History*, p. 99.
73. Stankevich, *Kastus Kalinoŭski*, p. 6.

The Scandinavian Countries and the January Insurrection

Emanuel Halicz

The question of the Scandinavian countries' attitude toward the 1863 Insurrection and the influence of the insurrection on the subsequent history of the countries of Northern Europe is not a new one; it was raised during the course of the insurrection itself by the distinguished polemicist and politician Julian Klaczko in his essays in the *Revue des Deux Mondes*. The literature on the subject is, however, meager and fragmentary. There are a few works by Swedish historians, concentrating mainly on the question of the attitude of Swedish society toward the insurrection, but there is a lack of any broader interest in the various aspects of Swedish foreign policy related to it. It is symptomatic of this that the Swedish historians did not use foreign archives, although, as can be seen from the works of Stanisław Bóbr-Tylingo,[1] there are many documents on Swedish policy to be found in these archives. The Danish literature treats the question of Denmark's attitude toward the Polish insurrection as marginal, and the Polish literature contains no treatises or books at all on the topic in which we are interested. Even the most thorough monographs on the insurrection fail us, particularly where the question of Denmark's attitude toward the Polish events of 1863 is concerned. The same applies to the studies which have appeared in Western Europe.[2]

There are various reasons for this lack of interest in the question. One is the tendency, which has still not been overcome, to view the events of nineteenth-century Scandinavia in isolation (this is particularly true of Scandinavian historiography); another is the underestimation of the role of small countries in the overall picture of European relations.[3] It is frequently overlooked that nineteenth-century Europe, although divided into separate states with different and often opposing interests, was politically a single entity, and every great European event influenced the fate of other countries (though this influence was not always direct).

In the present case I am concerned not just with the attitude of the Scandinavian countries toward the Polish insurrection, but chiefly with the influence of that uprising on the history of the Scandinavian countries. I am convinced that the year 1863 was of decisive significance for the subsequent political development of Europe and that its effects were felt directly, above all, by Denmark.

In this paper I shall use the term "the Scandinavian countries" to mean the states of Sweden/Norway and Denmark. I omit Finland because of its political status; it was, of course, part of the Russian Empire, and, apart from a group of émigrés resident in Sweden, Finnish society had no way of freely expressing its attitude toward the Polish question.

The question of the Scandinavian countries' attitude toward the Polish insurrection was integrally connected with the policy of the Scandinavian countries in the years after the Crimean War. The differences in political orientation between the two friendly Scandinavian states, which were looming during the last phase of the Crimean War, became deeper after the war. Their differing points of view on fundamental European questions stemmed both from the different historical experiences of Sweden and Denmark and from their geopolitical situations. I have in mind here their attitudes toward both Russia and Prussia. To Sweden Russia was a traditional enemy; this was a result of its historical experience and the conclusions it drew from the struggle for control of the Baltic Sea, reinforced as a result of the detachment of Finland from Sweden and the constantly unsatisfied appetite of the Russians. Denmark, on the other hand, had, not without reason, a reputation as a pro-Russian country, and even when it found itself between the devil and the deep blue sea during the Crimean War it made no fundamental move toward the Western states in order not to antagonize Russia.

Denmark and Russia were linked by political interests and dynastic ties, and for many years Russia had been regarded as the protector of Danish interests. The events of 1848–49 and the attitude of Russia toward the Schleswig-Holstein conflict confirmed this view. After the Russian defeat in the Crimean War, Russian policy, including its relations with Denmark, underwent a fundamental change brought about, on the one hand, by the Russo-Prussian rapprochement and, on the other, by the displeasure occasioned by the transformation of Denmark into a constitutional state ruled by a national-liberal group. The final factor was the spread of the political idea of Scandinavianism in Denmark, as in Sweden. Anti-Scandinavianism and fear lest the Danish straits and the entrance to the Baltic should come under the control of a single Scandinavian power brought Russia and Prussia together. In addition to this, Russia was grateful to Prussia for the position it took during the Crimean War. Russia saw Prussia as a conservative force capable of dealing with the liberal movement in Germany. All these factors, plus the desire to punish Austria for what Russia saw as its treacherous and shameful behavior during the recent war, caused Prussia to become the closest ally of Russia in Germany, and in consequence of this the government in St. Petersburg completely abandoned the position taken by Russia at Olomouc. This fundamental change, and the conclusions deriving from it, were ignored by the Copenhagen government, which continued to regard Russia as the guarantor of the London decisions of 1852 throughout the whole period following the signing of the Treaty of Paris. Although relations between Sweden and Denmark were very friendly and Sweden fully supported Denmark's policy on the question of the principalities and advocated the idea that the Eider frontier was the frontier of all the Scandinavian states, in practice there were bound to be differences between Stockholm and Copenhagen. This applied also to their views on the practical implementation of the idea of political Scandinavianism—what should be the political shape of the eventual union of the Scandinavian states and the future relations, degree of dependence, and forms of cooperation between them. These differences, which derived both from the different domestic situations and, in particular, from the external and geopolitical positions of the two Scandinavian states, are revealed especially in 1863 in the attitudes of Stockholm and Copenhagen toward Russia and the January Insurrection.

As far as Sweden's attitude toward the Polish insurrection is concerned, a variety of factors influenced its pro-Polish position. For Swedish society it was primarily humanitarian factors that were important; for the government, however, the reasons were mainly if not exclusively political. The government was continuing the policy initiated during the Crimean War and particularly after the conclusion of the treaty with Britain and France in November 1855, the provisions of which, although never put into effect, had not lost their relevance. The emergence of France under Napoleon III as the leader of Europe, and his nationality principle and its implications for Italy and Hungary and then for Poland too, the nationalistic celebrations in Russia in connection with the anniversary of the victory of Poltava, the hostile attitude of Russia toward Scandinavianism and, what was most fundamental for Sweden, the question of its claim to Finland, which was linked to Sweden by several centuries of common history—these were the political foundations on which pro-Polish attitudes developed. Once the insurrection broke out, these factors were supplemented by humanitarian considerations, as Swedish society was shocked by the barbarous treatment meted out by the Russian army both to the insurgents and to the defenseless civilian population in the areas affected.

An uprising which was regarded initially as an internal Russian affair came to be regarded in Stockholm, as in other European countries, after the conclusion of the Alvensleben Convention as a question of fundamental significance for the development of European politics. Reports of intended intervention by the European states reached Stockholm and fell on fertile ground. However, while the great majority of public opinion displayed its pro-Polish attitude and sometimes its readiness for active involvement in anti-Russian action, and this was supported by King Charles XV personally, the position of the government and, above all, of the minister of foreign affairs was from the start restrained. He was disturbed by the outburst of pro-Polish demonstrations throughout Sweden, which went far beyond humanitarian aid, and by the participation in them of politicians, intellectuals, and people from various walks of life, and he regarded them as unpleasant and even dangerous for the country. Ludwig Manderström picked his way adroitly between the pressure of general public opinion, the demands of the Western countries, and a dangerous course which might become a challenge to Russia. Hence the minister's statements intended to placate the Russian government, which was very hostile to all demonstrations in support of Poland, and his assurances to Russia that any statements in Western periodicals about an inevitable break in relations between Sweden and Russia were incorrect and that the Swedish government did not want its relations with the government in St. Petersburg to deteriorate. The minister did not wish the Polish question to go beyond diplomatic and general humanitarian intervention. He continually instructed the Swedish ambassador to St. Petersburg, Frederic Wedel-Jarlsberg, to this effect. In a telegram on March 2, 1863, for example, setting out his point of view, he asserted that the pro-Polish demonstrations taking place in Stockholm and other cities in Sweden were distasteful to the government and that he had faith in the good intentions of the tsar: "Nous avons trop de foi dans les motives élévés et généraux de cet Auguste Souverain pour n'être point persuadés qu'il ne laissera point s'arrêter par cette regrettable insurrection, dans la marche noble et éclairée que, depuis Son avènement, il a suivie a l'égard du Royaume de Pologne."[4] In a conversation with the Russian ambassador, Jakov Dashkov, Manderström maintained that since he had resided in Stockholm for so many years the ambassador should know perfectly well that the government was not in a position to do anything to prevent the demonstrations. The Swedish ambassador delivered a similar declaration to Alexander II. Caution was the principal byword of Manderström's policy, because, as he himself said, although he was for Poland he felt that lack of caution could lead the country into dangerous entanglements. The position taken by the minister of foreign affairs contrasted with the complete commitment of the king, a fact that did not escape the notice of the British ambassador.

The minister's cautious policy was influenced both by reports from Carl Wachmeister in London and Georg Nicolaus Adelswärd in Paris that there was little hope of joint military intervention by the Western powers against Russia and by information from Swedish military circles on fundamental gaps in the army's equipment in the event of a conflict.

Under the influence of the government, and in particular at the instigation of the minister of foreign affairs, articles appeared in the conservative press warning against an adventurist policy and agitation for war. There was no shortage of voices in society warning against Swedish involvement in a war against Russia, especially when the increasing wave of pro-Polish articles agitating for war caused panic in the stock markets and a collapse in Swedish securities' values.

All the same, under pressure from domestic public opinion and Western governments, the government dispatched notes to Alexander Gorchakov defending the Polish nation and its rights according to the provisions of the Treaty of Vienna. It called for the protection of the peace in Europe and declared itself opposed to bloodshed in Poland.

The Swedish authorities' attitude toward Polish affairs was put to the test again during the expedition of Colonel Teofil Lapiński on the *Ward Jackson*. Wanting to demonstrate their neutrality to Russia despite progressive public opinion in their own country, they complied with Russian demands for the confiscation of the vessel and its cargo.

Many factors contributed to this cautious policy by the government in Stockholm: fear of Russian reprisals, the inadequate military preparation of the country, and above all the rivalry between France and Britain, which frustrated all plans for war against Russia and the possible liberation of Finland. Unwilling voices also came from Finland itself, claiming that the population of the country remained basically loyal to Russia and that union with Sweden was not very popular there. The Swedish government's part in the powers' diplomatic intervention really ended with its telegrams and notes in March and April.

The separate policy carried on by the king behind the back of the government was another matter. He linked it with opportunities to implement his own political plans, which aimed at uniting the Scandinavian states, recovering Finland, and increasing his own royal power.

The king's dislike of Russia and his awareness that the reconstruction of Poland was in the interests of Sweden were the main reasons for his increased contacts with representatives of the Polish political émigrés beginning in 1862. These contacts had the common purpose of persuading France to go to war against Russia. How far these plans really aimed at coordination of the two countries' efforts and how far they were just ideas and soundings, particularly on the part of Napoleon III, is hard to say because of the lack of any archival evidence apart from the documents published by Bóbr-Tylingo in *Teki Historyczne* in 1960–61. At any rate, in the second half of 1863 the king returned to the idea of starting a war jointly with France against Russia in the spring of 1864.

If all these plans came to nothing, the chief responsibility, as Swedish historians correctly stressed, lies with France and Britain, since these powers were incapable of reaching agreement and acting in defense of Poland. Even the cautious Manderström saw Sweden's place as beside the Western powers in the event of such armed action by them in the Baltic. Sweden could not act on its own, but could only follow their lead.

Toward the end of 1863 Manderström did not hide the great danger threatening the country from Russia. He feared a surprise attack on Sweden in revenge for the policy pursued by Sweden toward the end of the Crimean War and in 1863. Faced with the prospect of an alliance between Russia, Prussia, and Austria, he severed the Swedish alliance with Denmark at the end of 1863, at the moment when Denmark was facing mortal danger and was under diplomatic and military pressure from the coalition of German states.

Norwegian society viewed the Polish events from the point of view of its own interests. Norway did not feel the Russian threat in the same way as Sweden and had no territorial claims against Russia. Only a small group of Norwegian Scandinavianists felt any solidarity with the anti-Russian disposition of the Swedes. Liberal circles supported the Polish nation's struggle for liberation chiefly out of fear of states that trampled on the rights of nations to political independence and freedom.

The Polish question was used by the liberal opposition to advance its political program, which aimed to abolish the office of governor, strengthen the parliamentary system and make the government subject to Parliament, and ultimately strengthen democracy in Norway. Solidarity with Poland was expressed by leading representatives of the liberal camp in the press and by meetings in Kristiania and other towns, especially in April 1863. The position taken by supporters of Scandinavianism in Norway coincided with that of the same camp in Sweden. They considered that diplomatic endeavors unsupported by force of arms would not free Poland. If France and Britain declared war against Russia, they argued, Sweden and Norway should take part in it. Such a war was in the interests of the whole of Scandinavia, which was threatened by Russia. Russia had already swallowed up Finland and threatened to invade Sweden and northern Norway. The main aim of action by the Scandinavian states must be the liberation of Finland, and the situation which had arisen in the Polish lands should favor that. Even if the attempt to free Finland failed, the very fact of the rise of an independent Poland would be of enormous importance for the Scandinavian countries. The rise of Poland would push Russia eastward and force it to switch to a defensive policy toward the European states. This would be important for Denmark, too, since the revival of a strong, free Poland could draw the Germans' attention away from Denmark. Starting from these premises, it was argued, the Scandinavian states ought to support the struggle for the liberation of Poland.

The majority of Norwegian society, however, regarded these principles with skepticism. It thought that war with Russia was mainly in the interests of Sweden, which sought to regain Finland. Norway was not interested in strengthening Sweden. Pro-Polish sympathies here did not gather the same momentum as in Sweden, chiefly because of differences in political objectives.

The most complicated attitude toward the insurrection was that of Denmark, and this remark applies both to Danish society and to the government. It was primarily the result of Denmark's political situation, in which the central problem for many years had been the conflict with Germany over Schleswig and Holstein, but there were other reasons as well.

The uprising in Poland and the course of the struggle in the initial period were misinterpreted by part of Danish society. There was a tendency to contrast the social character of the January Insurrection with the national character of the November Insurrection. In view of both the signs of strife between the peasants and the manor during the first period of the insurrection and the reluctant attitude toward it of the nobility, it was seen as a social rather than a national-liberation struggle. A section of the press opposed this position and emphasized the national character of the Poles' struggle, but it blamed Germany above all for everything bad that happened in Poland, since in its opinion the Russians were "children," a nation ruled by Germany and the Holstein-Gottorp dynasty since Peter the Great and Catherine II. Russia's friendship was much more dangerous for Denmark than Germany's hostility, it argued, and for this reason Denmark's place was beside the Western powers and Sweden.

The Danish government decided to make use of the insurrection to carry out its own political aims. After the rejection of John Russell's autumn note (the "Gotha Dispatch") Denmark found itself politically almost completely isolated in the international arena, but the outbreak of the Polish Insurrection appeared to create better prospects for it. Berlin and Vienna were so absorbed by events in Poland that for the moment they had lost interest in the Schleswig-Holstein question. After the conclusion of the Alvensleben Convention, Bismarck seemed to be in a difficult situation, the more so since Austria was in the opposite camp. Many of Denmark's ambassadors urged the government to take advantage of a favorable situation for the implementation of Carl Christian Hall's plan, known as "Dano-Eiderism."

In this context the Danish government's issue of a decree on March 30 establishing a new status for Holstein is understandable. This status was unfavorably received, not only by the population of the principalities, the conservatives in Copenhagen, and the German states, but also by Russia, which regarded it as an infringement of the 1852 Treaty of London. Both Britain and France considered the Danish government's move dangerous and urged caution. Edouard Drouyn de Lhuys regretted that the March 30 decree might unite Austria and Prussia, which had been split since the Polish Insurrection broke out, and advised Denmark to support Austria in German matters and make concessions to Vienna. Denmark's position was also contrary to Russell's suggestions. The French minister wrote the Danish ambassador in Paris on April 27 as follows: "Il faut avant tout que Vous Vous appliquiez à séparer dans cette question [the principalities] l'Autriche et la Prussie. Il faut que Vous tachiez de faire à l'Autriche certaines concessions. . . . Je dois en contester l'opportunité dans le moment actuel—vous ralliez vos ennemis tout en disséminant vos alliés."[5]

From then on, the disputes over Schleswig were always linked with Polish affairs. This is one of the sources of Danish sympathy with the January Insurrection. Denmark counted on directing Prussia's concern eastward and reducing its interest in the principalities. The political situation of Denmark was assessed by the moving spirit of the ministry of foreign affairs, Peter Vedel, in the following terms:

> Shortly after the start of the uprising two camps were formed in Europe, the Western states and Austria in one and Russia and Prussia in the other. For Prussia this alliance was very dangerous because of the prevailing view that France sought to achieve two of her traditional policy aims simultaneously—the reconstruction of Poland and the seizure of the Rhineland. Reports spread that Bismarck had doubly angered the emperor [Napoleon III] since by allying himself with Russia he had broken

the promise given to the emperor when the Rhine was "bought" in exchange for permission to rule northern Germany and perhaps for assurance against Austria. For Austria, on the other hand, a particularly favorable situation was created. Outwardly it looked very liberal, and there were also prospects of good will on the part of France and Britain. This gave her advantages in such matters as Italy and Germany and was a better starting point in our [Danish] question. But this too was a source of great danger for Denmark. We had to maneuver so that everything developed with no special conflict as long as relations between Austria and France did not deteriorate, and in our judgment that would happen in time, since Austria had no real intention of going to war against Russia. But at the same time we had to associate ourselves to some extent with the anti-Russian action in order to be in good standing with France and not to lose contact with Sweden. These were the two main elements in our policy, which was the product of the current situation.[6]

Here is the most authoritative explanation why the traditionally pro-Russian Denmark, which still expected Russian help if its conflict with the German states should intensify, finally decided, after two months had passed, to send notes to St. Petersburg. Denmark had rejected Russell's first proposal on the grounds that it had not been a signatory of the Treaty of Vienna of 1815. Only under renewed pressure from Britain and France, after many weeks of vacillation, did it change its position. Up to the last moment Hall hesitated and delayed. Who knows whether he did not finally succumb to the pressure from the Western states only when he learned that Sweden's April note had not been badly received by Gorchakov. To the Russian ambassador Hall apologized profusely that Denmark could not decline the invitation of the two Western powers, who were ready to assist it in its internal affairs.

The Danish government was afraid of the tsar's reaction. To avoid possible undesirable consequences, Vedel explained to Nicolaus Nikolay that the Polish question was foreign to Denmark and was of no interest to it. He did not conceal from Nikolay that it was essential for Denmark to maintain good relations with France, at that moment on good terms with Austria, which could be useful to Danish interests. Besides, added Vedel, if the Danish government were to decide to send a telegram through the intermediary of Otto Plessen, this would show what Denmark's real interest was and convey to the tsar its wish that he should enjoy complete success. Such a wish could not evoke displeasure on the part of the Russian government. In his report Nikolay adds: "He [Vedel] always controls the ministry, so I have cause to think that the government's decision will be in accordance with the ideas Vedel expounded."[7] In essence the government was guided by the principle of keeping the wolf fed and the sheep safe.

Formally, the Danish note of May 8 was reminiscent of the French and Swedish ones. It stressed factors such as humanitarianism, the solidarity binding the nations and governments of Europe, the disquiet of thinking people in all European countries, and the concern of second-rank states over the regrettable events in Poland. But in the second part of the note the Danish government emphasized that it wished Poland would lay down its arms before the magnanimous Alexander II and return to the path of peace. There were no such phrases in either the French or Swedish, let alone the British, notes. Furthermore, to remove any doubts and not to arouse any suspicion on the part of Gorchakov, Hall recommended that Plessen, who was on holiday in Baden, interrupt his holiday and travel to St. Petersburg to hand the note personally to Gorchakov. No one enjoyed a better reputation in St. Petersburg than the Danish ambassador, who had been there almost twenty years and was well known for his conservative and very pro-Russian views.

There was no particular irritation in St. Petersburg on account of the Danish note. Gorchakov received it reluctantly but without angry comment, and the answer he quickly addressed to the Danish government was couched in a supercilious tone. We read in the Russian reply: "Nous apprécions l'intérêt que le Cabinet de Copenhague témoigne pour la prosperité de l'Empire russe, et surtout le voeu, exprimé au nom de Sa Majesté le roi, de voir la Pologne déposer les armes devant la générosite de notre Auguste Maître et rentrer dans la voie d'un développement tranquille et fécond. Tel est aussi le plus cher désir de l'Empereur."[8]

In its content the Danish note was one of those of which the official publishing house of the Russian Ministry of Foreign Affairs was to write, many years later, that although the notes from some states were rather expressive of confidence in the Russian government, generally they looked like a diplomatic campaign against Russia.[9]

Russia attached no importance to the note, but nevertheless, because of the growing chauvinism in Russia, the very fact that it had been sent had an adverse effect on relations with Denmark. Articles appeared in the semiofficial *Journal de Saint Pétersbourg* in the summer which Danish diplomats regarded as ill-disposed toward Denmark and as taking a tendentious view of the dispute in the principalities. Even before this, Gorchakov had complained to Denmark that there were Danish sailors aboard the *Ward Jackson,* rather than Swedish, as Nikolay had initially reported. He did not add that the Russian ambassador in Copenhagen had been informed of the appearance of the ship in the Danish straits and of its movements by the navy minister, Steen Andersen Bille, who had done so *sua sponte*. The Russo-Danish estrangement in fact had to do not with these minor incidents connected with the Polish insurrection, but mainly with what was happening on the Copenhagen-Stockholm axis in the summer of 1863. The contacts between the monarchs of the two countries and, especially, between Hall and Manderström and the advanced stage reached in the talks on a military treaty between Sweden and Denmark greatly disturbed the St. Petersburg government. Any sign of Scandinavianism caused an immediate reaction on the part of Gorchakov.

The French and British governments treated the Danish note with understanding, in view of Denmark's difficult situation,[10] but there were critical voices in the West. In the *Revue des Deux Mondes* Klaczko ridiculed the Danish note and the phrases in which the Danish government wished Russia success in its fight against the insurrection and remarked that Denmark was the country which above all could complain about the abandonment of the Polish cause.

The sending of the Danish note coincided with an increase in pro-Polish agitation in Denmark that culminated in the second half of May. The demonstrations in favor of Poland organized by Danish Scandinavianists and liberals and the collection of money did not escape Gorchakov's notice, particularly as the list of contributors included the Countess Louise Danner, the morganatic wife of Frederick VII, and Augusta Hall, the wife of the head of the government.[10]

Denmark's policy toward the insurrection and the note of May 8 gave rise to a vehement debate, especially in the pages of the press. The national and liberal press passionately attacked the government, considering the note an unworthy and lamentable act. Instead of expressing sympathy for Poland in its struggle, commented *Danmark* on May 27, the government had expressed sympathy with the sufferings of Russia and called on the insurgents to capitulate, thus associating itself with the ignominious speech by Anthon Frederic Tscherning in the *Rigsraadet*. *Faedrelandet* protested that instead of wishing the tsar success in reasserting his rule over the whole of his territory, that is to say, the Kingdom of Poland, the government should have stressed the keen interest of small nations in the question of the observance of treaties, expressed the great sympathy felt by Denmark for the Polish nation, and wished it independence.

Just how distrustful the attitude of the liberal press toward the government's moves was is illustrated by the fact that both *Faedrelandet* and *Danmark* informed their readers that rumors were proliferating that, in addition to a note to St. Petersburg which simply associated Denmark with the French note, the government had sent a second note in which it expressed its regret that despite its regard for Russia it had been compelled to take part in the powers' diplomatic campaign. The papers added that they did not know whether or not this was true but that at any rate the rumors were consonant with the system.

In its "Weekly Review" on June 2, 1863, *Danmark* hit out in the following manner:

> We have more than once distinctly informed our readers that the Danish Nation generally feels the greatest sympathy for the desperate struggle of Poland for life and liberty. But it must be acknowledged that the above Dispatch of the government expresses sympathy for the sufferings of Russia, not for those of Poland. Foreign countries will therefore easily conceive the surprise and indignation which this document has excited in Denmark. But it has also called forth great apprehension. We are in a double position. Not only must our noble feeling for a noble land find vent at all hazards, but also we must establish beforehand the place we intend to occupy in case a general should fling the European states into two opposite camps. Should anything of this kind occur, the interest of Denmark, its instinct of self-preservation, quite as much as the far higher motives which animate a race so famous and so proud as our own, leads us to join the two other Scandinavian kingdoms in the ranks of those powers which will assist in establishing a free and independent Poland. It would be the greatest possible misfortune for this country if the policy of our ministry, in union with outward circumstances, were, at the decisive moment, to entangle us with powers and operations unfriendly to the chivalrous nations of Scandinavia and the West. We will hope that our cabinet's Dispatch of the 8th of May may not lead to results so disastrous. But it cannot be denied that there is great danger that this will take place. At all events, in the presence of our foreign readers, we must firmly and decisively and solemnly protest against this Dispatch's being considered as expressing the sentiments of the Danish people.

In its "Weekly Review" on June 23, 1863, *Danmark* described the political situation as follows:

> The most remarkable step in this direction for us Northmen—for all the Anglo-Scandinavian races—is the mighty movement toward a Scandinavian Union. This, and only this, can save the separate Scandinavian states from impending partition and absorption by Germany, on the one hand, and Moscovy, on the other. This alone can ensure to England an efficient bulwark, a natural ally, a future free from peril. Poland is now struggling for similar consolidation and independence, and with her success is bound up the "to be or not to be" of our whole Western freedom and civilization. Poland once masticated and assimilated by Russia, by fair means or foul,

Europe becomes inevitably Cossack. But Russia herself is determined to obtain a really national existence, to shake off her traditional slavery under an Imperial German bureaucracy, and give to her people rights and glory instead of a continuous course of bloody conquest and barbarous legislation.

The conservative press and the semiofficial *Berlingske Tidende,* on the other hand, praised the government's conduct, defended the content of the note, and argued that, despite what the liberal press said, the note was no different in content from that sent to St. Petersburg by the Swedish government. Besides, said *Berlingske Tidende,* a note from a small state could in any case have no influence on Russian policy.

It seems to me that the Danish note, the strength of which corresponded to the level of economic aid from the Danish population, cannot be viewed in isolation from historical conditions and cannot be regarded as evidence of sympathy for Poland on the part of the government, but was a move forced on it in a larger game in which its aim was to retain Schleswig.

It is also true that nowhere in Europe was the desire to support the Polish liberation struggle so strong that states, particularly such small ones as Denmark, were willing to put their existence at risk. Of course the Danish diplomatic move could not influence the behavior of Russia, but the question arises whether action of this kind, which became in a peculiar way a kind of approval of the policy and conduct of Russia, was necessary at all. Such action could not help Poland. Ultimately it did nothing for Denmark either. In the difficult situation in which Russia found itself, Gorchakov had no intention of putting pressure on Prussia in connection with the Schleswig question, "une question, dans laquelle les trois cabinets ont le même intérêt."

Danish Scandinavians saw a close connection between the Polish and Scandinavian questions. Poland was fighting against Russia and Prussia, which were enemies of Scandinavia and backed the anti-Danish forces in Schleswig-Holstein. They perceived the link between Gorchakov's attitude toward Denmark and the German countries and his attitude toward the insurrection. The Poles, wrote *Faedrelandet,* were the friends of Denmark, and what had happened to Poland in the eighteenth century (the partitions) was now threatening Denmark. The history of Poland and the Prussian sector provided many examples of what could be expected from the Prussians. Russia had changed its traditional policy toward Denmark on account of the situation in Poland. The rise of an independent Poland on Prussia's eastern frontier could be a real help to Denmark; it would improve Denmark's chances in its struggle for Schleswig.

Apart from propaganda for the Polish cause, however, action by national-liberal circles was confined to appeals to society to provide material help for the insurrection. In contrast to Sweden, any other help, such as political campaigns or public resolutions, was regarded as inadvisable and contrary to Danish custom.

Logical defense of the national rights of the Poles was obstructed mainly by the question of the German principalities. The cause of Polish liberation could be defended consistently provided that the German question in Schleswig was finally settled in accordance with the nationality principle. The national-liberal party lacked this consistency. Some politicians in the party saw this, but they drew only the conclusion that the claims of the German population were groundless, so as to justify their policy aim of linking Denmark and Schleswig closely and establishing a permanent state frontier on the Eider. Denmark's conduct toward the Germans, they asserted, could not be compared to the national oppression of the Poles in the Duchy of Poznań. Politicians far removed from national-liberal circles recognized this inconsistency. This can be shown by the speech of their political opponent, Tscherning, in the *Rigsraadet*, arguing that they could not support one group of rebels (the Poles) while they opposed another (the German population in the principalities).

The conservative parties, at heart pro-Russian, opposed the powers' diplomatic intervention, approached the Polish question almost exclusively from the humanitarian aspect, regarded the insurrection as the work of revolutionary European propaganda, and tried to convert the Polish-Russian conflict into a Polish-German conflict, arguing that it was inspired by Germany and that the tsarist dynasty was a German dynasty. They took a pessimistic view of the future of Poland (e.g., *Kronen*).

Faced with the increasingly tense situation and the threat of seizure of the territory of Holstein by the German Confederation, the Danish government picked its way between the Western states and Russia. Hall, who was personally nearer to the Western line, did not want to commit himself to it, and his closest colleagues were convinced that Russia would soon deal with the insurrection and everything would settle down as before. If this were to happen, Vedel argued, it would be very silly for Denmark to behave precipitately.

From the summer months of 1863 onward, Danish diplomats showed no great interest in the Polish question. Others, like Plessen, who was known for his conservative and pro-Russian views, reported from St. Petersburg on the course of events in the Kingdom of Poland almost in the spirit of the official Russian propaganda and warned against underestimation of Russian power and of the consequences should Russia adopt a more pro-German policy.

Hall's government was chiefly absorbed in the conflict with Germany and, it seems to me, failed to draw the appropriate conclusions from the changes in the Russian attitudes toward Prussia and Denmark. Hall accepted in good faith Gorchakov's declaration that Russia stood by the provisions of the Treaty of London, and he continued to count on Russian diplomatic assistance despite the growing evidence of Russia's hostile attitude toward Danish policy. Danish policy on relations with the Western states was inconsistent too; the mistake committed during the Crimean War was repeated. The whole of Hall's policy in 1863 was affected by intolerance of the German national movement in the principalities, a schematic and legalistic view of the conflict in the principalities, and, finally, misinterpretation of Russian intentions in relation to the Danish-German conflict. It is true that out of regard for state and dynastic interests Russia was in favor of maintenance of the integrity of Denmark and the status quo, but only as long as Denmark's main opponents were the national-liberal forces in Germany. The Polish insurrection and the new constellation of forces in Europe brought about a change in Russia's position. This does not mean that it fully supported Bismarck's policy, but it did not intend to oppose him, since he was the leader of the conservative forces in Germany. Denmark continually faced pressure for new concessions which were tantamount to capitulation to the demands of the German states.

When discussing the Polish question and the policy of the Scandinavian countries we cannot ignore the attitude of the Polish national-liberation movement toward the question of cooperation with the Scandinavian countries. From 1862 on, Polish émigré politicians paid particular attention to Sweden. This was illustrated by Colonel Władysław Jordan's mission to Stockholm. Its purpose was to take advantage of the anniversary of the battle of Poltava in order to arouse public opinion against Russia and its policy. In this it was successful. During the insurrection itself, Sweden played an important part in the Polish National Government's diplomatic activity, and the aim of both the [Konstanty] Czartoryski-[Walerian] Kalinka mission and that of Józef Demontowicz, the commissioner of the National Government, was to persuade the king, the government, and the society to help Poland and to take joint action with France against Russia. In the insurgents' plans Sweden was also to be the military base for the Polish insurgent detachments. The National Government did not attach great importance to Copenhagen, and there was no representative of the Polish government there. Not until the period of Romuald Traugutt's dictatorship did attention turn to Denmark as a result of the outbreak of war between Denmark and the German states. The Danish question occupies more and more space in the correspondence of Władysław Czartoryski, and Traugutt expected, especially after Austria's declaration of a state of war in Galicia in February 1864, that the insurrection would become an anti-German one too.

The January Insurrection, which in my opinion has not hitherto received the attention it is due, played a far from trivial role in the history of the Scandinavian countries. As far as its direct importance is concerned, the principal facts to be mentioned are its influence in activating the supporters of Scandinavianism in all three Scandinavian countries, the growth of anti-Russian feeling, especially in Sweden, and the popularization of both Poland's national-liberation struggle and its history and culture throughout the Scandinavian lands.

The political changes which occurred in Europe as a result of the Polish insurrection had a more fundamental influence on the history of the Scandinavian countries, particularly Denmark. The Russo-French understanding dating from the Treaty of Paris in 1856 lay in ruins. The Alvensleben Convention led to a momentary renewal of the coalition of the Crimean War period. The failures of French diplomacy were caused by changes in the constellation of forces: the break in the Anglo-French alliance and, after the November defeat of Napoleon III, Austria's abandonment of France and siding with Prussia and then Russia as well. The specter of a new Holy Alliance reappeared. France was now isolated on the continent of Europe, and the links between the three northern powers were strengthened. As a result of this, and of the collapse of the insurrection, Russia reestablished its international prestige, but to a great extent this was possible thanks to Prussia's attitude in 1863. Sweden, on the other hand, faced with the new constellation in Europe, abandoned the plan for close cooperation with France and military alliance with Denmark and also gave up its attempts to put the idea of political Scandinavianism into effect.

Denmark had to fight alone against the coalition of Prussia and Austria. Just as Britain was unwilling to cooperate actively with France to defend Poland in 1863, so France behaved similarly toward Britain during the Danish-German war in 1864. Russia, grateful for Prussian policy during the Polish insurrection, made no move to restrain Bismarck's aggressive plans. Alexander II told Plessen that Russia was not able to intervene in favor of Denmark because of the Polish Insurrection.[12] The adverse political situation in Europe, which was the consequence of the collapse of the insurrection, was a major cause of Denmark's defeat. Klaczko quotes Sir Andrew Buchanan's letter to Russell of November 28, 1863, as follows: "Les évènements qui passent en Pologne, malgré la réprobation des trois grandes puissances, ont aménè les Allemands à croire que personne ne s'opposerait par les armes à une oeuvre de spoliation contre le Danemark. . . . ." Klaczko adds his own comment on this quotation: "Si, au lieu d'être divisées et méfiantes l'une envers l'autre, les deux puissances libérales de l'Occident avaient été unies en ces années 1863-64, que de bien on eût pu faire, que de mal on eût empêché sur les bords de la Vistule, de l'Eider, et peut-être même des Potomac!"[13]

The collapse of the Polish insurrection had a serious adverse effect on the history of the Scandinavian countries. Despite all criticism of their policy toward that insurrection, however, the responsibility for these reverses does not lie with them.

Notes

1. Stanislaw Bóbr-Tylingo, "Napoléon III, l'Europe et la Pologne 1863-4," in *Antemurale 1863-1963* (Rome, 1963); idem, "Do tajnej dyplomacji Napoleona III (1863)," *Teki Historyczne* 11 (1960-61).

2. The literature on the January Insurrection as seen from the Scandinavian countries includes the following: M. J. Crusenstolpe, *Ett sekel och ett år af polska frågan (1762-1863)* (Stockholm, 1863); Tadeusz Cieślak, *Polska-Skandynawia w XIX i XX wieku* (Warsaw, 1973); Władysław Czartoryski, *Pamiętniki 1860-1864* (Warsaw, 1960); K. G. Fellenius, *Polska frågan i Sverige år 1863: Anteckningar ur polsk-svenska papper* (Stockholm, 1936); Carl Hallendorff, *Ilusioner och verklighet: Studier öfver den skandinaviska krisen 1864* (Stockholm, 1914); Einar Hedin, "Sveriges ställning i förhållande till Ryssland och västmagterna år 1863," *Historisk Tidskrift* 1922; Leokadia Kowalska-Posten, *Norwegowie a sprawa polska w roku 1863*, Komunikaty Instytutu Baltyckiego Gdańsk, no. 30 (1979); J. Klaczko, *Etudes de diplomatie européenne* (Paris, 1866); H. W. Münnich, *Polska frihetskampen 1863* (Stockholm, 1863); Erik Møller, *Helstatens fald*, vol. 1 (Copenhagen, 1958); N. Neergaard, *Under Junigrundloven*, vol. 2, no. 1 (Copenhagen-Kristiania, 1916); *Norge og den polske frihetskamp: Utgitt med innledning av R. Hammering Bang* (Oslo, 1937); Albert Olsen, "Danmark og den polske opstand 1863," in *Festskrift til Erik Arup den 22.11.1946* (Copenhagen, 1946); *Polonica: Kulturbilder från det äldre og nyare Polen* (Stockholm, 1937); Leokadia Posten, *De polska emigranternes agentverksamhet i Sverige 1862-1863* (Lund, 1975); and Stanislas Wędkiewicz, *La Suède et la Pologne: Essai d'une bibliographie des publications suédoises concernant la Pologne* (Stockholm, 1918).

3. Cf. E. Halicz, *Danish Neutrality during the Crimean War (1853-1856): Denmark between the Hammer and the Anvil* (Odense, 1977).

4. Skrivelser fran Stockholm till Petersburg, 1863, Riksarkivet, Stockholm.

5. Frankrig, Depecher 1861-64, Rigsarkiv, Copenhagen.

6. "Peter Vedels beretning om Danmarks udenrigspolitik fra sommeren 1862 til foraaret 1863," *Jyske Samlinger*, 1952–54, pp. 149–50.
7. V. Sjøquist, *Peter Vedel*, vol. 1 (Aarhus, 1957), p. 176.
8. Gorchakov's dispatch, May 5/17, 1863.
9. *Ocherk istorii Ministerstva Inostrannykh Del, 1802–1902* (St. Petersburg, 1902).
10. In order to neutralize possible displeasure on account of the tone of the note in Paris, Hall recalled in his telegram that it was the French government that had recommended that Denmark seek support from Russia in case the German states opposed the provisions of the Treaty of London.
11. Plessen to Vedel, May 14/26, 1863; Vedel to Quaade, May 14, 1863, 6498 Vedel, P.A.F.S. pk.12,5, Rigsarkiv, Copenhagen.
12. Plessen to Hall, November 28/December 10, 1863, Depecher Rusland 1863, Rigsarkiv, Copenhagen.
13. Klaczko, *Études de diplomatie contemporaine*, p. 448.

The Polish Insurrection of 1863 and the Czechs

Joseph F. Zacek

The Czech reaction to the Polish Insurrection of 1863 must be viewed within the broader context of Czech-Russian and Czech-Polish relations.[1] Until about the time of the French Revolution and Napoleon, Czechs and Russians had had very little contact with one another, a condition certainly conducive to misconceptions on both sides. When Russian troops arrived for the first time on Czech soil during the Revolutionary-Napoleonic period, they inspired widespread Russophilism among the Czech masses, who could communicate with them and—so contemporary correspondence, diaries, and memoirs tell us— found the "Great Slav Brother" stalwart, warmhearted, and friendly.[2] The Czech population was, in general, proud of the Russian victory over Napoleon (despite its genuine admiration for the latter, too), which it regarded as bringing great prestige to all of the Slavonic nations. This growing Czech Russophilism was apparently little affected by the signs of an increasingly harsh and repressive government in Russia and even by the Russian intervention against the Hungarian Revolution of 1848–49. (Official Czech policy during the Revolution was, after all, to maintain the integrity of the Habsburg Monarchy and to federalize it on the basis of the equality of all national groups within it, and Hungarian independence would, of course, have nullified that integrity.) In popular Czech thinking, Russia remained a "friend in reserve" throughout the nineteenth century and well into the First World War. Czech leaders were somewhat cooler and more critical, coupling warm affection for the Russian people with disapproval and fear of the autocratic, imperialistic Russian regime. In 1848, for example, František Palacký warned that neither a German nor a Russian "universal monarchy" was acceptable to the Czechs. After a disillusioning year in Russia (1843–44), the revolutionary journalist Karel Havlíček rejected the notion that either Russian culture or the government of "that despotic land" could serve as a model for the Czechs. But, despite their reservations, both men shared the feeling of the masses that Russia (within the broader nexus of "Slavonic solidarity"—*Slovanská vzájemnost*) provided the surest ultimate support for the Czechs against the perennial German threat, within as well as outside the Habsburg Monarchy. Palacký looked to a liberalized Russia to lead the Slavs to a happier future; Havlíček even declared that, forced to choose between German or Russian hegemony, he would take the latter.

The Czech-Polish relationship at the beginning of the nineteenth century was not as warm, despite the belief of many Czechs that the Poles were their "closest kin" among the Slavs (*národ nám kmenově nejbližší*), the long tradition of coexistence of their sovereign states, and occasional strong Polish influence on Czech historical developments, for example, on the origins of the Czech national revival at the end of the eighteenth century. Almost a thousand years of history had created significant differences, especially religious and social differences, and potential frictions between the two peoples. The Poles were proud, dedicated Catholics; the Czechs had had a deep experience with Protestantism (Hussitism) before they were forcibly returned to the Catholic fold. Although both were largely peasant peoples, the Czechs had lost their native nobility after the Thirty Years' War and were building a new, liberal, middle-class leadership from their own ranks. The Poles had been dominated by their selfish native aristocracy to the very end of their statehood and beyond. Czechs and Poles had sharply different attitudes toward Russia and different conceptions of "Slavonic solidarity." In the nineteenth century, these differences first bore fruit in the mixed Czech reaction to the Polish Insurrection of 1830–31. The competing considerations that plagued the Czechs then—loyalty to an unfragmented Slavdom led by its natural leader, Russia; sympathy for beleaguered fellow Slavs; and long-standing commitment to democratic and progressive principles—would continue to complicate their responses to Polish events throughout the century.

The popular leaders of the time, people of cultural rather than political eminence, split into three age-groups, each with its own attitude toward the Polish rebellion. "Czech Awakeners," led by Josef Jungmann, idealized Russia, gave loyalty to it their "highest priority," and condemned the Poles. Their pupils, the middle generation, were mixed in their feelings, though as a group they were more alive to contemporary continental currents of liberalism and nationalism. Jan Kollár, Pavel Josef Šafařík, and František Ladislav Čelakovský sided with the Poles. Palacký was ambivalent; though not unfriendly to the Poles (Kościuszko was one of his heroes), he disliked "revolutionary anarchy" as much as "universal despotism." The youngest generation (e.g., Karel Hynek Mácha, Karel Sabina, Josef Jaroslav Langer) was ardently Polonophile and deeply involved with the Polish events.

Some individuals actually volunteered to fight alongside the Poles. The Byronic Mácha collected supplies for the Polish belligerents and, like František A. Brauner, provided escape routes and safe-houses for Poles fleeing their homeland after the defeat of the insurrection.

Joint involvement in the Revolution of 1848 did not help to alleviate Czech-Polish differences. Their leaders agreed on the need to liberalize political and national conditions within the Habsburg Monarchy and cooperated at the Slavonic Congress in Prague, but they differed in their views on the acceptability (or desirability) of revolution in general and the Hungarian Revolution in particular and on the necessity of maintaining the existence of Austria.

The Polish Insurrection of 1863 found Czech society markedly different from what it had been in 1830. As a result of the Revolution of 1848 and its aftermath, the Czechs now had their own cadre of popular political leaders, a variety of political groups with different political orientations, and, in general, greater political experience and sophistication than they had had three decades earlier. It is generally assumed that Czech public opinion was overwhelmingly pro-Polish in 1863.[3] The clearest and best-informed reaction still came, predictably, from the political and intellectual leadership, but there is also record of a significant response among the masses (artisans, peasants, commercial people) in Prague and in the countryside, stirred up by the Young Czechs and especially by the Radical Democrats. Generally unaware of the nuances of difference among the Polish insurgents (between the "Whites" and "Reds," in general, and between the right and left wings of the "Reds," in particular), the Czech "lower classes" offered whatever occasional help they could, such as helping captured Poles escape from internment camps in Bohemia (Hradec Králové) and Moravia (Jihlava, Olomouc, Telč).

As in 1830, Czech spokesmen fell into three categories. On the right, the Old Czechs, a conservative-liberal coalition of bourgeois leaders of 1848 and some sympathetic Bohemian aristocrats led by Palacký and F. L. Rieger, were unequivocally pro-Russian. In their newspaper, *Národ,* they condemned the insurrection on the grounds that it provoked "fratricide" among the Slavic nations and threatened to weaken Russia, the acknowledged Slavic leader. Palacký even stated that a Polish victory would be "the greatest misfortune" for the Czechs (and for the Poles, too). Those who supported the Poles were, he felt, "revolutionaries by instinct," who feared growing Russian power and wanted to check it with a revival of Poland. Palacký contrasted the undemocratic views of the Polish "Whites" with those of Tsar Alexander II, who had given "twenty million souls" their freedom. Rieger rejected revolutionary claims for Polish "historical frontiers" in the Ukraine, Belorussia, and Lithuania, seeing them as a cloak for the desire of Polish feudal aristocrats to exploit the peasants of these areas. A small fringe of the Old Czechs led by F. J. Jezbera even defended the tsarist deportations of Polish rebels.

In the center were the Young Czechs, younger, of more liberal sympathies, and more "action-oriented."[4] They had split with the Old Czechs as early as 1861, and the Polish events of 1863–64 considerably widened the breach. Led by the brothers Julius and Edvard Grégr, Karel Sladkovský, and Prince Rudolf Thurn-Taxis, they expressed open sympathy for the insurrection and its aims (especially as given by the right wing of the Polish "Reds") and defended them in their newspapers *Boleslavan, Národní listy,* and *Pravda.* Some, like Emanuel Tonner and Josef Barák, made direct contact with the insurgents and cooperated actively with the passionately Polonophile, revolutionary left-wing group called the Radical Democrats.

The Radical Democrats, formed in the 1850s, were formally dedicated to bringing democracy and freedom to all captive nations.[5] They were centered in Prague and had strong contingents in Mladá Boleslav and Roudnice. Nominally under the leadership of Václav Frič, they were largely directed at long range (from Paris, Geneva, and other places) by his older brother Josef, who had emigrated in 1859.[6] Josef Frič, a revolutionary by profession with Europewide contacts and passionate antitsarist and anti-Habsburg feelings, was determined to integrate the Polish insurrection with a simultaneous one in the Habsburg Monarchy. An associate of Mierosławski (and later of Traugutt), Frič had advance knowledge of the imminent Polish outbreak and alerted his colleagues in Prague to it (as did various agents sent there from Poland, such as Jakub Sztejnik).

Of all Czech political groups, the Radical Democrats were the most active in supporting the Poles. They collected money, purchased arms and medical supplies, assisted couriers, refugees, and internees, and even tried to organize a legion of Czech volunteers (mostly students and apprentices), a thousand strong, to join the Poles on the battlefield. Josef Barák and others made several trips to Cracow to make the arrangements. When he was captured, the Prague police were able to uncover the network of such Radical Democratic pro-Polish enterprises and terminate many of them.

But the Radical Democrats continued with their conspiracy to correlate an uprising in the Czech lands with the events in Poland. Josef and Václav Frič met in Paris in May 1863 and with Thurn-Taxis in Heidelberg in December 1863 to set up a special group for the purpose called Dědici (The Heirs). In January 1864, representatives of the Young Czechs and Radical Democrats met in Prague, at the home of Thurn-Taxis, to discuss the formation of a new political party. The Freethinking Party, to be headed by Thurn-Taxis, was to have rather stolid bourgeois aims (e.g., the elimination of the privileges of the estates, the broadening of the franchise), but the Young Czech leadership split over the proposal. Even the Grégr brothers could not agree, Edvard being for it and Julius against. When the majority sided against it, the plan failed. Thurn-Taxis, pleading heavy financial losses, subsequently abandoned political life, confessing his previous political activities to the regime and requesting a pardon.

Josef Frič now attempted to combine the Polish insurrection and the Czech "revolutionary movement" with a Europewide upheaval to be centered at Turin, Zagreb, and Prague. In March 1864, with Tonner and others, he went to Dresden to confer with Polish representatives. There he detailed his plan to have the Czechs collaborate with Poles, Croats, Hungarians, and others to destroy the Habsburg Monarchy. He claimed, among other things, that the Czech revolutionary movement already numbered five hundred members, that a revolutionary government was in readiness in Prague, and that Czech troops were expected to desert from the imperial army and rally to the revolution. Frič's wild fabrications and fantasies were not put to the test. A month later, Traugutt was captured and the Polish Insurrection came to an end. By the time Traugutt was executed in August 1864, Frič was already busily negotiating with Garibaldi to hook up the Czech cause with that of the Italians.

Czech involvement with the Polish Insurrection of 1863 did little for the Poles. For the Czechs, it accelerated the pluralistic development of their domestic political life. It remained the high-water mark of Czech-Polish empathy and cooperation for the remainder of the century and even longer. Thereafter, relations between the two peoples worsened. The Poles resented the ostentatious pilgrimage of Czech leaders to Moscow in 1867, following the *Ausgleich,* and the growing Russophilism of the Czech people. For their part, the Czechs denounced the cooperation of Galician Polish leaders with Vienna and the piecemeal concessions they gained by it, at the cost of fracturing the "united Slavic opposition" within the Monarchy. Russian support and all-Slavic cooperation seemed to them to offer the only feasible solution to the Czech predicament within the Dual Monarchy. Not even T. G. Masaryk's unequivocal rejection of light and help from the East was capable of altering this popular conviction. On the eve of the First World War, many Czechs shared Karel Kramář's vision of a restored Bohemian kingdom under a Russian prince and waited patiently for the Cossacks to liberate them.

Notes

1. On Czech-Russian relations, see my "Czechs and Russians, 1848–1948," a paper prepared for presentation at the Rocky Mountain Association for Slavic Studies in Denver, Colo., in April 1982 and forthcoming in print. On Czech-Polish relations, see Josef Macůrek and Václav Žáček, eds., *Češi a Poláci v minulosti*, 2 vols. (Prague, 1964–67).
2. See Joseph F. Zacek, "The French Revolution, Napoleon, and the Czechs," in *Proceedings of the Consortium on Revolutionary Europe, 1980*, 2 vols. (Athens, Ga., 1980), 1: 254–63.
3. On the Czech response to the Polish Insurrection of 1863, see Václav Žáček, *Ohlas polského povstání r. 1863 v Čechách* (Prague, 1935); his "Češi a Poláci v době lednového povstání polského r. 1863," *Československý časopis historický* 11 (1963); and his contribution to Macůrek and Žáček, eds., *Češi a Poláci v minulosti*, 2:246–64.
4. The origin and development of the Young Czechs is treated comprehensively in Bruce M. Garver, *The Young Czech Party, 1874–1901, and the Emergence of a Multi-Party System* (New Haven, Conn., and London, 1978).
5. On the Radical Democrats, see Karel Kosík, *Česká radikální demokracie* (Prague, 1958).
6. On the stormy petrel Josef Václav Frič (1829–90), see Václav Žáček and Karel Kosík, eds., *J. V. Frič a demokratické proudy v české politice a kultuře* (Prague, 1956); and Václav Žáček, *Josef Václav Frič* (Prague, 1979).

The January Insurrection in Poland, 1863–1864, in the Light of British Consular Reports

Norman Davies

Although the reports of the British consuls in Warsaw have been known to historians for many years, they have only been used as a supplement to the general diplomatic correspondence. The published volume of consular documents is highly selective, and covers only the first four months of 1863.[1] The full value of the consular files as a rich and convenient source of Polish social, political, and economic history—with most of Polish and Russian documents translated into exquisite Victorian English—has not been realized. H. M. Consul in Warsaw during the January Insurrection, Colonel Edward Stanton, R.E., a veteran of the Crimea, was a professional military observer.[2] The Acting Consul and late Vice-Consul William Arthur White, who was destined to become one of the mandarins of the British diplomatic service, was a native of Poland and knew East European affairs from the inside.[3]

In the conflict between Russia and Poland, these mid-Victorian British officials provided as impartial a viewpoint as one might hope to find. In the period immediately after the Crimean War, when Great Britain and Russia had recently been at war, they shared the general revulsion of British public opinion against tsardom and most things Russian. At the same time, they shared the convictions, almost universal in diplomatic circles, that Russia under Alexander II was committed to fundamental reform and that any Polish rising against Russia could only end in bloody disaster. They also shared the fears common to the propertied class everywhere in Europe that any revolt against established order, however justified by local conditions, was bound to open the door to some general tide of crime, anarchy, and social revolution.

1. The Outbreak of the Insurrection

Following the notorious *branka* of January 1863, in which the tsarist authorities forcibly conscripted several thousand Polish dissidents for military service, the British consul wrote to London reporting the "complete success" of the operation and the impossibility of further resistance.[4] Yet within a couple of weeks he had changed his tone. On February 4, he reported the existence of three insurrectionary bands, the largest, some eight thousand strong, at Wąchock in the Holy Cross Mountains, under Langiewicz. The underground "National Government" was already raising its own taxes and recruits and issuing decrees—including one that had declared the tsar's chief minister in Poland, Marquis Wielopolski, to be an outlaw. "I must confess, my Lord," he told Earl Russell, the foreign secretary, "I was not prepared for an insurrection on so extensive a scale . . . [which] assumes daily more the appearance of a national rising."[5] Although the British observers were to hold their view that the odds always lay on ultimate defeat for the insurrection, they were repeatedly surprised by the Poles' resourcefulness and stamina. One month later, in March, Stanton was obliged once again to express his surprise at the "remarkable" performance of the insurrectionists. "Although it is impossible to suppose that the Poles can succeed," he wrote, "it is now evident that they can dispute the possession of the country."[6] Despite their expertise, the consuls had completely failed to predict the insurrection and had seriously misjudged its scale.

2. The Balance of Forces

For strategic reasons more connected perhaps with India than with Europe, the British government in London was eager to know the size and dispositions of the Russian garrison in Poland; and Colonel Stanton was able to provide a constant flow of information, partly from his own observations and partly from Lord Napier's dispatches concerning reinforcements sent from St. Petersburg. Stanton made light of the Russian commander-in-chief's complaints about the inadequacy of his forces, arguing that the Grand Duke Constantine's figure of 60,000 available men was a deliberate underestimate. By Stanton's first calculation in February 1863, Russian army strength in the Kingdom of Poland stood nearer 90,000 men, including 20,000 in Warsaw alone, with an extra 50,000 in neighboring Lithuania.[7] A detailed breakdown of these forces first made at the beginning of March, and naming each of the constituent regiments and units, had soon to be updated. On March 21, Stanton reported that Russian forces in the Kingdom totalled some 125,000 men, made up of 95,000 infantry, 12,000 regular cavalry, 10,000 Cossacks, and 8,000 artillery men with 200 guns.[8]

Against this large professional army, the insurgents could not possibly compete in terms of numbers. There was no certain means of calculating their strength. Stanton's first guess of a total of 13,000 men in February[9] was increased in March to 20,000.[10] But in shifting circumstances there could be no pretense at accuracy. In June, the estimated total was reduced to 10,000 insurgents actually in possession of arms.[11]

The disproportionate size of the Russian garrison in relation to its amateur opponents naturally led to the expectation of a quick victory. When the victory did not materialize questions were asked concerning both the composition of the tsarist army in Poland and the nature of its military operations.

3. Composition of the Tsarist Army

Although most Polish history books present the Russian army simply as a foreign army of occupation, the fact is that many thousands of Poles served under tsarist command both as volunteers and as conscripts. Following the abolition of the tsar's separate Polish army in 1832, numerous Polish officers and professional soldiers continued in the tsarist service—in the gendarmerie as well as in the army; while Polish landowners frequently acted as officers of the reserve. There were Polish regiments of the Imperial Guard. The introduction of the Russian system of a compulsory twenty-five-year draft to the Kingdom of Poland in 1834 brought an annual influx of Polish recruits, averaging some nine or ten thousand young men. Although the draft was suspended between the death of Nicholas I in 1855 and the outbreak of the insurrection in 1863, only one in ten of Polish enlisted men actually left the service, and the class of 1855, at the height of the Crimean War, had seen the largest single conscription (17,865 men) of young Poles from the Kingdom. According to detailed calculations made by Vice-Consul White, the "former Polish dominions of the Russian Empire" had supplied the tsarist army with over 600,000 recruits since 1834 (over 200,000 from the Kingdom alone),[12] and the majority of these men would still have been serving in 1863–64. Unfortunately, no estimate was made of the proportion of the tsar's Polish soldiers who were actually assigned to service in Poland or of the percentage of Poles in the ranks of the Russian garrison of the Kingdom. But circumstantial evidence points to the fact that their numbers were considerable and sufficient to cause anxiety to the authorities.

The loyalty of the Polish element within the Russian army was clearly suspect. As early as January, Lord Napier reported from St. Petersburg that when reviewing the Ismailovskii Regiment the tsar himself had made allusion to defections.[13] In a personal conversation in March, Alexander told Napier of his fears that "persons of a higher class" might be tempted to join the insurrection.[14] Although the facts would only emerge later, these fears were well founded. Numerous tsarist officers of Polish descent, were due to desert. The last "dictator" of the secret National Government, Romuald Traugutt, was the retired lieutenant-colonel of a tsarist artillery regiment and had served in the Crimea.[15]

Naturally enough, the leaders of the insurrection made every effort to suborn Polish soldiers. However, an insurgent decree of April 10 which had ordered all Poles in the army to defect immediately does not appear to have produced the desired result. A further decree, translated by White in June, threatened dire retribution against all who failed to comply:

> Since many Poles continue in the Muscovite ranks, and not only look with indifference on the national struggle, but even take an active part against it . . . all Poles remaining in the military service of Russia after 1 August next, within the boundaries of Poland as it existed in 1772, will be proclaimed outlaws, and as such will be deprived of all honours, and political and civil rights.[16]

Without means of enforcement, these decrees remained a dead letter; but they are indicative of a very genuine social and military problem.

Indeed, the complex nature of the social conflicts unleashed by the Polish insurrection cannot be fully understood without fuller analysis of the national composition of the forces of repression. J———K———'s revealing investigation into the composition of the tsarist gendarmerie in Warsaw after 1832 deserves to be emulated.[17]

4. Military Conscription

Quite apart from the numbers involved, the British diplomats showed great interest in the methods of military conscription. They all agreed that the "tyrannical" practices of Nicholas I's reign had been a major source of unrest, and they regretted that Alexander II's attempt in 1859 to introduce procedures on the French model had been abandoned. When in January 1863 the tsarist authorities reverted to their old habits, whereby the draft lists were drawn up by the police, the British officials denounced it without exception as a major provocation. Lord Napier fumed against this "barbarous recruitment by designation," "a malignant and I hope an expiring effort of the old system of despotic violence."[18] "The exercise of arbitrary military violence is out of all keeping with the humane and intelligent tendencies" of the new tsar.[19] "Is it wise," he asked, "to fill the Russian Army with revolutionary elements?"[20] In due course, he was to question the legality of the *branka,* uncertain whether the measure had really received the approval of the Council of State or not.[21] At this time, British diplomacy showed little sympathy for the Polish cause. Indeed, Lord Napier continued to believe that an independent Poland, which would be "a great Catholic military aggressive state," would be uncongenial to British interests and to the balance of power.[22] But he and his colleagues were in no doubt that the conduct of the tsarist government over military conscription was an affront to their hopes of "liberalization" and that it had accelerated the outbreak of the insurrection. They also held that trouble was simply being stored for the future. As Napier remarked, "For every patriot slain, silenced, or shut up, a hundred may perhaps be created in the new generation."[23]

Further indignation was caused by a government proposal to form a peasant militia to fight against the insurgents in the countryside. Stanton reported widespread fears that in this way, the tsarist authorities would stage another massacre of the propertied classes among the lines of the frightful Galician jacquerie of 1846.[24] Shortly afterwards, he noted that all the Polish co-opted members of the Council of State had resigned in protest.[25] The Russian authorities were clearly using their legal powers of military conscription to divide Polish society against itself.

5. The Nature of Military Operations

Slow progress in the tsarist campaign provoked inquiries into the strategy and tactics of the two sides. In the initial stages, Stanton observed that the "well armed and well supplied" Russian troops were "invariably successful when acting in any force."[26] But after the defeat of Langiewicz in open battle, he noted that the insurrectionary leaders had decided "to try the effect of partisan warfare carried on simultaneously by small bodies."[27] For this reason, he rightly considered that the government's view of the insurrection as being "nearly trampled out" was overoptimistic. Unlike several British civilians and journalists, who witnessed the fighting at first hand,[28] the diplomats in Warsaw had to rely mainly on official sources and descriptions in the local press. Even so, Stanton was able to paint some vivid pictures of the action, and at the same time to indicate the difficulties of bringing the insurgents into the open:

> A detachment under Maj-Gen Rall composed of three companies of infantry, 2 guns and 30 cossacks, and a second detachment under Col. Emanuel composed of 1½ companies of infantry and one squadron of hussars met on 14th inst. insurgent bands in the district of Pultusk [guberniya of Płock] and defeated them with heavy loss. . . . These bands being forced to retreat were met on 15th inst. close to the River Narew by Col. Valoniev with 2 companies of infantry, 2 sotnias of Cossacks, ½ squadron of lancers, as also a small detachment of rocketmen. The insurgents were defeated, and driven across the Narew. On the following day (the 16th) Col. Valoniev met the band of Trabczynski, 3000 strong posed in a forest, and after an engagement lasting about 2½ hours—in which an attempt was made by a party of scythemen to turn the flank of the Russian troops, but which was frustrated by the rockets and by a charge of the lancers, who had been held concealed,—the insurgents were totally defeated with the loss of their chief and upward of 1000 men: the Russian loss being 3 men killed and 12 wounded. Polish accounts of this action admit a loss on their side of 160 men and their chief.[29]

Apart from the usual discrepancy in casualty figures, what is significant here is that three large Russian units operating in concert could not pin down their opponents until on the third day of the engagement they stumbled on a major insurgent concentration, apparently by accident. The scythemen obviously indicated peasants fighting on the insurrectionary side. Despite their marked superiority in set combat, the Russians could not sustain their "flying columns" in the countryside indefinitely. In the later stages of the conflict, they opted for a war of attrition, concentrating their troops in the frontier zones, in the main cities, and along the lines of communication. In this way, they could deny the insurgents both assistance from abroad and bases for political activity and could afford to let them roam the countryside with impunity. In effect, the insurrection was militarily defeated long before the last insurgent group finally disbanded. Yet the struggle was less one-sided than might appear. In January 1864, Stanton quoted the official *Gazette* in Warsaw, which admitted 3,200 Russian casualties against 28,400 insurgent casualties and 6,295 prisoners of war.[30] Given the usual margin of mendacity in such matters, it was evident that the amateur insurrectionists had not submitted to Europe's largest professional army without a strenuous and sustained resistance.

6. Martial Law

Meanwhile, throughout the duration of the insurrection, the civilian population of the Kingdom was subjected to the rigors of martial law. Stanton disclosed the main provisions as published in the Warsaw *Gazette* on the orders of Baron von Korff, general-aide-de-camp and military chief of the Warsaw District:

> 1. All arms and ammunition to be handed in within three days;
> 2. All holders or distributors of seditious placards or printed matter to be punished by Court Martial as rebels;
> 3. A Curfew to be in force from 7 pm;
> 4. All persons remaining on the streets following notice of an alert to be exposed to the danger of military operations;
> 5. All houses occupied or used by the insurgents to be destroyed by artillery.[31]

The absurdly draconian nature of these rules, which permitted the authorities to shoot on sight, to sentence at will, and to bombard people's homes on suspicion, was hardly conducive to good order in the heart of a major European city. In the countryside, landowners faced sequestration if they absented themselves from their estates without permission of the military governor.[32] On the frontiers, all "military imports" which might aid the insurrection were stopped.[33] Even the symbols of sympathy for the insurrection were banned. Following the example of General Muravev in Lithuania, ladies in Warsaw were forbidden to wear black dresses, and gentlemen were ordered to replace their Polish caps with top hats—"the cylinders of civilisation," as General Berg called them.[34] In practice, martial law *à la russe* meant unrestricted terror at the whim of any sergeant or petty official.

In the course of their consular duties, Stanton and White became well acquainted with the rigors and vagaries of martial law. Already in January, they learned of the arrest of Henryk Abicht, and were hard pressed to explain how this well-known "revolutionary agent" had been issued with British passport, no. 47286, in London under the name of "John Bret."[35] They subsequently learned that Abicht had been hanged in front of the Warsaw Citadel.[36] In October, they were obliged to intervene with the gendarmerie on behalf of the British proprietors of Evans and Lilpop Ltd., Warsaw's largest foundry, who had been fined the colossal sum of 15,000 rubles (£2,300) for failing to prevent one of their workmen from secretly casting ammunition shells in their factory. Evans had been informed that under some (unpublished) "Rules of Siege," nonpayment of the fine would result not only in the closure of the foundry but also in the firm's obligation to pay the workers' wages during its closure. Stanton protested to the Diplomatic Chancery of the Kingdom, citing article 14 of the Russo-British Commercial Treaty of 1859, and by favor of Major General Trepon of the gendarmerie, the fine was quashed on appeal.[37] The arrested workman, William Algier, was shot in the factory yard as an example to his workmates.[38] Elsewhere, White had to deal with a British businessman, John Jacob Schweizer of Schweizer, Spong & Co. (varnish and color manufacturers) of Poole Street, Hoxton, who had the temerity to claim £200 compensation for items confiscated at the frontier station of Alexandrovsk (Aleksandrów).[39] It turned out that Schweizer's visiting cards were regarded as "printed matter" and therefore seditious. The import ban on military items was construed to cover "Horses, sheepskin coats, and other warm clothing" which might be used by the insurgents, although "flannel articles of superior quality, including shirts, jackets, drawers and socks" were inexplicably exempted.[40] For no good reason, British subjects captured in the company of insurgents and fully expecting summary execution or Siberian exile were released without penalty. Such was the happy lot of one H. F. Apel, of 46 Albany Street, Regent's Park, who had traveled to Poland "desirous of becoming acquainted with Polish affairs" and who had been taken prisoner with Lelewel's band, following the battle at Poręba near Terespol.[41] Alistair Macdonald of Dalelia in Moidart (Argyll), who had lingered in prison in Częstochowa, was sent home at General Berg's expense.[42] Arbitrariness, no less than brutality, was the hallmark of martial law.

7. Crime and Violence

Crime and violence invariably accompanies the breakdown of established order, and the January Insurrection was no exception. The "underground war," in which the insurrectionists were obliged to operate by stealth and deception and the Russian forces had to rely on spies, informers, and repressive police measures, was particularly conducive to mutual reprisals. The tsarist authorities complained that the insurrectionists had adopted the methods of common criminals. The insurrectionists charged that the Russians were guilty of indiscriminate violence far beyond the requirements of military operations. The British consuls noted the complaints of both sides but were particularly worried by reports of barbarities committed by the Russian troops or police. They had a strong feeling that not much by way of civilized behavior could be expected from rebels and lawbreakers, whereas the authorities had a moral duty to set an example by their conduct. In this, they were sorely disappointed.

For the most part, the British consuls were favorably impressed by the conduct of the insurrection and tended to discount official denunciations of "cette bande criminelle," as the tsar called it. The initial actions in January 1863, when numerous Russian detachments were ambushed, were described as "the murder of troops in cold blood,"[43] but it was soon accepted, with a civil war in progress, that such tactics were an unavoidable feature of warfare. The more extreme rumors—of alleged attempts to poison Marquis Wielopolski, or of women murdered by fanatical priests—were given little credence; and at the end of February, Stanton expressed his satisfaction about the absence of excessive violence. "As yet," he wrote, "I have not heard of any excesses committed by the insurgents," and he reported official sources, without quoting any proof, "that peasants have been hanged for want of sympathy for the national cause or for giving information to the troops."[45] Yet on two issues, the British counsuls did not conceal their horror. The fist concerned the activities of the underground National Government's secret police force, whom Stanton called "the hanging gendarmes." The second concerned terrorism. There were numerous attempts in Warsaw itself to kill the leading tsarist officials. When in September 1863, General Berg survived the nineteenth attempt on his life, from a shrapnel bomb tossed from the Zamoyski palace, Stanton condemned it in no uncertain terms as "a diabolical act."[46] Less violent aspects of politically motivated crime, such as the disappearance of the chief cashier of the Kingdom's treasury together with 4 million rubles in cash, were reported with a hint of amusement.[47]

When it came to the conduct of the tsarist authorities, the British consuls were in despair. They relayed numerous instances of needless cruelty. Stanton's fears were confirmed early on by his unusually detailed investigations into the case of Count Leopold Poteylo, a loyalist aristocrat, whose estate at Wojstawice(?) near Lublin was wantonly plundered by a Cossack regiment in an unprovoked attack in February. It is not clear why the British consul should have taken such trouble over this case, which presumably did not involve a British subject, but it is clear that the description of the storming of the mansion and the senseless killing and maiming of the count's house guests made a deep impression.[48] Obviously, if loyalist gentlemen could be treated in such a fashion, there was no hope that the tsarist authorities would behave humanely toward the lower classes or toward disaffected persons. When the insurrection was in its terminal stage, Stanton harbored no illusions that the Russians would show any restraint or mercy. As he told Lord

Russell, "nothing but the most abject submission will be considered sufficient to appease the desire for vengeance which appears now to be so deeply rooted in their minds."[49]

The dilemma which faced the British consuls was quite clear. On the one hand, as mid-Victorian officers and gentlemen, they instinctively sprang to the defense of law and order and could not bring themselves to condone the insurgents' lawbreaking. On the other hand, they could not accept the tsarist authorities' concept of the law, which was systematically used as an instrument of political control. Lord Napier had made the point in his denunciation of Russian conscription, where he in the official gazette openly admitted that "Legality is our Death." For this reason, although they could never actually excuse the insurgents, the British observers could also see that in Russian hands the law was not worthy of respect. Obviously, in the realms of the tsar, British standards of law and justice simply did not apply.

8. Social and Religious Issues

In their reporting on the insurrection, the British consuls betrayed the prejudice of their class in paying disproportionate attention to the affairs of the nobility. In Colonel Stanton's mind, the misfortunes of Count Poteylo were somewhat more newsworthy than the alleged atrocities committed in the countryside against the peasants. The fact that the Russian grand duke had snubbed some Polish nobles who attended his levée on the anniversary of the tsar's accession was clearly a political event of importance. In commenting on the politics of the insurrection, Stanton repeatedly states that "the socialist nature of the movement cannot be doubted" or that "the movement is deeply imbued with socialism" as if such revelations did not require further elucidation.[50] He constantly uses the term "the ultra-party" in reference to the insurrection's leaders and does not conceal his sympathy for the Polish "moderates," whose desire for reconciliation was ignored by both sides. He was aware of the church's difficulties under martial law and noted the interference with religious processions[51] and the banishment of Archbishop Feliński;[52] but he was at great pains to discount the Vatican's protests about the general persecution of Catholics. In a long memorandum on this subject, he stressed the relatively advantageous condition of the church in the Kingdom of Poland as compared to that in the Russian Empire proper.[53] White, who was a Catholic himself, endeavored to counter official charges against the alleged fanaticism of the Catholic clergy. He pointed out, for example, that the "friar Spleszyński" who was supposed to have incited the mob by the extreme violence of his sermon at the fateful funeral of General Savinski's widow in June 1861 was in fact a Protestant.[54] Considerable interest was shown in the emancipation of the serfs, although here the consuls seemed to be largely concerned with the effect of the measure on the life of the landowning class.

9. The Emancipation of the Serfs

Emancipation was a burning issue in Poland throughout the insurrection, as the insurgents competed with the tsarist government for the support of the peasantry. As White put it, the Polish serfs were "courted and intimidated" by both sides.[55] When the tsar's decrees on the subject began to be published and read out with great pomp and ceremony in Warsaw's old town square, Stanton was most impressed by the cynical political motives of the tsar's ministers. "The object of this complete Social Revolution," he wrote, "placing every possible impediment in the way of the landed proprietors, is to increase class animosity, by which they consider the Russian cause may be assisted."[56] On the final decree in April 1864, which fixed the terms of the cession of land and the arrangements for communal autonomy, Stanton commented, "Good management is being penalised."[57]

In this context, the case of John Bull, an English landowner residing at Janów in the district of Mińsk Mazowiecki, is most instructive. Bull had moved to Poland ten years before—presumably at the invitation of Count Andrzej Zamoyski, the local magnate, who was passionately concerned with agricultural improvement—and had farmed there through the period of the troubles. In 1859, he had resold the Janów estate, but had leased it back from the purchaser. In consequence of official legislation, he had been obliged to reorganize the estate on two occasions—in 1861, following Wielopolski's decree converting corvée labor into money rents, and in 1864, when all the leaseholders and laborers had to be given possession of their land. Quite apart from the disturbance involved, Bull felt aggrieved that the compensation which he received was entirely inadequate. As a result, he drew up a long statement summarizing the affairs of his estate in considerable detail and sent it to the British consul in Warsaw with a request for intervention with the Russian government and a claim for an indemnity. Bull claimed in effect that his losses were equal to two-thirds of his total property. Colonel Stanton was sufficiently impressed to forward the materials to Lord Napier in St. Petersburg. "I cannot guarantee

Mr Bull's figures," he wrote, [but there does appear to have been] "an injustice to a certain class of proprietor, trusting in the good faith of the government and [endeavoring] to improve the condition of the peasants and the agricultural resources of the country."[58] Even a cursory glance shows that Bull's figures were indeed hopelessly muddled, but the documents' value lies less in their mathematical accuracy than in their detailed survey of landholdings, mortgages, labor services, rents, dues, incomes, and indemnities. For the historian, the inside picture of a Polish estate at the moment of emancipation—written in English—is a rare item indeed and deserves to be published in full (see Appendix 1 of this volume).

10. Personalities

The consuls' files show that a surprising number of British subjects were caught up in the insurrection in one way or another, either as insurgents, like Abicht and Apel, or more frequently as travelers or adventurers, like J. J. Schweizer or Alistair Macdonald. Each of these files adds a human face and a human story to the generalized comments of diplomatic and commercial affairs. MacDonald's letter of farewell to his mother, for example, written in the full expectation of deportation to Siberia, is a period gem (see Appendix 2 of this volume).[59] More interesting from the Polish point of view are the instances when the British consuls came into contact with the affairs of actual Polish insurgents. Such was the strange case of Ludwik Żychliński, a prominent insurrectionary leader from Posnania.

In April 1864 toward the end of the insurrection, Colonel Stanton received a letter from one Arthur S. Malone, of Highfield House near Nottingham, asking for news of Żychliński's whereabouts, and enclosing a cutting from the German *Ostsee Gazette*.[60] From these accounts it emerged, to put it mildly, that Żychliński was something of a wild boy. The son of a Polish landowner in Prussia, he seems to have gone to England in 1860 after deserting from his regiment, the Bonn hussars. In England, according to the *Ostsee Gazette,* he married "a rich English heiress" in Plymouth, although the records of General Register Office suggest that he married a sixteen-year-old girl, Adeline Kate Maltby, a cousin of Malone, in Dover. A marriage certificate, dated October 27, 1860, describes the bridegroom as "Louis de Szeliga Zychlinski, 27 years, bachelor, Russian Baron, Captain —7th Imperial Guards, . . . son of Franz, Comte Zychlinski" and records a wedding solemnized at the Roman Catholic Chapel, Queen Elizabeth Square, Dover, in the presence, among others, of the Russian vice-consul.⁶¹ Soon afterwards, by Mr. Malone's information, Żychliński was divorced from Malone's cousin on the grounds of her "ill treatment" and was involved in an unspecified trial in Nottingham. Eventually he returned to Poland, fought in the uprising first in the region of Konin and then in Mazovia at the head of a group called "the Warsaw lads," and was captured by the Russians in February 1863 after a bloody battle and incarcerated in the Warsaw Citadel. Malone concludes by hinting that his family would not be too distressed if Żychliński's career came to a sudden end at the hands of summary Russian justice. In due course, Żychliński was sentenced to twenty years' penal servitude in Siberia.⁶²

It would be inaccurate to suppose that the colorful lifestyle of this one man was taken to be typical of the insurgent leaders as a whole. But there is no doubt that the British consuls viewed the insurrection as the work of irresponsible people; and Żychliński's apparently irresponsible conduct of his private affairs could have done little to contradict their negative opinion of the "ultra-party."

What the files do *not* show is that Żychliński's career was still more colorful than the British consul knew. He had already taken part in Garibaldi's expedition to Sicily, and between his departure from England in February 1862 and his return to Poland in 1863, he had crossed the Atlantic and had served as a volunteer NCO of the Union Army in Virginia, fighting at the Battle of Williamsburg under General McClellan in the regiment of "Les Enfants Perdus" of Colonel Felix Confort and receiving a wound during the siege of Richmond. His memoirs of the American Civil War had already been published in Prussia before his arrest by the Russians.⁶³ He survived Siberia, returned to Poland, and died in Brusna in 1891.⁶⁴

11. Support from Prussian Poland

On his return from leave in London in June 1863, Vice-Consul White spent ten days in Poznań. His lengthy report, which surveys the whole history of the Prussian partition, provides a comprehensive overview of the condition of the Poles in Prussia at that time. He noted that the influx of German immigrants and officials was causing great hostility. "The whole race feels more and more Polish," and "all the Poles in the Grand Duchy of Posen support the Insurrection" against Russia. Polish volunteers caught on the frontier were being tried in Prussia for conspiracy, and the Prussian army was cooperating with the Russians.⁶⁵

12. Repression

Long before the insurrection was crushed, the British consuls were noting instances of the Russian authorities' needless "barbarity" toward rebels and dissidents—of a wounded insurgent nursed back to health with great difficulty in order to be publicly hanged[66] or of leading officials arbitrarily transported into the depths of Russia.[67] Stanton pointed out that the insurgents were being driven to "the desperation to resist to the last." Later, the methods of the Russian repression were studied in some depth, in particular, the use of loyalty oaths, mass deportations, and the abolition of Polish institutions.

The loyalty oaths were first observed by Stanton in January 1864, although the Warsaw Police Department denied that they represented anything more than the "excessive zeal" of individual officers. "For some days past," Stanton wrote, "police agents have been going from house to house to collect signatures to an address of loyalty to the Emperor—a document . . . couched in the most abject terms and [which] commences with an admission of guilt."[68] One such document alone, he claimed, carried the signatures of 14,000 Warsaw citizens. In addition, corporate addresses of loyalty were being extracted from towns and villages. Where the peasants were illiterate, they had to leave their fingerprint. "It may be presumed," Stanton commented, "that considerable pressure has been employed in collecting even this very limited expression of loyalty to the Government."[69] There was further evidence that the loyal addresses were accompanied by heavy communal fines. The little town of Węgrów, for example, had to pay 4,000 rubles in 1864 for its assistance to the insurgents in the previous year.[70] Stanton succeeded in obtaining the French text of a loyalty oath exacted from members of the civil service in the Kingdom.[71] He also received information from the eastern guberniyas that the authorities were exacting petitions for the Kingdom's incorporation into the Empire.[72]

Deportation of people to distant parts of Russia could be effected without trial by confidential administrative measures, but the authorities made no secret of the practice. In November 1863, Stanton reported that the arrests involved "large numbers of all classes even young girls" and described them as "senseless" and "indiscriminate." He feared they would cause a revival of the insurrection.[73] Three months later, he had seen official, interim figures for the numbers sent to Siberia—31,573 from the Kingdom, including 4,762 from Warsaw alone, and three thousand young men drafted into the Russian army.[74] These figures were by no means complete and did not include the similar quota of deportees from Lithuania. Even so, from a total population of only

4.8 million (1861), they represented an enormous loss. Vice-Consul White compared them to the 10,000 Poles deported to Siberia in the twenty-five years of Prince Paskievitch's rule in Warsaw from 1832 to 1857.[75]

The Russification of Polish institutions also began at an early date. In April 1864, Stanton reported that the new head of the Kingdom's Department of the Interior, Prince Icherkaskii, had ordered all communications to subordinate civil authorities to be written in Russian.[76] Military officers were being commissioned to take over civilian affairs. In July, he remarked on the government's intention "to withdraw all the concessions of 1861–62 without any regard to the promises made by His Majesty," i.e., the tsar.[77] Polish officials were being replaced by Russians. The Administrative Council was being packed with Russians. Even the shops in Warsaw were being Russified. White, as a Catholic, paid particular attention to the attack on the church and to the abolition of 80 percent of Poland's monasteries, many of them officially closed for political causes.[78] Clearly, the process of destroying the Kingdom was well under way before any official decisions were published.

13. The End of the Insurrection

The British consuls were amazed that the insurrection continued for as long as it did. Already in July 1863, Stanton, expecting the authorities to negotiate, thought the end was near. "It is hard to believe," he wrote, "that the Poles may be sufficiently demented to wish to continue the hopeless struggle."[79] In November, he asked London for permission to go home on leave "since the Insurrection is likely to die out."[80] Yet in April 1864, he still had to admit that the insurrection was alive. "Incredible as it may appear," he confessed, "in a place so closely watched and guarded as Warsaw, . . . there is still a person calling himself the Revolutionary Chief of the Town."[81] That was the week when Traugutt was arrested. Not until June 1864 did the British consul risk a final judgment that "the Polish Insurrection is a thing of the past."[82]

The reports of the British consuls in Warsaw in 1863–64 by no means present a full picture of events during the January Insurrection. There were many aspects of which they took little account or about which they had no certain information. They had little firsthand knowledge of developments outside Warsaw and no access to the internal politics of the insurrectionary camp. They relied heavily on contacts within the tsarist administration of the Kingdom of Poland and on readings of the official press and public decrees. But the range of their interests was wide, especially with respect to military and social issues. Indeed, their awareness of the social implications of military events—of "War and Society"—was surprisingly modern. Their papers contain much more life and color than the more familiar General Diplomatic Correspondence of the time and deserve to be more thoroughly investigated.

By way of postscript, from the perspective of 1982, no one can fail to notice the echoes of the present situation in Poland. More than one commentator has seen General Jarulzelski as the Marquis Wielopolski of our own day, and the suppression of Solidarity by the state of war in December 1981 has much in common with the attempted suppression of the patriotic opposition by the *branka* of 1863. Apart from that, martial law, loyalty oaths, arbitrary arrests, the spectacle of an autocratic establishment trapped by the contradictory demands of reform and control, and the unedifying scene of Polish bureaucrats and soldiers dancing to the Russian tune are all too familiar. Judging from the historical precedent, even more tragic events could be in store if true dialogue continues to be ignored. Vice-Consul White, who had been raised in Poland himself, was particularly fearful of "the fiery patriotism" of Polish youth—"a dominant passion which brings each successive generation of Poles to an untimely grave."[83] Responsible leaders in Poland today could profit from their own history.

Notes

1. T. Filipowicz, ed., *Confidential Correspondence of the British Government respecting the Insurrection in Poland, 1863* (Cracow, 1912; Paris, 1914); a reprint of the Parliamentary Paper C3150 (London, 1863). (Hereafter CCB61P). The original correspondence is deposited in the Public Record Office, London, under Foreign Office, General Correspondence (Russia) = FO65.

2. Colonel, later General, Sir Edward Stanton, K.C.M.G., Royal Engineers (1827–1907), 1860–65, consul-general at Warsaw, then at Cairo; 1876–82, chargé d'affaires at Munich. See *Foreign Office List* (1863).

3. William Arthur White (1824–1891), born at Putawy (Poland). Vice-consul at Warsaw 1851–4, 1864 Consul-General at Warsaw and Danzig: 1887–91, ambassador to Constantinople—the first Catholic to be a British ambassador since the Reformation. See H. Sutherland Edwards, *Sir William White—His Life and Times* (London, 1902), especially chaps. 3, 4, 5. According to Edwards, the exceptional status of the British consulate in Warsaw, which pursued diplomatic and military functions in addition to the normal consular and

commercial activities, derived from the events of 1832, when Nicholas I wished to impress on the Western powers that the Kingdom of Poland was suspended but not abolished.
4. CCB61P No. 4, January 19, 1863.
5. CCB61P No. 28, February 4, 1863.
6. CCB61P No. 179, March 4, 1863.
7. CCB61P No. 180, March 7, 1863.
8. CCB61P No. 277, March 21, 1863.
9. CCB61P No. 28, February 4, 1863.
10. CCB61P No. 180, March 7, 1863.
11. FO 65/642, Stanton, No. 50, June 10, 1863.
12. FO 65/642, Calculations concerning Russian enlistment in the Kingdom of Poland since 1831. White to Earl Russell, May 2, 1863.
13. CCB61P No. 10, January 26, 1863.
14. CCB61P No. 210, March 11, 1863.
15. On Traugutt, see J. Zarzabowski, ed., *Traugutt—Dokumenty, listy, wspomnienia, wypisy* (London, 1970); also *Proces Romualda i cztonków Rządu Narodowego* (Warsaw, 1960–61), 4 vols.
16. FO 65/642, White, No. 56, June 21, 1863.
17. Ibid.
18. CCB61P No. 9, January 26, 1863.
19. CCB61P No. 25, February 7, 1863.
20. Ibid.
21. CCB61P No. 103, February 19, 1863.
22. CCB61P No. 370, April 6, 1863.
23. CCB61P No. 25, February 7, 1863.
24. CCB61P No. 181, March 9, 1863.
25. CCB61P No. 182, March 11, 1863.
26. CCB61P No. 28, February 4, 1863.
27. CCB61P No. 371, April 7, 1863.
28. E.g., W. H. Bullock (W. V. Hall), *Polish Experiences during the Insurrection of 1863–64* (Cambridge, 1864). The author traveled extensively through all three partitions and witnessed several military engagements in both the Kingdom and the Empire.
29. FO 65/642, Stanton, No. 65, July 28, 1863.
30. FO 65/665, Stanton, No. 4, January 5, 1864.
31. CCB61P No. 102, February 16, 1863.
32. FO 65/641, No. 34, April 17, 1863.
33. FO 65/640, No. 34, October 1863.
34. FO 65/642, Stanton, No. 55, June 30, 1863.
35. CCB61P No. 2, January 11, 1863. Polish revolutionaries apparently found little difficulty in obtaining British passports in London, and the consuls in Warsaw were repeatedly pressed by the Russian police to check doubtful papers issued in the name of "John Smith," "William Brown," "William Pitt," and so on. See FO 65/640, Stanton, No. 40, December 8, 1863. Henryk Abicht

(1835–64), a native of Vilnius, came to Poland in 1863 as an emissary of Herzen.
36. FO 65/642, Stanton, No. 52, June 17, 1863.
37. FO 65/640, Stanton, No. 30, October 7, 1863.
38. FO 65/643, No. 85, October 7, 1863.
39. FO 65/640, White, No. 5, January 15, 1863.
40. FO 65/640, Stanton, No. 38, November 1863.
41. FO 65/640, White, No. 26, September 29, 1863.
42. FO 65/665, Stanton, No. 22, May 19, 1864.
43. CCB61P No. 11, January 28, 1863.
44. CCB61P No. 110, February 23, 1863.
45. FO 65/642, Stanton, No. 50, June 10, 1863.
46. FO 65/643, Stanton, No. 80, September 22, 1863.
47. FO 65/642, Stanton, No. 51, June 15, 1863.
48. CCB61P No. 110, February 23, 1863.
49. FO 65/665, Stanton, No. 10, February 16, 1864.
50. CCB61P No. 11, January 28; No. 28, February 4, 1863.
51. FO 65/641, Stanton, No. 37, April 30, 1863.
52. FO 65/642, Stanton, No. 52, June 17, 1863.
53. FO 65/665, Stanton, No. 37, October 31, 1864.
54. FO 65/665, White, No. 2, December 3, 1864.
55. FO 65/665, White, No. 4, December 8, 1864.
56. FO 65/665, Stanton, No. 14, March 10, 1864.
57. FO 65/665, Stanton, No. 16, April 5, 1864.
58. FO 65/665, Stanton—Napier, June 8, 1864, pp. 180ff.
59. FO 65/665, Stanton, No. 22, May 19, 1864.
60. FO 65/665, April 20, 1864, Foreign Office to Stanton.
61. General Register Office, London. Registration District, Dover (Kent), 1860, No. 143.
62. FO 65/665, Stanton, No. 23, May 19, 1864.
63. Ludwik Żychliński, *Pamiętniki z wojny amerykańskiej 1862 r.* (Poznań, 1863).
64. Ludwik Żychliński (1837–91) later published further volumes of memoirs including *Pamiętniki przywodcy dzieci warszawskich* (1885) and *Przygody więznia politycznego* (1864). See *Wielka Encyklopedia Powszrchna* (PWN, vol. 12).
65. FO 65/642, White, June 24, 1863.
66. Frenczkowski. FO 65/642, Stanton, No. 52, June 1863.
67. Wotowski, "Attorney-General" of the Kingdom transported to Penza. FO 65/642, Stanton, No. 59, July 14, 1863.
68. FO 65/665, Stanton, No. 7, January 19, 1864.
69. Ibid.
70. FO 65/665, White, No. 3, December 6, 1864.
71. FO 65/665, Stanton, No. 14, March 10, 1864.
72. FO 65/665, Stanton, No. 8 (?), January 28, 1864.
73. FO 65/643, Stanton, No. 93, November 3, 1863.

74. FO 65/665, Stanton, No. 12, February 24, 1864.
75. FO 65/665, White, No. 4, December 8, 1864—undoubtedly a serious underestimate.
76. FO 65/665, Stanton, No. 15, April 16, 1864.
77. FO 65/665, Stanton, No. 28, July 11, 1864.
78. FO 65/665, White, No. 2, December 3, 1864.
79. FO 65/642, Stanton, No. 57, July 7, 1863.
80. FO 65/640, Stanton, No. 39, November 25, 1863.
81. FO 65/665, Stanton, No. 17, April 16, 1864.
82. FO 65/665, Stanton, No. 24, June 8, 1864.
83. FO 65/665, White, No. 4, December 8, 1864.

The Consequences of the January Insurrection

Zygmunt Mańkowski

Rarely does an event have only positive or negative consequences; most often we find a synthesis of the two. In defeat there may be elements of a future victory and in victory the germs of a future defeat. This should be kept in mind in considering the history of the January Insurrection of 1863 in the Polish territories. For more than a hundred years there has been controversy in Polish historiography about its significance, its aims, its prospects, and its consequences. Judgments and evaluations in the matter have undergone many changes under the influence of hindsight, research (during the last few years, with the help of historians from the Soviet Union, the fundamental authoritative materials for the history of the movement have been published), and the changing situation of Poland and the positions of its various political groups. In general, historical output on the insurrection is dominated by the view that of all the Polish attempts at liberation from the end of the eighteenth century until the end of the nineteenth it was the largest in territorial extent (including the territories of Lithuania, Belorussia, and the Ukraine), involved the largest number of active participants, and had the most significant consequences.

The Polish historiography on the subject is enormous, and it is impossible to characterize it here. Its crowning achievement is the comprehensive monographic synthesis published in 1972 by Stefan Kieniewicz. Kieniewicz's main thesis, which is contained in the final chapter (characteristically entitled "New Prospects Despite the Defeat") is as follows:

> To all appearances, the Polish question had hit bottom. The autonomy of the Kingdom underwent suppression, the Polish language was evicted from schools and offices, the Main School was closed. No one reckoned with the Polish question in the arena of international politics. The luminaries of Polish society, independently of their political views, were publicly expressing aspirations for independence. Such was the situation in the first ten years after the insurrection. A century later, it is a different story. The nation recovered its spirits very quickly. In the last three

decades of the nineteenth century there was a rapid demographic transition and an immense increase in the use of manufactured goods, urbanization, and living standards. Accompanying these economic processes was a rich development of the press, literature, the theater, and art and, what is especially important, precisely opposite to Gurko's and Apukhtin's Russification policy, an increase in literacy. There were different reasons for these processes, but they all manifested one thing: the very rapid progress of the Kingdom toward capitalistic development. However, the basic precondition for that development was the radical character of the freehold reform decreed in 1864.

Many Polish historians share this opinion today. For example, in a book published in 1973 entitled *The History of Polish Arms 1794–1938*, by E. Kozłowski and M. Wrzosek, it is said:

> Five times during the nineteenth century the Polish nation rose to fight, but each time it was repulsed. Yet these were the rungs it had to climb to reach a better future. . . . The 1863 Insurrection failed because of the superiority of the enemy and the consequences of its own errors; however, it was the longest of all national risings up to that time and gained more than all the previous ones put together. The freeholds in the Kingdom realized by the National Government paved the way for the development of a modern society and made clear the division with regard to class and politics.

At the same time, there are others who consider the insurrection a complete defeat. On the occasion of its hundredth anniversary in 1963, Henryk Wereszycki, who had previously written that "the January Insurrection ended as one of the greatest defeats the Polish nation sustained in the postpartition period," stated again,

> Surely most serious was the loss of the possibility of a regular national development in the Russian sector. Russification and postinsurrection persecutions caused material losses as well as casualties that can scarcely be counted or assessed. So great a defeat as the insurrection ultimately had to reduce national power. It was probably one of the stages of our historical degradation.

It is obvious that Polish historians from the beginning to the present have accepted the obvious defeat of the insurrection but differed in their assessments of its results. The problem is that now, with the revival of positivistic tendencies, the controversy over the results of the Polish national uprisings is inclined to return to earlier arguments. Formed under the influence of the defeat of the January Insurrection, the ideology of Polish positivism, with its complete renunciation of armed struggle for national goals and its concentration on economic welfare work, decidedly turned away from the tradition of the insurrection. Its main ideologist, Aleksander Świętochowski, wrote: "If the heroism of death is necessary to complete our national virtues, we already have it. Now we should only strive to obtain another one, less poetic but more profitable—the heroism of efficient life." The Polish positivists definitively broke with the romantic political ideas manifested by the uprisings, opposing to the cult of the Pole as soldier-insurgent the ideal of the Pole as social and economic worker. The watchword of "organic work" was to supplant the watchword of armed national struggle.

Both the significance and the results of the insurrection were quite negatively valued by Polish conservatives and, to some extent, people connected with the so-called national circle, the right wing of Polish political opinion. Accusations were common and very harsh. For example, Paweł Popiel, an outstanding conservative from Cracow, argued:

> The reckless perpetrators of these disasters will have to answer to God, country, and future generations. The blood of the most respectable Polish youth, the tears of so many mothers in the Kingdom and in Lithuania and the Ukraine should be on their consciences. They should be held responsible for the eradication of the Polish element, the confirmation of schism, the humiliation of the Catholic church, and the deterioration of church discipline among our clergy. It is difficult to lay responsibility on the enemy alone; it rests on those who, under outside influence and for alien aims, caused this unequal struggle without weapons, commanders, or allies.

What, then, were the real results of the insurrection? What part did it play in the history of the nation and the country? What was its influence on the regeneration of independent Poland in 1918? How did it affect the Polish political ideology of the turn of the century? How does the tradition of the insurrection survive in the consciousness of present generations of Poles? These are all important questions, and, though they appear in numerous monographs and studies, comprehensive and detailed answers to them have not yet been offered.

On its most direct and basic consequences, research is still in progress, but some general statements may be made. Probably about twenty thousand insurgents and people connected with the insurrection died in battle. Over fifteen thousand insurgents were taken prisoner. About six hundred seventy insurgents and conspirators were shot or hanged (many of them in public executions that made a strong impression and created a kind of neurosis). The number exiled to Siberia is estimated at thirty-eight thousand (38 percent from the Kingdom of Poland, 57 percent from Lithuania and Belorussia, 5 percent from the Ukraine), a tenth of them to penal servitude (that is, to more severe punishment) and the rest scattered over far parts of Russia. About ten thousand emigrated to the West. All this refers to the Russian sector only, but it is known that there were many arrests, sentences, and social degradations in the Austrian and Prussian sectors as well. These losses were especially severe in that they involved mainly the social element (representing various strata of society) that was the most active, patriotic, self-conscious, and educated. As Kieniewicz says, "The defeat of inspired hopes, the mourning of thousands of families, the consciousness of infirmity, the picture of the enemy sneering at the defeated nation—all this contributed at the end of 1864 to an atmosphere of despair."

To some extent, there were also material losses. During and after the insurrection the tsarist government confiscated at least 1,760 large estates and gave them to the victors (tsarist officers, officials, and even peasants). The Polish holders of a number of government estates were dismissed, and many of these, formerly influential national, economic, and social centers, became Russified. Many estates whose owners or staff had been involved in the insurrection fell to ruin. A second aspect of this phenomenon was taxation by the tsarist government, which involved many millions of rubles exacted by the most brutal of methods. In Lithuania alone, at least 14 million rubles were collected. It should be added that people in the regions of direct military operations bore in great measure the costs of the stay of the Russian army through confiscations and robberies. Polish society as a whole made great material efforts on behalf of the insurrection in the form of money, clothing, weapons, and so on.

Military operations, attacks by partisan units, fear and uncertainty, disruption of transport, and so forth, caused in some parts of the country, at least in the initial stage of the uprising, symptoms of crisis in industry, trade, and crafts. However, these were brief and had no important consequences.

Very severe losses were suffered by the Catholic church. Numerous restrictions were applied, and most monasteries and convents were liquidated. In November 1864 alone, over one hundred such institutions were closed by Russian decree. Uniate orders were dispersed, and some others (e.g., the Visitants) were forced to emigrate abroad.

Polish historiography has scrupulously recorded the Russian reprisals against the Congress Kingdom. Tsarist policy was directed toward the complete integration of the Kingdom into the empire—the obliteration of all the signs of political and structural separateness and full Russification. First of all, in the whole region embraced by the insurrection, a state of war was declared that—and this is important—was essentially never withdrawn. This enabled the government to use the strongest means of repression without orders or judicial process. From 1864 on the police and spy system was systematically developed. A special committee was created in St. Petersburg whose aim was the suppression of all the autonomous institutions in the Kingdom. In 1866 the secretaryship of state for the Kingdom, the so-called Council of State, and the autonomous commissions of the interior, religion and education, and justice and finance were abolished. All business matters were submitted to the central government of Russia. The Bank of Poland was also closed. The post of governor was replaced by that of governor general of the Warsaw Military District, thus linking civil and military functions in a single office.

In the cultural and social field, there was a ban on separate Polish educational, cultural, and even philanthropic organizations (unless a special license was granted). All publications, periodicals, printing houses, photographic shops, and so on, were censored. The complete Russification of administration and education followed in 1866. Russian law was instituted in the ten provinces (guberniyas), and Poles were dismissed from administrative and judicial posts. The Russian language became obligatory in secondary schools (with the exception of religious educational courses). In 1869, the Main School in Warsaw, the only Polish university in the Kingdom, was closed. The crowning blow was the replacement of the name "Congress Kingdom" (of Poland) with "Przedwiślański Kraj" (Vistula Country). Anti-Polish policy and Russification escalated over time, especially during the reign of Alexander III.

To the negative side of the balance should be added the influence of the disturbance on certain configurations in the arena of international politics and on world attitudes toward the Polish question. In this connection, historians and journalists (e.g., Stanisław Stomma of the Catholic *Tygodnik Powszechny*) have attempted to determine whether there was any chance for the Kingdom of Poland to become the "Polish Piedmont" (one outstanding Polish historian and journalist published in *Życie Literackie* an article entitled "Piedmont or Ashes?"), and some have stressed the fact that the Alvensleben Convention, by restoring the alliance of Russia and Prussia, buried any possibility of a rapprochement between France and Russia and thus any chance for improvement of the situation of the Poles through France's intervention.

One aspect of the depression caused by the failure of the insurrection was the appearance of the phenomenon of loyalism (or even Triple Loyalism) so severely condemned by contemporary and later generations of Poles. In the historiography this position has often been linked with class conditioning. Loyalist journalists and historians (for example, J. Szujski, S. Koźmian, K. Krzywicki) proclaimed the absurdity of efforts to attain independence and the necessity of abandoning insurgent ideas, condemned the January Insurrection decidedly, and pointed out that *liberum conspire* was no safer than *liberum veto*. Lech Trzeciakowski, the historian from Poznań, analyzing this phenomenon, writes, "All the facts [the activity of loyalists in the three sectors of partitioned Poland] showed clearly that servility, sometimes approaching treason, could be advantageous to the invader." It is worth noting, however, that in the course of an analysis in 1978 of the internal reasons for Poland's regeneration after the First World War, some historians (e.g., Kieniewicz) suggested that the loyalists had had some part in it, though only those who were convinced that loyalism might help the national cause. Therefore, this matter requires further research and consideration.

Summing up the opinions of Polish historians, the following matters and circumstances attract attention: The European powers were interested not in Poland's liberation, but in their own far-reaching aims. Their diplomatic interventions, according to Kieniewicz, "undertaken from selfish motives," brought Poland "no profit" and ended in "the success of tsarism and the unusual discredit of the governments of France and England." The insurrection and its suppression undoubtedly contributed in a way to the rapprochement of Russia and Prussia and affected the progress of events in the arena of international politics (Prussia's victories in wars with Denmark in 1864, Austria in 1866, and France in 1870–71). Kieniewicz sums up as follows:

> The insurrection fell. The police of the three invaders worked on eradicating the remnants of its organizations. Diplomats of the European powers who not long ago had been making use of the Polish question promptly began to forget about it. "People were tired of it," wrote the *Morning Herald*. "They were tired of a nation that talked all the time but whose deeds did not match its principles. . . . The Polish question had become boring."

Another negative result of the insurrection for the Polish question in the arena of international politics was the appearance, in the course of the polarization of views of different environments and personalities, of clearly anti-Polish attitudes. Here Prudhon ("Poland was always the most corrupt, aristocratic country and, what is more, completely undisciplined") and some outstanding Russian writers, among them Dostoevskii, are often cited.

In the estimation of the consequences of the January Insurrection by Polish historiography favorable ones have also been considered. Summing up "the active and adverse balance of the 1863 Insurrection," Wereszycki says,

Its main and unquestionable achievement is undoubtedly the granting of freeholds to the peasants on easier conditions than those of the Russian Empire. Furthermore, the liquidating of many economically inferior landowners' estates turned out to be advantageous for social, economic, and cultural conditions in the Kingdom. People driven from the farm turned to industry and trade; a new, modern sort of citizen came into being.

He goes on to point to the beneficial influence of postinsurrection conditions upon the situation of women (their emancipation as a result of positivistic ideas), upon the consciousness of the peasants (the struggle for souls), and upon education (the influence of the idea of "organic work").

In general, it is a firm conclusion of Polish historiography that the most important result of the insurrection was the solution of the agrarian question by giving the peasants the land they cultivated—which was not the solution the Russians attempted, but one devised by the insurrectionary authorities (Rosa Luxemburg understood it as merely attributable to Russia and drew far-reaching wrong conclusions from it). At present the majority of historians share the opinion that the emancipation of the peasants, which was more radical in the Kingdom than anywhere else in that part of Europe, opened the way for a swift development of capitalist relations, which meant economic advance for Poland and the swift spread of national consciousness among the masses.

This question is worth much more attention. The peasant problem has always been one of the most urgent issues in Polish history, and it is believed to have conditioned the opportunity for regaining independence. Polish historiography often associates the collapse of a national uprising with its neglect of the social question (Henryk Jabłoński). On the eve of the January Insurrection the peasants of the Kingdom, influenced by the reform introduced in Russia, manifested antifeudal resistance on an unprecedented scale. In order to draw them to the insurrection, the Provisional National Government abolished class differences and all kinds of privileges and proclaimed the immediate emancipation of the peasants. *History of Poland,* recently published in Cracow, presents the following view:

> The landowners were promised government compensation. The landless were promised 3 morgs of land from government estates provided they took part in the fight for liberation. The peasants were to retain their easement rights to the woods. Thus the resolutions represented a compromise—large landownership was preserved, the landowners were to be given compensation, and the problem of the landless was partially solved.

It was essential, however, to connect the matter of national liberation with the abolition of the feudal system. The resolutions pertaining to agrarian reform, in going far beyond any reforms of the tsarist government, offered the possibility of gaining the peasants' backing in the insurrection.

In *History of Poland*, published in Poznań in 1977, J. Topolski writes:

> The realization of the decree that granted freeholds to the peasants . . . determined the influx of peasant volunteers into the ranks of the insurgents. It depended on the attitude of the nobility, on the efficiency of the insurrectionary administration, and on the position of the peasants. . . . In spite of numerous difficulties, the agrarian decrees were put into effect. The peasants were almost entirely freed of labor obligations and land rents. . . . They were anxious, however, as they were not given documents of the abolition of the feudal charges.

Farther on, Topolski points to the postponing of the problem of the landless: "This gave rise to numerous encounters between the landowners and the poor. . . . Nevertheless, the agrarian decrees, though realized under rather difficult conditions, did embrace a considerable part of the peasantry."

After the collapse of the insurrection, the tsarist government faced a difficult problem; it learned that, as Kieniewicz has put it, "the decree which had granted freeholds to the peasants was an incontrovertible fact and the peasants would not give it up." Consequently, the tsarist government executed its own reform. The consensus of Polish historiography at present is that this was of great significance for the future of the nation. K. Grzybowski indicates that the agrarian reform accomplished by the insurrection prevented the tsarist government from solving the peasant question in a way similar to the English one (in which the peasant was a mere capitalist tenant) and "incorporated the masses of peasants as landowners into contemporary bourgeois society."

Another significant beneficial result of the insurrection that has long been emphasized by Polish historiography is the internationalizing of the Polish question. It has been generally noted that the 1863 Insurrection, as none before, aroused unprecedented interest in the Polish question in all of Western Europe. A variety of social circles (including both the aristocracy and the working class) and political circles (the democratic, the socialist), as well as such authorities as Kossuth, Mazzini, Garibaldi, Bakunin, Hugo, Marx, and Engels, became involved in the question. It is often mentioned that the tsarist government boasted of having repulsed "an attack by twenty nations" in favor of the Polish question. A letter "to Russian soldiers" written by Hugo in

February 1863 was a specific manifestation of the awakening of world opinion in defense of Poland:

> To murder a nation seems to be impossible. Like a star covered by clouds for an instant, it appears again before our eyes. . . . It is Poland that proves this. Poland is gleaming today . . . though not with full life, still with full glory. All the light has come back to her. She has been crushed and covered with blood, but now she stands upright and ravishes the whole world. . . . I wish the Poles to regain their independence, and I wish Moscow to regain her honor. . . . That is right, Poland will triumph. . . . Poland is a part of Europe's heart. Long live Poland!

These words resounded in Europe long afterward. Garibaldi said: "I understand the Polish question as the question of my mother country. I am glad to see the three sisters—Poland, Hungary, and Italy—working together, acting as an avant-garde bringing freedom to the people. . . ."

Polish historiography seems particularly interested in the attitude of the international working-class movement toward the question of an independent Poland. According to many historians, this is a broad complex of problems of real importance. In particular, the attitude of Karl Marx and Friedrich Engels toward the Polish question has been examined in detail by Polish historians. They say that both of them encouraged the aspirations of the Poles to regain their independence and drew them to the international working-class movement. In her recent work on the subject, Irena Koberdowa says:

> There has been argument among historians for a long time as to whether the Polish problem (i.e., the struggle for liberation) influenced the establishment of the International Workers' Association in 1864. Some denied it, while others sought to show that the origin of the first International dates to the mass meeting called in support of the January Insurrection in the Kingdom. Neither of these opinions is true. . . . In the middle of 1863, when the tension in international relations caused by the 1863 Insurrection portended an armed conflict, many Western European politicians representing the interests of the bourgeoisie began to withdraw from their pro-Polish positions and to accuse the Poles of anarchy, political ineptness, and so on. The working class, however, did not abandon its sympathy for the insurgents. On July 22, 1863, it organized an international mass meeting in London including a several-person delegation from Paris. Support for the Polish question was declared there, and it was there that the first negotiations among the workers' delegations with regard to establishing an international organization took place. The preparations took more than a year, and on September 28, 1864, during a London meeting called in order to discuss some French project, the International Workers' Association (the first International) was established. Thus, the Polish question was certainly related to the preparations

for establishing the first International, but the organization was not founded at the meeting called to manifest support for the January Insurrection. A group of Polish political émigrés joined the first International. . . .

The crucial aspect of the question is the part Russians played in the 1863 Insurrection and the influence of the insurrection upon Russian revolutionary ideas and upon the basis of Russian democracy. According to Kieniewicz,

> The alliance of the revolutionary movement in Russia and the Poles provided an opportunity for Herzen, Chernishevskii, and the members of Zemlya i Volya to criticize in public Russia's tradition of oppression of other nations. This alliance made the best sons of Russia assume a task that was beyond their abilities—an uprising simultaneous with that of the Poles in spring 1863. The task turned out to be unrealizable; the masses did not rise, there were not enough revolutionaries. Zemlya i Volya broke down and was almost immediately replaced by a new, more radical movement.

In its analysis of the facts connected with the liberation of Poland in 1918, Polish historiography often mentions the role of the national uprisings and especially the January Insurrection in that final victory. The main point of this analysis is the influence of the national uprisings upon the awakening of national consciousness in the society and their repercussions upon world opinion. They made the Polish question well-known everywhere. They called attention to the wrong done to Poland with regard to its right to independence and secured the support of wider circles of world opinion. They may also, as some Polish historians said on the occasion of the sixtieth anniversary of the liberation, have influenced the decisions of Lenin, Wilson, and others in 1918.

The January Insurrection had some significant effects. The origin of Polish positivism has been attributed to the collapse of the 1863 Insurrection. Polish positivism may pride itself on earlier beginnings (Barbara Skarga suggests that its origin should be associated with the period after the November Insurrection of 1830–31), but the belief seems general that the 1863 Insurrection was the turning point in the development of its identity and theory. In her 1971 book on positivism in Poland, Janina Kulczycka-Saloni says:

> The insurrection was unquestionably the threshold of that period. This turning point in the modern history of Poland is obvious to every researcher, and it was obvious to the people of the time as well. The contemporary novel is proof that the insurrection was a bloody turning point in the history of the nation, a disaster that changed completely the

course of the individuals' lives. . . . The problem of the 1863 Insurrection—the estimation of its course and results—becomes the dominant idea in Polish literature in the postinsurrection period and appears again and again up to the outbreak of the First World War.

Besides, the historians of literature say that the collapse of the insurrection revealed significant new objectives for the Polish people: avoiding biological extermination by helping all those who were threatened by postinsurrection repression, resisting attempts at denationalization, maintaining and even developing Polish culture, and developing the national economy to the level of modern European societies. Polish positivism is a phenomenon on a European scale, and it has been the object of detailed investigations and discussions within Polish historiography. Positivist ideas have surfaced again and again in Poland since the Second World War. Recently a new magazine appeared in Poland referring by its title to the main organ of the Polish positivists of the nineteenth century. The editors' foreword, in its first issue, reads as follows:

> We hand the first issue of *Przegląd Tygodniowy* [The Weekly Review] over to our readers referring to the traditions of the magazine which had a crucial influence upon the formation of Polish positivism. The positivists opposed the passive attitude; they believed that only an active attitude might provide a way out of the tragic situation in which Poland found herself after the collapse of the 1863 Insurrection. The fruit of their work is still alive in science, culture, education, literature, and even economics. The period of Polish positivism lasted about half a century. In view of its brief existence, the magnitude of the society's achievements, after long years of stagnation, is unbelievable. Therefore it is impossible to overestimate the importance of "organic work" and "the work from the basis." Not without reason, some historians have compared the significance of that epoch in Poland's life to that of the Renaissance.

This is an opinion that is now shared by a large group of intellectuals and certain social and political circles, though some of them do not fully accept it for class or other reasons. What is clear is that Polish positivism was a kind of reaction of the Polish elite to the situation after the collapse of the insurrection, a reaction that was fully justified and had many advantages. Skarga, in her profound work on the origin of Polish positivism, has pointed out that "positivism had a foot in both camps. On the one hand, it condemned obsolete feudal institutions and traditionalist theories. On the other, it opposed the socialists and the communists; in its program it remained within the framework of capitalist relations." The debate over Polish positivism continues, and the phenomenon itself (among the works of historians, Kieniewicz's *Dramat trzeźwych entuzjastów* [Tragedy of the Dispassionate Enthusiasts] seems fairly interesting) awaits further analysis from the point of view of its being the result of the 1863 Insurrection.

The tradition of the January Insurrection influenced in various ways the opinions and consciousness of the working-class movement developing in Poland. It turned out to be almost echoless as far as the internationalist wing represented by Ludwik Waryński is concerned. Nevertheless, it did propagate the idea, opposed by Marx, that patriotism and socialism are mutually exclusive and that the main object of socialism is the abolition not only of the capitalist system but of the state as well—that the slogan "Long live Poland!" should be replaced by "Workers of the world, unite!" This matter, which profoundly concerns Koberdowa in the recent work already mentioned, found expression in the well-known Geneva meeting in 1880. In a letter sent there, Marx, Engels, Lafarge, and Lessner stressed the fact that the *Communist Manifesto*'s program had not made the Polish question obsolete, though it looked different than it had fifty years earlier. In the past, it said, the Poles had fought bravely and died in the European democratic revolutions and national uprisings. Now, with the class struggle developing among the people, the revolutionary press should back it and the Polish working class should join in the efforts of "our Russian brothers." This could be an additional argument for repeating the slogan "Long live Poland!" In general, the active members of this movement (Waryński, Dłuski, Mendelson, Diksztajn) considered the Polish uprisings, including the January Insurrection, as associated with the gentry and antisocial. One of them, referring directly to the 1863 Insurrection, condemned the Polish propertied classes for the betrayal of national interests and for deceit in using patriotic slogans in an attempt to counteract the class struggle. Another current, the socialist one, took a different view of the national question and the results of the insurrection from the very beginning. Generally speaking, it recognized the consequences of the insurrection and the new social situation which had come into being as its result (or, rather, as the result of the agrarian reform) and argued that "the working class" or "the fourth estate" that had arisen through these changes could bring about national liberation and transform the social system. Some members of this wing (Józef Piłsudski) began to develop a new apologetics of the 1863 Insurrection, the debate over which is still going on.

It is impossible to speak briefly of the influence of the 1863 Insurrection upon Polish political ideas. Echoes of the insurrection appeared again and again in the years between the First and the Second World Wars (it was in this period that the apologetics developed), during the

Second World War (when the Polish underground movement drew upon the partisan experiences of that time), and even after the war. This matter calls for further profound and complex analysis. Some Polish researchers (e.g., A. Kijowski) say that all of the Polish uprisings were the product of "a bygone epoch," the epoch of Romanticism, and consequently produced entirely "dead ideas." At present, antiromantic tendencies are becoming more and more characteristic even of professional historians (e.g., Krasucki).

This analysis of the Polish historiography dealing with the 1863 Insurrection makes it clear that it includes both works that reject and works that glorify that phenomenon. The first to present a balanced estimation of the insurrection was Kieniewicz. Over the course of time, as our knowledge of this phenomenon has deepened, positive evaluations have come to predominate. The main positive results of the insurrection, according to Polish historiography, are the solution of the peasant problem, the internationalization of the Polish question, the strengthening of national consciousness (S. Bobrowski saw in the insurrection a means of preventing any gradual conciliatory Russification of the Poles), and the stimulation of the people in general. I shall end these reflections on the results of the 1863 Insurrection with a thought from the Polish poet and thinker C. K. Norwid: "The collapse that has living consequences is a victory."

New Editions of Sources on the Polish Insurrection of 1863

Stefan Kieniewicz

In the field of research on the nineteenth century, the January Insurrection of 1863 has been most favored, since the last war, with new editions of sources. The centenary celebrations in 1963 created an opportunity for collaboration between the Academies of Sciences of Poland and the Soviet Union. In 1957, the Institute of History in Warsaw and the Institute of Slavonic Studies in Moscow signed an agreement to publish, with the participation of the archival offices of the two countries, a critical edition of sources under the title *The January Insurrection: Materials and Documents*. Cooperation was essential to the success of the project, since a large part of the documents to be published had to come from Soviet archives and libraries. A joint commission was formed; some volumes were to be published in the U.S.S.R. and others in Poland, all under a common editorial staff.

Twenty-five years have elapsed since the beginning of our task, which is now approaching completion with the publication of the twenty-fifth volume. It seems appropriate to present this achievement to foreign specialists, who may not be aware of this new research tool for students of nineteenth-century Eastern European history.

An edition of sources is helpful to the student to the extent that it does part of his archival research for him. This goal can be attained in either of two ways: by publishing the whole or the essential part of a given archive or by collecting all the dispersed sources in a given category. Both methods have been employed in our editorial task. Most of the volumes of our series group specific types of documents, regardless of their contents. This guideline, however, proved hard to follow in the volumes devoted to regional problems and was the main difficulty with some of the volumes published in the Soviet Union, in particular.

One of the central items of the series is the pair of volumes dealing with the collaboration of Russian and Polish revolutionaries between 1856 and 1866.[1] This collection of documents covers practically the whole of the Russian underground's pronouncements on the Polish question (proclamations, news sheets, memoranda, bilateral agreements, and so on), as well as the most important depositions of imprisoned Russian and Polish revolutionaries. Long excerpts from the correspondence of the tsarist authorities concerning the suppression of Russian revolutionary movements are also included. The material has been arranged in eleven chapters: the Russian emigration and the Polish liberation movement; Russo-Polish contacts in the social movements of the early 1860s; the military organization in St. Petersburg; the Russian revolutionary committee in Poland; the Russo-Polish underground negotiations of 1862; the Russian emigration and the Polish Insurrection of 1863; Russian revolutionary democrats and the insurrection; the so-called Marienhausen affair; attempted agrarian upheavals on the Volga and in the Ural Mountains; and Russo-Polish contacts in the underground and in the Siberian deportation of 1864-66.

Two volumes have been devoted to the revolutionary events of 1861-64 in Lithuania and Belorussia and another two to those in the Ukraine.[2] In both cases, the official Russian documentation (reports of civil, military, and police authorities, depositions of prisoners) outweighs the testimony of the local Polish insurgents. The archival material, in large measure hitherto unknown to students, proved so abundant that only a selection could be included; additional documents have been taken into account only in the commentary. Each volume consists of a general section pertaining to the whole province and parts devoted to different guberniyas. Documents in languages other than Russian are accompanied by Russian translations.

Among the volumes published in Poland, the central place must be assigned to the documentation of the insurrection itself. These documents are numerous and dispersed; some were published in 1863-64 as leaflets, posters, gazettes, and so on, while a few appeared later, annexed to memoirs and diaries. The great majority have remained unpublished until now and scattered in dozens of archives and libraries in Poland and the Soviet Union, as well as in Prague, Vienna, Paris, London, New York, and Chicago. Some documents are still in private hands as family relics; many are in poor condition, having once been buried to conceal them from the police, and some are barely legible. The search for these documents has been arduous and deceptive. No sooner did one feel certain of having covered all possible areas of investigation than an important new document would turn up, calling for a supplement to the volumes already published. Many of these unpublished documents may seem trivial and of no great value, but collected they offer new opportunities for various areas of research.

The documents of the insurrectionary authorities can be found in the following volumes of our series:

1. Documents of the Central National Committee and the National Government, 1862–64:[3] the manifestos, legislative announcements, instructions, and correspondence of the insurrection's central authority and, in an appendix, the proclamations, orders, and correspondence of the insurrectionary chief of the city of Warsaw and the chief of the national police in Warsaw, as well as some documents of the central insurrectionary authorities of Lithuania and the Ukraine.

2. The correspondence of the National Government with the Polish diplomatic agent in Paris, Prince Władysław Czartoryski, first published in 1937, together with Czartoryski's reports from Paris.[4]

3. Documents of the War Department of the National Government 1863–64,[5] including its orders of the day, its regulations and instructions, and its correspondence. (This part of the National Government's documentation was detached on purpose in order to facilitate research on the conduct of warfare during the insurrection.)

4. Documents of the military commanders of the insurrection,[6] including their reports to the War Department and their correspondence with other authorities and private persons.

5. Documents of the civil administration of the insurrection in the Kingdom of Poland 1863–64.[7] (This type of documentation is unfortunately less well preserved, and we were able to collect only scanty fragments of papers emanating from local insurrectionary officials on the level of the province or district.)

6. Parallel documents of the insurrectionary authorities in Austrian Galicia,[8] including an interesting series of reports form Cracow and Lwów sent to Paris by the Galician agents of the Hôtel Lambert.

We lack a similar volume for Prussian Poland. Some documents of insurrectionary agents in Poznania have been included in the volume *Prussian Poland and the January Insurrection*,[9] which, however, is mainly composed of documents of the Prussian authorities.

The clandestine press of 1861–64 is represented by a full reprinting of fifty underground gazettes, numbering 304 issues[10]—a precious source for the history of insurrectionary propaganda. Many of these issues have been preserved as single copies only.

Another group of sources that is important but not easy to deal with is the depositions of imprisoned leaders of the insurrection. Oskar Awejde, Władysław Daniłowski, Zdzisław Janczewski, and Karol Majewski, while under investigation in the Warsaw Citadel, wrote extensive memoirs on the history of the movement and their own participation in it. The most important part of Awejde's *Zapiski* (Notes) was printed in 1866, in forty copies only, for the confidential use of the tsarist officials. Since only two copies of this very rare edition are known to exist, it was reprinted, with important annexes and ample commentaries, as the first volume of our series.[11] A shorter and earlier version of the depositions of the four prisoners named above, kept in the Jagiellonian Library in Cracow, was published outside our series.[12] Majewski's deposition is definitely the most interesting part of this volume. The major part of these depositions, however, is now kept in the Public Library in Leningrad, and the bulk of this is included in two further volumes of our series.[13]

The trial of Romuald Traugutt, the last head of the insurrection, and his collaborators ended in Warsaw in 1864 with five capital sentences. The documents of the trial, depositions of the defendants, and so on, are preserved in the Archiwum Główne Akt Dawnych in Warsaw; they too were published outside our series.[14]

It seemed fitting to give some place in our collection of sources to some material concerning the post-1863 emigration. The documentation involved is so abundant and varied that a careful selection was inevitable. Eventually we included one volume concerning the Zjednoczenie Emigracji Polskiej (Union of the Polish Emigration), a relatively large organization of the Polish left, in the years 1866–70.[15] The volume is entirely based on the Zjednoczenie papers preserved in the Polish Library in Paris.

In comparison with the insurrectionary documents, dispersed and threatened with destruction since their origin, the files of the tsarist authorities had a much better chance of being preserved in their entirety. Whereas the Warsaw archives suffered heavy losses in the course of the last war, the essential documentation concerning Russian policy versus Poland remains intact in the Soviet collections. We were able to include in our series the most important part of this documentation, namely, the correspondence of Tsar Alexander II with his viceroys in Warsaw: Prince Mikhail D. Gorchakov, General Nikolai Suchozanet, General Karl Lambert, General Alexander N. Lüders, Grand Duke Alexander N. Constantine, and Field-Marshal Fedor Berg. This exchange of telegrams and confidential letters, covering the period from January 1861 to May 1864, fills four volumes and may be considered one of the most valuable components of our series.[16] It enables us to get a privileged view of the top level of Russian politics of the time.

Two volumes of lesser importance contain the official correspondence of the autonomous authorities of the Kingdom of Poland. One of them concerns the patriotic movement of 1861 in towns outside Warsaw;[17] the other deals with the attitude of the peasants and the agrarian problem in the Radom guberniya (southwestern Poland) during the 1863 Insurrection.[18] Both editions are based on a limited number of archival units, with the aim of guaranteeing the full exploitation of a given set of evidence.

It is almost superfluous to mention that all documents are published in their entirety in the language of the original. Prefaces and tables of contents are in both Polish and Russian. Biographical data are relegated to name indexes.

It is obvious that even such a huge edition could not embrace the whole of the documentation available. In the domain of Polish documents, we were unable to include the rather numerous private correspondence, the files of the Roman Catholic church authorities, the enunciations of political parties unconnected with the National Government, and the major part of the correspondence of the insurrection's leadership with its agents abroad. With regard to the documentation of the partitioning powers, the Russian correspondence concerning the hostilities was left out of consideration. Nor was the very voluminous Austrian documentation taken into account. The political correspondence of the foreign consuls in Warsaw is a source very much appreciated by specialists of the 1863 Insurrection. A volume of French consular dispatches from Warsaw 1860–64 was published outside this series;[19] Austrian, Prussian, and British dispatches still await their turn.

Whatever its deficiencies, historians of the January Insurrection now have at their disposal a remarkable research tool in the form of so many volumes of printed sources. Needless to say, they can be used not just for the reconstruction of political and military events, but also for purposes of social and economic history. Language remains a major obstacle for foreign students; it should be accepted, however, that a thorough study of the January Insurrection is impossible without some ability to read Polish and/or Russian. The restricted volume of the edition, fewer than a thousand copies for most of the volumes discussed, is a serious disadvantage. Even in Poland and in the Soviet Union only a few public libraries are in possession of the entire series. What is more, the separate volumes lack a continuous numeration, and therefore it is difficult to be informed about the contents of the series. This is the main reason for the present communiqué, which may familiarize English-speaking specialists with a handy and not much exploited source of information on Eastern European history.

Notes

1. *Współpraca rewolucyjna polsko-rosyjska*, ed. I. S. Miller, 2 vols. (Mos-

cow, 1963), cxxii + 583, 794.

2. *Ruch rewolucyjny na Litwie i Białorusi 1861–1862* (Moscow, 1964), lxxii + 707; *Powstanie na Litwie i Białorusi 1863–1864* (Moscow, 1965), lvi + 586. (These two volumes are edited by a group of Russian, Lithuanian, Belorussian, and Polish historians.) *Ruch społecznopolityczny na Ukrainie 1856–1862*, ed. Gregory Marachov (Kiev, 1963), liv + 387; *Ruch społecznopolityczny na Ukrainie 1863–1864*, ed. G. Marachov (Kiev, 1964), l + 551.

3. *Dokumenty Komitetu Centralnego Narodowego i Rządu Narodowego 1862–1864*, ed. David Fajnhauz, S. Kieniewicz, Franciska Ramotowska, and Wiktore Śliwowska (Wrocław, 1968), lxxviii + 662.

4. *Polska działalność dyplomatyczna w 1863–1864 r.*, ed. Adam Lewak (Warsaw, 1937), xxxvii + 487. A second volume (ed. S. Kieniewicz, A. Lewak, and Henryk Wereszycki [Warsaw, 1963]) comprises the reports of Polish diplomatic agents from Vienna, Rome, London, and Berlin. Protocols of the Polish diplomatic bureau in Paris, 1860–64, as well as accounts of Czartoryski's interviews with French and British statesmen in the same period, were published by H. Wereszycki as an annex to W. Czartoryski, *Pamiętnik* (Warsaw, 1960).

5. *Dokumenty Wydziału Wojny Rządu Narodowego 1863–1864*, eds. Stanisław Chankowski and S. Kieniewicz (Wrocław, 1973), xxii + 400.

6. *Dokumenty terenowych władz wojskowych powstania styczniowego 1863–1864*, ed. S. Chankowski, S. Kieniewicz, and Leonard Ratajczyk (Wrocław, 1976), xxxii + 402.

7. *Dokumenty terenowych władz cywilnych powstania styczniowego 1862–1864*, ed. S. Kieniewicz, F. Ramotowska, and W. Śliwowska (in press).

8. *Galicja w powstaniu styczniowym*, ed. S. Kieniewicz, F. Ramotowska, and W. Śliwówska (Wrocław, 1980), xxxviii + 502.

9. *Zabór pruski w powstaniu styczniowym*, ed. Friedrich Gentzen, Zdislav Grot, and Franciszek Paprocki (Wrocław, 1968), lxxxvi + 371.

10. *Prasa tajna z lat 1861–1864*, ed. D. Fajnhauz, S. Kieniewicz, and W. Śliwowska (Wrocław, 1966), xlii + 640; pt. 2 (Wrocław, 1969), x + 555; pt. 3 (Wrocław, 1970), xx + 362.

11. *Zeznania śledcze i zapiski Oskara Awejde* (in Russian), ed. I. S. Miller (Moscow, 1961), xlviii + 663.

12. *Z. Janczewski, K. Majewski, O. Awejde, W. Daniłowski: Zeznania śledcze o powstaniu styczniowym*, ed. S. Kieniewicz (Wrocław, 1956), xxxiii + 313.

13. *Zbiór zeznań śledczych o przebiegu powstania styczniowego* (Wrocław, 1965), lx + 454; *Zarys powstania styczniowego, opracowany w Warszawskiej Komisji Śledczej* (in press). The editors for both volumes were S. Kieniewicz, Tatyana Koprejeva, F. Ramotowska, Zbigniew Stankiewicz, Yuriy Sztakelberg, and W. Śliwowska; the texts are in both Polish and Russian.)

14. *Proces Romualda Traugutta i członków Rządu Narodowego*, ed. Emanuel Halicz, 5 vols. (Warsaw, 1960), lxxxvi + 324, 345, 346, 285, 87. (The depositions are in Polish, the correspondence in Russian.)

15. *Zjednoczenie Emigracji Polskiej 1866–1870: Lewica na emigracji*, ed. Celina Bobińska (Wrocław, 1972), lviii + 398.

16. *Korespondencja namiestników Królestwa Polskiego,* January–October 1861 (Wrocław, 1964), xxxix + 374; October 1861–January 1863 (Wrocław, 1973), xxii + 400; January–August 1863 (Wrocław, 1974), xx + 412; August 1863–May 1864 (Wrocław, 1978), xxiv + 301. (The editors were Tamara Fedosova, Krzysztof Groniowski, S. Kieniewicz, Alexander Orechov, F. Ramotowska, Y. Sztakelberg, and W. Śliwowska; the correspondence is in Russian and French.)

17. *Ruch rewolucyjny 1861 roku w Królestwie Polskim: Manifestacje na prowincji,* ed. K. Groniowski, S. Kieniewicz, Klementyna Morawska, and W. Śliwowska (Wrocław, 1963), xxxviii + 282. (The correspondence is in Polish and Russian.)

18. *Chłopi i sprawa chłopska w powstaniu styczniowym: Materiały z terenu guberni radomskiej,* ed. Filomene Bortkiewicz, S. Kieniewicz, Z. Stankiewicz, and Czeslave Włodarska (Wrocław, 1962), xlvi + 307. (The correspondence is in Polish and Russian.)

19. *Raporty polityczne konsulów generalnych Francji w Warszawie 1860–1864* (in French), ed. Irene Koberdowa (Wrocław, 1965), xv + 563.

IV. Wars and Revolutionary Movements in the Balkans, 1850–70

Balkan Revolutionary Organizations in the 1860s and the Peasantry

Dimitrije Djordjević

In 1867 a secret revolutionary committee in Belgrade dispatched to its members a circular which read: "The war which resulted in the victory of the principle of national self-determination in Italy and Germany deeply moved all the nationalities living in these two empires. The gun of Königgrätz echoed from the Baltic to the Aegean as the true awakener of peoples."[1] Nothing could have been more fascinating for the nationalistic populace of the Balkans than the "promenade" of Garibaldi and his Thousand through southern Italy.[2] Indeed, it must have been a colorful spectacle when the Bulgarian revolutionary Georgi Rakovski drove in an aristocrat's carriage through the streets of Belgrade, Athens, and Bucharest, dressed in a pompous uniform and escorted by adjutants.[3] Garibaldi's hijacking of the two ships in the Genoa harbor in 1860 to transport his volunteers to Sicily inspired Hristo Botev sixteen years later to take over the *Radetzky* and force its captain to deliver his band to Bulgaria.[4]

The 1859 war for the unification of Italy, the 1859 unification of the Romanian principalities, and the 1866 Austro-Prussian War triggered a series of nationalistic upheavals in eastern and southeastern Europe. The Poles challenged Russian domination in 1863. After the bombing of Belgrade, Serbia was on the brink of war with the Ottomans. Hercegovinian and Montenegrin tribes waged war on the Turks from 1852 until 1858 and 1862, when Montenegro openly joined the belligerents. The Bulgarian national movement entered the dynamic phase that preceded the liberation of Bulgaria in the 1870s. After the setback suffered during the Crimean War, Greece resumed nationalistic activities, stimulated by the union with the Ionian Islands in 1864. In the 1866 Cretan uprising, followed by upheavals in Epirus and Thessaly, the Hellenic movement of the sixties reached its peak.[5]

The revolutionary fervor in the Balkans was the consequence of both foreign and domestic developments. Defeated in the 1848 revolution,

Hungarian and Polish émigrés, along with Italian nationalists and with the support of Sardinian and Prussian agents, forged a strategic diversion in the Balkans, the backyard of the Habsburg Monarchy, and as a result a new European map had to be drawn. Garibaldi was planning the landing of his volunteers on the shores of the Adriatic, and Count Ignatyev in Constantinople was reviving a Pan-Slavic movement badly shaken by the Crimean War. Consular agents, Slavophiles, and revolutionaries were traversing the Balkans seeking contacts with governments and with agitators among Balkan liberals and nationalists.[6]

Having missed two opportunities, in 1848 and 1853–56, Balkan nationalists were ready to grasp the new opportunity presented by the European wars of the 1860s. National romanticism was in full swing, and liberal ideas were penetrating Serbia, Romania, and Greece. National revolutionary organizations directed against the Ottoman Empire, having been restrained during and after the Crimean War, now reappeared. The Serbs were active in the northwest, the Greeks in the south, and the Bulgarians in the eastern parts of the peninsula.

I

The ideology of Balkan revolutionary organizations in the 1860s was strongly nationalistic. Conspiracy and the "imported revolution" were its methods in the domains under Ottoman rule.

Nationalism in the Balkans had acquired a political formulation as early as the 1840s in the Serbian Načertanije,[7] in the Greek Megali Idea,[8] and among the forty-eighters in Romania.[9] In the 1860s nationalism was deeply rooted in the elite of the Balkan societies of Greece, Serbia, and Romania and was prominent in the communities of the Bulgarian diaspora. In the early 1860s, after the unification, activity in Romania was largely directed toward the consolidation of domestic affairs and the stabilization of its international status. In Serbia and Greece, the revolutionary organizations that appeared in this period were mainly state-sponsored. In the absence of a Bulgarian state, Bulgarian activity developed in private circles.

The advantages of state sponsorship for the activity of national organizations are obvious. The revolutionaries enjoyed the support of state authorities and profited from (albeit limited) state financial and military resources. They could use the state's territory as a base for their activity, for the formation of bands, and as a refuge in the event of failure. However, state sponsorship had its disadvantages as well. The revolution had to adapt to the needs and interests of the state. The policies of Balkan governments were constrained by international pressures, the balance of European and Balkan powers on the Eastern

Question, and, above all, the risk of losing what they had gained. The requirements of *Realpolitik* inevitably restrained the dynamism of national revolutions. The politics of Balkan governments throughout the century confronted the same dilemma that had faced the Italian movement from 1848 until 1859: *fara da se* or *extero liberanda*. The first was questionable because of domestic weakness, the second dangerous because of the European interests involved in the Ottoman heritage.

Although the Balkan state became the promoter of national liberation and unification, national interest did not necessarily coincide with state interest. Besides the national, the state represented the interests of its own establishment, the courts, the military, and the bureaucracy. For Balkan governments, liberation of conationals meant their annexation to the state. National organizations became instruments of state policy, a kind of appendage to be used in diplomatic bargains or as means of applying pressure in foreign policy. In a letter addressed to Prince Michael in October 1861, Ilija Garašanin assigned to Serbian organizations the task of "dismantling Turkey and enlarging the frontiers of Serbia."[10] Captain Antonije Orešković, one of the main organizers of revolutionary activity, composed in 1863 a "Serbian War Plan" according to which "the uprising in Bosnia was not only to liberate the Bosnians from the Turkish yoke, but *much more than that* [my emphasis] to serve as an instrument for Serbia to accomplish her mission in the Balkans."[11] In another plan, conceived four years later, he envisaged the organization of an uprising in Bosnia but suggested that Serbia should not compromise itself during the first phase, but wait until the uprising developed. "Thus," he concluded, "Serbia will obtain an army by using more foreign [*sic*] than her own means."[12] An important task assigned to national organizations was supplying governments with intelligence on the situation in the Ottoman Balkans—the attitude of the population—and collecting data about Ottoman military strength and the deployment of army units. Garašanin instructed his agents to inspire petitions addressed by Bosnians to the Serbian government asking for unification with Serbia. He also advised them to oppose pro-Habsburg and pro-Croatian propaganda (which he identified) and to seek the support of local Muslims dissatisfied with the centralism of the Porte.[13]

In Greece, two Greek national societies could be distinguished: one in the Kingdom of Greece, the other centered in the Greek community of Constantinople and the Empire. This resulted in two different approaches to the accomplishment of Greek national goals. The role Piedmont played in Italian unification was contagious to Balkan governments. Their states had been born through wars and revolutions; the same mechanism had to be employed in their respective national unifications. Thus, Athens was to become the center for Cretans, Thessalians, Epirotes, and Macedonians. However, the Greek community in Constantinople, Thrace, and Asia Minor was too deeply involved in the social and economic structure of the Empire to espouse radical methods, which were considered not only highly unlikely to succeed but risky for the gains already achieved. The method they espoused was cultural and educational, aiming at Hellenistic self-preservation and gradual ascendance within the Empire. Essentially it meant coexistence with the authorities.[14] This dilemma in Greek national politics was reinforced by two further factors. The first originated from the limited resources of the Kingdom, which was unable to wage simultaneously battles in the north, in the Balkan hinterland, and in the south, on the islands (primarily Crete). The second resulted from the fear of the growing Pan-Slavism, especially when the Bulgarian struggle for the Exarchate challenged the Constantinopolitan Patriarchate.[15]

During the early sixties the success of the Italian Risorgimento captured the imagination of the youth of Athens. The radicals preached military action and territorial aggrandisement. The moderates advocated the postponement of military solutions until domestic economic and political development could guarantee success. The overthrow of King Otho in 1862 came from the European fear of his national radicalism and from the suspicion of domestic radicals of his readiness to follow the Megali Idea.[16] The unification with the Ionian Islands only briefly calmed the national ferment, which was fueled anew by the 1866 Cretan uprising.

Organizations promoting national revolution originated in private, nationalistic circles as well. They were expressed in various Pan-Slavic clubs (like the one in Serbia in 1861),[17] Greek *heterias* in the Ionian Islands, Athens, and Crete, and Bulgarian merchant communities in the neighboring Balkan states. Members were recruited among radical young intellectuals, professional revolutionaries, the irregular military, and desperate refugees from the Ottoman territories. Their own lives were the tokens they laid on the revolutionary gambling table. The private character of these organizations deprived them of state resources, equipment, and funds. In order to obtain these, they had to turn either to their government or to a foreign power, namely, Russia, both of which were reluctant to support private revolutionary initiatives. Most of the revolutionaries were liberals who opposed the conservative domestic policy of Balkan governments. The Serbian government was ready to subsidize the Bulgarian legion in 1862 because of the crisis over the Ottoman garrisons in Serbia, but this was more in the interest of

Serbia than of Bulgaria. While Romanian liberals had sympathy for the Bulgarian revolutionaries, Romanian governments sought to use the Bulgarian movement as a means of applying pressure on the Ottomans. The Russian Pan-Slavs were sympathetic, but official diplomacy, suspicious of revolutionaries of all kinds, favored contacts with governments. Left to themselves and facing a complex situation, the various Bulgarian national and revolutionary committees in the 1860s were confused and split over which strategy to apply: to seek freedom from Europe, from the neighboring Balkan states, from a dualistic arrangement with the Ottomans, or from a genuine revolution in Bulgaria proper. United Serbian Youth, a movement rather than an organization that originated in southern Hungary in 1866, expressed a wide range of ideas, nationalism, romanticism, liberalism, socialism, and revolutionarism among them. Nationalistic abroad, it turned political in Serbia, where the young liberals clashed with the authoritarian regime of Prince Michael.[18]

II

The need for conspiracy inevitably reduced the membership of Balkan organizations and limited the scope of their activity. The underground activity undertaken in the Ottoman territories or in the Habsburg Military Frontier, which was assigned the role of a springboard for the import of revolution into Bosnia, made impossible any profound penetration into the masses of peasantry. Activity was channeled through a network of committees which recruited agents or "apostles" and used codes and secret messages. A formal oath of allegiance to the organization was required. It usually bound the new member to secrecy, discipline, devotion to national goals, and readiness to make personal sacrifices.[19] While this conspiratorial atmosphere and risk might suit young romanticists and adventure-minded nationalists, it could scarcely appeal to peasants or the businesslike urban population. Only a few professional revolutionaries were involved; the majority were amateurs selling revolution along with the merchandise in their shops, lectures to their pupils, or services to their churches. Some were idealists, others tried to combine ideas with personal ambition.

The headquarters of organizations were located out of reach of the Ottoman authorities, in the Balkan states or, in the case of Serbia, in the Military Frontier. The Bulgarian committee operated either from Serbia or from Romania. The strategy was to import revolution into the Ottoman Balkans. Theoretically it emphasized sending in bands to mobilize the peasantry for a general uprising. A detailed plan for activity in Bosnia drawn up in Belgrade in 1867 recommended the "formation of bands out of reach of the enemy." Their high command was to stay in Serbia and wait until they had developed a successful uprising in Bosnia. The bands were to be recruited among volunteers in Serbia and among the refugees in Italy, "workers who will gladly exchange their hard daily labor for the life of a soldier."[20] A similar strategy was applied in Greece, where, during the Crimean War, Generals Grivas and Mamouris established their commands close to the Greek frontier and sent bands headed by army officers into Epirus, Thessaly, and Macedonia.[21]

The strategy of imported revolution proved to be a failure. Caratassos and Philaretos, though they had some local success, were unable to cause a general uprising in Macedonia and the Pindus area in 1854, and Leonidas Voulgaris failed to attain this goal in 1866 in Epirus and Thessaly. The bands introduced into Bulgaria by revolutionary committees shared a tragic fate. Those of Hadji Stavra in 1862, of Panayot Hitov and Filip Totio in 1867, and of Hadzi Dimitur and Stefan Karadja in 1868 failed to attract the expected support from the population and were isolated and destroyed.[22] Levski and Botev paid with their lives for similar unsuccessful attempts in 1873 and 1876 respectively.

III

The failure of Balkan nationalists to inspire a general Balkan uprising in the 1860s was primarily due to the social structure of the national organizations and their relationship to the peasantry.

The Balkan organizations of this period were made up of army officers, merchants, teachers, and intellectuals, priests, and refugees from Ottoman rule. A list of seventy-eight Serbian agents in the Military Frontier obtained by the government in 1863 may serve as an example; among them were twenty-seven merchants, twenty-four teachers, thirteen priests, two officers in the Austrian army, five state officials (mayors, postmen, clerks), two lawyers, and one woman (four were unidentified).[23] The organizer of the network was a captain in the Serbian army, Antonije Orešković, who had defected from the Military Frontier.[24] Austrian police reports mention the participation of officers and noncommissioned officers in the Frontier, priests, clerks, merchants, pharmacists, coachmen, barbers, porters, and criminals.[25] No report mentions the participation of peasants.

Planning, strategy, and leadership were assigned to the military. From the very beginning of modern Balkan statehood they assumed the messianic role of achieving national liberation. In the Balkans, military schools were established before universities.[26] Many Bulgarian nationalists had been trained in Russian army units operating on the Danube. The Balkan military introduced professionalism and elitism into the revolutionary movement. Officers inherited the haiduk or klepht tradition of popular movements but were influenced by their training and by technological progress in armament. They transformed the revolution into a military operation. Peasant upheavals, formerly spontaneous and sporadic, had to become organized, strategically elaborated, and coordinated activities in accordance with the rules of the military profession. The various plans that officers submitted for approval to the Serbian government in the 1860s give the impression of planning for a military maneuver. They project the main strategic lines of attack, the number of bands to be deployed, and the fortresses to be besieged. Some of them even include clerical expenses (*kancelarijski troškovi*). The people to be recruited on Ottoman territory were to be those with "an understanding of the military profession."[27]

In the developing Balkan societies, the military became part of the social elite and its technical intelligentsia.[28] Mainly recruited either among the offspring of leaders of previous revolutions (as in Greece) or among the families of the upper middle class, many of them were trained abroad, in aristocratic schools in St. Petersburg, in the Ecole Polytechnique, at St. Cyr, or in the Prussian Kriegsakademie. They brought home the approach to the peasant soldier as a disciplined element of the army unit. Professionally they had no understanding of the amateur peasant rebels who made up the core of revolutionary upheavals in the Balkans, and lack of sympathy was not far removed from distrust and rejection. Orešković, who had been trained in Wiener Neustadt, expressed his feelings in a letter to Garašanin in January 1863:

> The one who knows Bosnia and its population the way I do should trust me when I say that in Bosnia there is no possibility for a general uprising on the part of the Bosnians themselves. The reason is simple: because the uprising can never be organized. For such an uprising foreign elements are necessary, because the Bosnians are incapable and have no patriotism, real dedication, or will. In four hundred years of oppression the population of Bosnia has lost all its military capacity and manifests only disunity. They are not reliable . . . from there comes the saying that every Bosnian bum is sarcastically called a *voyvode*.[29]

Orešković also refused to place his hopes in the Serbian peasantry in the Military Frontier. Similar ideas were expressed by another military man, Toma Kovačević, who suggested a plan to Garašanin in 1862 and wrote: "The uprising in the regions which *we would like to conquer* [my emphasis] cannot successfully be raised by the Christians. They lack the basis, the capacity, and the means."[30] Consequently, he said, leaders would have to be recruited in Serbia or among those in Ottoman territories "sincerely devoted to the idea of unification of Bosnia with Serbia."[31]

Under the Ottomans, the church was the most important supporter of national consciousness. In the 1860s the Greek Patriarchate disposed of money and a network of clergy. Theoretically, the church was the best instrument for channeling a revolution because of the old confrontation between the Christian serf and the Muslim landlord. However, the Patriarchate was a part of the Ottoman establishment, with power and privileges acquired over centuries. Although it constantly struggled against Ottoman attempts to limit those privileges, a modus vivendi had been found based on mutual interests. National activity was directed toward cultural and educational rather than revolutionary goals. The clergy was made up of higher and lower priesthoods, with specific economic and social interests. The hierarchy was averse to any attempt at a violent overthrow of the Empire.[32] The Christians in the Balkans were in the process of polarization in terms of their national affiliations. The Bulgarian demand for the Exarchate raised the specter of Pan-Slavism. The Greek Phanariot bishops were alienated from their Serbian and Bulgarian parishioners. However, the lower priesthood, originating in and from the village, maintained close contact with the peasantry. Constant friction with Catholic authorities radicalized the Serbian clergy in the Military Frontier. The Bulgarian clergy fought for its own church, appearing among the leadership of peasant upheavals in Bosnia and Bulgaria from the 1830s until the 1860s. The priest Jovica Ilić led the 1834 uprising in Bosnia, the priest George Janković the 1841 uprising in Leskovac, and the priest Mita those in Berkovica in 1836 and 1837, to mention only the best-known.[33]

Another important factor in the Balkan national movements was the intelligentsia. In the 1860s it was largely the product of European schools and was imbued with liberal ideas absorbed during and after the 1848 revolution. This intelligentsia clashed with its predecessors, who were part of the nascent state establishment. Young liberals opposed the centralist, conservative structure of the Balkan state. They were idealistic, nationalistic, and revolutionary-minded. However, they loved their people in a romantic way, as an abstraction. When the peasants failed to respond to their idealized perception of the village, they turned on them with disdain. In this failure to establish contact with the peasantry they resembled their populist prototypes in Russia. That most of them were of middle-class origin could only add to the misunderstanding. Thomas Meininger, studying a group of 191 intellectuals of the period in Vozraždenije, found that 80 percent of them had been born in towns; 86 percent were offspring of well-to-do families and had come of age at the time of the Crimean War, while only 13 percent were of peasant origin.[34] The urban environment in which these young intellectuals had developed had influenced their philosophies. Their activity was extremely important for the formulation of national programs and the conduct of national politics in general, but for most of them direct understanding of peasants' needs did not equal their nationalistic fervor.

Besides intellectuals, modern nationalism found its main supporters in the developing middle class. However, in the Balkans of the sixties there was not one but several types of middle class. The economic development of the Ottoman Empire had given birth to a wealthy Balkan merchant class[35] with economic interests bound up with the markets of the Empire. This class was represented by Greek bankers in Constantinople, who controlled to a great extent the finances of the Empire, by the Bulgarian *chorbadzie* (wealthy non-Muslims) connected with the rich Bulgarian community in Constantinople, and by the Bosnian merchants who profited from the trade with the neighboring Habsburg Monarchy. This does not mean that these representatives of the middle class were immune to nationalism. In the sixties the Greeks of Constantinople and other urban centers initiated and subsidized educational and cultural associations (*syllogoi*) to promote Hellenism. The Bulgarian *chorbadzie* supported Bulgarian schooling, but by no means were they in favor of a revolutionary overthrow of the Ottoman Empire.[36] This idea found more support in the Balkan middle class of the diaspora and the Balkan states. This new middle class, formed in the Military Frontier, along the shores of the Danube and the Black Sea, originated from the economic traffic with Europe and was accessible to modern European ideas of nationalism. The Ottoman guild system and the general instability of the Empire hampered their economic interests and business prospects. It was this new middle class that recruited and subsidized Bulgarian activities from Romania. Greek activities in Epirus, Thessaly, and Crete were conducted from the Ionian Islands, Egypt, or Trieste. Serbian endeavors in Bosnia were channeled from the Military Frontier and southern Hungary.

However, the middle class was already polarized along specific national lines and socially and economically stratified, and its various components competed with one another. The revolutionary activity imposed by national needs and proposed by the liberal intelligentsia was a risky business. Prosperous merchants looked upon student revolutionaries with suspicion, if not disdain. "He has it in his head to become a great man, but he doesn't have money to live," said Hristo Georgiev, a Bulgarian merchant in Romania, of Karavelov, whom he hired to edit a journal.[37] Merchants involved in revolutionary activity often conducted the revolution the way they would operate their businesses. The rubric of "income" had to be balanced in their accounts with the rubric of "expenditures." We find in the Garašanin papers published by Vučković reports by merchants involved in revolutionary activity about their expenses for travel and national propaganda, accompanied by demands for more money. The leaders of national organizations were aware of this. In 1859 Garašanin instructed his agents to recruit followers among "priests, teachers (where they exist), village priors, distinguished family heads (*domaćini*) and *smaller merchants*" (my emphasis). He cautioned them not to recruit "rich merchants who lack patriotism and are ready for treason."[38]

In the Ottoman Balkans trade was concentrated in urban centers, with no retailers in the villages. Except for the Greeks, who were already entrenched in the Balkan city, the national bourgeoisie was struggling to penetrate the traditional *charshie* (market). The Slavic Balkan city, made up mainly of the Ottoman garrison and the Jewish, Armenian, Tzintzar, and Greek communities with an interpenetrating local element, was alienated from the peasant. A mutual distrust developed between the peasant consumer and the city supplier—between exploited and exploiter.

The Balkan émigrés from the territory under the Ottomans provided the best manpower for revolutionary activity. During the 1860s a wave of émigrés arrived in Serbia and Greece as a result of the colonization policy of the Porte, which had settled refugees from southern Russia in northern Bulgaria and the central Balkans after the Crimean War and moved Muslims into Bosnia after the withdrawal of Ottoman garrisons from Serbian cities.[39] The 1862 war with Montenegro and bad harvests in Bosnia contributed to the population movement. Thousands of Greeks escaped from Crete during the 1866–68 uprising. Among these Balkan refugees were former haiduks and klephts, smugglers and criminals, alongside of peasants.[40] Uprooted and desperate, they were ready to fight to return home. Some of them settled where land was available. Others joined Greek bands to operate in Thessaly and Epirus and the Yugoslav and Bulgarian legions organized in 1862 in Serbia. Some were willing to join the Sardinian army.[41] Defectors from the Military Frontier in Italy made up the Yugoslav battalion of the Hungarian legion in Italy[42] and supplied the army in Serbia with trained officers, many of whom were engaged in organizing revolutionary activity.[43]

IV

The success of nationalistic endeavors in the 1860s depended on the response of the majority of the population under Ottoman rule—the Balkan peasantry. The Balkan village lived its own life. The peasantry in Thessaly and central Bulgaria had benefited from the abolition of the timar system in the 1850s and lived in reasonably tolerable conditions. The peasantry in Bosnia and Macedonia suffered from Ottoman colonization in the 1860s.[44] The peasants living in the plains were more vulnerable to the feudal abuses of the landlords than the cattle breeders in the mountains. The bloody conflict between the local Muslim aristocracy and the central authorities in Bosnia from 1830 until 1851 affected the peasantry. The most successful upheavals in the 1850s and 1860s occurred in the tribal societies of Hercegovina, Montenegro, Epirus, and Crete. The tribe itself had attributes of a centralized, military organization, and Crete's insularity contributed to the cohesiveness of its inhabitants. In general, however, the Balkan village was socially, politically, and economically isolated and self-sufficient in its poverty. Peasant nationalism was on the level of religious and language affiliation to one's ethnic group. Those who lived closer to the newly established frontiers of their national states were more influenced by national politics. The more highly developed educational facilities of the Greeks contributed to their national awareness. For Serbs and Bulgarians, the free small peasant holding established in Serbia was attractive. Family ties and haiduk and smugglers' channels facilitated contacts across the frontier. Under the pressure of Ottoman maladministration and growing anarchy in the countryside, the peasant responded with ill-coordinated and spontaneous local outbursts. He was ready to welcome anyone who would free him from marauding bands and landlords' abuses, but he had neither the organization nor the arms to face the regular army and besiege the fortified city. The tradition of haiduk and klepht resistance was coupled with the fear of reprisals. The mighty sultan and his empire had for centuries stamped the psychology of the Balkan peasant.

Balkan revolutionary organizations failed to penetrate the Balkan village in the 1860s. The reasons were manifold: the need for conspiracy, elitism, military-professional approaches to the mechanism of peasant revolutions, the domestic instability and weakness of the Balkan states, and the constant fear of foreign European intervention. An additional factor, however, was the difference in nationalist goals between the organizers and the peasantry. For the young nationalists and romanticists, national revolution equaled political liberation and annexation of the Ottoman provinces to their respective states. This would, they thought, pave the way for the solution of social and economic problems. The revolutionary pamphlets and appeals of the time deal with nationalistic slogans without a single mention of peasants' socioeconomic needs. The peasant, however, was interested in changing the order of the day. For him liberation meant the abolition of feudal dues and state taxes, the acquisition of the land he tilled for his landlord, and the guarantee of his and his family's safety and security. Attempts made by politicians to find a compromise with the Empire for reasons of Pan-Slavic danger, dualistic Bulgarian-Ottoman combinations, and Serbian instructions to exploit Muslims in Bosnia in their opposition to central authorities were beyond peasant comprehension.

It was not only in the 1860s that Balkan nationalists failed to organize a synchronized and general Balkan uprising. This was the fate of other efforts made since the beginning of the century and later in the 1875–78 Eastern Crisis. The task proved to be impossible, and the Italian and German examples pointed to war, not revolution, as the instrument for national unification. The Balkan states were to realize their programs only half a century later. However, the revolutionary activities in the 1860s were not completely unsuccessful. They manifested the growing nationalism in the Balkans and expressed the revolutionary search for national solutions.

Notes

1. Circular from the Central Committee in Belgrade for the Unification of the South Slavs to agencies abroad, March 1867, Vojislav Vučković, *Politička akcija Srbije u južnoslovenskim pokrajinama Habsburške monarhije 1859–1874,* Srpska Akademija nauka i umetnosti, Zbornik za istoriju, jezik i književnost, vol. 27 (Belgrade, 1965), doc. 145, p. 283.

2. On the impact of Garibaldi's activity, see Ljiljana Aleksić-Pejković, *Politika Italije prema Srbiji do 1870. godine* (Belgrade: Narodna knjiga, 1979), p. 113.

3. Dimitur T. Strašimirov, "Komitetskoto desetiletie (epokha na komitetite), 1866–1876," in *Bulgaria 1000 godini (927–1927)* (Sofia, 1927), pp. 815–17.

4. Ivan Undzhiev, "Chetata na Khristo Botev: Formirane i boen pŭt," in *Aprilskoto vustanie 1876–1966* (Sofia: Institut za istoria, Bulgarska Akademia na naukite, 1966).

5. Dimitrije Djordjević and Stephen Fischer-Galati, *The Balkan Revolutionary Tradition* (New York: Columbia University Press, 1981), pp. 113–41.

6. Grgur Jakšić and Volislav Vučković, *Spoljna politika Srbije za vlade kneza Mihaila: Prvi balkanski savez* (Belgrade: Istorijski institut, 1963), pp. 94–99.

7. Paul N. Hehn, "The Origins of Modern Pan-Serbism: The 1844 Načertanije of Ilija Garašanin," *East European Quarterly* 9 (1975): 158–60.

8. T. A. Couloumbis, J. A. Petropulos, and H. J. Psomiades, *Foreign Inter-*

ference in Greek Politics: An Historical Perspective (New York: Pella, 1976), pp. 21-24.

9. Dinu C. Giurescu, *Illustrated History of the Romanian People* (Bucharest, 1981), pp. 341-66.
10. Concept of a memorandum addressed to Prince Michael, October 1861, Vučković, *Politička akcija Srbije*, doc. 44, p. 60.
11. Orešković in Belgrade, February 6, 1863, Ibid., doc. 56, p. 96.
12. Orešković's plan for operations in Bosnia, March 1867, Ibid., doc. 143, p. 263.
13. Ilija Garašanin's plan for the political activity of Serbia in Bosnia and its relations with the Croats, Belgrade, beginning of 1859, Ibid., doc. 1, pp. 1-4.
14. Evangelos Kofos, *Greece and the Eastern Crisis 1875-1878* (Thessaloníki: Institute for Balkan Studies, 1975), p. 29.
15. Couloumbis, Petropulos, and Psomiades, *Foreign Interference*, pp. 26-27.
16. Barbara Jelavich, "Russia, Bavaria, and the Greek Revolution of 1862-63," *Balkan Studies* 2 (1961): 125-50; also E. Prevelakis, *British Policy towards the Change of Dynasty in Greece 1862-1863* (Athens, 1953).
17. Milorad Ekmečić, "Pokušaji organizovanja ustanka u Bosni 1860-1862," *Godišnjak Istorijskog društva Bosne i Hercegovine* 9 (1957): 73-106; also Ljubomir Durković-Jakšić, "Prilog proučavanju propagandnog rada za oslobodjenje i ujedinjenje Jugoslovena 1860-1862," *Istorijski Zapisi* 21 (1964): 11-44, and Vojislav Vučković, "Neuspela politička akcija Matije Bana 1860-1861," *Istorijski Časopis* 9-10 (1959): 382-84.
18. Vaso Vojvodić, "Ujedinjena Omladina srpska i pripremanje ustanka na Balkanu 1871-1872," in *Ujedinjena Omladina srpska: Zbornik radova* (Novi Sad: Matica srpska, 1968), pp. 305-14, and Krumka Šarova, "Pripreme za ustanak u Bugarskoj i Ujedinjena Omladina srpska," Ibid., pp. 473-92.
19. The oath of allegiance was almost identical in organizations throughout the century. The Oath to Philiki Etaireia in 1814 reads: "I promise the homeland to be ever zealous and faithful, trying as much as is in my power to ensure its freedom, sacrificing for it if necessary all my feelings, all my beliefs, all my property in order that it regain its freedom and its former glory" (Gr. Kambourouglou, ed., *Istorikon Archeion Dionisiou Roma*, 2 vols. [Athens: Korinnes, 1901], 1: 1-3). The oath from the 1860s reads: "As the glorious rebellion which started in 1821 is not yet accomplished and the Greek provinces which still suffer under the villain yoke are not unified with the Kingdom of the Hellenes, we intend to organize a Society which has to unify all the endeavors. . . . In the name of the Holy Trinity and in the name of my Fatherland I swear to keep secret all matters which concern our Central Society without any personal benefit, having in mind only the goals for which the Society is longing" (D. Djordjević, *Tomou ton pepragmenon tou Diethnous Kritologikou Sinedriou* [Athens, 1975], p. 101).
20. Orešković's plan, Vučković, *Politička akcija Srbije*, doc. 143, pp. 264, 266, 268.
21. Driault Lheritier, *Histoire diplomatique de la Grèce*, vol. 2 (Paris, 1925),

pp. 381-402; W. Miller, *The Ottoman Empire and Its Successors* (Cambridge, 1936), pp. 220-21.
22. Dimitur Strašimirov, *Komitetskoto desetiletie*, pp. 781 ff.; *Istoria na Bulgaria* (Sofia: BAN, 1961), pp. 406-7. See also Djordje Ignjatović, "Beograd kao političko središte Bugara pre jednog stoleća," in *Oslobodjenje gradova u Srbiji od Turaka 1862-1867* (Belgrade: SANU, 1970), pp. 337-64 (esp. 347-48).
23. List of Serbian nationalists in the Military Frontier, Vučković, *Politička akcija Srbije*, doc. 57, pp. 101-3.
24. "Orešković, Antonije," in *Enciklopedija Stanoja Stanojeviča*, vol. 3 (Zagreb, 1928), p. 213.
25. Gödel-Lanoy to Minister of Foreign Affairs Mensdorf-Pouilly-Dietrichstein, 1865, transcript from the Haus- Hof- und Staatsarchiv, Vienna, Vučković, *Politička akcija Srbije*, doc. 72, pp. 125-48.
26. T. Veremis, "The Officer Corps in Greece 1912-1936," in *Byzantine and Modern Greek Studies*, vol. 2 (London, 1976), pp. 113-16; *Kratka Bulgarska enciklopedia* 1: 540; Georghe Romanescu, "The Formation of the National Army and Its Development Down to the War of Independence," in *Pages from the History of the Rumanian Army* (Bucharest, 1975), pp. 102-6; Vl. Belić, *Enciklopedija St. Stanojevića* 1: 394-95.
27. Toma Kovačević's project for an uprising against the Turks in Bosnia, Hercegovina, Old Serbia, and the Niš and Vidin Pashalick, Vučković, *Politička akcija Srbije*, doc. 47, pp. 69-80.
28. Veremis, *Officer Corps*, p. 114; also Victor Papacosma, *The Military in Greek Politics: The 1903 Coup d'Etat* (Kent State: Kent State University Press, 1977).
29. Orešković's plan of January 25, 1863, Vučković, *Politička akcija Srbije*, doc. 56, p. 97.
30. Toma Kovačević's project, Ibid., doc. 47, p. 71.
31. Orešković's plan, Ibid., doc. 143, p. 262.
32. Evangelos Kofos, "The Subject Greeks during the Eastern Crisis of 1875-1878," *Posebna izdanja Akademija nauka Bosne i Hercegovine* 30 (1977): 100.
33. D. Stranjaković, "Buna Hrišćana u Bosni 1834," in *Godišnjica Nikole Čupića* (Belgrade, 1931), vol. 40, pp. 122-69; V. Stojančević, "Narodnooslobodilački pokret u Niškom kraju 1833 i 1834/5 god.," in *Istorijski Časopis* 5 (1955): 427-35.
34. Thomas Albert Meininger, "The Formation of a Nationalist Bulgarian Intelligentsia 1835-1878," 2 pts. (Ph.D. diss.), pt. 1, pp. 122-25.
35. See N. Todorof, "La genèse du capitalisme dans les provinces bulgares de l'empire Ottoman au cours de la première moitié du XIX siècle," *Études balkaniques*, 1960, pp. 221-51.
36. See Kofos, "Eastern Crisis," pp. 31-33.
37. Meininger, "Formation," p. 382. To this Karavelov answered: "Let Mr. Hristo know that there are people in the world for whom ideals are worth a million times more than money . . . and even than life itself."

38. Garašanin's plan, Belgrade, beginning of 1859, Vučković, *Politička akcija Srbije*, doc. 1, p. 2.
39. Vaso Čubriković, "Politički uzroci seoba na Balkanu od 1860–1880 godine," *Glasnik Geografskog društva* 16 (1930): 26–48.
40. D. Djordjević, "Prilog proučavanju migracija iz Habsburške monarhije u Srbiju 60-tih godina XIX veka," in *Oslobodjenje gradova u Srbiji od Turaka 1862–1875* (Belgrade: SANU, 1970), pp. 313–35.
41. Astengo to Cavour, Belgrade, May 1, 1859, transcript from Archivio di Stato di Torino, Belgrade 1849–1859, Vučković, *Politička akcija Srbije,* doc. 13, p. 25.
42. The commander of the battalion was Major Vranješević, a defector from the Military Frontier (papers of Jovan Belimarković).
43. Ivan Pavlović, "Vojna granica i srpska vojska," *Glasnik Istorijskog društva u Novom Sadu* 9 (1936): 217–25.
44. See Vladimir Stojančević, *Južnoslovenski narodi u Osmanskom carstvu od Jedrenskog mira 1829 do Pariskog Kongresa 1856* (Belgrade, 1971).

The Bulgarian National Liberation Movement and the Wars in Europe in the Fifties and Sixties of the Nineteenth Century

Simeon Damianov

The third quarter of the nineteenth century was a turning point in the historical development of Bulgarian society. More than at any other time, its problems then were interpreted from a purely utilitarian standpoint, i.e., as they related to the practical tasks of the liberation struggle of the Bulgarian people. These tasks were many and differed in character, but in the final analysis they were subordinated to one fundamental goal which the epoch itself set before the Bulgarians: doing away with Ottoman rule. To this great nationwide imperative were subjected even the most peaceful forms of their legal struggle within the framework of the Ottoman Empire: their efforts to achieve cultural autonomy, to establish schools in which instruction would be given in the native language, to throw off the spiritual domination of the Patriarchate of Constantinople and the Greek clergy and restore the independence of the Bulgarian national church, and so on. These demands were but stages in or prerequisites to the effort to reject the political authority of the Sublime Porte and restore the state independence of Bulgaria, conquered by the Ottoman Turks at the end of the fourteenth century.

I

The period in which the revolutionary program of the Bulgarians crystallized coincided with the stormy upsurge of the concept of the nation. The revolution of 1848, which proclaimed the right of peoples to self-determination and political independence, was for them only an additional stimulus, for there was already an autonomous Serbian Principality at the beginning of the nineteenth century and the independent Kingdom of Greece had emerged in the twenties. The existence of these new states in the immediate proximity of the Bulgarians more than anything else accelerated their political evolution. Having taken shape as a nation in the modern sense of this concept as early as the eighteenth century, the Bulgarians took an active part in the liberation struggles of other Balkan peoples in the hope that after these had won independence they would help the Bulgarians escape from Ottoman domination.[1] The conviction of the need for an armed struggle, for the use of force against the foreign oppressor, had been deeply embedded in the Bulgarian national psychology long before the expression of the ideas of "Young Europe." The Bulgarians were convinced that they were conducting a just liberation struggle imposed on them by a conqueror who was trying to assimilate them at any cost.

Students of European Turkey in the thirties and forties of the nineteenth century, and the more recent epoch as well, are trying to press on us the notion of the Bulgarians as peaceful, obedient rayas—fully engrossed in their concern for material prosperity, lacking any political aspirations, and utterly indifferent to domination and government by another provided he did not rob them of the fruits of their labor and respected their faith.[2] This false notion of the Bulgarians, biased and often dictated by Turcophile considerations, is incapable of explaining their mass revolutionary manifestations over the long period of Ottoman rule, their participation in the Russo-Turkish wars in independent volunteer units incorporated into the Russian army,[3] and their numerous rebel movements—for instance, Velcho's conspiracy in 1835, the uprising in the Niš sanjak in 1841, the protracted struggle in the Vidin region in 1850, Dimitraki's revolt in the Kula area, Captain Nikola's plot in Turnovo in 1856, and so forth.[4]

Actually, the Bulgarians had never given up the idea of war as a way of achieving their national aspirations. The powerful surge of liberation and unification movements that shook all the multinational empires after the Crimean War only convinced them the more that uncompromising armed struggle was the only road to political independence. Naturally, in a society that was not homogeneous in its class composition, the views of the different social groups were characterized by nuances, differences in approach, even internal struggles over the effectiveness of one or another action that might be undertaken in connection with the major events of the time.

In order to support this claim with arguments, I will examine the attitudes of the most outstanding representatives of the Bulgarian national liberation movement toward the wars for the unification of Italy and Germany, the liberation struggle in Poland, and, above all, the manifestations of rebellion of the South Slavs. Once these are clear, it will not be difficult to understand how the Bulgarian leaders gave new meaning to the historical experience of the liberation struggles of other peoples and of the wars in Europe with regard to the liberation cause of the Bulgarian people and how they modified their foreign policy program in view of these events.

It was with the greatest attention that Georgi Rakovski, the universally recognized leader of the Bulgarian national revolution in the fifties and sixties of the nineteenth century, studied all the events in Europe that could have a negative effect on the Ottoman Empire, undermine its military might, and facilitate the liberation struggle of the Bulgarians. He was aware that Russia, irrespective of its defeat in the Crimean War, remained the only power that had declared itself against the status quo in the Balkans and therefore was the natural ally of the national liberation movement of the Bulgarians.[5] For the same reason, Rakovski showed marked sympathy for the heroic efforts of the Italian people for liberation and national unification. The liquidation of the possessions of the Habsburgs in Italy led to the weakening of one of the mainstays of despotism, violence, and national oppression in Europe—a monarchy that supported the integrity of the Ottoman Empire and was the natural enemy of the liberation struggles of the Central European and Balkan peoples. Austria's defeat in the war of 1859, in which Napoleon III was on the side of the Italians, was therefore regarded by Rakovski as the prologue to events of great significance for the Balkans.[6]

In connection with the help that France rendered to the Kingdom of Sardinia, Rakovski for a time showed marked confidence in the policy of Napoleon III. Unlike the other European states, which defended the "old monarchist law," France seemed to him a power that supported the principle of "national sovereignty."[7] Thus Roncière le Noury, the commander of the French naval squadron in the eastern Mediterranean, wrote to the minister of defense in Paris: "La guerre d'Italie a fait germer dans les esprits des idées nouvelles et un sentiment de nationalité, qui met tout son espoir dans l'Empereur."[8] At the same time, Rakovski was alarmed by the rapprochement between Austria and the Ottoman Empire in the name of the maintenance of the status quo—in particular, by the fact that the Austrian troops helped the Turkish armed forces in their campaign against the insurgents in Hercegovina.[9] It was with the greater satisfaction, then, that he looked upon Austria's new defeat in its war with Prussia in 1866. After Königgrätz a strong ally of the Ottoman Empire left the stage, although temporarily, and that was to the advantage of the Bulgarian people.

Rakovski declared himself in favor of all peoples who were trying alone to settle their destinies. He repeatedly dealt with the liberation struggle of the Polish people in his newspaper *Dunavski lebed* (Danube Swan), pointing out that the progressive Russian public also sympathized with that struggle.[10] At the same time he declared himself against the attempts of some Polish émigré circles to draw Bulgarians into the Catholic Union. The Bulgarian revolutionary warned the Polish émigrés who wanted to split the Bulgarian people religiously and politically that their activity might have bad consequences for them by depriving them of allies. "These brothers of our own flesh and blood have not been done any harm by the Bulgarians, but, on the contrary, they have always been received by them with an open heart and fraternal love," Rakovski wrote, pointing out that the Bulgarian people knew how to distinguish between nationality and faith and to defend their own political interests.[11] Rakovski's political sympathies were obviously with the left current among the Polish emigration, which was trying to win the country's freedom by armed uprising, and not with the right, aristocratic wing, which relied chiefly on the diplomatic and military action of the Great Powers, including the Ottoman Empire, and condemned the Bulgarians to remain under the sultan's rule.[12]

Even events far from the old continent were of interest to Rakovski when he felt that their consequences could affect regions nearer Bulgaria. Such was, for instance, the case with the conflict between Britain and the United States of America in connection with a British ship intercepted off the American coast. For Rakovski, the turn the dispute would take was important because, once engaged far away in the West, Britain could not pursue an active policy in the Near East, and this meant that in the event of complications in the Ottoman Empire the British government would not be in a position to defend the status quo in Turkey's interest.[13]

Throughout his turbulent life, Rakovski championed the establishment of a lasting alliance of the Balkan peoples on an anti-Turkish basis. He enjoyed the confidence of Prince Michael Obrenović in Serbia, Prince Cuza in Romania, and the Greek ruling circles. In Belgrade and Bucharest he tried to set up armed Bulgarian units (the First and Second Legions) which in a suitable international situation were to enter Bulgaria and, in combination with a popular uprising, achieve the country's liberation. In the course of his negotiations with Serbian, Greek, and Romanian leaders he became convinced that they were imbued with greater-state ambitions, laid claims to Bulgarian territories, and were trying to bend the Bulgarian liberation movement to their own political ends. Although a sincere adherent of the idea of a Balkan federation, Rakovski was compelled to give up the plans for joint actions of the Bulgarians with the Balkan governments of the time.[14]

In 1866–67, when the political crisis in Europe and the Balkans became more acute as a result of Austria's defeat and the outbreak of the uprising in Crete and when France and Russia undertook their demarche for reforms in the Ottoman Empire, Rakovski directed his attention exclusively to rallying the forces of the Bulgarian revolutionary emigration in Romania with a view to sending armed units into the Bulgarian lands. He drafted an "Interim Law for the People's Forest Armed Detachments for the Year 1867" to regulate the armed units and set up a special revolutionary organization ("Supreme People's Secret Civil Command") to prepare for the sending of the armed units of Panayot Hitov and Filip Totio to Bulgaria. Until the end of his life (October 9, 1867), Rakovski remained a partisan of the idea of Bulgaria's liberation by the incursion of armed groups (*cheti*) established in advance. He was convinced that, sent from abroad and in sufficient numbers, they could raise the people and lead them in a decisive fight against the enslaver.[15]

For a quarter of a century Rakovski headed the radical revolutionary current of the Bulgarian liberation struggle, the current of the so-called Young. The followers of his revolutionary ideology and tactics were chiefly poor exiles (*hushove*), i.e., political émigrés, deprived of property, living in Romania, Serbia, and Russia. At the same time, the liberal-bourgeois circles of the Bulgarian emigration set up another organization in Bucharest: the Secret Central Bulgarian Committee, headed by Ivan Kassabov, a former associate of Rakovski. This organization claimed to take a more realistic position on the national question than Rakovski's Supreme Command. Its leaders were deeply impressed by the defeat of the Habsburg Monarchy at Königgrätz in 1866 and the tendency in Vienna toward a compromise solution to the Hungarian national question along the lines of dualism. The idea of dualism seized the minds of the members of the Secret Central Committee to such an extent that they adopted it as a possible model for solving the Bulgarian national question within the framework of the Ottoman Empire.

It was not accidental that the Memorandum of the Secret Central Committee of 1867, addressed to the sultan and the European governments, caused such a stir in the press and in the chancelleries. Its authors argued that an arrangement like the dualism in Austria-Hungary, which concentrated the supreme power in the hands of a common head of state but granted a certain independence in internal life to the two basic national components, Austrians and Hungarians, was the most suitable answer to the Bulgarian national question. They suggested that Turks and Bulgarians form a Turco-Bulgarian monarchy within which an autonomous Bulgarian constitutional state, with its own parliament, courts of justice, and army commanded by Bulgarian officers, as well as Bulgarian administration, would be established. It was envisaged that this Turco-Bulgarian state would be headed by the sultan, who would be invited to be crowned in the ancient Bulgarian capital of Turnovo as tsar of the Bulgarians.[16] On account of its patent illusoriness, the idea of a Turco-Bulgarian state was left hanging; it was not accepted by anyone, and the Secret Central Committee ingloriously disappeared from the political scene.

The popularity, nevertheless, after Königgrätz of the idea of dualism may be judged by the fact that it was embodied also in the program of the third center of the Bulgarian emigration—the Benevolent Society or the so-called Committee of the Old, headed by Hristo Georgiev, which expressed the interests of the conservative grande bourgeoisie. In the political activity of the Benevolent Society the idea of dualism crystallized in the form of a Serbo-Bulgarian federative state. This organization in everything followed the suggestions of Russian diplomacy. "I foresaw," the Russian ambassador to Constantinople Count Ignatyev recalled later, "that the war in 1866 between Austria and Prussia would give such a strong impetus to the question of the nationalities that use of it would be made by those of the European governments which showed the greatest initiative, persistence, and felt the least embarrassed in the choice of means."[17] Until the middle of the sixties, Russia was engrossed in domestic transformations and opposed to any complications of the Eastern Question which might restore the Crimean coalition of the Western states against it. Immediately after 1856 it therefore chose to "freeze" the Balkan Question, and this for a long time condemned the Benevolent Society to political passivity. It took the positions of "evolutionism" and enlightenment.[18]

After Königgrätz, however, the situation seemed very favorable for a fresh advance by Russian diplomacy in the Balkans. In St. Petersburg they were in haste to be rehabilitated after their defeat in 1856. Count Ignatyev believed then that a large Slavic state capable of opposing the southward expansion of Austria-Hungary could be formed on the Balkan Peninsula. While again raising the question of the autonomy of the Bulgarians, the Russian government favored a Bulgarian-Serbian union and a South Slavic federation ("Serbo-Bulgaria" or "South Slavic Kingdom") under the scepter of Prince Michael Obrenović. The Benevolent Society in Bucharest drew up a "Program for Political Relations of the Serbo-Bulgarians (Bulgaro-Serbs) or for Their Cordial Relationship." Serbian Premier Garašanin accepted the "Program," pledging himself in this way to contribute to Bulgaria's liberation. At the same time, however, he was involved in secret negotiations with the Greek government for the division of certain Bulgarian lands. Count Ignatyev instructed the Russian consul-general in Belgrade to draw the attention of the Serbian government to the inadmissibility of these negotiations: "The bear has not been killed yet, and they have divided up its skin," he wrote.[19] The attempt to set up a federative Bulgarian-Serbian state failed, and the Benevolent Society again found itself in a political impasse.

Of greatest interest for the researcher is the attitude of the "Young" who succeeded Rakovski toward the idea of a federation after Königgrätz. From 1868 until his tragic death in February 1873, Vassil Levski was the undisputed leader of the "Young," although in the émigré circles in Romania the influence of Lyuben Karavelov was strong. Levski was the founder of the Internal Revolutionary Organization, which set itself the goal of arming and preparing the people for a general uprising, avoiding dependence on the policy of any external power. The experience to that time of Rakovski, the Secret Central Committee, and the Benevolent Society showed that only when the people were prepared in advance for armed struggle could the national revolution count on equitable partnership and cooperation from the external powers, Serbia in particular. Hristo Botev, who raised the national revolutionary ideology to its greatest heights, also adhered to this thesis.

It follows from this that the ideologists and founders of the Bulgarian national revolutionary organization, in stressing the necessity for preparing a popular uprising inside the country, were far from rejecting the possibility of external armed assistance—of an alliance of the internal forces of the revolution with anti-Ottoman external forces. The Bulgarian revolutionaries were realistic politicians, not adventurers. They were well aware that the Bulgarian people, deprived of arms, could not with their bare hands crush the centuries-old Ottoman Empire, which beyond everything else enjoyed the political support of most of the European states. Because at that time Russia was the only Great Power to pursue an unambiguous anti-Turkish policy, the hopes of the Bulgarian revolutionaries usually involved its military assistance.[20]

This became clear in 1870 when the Franco-Prussian War broke out. Leaving aside the lessons the Bulgarian revolutionaries drew from the Paris Commune, which had to do with combining the national liberation struggle with the struggle for social reconstruction,[21] I will dwell only on the effect of the Franco-Prussian War on the evaluations made by the Bulgarian revolutionaries of the prospects of their cause.

Some of the Bulgarian émigrés were deeply disturbed by France's defeat in the war. They had been convinced that, having helped Italy to realize its national unification and having in 1867 proposed a detailed project for reforms to the Sublime Porte, France, which had hitherto been regarded as the most influential power on the continent, could intercede for Bulgarian national interests as well. For this reason the news of France's collapse in the summer of 1870 had a shattering effect on them. "The Western war is weaving a shroud for my unfortunate motherland" were the dying words of the great revolutionary Ivan Kulin, one of the closest associates of Rakovski and Karavelov.[22]

However strange it may seem, the attitude of the most radical representatives of the emigration (Levski, Karavelov, and Botev) toward the defeat of France was quite different. They regarded the empire of Napoleon III as one of the most reactionary powers in Europe, the bulwark of the rule of the sultan, and its projects for reforms as only bluff, throwing dust in the eyes of the world public. Its collapse gave Russia an opportunity to declare the humiliating clauses of the Paris Peace Treaty of 1856 null and void. The decision of the Russian government, therefore, to reject these clauses unilaterally and to proceed toward the restoration of its naval fleet in the Black Sea was met with satisfaction by the Bulgarian patriots. A strong Russia with a more confident and independent foreign policy made it possible for the Bulgarians to hope that the end of the sultan's domination in European Turkey would come soon. If the "Old" in Bucharest undertook diplomatic action with a view to placing the Bulgarian Question before the London Conference of March 1871, convened for international-law recognition of Russia's sovereignty in the Black Sea, the "Young" were looking forward to a marked activation of Russia's policy in the Balkans and in the event of an uprising relied on Russia's military intervention in aid of the Bulgarians.

Levski clearly spoke in these terms. Irrespective of his republican ideology and his negative attitude toward the Russian tsar, who "persecutes and punishes with death the Russian republicans," the Bulgarian revolutionary declared in a most realistic way: "We do not refuse help even from the devil."[23] Karavelov, who also hated all despots, thought that the federation of South Slavs of which he dreamed should enter into a broader Slavic alliance relying on Russia.[24] "Russia's duty," he wrote, "is not to support the rotten empires and to think about their happiness, but to be Slav and to fight for the interests of the Slav tribes against a foreign element."[25] The socialist Botev was still more explicit in this respect: "Whatever anyone may say, I will say that the Christian nationalities on the Balkan Peninsula will find sympathy only in Russia."[26]

The Bulgarian national revolution, which reached its peak during the April Uprising in 1876, fully confirmed these forecasts of its leaders. When in the summer of 1875 the uprising in Hercegovina and Bosnia broke out, Botev, who at that time headed the Bulgarian revolutionary party, wrote in the newspaper *Zname* (Banner):

What South Slav heart will not beat faster at this signal of the revolution? What Bulgarian, what patriot will not start thinking and asking himself: 'What must we do?' . . . We must not wait. . . . We must rise and put an end to our loathsome and inhuman sufferings, we must square our accounts with the tyrants, help Hercegovina and ourselves, and show diplomacy that we are not animals, that we are not cattle, but a people capable of living and developing.[27]

And further: "Now is the time to call on the people to revolt and, by splitting the forces of the common enemy, to help ourselves and our brothers!"[28]

The people's uprising in Bulgaria in 1876 was the result of the great political crisis which had seized the Ottoman Empire. It was prepared by Levski's Internal Revolutionary Organization, but it brought about the intervention of outside forces as well. Russian military power played the decisive role both in the rescue of Serbia from certain collapse in 1876 and in Bulgaria's liberation in 1877–78. It was for this reason that in the days of the defeat of the uprising the revolutionary leader Georgi Benkovski, watching from the mountain peaks the burning villages in Trakia and the Sredna Gora area, declared with profound confidence and foresight, "I stuck a knife into the back of the tyrant; it is Russia's town now!"[29] The main strategic objective of the Bulgarian national revolution was realized with Russia's direct military help.

II

Thus, irrespective of their material or professional positions, the different strata of the Bulgarian society saw armed violence as the only possible means of political emancipation of the Bulgarian people. Even the Bulgarian Orthodox church was no exception in this respect. Although some of the bishops called on their flocks to respect the sultan's authority because, like any authority, it was "God-given," the Christian dogma that a war of liberation should be condemned from a moral viewpoint simply because it was connected with the use of force was alien to the clergy as a whole. Moreover, many representatives of the lower clergy, more strongly linked to the people, openly shared the revolutionary ideology and took part in the rebel struggle. All the Bulgarians, with the exception of a thin stratum of the grande bourgeoisie that was Turcophile and played a comprador role, subordinated their moral categories and religious ethics to their supreme patriotic duty to the nation.[30]

This explains why the wars fought for the unification of Italy and Germany in the fifties and sixties of the nineteenth century found a strong response among the leading figures of the Bulgarian national revolution and even in those circles of the patriotic bourgeoisie that did not share the revolutionary ideology. Garibaldi's exploits were an inspiring example for the Bulgarian patriots. The defeat of Austria in the wars in 1859 and 1866 and of France in 1870 put out of action two Great Powers which supported the Ottoman Empire. Russia's position in the Balkans was strengthened, and this was no doubt advantageous for the Bulgarians. The wars in Europe created more favorable prospects for the Bulgarian national revolution, and it was precisely from this standpoint that the Bulgarian public assessed them.

Notes

1. N. Todorov, *Filiki Etheriia i bŭlgarite* (Sofia: BAN, 1965); St. Doinov, *Bŭlgarskoto nationalnoosvoboditelno dvizhenie 1800–1812* (Sofia: BAN, 1979).
2. The first to formulate such views on the Bulgarians was the French diplomat Boislecomte, who passed through the Bulgarian lands in 1834 (Archives du Ministère des Affaires Etrangères, Paris, Mémoires et documents, Turquie, vol. 22, f. 28–42, pp. 287–97). Similar views were expressed by Ami Boué, *Turquie d'Europe*, vol. 3 (Paris, 1840), p. 99; Cyprien Robert, *Les Slaves de Turquie*, vol. 2 (1844), p. 237; Dr. Barrachin, "Maintien de l'équilibre européen, résultant de la régénération de l'Empire ottoman, assurée par le concours des Grandes puissances," *Revue orientale* (Paris, 1841), pp. 5–6.
3. In 1806–12 within the Russian army was formed the so-called Bulgarian National Army. In 1828–29, several thousand Bulgarians were again incorporated into the Russian army, and the uprising of the Bulgarian population in the area of Burgas and the Strandja Mountains facilitated the campaign of General Dibich and the capture of Adrianople. The most numerous was the participation of Bulgarians in the Russian army during the Crimean War (1853–56). The patriotic organization of the Bulgarian emigration in Romania, the Benevolent Society, directed by the wealthy banker and merchant Hristo Georgiev and Dr. Ivan Seliminski, formed volunteer units which took part in the Danubian campaign of the Russian army and then in the battles at Sebastopol. For details see V. D. Konobeev, *Bŭlgarskoto natsionalnoosvoboditelno dvizhenie: Ideologiia, programa, razvitie* (Sofia: Nauka i izkustvo, 1972), pp. 79–179, 180–271, 272–345; S. Damianov, "Russiia i bŭlgarskiiat vŭpros prez Vŭzrazhdaneto," in *Bŭlgariia i narodite na Sŭvetskiiat sŭuz prez vekovete*, Letopis na druzhbata, vol. 8 (Sofia: OF, 1981), pp. 453–88.
4. *Istoriia na Bŭlgariia*, vol. 1 (Sofiia: BAN, 1961), pp. 343–64.
5. Chr. Christov, "Le mouvement national de libération en Bulgarie et la politique de la Russie et des pays occidentaux," in *Etudes historiques*, vol. 1 (Sofia, BAN, 1960), pp. 285–315.
6. *Dunavski lebed*, no. 2, September 22, 1860. For the attitude of Rakovski

and the Bulgarians in general toward the liberation struggle of the Italian people, see D. Kossev, "L'unità d'Italia e il movimento di rivoluzione nazionale in Bulgaria nalla seconda matà del XIX secolo," in *Problemi dell'unità d'Italia: Atti del II convegno di Studi Gramasciani (Roma, 1960)* (Rome, 1962), pp. 201-2.
7. D. Kossev, "G. S. Rakovski za vŭshnata politika na chuzhdestrannite dŭrzhavi i na bŭlgarskoto natsionalnoosvoboditelno dvizhenie," *Spisanie na BAN*, 1967, no. 3-4, p. 66.
8. Archives du Ministère des Affaires Etrangères, Paris, Turquie, vol. 354, f. 240-41.
9. *Arhiv na G. S. Rakovski*, vol. 1 (Sofia: BAN, 1952), pp. 249-54. Cf. V. N. Kondrat'eva, "Sgovor Avstrii i Turtsii s tsel'u podavleniia natsional'noosvoboditel'nogo dvizheniia na Balkanah v 60-e godi XIX veka (Po konsulskim doneseniiam)," *Kratkie soobshteniia Instituta slavianovedeniia* 36 (1963): 44-60.
10. L. Widerszal, *Bulgarski ruch narodowy 1856-1872* (Warsaw, 1937), pp. 207-8; Ogn. Mazhdrakova-Chavdarova, "Natsionalnoosvoboditelnoto i revolutsionno dvizhenie v Evropa prez pogleda na G. S. Rakovski spored 'Dunavski lebed' (1860-1861)," *Istoricheski pregled*, 1970, no. 3, pp. 72-88; Kr. Šarova, "L'union des émigrés polonais (ZEP) et les mouvements de libération dans les Balkans," *Etudes balkaniques*, 1973, no. 4, pp. 50-71.
11. *Dunavski lebed*, no. 13, December 6, 1860.
12. V. Traikov, *Georgi Stoikov Rakovski: Biografiia* (Sofia: BAN, 1974), p. 215.
13. *Dunavski lebed*, no. 61, December 1, 1861.
14. D. Djordjević, "Projects for the Federation of South-East Europe in the 1860s and 1870s," *Balcanica* 1 (1970): 136-37; Traikov, *Rakovski*, pp. 226-27.
15. Traikov, *Rakovski*, pp. 332-33.
16. Al. Burmov, "Taen tsentralen bŭlgarski komitet," *Istoricheski pregled*, 1960, no. 2, pp. 41-42; no. 3, pp. 67-68.
17. "Zapiski grafa N. P. Ignat'eva," *Istoricheski vestnik*, SPb (1914): 59-60.
18. M. Dimitrov, "Komitetŭt na 'starite': 'Dobrodetelna druzhina," in *Bŭlgariia 1000 godini (927-1927)* (Sofia: BAN, 1930), pp. 761-62.
19. Gr. Jakšić and V. Vučković, *Spoljna politika Srbije za vlade kneza Mihaila: Prvi balkanski savez* (Belgrade, 1963), p. 492.
20. S. Damianov, "The Great Powers and the Eastern Crisis of 1875-76," *Southeastern Europe* 4 (1977): 200-216.
21. In the light of the experience of the Paris Commune, Levski wrote: "It is high time for an effort to win what we have sought and the brother Frenchmen are seeking, i.e., Young France, Young Russia, etc. At what cost and what losses? . . . Now is the time to prevent this evil. [Why should we] wage a second struggle? A brother to kill his brother, a son his father or a father his son? . . . Now it is easy and we can . . ." (Vassil Levski, *Dokumentalno nasledstvo* [Sofia: Nauka i izkustvo, 1973], p. 67). Still more determined in his inferences was Botev, who sent greetings by telegram to the Paris Commune and wrote the well-known "Symbol-credo of the Bulgarian Commune." In Botev's opinion, only the communist organization of society would save "all the peoples from

centuries-long sufferings and tortures through brotherly labor, liberty, and equality" (Hr. Botev, *Sŭbrani sŭchineniia*, vol. 2 [Sofia: Bŭlgarski pisatel, 1976], p. 5).
22. P. Kuzmanov, *Knez Ivan Kulin* (Sofia: Voenno, 1971), p. 310.
23. D. T. Strašimirov, *Vassil Levski*, vol. 1 (Sofia, 1929), pp. 26–27.
24. *Nezavissimost*, no. 44, July 21, 1873.
25. Ibid., no. 45, July 28, 1873.
26. Botev, *Sŭbrani sŭchineniia*, p. 340.
27. Ibid., pp. 133, 135.
28. Ibid., p. 167.
29. Z. Stoianov, *Zapiski po bŭlgarskite vŭstaniia* (Sofia: Bŭlgarski pisatel, 1962), p. 434.
30. S. Damianov, "Pravoslavnata tsŭrkva i bŭlgarskata natsionalna revolutsiia," in *Pravoslavieto v Bŭlgaria* (Sofia: BAN, 1974), pp. 153–91.

Serbia and the Wars of 1859 and 1866

Dragan R. Živojinović

The Italian wars of liberation and unification of 1859 and 1866 attracted wide attention and stirred substantial excitement in Serbia and among the Serbs of Austria and the Ottoman Empire. Furthermore, the major protagonists of these wars—the Kingdom of Sardinia, later the Kingdom of Italy, France, and Prussia—encouraged this unrest in Austria's backyard in order to relieve the pressure on themselves. The Italians especially endeavored to fan the spark of rebellion in Romania, Hungary, Bosnia and Hercegovina, Montenegro, and Bulgaria and to induce Serbia to declare war on Austria. The Danubian region and the Balkans became a theater of political machinations, intrigues, and plots. Agents and diplomats moved back and forth between Turin, Paris, and Berlin, on the one hand, and Belgrade, Cetinje, Bucharest, Galați, and Athens, on the other. They carried with them various plans and proposals, offering financial or, more frequently, only verbal support. In the aftermath of the Congress of Paris of 1856, this agitation threatened to disrupt the newly established balance among the Great Powers and open up the Eastern Question—something that virtually none of the Great Powers wanted.

Confronted with the approaching war between Austria and Sardinia, the Great Powers assumed different attitudes, thus revealing disagreements and opposing aims. France, under Napoleon III, seemed to be supporting Sardinia's ambitions even if that were to require a war with Austria. Russia as early as 1859 proposed a European congress to resolve the conflict, but Austria rejected this proposal. Britain, opposed to a reopening of the Eastern Question, supported Austria. Thus, the signatories of the Treaty of Paris, guarantors of Serbian autonomy, took opposite positions.

The debate among the powers encouraged the numerous peoples of Central Europe and the Balkans to hope for freedom and national unification. A war offered an opportunity to defeat Austria and subsequently bring freedom to the Italians, the South Slavs, and the Hungarians. An agreement was reached between Napoleon III and Prince

Camillo Cavour, the Sardinian prime minister, at a conference in Plombières in July 1858. Both statesmen were conscious of Austrian military power. Napoleon III warned Cavour that France and Sardinia would have to raise and deploy large armies. Cavour agreed, remembering the military campaigns of 1848-49 on the peninsula.

Anxious to ease the Austrian pressure on the Sardinian front, Cavour decided to work with Hungarian political émigrés to organize a rebellion in Hungary and began to prepare the ground for cooperation between the Hungarians, Slavs, and Romanians.[1] In January 1859, he submitted his plan to Napoleon III for his approval. The plan included agitation in Hungary; the dispatch of agents to Serbia and the Danubian Principalities to induce their rulers to help persuade their conationals living in Austria to cooperate, in the approaching war, with the Hungarians; transportation of arms and other equipment from Galaţi, Brăila, and Belgrade to Hungary, there to be used to equip an armed force of between twenty and thirty thousand men; and military operations along the Adriatic coast designed to divert the Austrian troops from Lombardy.[2] The plan was delivered to Napoleon III by György Klapka, a Hungarian general living in exile. In a covering letter, Cavour asked for French financial support for the realization of his plan. He argued that if it proved successful, it would be the end of Austria, which could not last long without its Italian, Hungarian, and Slavic provinces. Napoleon III approved the plan.

Cavour next decided to dispatch consuls to Belgrade and Bucharest. This idea came from Lajos Kossuth, the leader of the Hungarian émigrés, who believed that the Serbs would support this initiative wholeheartedly. The consul in Belgrade was to offer help to the Hungarians, follow Serbian policies, and exert an influence on public opinion. The election of Prince Cuza as ruler of Wallachia and Moldavia seemed to favor Cavour's plan. Cavour appointed as consul one of his secretaries, Francesco Astengo, who arrived in Belgrade on March 20, 1859, with instructions prepared by Klapka and approved by Cavour. The starting point was the claim that an agreement between the Serbs and the Hungarians was "virtually achieved" and that Astengo would secure their cooperation easily. He was to encourage every initiative which could bring the two nations into open rebellion against Austria and cooperate with the Russian and French consuls and prominent Serbian politicians. He was also to get in touch with the octogenarian Prince Miloš Obrenović and his successor Prince Michael. His work was to include the establishment of arms depots and transportation and distribution of arms along the Danube. The major depots were to be in Galaţi, from which the arms were to be transported to Iaşi and

Belgrade and on to Transylvania and the Banat-Bačka. The expenses were to be assumed by the Sardinian government.³

Cavour's plan had assigned a rather limited role to Serbia. Its territory was to be used as a depot for the shipment of arms to Hungary, while its politicians were to serve as mediators in an agreement between the Serbs and the Hungarians in Hungary. In his conversations with the Serbian politicians, including Princes Miloš and Michael, Astengo appeared to be open-minded and ebullient. He claimed that the Serbs were friendly to Sardinia and hostile to Austria, that they were watching carefully over the interests of their country, and that with a small effort a great deal could be achieved. In the course of a conversation on March 23, 1859, with Prince Miloš, in which the latter argued that Serbia and Piedmont ought to reach an agreement because they had "the same interests, the same hopes and hatreds," Astengo replied that he might soon have an opportunity to demonstrate this. Astengo then proceeded to explain Cavour's plan. Prince Miloš replied that he was not averse to cooperation but that Serbia's position did not offer much chance of success. Surrounded by hostile Austria and Turkey, Serbia could be deprived of all its contacts with the outside world. When Astengo went a step farther, adding that Sardinia expected from Serbia only "passive and covert cooperation" in supporting the movement in Hungary, Prince Miloš declined to say whether or not he would support Cavour's plan.⁴

Several days later, Astengo had two conversations with Prince Michael, who was about to leave Belgrade for Paris, London, Berlin, and St. Petersburg. Michael insisted that Serbia could not participate in the proposed operation because of the poor state of its army and its finances. Neither Michael nor Miloš was resolutely opposed to the stockpiling of arms along the Danube in Serbia, thus giving a practical answer to Astengo's question. During the following weeks Astengo traveled through Serbia, exploring its northern border region and getting to know people. His activities brought repeated protests from various consuls, especially the Austrian and the British, who suspected that he was plotting against Austria. Astengo's excessive eagerness apparently did not suit Cavour, who certainly did not want to reopen the Eastern Question. Astengo was ordered to be more restrained and to leave Belgrade for Constantinople.

The answers of Prince Miloš and Michael reflected Serbia's political isolation and economic weakness. After the Treaty of Paris of 1856, Serbia, Wallachia, and Moldavia came under the joint protection of the Great Powers, which meant that Russia had lost its dominant position there. The overthrow of the Karadjordjević dynasty by the Assembly of Saint Andrew in 1858 was disapproved by Austria and Turkey, and both worked to prevent the return of Miloš Obrenović to the throne. The last years of Alexander Karadjordjević's rule brought him into sharp conflict with Russia, while the internal opposition in Serbia was growing stronger. A lack of political acumen and internal disagreements tied up his initiative in questions of national policy. The young liberal intellectuals were becoming increasingly impatient with the prospects for the future. The plot of 1857 (Tenka) hastened the overthrow of the regime.

Serbia was a small state, and its economy was almost exclusively agrarian. According to the census of 1863, it had a little over a million inhabitants; by 1866 it had 1.2 million, including Serbs who had migrated from Turkey and elsewhere. More Serbs lived outside Serbia, in Austria and Turkey, than within it. Peasants constituted over 90 percent of the population, and there was a growing agrarian proletariat. Only 5.32 percent of the population was involved in crafts, 1.54 percent in commerce, and 3.06 percent in other activities.[5] Serbia's budget for 1860 was 19.1 million groš, with expenditures 1.4 million groš greater than income. Prince Miloš considered this unacceptable and asked the National Assembly to reduce the deficit by cutting back salaries in the bureaucracy. The Serbian army was small, about three thousand men, with obsolete arms and guns; only its gunpowder was locally produced. Thus, Serbia was unable to undertake any serious action in time of crisis without jeopardizing its very existence. Miloš's and Michael's sympathies for Sardinia and the demands of the younger generation were not enough. Besides, Prince Miloš believed that Serbia had been subject to Turkey for too long and argued that the Turks living in Serbian towns were an obstacle to his country's development and should withdraw. By the time of his death, Prince Miloš's goal was similar to those of the Italians, Romanians, Greeks, and Hungarians: the unification of all Serbs and the independence of the Principality.[6] However, he had no means to attain this goal. He was promised nothing in return for supporting Sardinia's proposal. Therefore, any overt action or participation in the war meant that Serbia would be exposed to attack by Austria and Turkey.

In order to clear up the situation, it was decided late in February that Prince Michael would travel to Vienna and other European capitals. He left Belgrade at the end of March; while in Vienna, he talked to numerous statesmen and diplomats. Austrian Foreign Minister Count Karl Buol appeared receptive to Michael's assurances of Serbia's neutrality. Viktor Balabin, the Russian ambassador, was not sure about the outcome of the Austro-Sardinian dispute and could not say whether it might extend to Turkey; he advised Prince Michael that Serbia should stand aside and not give any power cause for complaint. Michael continued to believe that Serbia should initiate secret military preparations and that war was imminent. Balabin asked the prince to monitor Astengo's activities in Serbia, since they might compromise the Serbian government.[7] The results of Prince Michael's visit to Paris were much the same. He was received by Napoleon III and Prince Napoleon. The emperor and his ministers advised Michael that Serbia should "preserve peace by all means" and avoid conflicts with the Austrian consul. They assured him of their support with regard to the withdrawal of the Turkish population from Serbia. The proposal that Serbia and France conclude an agreement in case "events should take such a turn as to facilitate the realization of Serbia's desire for independence and aggrandisement" was left unanswered, which was equivalent to refusal.[8]

During Prince Michael's stay in Paris, French-Austrian hostilities began, and soon the emperor left for the battlefield in Italy. The position of France was uncertain: England was opposed to the extension of the war to Turkey and threatened to enter the war on the side of Austria if this were to occur. Therefore, it was to be expected that the emperor would attempt to localize the war. The British ambassador to France, Lord Cowley, warned against stirring up unrest among the Christian population in Turkey. Michael assured the ambassador that Serbia would stand aside, although he mentioned that the treatment of the Christian population in Turkey was a constant source of unrest and agitation.[9]

The advice Prince Michael sent back to Belgrade reflected a consensus about the political course to be followed. One of the leading Serbian politicians, Ilija Garašanin, although out of the government, prepared a long memorandum about the Italian crisis and its possible consequences for Serbia. It is certain that Garašanin's memorandum was known to the responsible Serbian politicians, including the members of the government. In the memorandum, entitled "A Few Words about the War in Italy and the Consequences which Might Affect Serbia," dated May 1, 1859, Garašanin analyzed with a sure hand all aspects of the problem. His experience and his clear vision of the future gave the document exceptional value. Garašanin started from the premise that if the war remained limited to Sardinia, France, and Austria it would not pose a threat to Serbia. However, if Russia and Prussia came into the conflict, Britain and Turkey would side with Austria, and in that case, Garašanin believed, Austria and Turkey would disregard all international obligations and formalities and, exploiting Serbia's military weakness, occupy its territory. Since Serbia was unprepared militarily and the new regime was not firmly established, the invading armies would easily overwhelm any resistance. If that happened there would be no alternative for Serbia but to wait for a Great Power to decide, in its own interest, to liberate it. Another possibility was that the Great Powers, in concluding the eventual peace, might use Serbia to compensate one of their number. Garašanin recommended that the government, "without losing a single day," begin defensive and offensive military preparations for the invasion. He suggested that Russia and France be asked to explain their intentions toward Serbia and that the government act in complete accord with them. No ambiguous statements were to be accepted. Furthermore, Serbia should not undertake anything that might irritate Austria and Turkey; on the contrary, the government ought to seek to create the impression that it had no intention of doing anything.

That was not all. As a defensive measure, which might be used otherwise, Garašanin proposed a joint action and cooperation with Montenegro, an alliance with Greece, and preparations for a rebellion in neighboring countries. Garašanin believed that in the case of an Austrian invasion Serbia ought to support a rebellion in Hungary. Busy in Italy, Austria would not be able to send a single soldier against Serbia; Garašanin believed that Serbia would be able to resist a Turkish attack with its own forces and by fostering rebellion in neighboring countries. In the meantime, the Russian army would come to Serbia's rescue. He believed that Russian and French advice ought to be formally accepted but not blindly followed. Finally, he urged the government not to rush, but to exert complete control over any action that foreign agents and émigrés might prepare against Turkey, to establish its authority, and to invite a capable military officer to work on the organization of the Serbian army.[10] In recommending these preparations, Garašanin could not foresee that the war would end so quickly.

Prince Miloš, despite warnings from various sides, including those of the French consul Bernard des Essards, came to disregard the official advice of the French government. He told the consul that Serbia was carrying out military preparations and would move in the event of the extension of the Austro-Sardinian war, that he hated Austria, and that Serbia would act jointly with the Hungarians to destroy the Empire. The French consul, who took a reserved attitude, ascribed this behavior on the part of the elderly prince to the consul Astengo. Young, vigorous, and charming, the Sardinian consul had established numerous friendships among the Serbs; his relationships with the people were informal and friendly; he talked about the common destiny of the Italians and the Serbs and their struggle against Austria; he approved openly of Serbia's national aspirations. Astengo was a frequent guest at the court, and Prince Miloš called him "son" and had granted him Serbian citizenship. He also met young intellectuals, discussed problems, and prepared plans for the future. The myth of Cavour and the courageous initiative of a small state came into being; Serbia was to follow Sardinia's example.[11]

The Serbian press, including *Srbske novine* in Belgrade and *Srbski dnevnik* in Novi Sad on the Hungarian side of the border, carried long columns devoted to the events in Italy. The crisis was followed closely, creating the impression that war was imminent; Cavour's statements were taken verbatim from the foreign press. Before the war broke out there was evident fear that the crisis might end in a diplomatic compromise. *Srbske novine* was concerned that the compromise would include the Balkans and argued that such a solution was not realistic. Of course, the fear of Austrian interference was always present. The initiation of the military campaign dispelled such fears. *Srbski dnevnik* could not publish news about the course of the campaign in Italy because of the Austrian censors; *Srbske novine* published all the news that managed to reach Belgrade. Garibaldi and his successes in Lombardy were ever present, and the news of the Austrian withdrawal from Lombardy was greeted with enthusiasm. Enthusiasm for Sardinia and its victories was evident among the people everywhere; each success was celebrated in Belgrade cafés, outside the Sardinian consulate, and so on. Serbian army officers congratulated the French and Italian consuls for their armies' splendid victories. The Serbs celebrated these victories as if they were their own, and anti-Austrian feeling was rampant.[12]

Besides political agitation, the Serbian government had increased its troops and placed them in a state of alert. When the military commander of the Belgrade fortress asked why, the foreign minister replied that these measures were not directed against Turkey; rather, the government was concerned over an eventual Austrian defeat and the possibility of assisting in a rebellion of the Serbs in Hungary. The Turkish government decided, in response, to increase the number of troops in Bosnia and Bulgaria; its Belgrade garrison was increased to war strength. The Serbian government, faced with these threats, abandoned its military preparations and decided not to support the Hungarians. The French government asked the Serbian government to stop the implementation of Klapka's plan; there was widespread fear of a general European war. After the Austrian defeat at Solferino, Prussia mobilized its armies; Russia, concerned about the spread of revolutionary sentiments, advised Napoleon III to conclude a peace. Austria, worried about its position in Germany and the possible rebellion in

Hungary, accepted the proposal for a cease-fire, and an armistice was signed in Villafranca on July 11, 1859. The peace was concluded in Zurich in November 1859.[13] The armistice abruptly halted Sardinian activities among the Slavs and the Hungarians. Cavour resigned, and the new government instructed Astengo to stop his activities in Serbia against Austria. "The secret aim of your mission is over," wrote the foreign minister.[14]

The news of the armistice was received in Serbia with disbelief. It seemed inexplicable that an armistice should be concluded after such spendid victories. *Srbske novine* went so far as to claim that the news was Austria's invention. When it was confirmed, the general enthusiasm was replaced with sadness and bitterness toward France. No wonder that Sardinia was considered as a state deprived of the fruits of its victories on the battlefield. Sympathies for Sardinia grew even stronger, while anti-Austrian feeling remained as strong as ever.[15]

Serbia's restraint had permitted it to avoid a risky situation. The war had remained localized, and no other fronts had been opened up. In fact, the Serbian rulers had more urgent problems to cope with. Two neighboring powers—Austria and Turkey—were suspicious of the attitude of the Serbian government. The exchange of notes between Belgrade and Constantinople centered on the problems of refugees from Turkey and the problem of succession. Prince Miloš argued that Serbia had to receive refugees because the maintenance of peace in the neighboring provinces demanded it. In February 1860, he decided to send to Constantinople a deputation which would, among other things, demand the withdrawal of the Turkish garrisons from the fortresses in Serbia. It was believed in Belgrade that the European political situation warranted such a demand.[16] There was a widespread belief that a rebellion of large proportions would break out in the spring of 1860. This prospect posed a dilemma for the Serbian statesmen. Possible rebellion in Bosnia and Bulgaria loomed large before them, while threats and retaliation from Austria and Turkey menaced the very existence of the Principality. Russia had no intention of supporting Serbia's demands in Constantinople. Prince Miloš decided not to press the demand for the withdrawal of the troops, but instead requested the withdrawal of Turkish civilians living in Serbia. This was the only demand which was accepted by the Turkish government. The situation became tense when Prince Miloš died in September 1860.

In the meantime, the Kingdom of Italy was established with the unification of central and southern Italy. The remaining problems were the unification of the Venetian region and Rome with the new kingdom. Cavour tried to secure the cession of the Venetian region through negotiation with Austria. Mentioned as compensation in this connection were restless Bosnia and Hercegovina. Cavour also sought to exert pressure on Austria by negotiating with the Hungarian émigrés in order to prepare a revolutionary movement of the oppressed nationalities in Austria and Turkey, including the Serbs. If successful, this would weaken the Austrian ability to resist Italian pressure. The revolutionary fervor in Hercegovina and Montenegro was to be used as well. The project included incursions from Transylvania and the Banat and the landing of an armed force in Dalmatia. Serbia was again to be used as a depot for arms to be sent to the Hungarians. Thus, Hungary remained the major ally among the people of East Central Europe in Italy's struggle against Austria. The idea of a confederation headed by Hungary had enjoyed Cavour's support, and he endeavored, without much success, to secure support for such a solution in France and England. Thus, in order to get Venetia, Cavour attempted to induce Austria to look for compensations in the Slavic regions of Turkey. The Italian press openly supported such a combination, despite the fact that it touched the very essence of Serbia's national policy.[17]

The creation of the Kingdom of Italy stirred great interest and excitement in the Serbian public. Cavour's ability to exploit the political situation and revolutionary sentiments to achieve unification were received with wide acclaim. *Srbske novine* wrote on January 12, 1860, that the movement for national liberation in Italy had become so strong that no power could stop it. The coordination between the people, the army, and the king brought about unification in a way that was praised everywhere. A great deal of credit was given to the people's army. *Srbski dnevnik* also argued that Italy had achieved a great success. On the other hand, radicals, including Giuseppe Mazzini and the Republicans, were described in *Srbske novine* as dangerous elements, extremists, and a threat to the new state, while Cavour and Garibaldi were celebrated as wise and moderate. Cavour's external and internal policies—cooperation with one Great Power and struggle against leftist radicals—were considered a model for other nations to follow.[18] The press discreetly voiced the hope that the center of the future crisis would be the Balkans.

After Prince Miloš's death, Michael Obrenović assumed Serbia's throne. The success of the Italian unification had made a deep impression on Michael, who recognized that the strength of national sentiments was more important than the support of the Great Powers. He detested Serbia's and his own position versus the sultan and awaited the first opportunity to achieve independence. He firmly believed that Serbia could not count on substantial support from the Great Powers;

they always had some excuse, such as "European interests," for not supporting the liberation of the Slavs in the Ottoman Empire. This brought him to the conclusion that only the joint struggle of the Balkan nations might bring about complete independence. This would also bring them independence from the Great Powers. The desire of some of them to help Serbia was to be exploited craftily, always with a view to complete political freedom.[19] The example of the Sardinian kingdom loomed large in the background.

Prince Michael's ambition was to create a large state headed by Serbia. His first task was to prepare Serbia for war with Turkey, and therefore he was intent on creating a strong and well-equipped army. In order to do this he sought to concentrate all authority in his own hands[20] and to commit all the means available to the army and its armament. In the fall of 1860, Jovan Marinović was sent to various European capitals to ask for the help and cooperation necessary to smooth over any difficulties with Turkey over Serbia's demands. The primary one was the withdrawal of the Turks living around the fortresses, which was to open the way for the withdrawal of the Turkish garrisons. Without this Serbia could not undertake any action toward Bosnia or receive arms and other materials by way of the Danube and the Sava. Count Gorchakov, the Russian foreign minister, promised support for the request for the withdrawal of the Turks from Serbia provided it was peaceful. He also promised financial assistance under certain conditions. The French government promised to support the proposal for the withdrawal of the Turks living outside the fortresses as well. To the Serbs' disappointment, these two powers, the ones most sympathetic to Serbia, asked that any action be delayed. Thus, Cavour's invitation to join in the proposed Italian-Hungarian operation had to be declined.[21]

Despite the rejection of his proposals in Paris and St. Petersburg, Prince Michael decided to proceed with his plans for the withdrawal of the Turks from Serbia. The first step brought no results, but it did return Ilija Garašanin to power. Garašanin was well thought of in Paris and Constantinople. In the light of the rebellion in Hercegovina and the fact that the Great Powers were urging the Porte to introduce needed reforms, the moment seemed to him convenient to approach the Greek government about a joint action against Turkey. Confronted with the Serbian demands, the Porte adopted the tactic of protracted negotiations, and the Garašanin mission ended without result.

More successful was Prince Michael's effort to reorganize the Serbian army. The National Assembly, meeting on August 18, 1861, in Kragujevac (Preobraženje), adopted legislation establishing a militia. Serbia had a small standing army. The militia, to be available to serve in an emergency, was to be composed of all able-bodied men between twenty and fifty years of age. This meant an army of fifty thousand well-drilled soldiers, and the number could be increased if necessary. The army had been deficient in trained officers, technical means, and arms. The French major Hippolyte Monden was invited to organize the Serbian army.[22] The Turkish government protested these measures, claiming that they were an infringement of the Hatt-i Şerif.

From 1862 until 1866, there were numerous plans and initiatives to bring Serbia into the general framework of Italy's Balkan policy. In the summer of 1862, the Serbian government dispatched the special representative Miloje Lešjanin to Paris and Turin. His aim in the Italian capital was to collect information about Italy's policy toward Serbia. Garašanin wanted to explore the possibility of cooperation against Austria as a common enemy. Lešjanin was to point out that Serbia was lacking in arms and to see whether Italy was willing to help it obtain them. The outcome of Lešjanin's visit to Turin was a complete disappointment.[23]

The Polish Insurrection of 1863 seemed to increase the importance of Serbia in the eyes of the Italian politicians and diplomats, but it did not change their basic attitude, despite the fact that there were hints that Serbia in 1863 could have played a different role from that assigned to it in 1859. Mazzini wanted to involve Serbia in any action that might be undertaken concerning Venetia. He kept in touch with Serbian liberals, notably Vladimir Jovanović. He was charged with organizing a rebellion in Serbia and the Banat-Bačka region of Hungary, to be coordinated with one in northern Italy.[24] On returning to Serbia, Jovanović concluded that the moment for action had not yet arrived. Simultaneously, King Victor Emmanuel II urged a different course of action—an incursion against Austria in the Balkans and the Danubian region. Agents and representatives (among them Gerve de Sonna, General István Türr, Friggezzio) swarmed over Belgrade, bringing with them various plans and proposals.

Faced with the intensified campaign, the Serbian government decided to act on its own. Its agents in Bosnia and the Military Frontier had prepared plans for a rebellion in which units from the Frontier would participate. The Austrian secret service discovered these plans. At that moment, Garašanin was intent on cooperation provided the Italian government supported the action. The Italians operating in Belgrade insisted upon friendship and mutual interests and the need for cooperation but would not commit themselves to anything specific. In June 1863, Garašanin asked the Italian government to answer the following questions: Would Italy, in the event of a rebellion in Hungary, declare war against Austria (Garašanin believed that Italy should remain neutral), and would Italy commit itself to financial support of the Frontier regiments in Hungary? Garašanin appeared to be ready to support Italy's policy in Hungary if he received satisfactory answers to his questions. However, nothing came of it. Italy was not ready for an action that would reopen the Eastern Question or bring it into conflict with the Great Powers. From Turin came a reply that the whole action ought to be postponed until a more convenient moment.

In June 1864, Garašanin again approached the Italian government, this time with an offer to conclude a formal agreement between the two states. The details of the offer are not known; however, it is known that Garašanin asked certain territorial gains and an agreement between the Hungarians and the Serbs. It was most likely Bosnia that he demanded, as he wanted to prevent any transaction between Italy and Austria. As to the agreement, in the light of the Hungarians' refusal to enter into one with the Slavs, he sought to impose one with Italy's help.[25] Garašanin's proposal came at a convenient moment for Italy, as its agents in the Balkans were organizing an armed action in the Danubian area, but the plan was abandoned by the king. In September 1864, the Minghetti government resigned, and the new government formed by General Alfonso La Marmora decided to call a halt to revolutionary action. It declined to respond to Garašanin's proposal, and he was persuaded that Serbia could expect nothing from Italy.[26]

In the subsequent months and years until the outbreak of the Austro-Prussian war, the Italian government endeavored to avoid stirring up revolutionary movements in the Balkans. In 1865, it initiated negotiations to acquire Venetia, and Napoleon III supported the motion; intent on avoiding war between the powers, he wanted to cooperate with Prussia in order to force Austria to cede Venetia. Bosnia was mentioned as a compensation to Austria. Garašanin was aware of this and viewed it as a threat to Serbia's national interests. This suggestion clearly contributed to Serbia's very reserved attitude on the eve of the Austro-Prussian war.

Throughout these years the agitation in the Serbian press in the Principality and in Bačka-Banat was very intense. There existed a firm belief that the European (Italian) question could be tied up with the Eastern Question. Austria was considered an enemy of the Italians and the Slavs. Serbian public opinion held that the time had arrived for a thorough solution of the Eastern Question. The newspapers in Serbia believed that the policy should be to exploit the political situation and accomplish what was realistically possible. The press in Bačka-Banat took a different position, suggesting a more energetic policy in which the joint action of all the Balkan nations would defeat Turkey and bring freedom to all. Some of them advanced the idea of a confederation as well.[27] *Srbski dnevnik* rejected peaceful action as a means of achieving freedom; it argued for armed struggle and disregard of the Great Powers. The leading protagonist of this way of thinking was Svetozar Miletić, a leader of the Serbian National Party in Hungary. Miletić's arguments came close to Mazzini's solution to the Eastern Question. For supporting such ideas *Srbski dnevnik* was forced to cease publication.[28] *Sloboda*, published in Geneva by the Serbian liberal Vladimir Jovanović, carried this agitation even farther than Miletić. It was very critical of Serbian foreign policy and made frequent allusions to the conservatism of its protagonists. It openly argued for a military struggle, pointing to the example of Italy and inviting the Serbian government to follow that example.[29] During 1865 *Sloboda* ceased to exist as the liberal opposition became reconciled with the Serbian government.

The year 1866 was one of crucial importance for Serbia. The Austro-Prussian conflict was increasing in intensity, and at the same time Prince Michael's regime was becoming more oppressive. Demands for reform and the dissatisfaction caused by the requirements concerning the militia grew more intense. The Serbian ruling class was confronted with important policy decisions.

The European crisis seemed to take precedence over internal problems. Napoleon III's policies were inconsistent and vacillating, and the power of France seemed to be on the decline. Prussian power was on the rise, and Bismarck was intent on destroying the German Confederation. In April 1866, when it became clear that Austria would not accept the Prussian demand to annex Schleswig and Holstein, Italy and Prussia signed the Treaty of Alliance. At the same time, the overthrow of Prince Cuza attracted the attention of the Great Powers. In the course of the crisis Serbia had succeeded in remaining on good terms with Austria. Its relations with Turkey were also relatively peaceful, despite the fact that the problem of the fortresses had not been resolved. Stable relations with Austria and Turkey made the Serbian government attentive to the situation in Italy. The experiences of the past had made Garašanin realistic in his appreciation of Italy's policies toward the Balkans. He argued that Italy was not interested in supporting the Balkan Christians' aspirations for liberation[30]—that its aim was to create trouble along the Austrian frontiers in order to ease the pressure on the Italian front. Italy, he pointed out, was incapable of supporting the Balkan peoples materially and financially, and furthermore the political program of Serbia differed fundamentally from that of Italy. Serbia had to fight with Turkey, Italy with Austria; Serbia was not prepared to join in this latter struggle.[31] Thus, in Garašanin's view, Italy's intentions were not in accord with those of Serbia, and he was not ready to help Italy achieve strictly Italian goals. Moreover, he saw dangers for the Balkan peoples; in creating chaos in Turkey, Italy was preparing the ground for compensation for Austria's eventual loss of Venetia. Bosnia and Hercegovina were in Garašanin's mind.

When the Austrian government on April 27, 1866, ordered the mobilization of its troops, the Italians seemed ready to return to their old tactics. A cable was sent to the Italian consul in Belgrade asking the Serbian government to prevent the departure of the Frontier regiments for the Italian front. Garašanin replied that it was impossible to do this, as the network of agents had been abolished. He warned Consul Stephen Scovasso that Serbia would not accept any proposal by which Italy would acquire territory through compensation with Turkish territories inhabited by Serbs.[32] Scovasso argued that this was the moment for Serbia to attack Austria and went on to examine a plan for the landing of Garibaldians in Dalmatia. His proposals went unheeded by La Marmora; the Italian prime minister refused to consider the proposal for cooperation with the Hungarian émigrés.

In the middle of June 1866, Bismarck approved the proposal of a joint Hungarian-Serbian action against Austria.[33] La Marmora again refused to accept it. Prussian King William I showed a distaste for the idea as well, with the result that Bismarck was reluctant to propose it openly. It was only on June 17, 1866, when La Marmora left Florence for the front, that the new prime minister Baron Betino Ricasoli took the proposal under consideration. Several days later, on June 24, the Italian troops were defeated in the battle of Custoza, and this induced the government to speed up the action in Belgrade. Ricasoli sent Türr to Belgrade. In the meantime, the Prussian army had won its first victory over the Austrians in Bohemia, and the Austrian government offered Venetia to Napoleon III. This necessitated further clarification of the policy to follow. The Italian fleet was ordered to blockade the Adriatic, while a corps of marines was assembled in Ancona with the task of landing in Dalmatia. However, the defeat of the Italian fleet in the naval battle of Vis (Lissa) on July 20, 1866, brought the whole plan to nothing. On July 26, the fighting was interrupted on the Austro-Prussian battlefields and the negotiations for an armistice begun.

Ever since the beginning of the Austro-Prussian-Italian crisis, efforts had been made to get Serbia to side with Austria's enemies. Scovasso, Lobero, the Prussian vice-consul in Belgrade, and Antonije Oreškovic, an officer with good contacts with the Frontier officers, had tried hard to persuade Prince Michael and Garašanin to change their attitude. They were to be joined by Türr, who came to Belgrade in July. Türr's arrival was awaited with a certain uneasiness; Scovasso's requests had given a clear indication of the content of his proposals. The news of Italy's defeat at Custoza further confirmed Serbia's attitude. It was clear to Prince Michael and Garašanin that they could not count on Italy's help; its army had been unable to destroy Austria's fortifications in Venetia, march into the Tyrol, or land in Dalmatia. Besides, Prince Michael and Garašanin firmly believed in an Austrian victory. Garašanin openly expressed this opinion. Russia's advice strengthened Garašanin's resolve to remain neutral. In April 1866, Jovan Ristić, a diplomatic agent in Constantinople, informed Garašanin that Count Nikola Ignatyev, the Russian ambassador there, warned Serbia against acceptance of Italy's and Prussia's offers to join in an operation against Austria. He pointed out that the Turkish forces were stationed along Serbia's borders and might march into Serbia. Similar advice came from Vienna. The Russian ambassador there, Shchtakelberg, suggested that Serbia stay out of the conflict and prepare "for the great day of liberation," which would come soon.

On June 10, 1866, Bismarck spoke before the Prussian Crown Council about the joint Hungarian-Slav operation. It was decided that Richard Pfuel, councilor of the Prussian legation in Madrid, be sent to Belgrade. He arrived there early in July. In his conversations with Prince Michael and Garašanin, Pfuel explained that the Prussian government expected Serbia to support the planned Hungarian rebellion. The Serbian statesmen replied that Serbia could not become involved in a conflict with Austria as long as it was threatened by Turkey. Pfuel was told that even if that threat had not existed, Serbia would not initiate any action against Austria without prior agreement with the Hungarians. This came as a complete surprise to Pfuel. He subsequently demanded Serbian government consent for the passage of the Italian battalions across Serbia. This request was refused as well. Serbia could not allow itself to be squeezed between Turkey and Austria. If Serbia had been invited to join Prussia and Italy, in due time it would have prepared itself for action, claimed Garašanin. Therefore, Serbia could offer moral support only.[34]

The Austrian defeat at Königgrätz was not viewed as the end of Austria's resistance. Prince Michael and Garašanin were watching the events in Hungary carefully, and they came to the conclusion that no insurrection would take place there. When Türr arrived in Belgrade on July 25, his reception was even cooler than Pfuel's. While asking Serbia's support for the Hungarian rebellion, he gave no guarantees that Italy and Prussia would come to its defense or offer compensation.

Prince Michael and Garašanin wanted to send him back to Italy as quickly as possible in order not to make Austria suspicious. Despite clear rejection of their proposals, Türr and Orešković worked fervently to force Serbia to enter the war. Scovasso, acting in concert with them, was saying in Belgrade cafés that the government was unable to understand Serbia's national interests. Garašanin considered Italy's treatment of Serbia insulting. He wrote that Italy asked Serbia like a *bašibozluk* to enter the war. "When the war was over," wrote Garašanin, "our destiny would depend on circumstances; we might very well be dissolved like Garibaldi's volunteers."[35] The pressure on Serbia diminished in August, when Bismarck instructed Lobero to suspend all activity during the negotiations with Austria. Türr left Serbia soon thereafter.

The Austro-Prussian war caused uneasiness in Serbia. When it was over, the government realized that it meant a victory for the principle of nationality. There was a possibility that a similar opportunity might occur in the future and could be seized upon to realize Serbia's national program. Therefore, Serbia could not allow itself to be caught unprepared. A secret cabinet meeting held on July 28, 1866, was devoted to military preparations. It was decided that Serbia might enter into a war in a favorable international situation, when it was militarily prepared in cooperation with the Balkan peoples and when it had a just cause. It was decided that arming be speeded up and credits for it increased. A year was granted for these preparations. Also, the government was to enter into negotiations with Montenegro and Greece to prepare the ground for a joint action.[36] Soon thereafter, Serbia raised the question of the withdrawal of the Turkish garrisons from Serbia, and the next year the fortresses passed into Serbia's hands. With the departure of the Turks in May 1867, one of the major aims of Serbian foreign policy had been accomplished. Prince Michael's authority and reputation seemed to be at their highest point.

The outcome of the war attracted widespread attention in the press in Serbia and Bačka-Banat. There was consensus that the Prussian victory had opened the way for a solution of the Eastern Question in terms of the principle of the nationality, that is, without the interference of the Great Powers. *Vidovdan* in Belgrade insisted that it was inadmissible that the principles applied in Italy should be denied to the Balkan peoples. Here, however, the similarity of views ended. The question of ways and means of carrying out the program posed serious problems. The newspapers in Serbia, voicing the attitude of the government, argued for a diplomatic solution of the Eastern and the Serbian questions, that is, through an agreement among the Great Powers. *Vidovdan* argued for the confederation of the Balkan states and opposed a Yugoslav state. The example of Italy greatly influenced the thinking of the Serbian politicians. A diplomatic solution and conservatism in internal policy were seen as guarantees of success. *Vidovdan* was full of praise for the tactics of the Italian liberals and critical of Mazzini and his followers.[37] *Srbske novine* argued along much the same lines. As the semiofficial government newspaper, it went even farther in its conservatism, arguing that old political structures ought to be preserved and that the newly liberated peoples should join existing states. Autonomy should be the goal of a future constitution. Armed struggle and independence were not mentioned in *Srbske novine*;[38] this restraint was prompted by the ongoing negotiations with the Turkish government about the withdrawal of the Turks from Serbia.

The newspapers in Bačka-Banat, including the more conservative ones, appeared impatient with the policies of the Serbian government. Conservative *Srbobran* expressed its dissatisfaction with the Serbian attitude toward the uprising in Crete. It claimed that Serbia had to support the Cretans because Turkey could not be defeated without its participation. *Napredak,* usually moderate in its attitude toward the Serbian government, became impatient with Serbia's loyalty to Turkey at the time of the rebellion in Crete. The reason for it *Napredak* saw in the negotiations for the return of the fortresses. It expressed a belief in an imminent rebellion in the Balkans. Both newspapers demanded Serbia's armed intervention. *Srbobran* pointed to the example of Piedmont, which, although small, had succeeded in bringing the Italian people, divided under several rulers, into a unified state.

Zastava of Novi Sad, a voice of the liberal opposition both in Serbia and in Hungary, was very critical of Serbia's official policy. The Italian experiences were always in mind. The newspaper demanded that the Serbian government follow the desires of the people and not of diplomacy. The battle of Königgrätz, it was argued, was the beginning of the solution of the Eastern Question. Serbia could not develop within its borders, but had to struggle for the liberation of Serbdom, which would transform it into a large European state. Otherwise, it would become an object of compensation. *Zastava* refused to accept the claims of official Serbia as to its unpreparedness; once again, the example of Italy was pointed to: although defeated, Italy had achieved its goals by taking advantage of the opportunity offered by the Austro-Prussian war. *Zastava* approved the Serbian government's tactics in the question of the fortresses but argued that this question was insignificant in comparison with the larger question of Serbdom. Thus, the example of Piedmont was ever present in the minds of both supporters and critics of the

Serbian government. All the newspapers supported the idea of military action.

During 1866, there emerged another critic of the Serbian government and its policies: Ujedinjena omladina srpska (United Serbian Youth) (hereafter the Omladina). The guiding spirits of the Omladina—V. Jovanović, S. Miletić, and others—were followers of Mazzini. They created an organization and through various newspapers (*Srbski dnevnik, Sloboda, Zastava*) developed, defended, and spread Mazzini's revolutionary and democratic ideas and beliefs. Ideas about the common struggle of the Balkan nations for freedom became their credo. Young Italy and the Italian state became the models for Serbs. Since the Italian unification had been accomplished through national liberation, this was clearly acceptable for the Omladina and its leaders. Another point was a firm belief that Austria was an enemy to both Italy and the Serbs. This explains why the Omladina quickly came into open conflict with the Serbian government. It accused the statesmen of hindering the participation of the people in the struggle for national liberation.[39]

The Omladina also fought for the internal reforms and democracy in Serbia. For its members only a state with a liberal constitution and institutions could carry out a successful national policy. Again, Piedmont was the example. Therefore, the liberals of the Omladina were critical of Prince Michael's and Garašanin's authoritarian regime. They also disapproved of Michael's limited accomplishments in national policy, which were described as almost treachery. The Omladina believed that Serbian policy lacked energy and courage. Open conflict came in the summer of 1867, during the Omladina assembly in Belgrade. Hostility became mutual, with the Omladina leading the opposition to Michael's regime. This enmity increased in intensity until Michael's assassination in 1868. The Omladina argued that Michael was incapable of leading Serbia—that he was not ready to risk war, but instead used diplomacy to achieve small results. It expressed concern that the postponement of the armed struggle would diminish enthusiasm among the people and criticized the military reforms as slow and inadequate, the work of bureaucrats. The Omladina argued for a courageous stand vis-à-vis Turkey and accused Prince Michael of putting the management of national-revolutionary policy into the hands of old, conservative ministers.[40]

The wars of 1859 and 1866 had far-reaching consequences for Serbia and the Serbs. Certain characteristics appear evident. Both wars were important stages in the process of Italian unification; both were directed against Austria, although Italy's allies were different (France and Prussia). In both wars, first the Kingdom of Sardinia and then the Kingdom of Italy counted on the political and military support of Serbia and the Serbs, the Hungarians, and the Romanians. The Serbian army and the Frontier regiments were to carry out operations in the rear of the Austrian army and thus ease the pressure on the Italian front. In both wars, Serbia sought to persuade the Italians, the French, and the Prussians to pledge their political and diplomatic support for its national and territorial pretensions. Since none of the powers wanted to raise the Eastern Question, they refused to promise Serbia any territorial gains, and this, as well as its military unpreparedness and the fear of a Turkish invasion, persuaded Serbia not to undertake military operations.

In the light of the international situation and domestic conditions, the Serbian government did take some action. It began with the demand for the withdrawal of the Turks from Serbia and the surrender of the fortresses. This aim was realized in 1867. Awareness of Serbia's military weakness brought about the creation of a militia in 1861 and prompted national propaganda activities among the Serbs living in Austria and Turkey. Garašanin was sensitive to any transactions which might involve territories inhabited by Serbs. Bosnia and Hercegovina attracted his attention, and he sought to prevent their cession to Austria in return for Venetia.

The wars for Italian unification had important effects on Serbia's internal development. They provoked discussion of the authoritarian and conservative regime represented by Prince Michael and Garašanin and of Serbian domestic and foreign policy as a whole. Whether diplomacy or war was the key to the realization of national policy became the subject of endless debate. It became clear that, diplomacy having brought it only minor gains, in the next crisis Serbia would have to resort to arms.

Notes

1. For more details, see L. Chiala, *Politica segreta di Napoleone III e di Cavour (1858–1861)* (Turin-Rome, 1895); C. Durando, *Episodi diplomatici del Risorgimento Italiano dal 1856 al 1863* (Turin, 1901); A. Tamborra, *Cavour e i Balcani* (Turin, 1858), chaps. 3, 9; G. Jakšić and V. J. Vučković, *Spoljna politika Srbije za vlade kneza Mihaila: Prvi balkanski savez* (Belgrade, 1963).

2. Chiala, *Politica segreta,* p. 31; Durando, *Episodi diplomatici,* pp. 81–82; Lj. Aleksić-Pejković, *Politika Italije prema Srbiji do 1870. godine* (Belgrade, 1979), pp. 64–65.

3. Durando, *Episodi diplomatici,* pp. 84–85; Aleksić-Pejković, *Politika Italije,* pp. 65–66.

4. Tamborra, *Cavour,* pp.124–26; Jakšić and Vučković, *Spoljna politika,* p. 21.
5. *Državopis Srbije* (Belgrade, 1863–69), vols. 1–3.
6. Jakšić and Vučković, *Spoljna politika,* pp. 18–19.
7. Cukić to Lešjanin, Vienna, April 1, 1859, V. J. Vučković, *Politička akcija Srbije u južnoslovenskim pokrajinama habsburške monarhije 1859– 1874* (Belgrade, 1965), pp. 8–11, 12–14; Jakšić and Vučković, *Spoljna politika,* pp. 22–23.
8. Vučković, *Politička akcija,* pp. 22–24; Aleksić-Pejković, *Politika Italije,* p. 72. While in London, Prince Michael met with Kossuth. In his memoirs, the Hungarian leader wrote that Emperor Napoleon approved the idea of an agreement between Serbia and the Hungarians. This contradicts the contents of Michael's conversations with Napoleon III, Prince Napoleon, and Foreign Minister Walevski. See also J. Ristić, *Spoljašnji odnošaji Srbije novijeg vremena, 1848–1860,* vol. 1 (Belgrade, 1887), pp. 326–32.
9. Vučković, *Politička akcija,* pp. 22–23.
10. Papers of Ilija Garašanin, no. 1123, Archives of Serbia, Belgrade; Aleksić-Pejković, *Politika Italije,* pp. 73–75.
11. Tamborra, *Cavour,* pp. 156–58; Aleksić-Pejković, *Politika Italije,* pp. 76–77.
12. For more details, see Lj. Aleksić-Pejković, "Srpska štampa i ratovi za oslobodjenje i ujedinjenje Italije 1859–1866. godine," *Istorijski Časopis* 20 (1973): 258–65.
13. Jakšić and Vučković, *Spoljna politika,* pp. 35–36.
14. Tamborra, *Cavour,* p. 161.
15. *Srbske novine,* July 9, 1859; Aleksić-Pejković, *Politika Italije,* p. 82; Tamborra, *Cavour,* pp. 160–61.
16. Jakšić and Vučković, *Spoljna politika,* p. 43.
17. A. Tamborra, "Balcani, Italia ed Europa nel problema della Venezia (1859–1861)," *Rassegna Storica del Risorgimento* 4 (1957): 814–15; Aleksić-Pejković, *Politika Italije,* pp. 82–87.
18. Aleksić-Pejković, *Politika Italije,* pp. 87–89.
19. Jakšić and Vučković, *Spoljna politika,* pp. 50–51.
20. S. Jovanović, *Druga vlada Miloša i Mihaila* (Belgrade, 1933), pp. 145, 277, 313.
21. Aleksić-Pejković, *Politika Italije,* p. 104; Jakšić and Vučković, *Spoljna politika,* pp. 52–89.
22. Jovanović, *Druga vlada Miloša i Mihaila,* pp. 277–93.
23. Lj. Aleksić-Pejković, "Misija Miloja Lešjanina u Parizu, Londonu i Torinu u leto 1862. godine," *Istorijski Časopis* 21 (1974): 125–64.
24. For a complete analysis of Mazzini's contacts with the Serbs, see N. Stipčević, "Djuzepe Macini i Vladimir Jovanović: Poglavlje o italijansko-sprskim odnosima," *Prilozi za književnost, jezik, istoriju i folklor* 38 (1972): 163–201.
25. Aleksić-Pejković, *Politika Italije,* pp. 144–49.

26. Aleksić-Pejković, *Politika Italije,* pp. 150–54; Jakšić and Vučković, *Spoljna politika,* pp. 188, 194.
27. N. Petrović, *Svetozar Miletić i Narodna stranka: Gradja 1860–1885* (Sremski Karlovci, 1968), vol. 1, doc. no. 138–61.
28. Ibid., doc. no. 197–208; J. Skerlić, *Omladina i njena književnost* (Belgrade, 1906), p. 88.
29. V. Vuletić, "'Sloboda' Vladmira Jovanovića," *Zbornik za društvene nauke Matice srpske* 21 (1962): 137–54.
30. The Italian consul Scovasso admitted in May 1866 that Italy had always "neglected the Serbs," adding that Garašanin was not content with empty words (Aleksić-Pejković, *Politika Italije,* pp. 166–67).
31. *Pisma Ilije Garašanina Jovanu Marinoviću.* Sredio St. Lovčević, 2 vols. (Belgrade: SAN, 1931), 2: 168; Garašanin to Ristić, Belgrade, April 1866, The Garašanin Papers; Jakšić and Vučković, *Spoljna politika,* pp. 230–31.
32. Aleksić-Pejković, *Politika Italije,* pp. 167–70.
33. H. Wendel, *Bismarck und Serbien im Jahre 1866* (Berlin, 1927), pp. 23–27, 97, 99; J. Albert von Reiswitz, *Belgrad-Berlin, Berlin-Belgrad 1866–1871* (Munich, 1936), p. 55.
34. Jakšić and Vučković, *Spoljna politika,* pp. 260–63.
35. Garašanin to Lešjanin, Arandjelovac, July 28, 1866, Archives of Serbia, Presents, doc. no. 76/46; Jakšić and Vučković, *Spoljna politika,* p. 264.
36. On the military and political preparations, see Jakšić and Vučković, *Spoljna politika,* pp. 275–80.
37. Aleksić-Pejković, "Sprska štampa," pp. 257–58, 267, 279, 286, 287, 289.
38. See *Srbske novine,* September 15 and 29, October 1, 1866, January 21, February 21, March 5, 9, 1867.
39. Aleksić-Pejković, *Politika Italije,* pp. 196–97; *Ujedinjena Omladina Srpska: Zbornik radova* (Novi Sad, 1968); Skerlić, *Omladina i njena književnost,* pp. 106–26.
40. Jovanović, *Druga vlada Miloša i Mihaila,* pp. 383–402.

The Evolution of the Greek Army (1828–68)

Dimitris Michalopoulos

From the founding of the Greek state at the outset of the nineteenth century practically until the era of the Balkan wars, the lack of a strong army was one of the main reasons for the obvious weakness of the Hellenic Kingdom, particularly in the field of foreign policy. The fiasco of the 1854 "uprising," Greece's inability to participate in the Russo-Turkish war of 1877–78, and, obviously, the defeat of 1897 can be properly understood only in the light of the very low standards of the army. It may, however, appear out of character for a nation whose foreign policy was so manifestly inspired by an irredentist spirit and which to a great extent sacrificed its economic growth and social welfare in the name of this policy not to have developed a strong and effective army. In order to explain this aberration it is necessary to analyze the efforts made by Ioannis Kapodistrias, the regency, and King Otho to build up a military force.

The problem Kapodistrias was faced with on his rise to power in 1828 was whether to maintain and organize, as far as possible, the existing irregular army, which had borne the main burden of the struggle for independence, or to develop a regular army. He chose the first option, and the harsh experiences of his successors proved it to have been the right one. Thus, by a decree issued on February 7/19, 1828, the irregular corps were divided into chiliarchies, each consisting of about eleven hundred men. Each chiliarchy had the following officers: one chiliarch (commander), two pentacosiarchs (five hundred men each), ten hecatontarchs (one hundred men each), twenty pentecontarchs (fifty men each), forty eicosipentarchs (twenty-five men each), eighty dodecarchs (twelve men each), and one hundred sixty pentarchs (five men each). In addition to these there were, theoretically at least, two aides-de-camp, two secretaries, two priests, two doctors, two quartermasters, two paymasters, four ensigns, and four drummers or buglers. The privates numbered eight hundred.[1]

In addition to this reorganization, an attempt was made to endow this irregular army with the spirit of a regular European army: desertion, which had been the main problem of the Greek military forces during the 1821–29 period, became a severely punishable offense, as did unauthorized entry into and movement between military camps, stealing from civilians, and insubordination. The oath of allegiance required of soldiers was characteristic of the way in which the excesses of four centuries of partisan resistance to the Turks and eight years of fighting for independence were to be eradicated:

> I swear to obey His Excellency the Governor's [Kapodistrias's] orders and those of the commanders under whose command he may place me. I swear not to do harm to any of my fellow citizens, my coreligionists, or any other person. I swear not to murder or steal, not to seize and not to beat. I swear not to leave without the commanding officer's permission . . . and to obey the military laws and regulations, however severe they may be.[2]

Under these conditions, eight chiliarchies of irregulars were formed. At the same time, however, a large number of cadres of the French expeditionary force under the command of General Nicolas Joseph Maison, who had come to Greece in order to clear the remnants of the Ottoman forces out of the Peloponnese, were already enlisting in the Greek army. Under their initiative it was decided, in April 1829, to transform the chiliarchies into thirteen light battalions which in time of peace would patrol the borders and in wartime would make up the core of a regular army. In fact, it seems that Kapodistrias considered the organization of the irregular corps the first step toward developing a regular army. Knowing that the generation of the War of Independence would be unable to conform to the ethics and regulations of an army fashioned after the European models, he simply opted for the formation of a small force of regulars, who were somehow transformed into praetorians of the regime.

Greece had had a regular army in theory since 1822, but it had had one in practice only since 1825.[3] A colonel in Napoleon's army, Charles Nicolas Fabvier, had been appointed as commander[4] and, upon his resignation in 1828, had been replaced by a Bavarian colonel, Karl Wilhelm Heideck, who in turn was succeeded by various French officers. The regular army corps, which by the end of 1828 numbered 2,612 men,[5] was very short of both clothing and armament. By the 1830s there had been a slight improvement: there were four infantry battalions, subdivided into six companies each, one artillery battalion, and four cavalry companies. In addition to this, the following had been formed: one corps of engineers, consisting only of cadres, one quartermaster corps, a permanent court martial, and a central military academy for the training of officers, who, as a rule, belonged to the technical corps, along the lines of the French Ecole Polytechnique. An outward difference between regulars and irregulars was in the uniform. The latter wore the traditional fustanella (skirt), whereas the regulars wore something similar to the French uniform. The armament of the regulars was heterogeneous, being made up of donations from philhellenic organizations, the results of plunder, and a Russian donation of six thousand weapons.[6] The army (in fact only the irregulars, for the regulars were under Kapodistrias's personal control) and the navy came under the War Secretariat; the Greek colonel P. Rhodios was appointed as first secretary.

In September 1831 Kapodistrias was murdered, and after a period of unrest King Otho, second son of King Ludwig I of Bavaria, came to Greece in January 1833. Otho, however, had not yet come of age, and until he did so, on May 20/June 1, 1835, the country was run by a regency committee, whose members were Bavarian, under Count Joseph Ludwig von Armansperg. One of the regency's first undertakings was the reorganization of the armed forces. Over the objections of many prominent Greek politicians, it chose the opposite course to the one Kapodistrias had followed. Instead of strengthening the irregular corps, it chose to dissolve them and create a new regular army. This choice was influenced by the fact that Otho had brought with him to Greece thirty-five hundred Bavarian soldiers (four infantry regiments, two light cavalry companies, and one artillery company)[7] with the intention of casting them as the model for the organization of the new kingdom's infantry. In any case, on February 25, 1833, by royal decree, the regular army was set up as follows:[8]

Infantry: in place of Kapodistrias's dissolved regular battalions, eight new ones, each consisting of 728 men (staff plus six companies).

Cavalry: one regiment, with 681 men (staff plus six companies).

Artillery: six companies (100 men each), to which were added one company of drivers (126 men) and one company of technicians (132 men). A little later on, by a royal decree issued on July 9/21, 1833, the technical company was placed under the direction of the central arsenal, which was formed simultaneously.

Engineers: two companies of pioneers (86 men each).

It was during this year that the ranks of the military hierarchy were determined: sublieutenant, lieutenant, B-class captain, A-class captain, submajor, major or captain (cavalry), lieutenant-colonel, colonel, major-general, lieutenant-general, general. The soldiers' equipment was also decided upon: saber and bayonet-bearing weapon for the infantry, pistols, lance, and saber for the cavalry, and double-edged saber for the artillery and engineers.[9] In this manner the foundations were laid for a truly combatworthy regular army organized along Western European lines. These foundations, however, would shortly be undermined by the severe social problem created by the breakup of the irregular troops.

By royal decrees issued on March 2/14, 1833, all persons who had enlisted in the irregular units after December 1/13, 1831, were released and obliged to return to their places of origin. The rest had the choice of going home or joining one of the ten new skirmisher battalions that were formed on the same day.[10] In adopting these measures the regency opted for a solution to the army question opposed to that of Kapodistrias, the Bavarians wanting an abrupt, overnight transformation of the new kingdom's armed forces along Western European lines.

The idea was not a bad one, since Greece's need for a well-trained and well-organized army had been obvious from the moment it gained its independence. Furthermore, the presence of the Bavarian soldiers who had accompanied Otho represented, in terms of the conversion of the Greek irregulars into regulars, a far more effective factor than that of the troops of Fabvier and Heideck. Finally, the choice of December 1/13, 1831, as the cutoff date for those who could remain under arms was no accident: those who had enlisted after that date had done so for purely party reasons, with the objective of helping their preferred political faction during the civil strife which had lacerated the country after Kapodistrias's assassination.[11] Briefly, the regency was attempting to let the Greeks know that the military ethics which had characterized the resistance to the Ottoman oppressors and most of the operations during the War of Independence was a thing of the past.

The intent of these new measures was good, but in practice they proved devastating. In spite of the fact that it was decided that the national costume would be their uniform, the ten skirmisher battalions were subjected to the same regulations and the same penal code as the regular troops,[12] and this resulted in widespread reluctance to enlist in them.[13] While those who did not want to or could not be absorbed into the new formations were obliged to return to their homes, many of them came from areas which had remained outside the boundaries of the new state (Epirus, Thessaly, Macedonia, Crete),[14] nearly all of them had no other occupation, and most, rightly or wrongly, considered it degrading to have to take up another trade in order to earn a living.[15]

The results of this rash policy were soon apparent: groups of irregulars marched from Argos, their main base, to Nauplia, the country's capital, to demonstrate their opposition to the new measures. The Bavarian troops were ordered to disperse them with the threat of armed force, thus obliging many of the palikars to seek refuge in Ottoman territory, the land of yesterday's enemies.[16] The long-term consequences were more unpleasant. Many Greeks began to see the Bavarians more as an occupying force than as part of the Greek army.[17] In parallel, there was an increase in brigandage in the Greek mountains attributable to the unemployed irregulars.

Realizing its mistake, the regency attempted to correct the situation through a well-aimed measure: on June 1/13, 1833, it established a gendarmerie whose officers and rank and file came from the irregulars.[18] Even though only a few of the latter were able to enlist in the new corps (it was meant to number no more than twelve hundred men), this correct handling of the matter, after the bitter experience of the break-up of the irregular troops, made the gendarmerie the most combat-worthy section of the army. Armed with weapons supplied at low prices by the French government and with the bayonets so unpopular with the Greeks,[19] the gendarmes performed such varied duties as guarding the frontiers and policing the army in a manner which, during Otho's reign, enjoyed widespread acceptance.[20] The first commander of this corps, Fr. Graillard, was an old colleague of Fabvier.

When Otho came of age and personally took over the task of reigning on May 20/June 1, 1835, he immediately expressed the intention of making peace between the state and the fighters of the War of Independence. His ultimate goal was to extend the Kingdom's boundaries at the expense of the Ottoman Empire and to recover Constantinople. He believed that this could be achieved through a general Panhellenic mobilization along the lines of the 1821 uprising. Within the context of such a policy, the regency's regular army, which in any case lacked popular support, would be called upon to play only a secondary role. The brunt of any reckoning with the Turks would be borne by the Greeks of the occupied provinces, who would rise in revolt. Thus, the regular army in effect began to be neglected.

Indeed, in 1833 the army numbered 9,643 men;[21] by the end of 1842 this figure had fallen to 7,941. After the formation, in 1838, of a special corps of frontier guards for the protection of the borders, the regular army had the following structure:[22]

Infantry: five battalions, each divided into six companies, and eight frontier-guard battalions, each divided into four companies, a total of 6,240 men.

Cavalry: two squadrons, each divided into two companies, a total of 596 men.

Artillery: one battalion, divided into five artillery companies and one company of drivers, a total of 840 men.

Engineers: one pioneer company of 265 men.

During the same period the army had 562 horses, of which 542 belonged to the cavalry and 20 to the infantry.

Ten years later the armed forces had once again declined in numbers, this time to 7,575 men, with the following structure:[23]

Infantry: two line battalions, each with eight companies, two skirmisher battalions, each with six companies, and four frontier-guard regiments, each with six battalions, a total of 6,151 men.

Cavalry: one squadron of lancers divided into three companies, a total of 325 men and 277 horses.

Artillery: one battalion divided into one field-artillery and three mountain-artillery companies, as well as one technical company detailed to the central arsenal, a total of 553 men and 109 horses.

Engineers: in 1843 the pioneer company was dissolved, leaving this branch made up exclusively of cadres.

This force was complete only during maneuvers. The rest of the time, only the number necessary for the various guard duties were kept under arms. Furthermore, the veterans' phalanx (389 men) and company (157 men), though part of the army, were noncombatant units: the former, organized in 1835, consisted of chieftains and officers in the army of the War of Independence and was a purely honorary unit; the latter, formed in 1835 and taking its final shape in 1852, consisted of all those soldiers who had become disabled in the line of duty.

What were the origins of the officers and soldiers of this ever shrinking army? All matters concerning recruitment were regulated by 1837.[24] The army recruited volunteers and draftees. The former (those who enlisted before the date of their obligatory service), provided that they were over eighteen and under thirty, were allowed to choose the branch in which they would serve and to determine the length of their service.[25] Draftees were recruited for a period of four years. Conscription was effected through a lottery system at the municipal level among those included on special census lists[26] who were between eighteen and twenty-four years of age.

This system was rather unfair. The recruitment process mostly affected those from the lower stratum of society, since high-school and university students, priests, teachers, and doctors, as well as only sons, married men, the very short, and the physically handicapped, were all exempt from military service. Even after having been conscripted, a person could be released from service if he could pay someone to replace him. In this manner the uneducated sons of poor farmers were dragged through a long term of military service which often ruined their lives.[27]

Class distinctions were transplanted into the army: the wealthy could not only dress better than the others, but also avoid fatigue duty if they could pay someone to do it in their stead.[28] Finally, the volunteers, who during Otho's reign seemed to be the only soldiers who put some enthusiasm into their service, benefited from a rather lenient application of the regulations and had the possibility of being promoted to noncommissioned officers. In fact, those volunteers who wanted to and were deemed suitable could, after attending one of the schools which in 1840 were set up in every battalion,[29] become noncommissioned officers and then officers. To achieve the latter it became necessary after 1861 to attend the officers' training school established that year in Athens.[30]

The officer corps consisted of former noncommissioned officers (who had previously been volunteers) and graduates of the Evelpidon Military Cadet Academy. This academy had been established by Kapodistrias and was reorganized by the regency in 1834.[31] The students entered at a young age, no older than twelve, and during their studies in the first four forms were given the lessons normally taught in schools of the primary and secondary level. Upon graduating they entered the army with the rank of sublieutenant and, after 1861, warrant officer.[32] From the last years of Otho's reign on, their progress through the ranks was much the same as it is today: sublieutenant, lieutenant, captain, major, lieutenant-colonel, colonel, major-general, lieutenant-general, and general.[33]

Organized more or less along French lines,[34] the army by 1855 was still armed with a variety of weapons of French and Belgian origin. In that period an attempt was made to modernize and homogenize its armament: the artillery was basically supplied with twelve-pounder howitzers and six-pounder cannons and all of the infantry with rifles.[35] The armed forces' share of the national budget was three-elevenths between 1853 and 1859 and five-nineteenths between 1860 and 1863, about 6.5 million drachmas per annum.[36] Under these circumstances, the army was not in a position to be used as a foreign policy tool. Throughout Otho's reign, it was not once used in battle against external enemies,[37] though it played an active role in the domestic affairs of the country, as is witnessed by the coup of September 3/15, 1843, and the revolution of October 10/22, 1862. How can this be explained?

As I have said, Otho considered the founding of the Greek state the first step toward regaining Constantinople and believed that the extension of the Kingdom's boundaries could be achieved through the uprising of the subjugated Greeks. Consequently, he did not see Greece's military problem, as Kapodistrias and the regency did, in terms of whether to maintain an irregular or a regular army. His major preoccupation was with instigating revolutionary movements in the neighboring provinces and reinforcing them with Greek officers. This was clearly the case in 1854 during the uprisings in Epirus, Thessaly, and Macedonia.[38] In other words, the state ideology considered the entire nation as the national army, just as the War of Independence was the model for the liberation of the whole of Hellenism.[38]

The army thus took on an operetta-like character, with a number of officers which seems excessive[39] enjoying an undue social position. During most of Otho's reign it was charged with the maintenance of public order, in particular with the fight against brigands, a field in which little progress had been made by 1862 (the year of Otho's overthrow) and even later.[40] Military service, in spite of its reduction in 1859 to three years,[41] continued to be a burden to those who were drafted, especially because the system enabled the wealthy and the educated to avoid it. Furthermore, the very idea of the type of discipline a regular army necessitated was still foreign and incomprehensible to the Greeks.[42] To make matters worse, the systematic assignment of the army to the pursuit of brigands was, in effect, a tax on the rural population, since farmers were obliged to offer food and shelter to the detachments that were attempting to suppress the gangs.[43] Thus, it is worth stressing again, the army's role during the Othonic period was essentially one of active participation in the country's political life.

An analysis of this phenomenon is not within the scope of this paper. However, it is worth underlining the role that certain military or army-organized corps played in the coup of 1843, in the 1862 revolution, and in the turbulent interregnum period of 1862–63. The gendarmerie was, in 1843 and 1862, the most loyal protector of the throne.[44] On the other hand, a regular corps which had been formed in 1840 with the help of French officers[45] was instrumental in the overthrow of King Otho during the night of October 10/22–11/23, 1862, in Athens.[46] The national guard, formed in 1843 along Belgian lines,[47] played an important role in the fighting of February 8/20 and June 18/30, 1863, constituting the main force of the "progressive" Mountain party.[48] The artillery, also involved in Otho's overthrow, supported the "conservative" party headed by Dimitrios Voulgaris during the interregnum period.[49] Thus the division and polarization of the military (though the national guard was not a military corps in the strict sense of the term) was very clearly mirrored in the positions the gendarmerie and the national guard took in the country's political conflicts: the gendarmerie usually supported the throne or the conservatives, whereas the national guard was imbued with a progressive spirit.

The disturbances continued even after the accession to the throne of the new king, George I. These were partly the result of the granting to active army officers by the constitution adopted after Otho's overthrow of the right to be elected members of Parliament[50] and to take part in the country's political life. This, in turn, contributed to the disintegration of an army already so engrossed in politics that it had completely set aside its primary mission of defending the country. This would become clear after the outbreak of the Cretan uprising.

In 1866 the Greek element of the Cretan population revolted against Ottoman domination, demanding union with Greece. The latter was to support the Cretan struggle, but at the same time ran the risk of a war against the Ottoman Empire. In order to face this possibility the Kingdom needed, on the one hand, to be in a position to control the sea lanes of the Aegean and, on the other, to be able to deploy along its borders with Turkey a military force sufficient in both numbers and combat-readiness to confront the Ottoman forces of that region before reinforcements could be sent from other areas.

However, in 1866 this was impossible. In 1863 the Greek army numbered only 8,651 men and had the following structure:[51]

Infantry: twenty battalions, ten line and ten reserve, a total of 7,204 men.

Cavalry: one hipparchy, consisting of four companies, a total of 404 men.

Artillery: one battalion made up of five companies, a total of 669 men. The central arsenal also came under this corps.

Engineers: a double company of firemen, with 323 men.

The military band of the guard of Athens, with 51 men.

In the years that followed, the strength of the armed forces was increased somewhat: to 11,000 in 1864 and 12,000 in 1865 and 1866. These figures may be overstated, as they represent the levels set by the government and there are various indications that actual numbers were far lower. In terms of armaments, the infantry and the corps of engineers were supplied with 1857-model rifles, the cavalry with 1865-model carbines, and the artillery with 1829-model short-barreled arms.[52]

An intensive reorganizational drive was begun immediately by the government of Alexandros Koumoundouros, which came to power in December 1866. This was in keeping with his policies of reinforcing the Cretan struggle and increasing the country's preparedness for war. The "soul" of this endeavor was Colonel Dimitrios Botsaris, son of Markos Botsaris, the famous chieftain of the War of Independence, who was made minister of war. Botsaris at once grasped the magnitude of the problem and was quick to complete an impressive reorganization of the army. A law passed by Parliament in January 1867 set the level of the army at 31,300 men, including officers, noncommissioned officers, and musicians. Of these, 14,300 men were to make up the operational army, the other 17,000 being reserves.[53] In this manner, the army's manpower was in effect doubled—a logical step if one considers that the Kingdom's population, which in 1861 had been approximately 1 million, had by 1870 reached nearly 1.5 million.[54] Furthermore, the reserves, which consisted of regular recruits, volunteers, and in time of emergency all those who had already completed their service and were under the age of forty, were systematically organized and for the first time represented a sizable force capable of standing alongside the operational army.

Botsaris's major achievement, however, was to increase the army's numbers without a corresponding increase in the number of recruits.[55] He did this by creating a special corps of volunteers numbering two thousand men. According to his declarations in Parliament, this corps was to take on duties which had until then been improperly placed in the army's domain so as to enable the latter unhindered to devote its attention to the defense of the nation.[56] The formation of this corps of volunteers (i.e., professionals) raised a multitude of objections. Fears were expressed in Parliament[57] that it would attract men with shady backgrounds who, thanks to the special privileges which the government was prepared to grant them, would create a state of indiscipline and represent a source of insubordination and agitation within the army's ranks. Botsaris categorically refuted these suspicions, although he refused, in January 1867, to give further details on his ultimate goals for this corps. These goals were undoubtedly not limited to the creation of a unit which would simply assist the army. In fact, events were to prove him right.

By December 1867 four battalions of volunteers had been formed. The soldiers who served in these, the so-called evzones, received a substantial monthly salary,[58] had to purchase their own food, and wore the traditional Hellenic attire (fez, fustanella, and so forth). Thus, in spite of their high pay, these new battalions cost the state about one-third as much as the others, while their formation stimulated the tiny Kingdom's economy in that their uniforms were produced by traditional methods with domestic materials.[59] Over and above these economic benefits was the fact that through the evzones the idea of military service became acceptable to the Greek people. Until 1867 many draftees who lived in mountainous or remote regions, where their arrest was difficult, had refused outright to serve, and many islanders had fled to Turkey when they reached conscription age.[60] The first evzone battalions, however, became very popular, with many young men wanting to enlist in them.[61] Thus, Botsaris was able to find a final solution to the problem which Kapodistrias and the regency had confronted in different ways and which Otho had basically neglected. He formed a new corps which, although governed by the rules of the regular army, nevertheless maintained, thanks to its uniform, the appearance of the irregular units of the War of Independence, whose spirit it embodied. In 1867, therefore, the task which Kapodistrias had begun was finally completed. Botsaris's reorganization and augmentation of the army[62] was to enable Greece to face the possibility of a confrontation with Turkey without Otho's vague and utopian visions of a general uprising of the subjugated Hellenic element. In fact, it seems that the minister of war intended to transform the whole of the Greek infantry into evzones, apparently considering the formation of the original volunteer battalions the first, experimental stage.[63] This would have revolutionized the nature of the Greek army and would perhaps have been significant not only for Greek, but also for European military history.

However, in December 1867 Koumoundouros was overthrown, and his successor,[64] Dimitrios Voulgaris, chose to follow a totally different course in relation to the Cretan uprising. In the hope of ending the Cretan "episode," he systematically undermined Botsaris's reforms and once again reduced the army's numbers. Of greater significance was that Botsaris's plan to transform the infantry into evzones was definitively thwarted.

In retrospect, the nucleus of the battalions formed in 1867 remained and even grew. The brilliant performance of the evzones, especially during the Balkan wars of 1912–13 and the Asia Minor campaign of 1919–22, served to highlight the depth and soundness of Botsaris's vision. The solution of the regular-irregular dilemma as well as all the other problems that marked the development of the Greek army under Kapodistrias, the regency, and Otho was, because of Koumoundouros's overthrow, only a partial one. This in no way reduces the significance of the innovation of Botsaris, who should someday be recognized as one of the most prominent organizers of the Greek army.

Notes

1. Gh. Kremos, Νεωτάτη Γενική Ἱστορία ὡς τέταρτος τόμος συμπληρωτικός τῆς Γενικης Ἱστορίας τοῦ ᾿Α. Πολυζωίδου, vol. 2 (Athens, 1890), p. 953.
2. Ibid., p. 954.
3. Sp. Trikoupis, Ἱστορία τῆς Ἑλληνικῆς Ἐπαναστάσεως, vol. 3 (Athens, 1888), pp. 170–71.

4. On the reaction to the formation of regular army units in 1825, see Photakos, Ἀπομνημονεύματα περί τῆς Ἑλληνι κῆς Ἐπαναστάσεως (Athens, 1960), pp. 382–86.
5. Kremos, Ἱστορία, p. 955.
6. Army General Staff/Department of Military History, Ἱστορία τῆς ὀργανώσεως τοῦ Ἑλληνικοῦ Στρατοῦ 1821–1954 (Athens, 1957), p. 21.
7. Tr. E. Evanghelidis, Ἱστορία τοῦ Ὄθωνος βασιλέως τῆς Ἑλλάδος 1832–1862 (Athens, 1893), pp. 32, 35. Greece had undertaken to pay for this force.
8. Army General Staff, Ἱστορία, pp. 26–27.
9. Ibid., p. 28.
10. G. L. von Maurer, Ὁ Ἑλληνικός Λαός, trans. Olga Robaki, vol. 2 (Athens, 1976), p. 451.
11. Ibid.
12. Ibid., p. 452.
13. In any case, these battalions were very small, 204 men each (Army General Staff, Ἱστορία, p. 27).
14. Kremos, Ἱστορία, p. 1015.
15. Von Maurer, Ὁ Ἑλληνικός Λαός, p. 569.
16. Kremos, Ἱστορία, p. 1016; Gen. Makriyannis, Ἀπομνημονεύματα, vol. 2 (Athens, 1947), pp. 64–66.
17. This was clearly brought out during the Mani rebellion in 1834 (Kremos, Ἱστορία, p. 1051).
18. Von Maurer, Ὁ Ἑλληνικός Λαός, pp. 572–75.
19. Ibid., p. 573.
20. Cf. Ἡ στρατιωτική ζωή ἐν Ἑλλάδι (Athens, 1970), p. 77.
21. Officially, at any rate, and not including the gendarmerie (Army General Staff, Ἱστορία, p. 29).
22. Ibid, p. 33.
23. Ibid., p. 36.
24. "Νόμος περί Ἀπογραφῆς," Ἐφημερίς τῆς Κυβερνήσεως τοῦ Βασιλείου τῆς Ἑλλάδος, no. 40 (December 8, 1837), pp. 169–71.
25. Army General Staff, Ἱστορία, p. 31; Ἡ στρατιωτιή ζωή, p. 39.
26. Army General Staff, Ἱστορία, p. 31.
27. Cf. *Military Life*, pp. 218–19.
28. Ibid., pp. 41, 60–64.
29. Army General Staff, Ἱστορία, p. 31; *Military Life*, pp. 237–38.
30. Army General Staff, Ἱστορία, p. 40.
31. Von Maurer, Ὁ Ἑλληνικός Λαός, pp. 565–67.
32. Army General Staff, Ἱστορία, pp. 32, 41. In 1864 the academy's regulations were altered; youths fifteen to eighteen years of age were to be admitted and to attend for six years (five years after 1866) (ibid., pp. 47–48).
33. Ibid., p. 39.
34. Von Maurer, Ὁ Ἑλληνικός Λαός, pp. 563–64.
35. Army General Staff, Ἱστορία, p. 39.
36. Ibid., p. 42.
37. There was not even a mobilization plan (ibid.).

38. Cf. Άπομνημονεύματα τής υπουργίας Σπυρίδωνος Πήλικα, καθηγητού τοῦ Ποινικοῦ Δικαίου έν τῷ 'Οθωνείῳ Πανεπιστημειῳ, ed. Ioannis Pilikas (Athens, 1893), pp. 137, 156, 165-66.
39. The anonymous author of *Military Life* recounts that a little after the Crimean War a special office was created in the War Ministry for "officers without an army" (p. 262).
40. It must be pointed out that the gendarmerie was far more successful in the pursuit of brigandage (ibid., p. 77).
41. Army General Staff, Ἱστορία, p. 39.
42. Cf. Archives des Affaires Etrangères, Paris (hereafter AAE), Correspondance Polititique, Grèce, vol. 92 (1867), Gobineau to Moustier, December 18, 1867, f. 417.
43. Ή στρατιωτική ζωή, pp. 147-49.
44. Evaghelidis, Ἱστορία, pp. 201-3; AAE, Correspondance Politique, Grèce, vol. 84 (mai-octobre 1862), Bourée to Drouyn de l'Huys, October 27, 1862, f. 273.
45. H. Belle, "Voyage en Grèce (1862-1868-1874)," *Le Tour du Monde* 1876 (2d semester), p. 31.
46. AAE, Correspondance Politique, Grèce, vol. 84 (mai-octobre 1862), Bourée to Drouyn de l'Huys, October 27, 1862, f. 273.
47. "Διάταγμα περί συστάσεως Ἐθνοφυλακῆς," Ἐφημερίς τῆς Κυβερνήσεως τοῦ Βασιλείου τῆς Ἑλλάδος, no. 36 (October 16, 1843), pp. 179 ff.
48. Even though it remained theoretically neutral during the coup of February 1863. Cf. Πανδώοα [Pandora], Athens, vol. 13, April 1862-April 1863, p. 563; also see, in relation to the events of June 1863, a report by the chief of the national guard in Athens and Piraeus, P. Koroneos, in AAE, Correspondance Politique, Grèce, vol. 87 (mai-juillet 1863), Bourée to Drouyn de l'Huys, July 24, 1863, ff. 316-26. By January of 1863 a total of 4,901 men had enlisted into the national guard in the cities of Athens and Piraeus (the major points of growth of this corps), while another 1,080 were in training (Πρακτικά τῶν Συνεδριάσεων τῆς ἐν Ἀθήναις Β' τῶν Ἑλλήνων Συνελεύσεως, vol. 1, sitting of June 23, 1863, p. 453).
49. AAE, Correspondance Politique, Grèce, vol. 84 (mai-octobre 1862), Bourée to Drouyn de l'Huys, October 10, 1862, ff. 272-74; ibid., vol. 87 (mai-juillet 1863), Bourée to Drouyn de l'Huys, July 24, 1863, ff. 316-26.
50. See Article 71 (Πρακτικά τῶν συνεδριάσεων τῆς ἐν Ἀθήναις Β' τῶν Ἑλλήνων Συνελεύσεως, vol. 6, sitting of October 17, 1864, p. 570).
51. Army General Staff, Ἱστορία, p. 42. The army also had 424 horses: 44 in the infantry, 355 in the cavalry, and 25 in the artillery.
52. Ibid., p. 47.
53. Πρακτικά τῶν Συνεδριάσεων τῆς Βουλῆς, Περίοδος Α'-Σενοδος Β', sitting of January 18, 1867, pp. 100-101.
54. A. Mansolas, *La Grèce à l'exposition universelle de Paris 1878* (Athens, 1878), p. 13.
55. 4,500 in 1867 (Πρακτικά τῶν Συνεδριάσεων τῆς Βουλῆς, Περίοδος Α'-Σύνοδος Β', sitting of January 18, 1867, p. 101), of which 2,000 were destined

for the reserves. It is noteworthy that during the final decade of Otho's reign (1851-62) about 1,500 men were drafted annually (Army General Staff, Ἱστορία, p. 36). In 1864 and 1866 the figures was 2,200 and in 1865 it was 3,080 (ibid., p. 47).

56. Πρακτικά τῶν Συνεδριάσεων τῆς Βουλῆς, Περίοδος Α΄-Σύνοδος Β΄, sitting of January 16, 1867, p. 89.
57. Ibid., sitting of January 17, 1867, pp. 93-94; ibid., sitting of January 18, 1867, pp. 96-100.
58. Thirty drachmas per month (AAE, Correspondance Politique, Grèce, vol. 92 [1867], Gobineau to Moustier, f. 416). In comparison, a corporal's salary a little after the Crimean War was eighteen drachmas per month (Ἡ στρατιωτική ζωή, p. 245).
59. AAE, Correspondance Politique, Grèce, vol. 92 (1867), Gobineau to Moustier, December 18, 1867, ff. 416-17.
60. Ibid., f. 417.
61. Ibid.
62. In 1867 the recruitment law was changed significantly, restricting the categories under which military service could be avoided (Army General Staff, Ἱστορία, p. 46).
63. AAE, Correspondance Politique, Grèce, vol. 92 (1867), Gobineau to Moustier, December 18, 1867, f. 417.
64. After the short-lived government of A. Moraitinis.

The Crimean War and Greek Society

Dimitris Michalopoulos

The generally accepted idea that until the Crimean War the Greek political parties known as the "English," the "French," and the "Russian" were characterized by more or less blind allegiance to one or another of the Great Powers[1] is a gross oversimplification and a distortion of historical fact. Recent historical research has indicated that the political parties of Otho's reign (1833–62) had a more or less concrete social basis and a kind of ideology and program. On the basis of the information currently available, it seems that the "French" and "Russian" parties could be characterized as populist and the "English" as bourgeois; at any rate, the former drew their members primarily from the rural and, generally speaking, the ordinary Greek population (although the "French," consisting mainly of palikars, included a significant number of local primates) and the latter from among the bureaucrats and merchants.[2]

The "French" and "Russian" parties gave voice, sometimes demagogically, to the popular mentality and proposed solutions to national problems that did not threaten the traditional framework of Greek society. The Megali Idea—the notion of the liberation, through uprisings and armed struggle, of the Greeks under Ottoman rule and the transfer of the capital from Athens to a Turk-free Constantinople—was a basic element of the ideologies of both parties, although it was the "French" who championed the Idea after 1844 while the "Russians" assumed the cause of Orthodoxy. In contrast, the "English" party stood for the internal development of the country, the growth of trade, and the modernization of the army and the navy; only after these goals had been attained would it be ready to consider extending the boundaries of Greece at the Ottoman Empire's expense. Beyond this, the restraining or even abolition of absolutism and, after 1843, the espousal of constitutionalism were much more matters of principle for the "English" than for the other two parties. Its leader, Alexandros Mavrokordatos, briefly headed a government in 1841 and proposed to the king a set of reforms that would have limited the latter's power; when the king rejected them,

Mavrokordatos resigned.³ Three years later, on March 30/April 11, 1844, when the king had been obliged to grant the constitution that virtually the whole of the Greek population had demanded, Mavrokordatos was again instructed to form a government, the "first constitutional government" in Greece.⁴ This time he was prevented from implementing his reforms by opposition from the "French" and "Russian" parties. Accused of being "permissive" in religious matters and of undermining the constitution, he resigned on August 4/16, 1844.⁵

The "Russian" party's position on the constitutional question was ambiguous, although its leading figure Andreas Metaxas played an important role in the events of September 3/15, 1843, that led to the establishment of the constitutional monarchy. A characteristic opinion was that expressed by Theodoros Kolokotronis, a hero of the War of Independence and a known "Russian," in suggesting that Otho's granting of a constitution would lead to the foundering of the "homeland."⁶ Ioannis Kolettis, the leader of the "French" party, became prime minister on September 6/14, 1844, and immediately imposed a form of parliamentary dictatorship whose primary objectives were the restitution of luster to the crown's image, which had been tarnished by the coup of September 3/15, 1843, and—as he let it be understood, at least—the realization of the Megali Idea.⁷ The results of these policies became obvious when Kolettis died in 1847: not a single practical measure had been undertaken for the internal development of the country, and its international position and economic situation were shaky. In spite of this, Otho instructed Kitsos Tzavellas, Kolettis's minister of war, to form a new government in an attempt to maintain the political system that the "French" leader—whom the king regarded as his "master"—had imposed on the country.⁸

Thus, from the inception of the constitutional monarchy until 1854, the year of the occupation of Piraeus by French and British troops, the "English" party was practically out of power. In fact, all the governments of Greece up to March 1848 came from the "French" party, with or without the participation of "Russians" but with the support of the crown. The Kolettis government of mid-1845 was considered a coalition government of "French" and "Russians." From then until his death, Kolettis governed with "French" and sometimes "Russian" ministers. His successor Tzavellas included in his government the notorious "Russian" Georgios Glarakis. After Tzavellas's resignation in 1848, governments attached to the crown whose members came from the "French" and "Russian" parties ruled the country.⁹ Thus the rapid development of Greece along more or less Western lines—the essence of the "English" party's program—could not be realized. Why was this so?

From the time Otho attained his majority in 1835 until the Piraeus occupation, two broad political camps had been emerging: a "traditional" camp, consisting practically of the Peloponnese-based "Russian" and mainland-Greece-based "French" parties, and a "progressive" camp, whose main thrust came from the "English" party. The fact that the former parties were able to mobilize the masses provided them with a strong position in seeking the leadership of the country. The "English" party drew its support from the strata of Greek society that were to crystallize, by the end of Otho's reign, as embryonic *grande* and *moyenne bourgeoisies* but at the time were weak both in numbers and in political strength. Thus the governments headed by Mavrokordatos lacked the popular basis necessary to keep them in power—a basis made all the more indispensable by the crown's open mistrust of the "English" leader. The "traditional" camp therefore enjoyed a virtual monopoly of political power, and things began to change only under the pressure of the new conditions created in Greece by the Crimean War.

At the outset of the hostilities between Russia and Turkey, the tiny Kingdom of Greece followed the events closely and was already attached to the Russian cause. On January 15/27, 1854, an uprising motivated by the Greek Kingdom broke out in Epirus and rapidly spread to Thessaly, western Macedonia, the Olympus area, and Khalkidhiki. As a result, Piraeus was occupied on May 13/25 of that year by French forces, joined a little later by British troops, and a policy partial to the interests of the two Western powers was imposed on Greece.[10] Thus the Crimean War proved a traumatic experience for the Greek people: a national upheaval along lines that had long been considered appropriate for the realization of the Megali Idea—that is, the outbreak of uprisings in the Greek lands of the Ottoman Empire through the infiltration of armed groups from the Kingdom in parallel with a war between Russia and Turkey—resulted in the defeat of Russia and the occupation of Piraeus by Turkey's allies. This revealed the bankruptcy of Otho's policies and the need for far-reaching changes in both the political and the social structure of the country.

The presence of French and British occupation forces in Piraeus for almost three years (May 13/25, 1854–February 16/28, 1857) had socially beneficial results.[11] It spurred the industrial development that had been under way since 1848 and laid the foundations for the development of Piraeus into Greece's first industrial area by 1878.[12] In the country as a whole, there was a turn toward commerce and industry that undoubtedly had its impact on social structure. At the same time, Hellenism recognized that the Megali Idea could be realized through a peaceful process. After the Crimean War the Greeks of Constantinople, in particular, began to break away from Russia, until then considered their natural protector, because they suspected that tsarist diplomacy sought to undermine the authority of the ecumenical patriarchate.[13] The economic penetration of Turkey by Britain and France increased greatly, and the Greeks of the Ottoman Empire took advantage of this[14] and associated themselves with British and French capitalism. In the new situation the theory arose, first among the Greeks of the commercial centers of the Near East and the Diaspora and then in the Kingdom, that it was perhaps not necessary to defeat the Turks through the use of arms—that economic and intellectual supremacy would open the way for a less impressive but equally effective domination.

The Greco-Turkish commercial treaty signed on May 27/June 8, 1855, with the blessing of Britain and France[15] showed clearly the new orientation of the country's foreign relations and reflected the changes occurring in its domestic affairs. The program and, generally, the spirit of the "English" party were becoming more widely accepted, and this created a current that ultimately led to the fall of Otho. In fact, the latter, illogically seeking the realization of the Megali Idea through the use of arms, ended up being considered Russophile (and thus attracting the hostility of Britain) and devoted a very small part of his budget to the internal economic development of the country.[16] Furthermore, he had imposed a political system viewed as tyrannical. In short, he did not at all correspond to the emerging middle class's model of a king. The struggle between Otho and these emerging political elements began shortly after the departure of the occupation forces. While the prestige of the king had increased considerably because of the proud manner in which he had confronted the offensive attitude of the French, in particular, this was not sufficient to compensate for the obvious inability of his regime to deal with the new situation created by the country's economic development.

In the aftermath of the Franco-British occupation, the old "English," "French," and "Russian" parties disappeared from the political scene. No Greek wanted to bear the label of follower of one of these foreign powers after the disappointment and humiliation of the war.[17] From 1859 on, university students and professional people, along with bureaucrats and the young military, waged a dynamic struggle against Otho, whose policies they considered responsible for the economic backwardness of the country and the difficulties confronted by young lawyers and doctors.[18] This struggle ended in Otho's dethronement in October 1862.

This event was enthusiastically greeted by the whole of Hellenism—both the Greeks of the Kingdom and those in the Ottoman Empire and the Diaspora. Furthermore, it acted as a catalyst. The process that had begun with the occupation of Piraeus in 1854 was completed in 1862, and concurrently the political forces of the period became clearer. Shortly after Otho's departure, the Greek people elected Alfred, the son of Queen Victoria, their king.[19] The quasi-unanimity of this election—even though Alfred did not accept the crown—was the result of a show of force by those strata of Greek society I have referred to as the *grande* and *moyenne bourgeoisies*.[20] The economic development in progress since 1857 had allowed the crystallization of these strata, located mainly in the capital and in the commercial cities of Patras and Ermoupolis, and close contact between them and the *grands bourgeois* of the Ottoman Empire and the Diaspora.[21] The spearhead of these strata was the political group consisting of students and young professionals, bureaucrats, and military men. They were pro-British,[22] but with a dynamism quite different from that of Mavrokordatos's "English" party; they saw Britain not as the power on which Hellenism had to base its hopes, but as a model for the development of Greece.

The 1862 revolution ensured the rise of the successors of the "English"; Alfred's election ensured their political triumph. The tragic fiasco of the 1854 insurrection, foreign occupation, and Russia's defeat in 1856 offered them the opportunity to launch their offensive. They were enabled to do so partly by their growth, the result of the country's economic and industrial development. Nevertheless, for reasons beyond the scope of this paper, the accession of Queen Victoria's son to the Greek throne did not take place. Furthermore, it must be stressed that the dethronement of Otho had been accomplished not by the *grande* and *moyenne bourgeoisies* alone, but by a coalition of different classes and strata of Greek society. Would they continue to follow the bourgeoisies in their effort to "Europeanize" Greece along British lines? The course of the Greek state after 1862 rested upon the answer to this question.

Notes

1. G. P. Kremos, Νεωτάτη Γενική Ἱστορία ὡς τέταρτος τόμος συμπληρωτικός τῆς Γενικῆς Ἱστορίας τοῦ 'Α. Πολυζωΐδου, vol. 2 (Athens, 1890), p. 1057; T. Vournas, Ἱστορία τῆς Νεώτερης Ἑλλάδας ἀπό τήν Ἐπανάσταση τοῦ 1821 ὡς τό κίνημα τοῦ Γουδί (1909), 2d ed. (Athens, n.d.), p. 247.

2. J. A. Petropulos, *Politics and Statecraft in the Kingdom of Greece 1833–1843* (Princeton, 1968), pp. 119, 357, 371, 511 (but see, for a different view, p. 9).

3. M. D. Stasinopoulos, Σελίδες ἀπό τήν Πολιτική Ἱστορία τοῦ Νεωτέρου Ἑλληνισμοῦ (Athens, 1978), pp. 19–121. As far as the "English" party's pro-

gram is concerned, see N. Dragoumis, Ἱστορικαί ᾿Αναμνήσεις (Athens, 1874), pp. 321, 323-36.
4. Tr. E. Evanghelidis,Ἱστορία τοῦ Ὄθωνος βασιλέως τῆς Ἑλλάδος (Athens, 1893), p. 286.
5. Ibid., pp. 287-93; G. Aspreas, Πολιτική Ἱστορία τῆς Νεωτέρας Ἑλλάδος, vol. 1 (Athens, n.d.), pt. 1, p. 189.
6. N. Dragoumis, "᾿Απόσπασμα ὑπομνημάτων ἀνεκδότων," Πανδώρα 19 (1868-69):105; also Dragoumis, Ἱστορικαί ᾿Αναμνήσεις, p. 350.
7. Ἔκτακτον Παράρτημα τοῦ ἀριθμοῦ 40 τῆς Ἐφημερίδος τῆς Κυβερνήσεως τοῦ 1843. Ἡ τῆς Τρίτης Σεπτεμβρίου ἐν ᾿Αθήναις Ἐθνική Συνέλευσις. Πρακτικά, sitting of January 14, 1844, pp. 190-94; Evanghelidis,Ἱστορία, pp. 302-3; Dragoumis,Ἱστορικαί ᾿Αναμνήσεις,pp.311-21; General Makriyannis, ᾿Απομνημονεύματα, vol. 2 (Athens, 1947), p. 183.
8. Makriyannis, ᾿Απομνημονεύματα, vol. 2, p. 195.
9. I.e., the government of G. Kountouriotis, K. Kanaris, and A. Kriezis. The "Russians," after the resignation of their leader Metaxas from Kolettis's government in 1845, undertook a violent campaign against the latter, but this campaign did not signify a real difference in principles (even though it tended to be waged in the name of Orthodoxy) and is to be considered a commonplace of Greek political life (Petropulos, *Politics and Statecraft*, p. 429).
10. Evanghelidis, Ἱστορία, pp. 555-85. Under French and British pressure, Mavrokordatos was again called to form a government.
11. Among them the Tinan garden in Piraeus; see Henri d'Ideville, *Journal d'un diplomate en Allemagne et en Grèce: Notes intimes pouvant servir à l'histoire du Second Empire, Dresde-Athenes 1867–1868* (Paris, 1875), pp. 228-29.
12. A. Mansola, *La Grèce à l'exposition universelle de Paris en 1878* (Athens, 1878), p. 97.
13. E. K. Kyriakidis, Ἱστορία τοῦ Συγχρόνου Ἑλληνισμοῦ ἀπό τῆς ἰδρύσεως τοῦ Βασιλείου τῆς Ἑλλάδος μέχρι τῶν ἡμερῶν μας 1832-1892, vol. 2 (Athens, 1892), p. 86.
14. N. Svoronos, *Histoire de la Grèce moderne* (Paris, 1972), p. 58.
15. Πρακτικά τῶν Συνεδριάσεων τῆς Βουλῆς, Δ´Περίοδος–Β´Σύνοδος, sitting of June 9, 1855, pp. 392-405.
16. Archives du Ministère des Affaires Etrangères [Paris], Correspondance Politique, Grèce, vol. 84 (mai-octobre 1862), Bourée, French minister at Athens to Drouyn de l'Huys, French foreign minister, October 25, 1862, f. 254.
17. Evanghelidis, Ἱστορία, p. 586.
18. Ibid., pp. 608, 611; Fr. Lenormant, "La Grèce depuis la révolution de 1862. III. L'interrègne et la nouvelle royauté," *Revue des Deux Mondes* 52 (1864): 436.
19. Πρακτικά τῶν Συνεδριάσεων τῆς ἐν ᾿Αθήναις Β´ τῶν Ἑλλήνων Συνελεύσεως, vol. 1, sitting of January 22, 1853, pp. 449, 450.
20. The terms *bourgeois* and *grande* and *moyenne bourgeoisie* are used in this paper with some concern.

21. D. Michalopoulos, *Vie politique en Grèce pendant les années 1862–1869* (Athens, 1981), pp. 27–33.
22. Τό Μέλλον τῆς ’Ανατολῆς (Athens), January 16 and February 27, 1863.

War and Insurrection as Means to Greek Unification in the Mid-Nineteenth Century

Evangelos Kofos

Throughout the decade preceding the Crimean War, the Greeks were embroiled in a great debate over their national aims. By the end of the forties, a hazy consensus had emerged on what could be termed a national program. Its essence was the liberation and unification of all Greeks in a single national state. Since, however, there were conflicting views on who qualified as a Greek or what territories could be considered Greek-inhabited, the extent of this future state varied considerably. The confusion was compounded by the coining of the term "Megali Idea," which encompassed both the liberation program and grandiose schemes for the resurrection of the Byzantine Empire and the dissemination of Hellenic culture throughout the Balkans and the Middle East.[1] A brief discussion of the theoretical antecedents of the Megali Idea will contribute to an appreciation of the role of insurrection and war as a means to Greek unification.

The formative years of the Megali Idea, i.e., the forties, coincided with an animated debate over the nature, origins, continuity, and unity of modern Hellenism. The basic historical and even philosophical conclusions of this debate found their practical application in the formulation of the goals of the Megali Idea. The prevailing views could be summarized as follows:

Neo-Hellenism was viewed as descending in an unbroken line from classical antiquity, admittedly acquiring some scars during the Byzantine and Ottoman periods but certainly suffering no irreparable damage. Thus, the classical heritage—which included the Greek language—became for the modern Greek state a trust to be transmitted to the peoples of the East—an area vaguely defined as including the Balkans, Asia Minor, and even regions as far as Mesopotamia.[2]

At the same time, Byzantium was viewed as part of the heritage of the modern Greek kingdom. Considering themselves the heirs of that medieval empire, the Greeks believed that they were destined to lead the other nationalities in its revival.[3]

Apart from these two legacies, the recent experience of the War of Independence—which had resulted in the carving out of the Ottoman Empire of the first independent Christian state—had enhanced the view that the Greek kingdom, the only independent Christian state in the Balkans, was destined to play a leading role in the liberation struggles of all the enslaved nationalities of the Ottoman Empire.

Each of these legacies had its own impact on the shaping of the Megali Idea. The classical heritage attached to the Megali Idea a messianic, civilizing mission. The Greeks were to "Hellenize"—in the cultural sense—the other nationalities, bringing to them not only the values of the classical heritage, but also the Greek language. Borrowing the example of Catholic and Protestant missionaries, the advocates of this theory considered it their duty to "enlighten" the neighboring peoples through a voluntary peaceful and evolutionary process. Understandably, such a process would result in a regenerated East, a brotherhood of peoples sharing a community of culture and, possibly, of language. Of course, the rule of the Ottomans would have to cease.[4] The Byzantine heritage called for the gradual transformation of an alien empire—the Eastern Roman Empire—into an essentially Greek state in which a multiplicity of peoples would coexist. As the Ottoman Empire was showing signs of a steady internal decay in the early decades of the nineteenth century, the Greeks, rapidly ascending on the economic, social, and cultural ladder, could logically aspire to a leading role in transforming it into a Muslim-Christian state, admittedly with strong Hellenic features.

All these theories naturally laid emphasis on the peaceful advance of Hellenism across the lands of the Ottoman Empire. They had been popular among the Greek elites of the empire and the Diaspora prior to 1821. The War of Independence had dealt them a serious blow but had not shattered them entirely. The fact that freedom had been brought, albeit to a fraction of the Greek-inhabited Ottoman lands, not by an evolutionary or political process, but by an extended armed insurrection was to bear heavily on the tactics for the implementation of the Megali Idea in the years to come.

In the long run, the War of Independence affected the evolutionary concept negatively in two ways. On the one hand, the Ottomans came to realize that the emergence of Greek nationalism posed a serious threat to their domination. Thus Greek attempts at Greco-Turkish cooperation would henceforth be viewed with suspicion, to say the least. On the other hand, the achievement of the Greeks offered the other Balkan nationalities a model for their own national emancipation. Their national awakening, however, was bound to be detrimental to Greek efforts aimed at their Hellenization or, at least, their incorporation into a multinational state. These far-reaching implications were not visible, however, to most Greeks of the thirties and forties—an era of romanticism which encouraged the nurturing of schemes for achieving grandeur through a long, uninterrupted evolutionary process.

Putting aside, for the moment, such long-range delusions, the very establishment of an independent state through a revolutionary process had provided lasting encouragement to the unredeemed Greeks, particularly the Cretans and those of the border provinces, to adopt a similar course for their own liberation. The fact that they, too, had paid a heavy toll in human and material losses during the War of Independence and that large numbers of their compatriots lived in the Kingdom as refugees had resulted in the formation of strong pressure groups agitating for the adoption of such a course.

Understandably, irredentism was not among the major preoccupations of the first administrators of the Greek state, President Ioannis Kapodistrias (1828–31) and King Otho's Bavarian regents (1833–37). Struggling to build a state out of the ruins left by a devastating war of liberation and numerous civil conflicts, these leaders sought and, indeed, pleaded with the Great Powers for an extension of their territory. Their arguments were not so much irredentist as social and economic. For this reason, the first Greek envoys dispatched to European courts, in 1833–34, were instructed to demand the cession of Crete, certain Aegean islands, Epirus, and Thessaly on the grounds of building an economically and territorially viable state.[5] Similar views were echoed, a few years later, by the young King Otho, who as late as the Eastern crisis of 1839–40 pleaded with foreign diplomats for the cession of Crete "from the financial and geographical standpoint."[6]

A decade after its founding, the small independent Greek state was finding the task of reconstruction frustratingly difficult. The outbreak of the crisis of 1839–40 caught the Greek leaders not only materially and diplomatically unprepared, but without any comprehensive program. Their confusion was complete. Under the circumstances, it was neither the government nor the various political elites, but the veterans of the War of Independence and revolutionary elements among the refugee settlers in the Kingdom, as well as the Cretans, who jumped at the opportunity to raise the flag of insurrection.

The Cretans were a special case. As early as the War of Independence, they had formulated a concrete political program. Being in a state of military and psychological preparedness, they needed no guidance or prodding from outside to rise in revolt. In the Kingdom, however, the government had focused its energies on appraising the intentions of the powers with regard to territorial concessions. Thus the initiative had passed to revolutionary elements, which dispatched clandestinely armed bands across the borders. To the north, in Epirus and Macedonia, emissaries from the Kingdom endeavored to prepare the ground for a major insurrection, but the victory of the Ottoman troops over the Egyptian forces dealt a sharp blow to these erratic and ill-prepared initiatives.[7] The revolt in Crete met a similar fate. The island returned to the sultan's jurisdiction, and repressive measures forced thousands of new refugees to seek shelter in the Kingdom, swelling the numbers of their kinsmen already there since the War of Independence.

Insignificant though the military events of 1839–40 were for the Greek state, their repercussions on the shaping of a comprehensive national program were far-reaching. On the one hand, they brought the realization that the Ottoman Empire was experiencing recurring crises and that the young Kingdom had better be prepared to profit from them. On the other hand, they showed how pronounced and direct was the interdependence of the free and the unredeemed Greeks. The leaders of the Greek state could neither restrict themselves to the affairs of the Kingdom nor prevent, through legislative measures, the "eterochthones" (i.e., residents of the Kingdom originating in the unredeemed provinces or the Diaspora) from influencing Greek policies. Clandestine groups agitating in unison with their compatriots across the border could easily bypass the government and spark crises with serious consequences for the international relations of the Kingdom as well as for its internal political and social order. How unstable the latter was is shown by the fact that in 1843 a popular rising led to a major political crisis and the granting of a constitution. Under the circumstances, the king and the political leaders were compelled to turn their eyes from the most pressing internal problems of state building and focus them on ways and means of carrying out the Megali Idea.

The term "Megali Idea" had, of course, not even been coined prior to 1847, when Prime Minister Ioannis Kolettis pronounced it in Parliament.[8] Despite serious antagonisms over internal political and social issues, king, political leaders, intellectuals, war veterans, and revolutionaries found themselves surprisingly in unison with regard to national aims. They differed not on the validity of the Megali Idea, but on its translation into policy.[9] A debate started which was to last until the Megali Idea was carried to its conclusion in the first decades of the twentieth century. On this issue, the Greeks were divided into two broad camps: those who advocated an evolutionary process and those who insisted on an active course.

Briefly, the arguments of the first group centered around the idea of building a model state, economically and militarily strong and culturally advanced, that would act both as a magnet for the unredeemed Christians of the empire and as a suitable substitute, from the point of view of the powers, for the dissolving Ottoman Empire. Such a policy offered the advantage of preserving the corporate unity of the Greeks—as well as the Greek-oriented non-Greek-speaking Christians of the empire—until circumstances forced the powers to intervene. At that moment, the Eastern Question could be solved in one stroke, to the benefit of Hellenism. The advocates of this line believed in sparing no effort or resources in aiding the material and cultural ascent of the Ottoman Greeks so that, together with the Helladic Greeks, they would compose a powerful element that could be counted upon and could influence developments in the East. Understandably, to implement this policy a long period of peaceful, if not friendly, coexistence with the Ottomans was imperative.

The advocates of action—the "activists"—had no patience with such schemes. They considered chimerical the idea of building a model state—or even of maintaining a viable one—out of the underdeveloped, minute kingdom of the Peloponnese and Sterea. Instead, they argued for building a war machine at home and a revolutionary network in the Ottoman provinces. Seeing no reason to wait for the ideal combination of European powers acting jointly for the dissolution of the Ottoman Empire, they would seek alliances with those European powers or Balkan states or nationalities which, like the Greeks, appeared hostile to the maintenance of Ottoman territorial integrity. In the melee that would ensue, other European powers would be compelled to intervene—and, indeed, to intervene in support of the Greeks. In response to words of caution, the activists would point to the example of the War of Independence, when the Greeks rose in a massive revolt, sacrificed wealth, status, and their lives, but succeeded in the end in compelling the powers to assist them in establishing their independent state. In their view, the Kingdom needed only to pursue a similar course of confrontation with the Porte in order to achieve the liberation and unification of all the Greeks. Any gesture toward rapprochement or even working relations with the Porte was castigated as treason. Even the argument that uprisings ran the risk of destroying the unity of the Hellenic world was rejected on the grounds that armed agitation and revolutionary or war preparations cemented the ties between the Kingdom and the unredeemed Greeks, teaching the hard-pressed Christians to expect their future deliverance from the Greek Kingdom.

It is not an easy task to ascertain the social, political, economic, geographical, and even ethnic characteristics of the various groups that usually sided with the "activists," if for no other reason than that people of similar backgrounds often crossed the line separating "evolutionists" from "activists." Nevertheless, certain general patterns do emerge.

As already hinted, the group most likely to adopt the activist line was the war veterans, the palikars. A segment of them had of course been absorbed into the armed forces of the young Kingdom. A great number of them, however, finding it hard to adjust to rapidly changing circumstances, had turned into social parasites or outlaws—brigands. Whether in the army or in brigand bands, these elements of the population could be found in the vanguard of any revolutionary movement. Whenever an uprising occurred, the shift from marauding brigand to national freedom fighter was the rule rather than the exception. Indeed, it was a phenomenon that repeated itself throughout the nineteenth and even the early years of the twentieth century. It is no surprise that renowned veteran leaders such as Makryannis and descendants of War of Independence heroes (Karaiskakis, Kolokotronis, Tzavellas, and others) were among the most active irredentists of the mid-century period.[10]

This was particularly true of war veterans and their descendants from unredeemed lands now resident in the Kingdom: Epirotes in the northwest, Thessalians and Macedonians in the northeast, and Cretans in southern Peloponnese and the southern Aegean islands. Although special studies on this phenomenon are scarce or nil, even a superficial examination of the various revolutionary movements of the mid-nineteenth century confirms the view that the most energetic activists were to be found among this group. The old chiefs—*kapetaneoi*—remained focal figures among their compatriots, whether in the Kingdom or in their native lands. They were expected to provide guidance in peacetime and leadership during armed insurrections. Their word carried more weight than any government directive for their clansmen, who were expected to rally around them and form the backbone of armed bands.[11] Certainly, a significant number of bandits and other outlaws in the Kingdom as well as in the neighboring Ottoman provinces made their own calculations in joining the rebel bands (for "legal" booty, amnesty in the Kingdom, or guard posts in the Ottoman service after the conclusion of peace). Nevertheless, there is ample evidence that these social outcasts, frequently illiterate mountaineers or peasants, espoused the Greek national idea and threw themselves with astonishing courage into the battle against the Ottoman oppressor.[12] In the front lines of the activists were also second-generation young intellectuals, university students, and professionals descending from the ranks of first-generation eterochthones.

Among the Greeks outside the Kingdom, a dichotomy between evolutionists and activists appears to have followed fairly well-defined geographical patterns. Natives of Ottoman provinces adjacent to the Kingdom—including Crete—opted in a rather consistent way for insurrection and war. This was understandable. Liberation by direct confrontation with the Ottomans appeared to them feasible. Being, moreover, near the Kingdom, they were exposed at an early stage to the nationalist ideology and the nationalist stirrings emanating from Athens, and this accentuated their irredentism. In contrast, the Greeks living in provinces far from the borders of the Kingdom, in Asia Minor, Cyprus, and Thrace, tended to gravitate toward Constantinople. There, in the "captive center of Hellenism," the evolutionary ascent of the Greeks within the Empire was still the prevailing dogma. Macedonia, halfway between the two centers, found itself in crosscurrents. Thus southern Macedonians tended to associate themselves with the Thessalians and those in the north and the east with the Thracian Greeks.[13] Social and economic conditions in the countryside of European Turkey did not vary much from one region to another. The peasants of Thessaly were under similar deprivations as those of Macedonia and Thrace. As a result, banditry was common in all mountainous regions. In the border districts, however, during major crises—such as those of 1840, 1854, 1868, and 1878—the arrival of revolutionaries from the Kingdom often acted as a catalyst for the metamorphosis of bandits into freedom fighters.[14] This, however, would not be the case in regions remote from the Kingdom, where the Greek irredentist movement in its violent form could hardly reach the ranks of bandits.

Of the unredeemed Greeks, the Eptanesians, living under British rule, were a case apart. Their irredentist behavior would place them with the activists of the Kingdom and the adjacent Ottoman provinces. While they chose not armed revolt, but political agitation as their form of struggle, their objective was identical: the overthrow of foreign rule and unification with the Kingdom.

In the Kingdom, activists and evolutionists could to some extent be identified by their party affiliation. Most prominent activists belonged to the "Russian" party, since Russia projected among the Greeks the image of the deliverer of all Christians from the yoke of the sultan. While supporters of this line could be found within the "French" party, "French" partisans often opted for the diplomatic/political approach to the realization of the Megali Idea. Members of the "English" party were the strongest advocates of the evolutionary process.[15] Naturally, this attempt at classifying adherents of the Megali Idea on the basis of party affiliation should be viewed with caution, as the crossing of lines was common.

As for King Otho and Queen Amalia, their choice of the activist policy between the two Eastern crises (1840 and 1854) turned from simple opportunism to almost religious fanaticism. Indeed, during the Crimean War, the monarch's reaction left no doubt that he aimed at both territorial aggrandisement through insurrections and the resurrection of Byzantium with himself in the role of emperor—two goals which, pursued concurrently, were bound to defeat one another. There is no doubt that the king's choice of the activist line was considerably influenced by internal pressures, which threatened to evolve into antimonarchial violence and even revolution. Since the officers' corps and the rising young intelligentsia were in the vanguard of the activist movement, the king, in espousing their irredentist policies, hoped to divert their political activism away from his political absolutism.[16]

Understandably, Greece's international relations were influenced by the initiatives of its activist policy. So long as the unification program remained in the sphere of theoretical discussion or even long-range planning, the European powers would show some understanding and might even encourage it, in the hope of exploiting it to their own interest at the proper moment. When, however, uprisings broke out or war on Turkey was contemplated, practical politics would come into play.

Russia, bent on a policy of confrontation with the Ottoman Empire, looked favorably upon an active Greek policy. Greek-instigated uprisings in the Ottoman provinces could always play a useful diversionary role. The proposed schemes for a gradual increase of Greek influence within the Ottoman Empire were not to its liking, however, since they posed the possibility of a future threat to Russian dominance in Constantinople.

At times, Greek activists found encouragement and support among the Italians—who aspired to an escalation of disturbances in southeastern Europe in order to bring about their own Risorgimento—and even among the Austrians, who vied with the Russians for influence in the Balkans. Italian and Austrian support was, however, intrinsically connected with rapidly changing policy expediencies and could not be a sound basis for Greek policy options.

More solidly against an active policy were Britain and, to a lesser extent, France. Determined to maintain a viable Ottoman Empire as a bulwark to a southern advance of Russia, these Western powers conveyed to the Greeks, in no uncertain terms, their opposition to insurrectionary movements and/or threats of war.[17] To them, the Greek Kingdom and the unredeemed Greeks were a force in reserve—a trump card—to be used only in case of the total collapse of the Ottoman Empire. Then, a strengthened Greek state would emerge as a substitute bulwark to halt a Russian descent upon the Mediterranean. Even this remote possibility appeared improbable to the Greeks as they watched both powers struggling to render the empire viable through the introduction of administrative reforms.[18]

Under the circumstances, uprisings in the provinces and military preparations in the Kingdom were bound to come face to face not only with the military might of the Ottoman Empire, but also with the strong diplomatic pressure of most of the European powers.

Needless to say, the Balkan states or nationalities were enthusiastic supporters of the Greek initiatives. Pinning their hopes for achieving their own national unification on either a joint Balkan campaign against the Ottomans or a unilateral Greek military initiative which would offer them the necessary diversion to press the Porte for concessions, these Balkan nations sought to establish closer links with the Greeks in order to coordinate their efforts. On the Greek side, however, the idea of Balkan cooperation on equal terms had not yet matured. The prevailing notion was still the establishment of a large, multinational Christian state with the Greeks playing the dominant role.[19]

In this formative decade of the Megali Idea, the goals had been concretized, but the split over its implementation had widened. Nevertheless, the eruption of the Eastern crisis of 1853 found the Greeks emotionally —although not materially—prepared to opt for an active course.

Mobilization was carried out on two levels. Clandestinely, secret nationalist societies were engaged in preparing armed bands and spreading the insurrectionary ferment in the Ottoman provinces. At the same time, they sought to infiltrate the army—mainly the officers' and subofficers' corps—and to enlist the support of political leaders, including certain cabinet ministers, in order to press the government and the court to follow an active course. On the government level, appraisal of international developments convinced most leaders that Ottoman rule was nearing its end and that siding with Russia would either bring Greece direct territorial benefits or admit Greek claims to the European peace settlement. Such assessments—although misleading—found encouragement in the confused, emotional, even romantic climate that reigned at that time in the Athens court. For the king to run counter to the tide at a time when popular excitement, supported by the military, was assuming uncontrollable proportions would have been tantamount to political suicide. Otho chose to reject the counsel of neutrality of certain of his ministers and brushed aside menacing demarches by the British and French envoys. Indeed, he took over the supervision of the insurrectionary movements through his military aides at the court.

The revolutionary pattern that emerged during the mid-fifties had first been tested during the 1839–40 crisis. With many improvements, it would be repeated in similar crises in 1866–68 (the Cretan Revolution) and 1877–78. Briefly, it provided for almost total mobilization of the refugees from the unredeemed provinces and for the formation of armed bands, usually headed by members of the influential families of the respective provinces. Incursions by land or landings from the sea aimed at spreading the revolt northward—almost to the present northern Greek borders. The immediate aim was to capture certain border Thessalian and Epirote towns and proclaim the establishment of "provisional governments" for Epirus, Thessaly, and Macedonia. Then all these "governments" would proclaim the union of the respective provinces with the Greek Kingdom.[20] At the same time, a limited mobilization of the Greek army would offer moral support to the bands. If necessary, army units would cross the border into neighboring provinces and join them. For a small state to face the Ottoman Empire—even at war with Russia—with only eight thousand men in its regular armed forces was, to say the least, risky. Worse yet, the decision to base the whole campaign on the support of one power while the other European powers (and, indeed, the maritime ones) remained hostile was an affront bound to end in disaster.

The Greeks soon came face to face with reality. France and Britain did not hesitate to offer even naval cover to the Ottomans in order to crush the insurgents and the volunteers from the Kingdom. When such initiatives did not suffice, they landed troops and occupied Piraeus, while their navies set up a blockade of Greek ports. This dealt the death blow to the first attempt to put the active policy to the test with full government support. The crushing of the insurrections, the humiliation and economic losses, and Russia's defeat had far-reaching implications for the unification movement as a whole and for the active approach to its solution in particular.

In the neighboring Ottoman provinces, the punitive measures against the population recalled the half-forgotten cruelties of the period of the War of Independence. As a result, peasants and especially local leaders became extremely cautious about insurrectionary appeals by apostles from the Kingdom. In Constantinople, among the leadership of the subject Greeks—the clergy and the commercial and banking classes—the old concept of the evolutionary ascent of the Greeks within the empire acquired new impetus.

Back in Athens, the bitterness of defeat and the exposure of the impotence of the Kingdom led to a reappraisal of priorities. The hitherto discredited evolutionists assumed new influence. The prevailing idea now was that, since Greece could no longer solve the question of territorial expansion by revolution and war, it ought to establish good relations with the Ottoman Empire. With the signing of a commercial treaty including most-favored status for Greek commercial interests (which the other Balkan states did not enjoy) and the Hatt-i Hümayun reforms, which benefited both the Ottoman and the Helladic Greeks, a resurgence of optimism about the future growth of Hellenism soon softened the disillusionment over the debacle of the Crimean War. As the acceptance of this course acquired the support of influential economic, political, and even professional circles in the Kingdom, the advocates of the violent approach saw their ranks shrinking. Steady economic development in the Kingdom and in the Greek communities of the urban centers of the empire was the reward for and, indeed, the best proof of the validity of the new policy. Indeed, the commercial classes were experiencing a kind of territorial expansion of their activities even in non-Greek regions, where, along with their commercial undertakings, they were bringing Hellenic culture and even Hellenic national ideology to non-Greek Christians.[21]

Simultaneously with these developments, the post-Crimean War period saw the rapid rise of nationalism among the other Balkan peoples, particularly the Serbs and Bulgarians. The latter's confrontation with the Ottoman Greeks on the ecclesiastical issue introduced a new element into the methodology for implementing the national program. True, the menace of Pan-Slavism, which in subsequent decades assumed the dimensions of a national psychosis, had not yet penetrated into the Kingdom. Certain new politicians (Deligeorgis, for example), however, and a number of journals which had more direct links with the Ottoman Greeks began to base their arguments in support of the evolutionist approach on the future Slavic challenge to Greek positions in the mixed regions of Macedonia and Thrace. They were supported by the Ottoman Greeks in Constantinople, Thrace, and northern Macedonia, who were directly exposed to new developments in their immediate vicinity.

All these evolutionists exerted considerable pressure on King Otho to abandon his extremist irredentism. It is true that the monarch had shown signs of deep disillusionment not only at the failure of his policy in 1853–55, but also at the apparent shift in Russian policy, which in the post-Crimean War period appeared to espouse the interests of Christian Slavdom instead of those of the Orthodox Christians.

The evolutionist policy could flourish only in a climate of protracted peace. A series of events, however, changed all this. In the closing years of the fifties, the Italian Risorgimento came to its fruitful conclusion, the unification of Romania was successfully carried out, and the Montenegrin and Bosnian military confrontation with the Porte activated the Serbs in pushing forward their South Slavic Načertanije. Since all these developments appeared to the Greeks to bear a striking resemblance to their own unification program, they inspired a major reappraisal of tactics. In place of erratic, isolated military adventures which had the support of at most a single European power, a policy of joint undertakings with neighboring peoples was adopted. In this respect, the Italians and the Serbs appeared the most promising collaborators, and secret negotiations aimed at a military alliances with both took place from 1859 to 1862. Simultaneously with the official initiatives, revolutionary elements in the Kingdom (mainly among the most enthusiastic activists and antimonarchists) were equally energetic in approaching Italian and Balkan revolutionaries about joint military schemes in the Ottoman-occupied lands.

King Otho's dethronement in 1862 put an end to these initiatives. For a few years the evolutionary process maintained its momentum, but external developments prevented it from proceeding too far. In 1866, with the eruption of the Cretan Revolution, the pendulum once again swung to the activist course. In the years and decades to come, this pendulum continued to swing back and forth, indicating that the liberation and unification process had a long, uncertain way to go and that both activist and evolutionist approaches were necessary to bring the national program to its conclusion.

Notes

1. A brief discussion of this issue, with the relevant bibliography, appears in E. Kofos, *Greece and Eastern Question, 1875–1878* (Thessaloniki: Institute for Balkan Studies, 1975), pp. 17–20. A more recent, detailed review of Greek writings and contemporary Greek views on the Megali Idea is Nadia Danova, *Nationalniat vapros v Grtskite polititseseski programi prez XIX vek* (Sofia: Nauka i Izkustvo, 1980), pp. 10–18, 138–64.

2. The first American envoy to Athens, Tuckerman, correctly described this prevailing view when he wrote that the destiny of Hellenism was to Hellenize the vast stretch of territory "which by natural laws the Greeks believe to be theirs and which is chiefly inhabited by people claiming to be descended of Hellenic stock, professing the Orthodox or Greek faith, or speaking the Greek language" (Stephen Xydis, "Diplomatic Relations between the United States and Greece, 1868–1878," *Balkan Studies* 5 [1964]: 54).

3. The views of K. Paparigopoulos, G. Tertsetis, and N. Dragoumis, cited in Danova, *Nationalniat vapros,* pp. 178–79.
4. Danova (ibid., pp. 142–43) contends that similar notions prevailed in the early decades of the nineteenth century among the Germans, who believed in the civilizing mission of a large German state, and that these notions reached Otho's court through Bavaria and influenced the Greek monarch.
5. P. N. Pipinelis, *I Monarchia stin Ellada, 1833–1843* (Athens, 1932), pp. 116–17.
6. John Petropulos, *Politics and Statecraft in the Kingdom of Greece, 1833–1834* (Princeton: Princeton University Press, 1968), p. 349.
7. *Makedonia: 4000 chronia ellinikis istorias kai politismou* (Athens: Ekdotiki Athinon, 1982), p. 446; Elias Georgiou, "I Thessaliki epanastasis 1840–1841 kai i galliki politiki," *Thessaliki Chronika,* pp. 33–47.
8. *Istoria tou Ellinikou ethnous,* vol. 13, section by Constantine Dimaras (Athens: Ekdotiki Athinon, 1977), pp. 467–68.
9. Petropulos, *Politics and Statecraft,* pp. 346–47.
10. Petropulos (ibid., p. 357) writes: "The class permanently committed to a war policy of irredentism was the palikars. . . . Military implementation of the Great Idea provided the only hope of restoring to them the importance and power which they had enjoyed during the Revolution." Similar views are expressed for the Kolettis era by Maria Economopoulou, "Parties and Politics in Greece, 1844–1855" (Ph.D. diss., Somerville College, Oxford, 1982), pp. 103–5.
11. Referring to the composition of the insurgent forces in the 1854 uprising in Radovitsi, Epirus, Koliopoulos reports that on the Ottoman-held side of Epirus bands were composed not only of armed peasants, but also of former bandits and old chiefs, while on the side of the Kingdom, volunteer bands were formed of army and national guard officers and men and palikars, i.e., old hands, descendants of War of Independence fighters (Yannis Koliopoulos, *Listes* [Athens: Ermis, 1979], p. 77).
12. Ibid., pp. 81–82. Similar incidents were recorded in all the insurrectionary movements which occurred in various Ottoman-held provinces throughout the nineteenth century. For Macedonia in 1878, see letters from rebel/brigand chiefs in E. Kofos, *I epanastasis tis Makedonias kata to 1878* (Thessaloniki: Institute for Balkan Studies, 1969), pp. 331–41.
13. E. Kofos, "The Subject Greeks during the Eastern Crisis of 1875–1878," in *100ème anniversaire des insurrections en Bosnie-Herzegovine, dans d'autres pays balcaniques et de la Crise d'Orient de 1874 à 1878* (Sarajevo: Académie des Sciences et des Arts de Bosnie-Herzegovine, 1977), pp. 99–112.
14. Koliopoulos, *Listes,* pp. 71, 74, 76, 80–81; also consular reports in Kofos, *I epanastasis.*
15. See Petropulos, *Politics and Statecraft,* pp. 320–43, on the Philorthodox plot that arose within the ranks of the "Russian" party, and E. Georgiou, "I Thessaliki epanastasis," pp. 33–47, on the revolutionary ferment among "French" party adherents at the time of the Crimean War. For a discussion of this phenomenon in the forties and up to the Crimean War, including an

appraisal of Kolettis's attitude, see Economopoulou, "Parties and Politics," pp. 68–73, 100–105; Danova, *Nationalniat vapros*, pp. 84–126.

16. Danova, *Nationalniat vapros*, p. 167; Petropulos, *Politics and Statecraft*, p. 360.

17. France's policy in this respect is best described in Foreign Minister Drouyn de l'Huys's instructions to the French legation in Athens on the eve of the Crimean War, when he observed that Greece should gain the confidence of the powers by following "a prudent" policy, so that they would consider it, at the opportune moment, "the rock on which to build a more stable and permanent edifice" (E. Driault and M. Lhéritier, *Histoire diplomatique de la Grèce de 1821 à nos jours*, vol. 2, p. 383).

18. Danova, *Nationalniat vapros*, pp. 168–69.

19. Ibid., pp. 160–64; see also Dimitrije Djordjević, *Revolutions nationales des peuples balkaniques, 1804–1914* (Belgrade: Institut d'Histoire, 1965), pp. 49–54, 69–87.

20. D. Donda, *I Ellas kai ai Dynameis kata ton Krimaikon Polemon* (Thessaloniki, 1973), pp. 86–87; Economopoulou, "Parties and Politics," pp. 219–29.

21. Danova, *Nationalniat vapros*, pp. 180–83.

Greek Domestic Policies and the Irredentism of the 1860s: The 1866–1869 Cretan Revolution

Constantin Svolopoulos

For almost a century, Hellenism's longing for liberation was conspicuously expressed by the Cretans' struggle to rid themselves of Ottoman sovereignty. When Crete was left outside the bounds of the independent Greek state, despite its active participation in the Revolution of 1821, its Christian inhabitants were forced to undertake further lengthy and persistent efforts to achieve incorporation into free Greece (which came only at the end of 1912). If, apart from an analysis of the historical development of the matter, one were asked to produce simple and direct proof of the purely national character of the Cretan Question, one would only need to repeat Eleftherios Prevelakis's succinct observation: after Crete was united with Greece, the Cretan Question ceased to exist.[1]

The Cretan Revolution of 1866–69 tends to confirm this general point. Its outbreak is attributable to the violation of the principles of the Hatt-i Hümayun of 1856 and of the Firman of 1858, together with the Porte's imposition of particularly heavy taxation, but a more basic reason lay in the frustrated aspirations of the island's Christian inhabitants for union with Greece. A detailed account of the armed struggle is unnecessary here; the events have all been described before. It will suffice to note that its development attests to the unswerving tenacity and militancy of the revolutionaries despite their unfavorable circumstances. In January 1868, the Porte passed the Organic Law, affording equality of rights and justice to Muslims and Christians, but the revolutionaries remained unconvinced of the Turkish authorities' sincerity and, above all, dubious that their national aspirations would be satisfied. The revolutionary struggle gradually lost strength, however, and was ultimately crushed by the superior Turkish-Egyptian forces, especially given the Concert of Europe's condemnation of the Revolution and the intolerable pressure brought by the Porte and the Great Powers on Greece.² An examination of the events of the Revolution of 1866–69 provides an opportunity not only to emphasize the tenacity of the Cretans and to reaffirm the importance in the free Kingdom of the ideal of liberation, but also to point out certain obstacles to the achievement of Greece's national aspirations in general. A preliminary careful analysis of the developments indicates that the problems were intrinsic rather than purely circumstantial. Rather than being simply attributable to unfavorable diplomatic circumstances, the outcome of the Cretan uprising seems to have been a consequence of the inability of the promulgators of the Panhellenic policy to assemble the means for achieving their irredentist aims.

At first sight, the diplomatic circumstances did not necessarily seem negative. The Cretan problem was undoubtedly an organic part of the Eastern Question as a whole, but the satisfaction of Greek irredentist demands did not mean that corresponding concessions would have to be made to the other Christian countries of the Balkan Peninsula. At the same time, the Concert of Europe assumed the preservation of equilibrium and a certain respect for the Great Powers' unanimity; essentially, however, it was only Greece's three protecting powers—Russia, France, and Britain—that took any initiative in the Cretan Question. The vital question, therefore, was whether these countries were prepared to espouse the cause of Greek unification and to urge its acceptance by the Porte. Russia's attitude was positive: firmly opposed to the Treaty of Paris and the precept of Ottoman integrity, the Imperial Council of St. Petersburg supported either the union of Crete with Greece or the creation of an autonomous state along the lines of the Danubian principalities with a view to eventual unification. France apparently favored radical changes, influenced as it was in general by the broad trends of its European policy and in particular by developments in matters far more important for the Quai d'Orsay. The British attitude was firmly and unequivocally negative, on the principle that the preservation and strengthening of Ottoman power would provide the surest resistance to Russian pressure toward the Dardanelles and the eastern Mediterranean. This belief was certainly no basis for the rumors that sprang up concerning London's intention of imposing its exclusive control, or even sovereignty, on Crete; but it would be dangerous to maintain that this immediately unfeasible prospect was a more decisive factor than the principle of the preservation of Ottoman integrity. In any case, Britain's refusal even to discuss the annexation of Crete to Greece was enough to prevent the Great Powers from assuming any positive, and necessarily collective, initiative and to prevent any favorable development in the diplomatic sector.³

Crete's deprivation, under these circumstances, of effective diplomatic protection inevitably increased the importance of the means to maintain or extend the national armed struggle. The ratio of the opposing forces on Crete was decidedly unfavorable to the revolutionaries. In September 1866 the Greek consul in Hania estimated the Turco-Egyptian forces as numbering forty-two to forty-five thousand men, and in any appraisal of the Porte's military strength one should not forget that the Turks also had a fleet, modern weapons, and regular fresh supplies. Though the revolutionary forces consisted of hardy fighters who were brave and experienced in guerrrilla warfare, they were nevertheless considerably fewer in number and had no modern fighting equipment. Under these circumstances, the Turkish forces tended to retain control of the flat areas and the urban centers in particular, and the revolutionaries managed to maintain their own centers in the mountainous parts of the island and to harass the enemy's forces incessantly through the moral, organizational, and, above all, material support they were receiving from free Greece. From this point of view, Athens's support for the revolution has been judged by both contemporary observers and modern researchers to have been sufficient, other things being equal, to have kept the armed struggle going indefinitely.[4] The problem, however, was that to the extent that they insisted on providing active support for the revolutionary struggle on Crete the Greek governments of the time faced the possibility of armed conflict with the Ottoman Empire.

The minister for foreign affairs declared in Parliament at the end of November 1868 that the government's Cretan policy "has been cooling Greece's relations with the Ottoman government, so that the longer the struggle has lasted the more this coolness has increased. . . . in fact, our relations are already so changed that it seems that the Sublime Porte has decided to break off existing relations altogether."[5] The severing of diplomatic relations between the two countries was ensured when, on December 4, 1868, the Greek government rejected the Turkish ultimatum demanding not only the disbanding of the volunteer corps that had formed on Turkish territory, but also the disarming or the banning from Greek ports of the cruisers that were supplying the rebels with volunteers, food, and fighting equipment. Could Greece have found the diplomatic support that would have allowed it not to submit to the Porte's demands without an armed confrontation? An affirmative answer would require the protecting powers to have adhered to the principle of guaranteeing Greece's territorial integrity and independence—in accordance with the fundamental agreements of 1830–32 and the later ones of 1863–64—even in the event of its persisting in its intervention in

Crete. Any such hope was crushed once and for all when the six member powers of the Concert of Europe forced Greece to accept the terms of the Turkish ultimatum. Under these circumstances, Voulgaris resigned, and the Zaimis government that followed agreed to renounce all intervention in the Cretan Question, in accordance with the Porte's wishes and the demands of the Great Powers in their joint communiqué of January 20, 1869.

Might this backing down by the Greek government have been seen as a realistic adjustment to a situation brought about by its inherent inadequacies—an indication of political weakness leading to Greece's being insufficiently prepared for war? The answer to this vital question hinges on whether or not the Greek government was capable of calling up a military force prepared for an independent military confrontation with the Ottoman Empire. The Koumoundouros government had no hesitation in facing up to this latter possibility; thanks to an increase of some 25 percent in the national defense budget and to the unremitting organizational activity of Dimitrios Botsaris, the minister of war, the government succeeded in mustering a military force of thirty thousand—the largest since the founding of the independent Greek state.[6] But was it really feasible to continue the allocation of a significant proportion of the regular budget to military needs, and, above all, was this army capable of successfully standing up to the Ottoman military force? The opinions expressed on the occasion of the presentation of the latest budget in October 1868 were particularly critical: "The army, which is not adequately prepared for war, is using up almost a third of the budget, and future expenditure on its behalf for the supply of materials is going to cost us twice as much as its original value, since it will, of course, have to come from loans . . . the existing army is not only extremely costly for peacetime, but inadequately prepared for war."[7] This was the climate of opinion in the parliament formed after the elections of March 1868, and the army's inadequate preparation was also the definitive criterion of Voulgaris's policy, of the party which was to succeed Koumoundouros in power, and of King George I, who had assumed the initiative and the responsibility for this change of government. As a supporter of the king's policy, Alexandros Vyzantios wrote in January 1868: "The one side wanted to arm Greece in any way it could and to pay off the storehouses with all kinds of remnants; while the other side trembled lest this haste make Greece finally seem not like a fine ancient hoplite, but like a modern Don Quixote carrying a bayonet and wearing a basin for a helmet."[8]

If the country's military preparation was deemed inadequate, was there not a case for having recourse to foreign loans in order to meet this vital national requirement? A probable positive answer would presuppose a settlement of the outstanding differences with the holders of bonds from the War of Independence and the period immediately following. The inability of Greek governments between 1843 and 1878 to reach an agreement with their creditors had closed the door to international borrowing. Thus, with a view to meeting its financial deficit—60 million drachmas in the period from 1861 to 1878—Greece found itself obliged to conclude a series of internal loans on heavy terms, without even avoiding compulsory circulation.[9] But, even if foreign loans had been obtainable and internal loans available, was it desirable for the country's economic development and social progress to be mortgaged for the temporary advantage of preparation for war? On this topic the political leadership and public opinion were sharply divided, the two extremes advocating priority either for the military or for the domestic strengthening of the country respectively. Of course, the difference of opinion was not necessarily due to underestimation of one or the other factor on the part of either side. Rather, the one faction believed that territorial expansion was the main precondition for Greece's social and economic progress, while the other tended toward the view that only a solid substructure could ensure the success of a program of serious war preparation. This basic difference of opinion was also bound up with the protecting powers' policy toward the Greek Question: as a rule, Russia had advocated Greece's active participation in, or at least support for, enslaved Hellenism's struggle for liberation, whereas Britain had firmly, though without any immediate action on a practical level, given priority to the country's internal development as a prerequisite for realizing its daring national vision.

This dissension over the application of Greece's irredentist policy was particularly marked during the period of the Cretan uprising. While maintaining an appearance of neutrality, Koumoundouros adopted a policy of active promotion and vindication of national rights, which entailed support for the revolutionaries on Crete, military preparation in view of a war with Turkey, and extension of Greece's network of friendly relations in the direction of neighboring nations and peoples opposed to Ottoman sovereignty—Romania, Montenegro, Egypt, the Lebanese Maronites, and, above all, Serbia, with which Greece was to contract a bilateral treaty of alliance in August 1867 in Vöslau.[10] In order to set such an ambitious program in motion, the Koumoundouros government burdened the country with unforeseen expenditures, attempted to come to terms with foreign bondholders, and had direct recourse to domestic loans, all without, however, particularly encouraging results.[11] Voulgaris stood in opposition to Koumoundouros: without actually convincing anyone of his ambitions for a systematic and consistent program of domestic recovery, he was extremely circumspect in the face of any initiative in the direction of national demands on behalf of the unredeemed Greeks. In the case of the Cretan uprising he did not swerve from this policy; indeed, he sought the intervention of the protecting powers in order to have an alibi in the eyes of the Greek people for abandoning the Cretan revolutionaries. However, the fear of provoking unfavorable public opinion, coupled with the idea that it might be possible to take advantage of some favorable occurrence in order to promote an acceptable solution to the Cretan Question, prevented him, at least on the surface, from remaining aloof from the policy of his predecessors and in one or two cases led him to go even farther and adopt more active measures.[12]

The attitude of the protecting powers throughout the Cretan Revolution reflected the same basic differentiation of policy. Russia had encouraged both the Greek government and the Cretans in embarking on an armed struggle. On the opposite side, Britain not only had discouraged the resort to insurrection, but did not hesitate—frequently with the support of France—to exert pressure for a replacement of the Koumoundouros government with a cabinet determined to break off the support for the Cretan fighters. King George's espousal of the British line was in accordance with his extreme conservatism and his enforced sensitivity to British pressures and to the harsh experience acquired during the Crimean War: as he saw things, "Even if Russia were prepared to risk a war with the Western powers on behalf of Crete, it would be highly impolitic for [the king] to do so, for, were a Russian squadron to attempt the defense of Greece in war against Turkey, the immediate and certain consequences would be the destruction of the Russian and Greek fleets by the combined naval forces of England and France. . . . "[13] Referring to the "Cretan lesson," the British foreign secretary, for his part, observed at a later stage that the Greek governments should abandon their determined attempts to maintain alive the idea of territorial aggrandisement at Turkey's expense and reduce their military expenditures, since the guarantee of the three protecting powers was sufficient to allow Greece to manage with no military force other than the police; the sooner the Greeks abandoned this mentality, he argued, the sooner they would succeed in organizing their administration, putting their finances in order, and enhancing the material well-being of the country.[14]

In this brief analysis of the events concerning the Cretan Revolution of 1866–69 and the attitude of the Greek government toward them, I have tried to show the impact of the irredentist movement on war and society at the southernmost tip of the Balkan Peninsula. In conclusion, it can be argued that Greece's irredentist policy, which ran the risk of an armed confrontation with Turkey, conflicted to some extent with the need to pursue a consistent program of internal development; it should be added, on the other hand, that without the completion of the national unification program, any attempt at economic and social advancement within the narrow limits of the Kingdom was bound to have very poor results. Choosing the appropriate policy was such a difficult task that one wonders whether the Greek governments of 1856–70 were really faced with a dilemma or, rather, with an impasse.

Notes

1. E. Prevelakis, *I Megali Kritiki Epanastassis 1866–1869* (Athens, 1966), p. 7.
2. On the Cretan Revolution of 1866–69 see N. Tsirintanis, *I politiki ke diplomatiki istoria tis en Kriti Ethnikis Epanastasseos 1866–1868*, 3 vols. (Athens, 1950–51); I. Mamalakis, *O agonus tou 1866–1869 ya tin enossi tis Kritis*, 2 vols. (Thessaloniki, 1942–47); and "Aphieroma stin Kritiki Epanastassi tou 1866," *Nea Hestia* 80 (1966): 1473–1616. For an outline of the events, see Prevelakis, *I Megali Kritiki Epanastassis*; and N. Tomadakis, "I Kritiki Epanastassis 1866–1869," *Nea Estia* 80 (1966): 1488–1502. For a bibliographical view, see N. Tomadakis, "Simvoli es tin bibliographian ton Kritikon epanastasseon: B′. Bibliographia Epanastasseos 1866–1869," *Epetiris Etairias Kritikon Spoudon* 2 (1939): 128–238; M. Gregorakis, "Symboli sti bibliographia tis Kritikis Epanastasseos tou 1866–1869," *Paratiritis* (Hania), March 19–29, 1966, February 17–24, 1967. Of special interest is *I Kritiki Epanastassis, 1866–1869: Ekthessis tou en Kriti Proxenou tis Ellados*, 2 vols., ed. E. Prevelakis and V. Playanakov-Bekiari (Athens, 1967).
3. For details on the positions of the Great Powers, see D. Dontas, *Greece and the Great Powers 1863–1875* (Thessaloniki, 1966), pp. 63–155; D. Michalopoulos, *Vie politique en Grèce pendant les années 1862–1869* (Athens, 1981), pp. 190–202; K. Kalliataki, "Anglia ke Kriti, 1868," *Kritika Chronika* 25 (1973): 228–77. Older publications are E. Driault and M. Lhéritier, *Histoire diplomatique de la Grèce de 1821 à nos jours*, vol. 3 (Paris, 1925), pp. 180–320; and E. Kyriakidis, *Istoria tou Synchronou Ellinismou, 1832–1892*, vol. 2 (Athens, 1894), pp. 309–445.
4. Michalopoulos, *Vie politique en Grèce*, pp. 193–201.
5. *Praktika tou Synedriasseon tis Voulis*, 1st period, 3d session, 1868, pp. 561–62.
6. Michalopoulos, *Vie politique en Grèce*, pp. 193–95 (and see tables of expenses during the period 1863–69, pp. 231–41).
7. *Praktika tou Synedriasseon tis Voulis*, 1st period, 3d session, 1868, pp. 475–77, 509–10.

8. *Erga A. Byzantiou* (Trieste, 1893), p. 87.
9. A. Andreadis, *Mathimata dimossias economias: Ethnika daneia ke Elliniki dimossia economia,* vol. 1 (Athens, 1925), pp. 69–76, 79–81; A. Angelopoulos, *To dimossion chreostis Ellados* (Athens, 1937), pp. 20–22; T. Lignadis, *I xeniki exartissis kata tin diadromir tor Neoellinikou kratous (1821–1945)* (Athens, 1975), pp. 114–17, 119–20. See also A. Syngros, *Apomnimonevmata,* vol. 2, pp. 184–85.
10. S. Laskaris, "La première alliance entre la Grèce et la Serbie," *Le Monde Slave,* 1926, pp. 390–437.
11. For more general view of the policy of Koumoundouros, see Tsirintanis, *I politiki ke diplomatiki istoria,* vol. 2, p. 20; also Kyriakidis, *Istoria tou Synchronou Ellinismou,* pp. 417–23; and Michalopoulos, *Vie politique en Grèce,* pp. 193–98.
12. Dontas, *Greece and the Great Powers,* pp. 120–22; Michalopoulos, *Vie politique en Grèce,* pp. 198, 201.
13. Dontas, *Greece and the Great Powers,* pp. 129–30; see also p. 76.
14. According to unpublished sources presented in a lecture by Georges Dertilis in Thessaloniki in April 1982.

V. The Army and the Unification of Romania

The Impact of the Crimean War on the Government and Armed Forces of Romania

Ilie Ceauşescu

Emile Wanty, the Belgian military historian, characterized the Crimean War as "odd," and indeed he was correct.[1] The war presented numerous difficulties: the great distance between the theater of operations (Crimea) and the military bases of the Anglo-French-Piedmontese forces and the heterogeneity of the forces committed to battle (French, English, Turkish, Piedmontese, Russian), to mention only two. Both defensive and offensive tactics were affected by new technology, primarily because of the increased use of rifles. The Industrial Revolution had by this time produced steamships and many other kinds of machines, and the Crimean War played an important role in accelerating their application to the military sphere.[2] The conflict indeed recorded several firsts: a war correspondent was present on the battlefield, a telegram was dispatched in a war zone, and photographs were taken on the battlefield. All these firsts contributed to a more complete integration between war and the collective national consciousness, a development that made public opinion more sensitive to armed conflicts.[3]

In terms of international relations, the Crimean War was an episode in the continuing Eastern Question, the ongoing struggle in which the European powers tried to decide whether to maintain the Ottoman Empire. It was also an episode in the struggle for a general European balance of power.[4] Viewed from both of these perspectives, the war has an extensive literature.[5] Special emphasis has been given to the war's impact upon the balance of power among the Great Powers and to its role in hastening the unification of Italy and Germany.[6] But historians have paid only marginal attention to the war's impact on East Central Europe, and in particular they have slighted its consequences for the relationship between war and society. This essay focuses on precisely this aspect of the conflict.

National liberation and the renovation of sociopolitical structures were the two major goals of the peoples of East Central Europe. The

Greeks had won national independence in 1829, but each of the other peoples (Poles, Romanians, Hungarians, and South Slavs) was still fighting to shake off foreign rule and to lay the foundations of a modern society within the framework of a nation-state.

In Southeastern Europe, the Ottoman Empire's protracted crisis ensured the continued instability of the Istanbul-Vienna-St. Petersburg triangle. Even if the reform era (Tanzimat)[7] that was inaugurated in 1839 paved the way for the removal of an obsolete administrative structure, the "Sick Man of Europe" nonetheless recovered slowly, if at all. The struggle for the social and national emancipation of the empire's Christian peoples intensified, in the process creating a tense atmosphere that contained the seeds of an outbreak that might have significant international consequences.

In the meantime, the Habsburg Empire, badly shaken by the 1848 revolutions, had been rescued only by the intervention of tsarist Russia. Nevertheless, Vienna did not as a result fall into dependence on St. Petersburg. In the early 1850s, Tsar Nicholas I seemed to possess the means that would resolve the Eastern Question to Russia's advantage. But, though neither the Ottoman Empire nor Russia's rival, the Habsburg Empire, was in a position to withstand Russia's military might, Great Britain was determined to defend the integrity of the Ottoman Empire. The Anglo-Turkish trade agreement of 1838 had transformed the Ottoman Empire into a reliable client for British industrial products and also made it an important provider of cereals. For these reasons, any weakening of the Ottoman Empire threatened the economic interests of Great Britain and the security of its navigation routes in the Mediterranean. Britain benefited from the support of the France of Napoleon III, which had turned to London for a number of reasons, both domestic and international.[8] Thus Great Britain was in a position to carry out a policy consonant with its determination to prevent any attempt to partition the Ottoman Empire. As long as St. Petersburg insisted that "the collapse of the Ottoman Empire would inevitably occur immediately after its first serious clash with our [Russian] armies,"[9] conflict between Russia and Great Britain, the latter backed by France, was inevitable.

In East Central Europe the potential war was analyzed and appraised from two different perspectives. Revolutionary circles, on the one hand, were hostile to tsarist Russia because it had helped to suppress the revolutions in the Romanian principalities and Hungary. They therefore saw a war against Russia, whatever the aims of St. Petersburg's opponents, as performing a positive service for the cause of East Central European revolution. On the other hand, Russia's interests coincided with those of the Christian peoples of the Ottoman Empire in that both wanted to throw off the Ottoman yoke in the Balkans. This consideration earned Russia the support of those who thought Russia's presence in the Balkans would accelerate the disintegration of the Ottoman Empire, which was the precondition of the liberation and unification of the Balkan nations.

Greece provides a telling example of this attitude toward the Russian presence. After its independence had been acknowledged by the Treaty of Adrianople at the end of the Russo-Turkish War of 1828–1829, Greece sought to unify all the Greek lands, including Thessaly and Greek Macedonia. In Athens the Crimean War was seen as a timely opportunity to realize this goal, and, as a consequence, Greek public opinion favored Russia. In early 1854 an uprising led by Theodor Grivas and supported by the Greek authorities broke out in Epirus. The rebels besieged and conquered Metsovo in the Chalcidian Peninsula. In order not to prejudice the Greek authorities, this daring act was led by Greek officers who had resigned from the Greek army. Brave though the action was, it lacked coordination and failed in the face of the superior Ottoman forces. Great Britain and France, concerned about the security of their rear flank, intervened. An English-French fleet arrived in Piraeus (1854), where it remained until 1857, frustrating the Greeks' hopes of territorial gain.[10]

Serbia too hoped to take advantage of a new Russo-Turkish war. In order to prevent a Serbian military action, however, the Porte hastily issued a *hatt-i şerif* that renewed Serbia's autonomous status. This precaution proved unnecessary, for the Russian cabinet informed Prince Alexander Karadjordjević that Tsar Nicholas I did not want a Serbian "revolution." In fact, St. Petersburg did not want to embarrass Austria. Yet the Serbian leaders did not rule out the possibility of an Austrian intervention and therefore chose to remain on a war footing.[11]

The war began with the Russians' occupying Moldavia and Wallachia, a situation that stimulated the Bulgarian national liberation movement. A committee consisting mainly of Bulgarian merchants (such as H. Gheorghiev, H. Mustakov, and I. Bacaloglu) was set up in Bucharest. This committee was intended to stir up the Bulgarians and to contact Russian authorities in order to secure their support for the Bulgarian cause during the peace negotiations. The next year, a "Bulgarian Committee" (*nastoiatel'stvo*) was active in Odessa. These were the first political organizations of the Bulgarian bourgeoisie,[12] but their hopes were frustrated when the war's course proved unfavorable to the Russian cause. Russian misfortune robbed the Bulgarian actions of all effectiveness. During the Crimean War, but without any coordination with St. Petersburg, G. Rakovski's radical wing of the Bulgarian "Secret Society" was also active, seeking to initiate military actions by volunteer detachments.

The Crimean War's most significant impact on the social and national liberation movement occurred in the principalities of Moldavia and Wallachia, both of which witnessed major political and military developments.

The Romanian revolutionary emigration considered the war a good opportunity to implement the goals of the 1848 Revolution, which had been suppressed by the joint intervention of tsarist and Ottoman armed forces. Russia occupied Moldavia and Wallachia in the summer of 1853. The Russian commander, Prince M. A. Gorchakov, decided to use the armies of the two Romanian principalities as auxiliary forces of the Russian army. At the time, Moldavia had one "musketeer" and three "grenadier" companies, one battalion of lancers made up of two cavalry squadrons, an artillery battery, and three ships. Wallachia had three infantry regiments, four cavalry squadrons, an artillery battery, and three gunboats. The Romanian units took part primarily in the skirmishes on the banks of the Danube (Calafat, Olteniţa, Silistra, Gura Islomitel, Brăila, and so on). The Russian occupation authorities also started to organize a Romanian volunteer detachment.[13] In April 1854, in order to avoid military conflict with Austria, the Russian troops were withdrawn from the Romanian Principalities. Although the Russian commander's attempt to take Romanian troops with him in the retreat failed, the tsarist army nevertheless carried away part of the Romanian army's equipment. They left behind a "bill," in the amount of 17,590,190 lei.[14]

After the Revolution of 1848 was suppressed in the Romanian Principalities, many Romanian revolutionaries took refuge in the Ottoman Empire, which, because of its weakness, was seen as a less dangerous enemy than either the Habsburg or the tsarist empire. In addition to the Romanians, Hungarian and Polish revolutionaries were also active on Ottoman territory, and some of them even held command posts in the Ottoman Empire.

In Constantinople, the authorities, while taking every precaution, tried to use the activities of these revolutionary forces to serve the Porte's best advantage. On November 11, 1853, the Russian plenipotentiary in Constantinople, S. P. Buturlin, wrote to Prince A. S. Menshikov: "Making preparations for an invasion of Little Wallachia [Oltenia, that is], the Turks are carrying out revolutionary propaganda there, distributing encouraging proclamations that are subversive in nature, inciting the peasants against the tenants and the boyars. . . . These intrigues are conducted by Polish, Hungarian, Italian, and Sardinian immigrants. They have succeeded in winning the ordinary people's sympathy. What a lesson they teach us!"[15]

Buturlin's letter exaggerated the Porte's role in the evolution of revolutionary activities. In fact, the Ottoman Empire was as hostile to revolution as the Habsburg and Russian empires were. The revolutionaries undertook a whole series of actions from Ottoman territories without the knowledge or consent of the political and military authorities in Constantinople.

Faced with the situation created by the outbreak of the Crimean War, the Romanian revolutionary émigrés entertained three different views on the best way to achieve national liberation and unity. A group in Paris thought that, given the changes the war was to bring about, the preconditions for the realization of the social and national programs of the 1848 Revolution would emerge. A group that attached itself to the headquarters of Omer Pasha, the commander of the Ottoman army at Shumla, expected the reestablishment of the Romanian Principalities' autonomous status within the Ottoman Empire. A third group wanted to take rapid and energetic action against the Russians in cooperation with the local Ottoman commanders; this group's operational base was in Oltenia.[16] This province was chosen as the basis of Romanian military operation on the grounds that it had been the scene of revolutionary activities in the past—activities that had created a tradition of military organization, training, and warfare. These traditions can be traced back to the pandour corps that participated in the Russo-Turkish wars and in the 1821 Revolution of Tudor Vladimirescu in particular. The inhabitants of Oltenia had adhered en masse to the 1848 Revolution when an important military base was established in the region (the camp at Riureni, led by General Gh. Magheru). It was planned that General Magheru would again take command during the revolutionary actions that would coincide with the Crimean War.

Regardless of their options, all Romanian revolutionaries agreed on the need to set up one or more Romanian legions in order to support the Romanian political action with a military instrument and lend it a distinctive character. The group in Shumla, led by I. Heliade-Radulescu, contemplated using these Romanian military units within the Ottoman army. The other Romanian revolutionaries, such as D. Brătianu, C. A. Rosetti, N. Balcescu, and V. Magheru, wanted them to be engaged in independent revolutionary actions.[17] C. A. Rosetti paraphrased Descartes' famous words "Cogito, ergo sum," when he wrote to Ion Ghica (1854) about the necessity of the insurrection: "They fight, therefore they exist."[18] In other words, only through a military action could the Romanians focus international public opinion on their aims.

The efforts to organize a Romanian army corps had a significant corollary in the field of military thought. On June 22, 1853, D. Brătianu proposed the establishment of a commission charged with working on a book that would adapt partisan warfare to Romanian conditions. The task was assumed by George Adrian, a former Romanian officer who had taken part in the fights the Romanians waged in the Apuseni Mountains. In Brussels Adrian published a book entitled *Brief Study on Partisan Warfare, Followed by Instructions on Campaign Service and a Temporary Fortification Handbook: Translated from the French With Certain Alterations by G. Adrian, an Ex-Officer from the Principality of Romania*.[19] In writing the book Adrian had been guided—as he himself stated—by the belief that "our nation could never gain its freedom except through the force of arms" and that, consequently, it was absolutely necessary to be familiar with "at least the few rules laid down in this book," an indispensable condition enabling one "to render his homeland the most invaluable services in time of war."[20] Though the *Instructions on Campaign Service* was merely a translation, the part devoted to partisan warfare sought to adapt to Romanian conditions Karl von Decker's *On the Little War in the Spirit of Modern Strategy* (the French translation of 1845 was used). According to Adrian's book, the partisans were to be recruited from among military professionals, but the effectives of troops could be brought up to the required size by those who had received minimal training within the units of chasseurs, *dorobanți*, or militiamen. The actions of the partisans, whether independent or done in cooperation with the standing army, were to be carefully planned and carried out. Adrian's work also contains an idea much emphasized in today's theories of guerrilla warfare. It advocated an intimate relationship between the partisan fighter and the population among whom he carries out his fight. "The troop of Romanian partisans, fighting against the foreigner amidst its own fellow countrymen, must also support and facilitate, by every possible means, the assembling of those citizens who might be prompted by patriotic feelings to rise in defense of their homeland."[21]

A similar military plan was drafted by Cezar Bolliac, another Romanian revolutionary of 1848. Bolliac contemplated a wider involvement of the masses, however, and he wanted to involve the peasantry in particular.[22] Bolliac's plan called for the collaboration of Romanians from all the provinces then under foreign rule.

Both George Adrian and Cezar Bolliac drew their inspiration from the tradition and experience of the people's war for the defense of the homeland, which during the Middle Ages had been institutionalized in the "Greater Army."[23] It is worth remembering that these two revolutionaries combined tradition with innovation in their plans. They found in the history of Romania an efficient formula, one that was capable of ensuring victory in an unequal military conflict, that is, in a confrontation between belligerents with very disproportionate stores of natural resources.[24] Undoubtedly, their plans had to recognize that the new weapons and technology demanded increased professionalism and specialization. Their advice to appeal to the people as an inexhaustible source of strength should not be seen as mere revolutionary romanticism; instead it was a realistic utilization of a century-old experience, one that had secured the autonomy of the Romanian Principalities when they fell under Ottoman domination.

The political and military developments of the Crimean War did not allow these plans to be implemented, but the principles behind them nevertheless affected Romanian military thinkers considerably. After the creation of the Romanian nation-state in 1859, these ideas were in fact partially implemented. George Adrian became minister of war and in this position played an important role in drafting the Law on the Organization of the Army in 1869.[25]

Back in 1853, however, efforts to secure a popular basis for military organization had spawned violent social tensions in the Romanian villages. These tensions were a natural consequence of the burdensome corvée the peasantry had to perform for the landowners.

As a result of the close ties between the Romanian revolutionaries south of the Danube and those in Wallachia, the Frontier Guards in Oltenia rebelled in December 1853. Led by Grigore Scurtulescu, former representative of the peasantry in the Property Commission of 1848, they managed "to secure the participation of hundreds of villagers, young and old, women and children, armed with whatever they could lay hands on."[26] Nita Magheru and other revolutionaries arrived at the village of Gîrla Mare, where they hoisted the tricolor and issued a proclamation asking the population to join in the struggle for social and national liberation. The uprising was directed mainly against the great landowners and tenants. Although the action was cruelly suppressed by the authorities, the revolutionary excitement was not dampened.[27]

With the withdrawal of the tsarist armies, the revolutionary activity grew stronger. Simultaneously with the Turkish army's entry into the country, many of those who had emigrated after the Revolution of 1848, devoted advocates of the abolition of the feudal regime and of the union of Moldavia and Wallachia, returned home. They had entertained close relations with the Polish revolutionaries serving in the Ottoman army.

Among these were Michał Czajkowski (Sadyk Pasha), who became the military commander of Bucharest, and Klesczyński, the military commander of the town of Giurgiu. The Poles were fighting in Ottoman uniforms for the liberation of their own country. Czajkowski planned to recruit a *dorobanți* corps consisting of 3,000 infantrymen and 1,800 horsemen. Evidence of the Romanians' attachment to military traditions is provided by Czajkowski's remark that the very name *dorobanți* corresponded to an awareness of one's values, unlike "militia," which was a recent creation of the era of Organic Regulations.[28]

One of the most comprehensive and systematic projects for political and military organization drafted between the Crimean War and the Union of the Danubian Principalities was the memorial submitted to the Porte by General G. Magheru on May 12, 1854. The organization he envisioned was based on the Porte's reestablishment of the administrative autonomy of the Romanian Principalities on the basis of the old capitulations. The memorandum emphasized that the ruling princes should be chosen in free elections. Magheru also suggested that, for the duration of the war, the Porte appoint a military chief and a civilian commissioner to exert governmental authority over the two Romanian Principalities. A general assembly of the representatives of the people should be summoned to begin the reforms that would modernize the legislative and adminstrative institutions. Deeply concerned with the reorganization of the national army, General Magheru asked the Porte to provide 12,000 rifles, two artillery batteries, and ammunition for the military chief. Magheru planned first to set up volunteer units; later, a Moldo-Wallachian army of 80,000 men would be organized. Finally, this veteran of 1848 stressed that the Romanians' main purpose was to unite the two principalities under a single ruler.[29]

The revolutionary unrest that developed in Wallachia and Moldavia worried the authorities in Vienna, who believed that it posed a genuine threat to their empire. Claiming that these radical activists even embraced "socialist and communist ideas," Vienna made representations to the Porte demanding that they be arrested.[30]

The Porte indeed had no intention of tolerating revolutionary activities that might turn against itself and that had the potential to jeopardize its relations with Austria. Consequently, on June 14, 1854, the Porte agreed to the Convention of Boyadjy Keuy, which authorized Austrian troops to enter the Romanian Principalities. The Austrian occupation, which Lajos Kossuth called the "most terrible monstrosity of this century,"[31] put an end to the revolutionary activities. A. C. Golescu (Albu) expressed the great disillusionment of the revolutionaries who had hoped for a "war of the peoples" only to see it finally reduced into a mere "war of governments."[32]

The Treaty of Paris, which concluded the Crimean War, called for fundamental changes in Eastern Europe. It annulled the preponderance over the Balkans Russia had acquired in the treaties of Kuchuk-Kainardji (1774) and Adrianople (1829) and placed the integrity of the Ottoman Empire under the collective guarantee of the signatory powers. Moreover, by neutralizing the Black Sea, it deprived Russia of the right to station a war fleet in the Black Sea and to maintain fortifications on its shores. As a result, St. Petersburg lost its major means of putting military pressure on the Ottoman Empire. The treaty also instituted an international commission to oversee the free navigation of the Danube River.[33]

The treaty's provisions created a new political situation in which the political status of Moldavia and Wallachia became an issue of international concern.[34] Indeed, in the period between the promulgation of the Treaty of Paris and the Union of the Principalities, their status became a subject of protracted and fierce negotiations. Article 22 of the treaty placed the Principalities under the collective guarantee of seven European powers. It also stipulated that none of the guarantor powers could exert its prerogative unilaterally and that "no one is allowed to interfere with their [the Principalities'] domestic affairs."[35] The Russo-Turkish condominium over the Principalities that had been established by the treaties of 1774 and 1829 was now replaced by a collective guarantee. This was an important step toward independence, because the controversies among the seven guarantor powers meant they would be unlikely to take concerted action against the Romanians' struggle for national liberation. Article 23 of the treaty obliged the Porte to maintain an independent national leadership, as well as complete freedom of faith, laws, trade, and navigation in the Principalities.[36] Ad hoc assemblies were convened in Iași and Bucharest in order to canvass the people's views on the nature of their future government. Both assemblies demanded union, again demonstrating the yearning that had been a tradition in the two Romanian principalities for centuries. As Mikhail Kogălniceanu, one of the most outstanding spokesmen of the unionist trend, put it, "the foremost, the strongest, the most general national desires" of the population were observance of the autonomous status, the union of the two principalities into a state named Romania, neutrality of the Romanian territories, and the establishment of a representative assembly.[37]

These demands were proposed at the Paris Conference in May–August 1858, which adopted a convention on the international status and the domestic administration of the principalities. Their union into a single nation-state was not accepted, however. Nevertheless, a restricted union was permitted, but each principality had to preserve its own political structure (ruling prince, government, elected assembly), with a common Court of Justice and Cassation. Several articles regulated the organization of the armed forces. The two armies "would have identical organization, so that, if necessary, they could join to form a single army," and a common law on the organization of the army was to be drafted. The two armies were to be inspected annually by general inspectors who were to be appointed by the princes in Iaşi and Bucharest. "These inspectors will have to oversee the full implementation of the decisions meant to preserve those characteristics that would enable the militias to resemble two corps of a single army" (Article 42). In order to ensure unity of command and a Romanian military leadership, a commander-in-chief was "to be appointed by one of the princes (they would alternate this responsibility) when it became necessary for the militias to reunite. He will have to be Moldavian or Wallachian by birth, and he can be dismissed only by the prince who appointed him. In this case, the new commander-in-chief will be appointed by the other prince."[38]

The double election of Colonel Alexandru Ioan Cuza, commander of the Moldavian army, as prince of Moldavia on January 5/17, 1859, and as prince of Wallachia on January 24/February 5, 1859, bypassed the provisions of the Convention that had opposed the union of the principalities. The election of Cuza laid the foundations of the modern Romanian state.

The Union of January 24, 1859, fulfilled a century-old aspiration for unity which had known its first, though short-lived achievement in 1600 when Wallachia, Transylvania, and Moldavia were united under Michael the Brave, prince of Wallachia (1593–1601). The Union of 1859 was yet another proof of the irresistible force the historical legitimacy of a national cause can have, irrespective of obstacles. Thwarting any attempt of the Great Powers to establish spheres of influence or to divide the territory they inhabited, the Romanians firmly voiced their determination to unite in a single state: its foundations were laid in 1859, its independence won in 1877, and its full national unity accomplished in 1918.

The Union of 1859 resisted all enemy attempts to dissolve it because it answered the Romanian people's wish. It was rooted in century-old economic, political, diplomatic, military, cultural, and religious relations. It responded to an objective necessity: the making and development of the Romanian nation-state. The making of the modern Romanian state had considerable repercussions in Central and Southeastern Europe. Enjoying complete autonomy and being protected against the encroachments of bordering powers, Romania lent substantial and effective support to the social and national liberation movements in this part of the continent, particularly to those of the Hungarian, Bulgarian, and Polish peoples. A great many political and cultural organizations were established on the territory of Romania which prompted the national liberation and unity of the peoples of East Central Europe then under foreign domination. Romania also provided shelter to revolutionaries who were being hunted down by repressive authorities, thus enabling them to carry on their struggles.[39]

The struggle for social and national emancipation of the peoples of East Central Europe developed in the era of the Crimean War in forms according to specific local conditions. The widest in scope and the most important in terms of consequences was the struggle carried out in Moldavia and Wallachia. Even if the social aims of the 1848 revolutionary program had to be temporarily sacrificed, developments after 1859 favored the eventual realization of these goals.

From the military point of view, the Crimean War had forced a reappraisal of some matters of military organization. The foremost consideration was to achieve a military instrument that could serve the cause of the Romanian national struggle. The projects advanced and the steps taken to implement them all bore the stamp of the Romanian traditions of the people's war for the defense of the homeland. In all cases, however, there was also an attempt to absorb new technology and to adopt new principles of warfare.

In sum, the Crimean War was not that "war of the peoples" against absolutism that the revolutionaries of 1848 had intended but rather a "war of the governments." Nevertheless, it initiated a strong ferment among the peoples of East Central Europe, who saw this military conflict as an opportunity to promote their own social and national emancipation. The Paris Congress could not ignore the demands for the rebirth and unification of the Romanian Principalities. Utilizing the stipulations of the Paris Congress (1856) and Convention (1858), Moldavia and Wallachia were united on January 24, 1859, thereby laying the foundations for the modern Romanian state and army.

Notes

1. Emile Wanty, *L'art de la guerre,* vol. 2 (Verviers, 1967), p. 15.
2. Cf. *Voennaia istoriia,* ed. I. G. Bagramian (Moscow, 1971), pp. 54–55,

according to which the Crimean War made an important contribution to the development of military art.
3. Wanty, *L'art,* pp. 17–18.
4. L. C. B. Seaman, *From Vienna to Versailles* (New York, 1963), p. 27.
5. On this subject, see E. V. Tarlé, *Krimskaia voina,* 2 vols. (Moscow-Leningrad, 1950), and P. W. Schroeder, *Austria, Great Britain and the Crimean War* (Ithaca, 1972).
6. Seaman, *From Vienna to Versailles,* p. 31; Schroeder, *Austria, Great Britain and the Crimean War,* p. 423.
7. Mustafa Ali Mehmed, *Istoria turcilor* (Bucharest, 1975), p. 317.
8. Pierre Renouvin, *Histoire des relations internationales,* vol. 5 (Paris, 1954), pt. 1, p. 290.
9. *Istoria diplomaţiei,* ed. V. P. Potemkin, trans. from Russian (Bucharest, 1947, p. 175.
10. N. Iorga, *Istoria statelor balcanice in epoca modernă* (Bucharest, 1913), pp. 266–67; Charles and Barbara Jelavich, *The Establishment of the Balkan National States* (Seattle, 1977), pp. 78–80.
11. Iorga, *Istoria statelor balcanice,* pp. 265–66.
12. *Istoriia Bolgarii,* ed. N. P. Tretiskov, S. A. Nikitin, and L. B. Valov, vol. 1 (Moscow, 1954), p. 251.
13. Dr. Dorina N. Rusu, "Ţările române si forţelor militare în ajunul sî în timoul războriului Crimeei," in *File din istoria militară a poporului român,* ed. Ilie Ceauşescu, vol. 7 (Bucharest, 1980), pp. 45–49.
14. Ibid.
15. Tarlé, *Krimskaia voina,* 1: 221.
16. Iorga, *Istoria românilor,* vol. 9 (Bucharest, 1938), p. 247.
17. At length, Leonid Boicu, *Austria sî Principatele române în vremes Războiului Crimeei (1853–1856)* (Bucharest, 1972), pp. 129 ff.
18. Vintilă C. A. Rosetti, *Amintiri istorice* (Bucharest, 1889), p. 61.
19. A new edition edited by C. Antip, who also wrote an introductory study, was published by Editura Militară in 1972; see also C. Căzănişteanu, "Războiul de partizani în gîndirea militară românească din veacul al XIX-lea" in *File din istoria militară a poporului român,* ed. Ilie Ceauşescu, vol. 2 (Bucharest, 1974), pp. 28–32.
20. Adrian, *Idee repede despre războiul de partizani,* p. 8.
21. Ibid., pp. 15–16.
22. Cezar Bolliac, *Chois de lettres et mémoires sur la question roumaine, 1852–1856* (Paris, 1856); the draft is examined by Căzănîţeanu, "Războiul de partizani," pp. 33–34.
23. At length, *Oastea cea mare: Traditii înaintate ale luetei maselor populare din România pentru libertate si independentă naţională* (Bucharest, 1972); Ilie Ceauşescu, *The Entire People's War for the Homeland's Defence with the Romanians* (Bucharest, 1980).
24. Cf. Andrew J. R. Mack, "Why Big Nations Lose Small Wars: The Politics of Asymmetric Conflict," *World Politics* 27 (January 1975): 175 ff.
25. C. Căzănişteanu, *Apărarea naţională a României socialiste, cauză si operă*

a întregului nostru popor (Bucharest, 1974), p. 42. In 1861, Cezar Bolliac demanded "the general arming of the country, through the standing army, the militia, and the arming of the villages" (ibid., p. 43).

26. V. Dumitrescu, *Un episod din timoul resbelului ruso-turc din anul 1853–1854 sau revoluţia Seurtulescului* (Turnu Severin, 1888), p. 26; Boicu, *Austria sî Principatele,* pp. 131–32.
27. Apostol Stan and Constantin Vlăduţ, *Gheorghe Magheru* (Bucharest, 1969), pp. 190–93.
28. Stanislaw Lukasik, "Relatiunile lui Mihail Czajkowski—Sadyk Pasa cu românii," *Revista istorică română* 2 (1932), fasc. 2–3: 249 (the memo is dated October 29, 1854). M. Czajkowski also enclosed a "List of Romanian Officers Able to Serve in the New Organization of the Dorobanţi," ibid., pp. 249–50.
29. Stan and Vlăduţ, *Gheorghe Magheru,* pp. 199–200.
30. Boicu, *Austria sî Principatele,* p. 140; the consideration belongs to Alfon Wimpffen, on whom see N. Iorga in *Academia Română Memoriile Secţiunii Istorice,* series 3a, vol. 19, p. 250.
31. Boicu, *Austria sî Principatele,* p. 150.
32. Ibid., p. 191.
33. Renouvin, *Histoire,* pp. 269–97, and H. Temperley, "The Treaty of Paris, 1856, and its Execution," *Journal of Modern History,* 1932, pp. 287–414 and 523–43.
34. At length, L. Boicu, *Geneza "chestiunii româneşti" ce problemă internaţională* (Iaşi, 1978).
35. *Relatiile internationale ale României în documente,* ed. I. Ioneşcu, P. Bărbulescu, and Gh. Gheorghe (Bucharest, 1971), p. 330.
36. Ibid.
37. *History of the Romanian People,* ed. A. Oţetea (New York), p. 376. For the political developments of the period, see Dan Berindei, *Epoca unirii* (Bucharest, 1979), pp. 51 ff.
38. *Relatiile internationale ale României în documente,* pp. 340–41.
39. As regards the support lent by the Romanians to the national liberation movements in Eastern and Southeastern Europe, see P. Constantinescu-Iaşi, *Rolul României în epoca de regenerare a Bulgariei* (Iaşi, 1919); idem, *Studii istorica române-bulgare* (Bucharest, 1956); N. Ciachir, "România si popoarele balcanice (1856–1875)," *Revista română de studii internationale* 15 (1972): 127–53; C. C. Giurescu, *Viaţa sî opera lui Cuza-Vodă* (Bucharest, 1968).

Army and Society: Cuza's Military Reforms

Ilie Ceauşescu

"An advocate of the nationalities principle"[1]—this is the way Prince Alexandru Ioan Cuza described himself. His political opinions, fully reflected in a reign devoted to the foundation and consolidation of the modern Romanian state, represented the expression of a historical process characteristic of the period of transition from feudalism to capitalism: the founding of nations and of national states. In East Central Europe, a concurrence of historical factors delayed the establishment of national states, with the result that what Georges Weill so suggestively called "l'éveil des nationalités"[2] became a fundamental feature of European history in the nineteenth century. The elimination of state pluralism and of foreign domination—the main obstacles to the establishment of the national state—became the basic objectives of the movements of emancipation and national unity of East Central Europe.

The setting up of the Romanian national state in 1859 was part of the general trend toward national unification represented by the unification of Germany and of Italy in the latter half of the nineteenth century and the intensification of movements for emancipation and national unity in Poland and in the Balkans. Prince Alexandru Ioan Cuza played a part in Romania's history comparable, relatively speaking, to Cavour's in Italy or Bismarck's in Germany. His objective, the achievement of national unity, was the same; his means were different because the historical roots and conditions were different.

I

A period of paramount significance in the history of the Romanian people because of its broad efforts at renovating the structures of Romanian society, Cuza's reign (1859–66) has received a great deal of attention on the part of both Romanian and foreign historiography. Illustrative of the interest shown by the latter is the publication in the United States of America of two monographs on the period: T. W. Riker's 1931 volume *The Making of Romania: A Study of an International Problem 1856–1866,* once judged "the best-documented work of all those written by foreigners on the establishment of the modern Romanian state,"[3] and G. J. Bobango's 1979 book *The Emergence of the Romanian National State*. The reconstruction of the facts—grounded in rich and reliable Romanian and foreign sources—has been rigorous enough to reflect a true picture of the activities of this first leader of modern Romania. This essay has two objectives: to describe the military reforms initiated by Cuza and to point to the close relationship between these reforms and the exigencies of the process of modernization of Romanian society. In analyzing the military measures taken by Cuza it is important to identify the features generated by the conjuncture (the historical framework) within which they were taken and the fundamental structural features attributable to what Fernand Brandel has called "la long durée"—their connection with the evolution of the Romanian military system over the centuries.[4]

II

The union of Moldavia and Wallachia as a result of the double election of Alexandru Ioan Cuza as ruling prince of each was the logical-historical consequence of a century of development of Romanian society, which in spite of state pluralism (i.e., the existence of several Romanian principalities—Moldavia, Wallachia, Transylvania) had preserved the consciousness of its identity as a nation and the aspiration of regaining national unity. Emancipation and national unity were always linked in the program of revendications of the progressive sociopolitical forces of Romanian society, which found full expression in the generation of 1848, for renewing the socioeconomic structures of the society by removing the anachronistic elements, first of all in the field of agrarian relations, whose survival was made possible by the economic stagnation created by foreign domination.[5] The European political context created by the end of the Crimean War gave an international character to the status and organization of the Danubian principalities (which explains the discussion of them at the Paris Congress), thus permitting the Romanians of Moldavia and Wallachia to express their will for unity.

If national unity was to be achieved, a number of obstacles raised by the Great Powers would have to be removed. The Ottoman Empire considered the union of the two principalities a decisive step toward their independence; Austria was afraid of the effects of the emergence of a new state on the Romanians in Transylvania, where they constituted the great majority, for whom the achievement of union by their brothers beyond the mountains might be a sign of their own imminent liberation; from 1863 on tsarist Russia, whose efforts to include the young Romanian state in its political orbit had failed, sought to return to the situation existing before 1859 by annulling the union; England, concerned with the integrity of the Ottoman Empire, looked with suspicion, if not hostility, upon any action that might weaken the Turkish position in the Lower Danube area.

In the face of these obstacles, the two principalities succeeded in achieving their union by turning to good account the lacunae in the text of the Paris Convention and the conflicts among the guarantor powers (it is worth recalling that the France of Napoleon III embraced the nationalities principle and that Sardinia and Prussia were themselves involved in struggles for national unity). In its content and methods the union of 1859 had a revolutionary character. The union was a historical need, and it triumphed because of the efforts of the sociopolitical forces that recognized this.

For the young Romanian state the problem of the army was of vital importance. In the short term, the army had to defend the results of the act of January 24, 1859, against the foreign enemies of the union (the Ottoman and Austrian empires and, from 1863 on, the tsarist one), but in the long term it had to assist in the completion of the program of the national emancipation movement by winning independence and incorporating all Romanians, including those still under foreign domination, within the borders of a single state. Both short- and long-term objectives were likely to involve military conflict.

The need for organization of the army was recognized by the political leadership. Romanian newspapers of the period immediately following unification report a genuine debate on the organization of the national army.[6] Thus, under the eloquent title "Armare înainte de toate" (Arming first and foremost), the revolutionary writer Cezar Bolliac pleaded for enhancing military strength,[7] and a newspaper summarized the conclusion of the debates as "Ai armată . . . ai ţară" (You have an army . . . you have a country).[8] The intensity of these years' debates on the structure of the army was in no way an expression of militarism that might lead to a policy of expansion and annexation; rather, it gave voice to the general concern with providing the country with the military means of guaranteeing its security and integrity. "We do not arm ourselves," said an article in the Bucharest newspaper *Reforma,* "for conquest; we arm ourselves as the Serbs do, as the Montenegrins do, as our ancestors did, to educate ourselves, to make ourselves worthy of respect, to keep foreigners from invading the Romanian principalities with slavery and death; they must see armed breasts, not open arms; they must step on corpses, not flowers."[9]

The prevailing idea with regard to the organization of the country's armed forces was that territorial units including all citizens able to bear arms in the event of aggression were to be added to the standing army. This idea reflects the tradition of the people's war as it was practiced, with remarkable success, by the Romanians of the Middle Ages,[10] the idea of the "armed nation" promoted by the revolutionary generation of 1848, and, finally, the Prussian pattern of the *Landwehr,* whose popular roots go back to the period of Stein's and Scharnhorst's reforms, intended as preparation for a war of national liberation against Napoleon.

Cuza's military policy aimed at achieving some objectives of vital importance for the development of Romanian society: to consolidate the union; to defend the national territory against any aggression; to win independence; to achieve a unitary military structure corresponding both to the country's capabilities and to the requirements of modern warfare, grounded in the employment under new conditions of the tradition of the participation of the whole people in defending the country; and to develop a foreign military policy based on principles of equality and mutual respect and of support for the movements of national and social emancipation of East Central Europe.[12] The policy developed in two stages determined by domestic and foreign political conditions. The first (1859–61) was ruled by the necessity of strengthening the union in the international arena; during this period the fusion of Moldavian and Wallachian troops into a single army was achieved and the first steps were taken toward enhancing the country's military capabilities. The second stage (1862–66), coinciding with the apogee of Cuza's reforms (the agrarian reform of 1864), was marked by the modernization of Romanian military organization.

The fusion of Moldavian and Wallachian armed forces was facilitated by the similarity of the systems of military organization in the two Romanian principalities. An important event in the process of unification of the two principalities' armies, which had begun on March 1859 with an exchange of Moldavian and Wallachian units in Bucharest and in Iaşi, was the setting up of a camp in the Floreşti area between April and September 1859; here twelve thousand Moldavian and Wallachian troops trained together under a united command,[13] using new weapons recently supplied them. The camp at Floreşti played an important part in creating a single Romanian army.[14] Measures aiming at the unification of the command echelons followed. As long as the union remained only a physical one as a result of the double election, Prince Cuza was obliged to recognize two political-military entities, Moldavia and Wallachia. By appointing a single person, General Ioan Emanoil Florescu, minister of war of Moldavia and of Wallachia, he unified the two ministries, a measure which was consolidated soon afterward by the establishment of a single general staff with the mission of drawing up the standards for military training, preparing the mechanisms for military operations, working out a complete map of the country, and supervising the construction of military installations.[15] These measures were accompanied by a broad program of improvements in military training—the drawing up of regulations, the establishment of military schools—and the development of domestic arms production (the army arsenal was set up in 1862).

The second phase of development of Cuza's military policy centered upon the establishment of the legal foundations for the organization of the national army and other components of military power. The law, prepared by the Military Commission of the Legislative Assembly, whose secretary was Colonel George Adrian (the author of an interesting work entitled *Idee repede despre războiul de partizani* [A brief overview of partisan warfare], published in Brussels in 1853), relied on the 1848 principle of the "armed nation." Debated in an atmosphere of strain due to the violence of the conflict between the country's sociopolitical forces over the resolution of the agrarian problem, the draft bill was passed on February 7, 1864. It stipulated that the Romanian armed forces were to consist of the following elements: (1) the standing army, with its reserve; (2) the active militia, consisting of the border guards and the *dorobanți*; (3) the urban guard, to be organized in all the country's urban areas; (4) the inactive militia; and (5) the multitude. The urban guard, the inactive militia, and the multitude were to include all men aged seventeen to fifty except those already under arms; this gave them a profoundly popular character. At the same time, the law provided that military training to be included in the curriculum of the primary schools. It emphasized the defensive character of the military system being established.[16]

This law failed to receive Cuza's sanction because of his concern about the possible hostile reaction to it on the part of the guarantor powers and about the possibility that the urban guard might become an instrument of opposition to the government. The coup d'état of May 2 gave the prince the opportunity to implement his own reforms, and the new law on the organization of the military of November 27, 1864, set up a three-part structure for the country's armed forces: (1) the standing army, with its reserve; (2) the militias, consisting of the *dorobanți* and border guards and their reserves; and (3) the multitude. It also provided that six years of military service be compulsory for all men aged twenty to fifty. The arms provided by this law were infantry, cavalry, artillery, engineers, the Danubian flotilla, firemen, and administrative and logistical troops.

The balance-sheet of this remarkable policy was summed up by Prince Cuza himself, who wrote to Napoleon III on October 1, 1865: "Where I had found scarcely thirteen thousand men, recruited entirely from among the peasants, poorly armed and equipped and responding to commands in Russian and German, I have today twelve thousand *grăniceri,* eight thousand infantry and cavalry militia, and a standing army of twenty thousand recruited from among all classes of society, well-armed, well-equipped, and capable of being increased to three times its normal strength."[18] The military measures taken by Cuza provided strong military support for the union of 1859, modernized the Romanian military, and created the preconditions for the achievement of national independence in 1877.

Notes

1. P. P. Panaitescu, "Unirea principatelor române, Cuza-Vodă și Polonia," *Romanoslavica* 5 (1962): 80.
2. Georges Weill, *L'éveil des nationalités et le mouvement libéral* (Paris: Presses Universitaires de France, 1924).
3. Constantin C. Giurescu, *Viața și opera lui Cuza-Vodă* (Bucharest: Științifică, 1966), p. 15.
4. Cf. André Corvisier, "Le métier militaire en France aux époques de grandes transformations sociales," in *Commission internationale d'histoire militaire, Acta no. 5, Bucarest, 10–17.VIII.1980* (Bucharest, 1981), pp. 65–72.
5. For details, see Gh. Platon, *Geneza revoluției române de la 1848* (Iași: Junimea, 1980).
6. Teodor Popescu, "Gîndirea social-politică despre înarmarea maselor oglindită în presa civilă, dezbaterile parlamentare și legislația militară din timpul domniei lui Alexandru Ioan Cuza," in *File din istoria militară a poporului român,* vol. 1 (Bucharest: Militară, 1973), pp. 70–76.
7. *Naționalul,* April 5, 1859, Popescu, "Gîndirea social-politică," pp. 70–71.
8. *Reforma,* March 20, 1860, ibid., p. 72.
9. Ibid., August 1/13, 1860.
10. For details, see Ilie Ceaușescu, *Războiul întregului popor pentru apărarea patriei la români* (Bucharest: Militară, 1980).
11. David B. Ralston, ed., *Soldiers and States: Civil-Military Relations in Modern Europe* (Boston: Heath, 1966), pp. 93–94.
12. For details, see Ilie Ceaușescu, "Armata unirii: Politica militară a domnitorului Alexandru Ioan Cuza," in *File din istoria militară a poporului român,* vol. 7 (Bucharest: Militară, 1980), pp. 60 ff.
13. C. Toderașcu, "Tabăra militară de la Florești din vara anului 1859: Începutul contopirii oștilor Principatelor Unite Române," in *File din istoria militară a poporului român,* vol. 1 (Bucharest: Militară, 1973), pp. 49–68.

14. General Herkt, *Cîteva pagini din istoricul armatei noastre: Amintirile unui veteran în timpul serviciului* (Bucharest, 1902), p. 66.
15. V. Nădejde, *Centenarul renașterii armatei române* (Iași, 1930), p. 107.
16. Ceaușescu, "Armata unirii," pp. 79–80.
17. Ibid., p. 80; Giurescu, *Viața și opera,* pp. 219–20.
18. R. V. Bossy, *Agenția diplomatică a României în Paris și legăturile politice franco-române sub Cuza-Vodă* (Bucharest: Cultură Națională, 1931), p. 384.

The Role of the Army in the Modernization of the East Central European States: The Romanian Example

Constantin Căzănişteanu

The establishment of Phanariot rule in the Romanian lands at the beginning of the eighteenth century brought, among other things, a drastic reduction of their armed forces, to ordinary guard and ceremonial units only. In the first decades of the next century, however, with the intensification of the emancipation struggle and the gradual diminution of the Porte's domination, the national army revived. Although it was intended by its creators to guard the privileges of the ruling classes, the army became, through the very dialectics of its development, a symbol of the national regeneration to which Romanian progressives looked with sympathy and hope; a number of them, such as Nicolae Bălcescu, Mihail Kogălniceanu, C. A. Rosetti, and Alexandru Ioan Cuza, did not hesitate to wear the military uniform. Alongside the representatives of the progressive intelligentsia in the command cadres there were officers originating in the pandour troops for whom the memory of Tudor Vladimirescu and his 1821 battle for "justice and liberty" was still alive. In the process of development of the Romanian army there was a fusion of the tradition of popular struggle, represented by the pandours and volunteers, and the new sociopolitical forces' hostility to the anachronistic feudal regime and attraction to the bourgeois system. From both points of view, the modern army whose foundations were laid in the third and fourth decades of the nineteenth century became the embodiment of the Romanian nation's aspirations for national unity and independence and at the same time for social renewal. This is what explains the firm belief of numerous political personalities of the middle of the last century in the historical mission of the Romanian army as guarantor of the prosperity of the Romanian people. Nicolae Bălcescu, who laid the scientific foundations of Romanian military thought, wrote as early as 1844 that if "the Romanian nation is ever to achieve its rightful place among the nations of Europe, it will be through the regeneration of its old military institutions."[1]

It was only after the revolutionary events of 1848 that the army came to be recognized as a fundamental component of the movement for national and social liberation. While in all the states affected by the revolutionary wave of the period the army was the state's main instrument of repression, in the Romanian lands, especially in Moldavia and Wallachia, the army's position and consequently the revolutionary leaders' attitude toward it were different.[2] This attitude toward the army was encouraged by the evidence of the receptivity of military personnel to the renewal movements that had developed in the Romanian lands prior to the 1848 Revolution. There were numerous military men among the creators of the various drafts of constitutions concerning "the renewal of the homeland" and in the majority of the pre-1848 secret political associations or "conspiracies." Soldiers of the Transylvanian border regiments often participated in the actions undertaken by the peasants living in the neighborhood of their garrisons against the Habsburg authorities.

The belief in the army's historical mission and the military's steadfast support for all attempts at rebuilding Romanian society explain why the 1848 leaders considered the army, won over to the revolutionary ideals, a fundamental element within the general framework of the movement and made an effort to gather the entire army under the banner of the revolution. Some of the officers worked directly with the members of the revolutionary committee on the plan for the revolution: the units under their orders were ready to intervene at the appointed time. The rebels in Iași hoped that besides "all the inhabitants of their estates" some of "the militia" would join in the uprising.[3] Reports of the soldiers' dissatisfaction with official rule became more and more frequent, along with reports of "instigation" of those under the flag and even of the inhabitants and of the "disobedience" of certain officers affected by the "spirit of the uprising." The significance of these actions was recognized on the eve of the revolution by the Russian General Duhamel, who noted that the "officers were contaminated by the revolutionary spirit";[4] his notes elucidate, at the same time, why the revolutionary leadership considered the army its ally and not a supporter of the reactionary front. This state of mind persuaded the members of the revolutionary committee in Wallachia that in all the places where the insurrection was to begin—Islaz, Ocnele Mari, Telega, Bucharest—the military units and subunits had to be incorporated into the revolution to enhance the striking power of the masses.

The Romanian army did not disappoint the hopes placed in it, either at the beginning of the movement, when it fairly carried out the missions ordered by the revolutionary committee, or during the three months of revolutionary rule. The failure of the two counterrevolutionary plots of June 1848 was mostly due to the intervention of troops attached to the provisional government in Wallachia. Although some officers and subunits served the reactionary circles, on the whole the army supported the revolutionary government, and its establishment and maintenance, even for only three months, would not have been possible without that support.

After the 1848 Romanian Revolution had been suppressed, the main objective of the Romanian program of national liberation was the union of Moldavia and Wallachia as a first step in the process of gathering in all the Romanians then under foreign domination. In this struggle for unity the army gradually became a source of ferment, supporting, sometimes openly, the efforts of the unionist forces against the separatists, who played into the Great Powers' hands by acting in accordance with the principle *divide et impera*; in this way the army gave further evidence of its adherence to the national and social emancipation movement of the people from whom it descended and whom it defended and of its support for the modernization of the structures of Romanian society. The attitudes of the military in Iaşi and especially in Bucharest toward the struggle for union helped the elective assemblies in Moldavia and Wallachia to elect as ruling prince a single person, Alexandru Ioan Cuza. General Vlădoianu's call on the soldiers to serve the newly elected prince with "the unswerving fidelity and devotion that always characterized the Romanian soldier when it came to the nation's ruling prince and his homeland"[5] is evidence of this attitude. Subsequently the army's support contributed substantially to the consolidation of the union of January 24, 1859. Cuza himself, in one of his addresses to officers, underlined that "the dignified and decisive attitude of the Romanian army" had greatly contributed to the establishment of a single Romania.[6] On the other occasion he said that "the fusion of the armies was the first step toward the final union of the sister-countries."[7] In fact, the United Principalities' ruling prince, in harmony with the outlook of the 1848 Romanian Revolution's leaders, considered the army a reliable support in the difficult task of building a modern Romanian state.

First, the army had the duty of defending and consolidating the act of unification against pressures exerted by the Great Powers; Turkey, tsarist Russia, and Austria, in particular, did not look with favor on the emergence of a strong, united state on the Lower Danube. The Ottoman and Habsburg Empires' hostility toward the double election of Cuza meant that the diplomatic steps aimed at winning official recognition of the union had to be accompanied by military measures designed to demonstrate the Romanian people's determination to defend its rights with force. The two principalities' armies were concentrated in a common military camp in the Floreşti area (near Ploieşti) for the purpose of implementing the desire for unity expressed by Cuza's double election. In an address to the troops encamped at Floreşti, the prince gave them to understand the task that was being assigned to them: "It is to you that our country may someday owe its union."[9]

Further, the Romanian army's interests as a social-professional category linked to the bourgeoisie's advancement and the development of capitalism required the modernization of the society: the army's power and prestige depended upon the modernization of the equipment and the military, economic, social, and political structures of the Romanian state. Therefore the army represented a reliable support for the work of modernization, an objective vigorously pursued during Cuza's seven-year reign. The army was particularly helpful in crisis situations. The coup d'état of May 2, 1864, aimed at sanctioning the agrarian reform, led to the distribution of land to the peasants and the abolition of feudal servitude; on that occasion the soldiers were told that their patriotic duty was "to maintain public order" and to see that the will of the Romanian people (called to have their say in a plebiscite) was freely expressed. "Prove to be, as always, loyal defenders of order and discipline," the supreme commander told his troops. "I have always depended upon you, and you have always proved worthy of my trust. I have no doubt that this time, too, you will do your best to accomplish the task being entrusted to your patriotism."[10]

In conclusion, in contrast to the armies of other East Central European countries, from its reestablishment in the first decades of the nineteenth century until about 1870 the Romanian army was not a hindrance or a factor of instability in political life. Cuza's dethronement on February 11, 1866 represented the removal of a factor of domestic political confrontation; the ascension to Romania's throne of a foreign prince was intended only to eliminate the rivalries among the political groups concerned with controlling the succession. In this as in other situations, the military establishment was a fundamental element of the efforts to build a modern, united, and independent Romania.

Notes

1. N. Bălcescu, *Opere* (Bucharest: Academiei Republicii Socialiste România, 1952), p. 131.
2. Constantin Căzănişteanu, "Probleme militare în revoluţia română de la 1848," in *Revoluţia de la 1848 în tările române* (Bucharest: Academiei Republicii Socialiste România, 1974), pp. 131–42.
3. *Anul revoluţionar 1848 în Moldova* (Bucharest, 1950), p. 131.
4. Gh. Bezviconi, *Călători ruşi în Moldova şi Muntenia* (Bucharest, 1947), p. 387.
5. *Monitorul oastei*, February 15, 1859, p. 147.
6. Ibid., December 21, 1861, p. 568.
7. Ioan Popovici, *Organizarea armatei române*, vol. 2 (Roman, 1902), p. 256.
8. Ilie Ceauşescu, "Armata unirii: Politica militară a domnitorului Alexandru Ioan Cuza (1859–1866)," in *File din istoria militară a poporului român*, vol. 7 (Bucharest: Militară, 1980), pp. 60–95.
9. I. Lupaş, *Istoria unirii românilor* (Bucharest, 1977), p. 279.
10. *Monitorul oastei*, June 5, 1964, p. 253.

Foundations of the Independence Army: The Romanian Military in the Unification Era

Gerald J. Bobango

The centennial of Romanian independence, celebrated both in Romania and in the United States in 1977–78, gave rise to significant new research and writing on the origins and development of the Romanian armed forces in the nineteenth century. The army that ultimately conquered the nation's enemies and won independence at the Grivița redoubt and on the fields of Smirdan and Plevna was not a hastily contrived force, but had been many decades in the making, with roots deep in the nation's past. Between 1821 and 1878 it had incorporated modern elements of organization and equipment, some borrowed from the West and grafted onto native institutions and others indigenous.

Some excellent Romanian monographs on the evolution of Romania's military tradition have appeared in recent years, especially those of Apostol Stan,[1] Constantin Olteanu,[2] Teodor Popescu,[3] and Ilie Ceaușescu.[4] The limited circulation of Romanian-language studies, even in translation, in the West makes it appropriate to summarize for an English-speaking audience certain highlights of these works. Although Marcel Emerit's excellent study of the first French military mission in Romania appeared as long ago as 1966, the details of French assistance and impact on Cuza's army remain by and large unknown in American historical circles. My purpose here, then, is not only to review recent Romanian findings on the events which most contributed, during the era of Romanian unification (1859–66), to the creation of the army that, under Prince Charles I, would prove victorious in 1878, but also to suggest, on the basis of my studies of the Cuza period,[5] certain factors which perhaps ought to be subjected to further investigation.

Unquestionably the unification of the Danubian lands through the half-planned, half-spontaneous double election of Alexandru Ioan Cuza in 1859 was a critical moment in the evolution of modern Romania, one which laid the foundations of the nation-state and initiated a new stage in the country's historical development. From the beginning of Cuza's reign, the modernization of the armed forces was a major preoccupation of the governing circles, a sine qua non for consolidating the quasi-autonomy which the provinces had achieved in a few short years.

It is too early to say, as modern Romanian historiography does not hesitate to do,[6] that already in 1859 Romanians looked forward to the achievement of independence and even the realization of the "unitary national state" that became a reality only in 1918—although there are indeed foreshadowings of these things during the generally turbulent 1860s. More to the point is that, having experienced an Austrian occupation during the Crimean War and a Russian and Turkish invasion to crush the short-lived revolutionary outbreaks in Bucharest and Iaşi during 1848, and having lived with the constant threat of foreign intervention even after the double election whenever they seemed to be exceeding the limits the Great Powers had set for them, an army of their own seemed to be the surest guarantee that a maximum measure of the gains of 1859 might be preserved.

In Alexandru Cuza, moreover, Romania had a leader oriented to the role and importance of the military, for Cuza's military background was not negligible. Despite the cynical rejoinders of some that his rise through the Moldavian military was due solely to his political connections or sycophancy, in fact his record of accomplishment in various military capacities during the 1850s was real enough.[7] He had also lived for some time in France and been able to observe firsthand certain of those elements which he would later institute in his own country. If anything, more research on the influence of Cuza's military background and his pre-1859 career might well produce greater understanding of his military reforms as prince.

As early as February 25, 1859, Cuza's agent in Paris, Vasile Alecsandri, approached Napoleon III with a project for modernizing the Romanian armed forces. French assistance in such an effort would mean that Romania could bring fifty thousand men to the future aid of France in the event of war.[8] One has only to recall Napoleon's involvements in Sardinia, Italy, and Austria during the ensuing decade to realize how effective was this oft-repeated Romanian reminder of the value to France of a friendly—and well-armed—state east of Vienna. Alecsandri, for his part, worked this theme to the utmost. With pardonable exaggeration, he dangled before the emperor the vision of "nine million Romanians who, if Providence should grant their dream . . . would settle forever the Eastern Question."[9] Four years later Cuza himself addressed the emperor, stressing the same possibility of Romanian military aid to France in the Polish situation.[10] In his researches on the French Foreign Ministry, moreover, Emerit has discovered a second major French motivation to assist Romania, namely, the pressures brought to bear on the government in Paris by French capitalists such as those of the Periere, Talabot, and Godillot trusts, who saw the opportunity for intensive French penetration of the Danubian regions, along with the possibility of supplying the Romanians with millions of francs' worth of weaponry and munitions. Faced with increasing competition from arms manufacturers in Germany and Belgium, French entrepreneurs lobbied among Romanian officials, sent agents and journalists to the United Principalities to demonstrate their chassepot rifles, and in general carried on a multiplicity of activities that remain to be uncovered in Romania's archives.[11]

Even before the arrival of the French military mission, however, Cuza took steps toward solidifying the armed forces, the while blithely ignoring the spirit of the Convention of 1858, which intended that the two Romanian lands should have separate but parallel armed establishments. The convention, designed to serve as a constitution for the principalities at a time when the double election was as yet unforeseen, contained a series of measures (in Articles 42 and 45) providing for the identical organization of separate armies in Moldavia and Wallachia, with inspectors-general named by the respective princes who were to maintain the unitary character of their armies, concentrating them if need be to preserve internal order and the territorial integrity of the provinces. The size of the armies was increased by one-third over those ordained by the Règlement Organique of a generation earlier.[12] In fact, however, the armies were rendered nugatory by provisions that the commanders and inspectors-general be named alternately by the two princes and that any military action have the assent of both princes and of the Ottoman government as well. Thus the powers sought to prevent the creation of any real military power at the mouth of the Danube. It was true that by recognizing the Romanian military as henceforth intended to defend the borders of the provinces the convention had removed the limited internal militia or gendarme character attached to the army by the Règlement, but the cumbersome restrictions of the dual apparatus seemed to belie this intent.

Cuza's concentration of the two armies in April 1859 in the camp at Floreşti, once war had broken out in northern Italy and Turkish troops were gathering at Varna and Şumla, was the first step toward unification. The camp near Ploieşti contained some twelve thousand effectives. Although these forces had roughly only five thousand rifles and ten cannon, the move was symbolic of the new unified condition of the country. Its most important result was probably the sense of relative strength and unity of military discipline and spirit it created, and

Dimitrie Bolintineanu wrote that "the armies, seeing themselves gathered together in such a number for the first time, began to recognize and value their own military potential."[13]

By the end of the year Cuza had created a single general staff, and on May 30, 1860, Colonel Ioan Emanoil Florescu was named to head it. In the meantime, a unified military code had been worked out and adopted, combining the interior service regulations from Moldavia with the military penal code of Wallachia. Although the camp at Floreşti was a temporary measure, Cuza continued to perform symbolic gestures of mixing the two provincial forces, sending the Third Muntenian Regiment to Iaşi and a Moldavian regiment of musketeers, along with an artillery battery, to Bucharest. Besides the exercise in logistics and troop movement thus gained, the result was the frequent collaboration of men from the two provinces, many of whom had likely never before traveled to the other capital or mingled with men from the sister province. Such joint exercises thus contributed to the emerging sense of common identity and national consciousness. The spring and summer of 1860 saw this process completed. As his double election opened up the opportunity to perform dual operations having the same end in each province and, therefore, in the unified country, while yet technically not violating the letter of the Convention of 1858, Cuza ordered Florescu to assume command of the Ministry of War in both provinces, thus ipso facto uniting the two armies. By the end of August 1860, it was decided that the administration and supervision of the two forces would henceforth be unified under the control of the minister of war in Bucharest.[14] By this time uniformity of instruction, discipline, and accounting procedures had already been ordered for the two armies, and a law of May 13 had authorized bringing French military instructors into the country.[15] The end of 1860 found the two medical services united, with Dr. Carol Davila named inspector general, the beginnings of a fleet organized under Colonel Nicolae Steriadi, and the artillery from the two provinces reorganized into a single regiment of two divisions.

A final step was the consolidation of the former military schools at Iaşi and Bucharest into a single institution in Bucharest on July 22, 1861. Calling the new military college a symbol of "the indivisible union of Romanians," Cuza prepared to give his future officers the best training possible. Some one hundred fifty students were enrolled in the five-year program, and the best of these were sent, upon completion of their courses, to pursue additional studies in France. Between 1860 and 1864, more than sixty went abroad for this purpose.[16] During the wars which led to the unification of Italy, Cuza sent Romanian military missions to Maroc and to maneuvers at the French camp in Châlons.

Romanian officers also traveled with the Union forces at some length during the American Civil War.[17]

Too little attention has been paid to the use of the army purely as a modernizing force in Romanian society. Beyond the acquisition of up-to-date equipment and tactical knowledge, Cuza saw the reform of the military as a means of upgrading Romanian society. Thus even before the unification of the officers' schools, centers of instruction, termed "schools of the First Grade," for men in the ranks were created to provide reading, writing, and elementary computation skills for enlisted men, who in 1860 remained largely unlettered. Even more meaningful for the future, perhaps, were the School for Soldiers' Children and the higher-level Normal School for Writing, Gymnastics, Drawing and Instruction for Soldiers' Children. At a time when public literacy in Romania was nearly nonexistent, such centers formed the beginnings of an effort at broad-based education in a peasant society. In 1863 the School of Arts was opened to train men in technical occupations under army supervision. Students were required to work in state workshops for two years after the completion of their courses.[18] In the first few years of their existence, these schools were headed by officers drawn from the French military mission.[19]

With this groundwork laid in the administrative and command structure, Cuza proceeded along two lines: the physical enlargement of the armed forces and the acquisition of the best equipment possible. An estimate compiled from contemporary issues of *Monitorul oastei* by Teodor Popescu reveals that from some 24,948 effectives in 1859, of which approximately half were permanent army and half territorial troops (combining border guards and reserve militia troops), the number of men in all types of units had increased to 43,913, or nearly doubled, by 1865. Horses for the permanent army in the same period increased from perhaps a few hundred on the eve of union to 11,389.[20] By the end of Cuza's reign the Romanian army consisted of three territorial divisions, made up of seven infantry regiments, a battalion of chasseurs, a military police company, two cavalry regiments, an artillery regiment, an engineers' battalion, various fire companies in Bucharest and Iași, five squadrons and two companies of gendarmes, a modest fleet, administrative troops, ten battalions of border guards, and thirty-one squadrons of reserve militia.

Much of this growth was due, in addition to the general upward mobility made possible by the military school system, to the introduction of obligatory military service through a new law of recruitment of 1860. Military service was now compulsory for all citizens at age twenty, which represented a major new equality before the law of all social

FOUNDATIONS OF THE INDEPENDENCE ARMY   393

classes. Annual army contingents in each district were to be formed by the drawing of lots, which put an end to some of the abuses of the past, when the onus of service fell entirely on peasant sons or others without family wealth or connections. With the law of November 27, 1864, on the organization of the army, the age for compulsory service was fixed between twenty and fifty years, with active duty in the permanent army assigned to youths from twenty to twenty-six years of age. Active duty was four years, with two more in the reserves. Although, to be sure, abuses of recruiting and favoritism continued, undoubtedly the general level of morale and patriotic consciousness and the caliber of the troops was raised significantly through a combination of the enlistment laws, the establishment of military schools, and the high priority assigned by the state to training and outfitting its new armed forces.

Equally notable advances were registered in terms of supplying the new army with the implements of its craft. The acquisition of artillery was high on the list, and during 1862 Cuza purchased from Serbia 24 cannon and from Belgium an equal number of pieces of field artillery. A milestone was the passage by the Romanian Chamber on November 15, 1863, of a credit of 7.98 million lei for the purchase of 48 cannon, along with 40,000 rifles and the powder and shot to supply them. France, especially the firm of Alexis Godillot, was the major purveyor of all this weaponry. Between 1863 and 1865, 47,600 rifles, 700 sidearm pistols, 5,300 carbines, 4,000 muskets, 12,000 sabers, 200 Enfield carbines, and 48 cannon were purchased.[21] "At the time of my election," Cuza wrote to Napoleon III shortly after the delivery of this material, "the principalities possessed no more than four or five thousand Russian rifles . . . and about ten cannon of no value. . . . They possess today seventy thousand rifles . . . and my artillery numbers seventy-two."[22] Nor was the Romanian army to be dependent always on foreign supplies, for Cuza founded a national arsenal in 1863 and a number of armaments factories during the course of his reign.

Finally, mention should also be made of the series of unified instructional manuals, updated military codes, and theoretical publications which appeared in these years and served to regularize and nationalize the hitherto disparate and uncoordinated Romanian units. *Regulations for Exercises and Maneuvers* appeared in 1861, *On the Army's Service during Campaigns* in 1862, works on the command of and instruction of reserve troops when called to active duty during 1863, and so on. The important command bulletin *Monitorul oastei* first saw print during 1860, while *România militară* published its first number in January 1864 and the review *Almanahul militar* came out in 1865.

Unquestionably, the army forged by Cuza and Florescu, with the assistance of the French mission, was a far cry from the scattered ad hoc forces characteristic of the Danubian principalities prior to the double election. If this army still lacked experience and consolidation, nevertheless by 1866 it represented a force capable of resisting foreign intervention and defending the frontiers of the infant nation.[23] While still subject to the nominal suzerainty of the Ottoman Empire and theoretically to be governed in its ultimate acts by the majority rule of the seven guarantor powers who had created its new status at the Congress of Paris, in fact Romanian autonomy as a result of Cuza's reign was far more than a fiction. One of the factors weighing most heavily in the dramatic seven-year transformation from subject principalities to a state only a little more than a decade away from independence was the creation, in its broad outlines, of a viable Romanian military establishment.

Notes

1. Apostol Stan, *Renașterea armatei naționale* (Craiova: Scrisul Românesc, 1979), has been called "a fundamental work which constitutes the point of departure for every future investigation on the antecedents of the modern Romanian army" (cf. the review by Fl. Constantiniu in *Revue roumaine d'histoire* 19 [1980]: 75–77). Stan's excellent biography of Gheorghe Magheru (Bucharest, 1969) should also be consulted, along with shorter works such as his "Gărzile naționale în revoluția din 1848 în Țara Românească," *Studii* 18 (1965): 879–94.

2. Constantin Olteanu, *Contribuții la cercetarea conceptului de putere armată la Români* (Bucharest: Militară, 1979).

3. Teodor Popescu, "Modernizarea forțelor armate Românești în timpul domniei lui Alexandru Ioan Cuza," *Revista de istorie* 32 (1979): 79–102, is one of the best brief overviews of the military reforms under Cuza to appear recently, although the piece suffers from redundancy and severe lack of organization. Much of the information may be found in the thorough work on Cuza by Constantin C. Giurescu, *Viața și opera lui Cuza-Vodă* (Bucharest: Științifică, 1970). Any study of this topic will require also the use of the two-volume work by Major Ioan Popovici which appeared in Romania between 1900 and 1902, *Organizarea armatei române*. Its first volume, entitled *Schița istorică a organizării de la 1830–1877*, devotes some one hundred pages to Cuza-era reforms. Also in 1902 one General Herkt, a close collaborator of Cuza's in the area of artillery, published *Cîteva pagini din istorie armatei române*, covering the topic from the time of the Règlement.

4. The works of General Ceaușescu on Romanian military history, especially centering on the 1877–78 War for Independence, have become well known in America in the past five years. His stress on the historic concept of the "armed

nation" has shed light on the tradition of the citizen-soldier in Romania's military past and the important role of institutions such as the *dorobanţi* and *grăniceri* alongside the regular army. His works further have shown the integral connections between the military and the political and economic evolution of Romania. A recent example is "Le rôle de l'armée dans l'histoire du peuple roumain: son impact sur les facteurs politique, social et cultural en Roumanie et sur les relations avec d'autres pays (XX siècle)," *Revue roumaine d'histoire* 19 (1980): 371–88.

5. The most extensive monograph on the Cuza era in English in recent times is Gerald J. Bobango, *The Emergence of the Romanian National State* (Boulder: East European Quarterly, 1979). One must also study the older works by W. G. East, T. W. Riker, and R. W. Seton-Watson.

6. E.g., Popescu, *Modernizarea forţelor armate*, pp. 79–80, where the author indulges in one of the favorite fallacies of current Romanian historiography, that of writing "backwards history" wherein every act of the nineteenth century was deliberately taken in order to bring about the national unification accomplished in 1918.

7. Gerald J. Bobango, "Colonel Alexandru Ioan Cuza: The Making of a Hospodar," *Southeastern Europe* 2 (1975): 1–22.

8. R. V. Bossy, *Agenţia diplomatică a României în Paris şi legăturile politice franco-române sub Cuza-Vodă* (Bucharest: 1931), p. 165.

9. This is a statement which Alecsandri may or may not have actually made to Napoleon III, but which is representative of the rhetoric advanced at the time. Alecsandri repeats it only years later in *Convorbiri literare* 12 (2) (1878): 46.

10. Bossy, *Agenţia diplomatică*, pp. 291–96.

11. Marcel Emerit, "Le dossier de la première mission militaire française en Roumanie," *Revue roumaine d'histoire* 5 (1966): 576–77.

12. Popescu, *Modernizarea forţelor armate*, p. 84.

13. Gh. Romanescu and Gh. Bejancu, *Oastea româna de a lungul veacurilor* (Bucharest: Militară, 1976), p. 151.

14. *Monitorul oastei*, October 8, 1860, p. 583, and following issues.

15. Ibid., May 26, 1860, pp. 273–77.

16. Popescu, *Modernizarea forţelor armate*, pp. 92, 95.

17. Cf. Ilie Ceauşescu, "The American Revolution and Civil War as Echoed by the Romanian Historiography," *Revue roumaine d'histoire* 15 (1976): 687–94.

18. Popescu, *Modernizarea forţelor armate*, pp. 95–96.

19. Emerit, "Le dossier," p. 582.

20. Popescu, *Modernizarea forţelor armate*, pp. 99–100.

21. Ibid., pp. 96–97.

22. Romanescu and Bejancu, *Oastea româna*, p. 156.

23. Not directly cited herein, but necessary reading for any serious work on the subject, are the following additional sources: P. Baltagi, C. Soare, et al., *Pagini din gîndirea militară românească: Culegere de texte din lucrari apărute in perioada 1821–1916* (Bucharest: Militară, 1969); Eugen Bantea, "Aspects of the Correlation Materiél-Military Art in Modern Romania (1840–1940),"

Revue roumaine d'histoire 15 (1976): 669–85; articles by Dan Berindei, Ilie Ceauşescu, and Constantin Căzănişteanu, covering pp. 215–84 of Béla Király and Gunther Rothenberg, *War and Society in East Central Europe*, vol. 1 (New York: Brooklyn College Press, 1979); N. Iorga, *Istoria armatei românestii* (Bucharest: Militară, 1970), the revised version of the first and second editions of 1919 and 1930, respectively, ed. N. Gheran and V. Iova. V. Nădajde, *Centenarul renaşterii armatei româneşti* (Iaşi, 1930) is also useful, as is the anthology edited by Al. Gh. Savu, *Armata şi societatea românească* (Bucharest: Militară, 1980).

The Military and the Establishment of the Romanian National State: Reciprocal Influences, 1856–62

Mihail E. Ionescu

Two main points may be made about the Romanian military establishment in the period 1856–62—from the end of the Crimean War to the international recognition of the newly created state of Romania. First, the two Romanian principalities, Wallachia and Moldavia, whose fusion in 1859 gave rise to a new European political reality, Romania, already had modern military structures—armies with various arms that were capable of focusing the people's military defensive efforts against any foreign invasion; in other words, there was a Romanian army before the 1859 union. Second, the two principalities' armed forces had command echelons of some decades' duration whose political and social relations made them an influential element in the dynamics of the great events in the history of modern Romania; this was clearly revealed during the Romanian Revolution of 1848, when the army proved a remarkable component of the revolutionary wave. Thus the founding of the national state of Romania did not call for the building of an army from scratch. Rather, the emergence of the new state called for the development of this military force in a direction consistent with the state's fundamental needs. The role of the military is apparent in its attitude toward the union of 1859 and in the attitude toward the military of the political leadership of the period.

I

Within the principalities' armed forces, union—which had become a European question during and after the Crimean War[1]—was an imperative vigorously asserted. The thinking of the military command echelon stood out in bold relief in an essay by the officer Grigore Borănescu: "The sad state of things in Romania when it was deprived of its military institutions, when the country seemed to be only a great granary for invading armies, fully demonstrated to Romanians that only by armed force can we acquire the right to consider ourselves *among other free, independent nations* [my emphasis]."[2] The foreign military occupation of the principalities' territory during the Crimean War and the armed forces' inability, because of the international situation and the disproportion of numbers, effectively to resist it demonstrated the imperative need for a strong army and enhanced the military's prestige. Factors related to the military establishment's stability and its functioning in domestic and foreign fields led to the perpetuation within it of the aspiration for union that had been firmly asserted during the 1848 Revolution. The above-quoted essay by Borănescu sheds light upon this very obvious tendency: "How long will we go on depending on the foreigner's compassion and his intervention in our affairs? We are almost five million Romanians [in Moldavia and Wallachia], an intelligent nation, and thus we must want to live only on our own."[3] At the same time, the military expected the formation of the new state to be a decisive stimulus to the development of its own establishment. "This double election [of Alexandru Ioan Cuza in each of the two principalities]," wrote another officer, "offered the opportunity to set up a national army and gave stimulus to everyone's ideal of raising our army to the level of Europe's best."[4]

The military establishment's devotion to the cause of unification is clearly revealed by historical events. The first, of paramount significance, was the election of the United Principalities' first ruling prince, Alexandru Ioan Cuza, among the national army in which he served, achieving the rank of colonel. The second was the army's attitude toward Cuza's election in Wallachia on January 24, 1859. The army's commander-in-chief, General B. Vlădoianu, fully approved of the double election.[5] This meant that the army's influence was added to the popular will in Cuza's election as ruling prince of Wallachia. According to a report of the time, "all that night of January 23 and 24 was spent in continuous agitation by both people and government. Infantry and cavalry patrolled the streets, but at the same time groups of hundreds of people had agreed with the army that no blood was to be shed."[6]

Equally symptomatic of the military's support of unification was the influence upon the newly created state exercised by military leaders. Among Cuza's close advisers there were generals,[7] and one of them, Ioan Emanoil Florescu, became "one of Cuza's main supporters."[8] The fact that at no time in the period of 1856–62 was the military the source of any of the negative political initiatives so frequently seen under such conditions is eloquent of the unanimity of Romanian society with regard to unification.[9]

Thus the Romanian military was one of the fundamental forces in the establishment of the national state, both for reasons of its own, such as the desire for prestige and for the development and modernization of its structure, and for reasons of general national interest.

II

The idea that only a strong military establishment could ensure the achievement of union and the international recognition of the newly created state was a permanent part of the political ideology of the 1848 generation. Having been exposed in Bălcescu's essay before 1848 and put into practice during the Romanian Revolution of 1848–49, this idea frequently appeared again in the period of 1856–62. In the statements addressed by the revolutionary leaders of the emigration to the European governments prior to the Paris Congress of 1858, the assertion of the principalities' union was grounded in the idea of a military force with which the newly created state could effectively oppose the neighboring powers' expansionist tendencies in East Central Europe. In a memorandum addressed to the British government in December 1856 it was stated that "the importance of this state of five million Romanians, fully aware of their high rank, offers complete security for the future and the moral and material force necessary for its dignity and its people's interests to be respected."[10]

In 1859, Cuza, as chief of state, declared: "I want the army restricted for the moment to our needs for public order, to get ready for anything."[11] France, the union's great foreign supporter, also so advised.[12] Romanian public opinion, aware of the necessity for an adequate military force, made the army's consolidation its highest priority. The purpose of a strong military was explicitly defensive. The army had to prove—as Cuza himself declared—that "Romania really existed."[13] As one newspaper declared, "We are not by any means arming ourselves for conquest."[4]

The political leadership's orientation toward the military was apparent from the very moment of achievement of union. The fusion of the two principalities' armies was quickly implemented, and simultaneously steps were taken to develop their military structures and equipment. The latter, especially, meant mobilization of substantial material resources by the newly created state; the necessary funds, about one-third of the total budget, were almost unanimously voted by the country's parliament. The first step in the army's unification was achieved by the ruling prince's decision to take upon himself the tasks of supreme commander of the armed forces and to appoint a general staff.

Concurrently with the army's numerical enhancement, the needed organizational structures were quickly set up; administration and training were standardized.¹⁵ A law calling for compulsory military service for all the country's inhabitants was promulgated in 1860 with a view to reviving the old national soldierly establishments. Special attention was paid to the rapid development of the modern military personnel necessary for realizing the principle of the "armed nation," which, as a result of heated doctrinaire debates, had succeeded in winning numerous followers both in the military establishment and in the political leadership. In December of that year Cuza announced his decision to set up a "strong military that would be open to all Romanians and include them in the homeland's defense in the event of danger."¹⁶

From the first year of the union, the army was given a role of paramount importance. When foreign forces hostile to the unity of the Romanian state began to stir, the political leadership concentrated its troops at Floreşti (in Prahova County). This camp's location so close to Transylvania, in combination with the Habsburg Empire's anticipated defeat in the Franco-Sardinian-Austrian War, permitted a glimpse of another aspect of the stress laid on the strengthening of the army. It was considered not only a shield for the union, but also a strong instrument of the century-old ideal of the union of all Romanians within the borders of a single state.¹⁷

Of the dynamics of the relationship between the state and the army during the period of 1856–62, then, two things can be said: First, the army asserted itself, for general national as well as its own reasons, as one of the main factors in the implementation and preservation of the 1859 union. Second, among the priorities that guided the modernization of the state the consolidation of the military emerged as a necessary objective both for immediate and for future needs.

Notes

1. T. W. Riker, *Cum s-a înfăptuit România: Studiul unei probleme internationale, 1856–1866* (Bucharest, 1940).
2. G. Borănescu, "Necesitatea unei armate," in *Pagini din gîndirea militară românească 1821–1916* (Bucharest: Militară, 1969), p. 51.
3. Ibid.
4. General Herkt, *Cîteva pagini din istorie armatei române* (Bucharest, 1902), p. 58. A work issued in 1857, *O aruncătură de ochi asupra Unirii Principatelor Române*, argued that union would lead to an enhancement of the army's personnel and an increase in the financial means dedicated to the military establishment (see Tudor Gheorghe, "Contribuţia principatelor române la realizarea unirii—1859," *Buletinul Academiei Militare*, 1968, no. 1, p. 15.
5. *Lui C. A. Rosetti la o sută de ani de la naşterea sa* (Bucharest, 1916), pp. 25–26.

6. A. D. Xenopol, *Domnia lui Cuza-Vodă,* vol. 1 (Iaşi, 1903), p. 51.
7. Constantin Olteanu, *Contribuţii la cercetarea conceptului de putere armată la români* (Bucharest: Militară, 1979), p. 158.
8. Gerald J. Bobango, *The Emergence of the Romanian National State* (Boulder: East European Quarterly, 1979), p. 96.
9. When in March 1862 General T. Balş reported that a separatist petition addressed to Cuza was to be signed in his house, the prince admonished him: "When such a person holds public office, and especially when he is a soldier, he is not only a rebel, but also a traitor" (Xenopol, *Domnia lui Cuza-Vodă,* vol. 2, p. 315).
10. N. Corivan, *Din activitatea emigranţilor români în Apus (1853–1857): Scrisori şi memorii* (Bucharest, 1931), p. 133; cf. p. 139.
11. R. V. Bossy, *Agenţia diplomatică a României în Paris şi legăturile politice franco-române sub Cuza-Vodă* (Bucharest: Cultură Naţională, 1931), p. 142.
12. In February 1859 Napoleon III advised: "The Romanian nation, after this huge step forward, should stop here and organize the military force to get ready to confront events" (Riker, *Cum s-a înfăptuit România,* pp. 300–301).
13. *Mesagii, proclamaţii, răspunsuri, şi scrisori oficiale ale lui Cuza Vodă* (Vălenii de Munte, 1910), p. 105.
14. "Guvernul şi armarea," *Reforma,* August 1/13, 1860.
15. Ilie Ceauşescu, "Armata unirii: Politica militară a domnitorului Alexandru Ioan Cuza (1859–1862)," in *File din istoria militară a poporului român,* vol. 7 (Bucharest: Militară, 1980), pp. 62–66.
16. *Mesagii, proclamaţii, răspunsuri,* p. 20.
17. Riker, *Cum s-a înfăptuit România,* pp. 299–300.

Cuza, Florescu, and Army Reform, 1859–66

Radu R. Florescu

While it is presumptuous for a family member to speak of one of his forebears, my excuse is that I am not a *direct* descendant of General Ioan Emanoil Florescu; my grandfather Dumitru and General Florescu's father Manolache were brothers. The reason for this essay is that this "forgotten man of Romanian history," as army historian General Radu Rosetti has described him, is the only member of Cuza's inner circle whose biography has yet to be written, despite the fact that primary sources are readily available in his correspondence with most of the forty-eighters, his frequent speeches in Parliament (recorded in *Monitorul oficial*), abundant material in the Cuza archive, army legislation and orders of the day bearing his signature, and his extensive writings on all aspects of army reform, military tactics, and strategy.[1] Two explanations for this silence immediately come to mind: the unusual political rancor to which he fell victim and the fact that he worked in the shadow of larger-than-life military leaders—Prince Cuza and Prince Charles.

A comprehensive evaluation of General Florescu as "the organizer of the modern Romanian army" (to paraphrase the lines of the poet Vasile Alecsandri) would encompass the period when he served as secretary of state for war under Prince Charles from 1871 to 1876, the longest incumbency of that office in Romanian history.[2] For the purposes of this study, I shall focus on his army reforms under Cuza, beginning November 19, 1859, when he was first named secretary for war for both principalities, again from September 1862 to October 1863, and finally from June 1865 to January 1866 as secretary of the interior and permanently commander-in-chief of the army under Cuza.

A word about Florescu's professional training: after completing St. Sava, he entered the army at the age of fourteen in 1833, with the rank of "Junker," and was promoted to second lieutenant at sixteen. He spent the following four years at the Lycée Louis Le Grand in Paris and from age nineteen to twenty-two at the Ecole Militaire.[3] He joined the Second Infantry Regiment of the Line and became a full lieutenant at nineteen. Among his professors were General Jacques Aupick, Director of the Ecole d'Etat-Major, and Captain François Rocancourt, whose work *On the Duties of a Soldier* he translated into Romanian in 1844.[4] Returning to Romania, Florescu was advanced to the rank of captain in 1843 and, undoubtedly helped by his marriage to the daughter of the reigning Prince Bibescu, Ecaterina, soon became a major (at twenty-six),[5] a colonel (at twenty-nine), and a general under Cuza in 1860. By that time, he had served in two theaters of war: with the armies of General Lüders, helping to crush the Hungarian Revolution in Transylvania, and again under Lüders and Dannenberg against the English and the French in the Crimea.[6] Unquestionably Florescu was the best-prepared senior officer at the time of Cuza's election, with far more extensive experience in military affairs than his commander-in-chief.

Good-looking, vain, proud of his ancestry, with a well-rounded education, always receptive to new ideas, basically honest though disorderly in his private finances, Florescu shared the ideology of the forty-eighters, even though he was a political conservative. Above all, he believed in the soldier's oath to his commander-in-chief and was extraordinarily loyal to Cuza.[7] His relationship with Cuza represented a true partnership, and the two men in a sense complemented each other: they both believed that the army was the instrument for the implementation of the program of the unionists and that in the last analysis Romanian independence could only be gained through force of arms.[8] Although most of the army reforms that were instituted in the 1859–66 period bore the signatures of both men, it is reasonable to presume that Florescu, with the advantages of his army background, his greater mastery of administrative detail, and his extensive parliamentary experience, familiarity with military budgets, and excellent contacts with the French general staff, took the leading role and, very often, the initiative. By means of the new flag and the motto "Honor and Fatherland," Florescu aimed at destroying the last vestiges of Moldo-Wallachian particularism.[9] In his view the army was a source of national pride, an ingredient of nationalism, and an element of order in society, blind in its obedience to the commander-in-chief. Though a boyar, Florescu believed in the Napoleonic concept of promotion by merit and also that the strength of the army lay in its discipline, morality, and education. He believed in the traditional maxim of the "armed nation" and in the importance of sea power, defensive fortifications, and the artillery and the corps of engineers. He also spent a good deal of energy on army welfare, though in the eyes of some he devoted too much attention to pageantry and pomp in the belief that the army had to be a "good show" on the parade ground as well as on the battlefield. Florescu was often criticized for the extravagant military budgets he proposed to an unfriendly parliament often swayed by the flowery oratory of the Liberal party, to which he tried to respond with well-documented speeches, delivered in clipped sentences devoid of the conventional flowery rhetoric, in defense of his proposals.[10] He fought with as much tenacity for a yearly stipend for the post of bandmaster as for the three gunboats he deemed essential to strengthen the Danubian flotilla.[11]

Army reform during the period of the Cuza-Florescu partnership involved in the first instance the fusion, integration, and joint administration of two forces, the Moldavian and the Wallachian, which were organized as separate entities and had somewhat different traditions and institutions from the level of command to that of the local police force. It implied increasing the new national force to numbers far superior to those of what in fact had been police forces. It meant providing a new balance between the various services and arms; founding a joint navy and, in the case of Wallachia, a corps of engineers; making new rules for recruitment, promotion, reenlistment, pay scales, and exemptions from military service; establishing schools, uniforms, flags, insignias, decorations, garrison towns and fortifications; and, above all, securing the funds for modern weaponry to improve the army not only quantitatively, but also qualitatively.

Order of the Day no. 98, promulgated on May 30, 1860, conferred upon Florescu the title of commander (under Cuza) of the newly united Moldo-Wallachian force. By his nomination as sole secretary of war, the army became *de jure* the first institution in the country to be effectively united from the high command to the local garrison.[12] Florescu approached the task of implementing army unity during the early difficult days with the tact and diplomacy for which he was well known; he often adopted the pragmatic approach of choosing to preserve that branch or institution in each principality that was the most efficient. Thus the Wallachian penal code and the Moldavian model for garrison service were adopted for the whole army. In order to avoid sensitivities, it was necessary to balance off Bucharest and Iaşi: the Central Army Revision Council was set up in Iaşi, but the Criminal Court functioned in Bucharest.[13] There was particular concern for uniformity. The policemen and firemen of Moldavia were placed under military jurisdiction (Order no. 7251, 1860), as was already the case with these services in Wallachia.[14] This rapid organization of the unified army was all the more essential in view of Turkey's and Austria's reluctance to recognize the double election and the concentration of Turkish troops at Şumla. An improvised force of twelve thousand Moldo-Wallachian soliders under the command of the Moldavian General Constantin Milicescu was rapidly deployed at the camp of Floreşti while Cuza instilled in them a new sentiment of patriotism in the form of allegiance to the new flag and motto.[15]

Much of Florescu's work focused upon obtaining from Parliament the funds necessary to expand the army from two negligible forces to a size commensurate with the defensive tactical and strategic requirements of the newly established state. Florescu considered the infantry the "nucleus of an army," and in the course of 1860 he added two additional regiments—one from each principality, the Sixth Regiment of the Line in Moldavia and the Seventh Regiment of the Line in Wallachia—to the existing force.[16] The cavalry was strengthened by two squadrons, with the famous *lancieri* of Moldavia comprising the second cavalry regiment. As a cavalryman, he established a cavalry school modeled on Saumur in 1863. Deeply influenced by eighteenth-century French theories on the importance of firepower (and later by Count Helmut von Moltke's use of the Krupp guns during the Franco-Prussian War), Florescu organized Cuza's artillery: the separate artillery batteries and battalions from Moldavia and Wallachia were unified to form the first artillery regiment. In a nation ringed by the Carpathian Mountains one needed troops specialized in fighting on this kind of terrain; these were to be the *vănători*, one of Florescu's most successful initiatives.[17] To round off this notion of a unified command, it was essential to place all the irregular units that had never been part of the regular army, such as the *dorobanţi*, under the authority of the Ministry of War. With his reverence for history and knowledge of the crucial role played by the irregular forces in the history of both principalities, Florescu firmly believed in the notion of the "armed nation" in defense of the fatherland. However, he determined to integrate all irregular units into the national army in a series of legislative proposals submitted to Parliament from 1864 to 1866.[18] With relatively short lines of inner defense, ease of communication and transportation were crucial for the rapid deployment of the force in an emergency. With this in mind, Florescu created a Wallachian corps of engineers—there had already been one in Moldavia prior to union—and called it the first regiment of the corps of engineers. It was placed under the joint authority of the Ministry of War and the Ministry of Public Works.[19] Florescu continued with his road-building program even after he had left the War Office in his capacity of secretary of the interior and public works in the Nicolae Cretzulescu administration of 1866.

A great deal of discussion and acrimony ensued in the parliamentary debates centered upon providing the army with the equipment and fire power to transform it into a force to be reckoned with in the new balance of power shaping up in Eastern Europe, with an eye to asserting the nation's independence. As early as 1859, Cuza had sent Vasile Alecsandri and Stefan Golescu to approach Napoleon III for weapons under advantageous terms: 28,000 rifles and cartridges reached Galaţi in that year on a Piedmontese vessel.[20] By 1864, large quantities of weapons had reached the Danubian ports: 13,093 rifles for the infantry, 6,298 for the *vânători,* and another 30,000 guns used by the French spahis, 700 pistols, 4,314 swords, 1,998 bayonets, 1,600 lances, 46 bronze artillery pieces, and 16,000 cannonballs, all of them French-made.[21] However, Florescu ordered a number of 4- and 12-millimeter cannon and howitzers from Krupp—an indication of an interest in German weaponry that was to grow during his 1871-76 tenure at the War Office. Florescu's "Francomania" and later "Prussomania" were mitigated by the ultimate intention not to depend upon foreign powers for the bulk of Romania's armaments. The country, he thought, was well able to provide its own basic armaments, even if foreign technicians had to be engaged as advisors: cannon foundries, rifle factories, and munitions works had to be established in Romania itself. In February 1860, the building of the arsenal of Malmaison was begun. Florescu referred to it as "a system of power which would aid the development of the military."[22] This was followed shortly by the building of a powder and gun factory and of pyrotechnic works at Dealul Spirei for the development of explosive projectiles on the Belgian model for the artillery (under the command of the Belgian Major Herck).[23] The first artillery panoramic field lenses, later adopted by all the armies of the world, were invented by one of Florescu's officers, General Toma Ghenea. Horses for the cavalry and the artillery were thenceforth to be bred in Romania rather than purchased abroad.

Important as were numbers and weapon statistics, one of Florescu's greatest concerns was the quality of this new instrument of war. As a soldier who knew his profession down to the minutest brass button, he had great love and respect for the army and was deeply concerned about the welfare of both officers and men, a fact reflected in his numerous writings and in the law on the instruction of the army published in *Monitorul oastei* May 26, 1860. The education of the soldier or, better still, to paraphrase his words, "the transformation of the barracks into a school teaching basic skills such as reading and writing must be completed by the cultivation of high principles, religion and, above all, love of country."[24] For this purpose, textbooks were to be published by the Ministry of War containing patriotic readings involving such Romanian heroes as Stefan cel Mare and Mihai Viteazul and invoking great battles of the past in prose, poetry, and marching songs. Physical fitness was emphasized through gymnastics, as was target practice and even fencing. Instructors were recruited through the establishment of "model detachments" with officers and qualified soldiers entitled to serve on a rotation basis in all branches of the services.[25] Florescu founded a military school headquartered in Bucharest (it was temporarily moved to Iași in 1866 because of destruction of the building by fire). There were to be seventy candidates completing a five-year course, one-third on army scholarships. He kept a close eye on the recruitment of the teaching staff and the organization of the school and its curriculum, and careful instructions were laid down.[26] The new army paper, *Monitorul oastei,* was a Florescu initiative and aimed not only at providing news and information, but also at raising morale. Of lesser importance were *România militară* and *Anuarul militar al Armatei Române.*[27]

For the creation of the new elite cadres, Florescu realized that the training resources within the country were hardly sufficient. Article 6 of the new law provided four hundred thousand lei to send gifted young men abroad on military scholarships, almost without exception to France, Florescu's alma mater. Initially, eight candidates from the infantry were to be sent to St. Cyr, four from the cavalry to Saumur, six artillerymen and engineers to Metz, and a group of naval officers to the base at Brest.[28] Commenting upon his own achievement in a pamphlet entitled *Improvements Introduced in the Army during the 1859–1861 Period,* Florescu explained that some sixty postgraduates had completed their military training abroad, some of them acquiring actual war experience during maneuvers of the French army at Châlons and Toulon; others had been sent as "observers" in war theaters, for instance, during the Franco-Spanish campaigns in Morocco and the Austro-Italian war.[29]

Undoubtedly exaggeratedly impressed by the glitter of Napoleon III's army and its recent successes in the Crimea and in colonial wars, Florescu believed in the excellence of the French army, of which he was a product, and impressed upon Cuza the need of hiring French officers to act as military advisors. A mission led by Lieutenant Colonel Paul Lamy, a former French chasseur with African experience, was attached to Florescu's pet service, the *vânători.* Among other French military advisors were Intendant Gustave Le Clerc, entrusted with problems of administration, Captains A. Guérin and J. Bodin, who dealt with the artillery, and Captain Roussel, with the corps of engineers. By far the best-known French advisor was Carol Davila, an Italo-Frenchman originally invited by Stirbey in 1853, who was entrusted with the organization of military hospitals and ambulance services in 1860 and was given the rank of general in that year.[30]

Apart from education, the soldier's welfare was always close to Florescu's heart. Florescu was the initiator of a law on the endowment of the army passed in the first quarter of 1862 and dealing with pensions, rations, retirement, minimal standards in barracks, transportation, reenlistment, and rewards for excellence.[31] In order to provide a basic living standard for the wives and children of impoverished soldiers and for orphans, Florescu set up (by Decree no. 46, March 6, 1861) a division of troop children and wives—four children and two wives for each company, battery, and squadron. The children were accepted from age twelve and formed a special company under a sergeant-major, while the wives were hired for domestic services. Special schools for army children were founded at Iaşi in 1864 and included fencing and target practice in their curriculum.[32]

One of Florescu's strengths and perhaps also his chief weakness was his eye for detail; he devoted an inordinate amount of time to relatively secondary matters involving the army that could easily have been delegated to his subordinates. It would be impossible within the scope of this presentation to list the minutiae of army regulations in which he often took a very personal part. Just to cite one example, the administrative services of the army which were finalized in 1860 set up norms with regard to the way a soldier should answer a questionnaire, established rules for writing to military councils in conformity with formulae received from the Foreign Office, and regulated the lighting of barracks. Perhaps because of his own inordinate vanity, Florescu had a passion for uniforms, insignias, medals (he had repeatedly written to Baligot de Beyne, Cuza's French Secretary, and Vasile Alecsandri, Romania's diplomatic agent in Paris, to obtain the Legion d'Honneur for himself), service badges, stripes distinguishing ranks, regimental standards, flags, and commemorative plaques. He argued that the army must glitter; the uniform rounded off the importance he gave to the service, and a well-groomed and well-heeled private was a matter of personal pride. A commission for the uniformization of army dress was set up under his vigilant eye from 1859 to 1861, and from 1860 onwards we can speak of single uniforms. The medical corps was the first unit to be equipped with a uniform in 1859.[33] Florescu had a hand in designing mufti and formal dress for all branches of the services, both officers and men, his inspiration invariably being French models. For instance, in Order of the Day no. 4686, addressed to Cuza in 1861, he informed the prince that he had devised a uniform for the corps of engineers: tunic and trousers of blue cloth with two red stripes with small modifications for the various types of dress.[34] For the *vănători* he adopted a uniform involving a black hat, a brown jacket, black trousers, white shoes and spats.[35] Even brewers, members of the intendancies, were compelled to alternate daily with formal dress, and there were special outfits for mourning. No wonder the Romanian army acquired the reputation of being one of the gaudiest in Europe on the parade ground.

Fond as he was of pageantry, Florescu built an army that was hardly a paper tiger—a fact proven by mobilization and maneuvers executed in March 1860 under the trained eye of the heir to the Belgian throne, Leopold, Duke of Brabant. The tactical theme and the instructions to be carried out at the Floreasco camp from July 1 to August 10 under General Alexandru Macendonski were entirely planned by Florescu and represented substantial progress over the hasty mobilization which had taken place at Floreşti in 1859.[36] Florescu viewed the army as an apolitical force (he would deny soldiers and officers the right to vote) whose primary duty was the defense of order and unswerving loyalty to its commander-in-chief. As tensions among the peasants grew in Moldavia during the summer of 1863, when the electoral and rural laws were being discussed by Parliament, Florescu gave telegraphic instructions to the commanders of the gendarmes at Fălticeni and Botoşani (August 30–September 12) to march to the aid of the beleaguered gendarmes of Dorohoi.[37] During the hot summer of 1863, when the "monstrous coalition," profiting by Cuza's absence at Ems, made its first bid for power in Bucharest, Florescu in his capacity as minister of the interior ordered the troops to fire on the populace, leaving twenty dead and many wounded (August 2/14).[38] On his hasty return from Ems, Cuza congratulated the army but then dismissed the Cretzulescu government together with Florescu to calm spirits—a grave political error which probably cost him his throne.

Far more crucial was the use of the army in defense of the frontiers of the fatherland. Florescu instructed Romanian soldiers and sailors to refuse to present arms when a foreign ship of war docked at a Danubian port, a humiliating procedure that was a legacy of Ottoman tributary times. Both the army and the flotilla were under strict orders to oppose any violation of the border or the Danubian islands by Austrian or Turkish troops by force, as happened on February 4, 1860, when *grăniceri* under Lieutenant Simion Mihălescu fired on Turkish contrabandists. Similar orders were issued in September 1863 when sailors from some Austrian sloops fired upon the police at Turnu Severin (Drobeta).[39] More serious was the violation of Romanian territory by the Polish revolutionaries under Colonel Zygmunt Miłkowski, who tried to force their way through Romania on their way to Poland. Florescu ordered Colonel Ion Călinescu to fire on the Poles. A five-hour battle ensued, with many dead and wounded falling on both sides. This represented the first armed conflict involving the new army against a force greater in size. The Poles were defeated and surrendered their weapons.[40] Florescu received numerous congratulatory addresses concerning this bloody episode, though his opponents attributed his attitude to pro-Russian and anti-Polish bias.

Florescu, with his meager wartime experience, was no great master of strategy and tactics, overcoming his enemies by developing new concepts of war. Judging from his conservative treatises on military history and his Maginot-line defensive mode of thinking, it is conceivable that as a leader of men he would not have made the grade, though he wept unabashedly when he was cheated of the command of the army he had essentially shaped during the War of 1877–78. If not a war commander, he was essentially the less glamorous "organizer of victory"—the man who transformed what in essence were two police forces into a modern army with a unified command. In a letter to Napoleon III, Cuza described the situation confronting him in 1859: "Where I had found scarcely thirteen thousand men, recruited entirely from among the peasants, poorly armed and equipped and responding to commands in Russian and German, I have today twelve thousand *grăniceri,* eight thousand infantry and cavalry militia, and a standing army of twenty thousand recruited from among all classes of society, well-armed, well-equipped, and capable of being increased to three times its normal strength."[41]

With all his frailties, his innate conservatism, his love of pageantry, Florescu was a soldier's soldier who kept abreast of the latest scientific writings and innovations and of improvements in military hardware. With his administrative and parliamentary skill and his concern for detail, he laid the foundations of the Romanian army.[42] Contemporaries have described him as an organizer for whom the word "impossible" did not exist. The poet Vasile Alecsandri, a very close friend and collaborator who, together with Florescu, appears in the sculpture erected in the prince's honor in the center of Iaşi, was close to the truth when he composed a poem in honor of Florescu at the time of the War of Independence, one telling verse of which ran as follows: "For this lively young heroic army/Under Cuza and Carol/Was created through your efforts."[43] There can be no question that the placing of the Romanian army on a modern war footing during the Cuza period can be linked directly with its victories on the field of battle in 1877–78.

Notes

1. Radu Rosetti, "Un uitat, Generalul Ion Emanoil Florescu," *Analele Academiei Române, Memoriile Secţiunii Istorice,* 3d series, 19 (1937). A partial list of Florescu's writings includes the following: *Cîteva cuvinte asupra întrării în acţiune a trupelor noastre* (Bucharest, 1887); *Datoriile ostaşului* (Bucharest, 1876); *Discurs ţinut în Senat cu ocazia votării legii pentru contingentul armatei* (Bucharest, 1877); *Discurs relativ la creditul cerut pentru fortificaţii* (Bucharest, 1890); *Espunere de îmbunătăţirile cele mai însemnătoare introduse în armata Principatelor Unite de la 24 ianuarie 1859-1 iunie 1861* (Bucharest, 1861); *Fortificaţiunile* (Bucharest, 1889); *Osebirea între armatele vechi şi moderne* (Bucharest, 1890); *Studii şi pregătiri militare* (Bucharest, 1878); *Situaţiunea* (Bucharest, 1878); *Teoria dării la semn* (Bucharest, 1845); *Inalta ordonanţa din 21 august asupra serviciului armatei în campanie* (Bucharest, 1862); *Instrucţiuni extrase din legea reorganizării dorobanţilor din 1850 şi din alte dispoziţii ulterioare* (Bucharest, 1864); *Instrucţiuni extrase din legea reorganizării grănicerilor, promulgată în 1850 şi alte dispoziţii ulterioare* (Bucharest, 1864); *Instrucţiunea armatei bazată pe scoală* (Bucharest, 1885).

2. Very little has been published on Florescu to date beyond general references in standard biographies and monographs of the period. Among the scholarly articles are Radu Rosetti, "Un uitat, Generalul Ion Emanoil Florescu," *Academia Româna, Memoriile Secţiunii Istorice,* 3d series, 19 (1937); Ion Batalli, "Generalul Ion Emanoil Florescu, un précursor al armatei române moderne," *Studii şi materiale de muzeografie şi istorie militară, Muzeul militar central,* no. 9 (1976), pp. 75–78; *Generalul I. E. Florescu* (Bucharest, 1930); "Generalul Florescu," *Revista artileriei* 7 (1893): 205–16; Ionescu Gion, "Generalul Florescu," *Ateneul roman* 1 (1894): 879–903.

3. Batalli, "Generalul Florescu," p. 76.

4. *Datoriile ostaşului* (Bucharest, 1876).

5. Florescu fathered five children with his first wife Ecaterina Bibescu: Gheorghe (1848–72), Zoe (1859–63), Maria (1853–91), Eliza (1854–85), and Catrina (1858–1936). He later married Princess Alina Stirbey, but there were no heirs. The general also had one known illegitimate child, Ion Constantin Grigore, who was legitimized in 1881.

6. Florescu was decorated by Lüders in Order of the Day no. 77, April 30, 1850 (Rosetti, "Un uitat," pp. 8–9).

7. It was rumored that it was at Florescu's house that Cuza's election to the double throne of the principalities was determined. This was reported by the newspaper *Steaua Dunării.* Ion Brătianu's symbolic gesture in kissing Florescu on both cheeks following the election helps substantiate this story (V. Nădejde, *Centenarul renaşterii armatei române, 1830–1930* [Iaşi, 1930], p. 27).

8. Florescu was reckoned "the most faithful collaborator of Cuza" (Constantin C. Giurescu, *Viaţa şi opera lui Cuza-Vodă* [Bucharest, 1966], p. 13; Elena Pălănceanu, "Cu privire la măsurile luate de Alexandru Ioan Cuza între anii 1859–1861 pentru unificarea şi organizarea armatei," *Studii şi*

materiale de muzeografie şi istorie militară, Muzeul militar central, no. 10 [1977], pp. 287-92).
9. Academia RSR, Arhiva Cuza, vol. 3, f. 620.
10. For Florescu speeches, see *Monitorul oficial: Desbaterile Senatului şi Camerei Deputaţilor* (1862, 1862-63, 1864-65).
11. Florescu was concerned with the establishment of a Romanian navy. In 1861 he asked Parliament for funds for the construction of one destroyer, two transport barges, and twelve torpedo boats (Florescu, *Espunere de îmbunătătire,* p. 13). He was not successful, however, in obtaining funds to pay the salary of the director of military music (*Monitorul oficial,* February 16, 1863, pp. 6-7).
12. The article conferred the command of the general staff on Florescu. Article 5 stipulated that the Ministries of War in the two principalities were to be unified and that all ministerial decisions were to be published in *Monitorul oastei* (see *Monitorul oastei,* June 3, 1860, pp. 321-22).
13. As early as February 1860, Cuza decreed that the penal code of the Wallachian army serve as a model for both principalities and that Moldavian garrison regulations be applied in Wallachia. The decree was in fact due to Florescu's initiative (*Monitorul oastei,* February 27, 1860, p. 49).
14. *Monitorul oficial,* September 24, 1860, pp. 553-55.
15. Carol Davila (Biblioteca Enciclopedică), Academia RSR, Arhiva Cuza, vol. 3, pp. 613-14.
16. An Order of the Day dated September 9, 1860, established the third regiment of infantry (Sixth of the Line) in Moldavia; in Wallachia, an Order of the Council of Ministers of October 29, 1860, created the fourth regiment of infantry (Seventh of the Line) (*Monitorul oficial,* September 30, 1860, p. 565; see also *Monitorul oficial,* February 19, 1863).
17. The battalion of *vănători* (Alpine troups) was organized in 1860 by detaching the third battalion from the fifth infantry regiment and making it an independent unit specialized in mountain warfare (*Monitorul oficial,* 1, no. 36 [1860], pp. 565-68).
18. The law on the organization of the Romanian army of 1864 provided for "civil guards in all the major cities and a militia to be integrated into the army." It also introduced the notion of military instruction for those who had completed only primary school (Supplement no. 82 in the Parliamentary session of February 22, 1863 [XXXVII], p. 6).
19. *Monitorul oficial,* October 27, 1860, p. 713; Florescu, *Espunere de îmbunătăţirile,* p. 13. A special engineering course was introduced at the military academy for candidates for the corps of engineers.
20. *Documente privind Unirea Principatelor (Correspondenţă politică [1855-1859]),* ed. Cornelia Bodea, vol. 3 (Bucharest, 1963), p. 543.
21. D. I. Georgescu, *Istoria armatei române şi a războaielor poporului român* (Bucharest, 1929), p. 146; Ion Fetcu, "Armata româna în timpul domniei lui Alexandru Ioan Cuza 1859-1866," *Studii şi materiale de muzeografie şi istorie militară, Muzeul militar central,* no. 7-8 (1974-75).
22. *Monitorul oficial (Ţara Românească),* February 27, 1860, p. 64.

23. *Monitorul oficial (Ţara Românească)*, March 15, 1860, p. 283.
24. *Monitorul oficial (Ţara Românească)*, May 26, 1860, pp. 273-74. A good example of Florescu's approach to army schooling: "The soldier is not made for barrack life alone. These barracks are veritable schools where he can not only be taught conventional subjects, but complete his education by strengthening his spirit through love of fatherland, thus providing the force to defend it" (*General Florescu*, p. 50). A crucial work in which Florescu elaborates on the theme of military education is *Instituţiunea militară bazată pe şcoală*, in essence a speech he made at the Romanian Athéné in 1885.
25. Each "model detachment" was composed of elite soldiers from all the services. The "instructors" were commissioned and noncommissioned officers; e.g., for the infantry there were a battalion commander, a captain, the captain's aide (who might be a lieutenant), and two other officers in addition to four noncommissioned officers.
26. The new regulations concerning the military academy were based on Decree no. 1042, signed by Florescu on March 30, 1860. Many of the scholars were promoted to the military academy after completing a preparatory institute at Iaşi and Bucharest, upon termination of which they received the title of "sergeant." In addition to the military academy there were two military institutes, one at Iaşi, the other at Craiova (Maria Stan, "Contribuţii la cunoaşterea învăţămantului militar: Bucureşti în secolul 19lea," *Studii şi materiale de muzeografie şi istorie militară, Muzeul militar central*, no. 6 [1973], pp. 128-35).
27. The first military publication was edited by lieutenant Grigore Lipoianu and Ion Voinescu. It was first printed in Bucharest on July 23, 1859, under the title *Observatorul militar*, with the subtitle *Ziaru politicu şi ştienţificu*. It survived only until December of that year. It was followed by *Monitorul oficial*, a state publication which recorded parliamentary debates, particularly those dealing with army affairs. In 1860 *Monitorul oastei* became the official army newspaper for both principalities.
28. *Monitorul oastei*, May 26, 1860, pp. 274-77.
29. Order of the Day no. 30, *Monitorul oastei*, February 11, 1860. Florescu mentions the names of the military trainees who had been sent abroad to complete their apprenticeship.
30. Carol Davila (Biblioteca Enciclopedică), Academia RSR, Arhiva Cuza, vol. 3, f. 613-14.
31. *Monitorul oficial al României: Desbaterile Senatului şi Adunarii Elective a României* (1864-65), pp. 350-51.
32. *Monitorul oficial al României* 1 (1864): 50-80.
33. Christian M. Vlădescu, "Contribuţii la cunoaşterea uniformelor de cavalerie din perioada domniei lui Alexandru Ioan Cuza 1859-1866," *Studii şi materiale de muzeografie şi istorie militară, Muzeul militar central*, no. 1 (1968), pp. 58-59.
34. *Monitorul oficial*, January 1861, pp. 65-66.
35. *Monitorul oficial*, January 12, 1861, p. 34.
36. *Monitorul oficial*, November 19, 1860, pp. 764-65.

37. Cuza declared himself satisfied with the way Florescu handled peasant insubordination in Moldavia (Giurescu, *Viaţa şi opera,* pp. 336–41).
38. Cuza eventually granted the conspirators amnesty (Giurescu, *Viaţa şi opera,* pp. 336–41).
39. Academia RSR, Arhiva Cuza, vol. 9, f. 116; vol. 16, f. 123 and 126; vol. 22, f. 14.
40. Academia RSR, Arhiva Cuza, vol. 28, f. 5. Also see Giurescu, *Viaţa şi opera,* p. 178.
41. Gheorghe I. Brătianu, *Politica externă a lui Cuza Vodă şi dezvoltarea ideii de unitate naţională* (Bucharest, 1932), pp. 132–37.
42. Brătianu, who had little cause to like Florescu, was fair in his appreciation: "He was the most gifted young man with seductive manners, with a facility to understand and grasp ideas that would have taken others a serious effort to reach the same conclusions" (*General I. E. Florescu,* pp. 8–9). The Austrian Count Alphons von Wimpffen, who had spent the years 1854–56 as an observer in the principalities, saw Florescu as "a man with a rich experience, energetic, hardworking, honest in his personal life, and the best mind in the country" (Rosetti, *Generalul Florescu,* p. 9).
43. Vasile Alecsandri, "Epistola generalului Florescu," in *Generalul Florescu,* pp. 43–44.

Romania's Foreign Military Relations, 1859–66

Florin Constantiniu

The union of Moldavia with Wallachia on January 24, 1859, was an objective necessity imposed by the level of development of the Romanian nation, which called for a national state. Although modern Romania's foundations were laid on this date as a result of the double election of Alexandru Ioan Cuza as ruling prince of the two Romanian principalities, the new state was not independent, but only autonomous, and did not include all the Romanians of the ancient territory of Dacia. Therefore these two objectives remained part of the political program of the Romanian nation. The Crimean War (1853–56), modifying the balance of forces in Europe that had caused the 1848 Romanian Revolution to be suppressed, drew Moldavia and Wallachia out of the Turkish-Russian condominium and placed them under the joint guarantee of the seven Great Powers. The change in international status of Moldavia and Wallachia, and then of Romania as a result of their fusion, broadened the area of diplomatic maneuver for the newly created state to the extent that it could take advantage of the divergences among the guarantor powers, whose interests in the Lower Danube area it was difficult, if not impossible, to reduce to a common denominator.

The consolidation of the union, whose foreign foes awaited an opportunity to annul it, and the laying of the groundwork for the achievement of the other two fundamental objectives of the national political program became the main features of Cuza's policy. It has been fairly said that in international relations, whether peaceful or litigious, every state is represented by a diplomatic-military pair, one sitting down at the bargaining table and the other fighting on the battlefield when negotiations ultimately break down. Neither before nor after this point does their collaboration cease; it is only the priorities that change.

The close relationship between the political and military components of Cuza's policy is readily perceived.[1] In order to consolidate the union, to win the new state's independence, and to gather all the Romanians within its borders, a modern and effective military instrument was needed. The reorganization of the army, its provision with modern equipment, and the adequate training of its officers and enlisted men were fundamental to Cuza's military policy. In its implementation, however, external factors, both favorable and hostile, had to be taken into account. Romania's policy aiming at independence and unity developed within a precisely fixed historical context: it found support in some powers whose interests coincided at least partially with Romanian ones and faced hostility and the threat of opposition by force from others. The great neighboring empires, Ottoman, Habsburg, and tsarist, rivals among themselves for control over the Romanian territory, saw their policies of expansion and domination as being thwarted by a demographically and militarily strong Romanian state. A conflict in which the Romanian state faced these powers alone could only be an asymmetrical one.[2] A century-old experience, the struggle against Ottoman expansion and domination, had shown that in the case of an asymmetrical conflict the involvement of the entire people in the defense of its homeland was the most efficacious means of deterring the invader's efforts to destroy the Romanian political structures.[3] The idea of the "armed nation" enthusiastically promoted by the 1848 revolutionary generation therefore became the basis for the reorganization of the army. Cuza supplemented this idea with a broad system of foreign military relations aiming first and foremost at strengthening relations with the movements of national emancipation in East Central Europe, which of course supported Romania's goals of independence and national unity. The collaboration with the Hungarian revolutionaries consolidated Romania's position with regard to the Habsburg Empire and opened up the prospect of achieving the revendications sought by the Transylvanian Romanians, including their union with Romania. Through his relations with the Serbian and Bulgarian revolutionaries Cuza strengthened Romania's position vis-à-vis the Ottoman Empire. Finally, assistance given to the Polish revolutionaries helped to diminish the pressure of tsarist Russia. Of course, France remained the pivot of foreign relations, both political and military, and as early as 1860 had sent a military mission aimed at training and commanding exemplary units and organizing staffs and administrative and accounting branches. The activities of the French military mission were a valuable contribution to the development of the Romanian army. France was also the source of a great quantity of arms and military equipment: in 1859 the Alexis Godillot Company sold Romania ten thousand guns and contracted to deliver forty thousand more, along with forty-eight cannon, as well as to build a foundry in Romania; from 1865 on this company became the provider of all the supplies needed by the army for a dozen years.[4] France was the "great ally," but it was a remote one. It was capable of impeding the enemies' punitive actions within the framework of the joint guarantee or of being a last resort under crisis conditions, but it was too far away, both geographically and in its interests, to be able to offer the steadfast and effective support that could be provided —especially in such a period as the middle of the nineteenth century—by a very close neighbor.

Serbian-Romanian relations acquired new features during Cuza's reign: their similarity of status in relation to the Porte, their similar long-standing efforts to escape Ottoman domination, and, finally, their shared concern with pursuing independence with an adequate military instrument all drew them ever closer together. The episode of the transit of Russian weapons across Romania's territory to Serbia is very well-known: the movement of the convoy of five hundred carts loaded with sixty-three thousand guns and two to three thousand swords aroused intense emotion in European political circles and, after the intervention of the foreign consuls in Bucharest, especially the Austrian and the British, represented the subject of a conference of the guarantor powers' ambassadors convened in Constantinople. Cuza avoided compliance with the Porte's request for the sequestration of the weapons through a clever diplomatic maneuver and dilatory tactics. Serbia's gratitude—expressed in the touching dedication written on the sword offered by Michael Obrenović to his counterpart in Bucharest, "Amico certo in re incerta," as well as the twenty-four cannon presented to the Romanian artillery, measure precisely the dimensions of the service Cuza had performed for his ally. Serbian-Romanian military relations developed further through an exchange of delegations to share information on the level and means of modernization of the two armies.[5]

Romania's traditional support for the Bulgarian fighters against Ottoman domination continued to be extended them under Cuza's reign; he permitted the combatant detachment under the leadership of Georgi Rakovski to pass from Romanian into Bulgarian territory.

All these actions were part of a Balkan policy aiming at the disintegration of Ottoman domination through the liberation of the nations of that region controlled by the Porte. The Romanian prince's policy was detected by tsarist Russia, which, concerned over the consequences of Cuza's assistance to the various movements of national liberation, in 1863 proposed to the Ottoman Empire a joint action going so far as the military occupation of Romania. "The main reason," reported a Romanian diplomat in Constantinople who had learned of this step, "for the proposal of this [Turkish-Russian] alliance was the increasing tendency manifested by the ruling prince [Cuza] not only to avoid the sultan's suzerainty, but to draw after him Serbia, Montenegro, Bulgaria, and Poland as well."[6]

As I have said, Cuza recognized the convergence of interests between the young Romanian state and the revolutionary movements of national liberation directed against Vienna and St. Petersburg. In the very year of the achievement of union (1859), when Austria was frankly expressing its hostility toward Cuza's double election, the Romanian prince considered the possibility of a military action that would have served as a diversion on the eastern flank of the Franco-Sardinian-Austrian war. The camp at Floreşti was intended not only to facilitate the fusion of the Moldavian and Wallachian armies, but also to permit the concentration of troops ready for action beyond the Carpathians.

Cuza also increased the strictly military collaboration developed with the Hungarian revolutionaries, who, in accordance with the agreeement concluded with General György Klapka, were permitted to set up weapons depots at Bacău, Roman, Ocna, and Piatra Neamţ and promised twenty thousand of the thirty thousand guns to be ordered from France. By another agreement, the Hungarian revolutionaries promised to accord, after their victory, "the same rights, the same liberties to all Hungary's inhabitants, irrespective of their race or religion," and to convene a meeting in Transylvania to decide the administrative status of that province. The early end of the war as a result of the Piedmontese-French victories at Magenta and Solferino made these two agreements obsolete, but the relations with the Hungarian revolutionaries went on developing. In 1863 the Hungarian general István Türr requested, in the event of a new Italo-Austrian war, that a contingent made up of Hungarians from Romania who were to carry out an action in Hungary be armed with a thousand guns. Prince Cuza agreed on the condition that an agreement be reached between the Hungarian revolutionary circles and the Transylvanian Romanians.[7]

The same concept of support for the national emancipation movements that meant the weakening of the great neighboring powers also inspired the steadfast assistance given to the Polish revolutionaries. In this policy the incident of Costangalia—the conflict with a detachment of Polish volunteers led by Colonel Zygmunt Miłkowski that, having been landed by an English ship, tried to cross Romanian territory to come to the aid of the 1863 rebels—was a sad necessity imposed by the Polish fighters' imprudence. The actions of Miłkowski's detachment met with the disapproval of Władysław Czartoryski, the official of the Polish revolutionary national government, and the governments of France, Britain, Italy, Sweden, and Turkey; the Polish leader not only rejected the notion of offering Austria the territory of Romania in return for the

Polish territories under Habsburg domination, but also firmly pleaded for a Romanian-Polish military alliance. In response to this proposal, Prince Cuza offered Napoleon III his full military assistance if France should decide to make the events in Poland a *casus belli,* but the emperor had no such intention.[8]

The efforts made by the Romanian ruling prince to provide his country with a strong army and to support the movement of national liberation in East Central Europe disquieted the Great Powers. A passage from a letter from Prince A. M. Gorchakov, Russia's minister of foreign affairs, to the Russian ambassador in Vienna, dated January 18, 1864, is revealing:

> He [Cuza] wants . . . particularly to use, as he has already done and continues to do, the resources taken from the Orthodox church [a reference to the secularization of the monastic estates] for the purpose of arming beyond the country's needs and means, which can only serve ambitious and revolutionary purposes that no conservative country could approve of and that jeopardize the integrity of the Ottoman Empire and the tranquility of the neighboring countries.[9]

In another letter to the same person, dated February 18, 1864, Gorchakov describes Romania under Cuza's reign as "a revolutionary center" and warns of the consequences of the fact that "a government of relatively little importance and power is fearlessly and with impunity challenging European agreements."[10] It became apparent once again that a small state can be victorious in an asymmetrical conflict, in this case covering only political affairs.

This brief essay on Romania's foreign military relations during Prince Cuza's reign would not be complete without a mention of his desire that his officers become acquainted with the military experience of other armies. To this end he sent Captain Emanoil Boteanu to the United States of America in 1864 as an observer with the Union army in the Civil War; having been appointed to the Army of the Potomac under General Meade, Boteanu sent back many reports that were published in *Monitorul oastei.* After General Grant's victory he stayed on for another year to gather information on weapons manufacturing, arsenals, fortifications, and so on.[11] This is simply further evidence of the breadth of Cuza's military policy.

Notes

1. For details, see Ilie Ceauşescu, "Armata unirii: Politica militară a domnitorului Alexandru Ioan Cuza (1859–1866)," in *File din istoria militară a*

poporului român, vol. 7 (Bucharest: Militară, 1980), p. 60 ff.

2. Cf. Andrew J. R. Mack, "Why Big Nations Lose Small Wars: The Politics of Asymmetrical Conflict," *World Politics* 27 (1975): 175 ff.

3. Ilie Ceauşescu, *Războiul întregului popor pentru apărarea patriei la români* (Bucharest: Militară, 1980).

4. Idem, "Armata unirii," p. 84.

5. Constantin C. Giurescu, "Tranzitul armelor sîrbesti prin România sub Cuza-Vodă (1862)," *Romanoslavica* 11 (1965): 33 ff.

6. P. P. Panaitescu, "Unirea principatelor române: Cuza-Vodă şi polonii," *Romanoslavica* 5 (1962): 82.

7. Constantin C. Giurescu, *Viaţa şi opera lui Cuza-Vodă* (Bucharest: Ştiinţifică, 1962), pp. 123–26.

8. Panaitescu, "Unirea principatelor române," pp. 81–82.

9. Gerhard Hilke, "Russlands Haltung zur rumänischen Frage (1864–1866)," *Wissenschaftliche Zeitschrift der Martin-Luther-Universität Halle-Wittenberg* 14 (1965): 197.

10. Ibid.

11. P. Cernovodeanu and I. Stanciu, "The Romanians and the American Civil War," *Revue roumaine d'histoire* 19 (1980): 621–25.

Romanian Military Collaboration with East Central European Struggles for Emancipation and National Unity, 1856–66

Ioan Talpeş

The revolutionary years of 1848–49 had a decisive impact on the economic, social, and political development of the European peoples. The profound changes characteristic of bourgeois revolutions were assimilated by the whole of Europe, even where the revolutionary movements were suppressed in their very beginnings, before any violent confrontation. The persistence of anachronistic state forms—the absolutist feudal Ottoman, Habsburg, and tsarist empires—was marked, until their final collapse, by continuous adjustments to capitalist structures.

The Romanian people's collaboration with the peoples of East Central Europe arose out of the new situation created by the bourgeois revolutions pursuing freedom from foreign domination. The setting up of the modern Romanian state concurrently with the double election of Alexandru Ioan Cuza in the two principalities (on January 5, 1859, in Moldavia and on January 24, 1859, in Wallachia)[1] was decisive for this collaboration, causing the neighboring peoples to place their hopes in the United Principalities. Actions aiming at the liberation of the oppressed peoples within the Ottoman, Habsburg, and tsarist empires found a large audience in Bucharest, the Romanian government being fully aware of their importance for its own struggle for independence and for the liberation of all the Romanian lands still under foreign domination. Within this very complex context, ensuring the conditions that would permit "the Wallachian nationality, which represented the great majority of the inhabitants living in the region between the Lower Danube and the Dniestr, . . . to play an important part in the final settlement of the problems of these territories"[2] was of paramount significance in any military collaboration. Emphasizing the profoundly progressive character of the military collaboration between the Romanian people and the neighboring oppressed peoples, I shall briefly discuss some of the most significant moments of the 1856–66 period.

Both having been under Ottoman suzerainty and then subject to the provisions of the Paris Peace Treaty of March 18/30, 1856, under the guarantee of the seven Great Powers, Serbia and the United Principalities developed their military collaboration with a view to achieving the common goal of abolishing the Turkish suzerainty and liberating the territories under Habsburg domination. Though falling short of the broad collaboration that characterized the winning of complete independence (1877–78) and the setting up of unitary national states (1916–18), Romanian-Serbian collaboration in the period 1856–66 included an event with wide ramifications for both at that time and subsequently. This was the episode of the transit of weapons bought by the Serbian government across Romania's territory in November-December 1862. The very strained development of events in this instance was determined by the discovery of the five-hundred-cart convoy loaded with weapons and ammunition after it had entered Romanian territory; this discovery was made by the English and Austrian vice-consuls at Galaţi and was followed by imperative interventions of the Turkish, Austrian, and British governments with Prince Cuza. Although Cuza knew what his refusal could entail (the weapons transit might be seen as a violation of the provisions of the Paris Convention of 1858), he offered firm resistance to these foreign pressures and threats and took steps to ensure a favorable outcome of this action. In order to prevent any attempt on the part of the Turks, who had more than five thousand soldiers at Vidin, to capture the valuable shipment at the crossing-point on the Danube, the Romanian general staff set up a special detachment with the mission of protecting, at any price, the weapons transit.[4] The special importance of the Romanian government's stand, which helped the Serbian government to get a great quantity of weapons and ammunition (about sixty-three thousand guns, according to some sources),[5] can be fully grasped only in its relationship to the events of the summer of 1862, when, as a result of the Belgrade incident, the Serbians and the Turks were on the brink of war. In order to improve Serbia's situation, the United Principalities concentrated troops near its border with Serbia in response to the Turkish troops' concentration at Vidin. This was intended as "a demonstration in favor of the Serbs," as a military observer stated, and at the same time it harmonized with Cuza's view that "Romanians could not be neutral with regard to the struggle of the Balkan peoples."[7] Referring to the significance of the weapons transit in the Romanian-Serbian military collaboration, Garašanin, Serbia's minister of foreign affairs, declared: "Though Prince Cuza agreed only to the transit of arms meant for us through his territory, once we were in danger he proved ready to help us by all means and to keep his promise even at the price of sacrifice. . . . Therefore, we are proud to be the allies of a nation whose leader knows how to protect his rights so nobly against foreign aggression."[8] In March–April 1866, when, after Prince Cuza had abdicated, the seven Great Powers convened in Paris to discuss a possible separation of the United Principalities and Ottoman troops were concentrated near the Danube, the Serbian government expressed sympathy with Romania's declaration, and numerous Serbs sought to join the special corps of volunteers being set up under the command of General Gheorghe Magheru.[9]

Support for the Bulgarian people's efforts to achieve liberation from the Ottoman yoke was among the constant features of Romanian policy. Especially after 1859, many Bulgarian committees organizing the armed struggle against the Ottoman Empire were operating on Romanian territory. The leaders of the June 1862 Turnovo revolt, Hagi Stavri and Petre Kisimov, took refuge in Romania, and two years later Georgi Rakovski organized small groups of Bulgarian volunteers that crossed the Danube and attacked the Turkish troops. Rakovski was assisted in these actions by the Romanian government, Prince Cuza himself having promised him weapons for twenty-five groups of thirty-one men each.[10] In 1866, a "sacred coalition" was concluded between the supporters of the Romanian political leader C. A. Rosetti and the Bulgarian revolutionaries with a view to preparing the way for "a general revolution against the common enemy of the Christian peoples in the East."[11]

The military collaboration between the Romanian state and the Hungarian revolutionaries was a very active one. Because the pursuit of their common objective, the disintegration of the Habsburg Empire, was judged beyond the capabilities of the two parties, the Romanian-Hungarian military collaboration associated itself with actions initiated by France and Piedmont (later Italy). Soon after Cuza's election, negotiations between the Romanian government and the Hungarian revolutionaries—the former represented by Vasile Alecsandri and the latter by György Klapka—led to the conclusion of two conventions.[12] The first of these comprised the technical military conditions for collaboration in an insurrection in Hungary and Transylvania, Romanian territory being the staging area and supply base for the action.[13] The second convention opened with a declaration of principles according to which the Hungarian revolutionaries resolved to avoid the mistakes made during the revolution of 1848–49 by writing into Hungary's constitution "the same rights, the same liberties for all Hungary's inhabitants, irrespective of their race or religion; full freedom of worship and public education; separate Romanian and Serbian troops; and full equality in the army concerning the possibility of access to all ranks."[14] The rapid development of the Franco-Sardinian-Austrian hostilities and the beginning of the peace negotiations impeded the development of Hungarian military collaboration within the framework established by these conventions.

One of the concerns of the European progressives who considered Romanian-Hungarian military collaboration an essential part of the destruction of the Habsburg Empire, the implementation of the "brotherly concord" firmly emphasized the necessity that the Hungarians acknowledge the right of self-determination of the Romanians who represented the great majority of the inhabitants of Transylvania and the Banat. On October 15/27, 1861, J. A. Vaillant wrote to General Garibaldi, "Italy's liberator and inveterate pro-Romanian," revealing the Romanians' conditions for any collaboration: that Transylvania and the Banat be free to join the United Principalities and have universal suffrage. A little later, on December 5/17, 1861, approaching the same subject, the *Journal de Francfort* published an article noteworthy for its very title "L'indépendance constitutionelle de la Transylvanie." Similar conditions were also pointed out during the negotiations between General Türr and Prince Cuza in May 1863, when the latter stated that he was ready to give material and military assistance to a planned Hungarian diversionary action in Transylvania, but only after the Hungarians had come to an agreement with the Romanians beyond the Carpathians.[15] The Romanians went on helping the Hungarian revolutionaries who took refuge in the United Principalities, one of the essential problems on their agenda being the settlement of the nationalities problem in Hungary once it had been liberated from the Austrian yoke.

The complexity of Romanian-Hungarian relations—on the one hand their common objective of escaping Habsburg domination and on the other the discrimination against Romanians of the Hungarian nobility and the refusal of the Hungarian revolutionary leaders to acknowledge the right of the Romanians of Transylvania and the Banat to determine their own destiny—decisively limited the possibilities of the military collaboration. The intensification of the national conflicts within the multinational empire and the crisis created by the military defeats of 1866 led to the compromise concluded between the Austrian and Hungarian ruling classes in 1867 and the beginning of a new stage in the oppressed peoples' struggle for national emancipation.

The very complex situation of the Polish people, dominated by the Habsburg and tsarist empires and the Prussian kingdom, all of which were very much interested in perpetuating the existing situation and capable of maintaining that situation by force, inspired a cautious attitude on the part of the Romanians. The governments in Bucharest assisted the Polish emigrants in various ways, to the point at which the actions of some groups of emigrants jeopardized the very existence of the Romanian state. The incident in question was the attempt of 258 armed Poles under the command of Colonel Zygmunt Miłkowski to cross Romanian territory on the way to Podolia and Volhynia.[16] Considering that the action of the Polish detachment could entail the military intervention of the tsarist empire, and despite his own feelings, Prince Cuza, on July 1/13, 1863, ordered the prefect of Covurlui County to inform Colonel Miłkowski that "whatever our sympathies, we do not allow our country to be invaded by an armed force. . . . We had hoped for something better in return for the sympathy and hospitality they have always found in our country, and we regret that we must think of them as our enemies' instrument in behaving in this way."[17] After the incident of Costangalia created by the Polish commander's refusal to order the laying down of their arms, the Polish detachment, understanding that resistance would be in vain, obeyed the orders of the Romanian government. Colonel Miłkowski acknowledged in an open letter how generously they had been treated after they had laid down their arms and expressed his gratitude for this attitude.[18] In his turn, in September 1863, Prince Władysław Czartoryski thanked Romania's diplomatic representative in Paris "for the care he [Cuza] took of our fellow countrymen and for his own sympathies toward their cause."[19]

As a result of the intensification of unrest among the revolutionary emigrants within the United Principalities, in the summer of 1864 Russia and Austria concentrated troops on Romania's borders. In this very difficult situation, Prince Cuza sent the ministers of foreign affairs of France, Britain, Prussia, and Italy a circular in which he expressed Romania's stand toward the movements of national and social liberation in East Central Europe: "Our traditions of hospitality opened to them a safe refuge; I looked after their needs with all the freedom our poor resources permitted. If this is the reason for the military preparations being made by the two neighboring powers, I must declare that I shall not be able to yield to comminatory measures violating the public conscience."[20]

The Romanian people's military collaboration with the peoples of East Central Europe, manifested in the period herein analyzed in the assistance given by the Romanian state to the revolutionary movements of national liberation, represented the foundation for the success of the common struggle for national emancipation.

Notes

1. See Dan Berindei, *Epoca unirii* (Bucharest: Academiei Republicii Socialiste România, 1979); Leonid Boicu, *Geneza "chestiunii româneşti" ca problemă internaţională* (Iaşi: Junimea, 1975).
2. K. Marx and F. Engels, *Opere*, vol. 9, p. 10.
3. See T. W. Riker, *Cum s-a înfăptuit România: Studiul unei probleme interaţionale, 1856–1866* (Bucharest, 1940), pp. 74–76.
4. Academia RSR, Arhiva Cuza, vol. 10, f. 555–56.
5. Constantin C. Giurescu, *Viaţa şi opera lui Cuza-Vodă*, 2d ed. rev. and enl. (Bucharest: Ştiinţifică, 1970), pp. 145–47.
6. Academia RSR, Arhiva Cuza, vol. 10, f. 272.
7. Nicolae Ciachir, *România în sud-estul Europei (1848–1886)* (Bucharest: Politică, 1968).
8. Dan Berindei, "Les principautées roumaines unies et la lutte de libération nationale du sud-est de l'Europe," in *Actes du premier congrès international des études balkaniques et sud-est européennes*, vol. 4 (Sofia, 1969), p. 325.
9. Ciachir, *România*, pp. 82–83.
10. Ibid., p. 79.
11. Ibid., p. 83.
13. L. Kossuth, *Souvenirs et écrits de mon exil: Période de la guerre d'Italie* (Paris, 1880), pp. 236–38.
14. Ilie Ceauşescu, "Armata unirii: Politica militară a domnitorului Alexandru Ioan Cuza (1859–1866)," in *File din istoria militară a poporului român*, vol. 7 (Bucharest: Militară, 1880), p. 86.
14. Ibid.
15. Academia RSR, Arhiva Cuza, vol. 16, f. 301–9.
16. See Gheorghe Duzinchîevici, *Cuza Vodă şi revoluţia polonă din 1863* (Bucharest: Carteă Românească, 1935).
17. Giurescu, *Viaţa şi opera*, p. 183.
18. Academia RSR, Arhiva Cuza, vol. 17, f. 33.
19. Ceauşescu, "Armata unirii," p. 89.
20. Gheorghe I. Brătianu, *Politica externă a lui Cuza Vodă şi dezvoltarea ideii de unitate naţională* (Bucharest, 1932), p. 134.

VI. Habsburg Neo-Absolutism Against Hungarians: Secret Police Actions and Dragonnades

The War Without Arms: The Secret Service of the Habsburg Monarchy, 1849–65

Tibor Frank

Battles on visible fields have always been given more attention in historical research than less spectacular forms of conflict. It seems, however, perfectly legitimate to argue that one should give equal consideration to warfare of a different nature. The secret activities of states to control and prevent opposition activities may acquire a significance in terms of social and political importance and consequences not even paralleled by the major wars of the period. This, at least to me, is likely to have been so in the case of the Habsburg Monarchy during the post 1848–49 period, when the government was compelled to resort to a long and difficult rearguard action against a very large army of revolutionaries both at home and in exile—literally all over the then known world. This paper sets out to explain the warfare between the Habsburg government and its exiled enemies by way of secret service operations in the period between 1849 and 1865. I hope that a short presentation like this will justify my claim that this kind of "fighting" had social and political repercussions just as important as those of any of the armed conflicts of the period.

The emigration of the Hungarian revolutionaries after the suppression of the war of independence was anticipated by the imperial government in Vienna well before it began. As early as the beginning of July 1849 a memorandum reached Prince Schwarzenberg describing the probable plans of "the rebel leaders" in the event of what seemed their inevitable defeat:

> As the northern, western, and southwestern borders of the country are closed by the imperial-royal troops, it is almost impossible and certainly very dangerous to make a getaway there. It can almost be taken for granted that the escape would be directed to the south, i.e., to Turkey, where, because of the disorganized state of security measures as well as the great number of representatives and men-of-war of the various powers

means of escape are possible. And that the rebels will forever abandon their plans cannot be assumed. As soon as they find some shelter they will do everything in their power . . . to start subversion anew as soon as possible to attain what has so far eluded them. . . . The East would be the only place for the European democratic party to carry on agitation. The republican-minded Wallachians, the unstable and extremely sensitive Greek character, the constant uprisings in Bosnia and Bulgaria would all in fact afford a good deal of new territory for the agitators.

The author of this memorandum, an Austrian agent code-named Kiamil, suggested some suitable methods for averting this danger: "one should in due time set up fences, and this is the interest of the legitimate parties. This makes an extremely strict surveillance absolutely necessary, however difficult it might be because of the distance involved. Persons noted for their revolutionary tendencies must be constantly kept under control." Then comes a passage as to the likely methods of surveillance, containing in fact an almost complete program for Vienna:

1. Surveillance of the revolutionary leaders and observation of their communication with others, especially foreign ambassadors.
2. The establishment of a rather well-knit bogus association [club] in order to spy on conferences, decisions, and the supplementary sources of their realization.
3. The collection of information about emissaries dispatched to realize specific plans so that the government may know them as well as their smuggled correspondence.

"To promote success," the note ended, "it would be desirable to mix with the rebels in Pest and, what is more, to travel with them to the border—never alone and tailing them, but along with them—as it would be easier to gain their confidence through organizing a club, etc."[1]

Kiamil's plan seems to underline my assumption that the activities of the mid-nineteenth-century Habsburg secret service represented a direct continuation of the war of independence of 1848–49. The development of this new and powerful weapon by the imperial government rested, of course, on earlier foundations. The secret police, originally established by Joseph II, had become a government department by the 1800s. The Diet of 1805 had already found it necessary to legislate "in order to hinder noxious denunciations," and the king had consented to the Act. "Confidantes," as they were called, included distinguished gentlemen who served the Domus Austriaca with a feudal loyalty. They did, however, represent a smallish elite, as there were literally hundreds and hundreds of others spying on lower intellectual and moral levels. First- and second-class confidantes were served in turn by a host of petty informers during the reign of Francis: secretaries, lackeys, and chambermaids, all supported by local postmasters carefully copying "interesting" letters before having them delivered. The Austrian secret service was in full operation at the Congress of Vienna.[2]

It is perfectly understandable that this secret police system became even more important after the defeat of the 1848 revolutions. The police forces were reorganized: since the ill-famed *Polizeihofstelle* of Count Sedlnitzky had been dissolved by the victorious March of 1848, the police came under Alexander von Bach's Ministry of the Interior. His was the responsibility for building up in three years an extremely broadly conceived security system, both domestic and foreign, under the auspices of Prince Schwarzenberg, his patron. It was only after the powerful prime minister's early death in April 1852 that the police were removed from the control of the minister of the interior and placed under Baron Kempen in the new Supreme Police Authority.[3]

As István Hajnal has pointed out, Bach often emphasized "the great importance of the annihilating pursuit of the exiles. He presented this issue in terms of world order and accordingly sought to establish an international organization against revolutionary machinations." It was after the surrender at Világos (August 13, 1849) that Bach started to build his international network of agents, covering most European countries, and his people immediately began observing the exiles. At first, it was not at all easy to acquire their confidence; gradually, however, there appeared a considerable number of people among the exiled revolutionaries who, "with easy conscience or shattered in their beliefs during exile," began to work for Bach. Generally his agents sent their reports to certain addresses in Vienna. These served as the basis of weekly summaries compiled by the Ministry of the Interior for the direct use of the emperor. Certain parts of the reports were even read out in the original at cabinet meetings, where Bach tried to point out the extreme significance of the exiles in Turkey.[4]

It was thus not by chance that the busiest and most effective post of Bach's international system was set up in the East. While there were two or three agents watching exiles in most European centers (the number came to eight in Germany alone), in the East sixteen agents were working by the middle of 1850, and seven of them were still there a year later, just before the Hungarian leaders were to be released from Kyutahia.[5] The agents were organized in two concentric circles around Vienna: the ministry of the Interior made a subtle distinction between agents employed directly (*direkt verwendet*) and indirectly (*indirekt verwendent*). People in the first category knew the purpose and nature of their work and had an idea where their money came from; people in the second were left to speculate and had access to Vienna only via their liaison.[6]

The man who headed the "staff" in the East was the agent called Jasmagy, who sent his reports to Vienna marked Δ. A Viennese by birth and a technician by training, he entered the secret service in 1840 at the early age of twenty-four and was employed by the Austrian government in the East for a full twenty years. He worked first as interpreter for General Hauer in Serbia in 1841 and was later sent to Turkey to organize the surveillance of Hungarian, Polish, and Italian exiles. Jasmagy was a confidant of Bach as well as of Kempen, who gave him confidential tasks and listened to his narratives about secret missions to Bosnia and Hungary. He was also instrumental in finding the Crown of Hungary, which had been hidden by the revolutionaries on their departure. In 1859 he was responsible for organizing and managing the secret service of the Austrian territories in Italy. His annual salary of a thousand Austrian florins made him one of the best-paid members of the Austrian security forces. After the Austro-Hungarian Compromise of 1867 he was, on the advice of the Ministry of the Interior, recommended by the minister of finance for employment on the Turkish railways.[7] It is highly likely that Jasmagy himself was instrumental in organizing the whole Austrian system of agents in Turkey, employing the services of most of his fellow-members code-named Kiamil, Ali, Murat, Mehmed, Abdula, Said, and others.

It was one of the essential features of Bach's secret service that its members had no knowledge of the vast scope of the organization as a whole. They had no idea about other possible members: suspicion operated as a basic motive in the service—everybody spied on everybody else. Paradoxically, the secret service first of all tried to get information on itself: agents reported to Bach on each other and on members of the official diplomatic corps, while the Ministry of Foreign Affairs gathered data on those very agents and diplomats through its own channels. All this was characteristic not only of the lower levels of the organization, but also of the higher ones. The minister of the interior, and especially Kempen from 1852 onward, kept even members of the government under surveillance and reported, if necessary, to the emperor himself.[8] Thus mistrust and fear became the basic organizing principles of the autocratic regime.

One of the most telling examples of all this is the work of Gustav Zerffi. In the course of my recent studies of Zerffi's activities as a spy, first in Turkey (1849–51), then in Paris (1851–53), and finally in London (1853–65), it has become clear that this very able member of the ring of agents around Kossuth and other revolutionary leaders was almost the epitome of the means, skills, and methods of people working in this capacity for Vienna. Zerffi, better than perhaps anyone else of the period, was equipped with all the sophisticated armory of this Austrian war without arms. Few have ever had so good a command of languages, so very able a pen, so sharp and critical a mind, so enterprising a spirit—and so total a disregard for moral obligations and commitments. He achieved a career unique in Habsburg Austria.

Zerffi was employed indirectly by the Bach system as early as November 1849 and went on to dispatch to Vienna his numbered reports on the activities of the international (and especially of the Hungarian) communities of expatriates from Belgrade, Constantinople, Malta, Marseille, Paris, and London for more than fifteen years. He was diligent enough to produce almost two thousand intelligence reports in all. Zerffi, however, was more than an industrious observer: he skillfully managed to get himself involved in the affairs of exiled revolutionaries, such as Karl Marx, Lajos Kossuth, Gottfried Kinkel, and others, and tried to influence their activities, the better to follow his Viennese instructions. He went so far as to write anonymous pamphlets and even whole books to counteract revolutionary projects. The study of the subsequent volte-faces of this systematic turncoat illustrates the nature not only of Vienna's extremely well-organized intelligence network, but of Austrian autocracy as a whole.

Even Zerffi, though well-informed in most fields, had in the first period of his activities as an agent very little positive knowledge as to the exact nature of his work and its background. He had been a zealous participant in the 1848–49 revolution and as such was trusted only to a very limited extent, however willingly he cooperated with Vienna from 1849 on. He used the pseudonym Gustav Dumont and attached himself to the Sardinian consulate to avoid the harassment of the Austrian police while at the same time working as an agent for Bach under yet another pseudonym, Dr. Piali. Although one part of Austrian officialdom kept him at arm's length, his services were extensively used by another, the secret service. There are documents which refer to this almost unbelievable double standard, and they reveal one of the basic means of keeping people loyal in the government's service: fear. Dumont was forced to recognize that he had to work well for the government as Dr. Piali or he would have little chance of surviving. Whenever he got into trouble as a "political exile," it was only at the very last minute and in some very oblique form that the Ministry of the Interior came to his aid. The very methods he used for collecting information made Vienna suspicious: his constant mingling with revolutionary leaders appeared as dubious as it was useful.

Zerffi was quick to realize that the mere collection of data was not enough for his masters in Vienna and certainly earned far too little money for himself. This made him initiate an ingenious method whereby from simple informer he became a first-class agent. It is most interesting to see how this was established alongside developments in European politics: the gradual refinement of his techniques went hand in hand with the stabilization of counterrevolutionary systems throughout Europe in the 1850s.

One of the primary ambitions of this man was to establish close contacts with the higher echelons of the exiled community and specifically with its most important leaders. This was his principal motive in seeking to become intimate with Lajos Kossuth, governor-president of revolutionary Hungary in 1849. He sought not so much to establish personal links with the statesman as to collect information on him by sedulously monitoring the channels which connected Kossuth with the outside world. Zerffi realized that the easiest access to Kossuth's secrets was offered by his correspondence. Kossuth himself was well aware that his letters were closely watched by many people. In November 1850 he complained to his London representative Ferenc Pulszky that his correspondence "was surrounded by such an intricately woven web of espionage that to commit my plans, the details and interconnections of my work, to letters would be the most unguarded negligence."[9] Zerffi had an extremely important role to play in this "espionage" in that he had become friendly with Kossuth's agent in Belgrade, who enjoyed the full confidence of Kossuth, then living in exile in Asia Minor.

Kossuth's Belgrade agent, an Italian named Carossini, had served the Hungarian cause during the 1848–49 revolution and war of independence. Devoted and loyal to the Hungarian leader, he supported him in every way possible. Living at the Sardinian consultate, he was on friendly terms with both the British and the French. He had good relations with even the Russian and the Austrian representatives, as it was impossible to avoid him at soirées in the Serbian capital. Carossini had acquired some sort of semiofficial function as an attaché or secretary of the Sardinian consulate and consequently moved freely in the political and diplomatic circles of Belgrade. Kossuth attached such importance to this faithful follower that he even supplied him with official credentials to the Serbian government.[10]

Though generally on friendly and confidential terms with all the Hungarian exiles, Carossini kept his diplomatic secrets mostly to himself. He admitted one exception, however, and that was Zerffi. As Zerffi acquired the confidence of the Sardinian consul, he came to enjoy the hospitality of his house and, ultimately, to share accommodation with Carossini. For a long period Zerffi was in daily touch with the Italian, and it was only after something like eight months that Carossini realized with astonishment what had happened. Zerffi had acquired a key which gave him access to practically all Carossini's secret papers. Unlike many other Austrian agents, he did not steal or destroy documents; Carossini found everything where he had left it. Zerffi, however, was able to copy Carossini's whole correspondence and forward it to Vienna. In a report to the Ministry of Interior he boasted of having Kossuth's complete cipher, "to copy which I needed two or three weeks." It was only around June or July 1850 that Carossini was forced to admit to Kossuth that the man "for whom he did everything like a father for his son" had been quietly stealing his secrets.[11] Unfortunately, we possess none of the confidential reports Zerffi sent to Vienna in the pre-August 1850 period; however, it is highly probable that the Austrian agent made all the information acquired by Sardinian diplomacy in Belgrade available to Vienna. And as both Kossuth and the Austrian secret service considered the Sardinian consultate the crucial link in Kossuth's correspondence with Britain as well as with Hungary, Zerffi was able to monitor most of Kossuth's highly confidential correspondence in the first half of 1850 and keep Vienna posted as to his secret plans.[12]

This sort of surveillance, however, formed just part of his activities around the exiled Hungarian leader. One of Zerffi's most ambitious ventures was to cooperate with all the factions among the expatriates opposed in one way or another to Kossuth's personality or policies. To neutralize his enormous political influence, Zerffi did his best to contact all the major adversaries of the governor from Turkey via France to Britain. It is difficult to know whether or not Zerffi was following explicit instructions from Vienna here. It might have been his own idea to establish contact with practically all of the notable anti-Kossuth luminaries of the day. In trying to capitalize on the internal conflicts of the exiled revolutionaries he hoped to turn unfriendly relations into hostile relations and thereby to create sharp divisions within the community—to paralyze it from within.

A case in point was General Mór Perczel, to whom Zerffi offered his services in the form of weekly news bulletins. This was rather typical of his procedure: in several other cases he is known to have supplied fellow countrymen with information in the hope of receiving money, confidential services, or information in return. Zerffi's bulletins, similar in nature to the intelligence reports he sent to Vienna, allowed him to get into direct and regular contact with important people. Perczel was extremely important for Vienna, as his anti-Kossuth stance and intrigues made him an almost natural—if unconscious—ally of Vienna in its endeavors to counteract Kossuth. The general showed a particularly strong desire to lead the Hungarians and was hurt by Kossuth's unrivaled popularity. This led him to cultivate connections with practically everybody known to oppose Kossuth. As one of Bach's agents in the East accurately observed, Zerffi's services to Perczel and his openly declared hostility to Kossuth were strongly related: "Zerffi works in Constantinople as one of the most zealous partisans of Perczel. He is a decided adversary of Kossuth's and has a very skillful pen which is particularly suited to counteract the subversive plans of the former in both word and action."[13]

This method of inciting revolutionary leaders against each other was perfected by Zerffi in due course. An idea which he seems to have discovered for himself in Constantinople proved to be a centrally directed principle for action by the time Zerffi reached Paris in 1852. His ambition is quite clear by this point: to widen existing conflicts among the exiles and to divide and discredit their leadership, in sum, and as a result, to paralyze the political strength of the anti-Austrian forces in exile. All this was no longer to be achieved through the isolated zeal of individuals; it was almost certainly coordinated in Vienna.

One of Bach's chief agents in London, Berndt, was completely devoted to this kind of activity; he instructed subordinate agents "to carry on the project already started on the discrediting declarations made by Hungarian exiles about each other. Nothing else can so spoil their chances. What was written about Kossuth by Szemere has been duly distributed. Disunity is at its height."[14]

The method was of course by no means an invention of the Austrian Ministry of the Interior: creating internal tension was a trusted method of other secret services as well. For example, Kossuth himself knew of a similar scheme organized by the Russian police, "who ordered Count Lanczkoronsky to go immediately to Mexico and increase the disturbances there."[15] It is, however, remarkable to see the singularly precise way in which the foreign agents of the Austrian secret service were guided through the vast field of European power politics and the international underworld. As to Zerffi, an overview of Vienna's international espionage network written in April 1852 reveals "that his attraction to political intrigue makes him particularly suitable to play the role allotted to him against [Bertalan] Szemere, Kázmér Batthyány, and [Lajos] Kossuth."[16] This highly confidential document makes it quite clear that members of the Austrian secret service had specific functions which were elaborately planned and administered by the Ministry of the Interior in Vienna. For his work a man like Zerffi, for example, received a regular monthly salary of two hundred Austrian florins, which was occasionally supplemented by a bonus of twenty florins for "special services."[17] This sum was paid out partly for his services in disrupting the exile community and partly for the uninterrupted flow of his intelligence reports. Two examples of these "special services" are his efforts concerning Bertalan Szemere, the exiled prime minister of 1849 Hungary, and his role in what came to be known as the Kossuth banknote case.

Szemere was generally considered the most fervent, even angry, critic of his governor and did his best to discredit him in international opinion.[18] An almost uncontrolled hatred for Kossuth permeated Szemere's correspondence and made him seek out friends almost exclusively among Kossuth's political opponents. He found just a handful, as almost all of the members of the Hungarian community in exile recognized that they should retain Kossuth as their leader even if some, at least, had their reservations about him. To oppose Kossuth was seen by most of them as the equivalent of helping Vienna. This was quickly understood by the Austrian agents János Bangya and Gustav Zerffi, who offered Szemere help in compiling a book to discredit Kossuth in 1852.[19] News of the completion of the manuscript reached Vienna extremely quickly: one of Bach's reports even informed the emperor of this.[20] Bangya and Zerffi aided Szemere in his efforts to reveal Kossuth's weaknesses by undertaking to translate, copy, and eventually publish the manuscript. By doing so they placed the exiled Hungarian prime minister under their close control. Bangya, himself one of the most infamous characters in the Austrian service, even tried to exert influence directly in the actual wording of Szemere's pamphlet and in softening the anti-Habsburg rhetoric.[21] Both Bangya and Zerffi were instrumental in establishing contacts between Szemere and Karl Marx, who were supplied by them with an astonishing armory of anti-Kossuth references.[22]

Yet another type of "special service" to the Austrian government was offered by Zerffi in case of the Kossuth banknotes. Kossuth, who was weighing the chances for a new revolution in Hungary, had Hungarian banknotes to the value of 20 million forints printed in London at the printing firm of Day and Son.[23] This grand scheme could not be kept secret. Kossuth himself suspected that there were Austrian agents in his immediate vicinity. "That the Austrians have ordinary spies and informers among us is a fact, an established fact, the Agency is pretty well organized (why not? we would also do it in the same situation)."[24] The Austrian embassy in London knew of the venture at the very beginning of 1861 and immediately saw to having the project stopped. Councillor

Felix von Wimpffen was entrusted by Ambassador Count Rudolf Apponyi with the task of handling the Home Office.[25] As a result, the British police began an investigation. The British government had no desire to intervene directly and advised the Austrian embassy on behalf of the emperor to prosecute Kossuth and the printing firm for producing banknotes.[26]

Kossuth immediately realized that the case had a tremendous potential impact on international opinion for the simple reason that it provided an opportunity for a public airing of the Hungarian cause. He reckoned on very systematic press coverage of the case and hoped to refute the Austrian accusations one by one:

> He [Francis Joseph] says he is King of Hungary—untrue—he says that he alone enjoys the privilege of printing paper money in Hungary—untrue—he says the arms of Hungary cannot be used without his consent, untrue. . . . All this might cost me £1,500–2,000, so my solicitor tells me. But think of the impact, the triumph once we defeat him in an English court—and it is reported by all the papers of the world—This equals a few battles won.[27]

The battle, however, was lost. Kossuth made tremendous efforts to establish a solid legal case, recalling all the possible historical facts supporting his claims. Responsible for the legal arguments was János Ludvigh, one of the best lawyers among the exiles. Nevertheless, the case was lost in London because the court did not accept Kossuth's arguments, however ably they were put. The governor was right on one thing, however, and that was the surprisingly great attention the subject attracted both in Britain and elsewhere. The court proceedings were fully treated by the leading dailies, including the *Times,* which published all the major documents produced on both sides. The case was also brought to the House of Commons, where the prime minister was compelled to answer questions put by M.P.'s sympathetic to the Hungarian side. The court proceedings were supplemented by what amounted to a war in the press. Open letters, pamphlets, offprints of articles were circulating in London throughout the spring of 1861, most of them supporting the governor in one way or another.[28]

There appeared, however, one publication supporting the other side. A pamphlet of some thirty pages was published to back the emperor and denounce Kossuth. This piece of counterpropaganda was all the more dangerous in that it was published by the publisher Nikolaus Trübner, usually considered a friend to revolutionaries of all countries. The anonymous pamphlet was written by Zerffi, who did a formidable job.[29] He collected practically all the documents that seemed relevant for a refutation of Kossuth's arguments. He set out to argue that Hungary had never been independent within the Habsburg Empire and that Francis Joseph was the rightful heir of Ferdinand V—a point most emphatically disputed by the Hungarian governor, who came forward with the claim of being the only legitimate, duly elected leader of Hungary.[30] Zerffi not only put forward this kind of historical-legal argument, but went on to attack Kossuth by referring to his "want of character and courage and his utter contempt for truth as a political agitator."[31] At the end he warned the British public to reject Kossuth's claims to be a liberal—the coup de grace in the age of mid-Victorian liberalism:

> And now we come to the principal object of this pamphlet. We protest most solemnly, in the face of the English or any other press in the world, against the insinuation that Kossuth represents even the shadow of the liberal principles of any country. The liberals . . . do not carry on any dubious bank-note business on their own account. The liberals desire a strict observance of the laws, from the Emperor to the lowest beggar; and do not employ any pettifogging lawyer-tricks to distort or avoid them. The liberals respect their word; they never deny their own assertions, and always honour their signatures. The liberals speak the common language of right and truth, hate all diplomatic ambiguities, and never believe that nations can be made free by artifices à la Talleyrand and Louis Napoleon. . . . The Hungarian liberals . . . prefer a firm union with the element of civilization and humanity, to a mere vassalage to the northern colossus, and are willing to become great as a part of the powerful German nations. With these liberals M. Kossuth and his followers have nothing in common.[32]

The author of these denunciations was not bold enough to sign his own name for the British public. He was, however, more open to his masters in Vienna. On April 23, 1861, he sent a private letter to the emperor himself, duly signed, arguing that "he had been indefatigable in his efforts to work for the unity and greatness of Austria for ten years in the interest of His Majesty's revered House and the Empire."[33] This "subtle" reference was quickly understood in Vienna. The Ministry of Foreign Affairs suggested to Police Minister Mecséry (Kempen's successor) that Zerffi should be adequately rewarded. The undersecretary of state for foreign affairs drew attention to the fact that Zerffi had "exerted influence on the favorable outcome of the Kossuth note case."[34] Mecséry, however, was not at all moved. He reminded the undersecretary of Zerffi's "revolutionary" past and emphasized that Zerffi "did not seem suitable to receive recognition of any other sort" than the moderate sum of ten pounds.[35] The Austrian ambassador in

London was also informed of the decision and was warned to refuse any further claims Zerffi might make on him.[36] This, of course, was in strict accord with the Austrian (as well as international) practice of keeping the secret service completely separate from the diplomatic world: the two were supposed to have no links whatsoever. The embassies were repeatedly warned throughout the 1850s not to maintain any intercourse with members of the intelligence service, who were not even allowed to enter Austrian missions in foreign capitals.[37]

The history of the Austrian secret service cannot be fully written without further detailed research into the exact workings of that intricate machinery. Studies of the activities of individual agents, however, reveal a great deal of the means, methods, and techniques used by the Austrian Ministry of the Interior in a period of relative tranquility in Europe. I have tried to present a handful of the most typical weapons used constantly and by many people in what was a highly unconventional warfare. Unusual as it was, that war without arms had an enormous impact on mid-nineteenth-century politics in East Central Europe, paving the way for both future political settlements and the armed conflicts that were to arise later.

Notes

1. Kornél Tábori, *Titkosrendőrség és kamarilla* (Budapest, 1921), pp. 139–40.
2. Edit Mályuszné Császár, "Schedius Lajos politikai magatartásának ürügyén," *Irodalomtörténet* 59 [9] (1977): 201–3; August Fournier, *Die Geheimpolizei auf dem Wiener Kongress* (Vienna, 1913).
3. J. K. Mayr, ed., *Das Tagebuch des Polizeiministers Kempen von 1848 bis 1859* (Vienna-Leipzig, 1931), pp. 34–37; Waltraud Heindl, "Probleme der Edition: Aktenkundliche Studien zur Regierungspraxis des Neoabsolutismus," in *Die Protokolle des Österreichischen Ministerrates 1848–1867*, pt. 3, vol. 1 (Vienna, 1975), pp. xxxvi–xxxvii.
4. István Hajnal, *A Kossuth-emigráció Törökországban*, vol. 1 (Budapest, 1927), pp. 327–28, 332; Dénes Jánossy, *A Kossuth-emigráció Angliában és Amerikában*, vol. 1 (Budapest, 1940), pp. 461–63; Lajos Steiner, *Beniczky Lajos bányavidéki kormánybiztos és honvédezredes visszaemlékezései és jelentései az 1848/49-iki szabadságharcról és a tót mozgalomról* (Budapest, 1924), pp. 705–6; Tábori, *Titkosrendőrség*, pp. 174–76; Christoph Stölzl, *Die Ära Bach in Böhmen: Sozialgeschichtliche Studien zum Neoabsolutismus 1849–1859* (Munich-Vienna, 1971), pp. 257–67; György Szabad, "Az önkényuralom kora (1849–1867)," in Endre Kovács, ed., *Magyarország története 1848–1890* (Budapest, 1979), pp. 458–60. For the history of

secret service operations in Hungary, see Sándor Takács, *Kémvilág Magyarországon* (Budapest, 1980).

5. A list of agents of June 1850 was attached to a report numbered 7249/A, dated July 26, 1851, Allgemeines Verwaltungsarchiv (Vienna), Nachlass Bach, Karton 29, "Polizei: Staatspolizei."

6. G. Zerffi's secret report no. 205, dated Constantinople, August 20, 1850 (unsigned), Haus-, Hof- und Staatsarchiv, Ministerium des Aussern, Informations Büro, Karton 19, 3016/A, ad 7756/A; a summary report on agents in foreign countries dated Vienna, April 19, 1852, is in the Allgemeines Verwaltungsarchiv, Nachlass Bach, Karton 29, "Polizei: Staatspolizei."

7. Department 2 to the Ministry of Finance, Vienna, July 24, 1869, Haus-, Hof- und Staatsarchiv, Ministerium des Äussern, Informations Büro, Praesidial Sektion, Dept. 2, 1869:1439; Hajnal, *A Kossuth-emigráció,* pp. 333–37; Mayr, *Tagebuch,* pp. 274–75, 301, 303, 322–23; Tábori, *Titkosrendőrség,* p. 141; Miklós Perczel, *Naplóm az emigrációból* (Budapest, 1977), p. 131; L. Kossuth to L. Böck, Shoumla, December 28, 1849, Hungarian National Archives, Budapest, R 90, I. 614.

8. Mayr, *Tagebuch,* pp. 43–44.

9. Kossuth to Pulszky, Kyutahia, November 8, 1850, Hungarian National Library, Budapest, MS Collection, Fond 8/537.

10. Á. Schoepf to L. Kossuth, Pest, October 14, 1848, Hungarian National Archives, H 2 (OHB: Kossuth Polizei Akten), 59: 232; Dispatches of Foreign Minister Count Kázmér Batthyány to G. Carossini, Hungarian agent in Belgrade, Hungarian National Library, MS Collection, Fond 27/61; Politische Wochenberichte, Vienna, February 14, 1852, Allgemeines Verwaltungsarchiv, Nachlass Bach, Karton 28; Hajnal, *A Kossuth-emigráció,* pp. 372, 368.

11. G. Carossini to Kossuth, Belgrade, July 5 and September 27, 1850, Hungarian National Archives, R 90, I. 823, I. 918; G. Zerffi's secret report no. 218, dated Constantinople, October 23, 1850 (unsigned), Haus-, Hof- und Staatsarchiv, Ministerium des Äussern, Informations Büro, Karton 19, 3686/A, ad 7756/A.

12. Kossuth to Pulszky, Kyutahia, December 21, 1850, Hungarian National Library, MS Collection, Fond 8/537; Tábori, *Titkosrendőrség,* p. 151.

13. "Die ungarische Emigration im Oriente ('Memorial')," no date or place, Allgemeines Verwaltungsarchiv, Nachlass Bach, Karton 23, "Polit. Flüchtlinge," ffol. 11–12.

14. Tábori, *Titkosrendőrség,* p. 225.

15. J. Bangya to Kossuth, Paris, February 4, 1853, Hungarian National Archives, R 90, I. 2090.

16. Report on agents in foreign countries, Vienna, April 19, 1852, Allgemeines Verwaltungsarchiv, Nachlass Bach, Karton 29, "Polizei: Staatspolizei."

17. "Uebersicht sämtlicher mit dem Dienste der staatspolizeilichen Agenturen in In- und Ausland verbundenen Auslagen," Vienna, April 19, 1852, Allgemeines Verwaltungsarchiv, Nachlass Bach, Karton 29, "Polizei: Staatspolizei."

18. Sándor Maller, "Marx és Szemere," *Századok* 90 (1956): 668–69; Klára Málek, *Szemere Bertalan az emigrációban* (Pécs-Balatonfüred,

1940), pp. 20-22; Hajnal, *A Kossuth-emigráció,* p. 384.
19. Bartholomäus Szemere, *Graf Ludwig Batthyány, Arthur Görgei, Ludwig Kossuth: Politische Characterskizzen aus dem ungarischen Freiheitskriege* (Hamburg, 1853).
20. Politische Wochenberichte, Paris, April 17, 1852, Haus-, Hof- und Staatsarchiv, Gend. Dept. 1852, Fasz. 8, fol. 77.
21. Bangya to Szemere, London, March 29, April 3, May 5, 1852, Hungarian National Library, MS Collection, "Levelestár"; September 24, November 1, 1852, University Library, Budapest, MS Collection, Litt. Orig. 583:25. On Bangya, see R. Rosdolskyj, "Karl Marx und der Polizeispitzel Bangya," *International Review for Social History* 2 (1937): 229-45.
22. Tibor Frank, "Marx and Hungary: A Missing Link (1852-1853)," *Austrian History Yearbook* 15-16 (1979-80): 83-99.
23. Lajos Kossuth, *Irataim az emigrációból,* 3 vols. (Budapest, 1880-82), 3: 367-90; Hungarian National Archives, R 115.
24. Kossuth to D. Ihász, London, February 18, 1861, Hungarian National Archives, R 125, 2.
25. Waltraud Hirsch, "Felix Graf Wimpffen (1827-1882): Ein österreichischer Diplomat der franzisko-josephinischen Epoche" (Ph.D. diss., Vienna, 1969); Tibor Frank, *The British Image of Hungary 1865/1870* (Budapest, 1976), pp. 79, 92-95.
26. S. Mednyánszky to Gy. Klapka, February 18, 1861, Hungarian National Archives, R 295; Bill of Complaint, London, February 27, 1861, Hungarian National Archives, R 115, II. S. 5-10.
27. Kossuth to J. Ludvigh, London, February 28, 1861, Hungarian National Archives, R 115, II. S. 5-11.
28. Affidavit, no. 1, of Louis Kossuth, March 16, 1861, *Times,* March 26, 1861; cf. Kossuth, *Irataim,* 3: 445-50, 397, 507; see also Kossuth's own collection of clippings, 1859-63, Hungarian National Library, R 90, I. 2972.
29. [G. G. Zerffi], *The Emperor of Austria versus Louis Kossuth: A Few Words of Common Sense, Based on Documentary Evidence and Historical Facts, by an Hungarian, Author of "Civilization in Hungary"* (London: Trübner, 1861).
30. Ibid., pp. 3-8, 10-14.
31. Ibid., pp. 15-16.
32. Ibid., pp. 27-28.
33. Zerffi to Emperor Francis Joseph, London, April 23, 1861, Haus-, Hof- und Staatsarchiv, Ministerium des Äussern, Informations Büro, Actes de Haute Police, 1861, London, Karton 57, 364/g.
34. Koller to Mecséry, Vienna, May 10, 1861, Haus-, Hof- und Staatsarchiv, Ministerium des Äussern, Informations Büro, Karton 174, 3247/BM/1861.
35. Mecséry to the Minister of Foreign Affairs, Vienna, May 14, 1861, Haus-, Hof- und Staatsarchiv, Ministerium des Aussern, Informations Büro, Karton 174, 3247/BM/1861.
36. Koller to Apponyi, Vienna, May 19, 1861, Haus-, Hof- und Staatsarchiv, Gesandtschaftsarchiv, London, Weisungen 1861-62, Fasz. 99, 391/g; see Apponyi to Rechberg, London, April 19, 1861, Haus-, Hof- und Staatsarchiv,

Ministerium des Äussern, Informations Büro, Actes de Haute Police, London, 1861, Karton 57, "Kossuth Noten," 300/g.

37. Buol to Kempen, Vienna, June 10, 1852, Haus-, Hof- und Staatsarchiv, Ministerium des Äussern, Informations Büro, Fasz. 24 (1852), 29/BM, 350/g.; Konfidentenwesen in genera, Vienna, April 5, 1853, Haus-, Hof- und Staatsarchiv, Ministerium des Äussern, Informations Büro, Actes de Haute Police, 1853, Interna, Fasz. 24, 207/g.; Colloredo to Buol, London, May 2, 1853, Haus-, Hof- und Staatsarchiv, Ministerium des Äussern, Informations Büro, Actes de Haute Police, copy in Hungarian National Library, MS Collection, Fond 27/57/725.

Habsburg Dragonnades in Hungary, 1861–62

Éva Somogyi

Ever since the Napoleonic wars, the Habsburg Empire had been accumulating budget deficits year after year, and its debts further increased with its defeat in the 1859 war. Its modern centralist, neoabsolutist state bureaucracy aimed at restoring order to an empire profoundly disturbed by the revolutions of 1848–49—at holding in check the forces of change. At the same time, the empire entertained Great Power ambitions in international relations, and this cost a great deal of money. Throughout the first two postrevolutionary decades the bureaucracy engaged in a hopeless struggle to attain a balanced budget and stabilize the empire's finances. Harm-Hinrich Brandt, in a recent monograph, argues convincingly that the state deficit of the time was not a consequence of the system of taxation, but a result of the fact that the centralist state's massive financial needs surfaced long before the development of the modern economy required to fulfill them.[1] Under the circumstances, it is understandable that efforts to improve the empire's credit and raise the necessary state income dominated the postwar political maneuvering.

The emperor convoked an enlarged Reichsrat in the spring of 1860 to supervise the empire's finances.[2] In July he agreed to impose new taxes only with the consent of the Reichsrat and to borrow only with the consent of his state counselors.[3] The process of reining in the absolutist state was not, however, free of conflict between opposing forces.[4]

The promulgation of the October Diploma was the first comprehensive attempt to resolve the crisis of the absolutist state.[5] The Diploma introduced structural changes into the empire. It abandoned strict centralism and, in an effort to pacify Hungary, restored portions of the Austro-Hungarian dualism that had been characteristic of the Habsburg Empire for centuries. Hungarian governmental institutions that had been dormant for twelve years were revived, among them the Hungarian National Assembly, the county assemblies, and the executive branch of the central government of pre-1848 Hungary, consisting of the Court Chancellery, located in Vienna, and the Viceregal Council or Consilium, located in Buda.[6] The Diploma was a step toward the elimination of absolutist rule that was consistent with the emperor's repeated statement that he would never permit the establishment of a Western-type constitution calling for a popularly elected parliament, which would limit his power. Thus it recognized neither the provincial legislatures' nor the Reichsrat's right to levy troops or impose taxes, although these fundamental prerogatives of a constitutional government were deeply rooted attributes of the Hungarian feudal legislative system.

The imperial government as reconstituted in 1860 reflected conflicting views on the governing of the empire. Count Agenor Goluchowski, the prime minister, and Minister without Portfolio Count Antal Szécsen were framers of the Diploma. Count Johann Rechberg, the minister of foreign affairs, was another proponent of a system of government that would restore the power of the aristocracy and grant greater autonomy to the provinces, and Baron Mecséry, the minister of police, held similar views. Other cabinet members championed a liberal-bureaucratic-centralist government, among them Ignaz von Plener, the minister of finance, Joseph Lasser, the minister of justice, and Count August Degenfeld-Schönburg, the minister of defense.[7] When Plener received the news of the drafting of the Diploma, he tried to warn Rechberg against its promulgation. Calling attention to the increased financial needs of the army and the consequent inevitability of state borrowing, he argued that the planned reorganization of the government would be detrimental to the empire's financial status: "Without a recognition of the unity of the empire, without an imperial constitution, the financial task in Austria (at least as far as my limited energies are concerned) would be impossible to accomplish."[8] Plener offered his resignation, and when Francis Joseph routinely declined to accept it he became the opposition within the government.[9]

The events of the following few weeks proved Plener's fears to have been to some extent justified. The October Diploma was incapable of contributing in the smallest way to the solution of the empire's financial problems; on the contrary, it added to the difficulties. In November, Hungarian county assemblies were elected all over the country. They promptly declared the absolutist government's tax assessments illegal because they had been assessed without parliamentary consent and called on the population to refuse to pay taxes.

The refusal to pay taxes was a clear demonstration that the Hungarians considered what the Diploma granted them too little. The Hungarian politicians who had acted as midwives for the Diploma tried to assure their Austrian colleagues that the events unfolding in Hungary were both natural and temporary. György Majláth, president of the

Viceregal Council, stated in his December 14 report to the Chancellery:

> In Hungary the excessive amount of direct taxes and the various fees that have had to be paid in all areas of everyday life have jointly created conditions that have turned the nobility—which, after all, is unaccustomed to paying taxes—into an enemy of the current government. [The same factors], despite the government's democratic tendencies, have made the people indifferent toward it, dissatisfied, and prey to agitators.
>
> It was therefore foreseeable that when the government's power weakened and the country felt it might have a chance at a return to the old form of government, which demanded less taxes, the payment of taxes would decline.... [it could also have been expected] that here and there resistance would occur.
>
> This natural response was intensified in no small degree by the state of the public mind created by the initial deliberations of the county assemblies. This situation has just reached a climax, but I doubt that it will last long.[10]

Majláth is obviously referring here to the events that had occurred three days before at Pest, where the county assembly in its December 11 session had protested against a governmental decree which required county officials to collect taxes even before they had been endorsed by Parliament.[11] This was the beginning of a virtual tax war that lasted long after the Diploma had expired and the parliament convoked in the spirit of the Diploma had adjourned.

The Hungarian members of the government did what they could within their authority to enforce tax collection. The Viceregal Council sent Pest a decree on January 2 declaring an emergency and ordering the collection of taxes. The decree was intended to instruct not only the officials of Pest, but all the other counties' recalcitrant officials.[12] The Chancellery sent a strongly worded royal edict to all counties on January 16.[13] These efforts were, however, of no avail. Also without result was a February 14 conference between the chancellor and the newly appointed county high sheriffs aimed specifically at the resolution of the conflict. The refusal to collect taxes was both a dramatic sign of the failure of the champions of the Diploma and an excuse for the Viennese government to launch another political assault.

Ever since November, Plener had done everything he could to use the specter of a potential state bankruptcy to promote a different political formula. According to Brandt, it was Plener who was responsible for the abandonment of the Diploma. At the ministerial council meeting of January 5, Plener argued that since taxes could not be raised and no more paper money could be printed, new state loans had to be floated. Favorable loans could be gained, however, only with parliamentary guarantees. The next day Plener vigorously denounced the Hungarians for creating the new financial crisis by refusing to pay their taxes. Under the circumstances, he said, there was no sense waiting for the Hungarian Parliament to decide to recognize the imperial structure:

> To fulfill the universal and loudly expressed wish of the population of the other [than Hungarian] provinces [crown lands] and, in particular, to satisfy the requirements of the minister of finance—who, by the way, will provide money if sufficient guarantees are secured—common representation should be granted to the German-Slavic provinces, extending to them the same prerogatives as are enjoyed by the Hungaians. That is the only correct way; nothing else will work.[14]

The ministerial council for the time being made no decision on this suggestion, but the very fact that there was open discussion of the necessity for a constitution based on representation meant a departure from the concepts of the Diploma. Plener's efforts were concentrated on the establishment of an imperial constitution and a single parliament for the entire empire, which by its nature would have destroyed the separate status of Hungary that the Diploma, although unacceptable to the Hungarians in other ways, secured for it. The nature of the change was defined, in an oversimplified way, decades later by the then ninety-one-year-old Plener as follows: "People have long looked for other reasons for the hasty transition from the October Diploma to the February Patent. In fact, the state's finances were the only reason."[15]

Early in February, Plener took steps to set up the machinery for collecting taxes without the cooperation of the Hungarian county and communal governments.[16] He had the Hungarian Royal Chamber—which was under his jurisdiction—draft a plan for tax collection in Hungary. Special tax committees were to be formed to tour the country and, village by village, collect the taxes due and in arrears. Each committee was to consist of two tax experts and eight gendarmes to guard the money; in the event of need, the committee might seek the assistance of the regular army. A committee was to stay in a village for three days, and if during this period the taxes had not been collected, the military was to take over the task. The size of the army unit assigned was to be in direct proportion to the amount of uncollected taxes. The support of the occupation force was the responsibility of the village involved. The military was to stay until at least two-thirds of the tax had been collected.[17] Stefan Malfér, in a recent study based on the minutes of the ministerial council and the archives of the Ministry of Finance, points out that this tax collection by the military was in several respects based on Austrian law. In Austria the concept of tax collection by the military was accepted throughout the life span of the Habsburg Monarchy, although it was put into practice only during the era of neoabsolutism. In Hungary, in contrast, tax collection by the military was illegal.[18]

During the consultations preparatory to this extraordinary tax collection, the Hungarian members of the government proposed that in order to break down resistance the government should urge Hungary's Prince Primate, the bishops, and the county high sheriffs to pay their own taxes promptly and thereby set a good example for the rest of the population. Nonetheless, Vice-Chancellor László Szőgyény-Marich accepted the idea of tax collection by imperial tax officials, even assisted by the military if necessary, on the condition that they spoke the local native tongue and executed their duties politely and with circumspection.[19] On March 23, 1861, ministerial council Chancellor Baron Miklós Vay consented to Plener's proposition, specifying that "only in case of real obstinacy should the military be called in. In general the [civilian] tax organizations should perform the duty with all possible courtesy."[20]

On April 24, when the Hungarian Parliament was already in session—in other words, when it would have been able to make decisions on taxes and their collection—the Viceregal Council dispatched decrees to the county governments instructing them that, in order "to implement the resolution of His Most Sublime Majesty on the assessment and collection of taxes, if the municipalities refuse to cooperate [the task] will be handed over to the imperial-royal district financial directorates, which will carry it out with military assistance if necessary."[21] The Hungarian members of the government could not, if they wished to maintain their positions, withhold their cooperation from these emergency actions.[22] By April 30, 10 percent of the taxes due had indeed been collected.[23]

The tax issue and the measures introduced in connection with it demonstrate the chaos that existed. Government in Hungary was tripartite. One branch consisted of the county governments revived on the basis of the laws of 1848 and concerned to put those laws into practice. The second was the imperial government, which from the day of the appointment of Anton von Schmerling as prime minister was dominated by advocates of a centralized empire like Plener.[24] The third was the Hungarian government's central executive institutions, the Chancellery and the Viceregal Council, both of which acted in terms of the October Diploma. These three branches of government could not and indeed did not want to cooperate. The proponents of the October Diploma were desperately trying to hold onto their positions. The adherents of the 1848 laws continued to refuse to assess and/or collect taxes. The military was controlled by the champions of a centralized empire. The outcome of the struggle among these three branches could scarcely be in doubt. On April 22 Plener received authorization to commence the emergency tax collection,[25] and as a result a small war began between the financial authorities controlled by Vienna and the military, on the one hand, and the Hungarian county administrations and the population, on the other. The county assembly of Pest passed a resolution, based on Act no. 1 of 1504, making it treason for an official to cooperate in any respect whatsoever with the tax collection.[26] Torontál County was the first to dispatch a grievance to Parliament. The document stated that on April 28 at Nagybecskerek, the commander of a military unit dispatched from Temesvár had demanded that the city magistrate collect the overdue 1860 taxes and the taxes due for the first half of 1861. He had given the city officials six hours to decide, and when the civilian authorities failed to act the military had collected the taxes. The county's grievance was received by Parliament on May 3. From then on, such grievances came day after day. By mid-May Parliament had received grievances from Esztergom, Csongrád, Debrecen, Nyitra, and Zenta.[27] The passionate resolution of the county assembly of Pest had a nationwide echo:

> It is difficult not to wish that God would put an end to the days of a government that constructs jails for poor, honest debtors while it refuses to pay its own debts. . . . God have mercy on a government that is destroying the general welfare and multiplying the number of beggars and servants in a country that was once rich.[28]

The cruelties of the dragonnade, used for the purpose of tax collection, were so excessive that even the chancellor felt obliged to write Szőgyény-Marich in May that in Nyíregyháza the houses of citizens had been overrun by twenty to thirty cavalrymen, and "all his possessions having been confiscated, the owner had to abandon his devastated house."[29] Minister of Defense Degenfeld reported to the ministerial council on June 26 that the tax-collecting soldiers often committed inadmissible violence against the population.[30]

Soon it became obvious that the dragonnade was not without danger for the government itself. The chancellor wrote that the action was distasteful to the soldiers, since "those who are quartered in homes fraternize with the people."[31] The minister of defense went even farther, stating that "any army that has to carry out such a task for very long will eventually stand condemned both militarily and morally."[32] The minister refused to increase the number of soldiers engaged in tax collection and warned against giving the quartered soldiers any license to extort goods from the population beyond their own legal meals.[33] These warnings resulted in the suspension, on August 6, of the dragonnade in rural areas for the duration of the harvest. The suspension expired on September 15.[34]

At the end of the summer the policies of the October Diploma were discontinued. The monarch dissolved the Hungarian Parliament, which insisted on the validity of the laws of 1848. Subsequently the governments of counties, districts, and municipalities were also banned. On November 5, 1861, a provisional government called the Provisorium was imposed on Hungary, and an appointed administrator was vested with extraordinary absolute powers. This meant a return to the neoabsolutist regime of the 1850s. In place of the autonomous regional and local governments that had led the popular resistance there was now an obedient governing structure that made it possible for tax collection to increase substantially by the end of the year.[35]

Military tax collection was not, however, immediately abandoned. By February 1862 the minister of defense openly opposed the continuation of the dragonnade, which he said had been very harmful not only for the military, but also politically. The soldiers were often brutal to citizens who were unable to pay their taxes, and this had created bitterness even in circles that had not necessarily been hostile to the government before.[36] Chancellor Antal Forgács[37] argued that, while the dragonnade had been necessary, the people were now willing to pay their taxes if they could. He listed instances in which the tax collectors had overstepped the limits of their authority and argued that it was time to return to legality by restoring the responsibility for tax collection to the county high sheriffs. The ministerial council nonetheless resolved that for the time being tax collection should remain in the hands of the imperial officials, with the military to be used only in extreme cases. Three months were to pass before, on April 22, tax collection by the military was ended.[38]

Thus taxes that were illegal because they had not been voted by Parliament were collected in Hungary between April 1861 and April 1862 with the assistance of the military. Was this simply a mournful episode of a mournful year, or the slow choking to death by the military of a mass movement? Probably much more was involved. The issue was a profound one not only because financial matters were so extraordinarily important during the governmental reform experiments of 1859. More than this, the refusal to pay taxes was a painful but irrefutable demonstration of Hungary's rejection of the compromise offered it by way of the October Diploma. Besides, a contradiction surfaced here that came to be characteristic of the 1860s. Plener was a constitutionalist politician who often referred to 1849 and who criticized Schmerling for being too willing to yield to the absolutist tendencies of the monarch.[39] Yet he himself employed the most unconstitutional means of government, the dragonnade, simply because he had no other means of defending the interests of the centralized monarchy against Hungarian efforts to regain their autonomy within the Habsburg Empire. The Hungarian conservative camp that produced the Diploma was crushed by the tax crisis. In any case, Szőgyény-Marich complained that the Austro-German ministers were conspiring against the Hungarian conservatives,[40] and Brandt confirms his assertion.[41] This was the first spectacular fiasco of the constitutional centralist empire; it demonstrated without any doubt that any "constitutional" pattern of government of the empire that disregarded Hungary's historic rights could only be introduced by military force.

Notes

1. Harm-Hinrich Brandt, *Der österreichische Neoabsolutismus: Staatsfinanzen und Politik 1848–1860*, Schriftenreihe der Historischen Kommission bei der Bayerischen Akademie der Wissenschaften no. 15 (Göttingen, 1978).
2. Imperial Patent of March 5, 1860 (Edmund Bernatzik, *Die österreichischen Verfassungsgesetze* [Vienna, 1911], pp. 217–20).
3. Imperial Patent of July 17, 1860 (Bernatzik, *Die österreichischen Verfassungsgesetze*, p. 221).
4. Anton von Schmerling, *Denkwürdigkeiten*, Haus-, Hof- und Staatsarchiv, Vienna, Nachlass Schmerling-Bienerth. See also Count Johann Rechberg, Minister of Foreign Affairs, to Count Franz a. Thun, Austrian Ambassador at St. Petersburg, on February 10, 1861, Haus-, Hof- und Staatsarchiv, Vienna, Politisches Archiv 1, Nachlass Rechberg K. 527.
5. For the Diploma and related documents, see Bernatzik, *Die österreichischen Verfassungsgesetze*, pp. 223–43, and Kaiserlisches Diplom vom Oktober 20, 1860, RGBF no. 226, zur Regelung der inneren staatsrechtlichen Verhältnisse der Monarchie. For recent analysis, see György Szabad, *Forradalom és kiegyezés válaszútján 1860–1861* (Budapest, 1967), pp. 77–80; Éva Somogyi, *Abszolutizmus és kiegyezés* (Budapest, 1981), pp. 121–25; C. A. Macartney, *The Habsburg Empire, 1790–1918* (New York, 1969), pp. 569–87; Robert A. Kann, *The Multinational Empire: Nationalism and National Reform in the Habsburg Monarchy, 1848–1918*, 2 vols. (New York, 1950), 2: 88–124.
6. On the pre-1848 central executive branches of the Hungarian government reestablished by the October Diploma, see Béla K. Király, *Hungary in the Late Eighteenth Century: The Decline of Enlightened Despotism* (New York, 1969), pp. 90–102.
7. On the members of the ministry, see Josef Redlich, *Das österreichische*

Staats- und Reichproblem: Geschichtliche Darstellung der inneren Politik der habsburgischen Monarchie von 1848 bis zum Untergang des Reiches, 2 vols. (Leipzig, 1920–26), 1: 468 H. On Plener, who played a dominant role in the events of this period, see Mechtild Wolf, *Ignaz von Plener: Vom Schicksal eines Ministers unter Kaiser Franz Joseph* (Munich, 1975), pp. 21–37. On Count August Degenfeld-Schönburg, see Walter Wagner, *Geschichte des k. k. Kriegsministeriums I. 1848–1866,* Studien zur Geschichte der Österreichisch-Ungarischen Monarchie, no. 5 (Graz, 1966), pp. 174–98.

8. Plener to Rechberg, October 11, 1860 (Brandt, *Die österreichischen Verfassungsgeschichte,* p. 969).
9. This was revealed by Plener's behavior at the October-December 1860 meetings of the ministerial council (Albert Berzeviczy, *Az abszolutizmus kora Magyarországon,* 3 vols. (Budapest, 1932), 1: 119, 142, 170. See also Wolf, *Ignaz von Plener,* pp. 24–30.
10. Oszkár Sashegyi, ed., *Munkások és parasztok mozgalmai Magyarországon 1849–1867* (Budapest, 1959), pp. 318–19.
11. Ludwig Karl Klauhold, *Der ungarische Verfassungsstreit urkundlich dargestellt: Beilage zu Aegidi. Das Staatsarchiv. Sammlung der officiellen Actenstücke zur Geschichte der Gegenwart* (Hamburg, 1862), pp. 41–42.
12. Ibid., pp. 47–49.
13. Ibid., pp. 49–52. For the origin of the monarch's Patent of January 16, see *Szőgyény-Marich László országbíró emlékiratai* (Budapest, 1918), p. 71.
14. Brandt, *Der österreichisches Verfassungsgeschichte,* pp. 985–87.
15. Ibid., p. 968.
16. Oszkár Sashegyi, *Az abszolutizmuskori levéltár* (Budapest, 1965), p. 80.
17. Stefan Malfér, "Steuerwiderstand und Steuerexekution in Ungarn 1860–62," in *Österreichische Osthefte* 1982 (forthcoming).
18. Ibid. The administrator of Szabolcs County considered the need for forcible tax collection as follows: "Under the present circumstances, in my modest opinion, there is no other way but to introduce the method of tax collection into our country which has long existed in the other crown lands. Taxes should be collected by the military. The method should be that anyone who has not paid his taxes should supply food and pay fees to be increased from time to time for the soldiers billeted in his home. The soldiers should remain until the person who unquestionably is capable of paying pays his debts" (Sashegyi, *Munkások és parasztok,* pp. 317–18). Armed protection was necessary not only for the money, but also for the tax collectors' persons; they were often attacked by the villagers (ibid., p. 317).
19. Sashegyi, *Abszolutizmuskori levéltár,* p. 80.
20. *Die Protokolle des österreichischen Ministerrates 1848–1867, Abteilung: Die Ministerien Erzherzog Rainer und Mensdorff,* 5 vols. (Vienna, 1977–81), no. 37, 1: 219–23.
21. Klauhold, *Der ungarische Verfassungsstreit,* p. 117.
22. Indeed, they had been willing to take this action much earlier. Majláth had

considered the collection of taxes by the military permissible (Sashegyi, *Munkások és parasztok*, p. 318), and Chancellor Vay had proposed tax collection by the military in order to crush the resistance of Pest and Pozsony Counties (*Szőgyńy-Marich országbiró,* p. 67.
23. Malfér, "Steuerwiderstand," p. 319.
24. The emperor dismissed Goluchowski on December 13, 1860, and appointed Schmerling as his successor.
25. Malfér, "Steuerwiderstand," p. 318.
26. Klauhold, *Der ungarische Verfassungsstreit,* pp. 117–18.
27. Ibid.
28. Berzeviczy, *Az abszolutizmus kora,* 1: 270; *Szőgyény-Marich országbiró,* pp. 105–6. Pest County claimed that services rendered in the past for the supply of imperial army units garrisoned in the county had not been paid and demanded payment of these arrears. This is what is meant by the phrase "refuses to pay its own debts" (Szabad, *Forradalom és kiegyezés,* pp. 532–34). The monarch became aware of this controversy through the daily press, which printed municipal resolutions. The ministerial council discussed the matter on June 13, and a royal commissionaire was dispatched to investigate the origins of the resolution (*Die Protokolle,* no. 82, 5: 127–30).
29. Vay to Szőgyény-Marich, May 28, 1861 (*Szőgyeny-Marich országbiró,* p. 330).
30. *Die Protokolle,* no. 99, 5: 247.
31. *Szőgyeny-Marich országbiró,* p. 329.
32. *Die Protokolle,* no. 102, 5: 263.
33. Ibid., pp. 279–80.
34. Klauhold, *Der ungarische Verfassungsstreit,* p. 120. For the minutes of the June 28 ministerial council that discussed the suspension of military tax collection, see *Die Protokolle,* no. 102, 5: 260–64.
35. Plener's report to the August 2 ministerial council; see also Malfér, "Steuerwiderstand."
36. Minutes of the February 5, 1862, meeting of the ministerial council.
37. Vay, who was committed to the October Diploma, was removed from the office of chancellor and replaced by Forgács on July 18, 1861.
38. Malfér, "Steuerwiderstand."
39. On Plener's constitutionalism and his controversies with Schmerling, see Wolf, *Ignaz von Plener,* pp. 33–36; Éva Somogyi, *Vom Zentralismus zum Dualismus: Der Weg der deutschösterreichischen Liberalen zum Ausgleich 1861–1867* (Wiesbaden, 1983), pp. 6–9.
40. Szőgyény-Marich writes, "The Austrian ministers continually blamed us for the virtual cessation of taxes from Hungary and even said that if we could not enforce order, they would do it" (*Szőgyény-Marich országbiró,* p. 71).
41. Brandt, *Der österreichische Verfassungsgeschichte,* pp. 979–80.

VII. Hungarians under Foreign Flags against Habsburg Absolutism

Military Organizations of the Hungarian Exiles, 1859–67

Lajos Lukács

The manifold international activity of the Hungarian emigration of 1848–49 included both political maneuvers and military preparations for a desired new war of independence. The international situation in the era of reaction of the 1850s offering no prospect for solving the Hungarian question, a major military project could, of course, scarcely be planned, although military cadres did exist. While this period was unfavorable for the realization of the aims of the Hungarian émigrés, activity on their part with regard to international conflicts can be traced in several places in the Old and New Worlds. This study will not be extended to individual or group military actions and organizations of émigrés from Turkey to Cuba, the best and richest examples of which may be drawn from the history of the United States Civil War. No one could contest the international importance of the heroic behavior of the Hungarian refugees who fought—although not in the framework of an independent Hungarian organization—for the great truths of social progress and sacrificed their lives for the unity of the American states and the success of the abolition movement, among others Gyula Stahel-Szamvald, Sándor Asbóth, and Károly Zágonyi. Our present task, however, is to examine military achievements of another kind in the history of Hungarian emigration, trying to answer the questions where, to what extent, and under what circumstances independent Hungarian military corps were established. There Hungarian legions played a role in the period examined: the Hungarian legion in Piedmont, formed in 1859, the one formed under Garibaldi in 1860 in Sicily, and the one that became operative in 1866 in Prussia. Each of these deserves the historian's attention in itself, and a look at the literature shows that attention and interest have been accorded equally to all three.[1] While the legions of 1859 and 1866 appeared at a crucial historical moment and undertook promising activity amidst great interest and expectation, the character of the wars against Austria limited their development; the Hungarian legion of 1859 functioned for only a few months and the legion of 1866 for a few weeks.

The most conspicuous feature of the second legion, formed in July 1860 in Sicily, is that it took shape not with the authorization and financial support of official governments and on the initiative of the leadership of the Hungarian emigration but in the course of a revolutionary movement for the liberation of southern Italy, with the assistance of Garibaldi and within the framework of his movement. Although there were some personal connections among the staffs of the legions of 1859 and 1860, they differed in many respects, and the latter was no continuation of the former. Nor did the Hungarian émigrés who assembled under the flag of Garibaldi become members of the legion. Some of them, especially those with considerable military experience, were given command of independent Italian units; here I think of General István Türr, Commander of the Fifteenth Division, Major Lajos Tüköry, who died the death of heroes, Brigadier General Nándor Éber, Lieutenant Colonels Lajos Winkler and István Dunyov, and Major Gusztáv Frigyesy, among others.[2] The legion was founded by a dictatorial decree in Palermo on July 16, 1860, and headed by Lieutenant Colonel Adolf Mogyoródy; the Hungarian hussar unit formed somewhat later and temporarily constituting a separate group was led by Lieutenant Colonel Fülöp Figyelmesy. Garibaldi's forces included other international troops as well, such as the Swiss Rifle Company, later annexed to the Hungarian legion, the French legion called the "Compagnia La Flotta," and the British legion under the leadership of Major Carlo S. Smelf.[3] The Hungarian legion was a redshirt unit advocating universal national liberation. Without distinction of nationality, it accepted anyone who undertook to serve this noble cause.

The situation was different in 1859; the basic principles of the organization of the Hungarian legion were prescribed by Napoleon III and Victor Emmanuel II, who of course had no intention of giving it any revolutionary character. This was very clearly indicated by the fact that Polish émigrés were not to be accepted. This kind of obstacle would have been incompatible with the democratic character of Garibaldi's War of Liberation, with its revolutionary program and its aim of the liberation of Rome. Garibaldi had deep contempt for the part Napoleon III had been playing in Italy, where he had been garrisoning troops in Rome since 1849 in order to ensure the maintenance of secular power for the Papal State.[4] The Hungarian legion of 1860 was identified with Garibaldi's objectives, although being part of the legion did not necessarily mean a thorough understanding and acceptance of the program and social content of his movement, much less of the far-reaching Garibaldian and Mazzinian efforts in opposition to the monarchist approach to the achievement of Italian unity.[5] The political connections of the 1859 Hungarian legion in Piedmont were of quite another nature. The leadership group of the Hungarian emigration, the Hungarian National Directorate, was established in May 1859 following a rather long period of division among the exiles. Lajos Kossuth, György Klapka, and Count László Teleki, who shared the responsibility of leadership, had been in disagreement since the beginning of the 1850s. Mutual concessions had to be made for the compromise achieved in 1859, including both the limitation of single-person leadership of the emigration and the accommodation of different views on the nationality problem. When in 1859 Napoleon III was willing to grant an interview to Kossuth—though under strictly defined conditions—the principal stipulation was the full and final break of Kossuth with the international republican and democratic movements, above all with Mazzini, who strongly opposed cooperation with the French emperor.[6] The effectiveness of this new and venturesome émigré tendency was severely tried by the outcome of the 1859 war; as became evident with the early armistice, the settlement of the Hungarian problem had not been included in the international politics of the French emperor. The Hungarian legion of 1859 was subordinated to the general political tendencies of the emigration, and therefore the conditions of the Italian-French-Austrian armistice led to its dissolution. A demand began to develop within the emigration for another orientation than French imperial power and its alliances and for a closer connection with the developing national movement in Hungary.

This attitude was expressed in an orientation toward the Garibaldi movement. The general democratic movement of the 1860s in Europe and America provided the background for this development. The circumstances in which the Hungarian legion was founded in 1860 point to the fact that the official leadership of the Hungarian emigration had little to do with it. Long months had passed and the Hungarian legion had already arrived in Naples before the leading circles of the emigration learned of its formation. In Kossuth's opinion, it would have been more proper to reserve the Hungarian military forces for tasks more directly connected with the program of liberating Hungary. Kossuth believed that what was happening in Italy could be only of secondary importance from the point of view of the Hungarian cause.[7] In 1860, the Hungarian National Directorate was still devoting all its energies to the maintenance of its previous political orientation, though at the moment it did not meet with full approval in Paris. Cavour, afraid that Austria would seek revenge and worried about the spread of the Mazzinian-Garibaldian movements, sought to draw prominent Hungarian exiles into the wake of Piedmontese politics, and the Hungarian emigration's leadership was not averse to this idea. Thus it happened that while fresh Hungarian legionnaires were marching in their red shirts under the hot sun of Calabria and lining up along the ramparts of Naples and on the Volturno, Cavour was paid a quick, confidential visit by Kossuth, Klapka, and Teleki in Turin. They asked for support and got encouraging promises of military and financial aid from Piedmont in connection with a possible war against Austria. In the meantime, Kossuth wrote to Garibaldi, at Cavour's request, warning him to give up his plan to attack Rome because it would arouse the fury of Napoleon III.[8] The intervention of the Piedmontese armed forces in September 1860 was a clear indication of Cavour's intention to thwart Garibaldi's plans not only through political action, but with all the military force of the Piedmontese monarchy. On that occasion the war against Austria came to nothing, but the Piedmont monarchy reaped the rewards of the successes of the Italian unification movement led by Garibaldi, annexing the fallen Kingdom of Naples, the foundation of the United Kingdom of Italy.[9]

The fate of the Hungarian legion of 1860 was inseparably connected with the general historical turn of events in autumn 1860, with the retirement of Garibaldi and the disbanding of his army in November. Paris demanded that all Garibaldian international units be disbanded, and this was done with the exception of the Hungarian legion. Its escape from this fate was due to Kossuth's personal intervention; he took political responsibility for ensuring that the legion would adjust to the changed situation and adhere to the conditions of the Piedmont monarchy. With this the Garibaldian period of the legion's history ended and a new phase, in many respects uncertain and dangerous, began.[10]

Changing from Garibaldi to Cavour had far-reaching consequences. The Hungarian National Directorate took over political control of the legion, and, as can be seen from the correspondence of Klapka and Kossuth, they intended to take strong measures to coordinate the legion with the claims and aims of the Directorate, giving every assistance to the Italian monarchy in changing the legion's function in accordance with these new claims. This Piedmontization did not proceed without complications, failures, and crises. Kossuth could scarcely have foreseen that the arrival of Antal Vetter in Naples as his appointed leader of the legion would not lead to the desired unity and calm, but cause further trouble. The appointment of Colonel Lajos Sréter, aided by General Türr, also had serious consequences, and both leaders were overthrown in May 1861.[11] Over and above these events, a series of complications was caused by the distrust and latent conflict between the official Hungarian émigré leadership and Türr. This conflict was not basically ideological, because the former Garibaldian general had thrown his glorious red shirt away and changed to the gold-braided uniform of the Piedmont generals. This change was not, however, immediately recognized among the legionnaires. Many of them connected their feelings against the monarchy and their distrust of the official leadership of the emigration with the well-known, respected figure of Türr. This is why it could seem to Klapka while in Naples that Türr would be pleased with the role of a kind of Garibaldi in Hungary. Even if such tendencies had arisen in the general with his growing popularity, he had always accepted the older leadership of the emigration, though he kept his distance from it politically and personally. He was the more able to do this because of his high military position, and, of course, his marriage to the niece of Napoleon III ensured his financial independence.[12]

When in May 1861 there was a major purge of legionnaires sympathizing with Garibaldi, the unity of the emigration and the leadership seemed unbroken. When Türr took over, he had not only the commission of the Turin government, but also the sanction of the Hungarian National Directorate (without László Teleki at that time). Kossuth found it reassuring that Colonel Dániel Ihász, one of his confidential followers, had been made commander-in-chief of the legion. Türr was inspector general. After the purge, a special depot was established in Acqui, in northern Italy, for the officers who had to leave the legion, and they were taken under the supervision of the Ministry of the Interior and granted a rather small stipend.[13]

What followed could hardly reduce the dissatisfaction of the members of the legion. Volunteers continued to arrive in Italy. By the spring of 1862, its strength had reached 1,146. The main contradiction was that its function and practical application were not in accord with the noble program for which the legionnaires had joined Garibaldi; they were looking for an opportunity to fight against Austria, and so were the exiles who joined them later. The Kingdom of Italy, preoccupied with pacifying the newly annexed southern part of the country, controlling the dissatisfied peasantry, and attempting to eradicate the flourishing brigandage, was for the time being not interested in waging war against Austria for Venetia. Furthermore, the international conditions for such a project were lacking; after 1859, Paris did not want a military confrontation with Austria, and this fact also calmed its Piedmont allies. The crisis of 1859–61, and within this the growth of Hungarian national resistance, pressed even the Austrian government toward concessions rather than toward a war of revenge. In this special situation, lasting up to the war of 1866, the maintenance of a Hungarian legion was increasingly problematic. If in Turin there was insistence on maintaining the legion, it was not only because of Kossuth and Klapka, who had always been concerned with it, but because more and more it had become the meeting place for émigrés of the most varied nationalities. This made it possible for the Italian government to control the émigrés, always considered dangerous and sympathetic to extreme radicalism. Thus the Hungarian legion proved to be an effective means of military and political supervision of foreign exiles in Italy.[14] The Italian government made no secret of this, but the development of events cast a stronger light on it. When the legionnaires, tired, disillusioned, and embittered, sought to leave their service, referring to their basic right as volunteers to do so, the true intentions of the Italian government became evident. When in the summer of 1862 Garibaldi unfurled his flag again in Sicily and adopted his slogan "Roma o morte," his call did not fail to affect the circles of his sympathizers. The desire to change their unbearable situation increased among the dissatisfied members of the Hungarian legion, as was clearly shown by the opposition movements that broke out in the spring of 1862, by the laying down of arms, by the replacement of commanders, and by announcements of intentions to retire. Minister of War La Marmora told the legionnaires wishing to retire that they could choose among only three possibilities: remaining in service, returning to Turkey, or being given back to Austria. Anyone who happened to reject all of these would be deported to Sardinia or sent to military prison. The rebellion was vigorously put down; there were mass imprisonments in the dungeon of the Forte del Carmine in Naples, nearly the whole legion was disarmed, and the captive volunteers were transported, escorted by carabinieres, to the fortress of Alessandria in northern Italy. With these events closed the second period of the history of the legion, full of tragic elements, and with it came the downfall of Dániel Ihász.[15]

The legion was formally disbanded, but reorganization began at once. Directed by the highest circles, an investigating committee of Hungarian officers was set up, its president being General Count Gergely Bethlen and its patron General István Türr. A severe and consistent purge ensued, lasting from September to November 1862. Ruthless measures were undertaken against all who had taken part in the revolt of the legionnaires, in the organizations for Garibaldi, and in antigovernment actions. The intentions of official circles were shown by the expulsions, internments, and imprisonments. Many were transferred from the legion to newly established depots, called officers' schools, in Cuneo controlled by the Ministry of the Interior.[16]

At the head of the reorganized legion was Colonel Károly Földváry, who with his cruel rigor and opportunism intensified the disadvantageous consequences of the events of 1862 for the legionnaires. Being jealous of his military position, he was hurt by the occasional interventions of the political leaders of the emigration. He was closest to Türr, whose absolute confidence he possessed. At the same time, he cultivated his connection with Kossuth, though there was much protocol and insincerity in it. Kossuth took it amiss that his intimate Dániel Ihász was not honored with a promotion to general and that Colonel József Telkessy was put at the head of the legion for some months until Földváry took over. Kossuth's position became rather awkward; the Hungarian National Directorate had practically broken up, Klapka had gone his own way, and Kossuth had to take care that the Italian government continue to consider him the official leader of the Hungarian emigration. Concerned with maintaining unchanged his political influence over the legion, he would have preferred to have Ihász followed by a confidential associate of his own. He therefore promoted the appointment of the Italian brigadier general Károly Eberhardt as leader of the Hungarian legion. This latter, though in 1860 he had fought at Garibaldi's side, had broken with his redshirt past for the sake of his career, and a bright future was expected for him in the army of the Italian monarchy. He was, however, unable to take over the direction of the legion because he was chosen to direct a concrete military action against Garibaldi, which was carried out on August 29, 1862, at Aspromonte to the full satisfaction of his superiors.[17]

As Kossuth later acknowledged, this turn of events favored Földváry's position. Kossuth soon recognized that things had changed, not only in his relation to the legion, but also in the attitude toward him of the Italian government. The process that was taking place in the Hungarian emigration in the 1860s led to isolation and loneliness for Kossuth. New stars appeared among the émigrés. György Komáromy and Count Tivadar Csáky were not only associated with the noble-liberal group in Hungary, but also had a strong influence on Türr, Klapka, Éber, and Földváry. This latter, parallel to his letters to Kossuth, sent reports with the same content to Csáky, acknowledging his authority both in Hungary and with the emigration. Csáky and Komáromy established close relations with leading Italian circles, in which their home connections were greatly appreciated and they were given protection and significant pecuniary assistance.[19] In this changed atmosphere the situation of the legionnaires further deteriorated and their defenselessness increased. Although the shift of the legion in 1863 from Alessandria to the Adriatic coast first offered them the hope of being nearer the expected enemy, Austria, it ended in disappointment. The legion was scattered again; the infantry was stationed in Ancona, the hussars in Senigallia, the rifles in Jesi, the artillery in Veneria Reale in Piedmont. The employment of the legionnaires was a rude insult to their original noble goals. They were ordered against peasants in rebellion and striking workers. In 1865 they had to fight once again against brigandage in the south, the task which had so offended them in the past. From Chieti they were entered into action against brigands in the awesome landscape of the Abruzzi. With the hardships of everyday life aggravated by the difficulties of a cruel nature, dissatisfaction increased from day to day. The volunteers came to recognize not only that the fight against Austria was being postponed, but also that the Italian government was using them to maintain public order. Under these circumstances it is perfectly understandable that desertions and insubordination were common, expressing the disappointment of the legionnaires, their desire to leave and, if there seemed no other way out, to return to their country. This absolute right of volunteers was appreciated neither by the leadership of the legion nor by the Italian military authorities. Legionnaires wishing to leave were prevented, if necessary by force. Military tribunals were set up; the military prisons of Ancona, Chieti, and other towns were filled with legionnaires, many of whom spent more time in prisons than in the legion. The desertions indicated the irreversibility of the process of disintegration of the legion; not even the harshest reprisals could stop it. Illness, death, and suicide thinned the ranks of the legionnaires. The events in the Hungarian legion in Italy reflected, though in an extreme and brutal way, the instability and hopelessness of the general situation of the Hungarian emigration.[20]

Numerical data on the composition of the Hungarian legion in Italy are not without interest. Scarcely 70 set off from Palermo; at the Volturno by October 1, 1860, their number exceeded 300. In spring 1862 the legion counted nearly 1,200 members. From this time on its numbers diminished. The events of autumn 1862 reduced its strength by half. The constant core of the legion was small; there were fluctuations both among officers and in the ranks, and the number of enlistments and retirements was very large. By the outbreak of the Austro-Prussian War in 1866, the legion amounted to about 400 men. Considering all who served in the legion between July 1860 and autumn 1866, however, the least we can speak of is 2,600 persons, about 2,400 in the ranks and the rest officers. This division, however, cannot reflect the complexity of the composition of the legion. Because of the limited possibilities for officers' appointments, many who had been officers in the Hungarian, Austrian, and perhaps the Turkish armies had to serve as warrant officers or common soldiers. As a result, there was worked out in the legion the so-called aggregated officers' assignments, for those who had previously been officers but in the legion were mainly sergeants, sergeant-majors, or supply sergeants. There were also many who wanted to join the legion but were not accepted; they were placed in various depots for officers, at first in Sorrento, later in Acqui, and finally in Cuneo. These officers constituted the main reserve for new appointments, but in many cases men who had served in the ranks were preferred. Considering the officers' depots as well, it could be said that the number of émigrés in military and semimilitary organizations in Italy in the 1860s was about 3,000. The majority of Hungarian émigrés were concentrated there, and the Hungarian legion constituted the mass base of the Hungarian emigration. At the same time, it is not to be forgotten that though the legion was called Hungarian, its composition by nationality was very complex. No doubt the officers were mainly Hungarian, but there were also officers from Croatia, Romania, Austria, Bohemia, and Italy. The men of the rank and file varied widely in nationality. After the disbanding of the Garibaldian troops in November 1860, the Swiss Rifle Company was joined to the Hungarian legion, and the base of this group was composed of Swiss, Austrian, and German elements. It may be roughly estimated that half of the common soldiers were not Hungarians; these included a fair number of Italians, Austrians, Germans, Bohemians, Moravians, Poles, Croatians, Romanians, and people of other nationalities. Most of the nations of Europe were represented in the Hungarian legion, including England, France, and Finland. Thus it could be said that the Hungarian legion was basically an international, though from the mid-1860s on the Hungarian elements tended to be the more lasting ones. The uncomfortable incidents of the period of Földváry inspired distrust of the leadership in the non-Hungarians and encouraged them to retire. It is not irrelevant that the majority of the troops represented the generation that had spent its childhood among the events of the 1848 Revolution and sought, by joining the Hungarian legion, to follow its fathers' example. Enthusiastic and confident when they arrived, after their bitter experiences they were the more critical and wanted to leave as soon as possible.

While the Austro-Prussian War again held out hope, the ensuing events caused further disappointment for the legionnaires, both in Italy and in Prussia. The Hungarian legion organized in Prussia experimented unsuccessfully with the aim of overrunning Hungary; it was not prepared for this war, and the action coincided with the Prussian-Austrian armistice. The Hungarian legion in Italy was only after a long quarrel withdrawn from the Abruzzi but was not allowed to take part in battles against Austria. On arriving in Bologna it was assigned to hospital service, which had a terrible effect on the volunteers and amounted to the last straw. These events destroyed what was left of the basis for existence of the Hungarian legion, and its disbanding was only a matter of time. Many of the legionnaires sought to leave the place of their disappointments as soon as possible. The experiences of the wars of 1859 and 1866 established the truth of the ever more limited possibilities of resolving the Hungarian national question for a whole generation, but the experiences of the émigrés in Italy and in particular in the legion were decisive for them.[21] Unwillingly they may have come to the conclusion that the possibility of realizing the far-reaching program of the emigration had not been created. Thus, without being in accord with the agreement expressed in the Austro-Hungarian Compromise of 1867, they had no choice but to make the best of the opportunity offered by its wide-ranging amnesty and return to their country. There remained for them the possibility of working for social development—though within a narrow range—in dualistic Hungary. Social progress in their homeland found new support in the former émigrés and legionnaires. Between the generation of 1848 and the later ones the continuity was unbroken, although the everyday struggle lacked the romanticism of the legionnaires and exiles. The international experiences of the exile gradually accumulated in the consciousness of a series of generations, and assimilating this lesson was a precondition for the determination of the new tasks of a changing society.

Notes

1. General György Klapka became commander-in-chief of the Hungarian legion in Piedmont in 1859. The First Infantry Division was led by Colonel Miklós Nemeskéri Kiss and the Second by Colonel Dániel Ihász. Most of those registered had been prisoners of war, but only formally so. Thus about 3,200 were recorded, but they were not employed in action. See Eugenio [Jenő] Kastner, *Il contributo ungherese nella Guerra del 1859* (Florence, 1934), pp. 216 ff.; idem, *Iratok a Kossuth-emigráció történetéhez, 1859* (Szeged, 1949), pp. 120 ff.; Attilio Vigevano, *La legione ungherese in Italia (1859–1867)* (Rome, 1924), pp. 41 ff. General György Klapka was also commander-in-chief of the Hungarian legion in Prussia. The inspector general was Antal Vetter. General Count Gergely Bethlen was in charge of the cavalry, Colonel Adolf Mogyoródy was commander of the infantry, and Lieutenant Colonel György

Schreter was commander of the hussars. The number registered exceeded 1,500 including prisoners of war. See A. Kienast, *Die Legion Klapka: Eine Episode aus dem Jahre 1866 und ihre Vorgeschichte* (Vienna, 1900), pp. 70 ff.; Ludwig Abafi-Aigner, "Die ungarische Legion in Preussen 1866," *Pester Lloyd,* April 16–17, 1897; Eduard Wertheimer, *Bismarck im politischen Kampf* (Berlin, 1930), pp. 23 ff.; Imre Gonda, *Bismarck és az 1867-es osztrák-magyar kiegyezés* (Budapest, 1960), pp. 32 ff.

2. Lajos Lukács, *Garibaldi e l'emigrazione ungherese, 1860–1862* (Modena, 1965), pp. 102 ff.; idem, *Garibaldival a szabadságért: Dunyov István élete és működése. 1816–1889* (Budapest, 1968).

3. See C. S. Forbes, *The Campaign of Garibaldi in the Two Sicilies* (Edinburgh, 1861); Carlo Pecorini-Manzoni, *Storia della 15ª Divisione Türr nella Campagna del 1860 in Sicilia e Napoli* (Florence, 1876), pp. 131 ff.; George Macaulay Trevelyan, *Garibaldi and the Making of Italy* (London, 1911), pp. 124 ff.; Angelo Tamborra, "Garibaldi e l'Europa," in *Atti del XXXIX Congresso di Storia del Risorgimento Italiano, Palermo-Napoli, 17–23 ottobre 1960* (Rome, 1961), pp. 445 ff.; "On the Organization of the Legion of 1860," *Archivio di Stato di Torino,* Sez. I, Esercito Italia Meridionale 15ª Div.

4. See Giuseppe Garibaldi, *Memorie autobiografiche* (Florence, 1888), pp. 331 ff.; Cesare Abba, *Da Quarto al Faro: Noterelle d'uno dei Mille* (Bologna, 1862); idem, *Da Quarto al Volturno,* 4th ed. (Bologna, 1899); Enrico Emilio Ximenes, *Epistolario di Giuseppe Garibaldi: Con documenti e lettere inedite (1836–1882),* 2 vols. (Milan, 1885).

5. See Lajos Lukács, *A magyar garibaldisták útja: Marsalától a Porta Piáig 1860–1870* (Budapest, 1971), pp. 192 ff.

6. See Luigi Chiala, *Politica segreta di Napoleone III e di Cavour in Italia e in Ungheria: 1858–1861* (Turin-Rome, 1895); Lajos Kossuth, *Irataim az emigrációból,* 3 vols. (Budapest, 1880–82); *Kossuth Lajos iratai,* ed. Ignác Helfy and Ferenc Kossuth, 13 vols. (Budapest, 1894–1911), 1: 209 ff.; idem, *Memoirs of My Exile* (London-Paris-New York, 1880).

7. See *A Kossuth-emigráció szolgálatában: Tanárky Gyula naplója 1849–1866,* ed. Jenő Koltay-Kastner (Budapest, 1961), pp. 169 ff.

8. Kossuth, *Irataim,* 1: 549 ff.; cf. *Camillo Cavour's gedruckte und ungedruckte Brief: Gesammelt, erläutert und mit einer Biographie versehen von Luigi Chiala,* 4 vols. (Leipzig, 1884–86), 3: 345 ff.

9. See H. Bolton King, *A History of Italian Unity, Being a Political History of Italy from 1814 to 1871,* 2 vols. (London, 1899), 2: 166 ff.; Giorgio Candeloro, *Storia dell'Italia moderna,* vol. 4, *1849–1860* (Milan, 1966), pp. 492 ff.; Denis Mack Smith, *Cavour and Garibaldi* (Cambridge, 1954), pp. 175 ff.

10. Lajos Abafi, "Az olaszországi magyar légió történetéhez," *Hazánk* 10–11 (1888–89).

11. See Lukács, *Garibaldi e l'emigrazione ungherese,* pp. 134 ff.

12. See "Klapka tábornok naplója," in Kossuth, *Irataim,* 3: 223 ff.; E. Kastner, "Étienne Türr en 1860," *Revue de Hongrie,* 1929; *L'opera di Stefano Türr nel Risorgimento Italiano (1848–1870) descritta dalla figlia,* 2 vols. (Florence, 1928).

13. Türr to Kossuth, Turin, May 29, 1861, National Archives, Budapest; see also Kossuth to Türr, London, May 2 and 6, 1861, Kossuth collection, II.S.2.-113; Türr papers, no. 1636.
14. See G. Candeloro, *Storia dell'Italia moderna*, vol. 5, *1860–1871* (Milan, 1970), pp. 119 ff.; Franco Molfese, *Storia del brigantaggio dopo l'Unità* (Milan, 1966), pp. 57 ff.; Adolfo Omodeo, *Difesa del Risorgimento* (Turin, 1955), pp. 268 ff.; Giulio Adamoli, *Dal Volturno ad Aspromonte: Commemorazione del colonnello Giacinto Bruzzesi* (Milan, 1907), pp. 79 ff.
15. Adolf Kunfy, *Itáliában a magyar légiónál* (Budapest, 1910), pp. 22 ff.; Vigevano, *La legione ungherese in Italia*, pp. 95 ff.; Lukács, *A magyar garibaldisták útja*, pp. 142 ff.; "A légió 1862. évi mozgalmaihoz," Az olaszországi magyar légió iratai, 1860–62, War History Archives, Budapest.
16. Türr papers, no. 83; Kossuth collection, II.S.2.-470, National Archives, Budapest.
17. See Lukács, *Garibaldi e l'emigrazione ungherese*, p. 170.
18. Földváry to Kossuth, Ancona, April 24, 1865, Kossuth collection, II.S.2.-642/a, National Archives, Budapest; Földváry to Count Tivadar Csáky, Chieti, September 20, 1865, Csáky papers, National Archives, Budapest.
19. See Kienast, *Die Legion Klapka*, pp. 51 ff.; Alfonso La Marmora, *Un po' più di luce sugli eventi politici e militari dell'anno 1866* (Florence, 1876), pp. 37 ff.
20. Földváry to Kossuth, Ancona, February 15, 1864, Kossuth collection, II.S.2.-618, National Archives, Budapest; Földváry to Türr, Ancona, April 13, 1864, Türr papers, no. 1475, National Archives, Budapest; cf. Lukács, *A magyar garibaldisták útja*, pp. 215 ff.; Vigevano, *La legione ungherese in Italia*, pp. 172 ff.; Molfese, *Storia del brigantaggio*, pp. 311 ff.; "A brigantaggio elleni küzdelemhez," Per il Brigantaggio delle provincie Meridionale (1863–66), Archivio Centrale dello Stato di Roma.
21. See Kossuth's *Irataim*, 1: 403 ff.; Luigi Chiala, *Ancora un po' più di luce sugli eventi politici e militari dell'anno 1866* (Florence, 1903), pp. 76 ff.; on the returning legionnaires see Haus-, Hof- und Staatsarchiv (Vienna), Informations Büro des k. k. Min. d. Ausseren, B. M. Acten 1862–66.

The Hungarian National Directorate and the 1859 War

Thomas Kabdebo

After its military defeat in the 1848-49 war, Hungary endured a period of Austrian terror and administrative repression with a combination of passive resistance and concealed tenacity. Its institutions—the county system, the Diet, the judiciary—survived a deep-freeze of variable length that was showing signs of a general thaw by the beginning of 1859. However, the political will of the Hungarian nation could not manifest itself in independentist postures. The most such able politicians as Ferenc Deák and Gyula Andrássy could hope to achieve, at least for the time being, was a return to constitutionalism.[1]

Meanwhile, the Hungarian emigration of 1849, divided though it was, had continued fighting for what each faction understood to be the "Hungarian cause." The most influential and largest group consisted of Kossuthists living in diaspora in various countries of Europe and in the United States. Kossuth had one clear aim—to liberate Hungary—and in this purpose he invested every effort. In the earlier stages of his partly public, partly clandestine revolutionary fight, he had recruited and carried with him the ablest of the Hungarian emigrants living in the West: General György Klapka, Count László Teleki, and Ferenc Pulszky. The "Hungarian cause" in Kossuth's hands had gone through a public fund-raising stage (in England and America, 1851-52), a Mazzinian conspiratorial phase (1853), and an early diplomatic phase (1854-55) in which the Kossuthists had tried, unsuccessfully, to unite the Hungarian cause with France's and England's contest against Russia in the Crimean War. Now, in 1859, a different opportunity knocked on the door.[2]

From the Hungarian point of view, the first initiative came from Klapka. The successful general of the Hungarian war had come to England, after the memorable defense of Komárom (Komorn), in 1850. Having written a best-selling military account of the war[3] (and the best to date), he had undertaken a number of successful political and commercial ventures. In 1856 he had organized the resistance of Neuchâtel against Prussian claims. As a consequence of this operation, he had become, in 1857, the president of the Banque Général de Suisse and had traveled to Constantinople to set up trade routes. Since the Paris Congress of 1856 that had settled the affairs of the Crimea, he had had various connections with the ministers of Piedmont. In the summer of 1858 Klapka met Teodoro Santa Rosa, one of Cavour's junior ministers, to sound him out on ways of connecting the cause of Italy's liberation with a possible Hungarian uprising. Since the Italian-French alliance was an established fact and their waging war on Austria a distinct possibility, Klapka, equipped with Cavour's recommendations, went to see Prince Napoleon[4] in December 1858.

"Plon-Plon," the Red Prince, as Prince Napoleon was fondly called, was a devotee of the ideal of self-determinant nationalities. He had been in correspondence with Cavour since the early part of 1858.[5] Having met Klapka, he established a link with Kossuth through Dániel Irányi, Kossuth's trusted agent. Earlier, Kossuth had learned from Mazzini of a meeting between Cavour and Napoleon III and the terms of a French-Italian alliance. In the event of defeating Austria in a future war, Lombardy and Venetia were to be ceded to Piedmont, while Nice and Savoy were to be attached to France.[6] In his letters to Kossuth, Prince Napoleon urged the Hungarian leader to abandon Mazzini and put his trust in the emperor of France.[7] Meanwhile, Cavour had to make sure that the emperor approved of the "Hungarian connection." The approval in principle was transmitted to Cavour by Count Nigra on December 13, 1858, and his meeting with Napoleon III on February 17, 1859, dispelled any doubts he might still have had.[8]

At the same time Klapka was busy trying to involve all interested parties in the projected bond. At a meeting with Cavour on January 6, 1859, he sketched the idea of a Hungarian legion in Piedmont. Shortly afterward the king, Victor Emmanuel II, assured him that war between Austria and Italy was inevitable. On January 10, 1859, Klapka met Prince Napoleon in Paris and was promised money as well as ships to transport the Hungarian legion across the Adriatic to the Dalmatian coast. After January 16, Klapka met Kossuth in London, and they agreed that, to start with, Kossuth would have a propaganda role and would only effectively become leader once Hungary had entered the field of action.[9]

In February 1859, when the friendship between Austria and France had already cooled considerably, Count László Teleki was staying in Tours. Formerly a left-wing orator of the Hungarian Assembly and the able ex-ambassador of independent Hungary to France, he was living, at the time Klapka approached him, in semiretirement. With Klapka's persuasion and Kossuth's written assurances, Teleki was mobilized; the count and the general went together to Genoa at the end of February. Between them a contingency plan was hatched: Hungary should be liberated[10] during the forthcoming anti-Austrian war. Kossuth would be in overall (if nominal) charge of whatever Hungarian army the emigration could muster; Klapka would try to take an interventionary force through Romania to Transylvania; Teleki would organize the conspiratorial/revolutionary movement in Hungary.

The good news spread quickly among the Hungarian emigrants. At the close of winter some leading figures began to rally around Kossuth: the devoted Dániel Ihász, the fearless Colonel Mednyánszky, the skillful Frigyes Szarvady. In March 1859 Klapka met Alexandru Ioan Cuza, the ruling prince of Moldavia and Wallachia, in Constantinople and gained his support for the "plan." They agreed that Hungarian arms would be stockpiled in the principalities.[11]

In April Teleki left Tours for Paris. On April 29 he met Prince Napoleon, who asked him to try to unite the Hungarian emigration. Teleki or the turn of events did have a limited success: Dániel Irányi and Miklós Nemeskéri Kiss forgave one another, and Mór Perczel made an attempt to cooperate,[12] but there were others who, having quarreled with the Kossuthists, had already returned to Hungary or, like Kázmér Batthyány, had died unreconciled. Kossuth wrote a memorandum to both Napoleon III and Cavour asking each to issue a proclamation to the Hungarians with the expressed intention of a possible liberation.

At the beginning of 1859, Ferenc Pulszky, formerly the Hungarian plenipotentiary in London, noted in his diary that Emperor Napoleon III in his New Year's greetings to Hübner, the Austrian ambassador in Paris, had expressed his sorrow over the gradual estrangement between Austria and France.[13]

Further news came from France via Nemeskéri Kiss, who had moved to Paris and married the sister of Thouvenel, Napoleon's adviser on foreign policy and future foreign minister. The French-Italian alliance was an extension of a bond left over from the Crimean League, an expression of Napoleon's gratitude to the House of Savoy for services rendered. The bond was further strengthened by Prince Napoleon's betrothal to Princess Maria Clotilde, daughter of Victor Emmanuel II, and its significance was discussed by F. W. Newman and his Hungarian friends in 1858.[14]

Differences of opinion had arisen in the past among the leaders of the Hungarian exiles, mainly about the leadership of Kossuth, but now a united political stand was needed. This was put to Klapka by Cavour, who understood Kossuth's immense political appeal among the Hungarian masses. Napoleon, still keenly remembering the time he refused the revolutionary leader in 1851, was bent on enlisting his support.[15] It was hoped by the allies that in a war with Austria a proclamation issued by Kossuth to the Hungarian soldiers fighting on the Austrian side would make them desert their ranks. Kossuth instructed Pulszky to rally the German emigrants for an anti-Austrian demonstration in which Vogt's[16] line of argument—that the dissolution of the Habsburg Empire was in the true interest of all Germans—could be put to them.

The tactics Kossuth adopted were to alienate Austria from its friends. This emerged more clearly when he met both Teleki and Klapka in London and was preparing to go to Napoleon with an offer to exert his influence in ensuring the neutrality of Britain in the event of war. He wrote to Pulszky on May 2, 1859: "Teleki and Klapka arrived today claiming that in the name of the Emperor . . . the Prince [Napoleon] had asked them to come and invite me to go over [to Paris] and confer with the ruler. . . . I shall see whether they will insist on such details which only pretend the acceptance of my principles and simulate agreement between us."[17] Kossuth rightly guessed that Napoleon would try to persuade him to issue a proclamation to the people of Hungary to revolt against Austria.

Before their departure, Pulszky met Klapka, Teleki, and Kossuth.[18] On May 7, 1859, he recorded the receipt of a letter informing him that the meeting had taken place. Next day, Pulszky saw the three Hungarian leaders back in London and recorded Kossuth's interviews with Prince Napoleon, which took place on May 5, 1859, and with the emperor on the following day, as reported by Kossuth on May 8, 1859.[19] On the night of May 6 the Hungarian National Directorate was formed by Klapka, Teleki, and Kossuth for the liberation of Hungary. As president, Kossuth sought guarantees from Napoleon to equip a French expeditionary force which would land on the Dalmatian coast and march on Hungary before he was prepared to send a proclamation into the country. Napoleon gave no firm promise, but granted money for propaganda purposes, for arms, and for the organization of a Hungarian legion. They were in complete agreement with regard to Britain. Kossuth promised that as soon as he was back in London he would start a campaign advocating British neutrality.

Pulszky had already tested the ground. On April 30 he had contacted Charles Gilpin, an admirer of Kossuth and a supporter of the Hungarian cause. Gilpin was a publisher and a member of Parliament for Northampton in Cobden's party, with well-established connections with the

Manchester group of liberals, on the one hand, and with Palmerston's Whigs, on the other. He promised his support to Pulszky if and when Kossuth wanted a public meeting. On the night of May 8 Pulszky visited Grant, the editor of the *Morning Advertiser,* to inquiry how well-disposed the British newspapers were to the idea of neutrality. Grant promised his support, and so did Walker, the editor of the *Daily News.*

Pulszky and Kossuth considered that Napoleon could count on the throne but not on the Derby government, well known for its support of Austria. Since the end of March, Lord Augustus Loftus, the British ambassador in Vienna, had made proposal after proposal that the Great Powers simultaneously disarm.[20] As these had been of no avail, there was mounting fear of British mobilization in support of Austria. Elections were held on May 20, resulting in the return of 302 Tory, 263 Whig, and 90 independent Cobdenite members. It was obvious that when Parliament reassembled on the last day of May the vote of the Cobdenites would decide the fate of the government.

Kossuth and Pulszky concentrated their propaganda efforts on the ten days between the election and the reassembly of Parliament. As in the past, the organization was left to Pulszky. He went to Bradford on May 12 and spoke to the mayor. Next day he moved on to Manchester, while Kossuth himself, with the help of Gilpin, made arrangements with the municipal authorities in London. Pulszky's entry in his notebook on May 18 reads as follows: "News confirming that in Bradford, Glasgow, Manchester everything is all right, meetings on 24, 25, 27 May." The first meeting was held at the London Tavern on May 20. The Lord Mayor was chairman, and Kossuth, Pulszky, Gilpin, White (member of Parliament for Plymouth), Nicholay, Newman, and the Reverend Newman Hall took part. A resolution was passed that "England would not under any circumstances whatever violate the principles of non-intervention."[21] The meeting at Manchester Free-Trade Hall on May 24 was reported quite favorably in the *Times* of the following day, and the next two meetings in Bradford and in Glasgow had similar receptions.[22] The favorable reports in the *Times,* which had been notoriously anti-Kossuth in the past, may have been due to two factors: a genuine support for neutrality and the influence of Hungarians such as Ede Horn and Nándor Éber, who were employed as correspondents at the time of the outbreak of Austro-French hostilities. It would be difficult to decide whether Kossuth in fact had a modest and indirect share in the eventual overthrow of the Tory government, as has been claimed by some Hungarian historians,[23] or just happened to support a policy that won the day on June 11, 1859.

Italy's position at the outbreak of hostilities may be sketched this way:

in Lombardy-Venetia the vigorous military rule of Radetzky and his successors prevailed. Tuscany, nominally under the Grand Duke, was, through its liberal, cautiously moving government, favorably disposed toward Cavour. In Rome, the Pope, once a liberal, had completely alienated himself from Piedmont and the French alliance. For King Ferdinand of Naples, any move toward a possible unification of Italy was anathema. The Italian war caused internal turmoil in every part of the peninsula.

Victor Emmanuel II opened the Piedmontese Parliament with a speech that echoed the New Year's resolutions of his French ally: "We are not insensible to the cry of pain which rises toward us from so many parts of Italy."[24] The speech was soon followed by action. On January 19, 1859, a treaty—the military convention—was contracted between the allied powers. Volunteers were flocking into northern Italy from the Papacy, the Duchy of Tuscany, and all over Italy—the largest contingent led by Garibaldi—and from Western European countries, from which also came a growing number of Hungarians.

The war commenced on April 29, 1859, with the Austrian invasion of Piedmont. On May 1, Victor Emmanuel put himself at the head of his army; on May 12, Napoleon followed his example.

> On the 20th the Austrians were beaten at Montebello; on the 30th at Palestro, both victories being specially Piedmontese: on June 4, the French, after crossing the Ticino at Turbigo, won the battle of Magenta, and thus freed Milan; on the 8th they conquered at Melegnano, after a tremendous and sanguinary struggle. The Allies then advanced towards the Mincio; but, before they crossed it, the Austrians once more confronted them in full force at Solferino and San Martino, on June 24. The battle was on an enormous scale, and the victory was won with difficulty, mainly by the valour of the French and Piedmontese soldiers.[25]

Solferino was virtually the last real battle of the war, and on July 6 the allies submitted proposals to and on the 11 agreed with the Austrians on an armistice. Lombardy (exclusive of Mantua and Peschiera) was ceded —via France—to Piedmont; the peace treaty was to be concluded later in Zurich. Finally, France received its prize; Nice and Savoy were ceded to it by the Treaty of Turin on March 24, 1860. Meanwhile, the architect of all the background diplomacy, Cavour, resigned in disgust. He had been fighting for the unification of Italy, not just for limited gains. Before considering the reasons Napoleon, the senior partner of the alliance, had pressed for the armistice at Villafranca, we shall examine the role the Hungarian National Directorate played behind the scenes and in the war effort.

The Hungarian National Directorate was formally launched on

May 6, 1859, in Paris, though it had existed in spirit since March 19, when Teleki had approached Kossuth in a friendly, conciliatory letter, offering cooperation.[26] In their meeting on April 29 (the first day of the war), Klapka and Teleki had proposed to Prince Napoleon the plan of a three-pronged attack: a French force was to land at Fiume, Transylvanian guerrilla warfare would be fomented with local support, and a Hungarian emigrant force would cross the Danube. On May 2 Klapka and Teleki came to London to talk with Kossuth. The next day the three of them went to Paris. On May 5 they met Prince Napoleon during the day, and Kossuth conferred alone with Napoleon in the evening about the plan Klapka and Teleki had proposed earlier. Napoleon attempted to avoid the question of guarantees, for which Kossuth was ardently pressing, and asked Kossuth to assume that he would get those guarantees and issue proclamations to the people of Hungary and to the Hungarian soldiers in the Austrian army.[27] Kossuth was adamant and, for once, ready to give the same answer, in summary fashion, that he had already preempted, as it were, in an earlier declaration to the Hungarian emigration. Hungary's participation, to the extent Kossuth was able to foresee it, would depend on a guaranteed agreement with Napoleon the mainstay of which would be a French interventionary force.[28]

Yet, the Kossuth-Napoleon meeting was not a stalemate. On May 6 Kossuth met Prince Napoleon, asked for a loan of two hundred fifty thousand francs, and got, as the first installment, fifty thousand.[29] On May 8 Kossuth was back in London, while Klapka went to Genoa and then to Turin to meet Cavour. It is probably because of their meeting that on May 15 leaflets were distributed among the soldiers in Pest urging them to desert. On May 17 Teleki wrote to Klapka that the first shipment of arms was on its way to Moldavia.

Invited by the cause but not by the Directorate, General Mór Perczel appeared in Italy in mid-May and on the twenty-first issued a proclamation to the Hungarian soldiers fighting on the other side: "You are the best soldiers of the Austrian army. Come over to the Hungarian flag on the Italian side."[30] A Hungarian flag had indeed been flying among the Piedmontese, and it received a new status on May 24, when the Hungarian legion was formally launched.[31]

A few days earlier three colonels, Dániel Ihász, Miklós Nemeskéri Kiss, and Gergely Bethlen, had been meeting in Genoa: they were to be the commanding officers of the legion. On May 20 another invitation to desert was published, this time by László Teleki in the name of the Directorate. Meanwhile Pulszky, the secretary of the Directorate, had received the second installment of the French loan, another fifty thousand francs.[32] Recruitment for the Hungarian legion was pursued vigorously. In the battles of Montebello and Palestro the French took 1,000 prisoners, from whom Teleki selected 126 Hungarians for the Genoa legion. On June 10, Victor Emmanuel II declared the Hungarian legion part of his army, and the next day the soldiers and officers repaired to Acqui. Klapka was named general of the "Hungarians," who, on June 27, amounted to 880 men. Since July 14 the legion had only 400 men, half of whom were emigrants (such as István Türr, who had come from Turkey to join up and was among the first wounded, or Colonel Mogyoródy, who led a Hungarian emigrant contingent from Britain), the difference was largely made up of prisoners from the Battle of Magenta, selected from Milanese and Bergamese camps.

Sometime in June a French ship unloaded 180 carriageloads of weapons on the Danube near Galaţi, intended for the Hungarian border. The Austrians were taking no chances: because of the growing internal unrest in Hungary, they kept five fully armed infantry regiments, thirty cavalry squadrons, and four batteries near Vienna.[33]

On June 16 Kossuth left London for Italy. As president of the Hungarian National Directorate, he left Pulszky the following instructions:[34] (1) to keep a close watch on the changes in the government's foreign policy and report to the Directorate thereon, (2) to maintain contact with the friends of Hungary in Britain, with a view to holding further meetings when necessary, (3) to maintain contact with the newspapers, (4) to contract for certain printing machines for the eventual production of paper money, and (5) to deal with Kossuth's correspondence in his absence. The newspapers Pulszky maintained contact with were the *New York Tribune,* the *Morning Advertiser,* and the *Daily News.* He relates in his memoirs that on one occasion Grant of the *Advertiser* said to him excitedly that he must have been misleading him about the feelings of the Hungarians in Austria, since the field marshal of the Austrian army was a Hungarian aristocrat, Count Ferenc Gyulay:

> I was slightly annoyed and answered in jest that an Englishman could understand neither the stupidity of the Viennese nor the patriotism of a Hungarian. The Field Marshal will outdo even Brutus and, relinquishing his fame and military honor, will let himself be beaten by the French army. As it happened, in three days' time, the news of the Battle of Magenta reached London, and duly the *Morning Advertiser* extolled Hungarian patriotism, which recalled the legends of ancient Rome.[35]

Kossuth arrived in Genoa on June 21. On the twenty-second he delivered a rousing speech to the soldiers of the Hungarian legion. Two days later—on the day of the Battle of Solferino—he met Cavour,[36] and the two agreed, in principle, that Hungary's and Italy's liberation was a joint ongoing concern. On July 3 Pulszky published extracts of a long letter[37] from Kossuth describing his reception in Italy. The letter was sent from Parma on June 27, 1859, three days after the victory of the allies at Solferino. Before the battle, the letter informs us, Klapka and Kossuth issued proclamations to the Hungarian soldiers in the Austrian army to desert their ranks and come over to the allied camp, where a Hungarian legion was being organized to fight for the liberation of Hungary. In the letter Kossuth implied that the Austrian defeat was partly due to the success of these proclamations; over three thousand Hungarian soldiers and officers had surrendered their arms and come over.

Kossuth met Prince Napoleon again, this time at the French headquarters at Magenta, on June 30. He adamantly refused to issue a proclamation for rebellion *within* Hungary before a French army had landed on the Dalmatian coast. On July 3 Kossuth and Napoleon III met at Valeggio.[38] Kossuth, perhaps slightly overstating his role in the victory of the neutrality advocates in England, claimed that a French diversion into Hungary would not change Palmerston's attitude toward the war. A letter dated June 24, 1859, from Pulszky, who had consulted R. Monckton Milnes, undersecretary of state for foreign affairs, contained a warning: "they went here to pacify at any price and are afraid of the Hungarian diversion."[39] Napoleon knew even more about the British attitude, however. He received Kossuth with a telegram from the British foreign minister, Lord John Russell, which confirmed the British declaration of neutrality but warned the emperor, "with special regard to the trip of the Hungarian statesman published by the press,"[40] that his support of the Hungarian independence struggle would provoke the Germans. The emperor spoke of his fears of possible Prussian and Bavarian action on the side of Austria that might compel him to make peace with Austria. Otherwise he was firmly decided to make Hungary independent.

Even though there was to be no French expeditionary force, Kossuth's hopes were kept alive, and he also derived encouragement from the shipment of French arms to the Balkans. Accordingly, he sent instructions to Pulszky about ordering cloth and boots for the Hungarian legion in Italy and reminded him about drawing up a contract for a banknote press. His idea was that, in the event of liberating the country from Austrian rule, he should issue new banknotes—as he had in 1849—as the only legal tender in independent Hungary. When Pulszky received Kossuth's instructions about the boots and clothing for the army, he went to Bradford to order the goods. Before he set off, he called at the Sardinian embassy, where he learned that French troops occupied Lussin Piccolo, near Fiume. He began to believe "that it will be Fiume next, and here, on Hungarian land, they will set the Hungarian tricolor flying and issue the proclamation that will involve Hungary in the war."[41] We should note that this appeared a realistic possibility to most contemporaries, especially when on July 6 and 7 two French warships bombarded Zara.[42] "With these hopes I traveled to Bradford, where, within a few hours of my arrival, I learned the news of the armistice, whch soon ended the war. I went back to London immediately. . . . our hopes evaporated again, at a time when it seemed they were about to be fulfilled."[43]

On July 11, 1859, Francis Joseph and Napoleon III met at Villafranca, and the terms of peace soon transpired. On July 18, 1859, Kossuth wrote to Pulszky from Aix-les-Bains, Savoy.[44] He described how Napoleon had sent him a message on July 14 saying that his hand was forced to make peace with Austria. Kossuth rushed to Turin on a call from Cavour. Cavour told him of his resignation: "I feel dishonored. How could I sign a peace which makes my king a confederate with the Austrians and with the Pope? Which gives back Tuscany and Modena to the Princes who had escaped? Never! . . . *Mais ça ne sera pas. Cette paix ne s'executera pas. Moi je me ferai conspirateur, revolutionnaire s'il le faut.*"[45] Kossuth, on his part, stipulated that those soldiers of the Hungarian legion who wished to go back to Hungary should be free to do so. He insisted that a guarantee of total amnesty for them be included in the final peace treaty. This was promised by Cavour, communicated to Napoleon, and accepted without qualms by Francis Joseph, still afraid of a revolt in Hungary and desirous of making conciliatory gestures. The legion, 3,145 strong on July 8, was disbanded by a proclamation issued by the Directorate on July 16. A hard core remained in the service of the king of Sardinia, forming a contingent called the Hussars of Piacenza, and when the banner of Italian liberty was unfolded again former officers such as Türr and Lajos Tüköry joined forces with Garibaldi.[46]

Kossuth traveled to Switzerland, where he met his wife and children. Teleki went to Zurich to monitor the peace conference to make sure the guarantees for the Hungarian soldiers were kept. Klapka left Turin and occupied himself with finding employment for the exiles who did not want to return to Hungary. He entered into long negotiations about the fate of the weapons stored by Prince Cuza. The Hungarian National Directorate still existed, anchoring its hopes in the future, when and if Cavour returned to power. Kossuth, as president, received a hundred thousand francs severance pay from Napoleon, which he wanted to put to the best use. On September 24 he returned to England with the idea of keeping the Hungarian question alive with a press campaign on an international scale.

There remain two questions to be discussed, by way of summary: Did the activities of the Hungarian National Directorate directly contribute to the victory of the allies? Did the "Hungarian diversion" play a role in the swift conclusion of the hostilities? Analysts of the final battle emphasize that it was a full-scale collision of the two armies. Whereas the Austrian wings—where, among others, the Hungarian and Croatian divisions were placed—held on, the center eventually collapsed. Earlier, after the Battle of Magenta, about four hundred Hungarian soldiers—formerly in the Austrian army—had joined the Hungarian legion. The majority of these were not "deserters," but prisoners of war whom the Hungarian Directorate had liberated from hospitals and camps. After the Battle of Solferino, over two thousand more Hungarians joined the legion under similar circumstances. The allies had taken six thousand prisoners. A third of these were Hungarians, which was indeed a very high ratio, but if we compare the number of prisoners to the total number of Austrian casualties, which was twenty-two thousand, the number of prisoners was not high.[47] I have found little direct evidence for Kossuth's claims of mass desertion in contemporary reports, such as the *Times* reports from Solferino, Villafranca, from the Austrian headquarters in Verona, or from Vienna. There was, however, an unusually large number of persons missing from the various regiments of the Austrian army, totaling nine thousand (against two thousand for the allies),[48] and although no one was able to make a nationality head count the regiments that must have suffered most from deserters were the Hungarian ones. The Hungarian regiments of the line were the Lichtenstein, Thun, Ferdinand d'Este, Archduke Joseph, Archduke Ernest, Archduke Francis Charles, and Prince Wasa; the *Times* reported that they "held their peace but their countenances show that they feel their vantage."[49] From Vienna, the *Times*'s own correspondent wrote on July 6 that "Archduke Albert has proclaimed . . . that persons attempting to debauch these soldiers [i.e., to persuade them to desert] . . . will be put to death." It was more difficult to be taken prisoner than to fight halfheartedly and wander off in another direction. Yet nothing in the contemporary records indicates that the outcome of the Battle of Solferino or any other battle of the war was heavily influenced by the behavior of Hungarian soldiers, most of whom must have read or heard of the Directorate's proclamations.

Historians of the period showed some awareness of Kossuth's diplomatic role on the side of the allies.[50] If the Directorate had little actual influence over the outcome of the battles, its existence, activities, and revolutionary potential were a major threat that both the Austrian secret police and Austrian diplomacy had to reckon with. It had influenced British neutrality. On the one hand, Francis Joseph felt pressed by it to make a swift peace treaty, cut his losses with the allies, and make a conciliatory move toward the Hungarian constitutionalists; on the other hand, "the Hungarian diversion" was also a factor in Napoleon's decision making. Among the internal causes of the French approach to Villafranca Albert Thomas has listed pressure from French Catholics and the mounting costs of the war, both in money and in human wastage. One may list a third cause: the French had calculated certain territorial gains, and once these were in sight they lost interest in prolonging the hostilities. There were two major external causes: the Prussians adopted a threatening diplomatic posture,[51] and the English delivered oblique warnings about British neutrality. The fact was that in 1859 Russell pursued the same foreign policy that Palmerston had in 1849. Their cornerstone was a strong Austria, and a Hungarian diversion that might disrupt Austria was as dangerous in 1859 as it had been in 1849. As the Hungarian cause was thus enmeshed in a geopolitical net, the liberation of Hungary was not a real option, but only a diplomatic lever.

Notes

1. A. Berzeviczy, *Az abszolutizmus kora Magyarországon, 1849–1865*, 4 vols. (Budapest, 1922–37), is still the definitive monograph on the subject.
2. Gy. Szabad, *Kossuth and the British "Balance of Power" Policy 1859–1861*, Studia Historica Academiae Scientiarum Hungaricae, no. 84 (Budapest, 1960).
3. Gy. Klapka, *Memoirs of the War of Independence in Hungary* (London, 1850).
4. T. Ács, *A genovai lázadás* (Budapest, 1968), pp. 17–18.
5. J. Koltay-Kastner, *A Kossuth-emigráció Olaszországban* (Budapest, 1960), pp. 58–59. On the three-cornered secret diplomacy, see L. Chiala, *Politica segreta di Napoleon III e di Cavour in Italia ed in Ungheria (1858–1861)* (Turin, 1895).
6. F. Pulszky, *Életem és korom*, 2d ed. (Budapest, 1884), 2: 186.
7. L. Kossuth, *Irataim az emigráczióból*, 14 vols. (Budapest, 1891–1914), 1: 87–88.
8. *Carteggio Cavour-Nigra, a cura della R. Commissione Editrice*, 2 vols. (Bologna, 1926), 2: 116–18.
9. Koltay-Kastner, *A Kossuth-emigráció Olaszországban*, p. 74.

10. Klapka, Aperçu général des forces présomptives dont la Hongrie peut disposer en cas de guerre (Memorandum to Napoleon III), p. 77.
11. E. Ollivier, *L'empire libéral* (Paris, 1899), 3: 425–27.
12. Which was ultimately unsuccessful; see Teleki to Kossuth, June 5, 1859, in L. Teleki, *Válogatott munkái* (Budapest, 1961), 2: 143.
13. T. Kabdebo, "Francis Pulszky's political activities in England, 1849–1860" (M. Phil diss., University of London, 1969), p. 224.
14. F. W. Newman, *Reminiscences of Two Exiles, Kossuth and Pulszky and Two Wars, Crimean and Franco-Austrian* (London, 1888), p. 110. Professor Francis Newman, the brother of Cardinal Newman, was a friend of Pulszky, Kossuth, and the "Hungarian cause."
15. D. Jánossy, *A Kossuth-emigráció Angliában és Amerikában, 1851–1852*, 2 vols. (Budapest, 1940–48); vol. 1, chap. 1, deals with Kossuth's route after his liberation.
16. Charles Vogt, a friend of Kossuth, was once a member of the Frankfurt parliament and was a well-known liberal in London (Kabdebo, "Pulszky's political activities," p. 119).
17. F. Pulszky, Notebook, f. 4, National Széchényi Library, Manuscript Department, Quart. Hung. 2501.
18. Ibid., May 3, 1859.
19. Ibid., f. 5–6, and two separate sheets loose in the notebook; cf. Kossuth's own account of this interview (L. Kossuth, *Memoirs of My Exile* [London-Paris-New York, 1880], pp. 155–81).
20. Great Britain. Public Record Office. Foreign Office, 7, vols. 563, 569, esp. dispatches of Loftus to the Earl of Malmesbury, March 28 and 29, 1859.
21. Report in the *Daily Mail,* May 21, 1859. The *Daily News* gave a full coverage to the meeting on the same date. Pulszky's clippings are inserted in his notebook.
22. *Times,* May 25, 26, and 27, 1859.
23. Ács, *A genovai lázadás,* pp. 98–101; C. M. Macartney (*The Habsburg Empire* [London, 1968], p. 494) quotes F. A. Simpson, who, in his *England and the Italian War of 1859,* noted that "it was Kossuth . . . far more than any single Englishman, who kept England out of the war."
24. E. Masi, "Cavour and the Kingdom of Italy," *Cambridge Modern History* (Cambridge, 1909), 11: 381.
25. Ibid., p. 383. It cannot be forgotten, however, that the Austrian Eighth Corps, under Lajos Benedek, repulsed the Sardinian Third, Ninth, and Eleventh Corps and counterattacked but was ultimately checked by the collapse of the Austrian Seventh Corps at Carriana (see the *Times,* July 25).
26. Teleki to Kossuth, marking their reconciliation, Paris, March 19, 1859, in Teleki, *Válogatott munkái,* 1: 142.
27. Kossuth, *Irataim az emigráczióból,* 1: 211–12.
28. Ibid., pp. 177–78.
29. *Carteggio Cavour-Nigra,* 2: 189.
30. Ács, *A genovai lázadás,* p. 89.
31. A. Vigerano, *Legione ungherese in Italia* (Rome, 1924), p. 45.

32. Gy. Tanárky, *Naplója* (Budapest, 1961), p. 13. (Tanárky was Pulszky's secretary.)
33. Koltay-Kastner, *A Kossuth-emigráció Olaszországban,* p. 146.
34. Pulszky, *Életem és korom,* 2: 194.
35. Ibid., p. 192.
36. Koltay-Kastner, *A Kossuth-emigráció Olaszországban,* p. 150.
37. *Daily News,* no. 4099; Tanárky, *Naplója,* pp. 74–77.
38. Kossuth, *Memoirs,* pp. 321–26.
39. Szabad, *Kossuth,* p. 19.
40. Ibid., pp. 20–21.
41. Pulszky, *Életem és korom,* 2: 192.
42. *Der Krieg in Italie* (Vienna, 1876), 3: 224–26.
43. On the same day Pulszky wrote to Newman: "I have still no other news from Kossuth but a telegraphic message dated Turin, July 15, when he was in despair about the extent to treachery which he could not at once believe" (Pulszky to Newman, July 18, 1859, National Széchényi Library, Pulszky Collection).
44. Pulszky, *Életem és korom,* 2: 201–2.
45. Ibid., p. 203. Kossuth quoted Cavour in Hungarian and then in French.
46. Koltay-Kastner, *A Kossuth-emigráció Olaszországban,* p. 168; Kossuth, *Irataim az emigráczióból,* 1: 476–78; 3: 480.
47. *Times,* June 27, reporting from Solferino, and July 25, reporting from the Austrian headquarters in Verona.
48. A. A. Ducrot, *La vie militaire,* 2d ed. (Paris, 1895), 1: 343; A. Chenu, *Rapport médico-chirurgical sur la campagne d'Italie* (Paris, n.d.), p. 225.
49. *Times,* July 7, 1859.
50. A. Thomas, "The Liberal Empire," *The Cambridge Modern History* (Cambridge, 1909), vol. 11; Macartney, *Habsburg Empire,* pp. 489–94.
51. Masi, "Cavour," p. 384.

Hungarian Armed Units in Italy, 1848–67 and the Sardinian Army (1859–1867)

Paolo Santarcangeli

The presence of foreigners in fighting armies is a phenomenon as old as warfare itself. Allies have furnished auxiliary units to their fighting partners. Individuals have been motivated by the spirit of adventure to serve in foreign forces. Unscrupulous rulers have sold men as cannon fodder to others. Poverty-stricken men have been enlisted as mercenaries in Italy, Scotland, Germany, Switzerland, Sweden, and other countries. In the seventeenth and eighteenth centuries, foreigners were recruited to serve in princely bodyguards, being considered more reliable than natives. All these, however, had nothing to do with the individuals' own feelings and loyalties. The great change came in the late eighteenth and early nineteenth centuries, when, under the influence of the Enlightenment and nationalism, the individual's desire to offer his life and sword to the cause of liberty became a motivation for serving under a foreign flag. Such volunteer foreigners fought shoulder to shoulder with the rebels in America, on the plains of tsarist-occupied Poland, in the historic land of ancient Hellas, then under the yoke of the Porte, and in the various national liberation movements of the Habsburg Empire. The names of Lafayette, Kościuszko, Byron, Bolivar, Garibaldi, Türr, and Klapka represent the scope of this phenomenon.

Before the formal entry of the United States into the First World War, many American citizens flowed, from similar motives, to the banners of Britain, France, and Italy. Again, at the outbreak of the Spanish Civil War in 1936, many foreign volunteers joined the banner of the Spanish Republic. Although this phenomenon is infrequent today, it was widespread in late eighteenth- and nineteenth-century East Central Europe. This essay deals with the Hungarians' participation in the wars of liberation Italians fought against the Habsburgs between 1848 and 1866.

Italian-Hungarian relations have long been rich in common ideas and mutual sentiments. The attraction of the two nations to each other has often been mentioned by both Hungarian and Italian historians, and the political regimes of both countries through much of the interwar era favored this interest even though it sometimes meant a distortion of reality. During the nineteenth century, up to the Austro-Hungarian Compromise of 1867, the liquidation or at least the weakening of the Habsburg Empire was a common interest of Italians and Hungarians, being a precondition for Italy's unification and for the reestablishment of full domestic self-government in Hungary. The prevalence of foreign capitalism and the expansion of international trade played a prominent role in the political evolution of both nations, although in both the economy was still predominantly agrarian with remnants of feudalism.

Giuseppe Mazzini was aware of these conditions as early as 1832, and he counted on the cooperation in the impending struggle against the Habsburgs not only of the Hungarians, but also of the Slavs. In the spirit of Italian-Hungarian cooperation against oppression, the Provisional Government of Lombardy and Terenzio Mamiani of the Republic of Rome appealed to the independent government of Hungary in 1848 for joint action against Austria and for the desertion of Hungarian military units garrisoned in Lombardy-Venetia. It is not the aim of this essay to describe these events fully. I shall mention only that Count László Teleki, Lajos Kossuth's envoy in Paris, established effective contact with the revolutionary government of the Republic of Venice as well as with Piedmont and sent László Splényi to Italy, where he was recognized as the Hungarian envoy. Splényi succeeded in getting the Kingdom of Sardinia to recognize the new Hungarian government; it was the only state in Europe to do so. Vincenzo Gioberti, premier of Sardinia in December 1848, agreed to the establishment of a Hungarian unit in Piedmont and of an Italian unit in Hungary, contemplating a joint Italian-Hungarian military action.[1] Alessandro Monti was sent to Hungary as Sardinian envoy extraordinaire and later became the commander of the Italian legion in Hungary. After the defeat at Custoza, the battle of Novara, and the armistice at Villafranca, Monti was instructed by his government to return to Sardinia. He disobeyed and participated in the Hungarian War of Independence until the bitter end. When the fighting ended, the four hundred and fifty survivors of the Italian legion (of the original fifteen hundred) crossed the Hungarian border at Orsova to safety in the Ottoman Empire.

It is not well known that in 1849, while Italians were fighting for the independence of Hungary, a Hungarian cohort consisting of soldiers who had defected from the Habsburg army in Italy was deployed in defense of Murano by the government of the Republic of Venice and fought there until the capitulation of the republic. When, after the

Battle of Custoza, King Charles Albert was compelled to retreat across the Ticino and to sign the armistice of Salasco, the city of Venice decided to continue its resistance with a small army of volunteers: the decree of October 23, 1848, of the new Republic of Venice foresaw the formation of a Hungarian corps as part of this policy. This corps, called initially (and rather ambitiously) the Hungarian legion and later the Hungarian cohort, was put under the command of Captain Lajos Winkler and never exceeded 70 members. With an Italian and a Swiss company, it was entrusted with the defense of the island of Murano, a lengthy and boring commitment that ended with the surrender of Venice on August 24, 1849. The cohort was disbanded, and with the amnesty for former Austrian soldiers its members dispersed into exile.

These events had their political aspects. In 1849 Kossuth, having been informed of Venice's continuing resistance, wrote a letter (from Debrecen on April 20, 1849) to Daniele Manin, president of the Venetian provisional government, in which he said that, after "the treason of the House of Austria" and the Russian army's invasion, the National Assembly of Hungary had proclaimed the total independence of their country, electing him (Kossuth) governor and chief executive, pointed to the common interests of the "two independent and free peoples of Venice and Hungary in the fight against the same tyranny," and announced the appointment of János Bratich as his envoy extraordinaire to the republic. Manin in turn appointed Ludovico Parzini Venetian plenipotentiary to the Hungarian government. The two envoys met at Ancona and signed for their governments on June 3, 1849, a military alliance in which the two states agreed to develop a joint military action, to form a Hungarian legion in Venice, and to refrain from signing any separate peace treaties. This alliance, which came too late, proved of no noticeable advantage to either partner.

The revolutions of 1848–49 fulfilled the aspirations neither of the Italians nor of the Hungarians. During the next two decades, there was an increasingly close relationship between Italian and Hungarian champions of their nations' liberty. Kossuth and Garibaldi, the two national leaders, were very popular in both countries, and there was a considerable flow of publication from one country to the other. The connection between Kossuth and his followers and Mazzini was also intensive. The former was triumphantly acclaimed during his short visit to La Spezia aboard an American vessel. Soon both Mazzini and Kossuth assumed leading roles in the European Central Democratic Committee in London.

In the 1850s, the Hungarian soldiers who had been drafted into Austrian regiments garrisoned in Italy were defecting in increasing numbers, and others had escaped to Italy from elsewhere. These Hungarian refugees in Italy participated in the abortive revolution in Milan in February 1853 and in other actions launched by their Italian comrades against the Habsburg oppressors. After 1849, Milan was one of the centers of what we would today call an anti-Habsburg resistance movement. The sources on the political aspects of this movement are very poor, being mostly confined to the writings of Kossuth's followers and individual Hungarian refugees. The silence on the Austrian side is quite understandable, the shock of 1848–49 being too fresh to encourage any investigation of the morale of Hungarian military units of its army in Lombardy-Venetia, but research in the military archives of Vienna might reveal data as yet unexplored.

Italian-Hungarian anti-Austrian activities reached their peak in 1859–61, during the renewal of the war for Italian unity. The deep crisis of Habsburg absolutism that surfaced in this period both allowed and demanded the establishment in Turin of the Hungarian National Directorate, which negotiated with the French and Sardinian governments on joint operations. Very soon, however, Kossuth and his followers had to recognize that for the Piedmontese political leadership the Hungarian-Sardinian alliance was more a pragmatic tactical operation to be used against Austria than a sincere pact to promote a common struggle of oppressed peoples against absolutism. In other words, Cavour was inclined at that moment toward compromise. The Hungarians' reaction to this *Realpolitik* was a renewal of their sympathies for Garibaldi and mistrust of the government of the Kingdom of Sardinia. This explains the passionate participation of many Hungarians in the expedition of the Thousand, the increasing influx of volunteers into Garibaldi's army, and the unprecedented popularity in Hungary of Garibaldi, the "hero of two continents."[2] The Austrian government was seriously alarmed at the idea of a second Hungarian revolution, supported by Italian forces.

The political situation immediately following the crisis of 1859–60 was increasingly unfavorable to a revolution in Hungary. There was substantial public support for the liberals, guided by Ferenc Deák, who sought to regain self-rule for Hungary through a compromise with the dynasty rather than through revolution. The Piedmontese political agent Giuseppe Giacomelli, who was sent to Hungary to report on the political situation, understood these circumstances very well: "Hungary is interested in staying with a powerful Austria, since it could not survive without the support of a strong empire. . . . Therefore, Italy must abandon its hope of achieving any success on the Danube."[3] The circumstances, however, had been quite different earlier in the decade.

Ever since the Congress of Paris, Cavour had favored plans similar to

Mazzini's and Gioberti's for Hungarian-Italian cooperation in the event of war against Austria. To prepare for such cooperation, he met soon after his return from Paris to Turin in 1858 with the Hungarian general György Klapka. Cavour and Klapka discussed ways of encouraging soldiers from the Hungarian regiments of the Habsburg army to join a Hungarian legion. Once the principles so important to Kossuth—that any warlike action of Hungary against Austria had to be part of a general campaign rather than simply a diversion and that the king of Sardinia would never sign a separate peace treaty with Austria—had been accepted, a preliminary accord was reached whose main elements were the following: the reestablishment of the Hungarian legion in Italy; the setting up in Italy of an initial stock of Hungarian military uniforms for four thousand; a secret entente with Prince Michael Obrenović of Serbia and Prince Alexandru Cuza of the Danubian principalities to promote a military action in Hungary; the furnishing to the Hungarian National Directorate by Piedmont of fifty thousand shotguns, two batteries of artillery with ammunition, and three thousand swords, along with thirty thousand francs to pay for the transport of this material to Serbia and the Danubian principalities; and the provision to the committee of an initial sum of three hundred thousand francs for its use in obtaining the cooperation of the Serbians and the Romanians and in making contacts with Hungary and further funds to enable it to issue Hungarian paper money. Once the financial basis for the stability of the legion had been established and the willingness of Cavour to cooperate had been determined, Klapka was sent to East Central Europe to meet with Princes Michael Obrenović and Alexandru Cuza.

Kossuth, however, placed some realistic conditions on his approval of the project in order to prevent exploitation of the Hungarian patriots by Italy and France.[4] In May 1859 he met with Napoleon III, who gave him some verbal assurances that did not satisfy him. Circumstances nevertheless forced him to give his halfhearted consent. These uncertainties justified the hesitation of the leaders of the Hungarian political emigration. Uncertainties also marred the policies of the Piedmontese government. These controversies inevitably had a negative effect on Hungarian armed participation in Italy's war on Austria.

In the same month, under the signatures of Klapka and Mór Perczel, a manifesto was addressed to the Hungarian components of the Habsburg army in Italy urging them to desert and join the Sardinian army, in which they were to serve under the Hungarian banner. Subsequently, a Sardinian royal decree issued on May 12, 1859 (published on June 10), established a Hungarian legion. A trusted friend of Kossuth, Colonel Dániel Ihász, was dispatched to Genoa to establish the headquarters of the Hungarian legion at the headquarters of the local divisional command. The legion's headquarters immediately proceeded with the recruitment of volunteers. The first men to join were mostly prisoners taken at the battle of Marengo.[5]

Kossuth's comment on the royal decree was justifiably bitter:

> [The decree] makes our soldiers a legion of mercenaries in the service of Piedmont for the duration of the war. Not a word about the national destiny, not a word about the Hungarian flag as a symbol of our nationality. Nothing that indicates our Hungarian character. . . . It would be impossible for me to describe the indignation this decree has caused within our ranks. Everyone agrees that it cannot be accepted![6]

On the intervention of Klapka and some of his fellow officers, Cavour accepted most of the Hungarian demands; the name of the legion was even changed to "Hungarian Army in Italy." Subsequently Klapka and Ihász proceeded in earnest with recruitment for the army. By July the Hungarian Army in Italy contained five and then eight battalions organized into two brigades, with a total of some thirty-two hundred men.

It could not have been foreseen that the Hungarian Army in Italy would have so short a life-span. Because of the dramatic change in the political situation, it did not even reach the theater of war. Napoleon's actions were dubbed treason in Italy, but according to Jenő Koltay-Kastner this was because the difficulties he faced were not sufficiently appreciated.[7] The armistice of Villafranca unexpectedly ended the war and dashed the hopes of Cavour and Kossuth. The liquidation of the Hungarian unit began. A majority of the soldiers were transferred to the Austrian military headquarters at Pescara starting in September for return to Hungary. An amnesty for the returnees was obtained, under pressure by Kossuth, by Alfonso La Marmora, the Sardinian minister of defense, and they were also excused from any further military service in the Habsburg armed forces.[8] Nonetheless, many Hungarian legionnaires went elsewhere. Approximately a hundred volunteered for the Hungarian legion formed by Garibaldi for his expedition to Sicily against the Bourbon regime.

On July 16, 1860, Garibaldi issued a decree in Palermo establishing a Hungarian legion. By September 30, the combat force of the legion had increased from 51 men to over 200, about equally divided between infantry and light cavalry or hussars. The legion was incorporated into the Second Brigade (under the command of the Hungarian general Nándor Éber) of Garibaldi's Fifteenth Division (under the Hungarian colonel, later general, István Türr). It was surprised by the Bourbon army on the morning of September 15 near Santa Maria Capua Vetere and sustained the attack with great gallantry. A much harder fight somewhat later in the same place has gone down in history as the battle of the Volturno, one of Garibaldi's most brilliant victories. In it the Hungarian legionnaires fought with great gallantry, suffering heavy casualties and earning the praise of their commanders; Garibaldi's order of the day of October 3, 1860, read in part: "It was fine to see the Hungarian veterans move to fire with calm and orderliness of maneuver; their fearless valor made a great contribution to the defeat of the enemy."

In August 1860, Cavour was preparing for the invasion of Marche and Umbria that he considered a necessary response to Garibaldi's campaign in the south. He realized that such a military operation might provoke the renewal of war with Austria and on September 13 called the attention of General La Marmora to this possibility. With a view to encouraging a revolutionary movement in Hungary that might weaken the Habsburg Empire, he resumed contact with Kossuth, Teleki, and Klapka and recommended to them that the Hungarian legion in Italy be reestablished. Immediately following the transfer of power from Garibaldi's command to the royal army in November 1860, Cavour speedily effected the incorporation of Garibaldi's legion into the royal army. Additional recruitment was carried out to strengthen that army.

On November 9, 1860, General Sirtori, the new commander of the Thousand, announced the transfer of command from Garibaldi to himself as follows: "This is the third time that General Garibaldi has entrusted me with the command of the army, and for the third time I hope soon to give it back to the great man whom all of us love as a father, or even the father of a nation." These words suggest the uneasiness of the Piedmontese general. A good number of Garibaldinis found the transfer to the regular army incompatible with Garibaldi's project and consequently left their units, which in the end were practically reduced to officers. The Hungarian legion was an exception, although its numbers were also reduced substantially by the extremely chaotic disciplinary and legal aspects of their transfer and their dispersal into many separate units in different garrisons. The losses were partly compensated for by new enrollments that brought the total membership of the legion in July 1861 to some seven hundred men. The eventual liquidation of the legion came only after its transfer to Piedmont in August 1861.[9]

The unification of Italy under the Kingdom of Savoy and the recognized leadership of Piedmont generated enthusiasm and hope in northern and central Italy. In the south, however, it gave birth to a vast movement of reaction rooted in the cultural differences between North and South. In the provinces south of Rome, a number of strong and well-armed guerrilla bands arose against which ordinary police actions proved inadequate. The strength of these bands, whose members were called "brigands," varied from region to region and from one moment to another. Led by fanatical, cruel, and resolute chiefs and supposedly acting for God, religion, justice, and legitimate thrones, they became a serious threat to the unity of the new kingdom. The government was forced to apply military measures that developed into virtual civil war operations.

It was in this tragic crisis that the Hungarian legion, as a component of the Sardinian army, was now employed. The Hungarians were obliged to participate in the clashes of Montefalcione, Ruvo, Fosse della Neve, Montemilone, Lariano, Praiano, and Amalfi. In June 1861, the "reactionaries" of the province of Avellino issued a secret order of insurrection; in several communes (Montemiletto, Montefusco, Montefalcione) the rebels took over, and the intervention of the military command in Naples was requested. Together with other units, the Hungarian legion (quartered at Nocera de Pagani under Ihász), was ordered to move toward Avellino with a force of some 300 infantry and 120 cavalry. On July 10, along with other units, it attacked Montefalcione and liberated a number of other villages and towns. The efforts of its cavalry, in particular the charge of Montemilone and the clearing of Lariano and Praiano in June 1862, eventually eliminated the resistance groups in that region. Even more important was the liberation of the important coastal city of Amalfi. Major Reinfeld, commander of the battalion involved, was proclaimed an honorary citizen and "patrician" of that city.

Civil wars are usually bloody, cruel, and ruthless, yet the Hungarians were not accused of deeds of unnecessary cruelty. On the contrary, members of the legion were deeply disgusted at being required to fight Italians, whom they felt might be innocent victims of a tradition rather than enemies. This kind of armed struggle could not have been more alien to the Hungarian legionnaires' original goals. Their distasteful mission and other instances of mismanagement of their affairs by the Italian government brought the Hungarian troops to the verge of mutiny. At last, Generals Klapka and Türr had to intervene, recommending the dismissal of the most riotous elements and the transfer of the rest to the north. These recommendations were realized when, in Palermo in July 1862, Garibaldi stirred up the population to an untimely and unprepared campaign against Rome and the Papal State and called on the Hungarians to join him in that expedition. Under the pressure of these new tensions, the coherence of the troops weakened and their numbers diminished.

Nevertheless, the Hungarians—or at least some groups of them—responded to Garibaldi's call. A squadron of hussars quartered at Lavello left its officers during the night and went, fully armed and equipped, to Nocera, where it joined other Hungarian units on August 3, 1862. Another squadron, quartered near Melfi, was officially authorized by the Italian colonel in command to leave Nocera in order to avoid the appearance of a mutiny, and for the same reason the prefect of the Basilicati region gave free rein to the infantry battalion of the legion. These events provoked the furious reaction of the general in command of the military department of Naples, who asked his minister to order the immediate transfer of the legion to Naples. But Garibaldi, with his three thousand volunteers, in spite of King Victor Emmanuel's disapproval and the risk of triggering a war, had already launched his action against Rome.

Strangely, the Italian generals, probably sympathizing with these actions in their hearts, allowed Garibaldi's troops free passage. The troops met with enthusiasm along their way and were even blessed in church by a Catholic priest fearful of the end of the Pope's temporal power. The campaign ended on August 8, when it was stopped by Colonel Pallavicini, commanding two infantry regiments and two battalions of Bersaglieri. Garibaldi himself was wounded in both legs.

Fewer than eight hundred men remained in the legion, and these were disarmed, not without incident, and transported from Nocera to the port of Salerno. From there they were sent to Genoa and thereafter, in a state of semicustody, to the Piedmontese fortress of Alessandria. Thus the Hungarian legion came to an end, a victim of unfair treatment and the requirement of combat for which it had no motivation.

For reasons of foreign policy and good will toward the Hungarian exiles, the Italian government once more planned a reorganization of the Hungarian legion. General Türr was commissioned inspector general and charged with the task. The legion was organized as a brigade composed of infantry, light infantry (*cacciatori*), hussars, and artillery. Within the legion, German and Slav nationals formed a Serbian-Croatian company. The soldiers of the legion were made equal with the military personnel of the Italian army. Italian army regulations were to apply to them, and the minimum length of service was to be one year. These regulations were promulgated in a royal decree on November 9, 1862. Two special commissions were appointed, one to screen personnel and the other, under the presidency of the Italian lieutenant general Pianell (and, though named after him, composed entirely of eight Hungarian officers), to prepare clearly defined norms for the evaluation of titles and years of service and for the regulation of the officers' ranks in the legion. The latter commission completed its task very quickly (January-February 1863), and its decisions were immediately sanctioned by the Italian Ministry of War. The list contained the names of sixty-seven officers; Colonel Károly Földváry was nominated for the command.[10] The uniforms of the Italian army were adopted with modifications involving such traditionally Hungarian features as blue and red colors and braided loops (*vitézkötés*). The various corps were to be deployed in a number of important garrisons in Piedmont.

The new regulations aimed to guarantee the legion's discipline and its correct utilization by ensuring legal protection. All this aimed at stability, which was attained only gradually after a new sequence of restlessness and mutinies. As Vigevano, the careful historian of the Hungarian legion and a member of the general staff's historical office, observed,

> The Hungarian legionnaires were too bored with barracks life, too much imbued with Garibaldian memories and Mazzinian ideas, too much subject to the passions and plans of exiles, too much exposed to outside suggestions of conspiracy and intervention to endure in a state of complete passivity. . . . They were soldiers, of course, but . . . above all they were Hungarians, evidently ready to grasp any hope of return to their homeland and of an immediate solution of the Hungarian problem.[11]

An exile military organization living in a foreign land without realistic hope of engaging in action and returning to its homeland is a contradiction, and the Hungarian legion in Italy was no exception. Rifts, restlessness, and riots were frequent. The ringleaders were purged and the legion once again redeployed in various garrisons of Marche from April 1864 to June 1865. This, however, did not change its basic status and circumstances, and consequently the disorder continued. In October 1864 General Cialdini, commander of the region, recommended that the Ministry of War dissolve the legion. Political necessity overruled military considerations, however, and the legion remained in existence. The Italian government still had an unsolved problem with Austria, and the blood of the Hungarians might still be needed to realize Italian interests.

Obviously, the legion's numbers declined under the pressure of all this turmoil—by December 1863, in contrast to the total of 1,805 the organizational regulation would have permitted, to approximately 650 and by the following year to 600 (a number not at all negligible in view of the fact that the last war had been fought five years earlier). In June 1865 the government decided once again to misuse the legion in a mission against Italian "brigands." It was sent south, to the Abruzzi, where it remained until July 1866. Between June and July 1865, all the units of the legion (with the exception of the mountain artillery battery) were transferred to different garrisons of that region, and in October they were engaged in a series of small, brief, and frequent clashes against the guerrilla bands. These actions, in which the Hungarians demonstrated their best military qualities, continued until June 1866. The satisfaction with the legion's behavior in the field is reflected in two official statements by Lieutenant Griffini (under whose command the units were serving), both expressing appreciation for their zeal, good will, and discipline. Nonetheless, the ugly scenes of the first such campaigns were repeated, and the Hungarians' losses reduced their strength to some 500.

The declaration of war against Austria by King Victor Emmanuel II, ally of the king of Prussia, on June 20, 1866, seemed, finally, to give the legion the mission for which it had been created. This lifted the legionnaires' spirits and aroused new hopes and expectations. In compliance with the urgent request of Lajos Kossuth, the legion was recalled to Piedmont, its name changed to the "Hungarian Auxiliary Legion," the legal protection of its members reaffirmed, and its organization established. Two battalions, a Serbian-Croatian company, and two cavalry squadrons were formed, a total of 1,881 soldiers. This new arrangement was also doomed to a short life.[12] The armistice between Austria and Prussia and the intervention of Napoleon III, followed by the armistice between Austria and Italy on August 12, 1866, and the Treaty of Vienna, put an end to the hostilities, and the Hungarian legion once more was without a raison d'être.

The new balance of power in Europe and the fundamental change in the constitutional status of Hungary convinced the leaders of the Hungarian exiles that their last chance for the liberation of Hungary from Habsburg dependency had been lost, for a long time if not forever. With the conclusion of the Compromise of 1867, it was easy to predict that Kossuth's goals would not be realized. Thus, the very existence of a Hungarian legion in Italy became an anachronism, since from now on its components were to be considered—at least in theory—potential opponents of their fellow countrymen in the fatherland, integrated into the Austro-Hungarian monarchy.

Kossuth, before retiring once more into silence and sorrow, carefully intervened, with a letter to the Italian minister of war on August 20, 1866, in favor of his loyal followers. He asked, in the event of dissolution of the corps, for full Austrian amnesty for its members; their enlistment, if required, into the Italian army without any distinction between prisoners of war, deserters, and émigrés; and a proper bonus plus civilian clothes and free transportation to the localities of their choice for the others. All those officers who could not receive or refused amnesty were to retain the rank they had held in the legion. These requests were fully granted, and the legion was disbanded by a royal decree on January 23, 1867. Before leaving his command, Colonel Földváry deposited the flag of the infantry and the standard of the cavalry at the Royal Armory in Turin. On February 1, 1867, the Hungarian Auxiliary Legion ceased to exist.

In the words of Vigevano, "In the heart of every member of this corps was hidden a romance of love and loneliness, of victories and defeats, of richness and misery, of glorification and discomfort, of pleasure and pain, of struggle and weariness, of dedication and rebellion."[13] In spite of the difficulties I have mentioned, they fully deserved the gratitude of the Italian nation that had welcomed them, in a period of great upheaval, into the ranks of its own army.

Notes

1. Attilio Vigevano, *La legione ungherese in Italia (1859–1867)* (Rome, 1924), pp. 4, 5, 28–33. See also Tivadar Ács, "A magyar legionisták életrajz gyűjteménye," in *Magyarok és a Risorgimento* (Budapest, 1961); F. Bettoni-Cazzago, *Gli italiani nella guerra d'Ungheria, 1848–1849: Storia e documenti* (Milan, 1887); Luigi Chiala, *Politica segreta di Napoleone III e di Cavour in Italia e in Ungheria, 1858–1861* (Turin, 1895); Ernő Hartai, "Az 1859. évi olasz-osztrák háború és az olaszországi magyar légió," *Hadtörténeti Közlemények* 1954, no. 1; Lajos Lukács, *Garibaldi e l'emigrazione ungherese* (Modena, 1965); idem, *A magyar garibaldisták útja Marsalától a Porta Piáig, 1860–1870* (Budapest, 1971).
2. Péter Hanák, "Rapporti storici Italo-Ungheresi verso la metà del secolo XIX," in *Études des délégués hongrois au XXe Congrés Internationale des Sciences Historiques, Rome, 4–11 Septembre 1955* (Rome, 1955), pp. 232 and passim.
3. Chiala, *Politica segreta*, pp. 196–99. See also Vigevano, *La legione ungherese*, pp. 218–91.
4. Lajos Kossuth, *Souvenirs et écrits de mon exil* (Paris, 1880).
5. Vigevano, *La legione ungherese*, pp. 48 ff.
6. Kossuth, *Souvenirs et écrits*, pp. 228–29.
7. Jenő Koltay-Kastner, *L'Ungheria libera nel Risorgimento Italiano* (Rome, 1925); idem, *Il contributo ungherese nella guerra del 1859* (Florence, 1934); idem, *A Kossuth-emigráció Olaszországban* (Budapest, 1960), pp. 158–62.
8. Vigevano, *La legione ungherese*, p. 63; see also the cable of Emperor Napoleon III to King Victor Emmanuel II, dated September 14, 1859.
9. Vigevano, *La legione ungherese*, pp. 95 ff.; 100–106.
10. Ibid., p. 143.

11. Ibid., pp. 160–61.
12. Koltay-Kastner, *A Kossuth-emigráció Olaszországban,* pp. 259–66, 283, 301–2.
13. Vigevano, *La legione ungherese,* p. 215.

Defeat at Solferino: The Nationality Question and the Habsburg Army in the War of 1859

István Deák

The War of 1859 was the first conflict in modern times in which the Habsburg Empire was unequivocally defeated. There had been major setbacks for Austria, of course, during the Prussian wars of the eighteenth century and during the Napoleonic wars, along with the humiliating peace treaties, but after each of these setbacks the empire had rebounded quickly and resumed its struggle against the enemy. Thus, the Prussian wars ended honorably for Austria, and the Napoleonic wars brought a splendid victory. This time there was to be no recovery: Austria's war against Sardinia and France ended in irrevocable defeat and was to be followed by an even greater disaster in the war of 1866 against Prussia. The fact that the Sardinian conflict had been lost by a young and ambitious emperor, who had taken personal charge of the campaign, only increased the magnitude of the tragedy. What is more, the defeat had occurred at a time when Francis Joseph was attempting to create a unitary, centralized, and authoritarian state. The war now made it clear that Austria was in no position to imitate the modern nation-states; if she was to survive at all, it could only be through a series of compromises with the other Great Powers and with at least some of its domestic national movements. True, the empire could have continued the war even after the defeat at Solferino from behind the protective shield of the Quadrilateral, a system of near impregnable fortresses in northern Italy, but the general discouragement was so great that when the French emperor suddenly offered an armistice on fairly generous terms, the Austrians accepted with a sigh of relief.

The explanations which have been offered for the Austrian military defeat are many and diverse. Historians customarily credit such things as (1) the ineptitude of the Austrian leadership from the commander-in-chief, Feldzeugmeister Count Franz (Ferenc) Gyulai, down to the careless, overconfident, dissipated or just plain stupid junior staff officers; (2) the Habsburg army's maniacal insistence on spit and polish, on parade and drill, rather than on modern combat techniques; (3) the insufficient training of the troops, which meant that young recruits were forced to march into the precision fire of the French Guards without having ever fired a live round; (4) the breakdown of transport and supply, which resulted in soldiers' arriving in Italy sick and exhausted and having to storm into battle hungry or with only a bit of cold food in their stomachs; (5) the financial weakness of the empire, which was, incidentally, the major reason for its unpreparedness; (6) the pacifist inclinations of many a cabinet minister, especially the liberal minister of finance, Baron Karl von Bruck; (7) the opposition of Austro-German liberals to the emperor's authoritarian experiment; (8) the hostility of Russia, still wincing from the bitter experience of the Crimean War, and the indifference, verging on hostility, of Prussia and the other German states; (9) the acute discontent of many ethnic groups, particularly the Hungarians and Italians, but also the Poles and Croats, and, last but not least, (10) the alleged apathy, unreliability, and even outright insubordination of many Habsburg soldiers, especially those of Hungarian and Italian nationality.[1] It appears that any one of these causes should have been sufficient to finish off the Austrians.

The causes of the defeat were, of course, interconnected. Some historians have even argued that Austrian tactics were gravely hampered by the fear of internal revolt. The American historian Gunther E. Rothenberg, for example, contends that the High Command was reluctant to introduce the new rifled arms, because this precision weapon would have required open-order tactics, and open-order tactics would have facilitated desertion. So the High Command found it better to do nothing.[2]

My concern is not with the first nine of these explanations or with the ultimate cause of the empire's defeat, but only with the ethnic question in the Habsburg army. In other words, I wish to look at the combat behavior of the two ethnic groups which, at the time, had the weightiest reasons—ten years after the suppression of the Hungarian and the Italian revolutions—to be dissatisfied with Habsburg rule. The presence or absence of national consciousness among the rank and file of 1859, which I assume would find expression in the combat performance of the nationalities, should provide us with an important clue for solving the riddle of nineteenth-century East Central European nationalism.

Those who uphold the thesis of profound ethnic dissatisfaction in the empire note that 156,000 regulars had to be stationed in Hungary during the War of 1859 to collect tax arrears and to keep the population down.[3] Others note that, because of the threat of a French naval assault on the

Adriatic coast and the possible landing of Hungarian and South Slav exiles there, several first-class army divisions had to be diverted to Dalmatia. Had the local population been more reliable, these historians argue, far fewer troops would have been needed to scare off the French fleet.[4]

Even more important, historians point out, several Austrian units were so unreliable that they had to be withdrawn quickly from the theater of operations. Other large units deserted to the enemy in the middle of the fiercest battle, thus dragging the rest of the army down to defeat.

Historians of the 1859 war are usually quite specific in pointing to the army units that performed less well in battle than others: Count Eduard Clam-Gallas's First Army Corps and two Hungarian infantry regiments, the Nineteenth and the Thirty-fourth. The First Army Corps is said to have been the one large unit that had to be withdrawn from the combat zone because of the unreliability and rebelliousness of its Hungarian troops; and the Nineteenth and Thirty-fourth Infantry Regiments are said to have suffered from an extraordinarily high number of desertions on the battlefield.[5] All in all, writes C. A. Macartney, desertion from these and other units reached a total of 15,000 men, six percent of the Austrian effectives in Italy.[6]

Documentary evidence shows the story to be more complex than it was generally assumed. For instance, while it is perfectly true that the First Army Corps consisted mainly of Hungarians and Italians, it is also true that it participated in every major engagement of the war, and it was dissolved, along with another much tried army corps, only after the battle of Solferino on June 24, 1859, that is, after the final battle of the war. Even then, all the regiments of the corps, with the exception of one, continued to serve in Italy.[7] Let us now investigate the behavior of the units making up this army corps.

At the time of the battle of Solferino, the First Army Corps consisted of 20,620 men, including the combat-ready battalions of the Sixteenth, Twenty-ninth, Forty-eighth, and Sixtieth Infantry Regiments, the Second and Fourteenth *Feldjäger* (light infantry) Battalions, the First and Second Battalions of the Banat *Grenzer* (Border) Regiment, and two squadrons of the Twelfth Haller (formerly "Palatinal") Hussars.[8] With the exception of the two *Feldjäger* battalions and the two Croatian Border Guard battalions, all of these units were Italian or Hungarian. The Sixteenth Infantry Regiment was recruited in the province of Venetia, while the others came from Hungary. Significantly, the First Army Corps' Hungarian regiments were generally not recruited from among the national minorities in Hungary: the majority of them were

Hungarian-speaking. Only the Twenty-ninth Thun-Hoenstein Regiment, with its staging (recruiting) area in the Banat, in southeastern Hungary, was of mixed ethnic composition: Germans, Hungarians, and Serbs. The regiment suffered heavy losses at Solferino, and its officers and men were awarded an extraordinary number of medals for gallantry.[9] The Forty-eighth Erzherzog Ernst and the Sixtieth Gustav Prinz von Wasa Infantry Regiments were quintessentially Hungarian, the first with its staging area around Nagykanizsa in Zala County, and the second with its staging area around Eger in north-central Hungary. The two regiments had long and colorful histories.

As was almost always the rule among Hungarian regiments in 1848–49, the First and Second Line Battalions (*Linienbataillone*) of the Erzherzog Ernst Infantry Regiment fought for the emperor under Radetzky in Italy, while the Third or Reserve Battalion of the same regiments fought against the emperor in Hungary. This was not surprising in view of the fact that early in 1848 the line battalions of most Habsburg regiments had either been dispatched to or were already stationed in northern Italy; on the other hand, the reserve or third battalions of the Hungarian regiments had fallen under the authority of the new, constitutional Hungarian government. As their regimental history notes with some pride, every unit of the Erzherzog Ernst Regiment fought well in 1848–49, no matter on which side it served. In 1859, all the combat-ready units of the regiment, including trained reserves, were thrown into battle in Italy. Its wartime casualties, amounting to 62 killed, 347 wounded, 235 taken prisoner, and 161 missing, were no embarrassment to the regiment, especially since the Erzherzog Ernst Regiment stood in the very center of the fighting at Solferino, where losses and general confusion were the greatest. The two Gold, twenty-seven Silver First Class (Large Silver) and fifty-two Silver Second Class (Small Silver) medals awarded to the rank and file of the regiment represented one of the highest numbers, proportionately, awarded to any regiment. Those decorated, almost without exception, had Hungarian names. It is true, however, that of the 235 taken prisoner, at least 210 subsequently joined the Hungarian legion constituted behind the Franco-Sardinian lines.[10]

The Sixtieth or Wasa was one of the very few infantry regiments which had fought almost entirely on the Hungarian side in 1848–49. This was not solely due to the circumstance that the entire regiment was present in Hungary early in 1848: in a memorable incident, during the Croatian invasion of Hungary, in September 1848, the officers of the regiment's first battalion had actually voted in favor of defending the new Hungarian regime.

Having thereby dishonored itself, from the Habsburg point of view, the Wasa Regiment was punished after 1848–49 by being completely reorganized, a bad prospect for the regiment's role in the turmoil of 1859, when there was some real trouble with the Wasa. Attached to the First Army Corps, the Wasa suffered greatly at Magenta on June 4, where "it fell into total confusion," allegedly because of the contradictory orders it had received.

The confusion was repeated at the Battle of Solferino, where the enemy drove the Wasa, along with others, into the Castell, a militarily worthless structure from which escape was almost impossible. In the general stampede, the commander of the regiment, Colonel János Máriássy, was wounded and captured by the French. During the subsequent withdrawal, soldiers of the Wasa fired on each other in the dark. The regiment suffered heavy losses at Solferino, including 56 killed, 249 wounded and 548 missing. Of the last group, 311 returned from the Franco-Sardinian captivity after the war. According to another document, at least 368 men joined Kossuth's Hungarian legion while in captivity. "The accomplishments of the Regiment were meager," their regimental historian notes sadly, and he adds: "The Regiment did not fully do its duty" in the War of 1859. For this, the historian blames the regiment's many untrained recruits and the fact that the officers of the regiment spoke no Hungarian. In this politically unreliable unit, the basic principle of the Habsburg army was neglected, namely, that the officers and the NCO's be able to communicate with the men not only in German but also in the regimental language.[11]

Let us continue the examination of the First Army Corps. Its Sixteenth Baron Wernhardt (formerly Zanini) Regiment hailed from Treviso, and thus its rank and file were Italian. Back in 1848, the first two battalions of the Sixteenth Regiment were stationed in Hungary and ended up playing a rather controversial role there. Although obliged by the so-called April Laws to swear loyalty to the new Hungarian government and generally sympathetic to the Hungarian cause, the Sixteenth Regiment seemed to have had only one desire: to be allowed to go home. When the war in Hungary made this impossible, some units of the Sixteenth Regiment went over to the Austrians, as, for instance, at the Battle of Kápolna in February 1849; other units attempted to stay neutral in the war between Austria and Hungary, as did the battalion garrisoned in the fortress of Eszék. Meanwhile, the Third Battalion and the Grenadier Battalion of the Sixteenth Regiment, both stationed in northern Italy, either voluntarily joined the Venetian revolution or were handed over to the new Venetian Republic of Daniele Manin under a curious agreement concluded between the Venetians and Austria.

With such a historical background, it would have been quite logical for the Sixteenth Regiment not to want to fight against their Italian compatriots in 1859. Yet the opposite happened. The regiment behaved with courage at Solferino, for which its rank and file were decorated with an extraordinary number of medals. Those cited for gallantry almost all had Italian names.[12] As we shall try to demonstrate later, in the matter of loyalty there was a considerable difference between Lombard and Venetian units in 1859. If was as if the Lombard regiments had had advance intelligence of their postwar cession to Sardinia-Italy, while the Venetians knew that they would have to wait until 1866.

All in all, then, Clam-Gallas's First Army Corps was not one of the best of the Austrian campaign. What matters, however, is that contrary to historical lore, the army corps *was* there and that it performed creditably.

The story is not very different with regard to the two commonly indicted infantry regiments, the Nineteenth and the Thirty-fourth. Rather than deserting en masse, the soldiers of the Nineteenth Kronprinz Rudolf (until 1858 called Schwarzenberg) and the Thirty-fourth Wilhelm Prinz von Preussen Regiments were killed en masse in northern Italy. One wonders why the usually very accurate Wilhelm Gründorf von Zebegény, himself a participant in the war, and others after him insisted on the fundamental disloyalty of these two regiments. According to Gründorf, the two regiments suffered 1,200 missing at Solferino, which prompted the commander of the Prinz von Preussen Regiment, Colonel Sándor Benedek (not to be confused with Lajos Benedek, commander-in-chief in 1866), to tell his troops that they deserved to be decimated for cowardice.[13] Documentary evidence does not support Gründorf's contentions.

The Nineteenth or Kronprinz Rudolf Regiment was from the area of Győr, and the great majority of its conscripts were therefore Hungarian. In 1848–49, the regiment's first, second, and grenadier battalions fought for the Austrians in northern Italy; its third battalion fought against the Austrians in Hungary. In 1859, all the combat units of the regiment were incorporated into the Ninth Army Corps and suffered substantial losses in the war. Casualties at Solferino numbered 32 killed, 183 wounded, but only 64 missing. Of the latter, 31 returned from service in the Hungarian legion after the war.

As for the Thirty-fourth or Prinz von Preussen Regiment, with a staging area at Kassa, it consisted of Hungarians, Slovaks, Ruthenians, and presumably some Germans and Jews. In 1848–49 the entire regiment fought on the Hungarian side, except for its grenadier battalion, which distinguished itself under the imperial flag in northern Italy.

Here, too, was a regiment that might well have been expected to behave erratically in the war of 1859, yet the opposite seems to have been the case. The regimental historian of the Thirty-fourth Regiment probably exaggerates when he writes that the regiment stormed into battle at Solferino shouting "Éljen a király!" (Long Live the King!), but regimental casualty statistics speak clearly enough.

Of the Regiment's 703 casualties at Solferino, only 271 represented missing soldiers, a low figure considering that the battle was lost and that the Austrians listed as missing everyone who could not be positively identified as dead.[14]

It is clear that the units singled out by historians were not significantly different from the others. Consequently, they could not have been a major cause of defeat. What remains to be answered is whether ethnic discontent existed in the army as a whole, and if so, how much it influenced the conduct of operations. This is the question which the second part of the essay will attempt to address.

In 1848–49 approximately one out of every ten Habsburg army officers and one out of every ten conscript soldiers served on the rebel Hungarian or Italian side. Many of these military rebels in the Kossuth, Manin, or Charles Albert camp were there not by choice, but by the force of circumstance. Still, there were enough volunteers to combat the emperor-king's forces to provoke the greatest internal crisis in Habsburg army history.

Unfortunately for historiography, the Austrian High Command did not even attempt to analyze the causes of the crisis after the war; it was content to punish the guilty and to reorganize the treasonous regiments. But had there been such an analysis, the emperor and his generals would probably have been quite satisfied with its outcome. Aside from the Russian army, it was undoubtedly the career officer corps as well as the monarch's German and Slavic peasant soldiers who had saved the monarchy. The army overcame its great crisis, and by 1850 was at the peak of its power and prestige. By quickly and efficiently mobilizing an army of half a million men, Austria was able to force Prussia into a political surrender in that same year.[15] Then, gradually, everything went wrong. Unlike the Prussian army, the Austrian army was not modernized, chiefly because of the shortage of funds. Far too much money was wasted on a useless mobilization during the Crimean War (in 1855, the military budget amounted to 257 million gulden), and then the debt service forced the depreciation of the paper currency and with it substantial military budget cuts. By 1858 defense expenditure was down to 122 million, meaning that of all the great powers, Austria spent proportionally the least on her soldiers.[16]

In July 1858, Napoleon III and Cavour met secretly at Plombières in France and plotted how to provoke Austria into war. Misled by the optimism of his civilian ministers, especially Foreign Minister Count Karl Buol, Francis Joseph hesitated to mobilize at first. When he finally sent his ultimatum to Sardinia, on April 19, 1858, his army was far from being ready. Francis Joseph refused to believe that neither England, nor Russia, nor the German states would rush to his aid. The Sardinians rejected his ultimatum, of course, and on April 26 Austria was at war with both Sardinia and France. There followed a ridiculously cautious campaign by Commander-in-Chief Gyulai; then the battle of Magenta on June 4, which Gyulai could have turned into a victory, but which he used rather as an excuse for the evacuation of most of Lombardy. On June 17, Francis Joseph assumed personal command and continued the blunders of Gyulai. On June 24, at Solferino, the war was lost. Then came a relatively favorable preliminary peace at Villafranca on July 11, and a less favorable treaty at Zurich on November 10. In the end, Lombardy was lost but not the Quadrilateral or Venetia.

In the war almost one million Austrians had been put into uniform, but owing to limited transportation facilities, only about a third of them were moved to Italy. Still, at Solferino, 133,000 faced an only slightly larger Franco-Sardinian army. In the same battle, the Austrian artillery had 413 guns against the enemy's 370, but the French rifled cannon was definitely superior. Earlier, at Magenta, the Austrians had had a net preponderance in men, and an overwhelming superiority in guns and in cavalry.[17]

The Austrian High Command had gone to war expecting the worst from some of its nationalities. As early as February 19, 1859, First Adjutant General Count Karl Ludwig Grünne, the real head of the army, demanded that, in case of mobilization, the fourth battalions of the nine Italian infantry regiments, and all the soldiers on furlough from these regiments, as well as those from other units which received their recruits from northern Italy, be immediately removed from that area. Otherwise, he argued, these troops would be lost to the enemy immediately.[18] The civilian ministers, especially Buol and Minister of Interior Baron Alexander von Bach, who had long insisted that peace not be endangered by preparations for war, became by April very gloomy and urged the military to assume full responsibility. On April 27, Buol declared that Austria had been abandoned by all, and must fall back on itself, as it had done under Maria Theresa. In his reply, Grünne stated angrily that the situation was completely different now, as the Hungarians were far less loyal than they had been in 1740.[19] The individual who distrusted the Hungarians most was Archduke Albrecht, Commander of the Third Army Corps and of the Hungarian *General-Kommando*. He wrote on June 7, 1859, that as soon as the fifth depot battalions of the Hungarian regiments were formed, and at least half equipped, they should be removed from Hungary. Otherwise, unfavorable news from the war might cause them to join an eventual Hungarian revolt. Nor, he continued, should these battalions be sent to Italy but, rather, to some other part of the monarchy. Albrecht held the Transylvanian regiments to be more reliable because of the presence of Saxons and Romanians in their midst.[20]

Albrecht's insistence that the Hungarian reservists be removed from Hungary and replaced with reservists from other provinces was one of the rare concrete instances of the monarchy's alleged policy of "divide and rule." Actually, there really was no such policy, and troops were used whenever needed, regardless of their nationality. Even in the above-mentioned case, Albrecht's wish could not be fulfilled, mainly because of the rapid conclusion of the war. The Archduke had, incidentally, also warned against sending Italian troops to Hungary, where, he feared, they might join an eventual revolution.[21]

Not everyone shared Albrecht's pessimism with regard to the Hungarians and Italians. In a long report prepared for the emperor on March 29, 1859, on the morale and quality of the troops, Feldmarschalleutnant Karl Baron Schlitter, Count Grünne's adjutant, judged the army's spirit to be generally excellent. In his review of the infantry, Schlitter listed thirteen regiments as especially valuable, among them the Transylvanian Thirty-first and the Hungarian Thirty-Seventh and Sixtieth (Wasa!) Regiments. Schlitter found fault only with the elite Fourth Deutschmeister Regiment and with the Fifty-eighth Galician Infantry Regiment. The latter included 250 Jews who, in Schlitter's enlightened opinion, were "von Haus aus schlecht." In the cavalry, Schlitter singled out the hussars, all of whom were from Hungary, for special praise, but he called the Eleventh Württemberg Hussars, who were from the Banat, unmanageable because the rank and file spoke five different languages. Schlitter suggested that the number of Serbs and Romanians in the regiment be reduced because "these people have no talent for cavalry service."

Schlitter considered only two Jäger battalions of Dalmatian origin to be politically unreliable, and his complaint was generally far more with the training of the officers than with the quality of the troops. He particularly bemoaned the grave lack of "*Sprachtalent*" among the career officers.[22]

Historical evidence has proven Schlitter more correct than Grünne or

Albrecht, at least with regard to the Hungarians. In the voluminous documentary collection of the Austrian War Archive, there seems to be no evidence of rebellion or mass desertion by Hungarian troops. Nor did the population revolt in Hungary.

Today it is very difficult to explain the disciplined behavior of the Hungarian soldiers in the Italian war: one can only suggest such reasons as fear of punishment, the realization of distance from home, or political ignorance. Contemporary military observers argue that a few warm words pronounced in their mother tongue worked wonders with the Hungarian soldiers. Gründorf writes that one could make the Hungarians "bring the Devil back from Hell" by addressing them in their own language, sometimes which, however, hardly ever happened.[23] And Feldmarschalleutnant (later Feldzeugmeister) Ludwig (Lajos) Ritter von Benedek, commander of the Eighth Army Corps, it was reported, turned his part of the battle of Solferino into a victory when he stopped the retreat of his troops at San Martino by riding up to the Thirty-ninth Dom Miguel Regiment and crying: "Rajta vitézek—én is magyar vagyok!" [Forward, brave soldiers!—I am also a Hungarian!] This allegedly moved the Miguels to turn around and storm forward like lions.[24]

The situation was quite different with the Italian soldiers of the Habsburg army, especially the Lombards. Reports about the unreliability of certain Italian units had been arriving sporadically in Vienna well before the outbreak of hostilities. Whether these reports were more numerous than could normally have been expected, and whether they were true, is difficult to say. There were reports, for example, that some Italians of the Fifty-fifth Bianchi Regiment walked down the street of Graz arm in arm with Italian students, all singing "Corriamo conscritti Italia salvar!" [Let us run, conscripts, to save Italy!].[25] Likewise, when soldiers of the Forty-fifth Erzherzog Sigismund Regiment marched across the city of Görz (Goricia) near Trieste, they were said to have shouted "Evviva l'Italia, evviva il Re Vittore Emanuele!"[26] It is worth noting, though, that in his follow-up report, the military governor of Trieste firmly denied that this had taken place, arguing that, if anything had happened at all, it had been the work of a few drunks. The governor claimed to have witnessed personally the excellent spirit of the Forty-fifth Regiment, as well as of the Twenty-sixth Grossfürst Michael Regiment.[27] Another, rather typical complaint came from the commune of Libschitz in Bohemia, where 67 men of the Venetian Sixteenth Regiment (of the First Army Corps fame!) were said to have declared that, in case of a war, they would not fight, but rather hold their rifles "bei Fuss" [at rest]. Since the denunciation came from a single local official in retirement, and since the soldiers had allegedly communicated with him "partly in German and partly in sign language," His Imperial-Royal Majesty's *Militärkanzlei* wisely decided to put the file "ad acta."[28] True to the traditions of the Austrian bureaucracy, this momentous denunciation by former Councilman Keiř traveled from the commune of Libschitz to the Viceregal Council in Prague, from there to Feldmarschalleutnant Baron Menzinger of the Bohemian *General-Kommando*, and thence to the Military Chancellery in Vienna, where it was finally set aside. In this case, though, Francis Joseph did not make a personal note on the report, as he did with so many others.

After the war had begun in earnest, desertions increased as well. By June it had become quite customary for Italian battalions on the march to report the nightly disappearance of scores of soldiers, including a handful of NCO's. Thus, on June 4, the Thirteenth Infantry Regiment (recruiting area: Padua) reported ten soldiers missing; two days later the Regiment reported 40 more deserters.[29] On the night of June 8, the Forty-third Infantry Regiment lost 11 men who absconded with all their equipment; between June 9 and 13, the regiment lost another 27 men.[30] On June 18, the Commander of the Forty-fifth Regiment reported "a never ending stream of desertions" from his unit, "so far a total of 236 men."[31] The reports stated repeatedly that the deserters were extremely difficult to catch because they were hiding out with friends and relatives: "in Lombardy no one wants to help the authorities." On June 19, the Commander of the Twenty-sixth Regiment reported, in addition to the disappearance of 80 men, an attempted mutiny by two whole companies.[32] Italian Jäger battalions in Dalmatia must have been particularly unruly, and the commander of the coastline, Feldmarschalleutnant Nagy, clamored for their removal into the hinterland. The request was rejected by Archduke Albrecht with the argument that he had "even more Italians."[33]

The hunting down of deserters brought only meager results. During the war the death penalty was applied only in such units where martial law (*Standrecht*) had been specifically proclaimed, which meant a small fraction of the army. Before the war, insubordination was punished by imprisonment, assignment to disciplinary companies, or caning. Thus, on February 3, 1859, Gyulai reported to Grünne that a mutineer by the name of Luigi Fabretto from the Twenty-second Infantry Regiment had been sentenced to 15 months in irons, with one day a week on bread and water. Three of his accomplices from the Erzherzog Sigismund Infantry Regiment were each given "20 *Stockhiebe*" (20 strokes with the cane).[34] After the outbreak of the war, deserters were executed, but there were probably no more than a few dozen such executions. For example, on

July 1, the High Command was told of nine Italian deserters from the Alemann and Michael regiments whom the military gendarmes had caught, and who had been duly court-martialled and put to death with "lead and powder."[35] On July 30, Colonel—later Major-General— Count Leopold Gondrecourt (subsequently Crown Prince Rudolph's near-sadistic tutor) reported the execution of one Giuseppe Casotto of the Seventeenth Company of the Thirteenth Prinz Hohenlohe-Langenburg Infantry Regiment. Casotto had fled from Tyrol to Bavaria, had shot and wounded a Bavarian border guard, and was then returned to Austria and shot on July 16 in "semi-secrecy, so as to prevent Casotto from playing the role of a public martyr."[36] The execution must have been one of the last ones of the war, as by mid-July the *Standrecht* had been cancelled,[37] and subsequently all deserters and mutineers were pardoned. In any case, all Lombard soldiers had to be turned over to Sardinia in accordance with the preliminary peace treaty.

What all this shows is that the generals viewed the majority of the Lombard soldiers, and perhaps a minority of the Venetians, as unreliable. It shows also that hundreds and perhaps even as many as a few thousand Italians actually did desert. This, however, could have had but a minor effect on the Austrian war effort.

There remains to be told the curious history of the Hungarian legion, one that testifies more to the difficult life of little men caught up in a historical turmoil than to the growing national consciousness of the Hungarian peasant soldiers.

The Kossuth emigration had become both disillusioned and contentious by the late 1850s. Then, suddenly, its hopes were lifted with the news of the coming Franco-Sardinian war against the Habsburgs. On May 5, 1859, Kossuth met with Napoleon III, offered him assistance in securing the benevolent neutrality of Great Britain in the war, and promised a Hungarian national uprising, though only if the French were to land on the Adriatic coast. Encouraged by his audience with the French emperor, Kossuth, along with Count László Teleki and General György Klapka, formed a "Hungarian National Directorate" the next day. The Directorate, with its seat in Genoa, cultivated fruitful contacts with Romania and Serbia, agreeing to help these countries achieve their national aims, acknowledging Transylvania's right to decide her own future, and proclaiming a Romanian, Serbian, and Hungarian confederation as a goal for all East Central European revolutionaries. All these were laudable ideas, but in Hungary the political leadership had already given up on complete independence; nor was it willing to grant self-government to the nationalities in Hungary or to allow Transylvania to secede and join another country.

On May 20, Klapka and General Mór Perczel, another general of 1848–49 fame, issued a manifesto to the Hungarian soldiers in Italy, urging them to desert and join a soon-to-be-formed Hungarian legion. The manifesto offered immediate promotion to every deserter, as well as an unspecified gift, but only handful of Hungarian soldiers were able to respond to the call.[38] On June 6, the legion numbered 120 men; a week later there were 300, mostly old-time émigrés. Then the prisoners of war began to pour in, and the situation changed remarkably. At the order of the French High Command, every Hungarian prisoner of war was to be transferred to the legion, but the French did not quite know how to identify a Hungarian. Their ultimate solution was based on a very simple criterion: all those who wore Hungarian-style "pantalons collants" [tight pants] were to be considered Hungarian. Reality, however, was more complicated. Colonel Dániel Ihász, first commander of the legion, wrote to Kossuth on June 6: "The Austrians had craftily mixed the different nationalities together. As a result, there are masses of non-Hungarians in the Hungarian regiments, all wearing tight pants and laced boots. These people are sent to us as well." On the other hand, Ihász wrote,[39] "Hungarians serving in non-Hungarian regiments are prevented from joining the Legion."[40]

Actually, the Austrians had not deliberately shuffled the troops and the uniforms: because over one-half of Hungary's population was of non-Hungarian nationality, the Hungarian regiments were likewise multinational. Even some of the Croatian regiments traditionally wore Hungarian-style uniforms.

The continuous arrival of prisoners of war caused the legion to grow to 4,000 by July 4, but it still had seen no action. Then came Villafranca, and with it the end of Hungarian revolutionary hopes.

The preliminary peace treaty guaranteed a complete amnesty and an immediate discharge to all the NCO's and conscripts of the Habsburg army who had joined the Hungarian legion. But negotiations for their return dragged on, and the discouraged legionnaires began to yearn for home. When, on September 12, Colonel Miklós Nemeskéri Kiss, another commander of the legion, complained to Kossuth that 160 of his soldiers had already deserted,[41] it was decided to disband the legion. At first, the Hungarian émigré leaders were greatly concerned whether the Austrians could be trusted,[42] but, as it turned out quickly, Francis Joseph firmly intended to keep his promise of a complete amnesty. Soon indignant letters began to be sent to headquarters by local Austrian commanders about the arrival of former Hungarian prisoners of war "wearing conspicuous, well-tailored, dark blue or light blue [i.e., Sardinian army] overcoats, or Piedmontese civilian outfits of Attila-like [i.e., Hungarian] style."[43] This, the generals complained, might create an unwanted sensation at home. Moreover, many of the former legionnaires belonged to the classes of 1857 and 1858, which meant that they had been slated to remain on active duty. By discharging them, the army was favoring them over the loyal recruits. Finally, several of the returnees had been given officers' commissions in the Hungarian legion. "Some of them arrived with 800 gold francs in their pockets, which, they claim, was a gift from His Majesty the King of Piedmont." Clearly, the Habsburg generals argued, the money was for anti-Austrian propaganda purposes.[44]

In the end all of the former legionnaires were discharged and sent home. Those whom the army questioned before their release stated that they had been captured in the heat of battle and subsequently impressed into the legion.[45] Such depositions were of course nearly worthless. What these events showed was that, while there must have been many genuine volunteers in the Hungarian legion, and while thousands of Hungarian émigrés fought for Garibaldi later on, the majority of the 1859 conscripts were simple victims of events beyond their control.

Why do soldiers fight? Why and when do they desert? What is the proportion of defectors among prisoners of war? At what point is it honorable to surrender? What is the difference between rational behavior and cowardice? Between heroism and recklessness?

The Austrian army in Italy did its duty. Its soldiers died by the thousands, because they knew no better or because they felt that the monarchy was worth defending. The evidence does not prove the charge of massive insubordination by the Hungarian soldiers; the insubordination of a significant part of the Italians was a reality, but that is easily understood if one considers that Lombardy was never an integral part of the monarchy, and that even the simplest soldier could guess, by 1859, that the empire would not be able to hold on to that province.

The nationality question did indeed exist in the Habsburg army, but it affected only a segment of the Italian regiments. Even if we assume that one half of all the Italians were in a rebellious mood, this means that only one half of nine infantry regiments out of a total of 62 line infantry regiments were unreliable, amounting to only about seven percent of the total effectives. The situation was rather similar in the 25 *Jäger* battalions, but quite different in the artillery, from which there were almost no defections, and in the 12 border guard regiments, which contained almost no Italians. About the cavalry we know little, as the monarchy's 40 cavalry regiments played only a very secondary role in 1859. All in all, then, it is safe to conclude that it was not because of ethnic discontent in the military that Austria lost the war. The latter was brought about by a hesitant leadership, both civilian and military which was reluctant to accept war, and did not expect victory. The war was fought by an ill-led and ill-trained army against an enemy which was, particularly in the case of the French, superior in leadership, experience, and weaponry. Political opposition in Hungary also weakened the war effort, although to what extent is not easy to say.

Undoubtedly, it was the career soldiers, officers and NCO's, who kept the army—and thus the empire—together in 1848–49 and in 1859. The professional officer corps,[46] probably about 15,000 strong in 1859, was a state within a state, a society within a society. To a large extent of non-"Austrian" origin (Gunther E. Rothenberg writes that 52 percent of the officer corps was recruited from outside the country, mainly from Germany[47]), the officer corps included many Englishmen, Irishmen, Walloons, Frenchmen, Spaniards, and, of course, Germans in its ranks. Of those who had been born in the monarchy, a large proportion consisted of German settlers in Hungary and Transylvania, as well as Czechs and Croats. Socially, the infantry officer was more often than not the son of an NCO, a craftsman, a petty clerk, or a farmer. Artillery officers tended to come from the middle classes, and only the cavalry included a large number of officers of aristocratic origin. Most officers lived in garrison towns, isolated by their poverty, their peculiar cultural and social heritage, their inability to master the local language, and their unwillingness to embrace the particularist nationalism of the local middle class. It is a little-known fact that the officers, the pride of the monarch and the monarchy, were all but unacceptable as marriage partners among the educated classes. On the other hand, they were forbidden to marry below their rank.

The peculiar situation and isolation of the officer corps was characteristic of the last hundred years of the monarchy. The revolution of 1848–49 proved to be a traumatic experience, catching up many officers in its legal and political web. Only a small part of the so-called rebel or revolutionary officers intentionally opposed the emperor-king in the name of some revolutionary ideology. This is not to cast doubt on the patriotic fervor of the nearly 200,000 Hungarians who took up arms in the War of Independence. It is only to say that the 1,000-plus career officers who led the Hungarian *honvéd* army were probably the least radical members of the Hungarian army.

In 1859, there could be no question of overlapping or conflicting authorities and loyalties. The Hungarian and Italian nationalists were located outside the monarchy, and their appeals had no noticeable effect on the officers.

The officer's fatherland was the regiment: it was his true nationality. In the words of the great Austrian novelist, Joseph Roth: "The old Imperial and Royal Army had its own brand of patriotism, as well as a regional patriotism, a regimental and battalion patriotism."[48] It is no coincidence that regimental names and numbers so often figure in historical accounts. Boasting of a great historical tradition, even if there happened to be none, the regiment bore its name and regimental colors with enormous pride. The officers of each regiment engaged in a kind of sporting competition with each other, even on the battlefield. At Magenta and Solferino, the junior officers marched to their deaths with dignity and pride, and their German, Czech, Hungarian, Croatian, or Romanian rank and file marched behind them with little complaint.[49]

High Military Ranks and Commands in the Habsburg Monarchy

Rank	Abbreviation	U.S. Equivalent	Command
Feldmarschall	FM	General of the Army	Rare rank. Given to such successful generals as Radetzky
General der Infanterie General der Kavallerie Feldzeugmeister	GdI GdK FZM	General or Lt. General	Army (e.g. FZM Count Gyulai was commander of the 2. Army in Italy)
Feldmarschalleutnant	FML	Major General	Army Corps or Division (e.g., FML Clam-Gallas was in command of the I. Army Corps. Both his divisional commanders were also FML's)
Generalmajor	GM	Brigadier General	Brigade (e.g., GM Hoditz was commander of one of the 4 Brigades in the I. Army Corps)
Oberst	O	Colonel	Regiment
Oberstleutnant	OL	Lt. Colonel	Independent Battalion (Jäger, Grenadier)
Major	M	Major	Battalion

A peacetime regiment consisted of three (active) battalions, a wartime regiment of four field and one depot battalion. The January 25, 1857 "Organisations-Statut" of the Army set the peacetime strength of an infantry regiment at 2830 men, the wartime strength at 6886 men. See Alphons Freiherr von Wrede, *Geschichte der K. und K. Wehrmacht*, 5 vols. (Vienna: L. W. Seidel and Sohn, 1898), vol. I, p. 51n.

DEFEAT AT SOLFERINO

Notes

1. For characteristic enumerations of the many causes of Austrian defeat in 1859, see Egon Cesar Conte Corti, *Mensch und Herrscher: Wege und Schicksale Kaiser Franz Josephs I zwischen Thronbesteigung und Berliner Kongress* (Graz-Vienna-Altötting: Styria, 1952), pp. 229–35; Heinrich Friedjung, *Der Kampf um die Vorherrschaft in Deutschland 1859 bis 1866*, 2 vols. (Stuttgart: Cotta'sche Buchhandlung, 1898), 1: 29–30; Wilhelm Ritter Gründorf von Zebegény, *Memoiren—eines österreichischen Generalstäblers, 1832–1866* (Stuttgart: Robert Lutz, 1913), pp. 139–52; C. A. Macartney, *The Habsburg Empire, 1790–1918* (New York: Macmillan, 1969), pp. 485–99; Oskar Regele, *Feldzeugmeister Benedek: Der Weg nach Königgrärtz* (Vienna-Munich: Verlag Herold, 1960), pp. 120–94; Gunther E. Rothenberg, *The Army of Francis Joseph* (West Lafayette, Ind.: Purdue University Press, 1976), pp. 54–55; W. Rüstow, *Der italienische Krieg 1859* (Zurich: Friedrich Schultess, 1859), esp. pp. 329–37 (note that Rüstow gives only military reasons for the defeat); E. v. Steinitz, "Magenta und Solferino," *Militärwissenschaftliche Mitteilungen* 60 (1929): 476–87; finally, K v. Land, *Ursachen der Misserfolge der österreichischen Armee in den Feldzügen 1859 und 1866* (Vienna: L. W. Seidel und Sohn, 1912).
2. Gunther E. Rothenberg, *The Military Border in Croatia, 1740–1881* (Chicago: University of Chicago Press, 1966), p. 161.
3. Macartney, *The Habsburg Empire*, p. 487.
4. On the Dalmatian coastal defenses, see Rothenberg, *The Military Border*, pp. 162–63.
5. See, for instance, Friedjung, *Der Kampf*, 1: 29; Gründorf, *Memorien*, pp. 144–45; and Rothenberg, *The Army of Francis Joseph*, pp. 54–55.
6. Macartney, *The Habsburg Empire*, p. 493.
7. The activities of the First Army Corps at Magenta on June 4 and at Solferino on June 24 are described in, among others, Rüstow, *Die italienische Krieg*, pp. 209–36 and 263–37, and Karl Edler von Prybila, *Geschichte der Kriege des k.u.k. Wehrmachts von 1848–1898* (Graz: Rudolf Brzezowsky und Söhne, 1899), pp. 334 and passim. An Austrian "Ordre de Bataille," signed by FZM Hess at Verona on June 28, 1859, no longer lists the First Army Corps as being in Italy; one finds, however, almost all of its regiments incorporated in the Eighth Army Corps or garrisoned at Verona. The Sixteenth Wernhardt Regiment of the First Army Corps and another Italian regiment, the Forty-fifth Erzherzog Sigismund, were the only regiments sent after Solferino. See Kriegsarchiv, Vienna, Kriegministerium Präsidialbüro 1859 (hereafter KM Präs. 1859), no. 2751.
8. See the table in Rüstow, *Der italienische Krieg*, p. 408.
9. See Major Alfons Freiherr von Wrede, *Geschichte der k. und k. Wehrmacht*, 5 vols. (Vienna: L. W. Seidel und Sohn, 1898), 1: 323–29, and Rudolf von Hödl, *Geschichte des k.u.k. Infanterieregiments Nr. 29* (Temesvár, 1906), pp. 402 ff.
10. On the Forty-eighth Ernst Regiment, see Wrede, *Geschichte* 1: 452–57, and Alexander Hold, *Geschichte des k.k. 48. Infanterie-Regimentes von seiner*

Errichtung im Jahre 1798 an (Vienna, 1875), pp. 288, 363, and passim. On the prisoners of war who joined the Hungarian legion and who ultimately returned to Hungary, see the report of the "III. Armee und Landes-General-Kommando für Ungarn," Ofen [Buda], October 28, 1859, KM Prás, 1859, no. 3777.

11. On the Sixtieth Wasa Regiment, see Wrede, *Geschichte* 1: 538–42, and Coloman Rupprecht von Virtsolog, *Geschichte des k.k. 60. Linien-Infanterie-Regiments, gegenwärtig Gustav Prinz von Wasa* (Vienna, 1871), pp. 418–64. The particular quotations are on p. 453. On the Wasa incident in September 1848, see Istvan Deak, *The Lawful Revolution: Louis Kossuth and the Hungarians, 1848–1849* (New York: Columbia University, 1979), p. 165. Statistical data on Wasa soldiers back from the Hungarian legion are to be found in KM Präs. 1859, no. 3777.

12. On the Sixteenth Regiment, see Wrede, *Geschichte,* 1: 218 ff. Also Karl Sirowy, *Kurze Geschichte des . . . Infanterie-Regimentes . . . Nr. 16* (Zagreb, 1903), pp. 12–15. On the curious history of the Sixteenth Zanini in 1848–1849, see, among others, Deak, *The Lawful Revolution,* pp. 193 and 249.

13. Gründorf, *Memoiren,* pp. 144–45.

14. On the Nineteenth and the Thirty-fourth Regiments, see Wrede, *Geschichte,* 1: 249–55, and 359–65. Also Viktor Weissenbacher, *Geschichte des k.u.k. Infanterie Regimentes Nr. 19 . . . von der Errichtung in 1734 bis 1896,* 2 vols. (Vienna, 1896), 2: 548–49 and 596–612, and Julius Kreipner, *Geschichte des k. und k. Infanterie-Regimentes Nr. 34 für immerwährende Zeiten Wilhelm I . . . von Preussen, 1733–1900* Kassa, 1900), pp. 568 ff. and 612–30. On Hungarian legionnaires originating from the Nineteenth Infantry Regiment, see KM Präs. 1859, no. 3777. The same document shows no one from the Thirty-fourth Regiment having returned from the Hungarian legion after the war.

15. Rothenberg, *The Army of Francis Joseph,* pp. 48–49.

16. Macartney, *The Habsburg Empire,* p. 492, and Rothenberg, *The Army of Francis Joseph,* pp. 38–52.

17. Regele, *Felzeugmeister Benedek,* p. 143, and Corti, *Mensch und Herrscher,* p. 229. Prybila's figures (*Geschichte,* p. 364) differ somewhat from those of Regele and Corti.

18. Minister-Conferenz-Protokolle dem Feldzug 1859 betreffend, Conference on February 19, 1859, Kriegsarchiv, Vienna, Kriegsministerium, Archiv der Militärkanzlei Seiner Majestät des Kaisers und Königs (hereafter MKSM), Sonderreihe 7 (hereafter SR 7).

19. Minister-Conferenz-Protokolle, Conference on April 27, 1859, MKSM, SR 7.

20. General of Cavalry Archduke Albrecht to "Feldmarschalleutnant und General-Direktor beim Armee-Ober-Commando Freiherr von Eynatten," Vienna, June 7 and 9, as well as July 5, 1859, KM Präs. 1859, nos. 2484, 2595, and 2797.

21. Albrecht to Eynatten, Vienna, July 5, 1859, KM Präs. 1859, no. 2798.

22. FML Schlitter to Francis Joseph, Vienna, March 28, 1859, MKSM 1859, no. 1525.

23. Gründorf, *Memoiren*, p. 145. See also Lang, *Ursachen*, p. 29.
24. Regele, *Geschichte*, pp. 142–46 and 182.
25. FML Count August Degenfeld to "Militärkanzlei Seiner Majestät," Graz, January 8, 1859, MKSM 1859, no. 118.
26. Report from Trieste on March 27, 1859, MKSM 1859, no. 1310.
27. FML Mertens, Trieste, March 29, 1859, MKSM 1859, no. 1338.
28. FML Baron Menzinger to the Military Chancellery in Vienna, Prague, May 26, 1859, MKSM 1859, no. 3292.
29. Reports to the I. Armee Commando in Mantua, Mantua, June 4, and Verona, June 6, 1859, KM Präs. 1859, no. 2521, also MKSM 1859, no. 3791.
30. Baron von Kempen to Grünne, Vienna, June 10, 1859, MKSM 1859, no. 3865. See also MKSM 1859, nos. 4325 and 4650.
31. MKSM 1859, no. 4642.
32. Colonel Waldstätten to the Second Army Command in Trieste, June 19, 1859, no. 4655.
33. There is voluminous documentation on the Italian Jäger Batallions in KM Präs. 1859, nos. 2652, 2676, and 2745, as well as in MKSM 1859, no. 5731. For other characteristic reports on "Unruhen" (unrest) and "Deserteure," see KM Präs. 1859, nos. 3473, 3865, 4108, 5242, 5305, and 5332.
34. Gyulai to Grünne, Milan, February 3, 1859, MKSM 1859, no. 447.
35. FML Degenfeld to the High Command at Verona, MKSM 1859, no. 5224.
36. Colonel Gondrecourt, Linz, July 30, 1859, MKSM 1859, no. 6038.
37. FZM Hess to the High Command in Verona, July 18, 1859, MKSM 1859, no. 5722. See also KM Präs. 1859, no. 2923.
38. Lajos Kossuth, *Az 1859-ki olasz háború korszaka*, which is the first volume of his *Irataim az emigráczióból*, 13 vols. (Budapest: Athenaeum, 1880), pp. 344–45, and Endre Kovács, *A Kossuth-emigrácio és az európai szabadságmozgalmak* (Budapest: Akadémia, 1967), p. 105.
39. Hungarian-style tight pants were the source of another, more tragic confusion in the war. Henri Dunant, founder of the Red Cross, wrote in his *Un souvenir de Solferino* that the Croatian soldiers of the Austrian army were guilty of some terrible atrocities. Because of this, the French tended to give no quarter to the Croats. "They [the French] argued that these 'pantalons collants' always killed their captives. But the captives [of the French] were not Croats; they were Hungarians. True, the uniforms were similar, but in reality the Hungarians are not at all cruel. I was able to explain this to the French, and thus managed to free a number of terrified Hungarians from their cluthes" (Henri Dunant, *Solferinói emlék*, trans. Éva Deák-Veress [Budapest: Magyar Vöröskereszt, 1978], pp. 20–21).
40. Iházs to Kossuth, Genoa, June 6, 1859, in Kossuth, *Az 1859-ki olasz háború*, p. 349.
41. Nemeskéri Kiss to Kossuth, Asti, September 12, 1859, in Kossuth, *Az 1859-ki olasz háború*, pp. 502–4.
42. Klapka to Kossuth in Paris, Torino, September 8, 1859, in Kossuth, *Az 1859-ki olasz háború*, pp. 499–500.

43. FML Degenfeld to "Armee Ober-Commando" in Vienna, Verona, September 21, 1859, KM Präs. 1859, no. 3476.
44. Ibid.
45. See KM Präs. 1859, nos. 3396 and 3777, as well as MKSM Sonderreihe.
46. I regret to say that my research so far has given me no significant information on the career sergeants and other NCO's of the Habsburg army. But clearly, they must have played a crucial role.
47. Rothenberg, *The Army of Francis Joseph,* p. 42.
48. Joseph Roth, *Die Kapuzinergruft* (Cologne: Kiepenheuer und Witsch, 1972), p. 70.
49. Officers were much less likely to be captured than their men. Here are the Austrian casualty statistics for Solferino: killed: 94 officers (15 percent), 2,198 men (10 percent); wounded: 500 officers (78 percent), 10,307 men (49 percent); missing and captured: 45 officers (7 percent), 8,593 men (41 percent). See Prybila, *Geschichte.*

VIII. The Compromise of 1867 and the Reestablishment of the Hungarian *Honvédség*

The Military Compromise of 1868 and Hungary*

Gunther E. Rothenberg

Discussions of the *Ausgleich* of 1867 generally focus on the complex political and economic arrangements between Austria and Hungary and pass over the dispute over Hungarian demands for a separate military establishment that threatened to block both the negotiations and implementation of the accord. The leading Hungarian negotiator, Count Gyula Andrássy, described the problem as the "sword of Damocles suspended over our heads,"[1] while the joint war minister, Feldmarschall Leutnant Baron Franz Kuhn, claimed that the "future existence of the Habsburg Monarchy" depended on a "satisfactory resolution of the army issue."[2]

The issue was of long standing. Ever since 1526, when Ferdinand I assumed the Crown of St. Stephen, Hungary had aspired to an independent military establishment. With most of the country under Turkish rule, however, the question became acute only after the Treaty of Karlowitz, when the Habsburgs tried to introduce greater centralism into the (1699) liberated kingdom, including the raising of standing forces. These efforts were strenuously resisted by the "ruling nation," that is, the magnates, lesser nobles, and clergy who alone were represented in the Diet and furiously defended their privileges, above all exemption from all taxes in return for their service in the anachronistic feudal levy, the *insurrectio*. In the end, as part of the negotiations leading to acceptance of the Pragmatic Sanction, a solution was found. In 1715–22 the Diet accepted the principle of a standing royal army but retained control over recruitment and supply and specifically reaffirmed the tax-exempt status of the nobility. Also left unresolved was whether the Diet had accepted a unitary Habsburg army or merely agreed to a joint defense.[4]

At that, Hungary's support was limited. During the Prussian Wars, despite fervent protestations of loyalty and devotion, the country provided only a few regiments, and a diet convoked in 1764 to raise the country's contribution to army finances and to convert the *insurrectio* obligation into a cash subsidy refused to act. Even so, Maria Theresa refrained from an open confrontation. "In the Kingdom of Hungary," she wrote, "I did think it better not to introduce any changes. . . . special considerations apply in the case of the Hungarians."[5] Joseph II was less cautious, and when he tried to enforce reforms there was a noble revolt during which the Diet of 1790 openly called for a separate Hungarian army.[6] The pacific Leopold II ended the revolt by a mixture of threats and concessions, and by 1792 the struggle between the Hungarian ruling nation and the crown had resolved itself in an uneasy truce. Hungary's contribution to the military establishment remained disproportionate compared with that made by the hereditary lands, and "even in time of crisis the Habsburg had to negotiate and cajole for manpower and supply rather than the command."[7]

Hungarian support remained limited during the wars against the French Revolution and Napoleon. Although *insurrectio* was called out four times, it fought only once, in 1809, and then with poor results. Moreover, the Hungarians seemed determined to exploit the Habsburg Monarchy's difficulties for their own ends. In 1802, when Archduke Charles was attempting to reform the military establishment, the Diet rejected his request for the introduction of selective conscription, a larger recruit quota, and a higher financial contribution. Instead, it raised conditions which Charles regarded as nothing less than an attempt to gain control over its military contingents.[8] Matters did not improve during the next decade. In 1809 the Diet flatly refused to consider introducing the national guard (*Landwehr*) in the kingdom, and by 1812 John Harcourt King, the well-informed British agent in Vienna, reported that Hungary could not be relied upon to support the imperial government. "The ill-will of the Hungarians," he noted, "is deeply rooted."[9]

Victory over Napoleon and the regime of Chancellor Metternich did not diminish Hungarian desires for an independent army, though for two decades there was little overt agitation. In 1839–40, however, there once again were demands that all troops raised in Hungary wear the national insignia, use the Hungarian language of command, and be officered only by Hungarians.[10] The authorities in Vienna were perturbed but believed that the regular army, above all the troops of the predominantly Slavic Military Frontier, would provide an adequate counterweight against Hungarian nationalism.[11]

But in March 1848 the situation suddenly changed. Revolutions in Pest-Buda and Vienna overthrew the regime with surprising ease; Hungary became legally independent, though maintaining a personal union with Austria in the person of the king. By August, however, the formation of a separate Hungarian army precipitated a break with the sovereign, followed by civil war in which the Austrian army, albeit with Russian help, finally prevailed.[12] The specter of an independent and rebellious Hungarian army had long haunted the dynasty; now it had become a reality. Henceforth maintenance of a unitary army became an even greater priority.[13] In regarding the army primarily as the guarantor of the dynasty, however, the Habsburg Monarchy failed to recognize that the new forces unleashed by the industrial revolution required mass armies based on the socioeconomic potential of the entire population. Locked into the rigid dynastic posture of an *ancien régime* force, the army deteriorated as a fighting instrument. The Italian debacle in 1859 induced the dynasty to make efforts to conciliate Hungary, while the unexpected and sudden defeat of 1866 convinced the Emperor Francis Joseph that he had to come to an overall accommodation with the Hungarians, and this required a reopening of the army question.

Negotiations actually had begun before the war, and the Hungarian Parliament had been reconvened in December 1865. To conduct the negotiations, the Parliament named a Committee of Sixty-Seven which in turn created a Select Committee of Fifteen with Andrássy and Ferenc Deák as its most prominent members and guiding spirits. War interrupted the negotiations, but when they were resumed in July 1866 the new situation created by Königgrätz emboldened a committee minority, led by Kálmán Tisza, to make extreme demands. The Pragmatic Sanction, they claimed, required only a common defense, not a unitary army. Andrássy and Deák, however, realized that even now, Francis Joseph would never consent to a complete division of the military establishment, and, supported by a committee majority, they urged the continuation of a unitary army in return for substantial military concessions. When these differences of opinion could not be reconciled, the Select Committee agreed to shelve the army issue temporarily in order not to disrupt the progress of the political negotiations.[14]

Despite his seeming moderation, Andrássy, now prime minister designate of the new Hungarian government, was determined from the outset to assert his country's claims in military affairs. The occasion came soon enough. Defeat had convinced the emperor and his generals that the army had to be enlarged and placed on a broader base. Greatly impressed by Prussia's capacity to raise large conscript armies, Vienna resolved to introduce universal military service. On September 25, 1866, Field Marshal Baron Heinrich Hess proposed such a step, including a basic six-year service obligation, with different terms in the various branches, and a minimum of two years of active duty, followed by a reserve and national-guard liability for all men between the ages of twenty-one and forty.[15] The plan, with some modifications, was supported by John, the acting war minister, who called for an active-duty tour of three years, providing a line army of six hundred thousand men.[16] Even Archduke Albrecht, the son of Archduke Charles, recently victor at Custoza, commanding general of the armies, and long an advocate of the traditional dynastic army, changed his tune and demanded universal conscription.[17] Francis Joseph agreed. In December 1866, he issued an order introducing general conscription throughout the empire, that is, in both Austria and Hungary. At this Andrássy protested at once. The order, he declared, was a "flagrant violation of the nation's rights," and any such basic change in the military system could be accomplished only by constitutional process.[18] In the face of this protest, the emperor, who also wanted to resolve the political issue with the least possible delay, retreated. In February 1867 the decree was annulled for the Hungarian parts of the empire; on November 10, 1867, it was cancelled in Cisleithania.[19]

Retraction of the conscription decree reopened the negotiations between Andrássy and his Austrian counterpart, Count Friedrich Beust. Prodded by Andrássy, the Select Committee agreed in January 1867 to accept the old interpretation of the Pragmatic Sanction. The sovereign, it declared, retained exclusive command over the actually embodied army, while the Hungarian parliament would be responsible for recruitment, supply, and quartering within the kingdom.[20] This interpretation in turn was accepted by the Committee of Sixty-Seven on February 6, and on February 17, 1867, parliamentary government was restored in Hungary. Andrássy assumed office as prime minister.

The final version of the *Ausgleich* document, accepted by Parliament on May 29, 1867, by a vote of 209 for, 89 against, and 83 not voting, reflected the formula agreed to by the committee, though the language adopted was, perhaps deliberately, vague. Articles 2, 4, 5, 8, and 9 stressed the common defense obligations, with many references to past accomplishments and the Pragmatic Sanction. Article 11 stipulated that "in accordance with the constitutional prerogatives of the sovereign, all matters relating to the unified command, control, and internal organization of the entire army, and also of the Hungarian army as an integral part of the entire army, are recognized as being reserved for the disposition of His Majesty." Replacements, terms of service, quartering, and financial support were declared subject to the approval of the Hungarian parliament (Article 12), while Article 13 stated that all basic changes in the military system affecting Hungary required the consent of the Hungarian ministry. Article 14 declared that the Hungarian ministry and parliament would pass the necessary legislation concerning the status, duties, and rights of individual members of the Hungarian army, and, finally, Article 27 stated that "a joint ministry, to deal with matters of common concern and not falling under the jurisdiction of either the government of the lands of the Hungarian crown or those of the other lands of His Majesty, should be created."[21]

The complicated language probably was designed not only to silence nationalist Hungarian opposition, but also to stifle the protests of the ultra-conservative Habsburg generals. If so, it did not entirely succeed. Reference to a "Hungarian army as an integral part of the army" was enough to arouse the opposition of the conservative soldiers led by Archduke Albrecht. On February 20, 1867, he issued an order denouncing "military separatism." He accepted the establishment of the Hungarian Ministry of Defense within the Hungarian cabinet taking office the same date but asserted that the "army has not changed in the close unity of its components."[22] He fought the concept of a separate Hungarian army at court and in the ministerial councils and even took the extraordinary, in many ways radical, step of taking his case to the public in a number of pamphlets attacking "political machinations and the glorification of traitors" and claiming that the various peoples of the Habsburg Monarchy cherished the traditional unifying *Armeegeist* and rejected the divisive Hungarian *Regimentsgeist*.[23] In Hungary these attacks, seconded by some senior officers like General Karl Moering, aroused misgivings and provided the opposition parties with ammunition for their own purposes. Motion after motion was introduced in the Pest parliament attacking the government for its failure to obtain a truly independent national army and delaying the introduction of legislation for a new recruiting system based, at least in principle, on universal military service.[24]

This deteriorating situation placed the entire *Ausgleich* in question. After all, the emperor had agreed to these considerable concessions only in the hope of gaining a permanent truce with his most troublesome challengers and to secure their unquestioning cooperation in restoring Austria's position as a Great Power. This required, above all, army reform and speedy augmentation of fighting strength. As Vienna grew more and more impatient about the stalled army reform, the delay raised the specter of a serious confrontation between the two halves of the monarchy. Moreover, there existed serious differences within the imperial generalcy regarding the exact future character of the army—its recruitment, terms of service, composition of the various branches, strength, and so on. To obtain agreement on these questions, a precondition for resolving the impasse with the Hungarians, Francis Joseph on December 26, 1867, established a council of senior officers—Generals

Baron Wilhelm Ramming, Baron Joseph Maročić, Baron Ludwig Gablenz, Baron Leopold Edelsheim-Gyulai, Baron Franz Kuhn, Moering, Baron Joseph Wilhelm Gallina, and Georg Grivčić, as well as Admirals Wilhelm v. Tegetthoff and Baron Friedrich Pöckh. It was a sign of the changed times that he instructed them, on the one hand, to observe the new constitutional framework but, on the other hand, to zealously guard the unity of the army and to preserve the old traditions.[25] Many, though by no means all, of the generals on the council belonged to a "liberal-centrist" group which shared Albrecht's aversion to separatist nationalist aspirations but at the same time opposed a purely dynastic army. Their leader was Feldmarschall Leutnant Baron Franz Kuhn, who by the time the council actually met late in January 1868 had replaced John as joint war minister.[26]

Francis Joseph had informed the Austrian and Hungarian prime ministers of his instructions to the council. Moreover, he sent the trusted head of military chancery, Colonel Friedrich Beck, to negotiate directly with Andrássy. At the outset of his mission, Beck was a determined supporter of a unitary army. In several memoranda he tried to convince Andrássy that an independent army would isolate Hungary and provoke similar demands from the Slavic nationalities in the Dual Monarchy. As for the demand for Hungarian language of command in Hungarian units, Beck pointed out that Hungarians comprised over 14 percent of the rank and file in only fourteen out of the sixty-four infantry regiments and less than 10 to 12 percent in Jäger artillery, engineer, and signal formations; only the fourteen hussar regiments were 80 to 100 percent Hungarian-speaking.[27] Andrássy, facing an angry opposition and an aroused country, would not be diverted from his demands for further concessions. He was prepared, however, to offer some concessions of his own. There should be, he proposed, a joint (k.k.) army controlled by the emperor as well as separate Austrian and Hungarian national guards (*Landwehr* and *honvédség*) controlled by the respective ministries of defense. Moreover, Andrássy agreed to the German language of command for the joint army and promised, though here it would seem that he misled Beck, that he would not press for the dissolution of the Military Frontier, long an objective of Hungarian policy.[28] Perhaps Beck was overanxious to reach an agreement, but he was favorably impressed and noted in his report that, given the temper of the country, the prime minister's position was most courageous.[29]

In Vienna, however, Albrecht was not so easily convinced. The national guards, he argued, would provide training for subversive elements, and at the same time their existence would induce the two parliaments to reduce appropriations for the joint army, the only reliable force safeguarding the established order.[30] Similar fears and objections were voiced by the council of generals. Some officers declared that, regardless of the imperial desires, the unity of the army and its historic legitimacy had to be preserved and that no concessions should be made just to preserve the Andrássy cabinet from its parliamentary opposition. A break with Hungary, Moering asserted, was probably unavoidable in any case, and he compared Andrássy's assurances to those made by the Prussians at Gastein just before the outbreak of war in 1866. Feldmarschall Leutnant Baron Ludwig Gablenz replied that this went against the expressed wishes of the emperor, but Feldmarschall Leutnant Count Karl Bigot de St. Quentin countered that the army was the last and only secure support of the monarchy and had to be preserved in its traditional form at all costs. Only a minority, led by Feldmarschall Leutnant Baron Rudolf Rossbacher, favored Andrássy's proposals, mainly because the mix of a regular joint army with separate national guards promised to be cheap, always an important consideration in Vienna. In the end, however, the habit of obedience reasserted itself, and the generals bowed, albeit reluctantly, to the imperial wishes. On March 23 they reported their basic acceptance of the Hungarian proposals.[31]

But this was not yet the end of the complications. To attract popular support, the Hungarian government planned to re-create the revolutionary army of 1849 in organization, uniforms, flags, and drill, and this was totally unacceptable both to Francis Joseph and to the military leadership. For eleven days, from April 18 to April 29, 1868, there were conferences in Pest-Buda attended by the ministers of defense, Kuhn, Beust, Andrássy, the joint finance minister Franz Baron Becke, and others and presided over in person by the emperor, who instructed all participants that the deliberations were to be strictly confidential. At issue were the Hungarian plans for the *honvédség* and the nature of the joint army. Attempting to make matters more palatable to the emperor and his ministers and generals, Andrássy emphasized the past loyalty of the Hungarian regiments and argued that if the concessions were made, Hungary within ten years would raise its contributions from 30 to 40 percent of the joint military budget.[32] It is only fair to point out that this never happened as long as the Dual Monarchy existed.

In any case, the conference deadlocked, but once again the diplomatic Beck, who had participated as secretary, came to the rescue. In personal discussions with Andrássy he found a solution. The *honvédség* would be patterned after the joint army in organization and uniforms, but it would be authorized to employ distinctive insignia and flags and the Hungarian language of command. Its oath of allegiance would be to the king as well as to the national constitution. The solution was acceptable to the emperor and pleased Andrássy, who on June 17, 1868, congratulated Francis Joseph on the "resolution of a problem that . . . in the past has bitterly divided the Monarchy."[33]

Congratulations, however, were premature, because Andrássy, still confronted with a clamorous opposition, promptly raised additional obstacles. Above all, he now demanded that the *honvédség*, originally restricted to infantry and cavalry, must receive its full allocation of artillery. But this would have given the Hungarian units equal combat potential with the joint army, and with 1848–49 still vivid in his memory the emperor, strongly supported by Kuhn and Albrecht, refused.[34] At this point, Andrássy, always a political realist, decided that he had reached the limit of the concessions immediately available, and, in order not to jeopardize the political settlement that had given Hungary complete parity within the Dual Monarchy he rammed the military settlement through Parliament. However, and this was an ominous portent of things to come, in order to quiet the vehement objections of the opposition he had to promise that the government would continue to pursue greater military autonomy with all available means.[35]

At the same time, similar legislation was piloted through Parliament in Vienna, though here, too, there was substantial opposition. Most important, however, was the recalcitrance of the military leadership, which was still suspicious of the ultimate intentions of the Hungarians. In August 1868, during a tour of inspection in Croatia, Albrecht made a symbolic pilgrimage to the grave of Ban Baron Josef Jelačić, the man who in 1848 had opened the military intervention against Hungary.[36] The meaning of this action was not lost on either Vienna or Pest-Buda, but this was 1868 and not 1848. The emperor, "who always maintained and protected . . . the compromise law from a strictly Hungarian point of view,"[37] would not tolerate any further obstruction. Once both parliaments had passed the necessary legislation, he acted to make the soldiers accept the new situation. On December 5, 1868, a carefully worded order of the day, written and rewritten several times by Beck, was issued:

> A new element, the *Landwehr* (*honvédség*), today joins the army as a valuable augmentation of the common defense. . . . [The new organizations] serve the same purpose as the army . . . , and I expect that all officers . . . , and in particular the generalcy, will do their utmost to further the bonds between all components of My Army and that they will strengthen the spirit of order and discipline and combat any potentially divisive and dangerous influences from the very outset.[38]

The order achieved its purpose and settled, for the moment at least, any attempts by the military leadership to oppose the new order. At the same time, however, it glossed over the full extent of the Hungarian victory. The statement that the national guards merely augmented the army evaded the fact that from the outset Pest-Buda never considered the *honvédség* merely as a second-line homeguard, but rather regarded it as the first step toward a fully equipped national army receiving liberal support from Parliament. Moreover, the initial victory merely whetted the appetite for further gains. By 1869, Andrássy, disregarding the promise he had made to Beck, began to press for the dissolution of the Military Frontier, and, despite objections from the military, Francis Joseph conceded the point that the introduction of general conscription and the new status of Hungary had made the institution obsolete. Demilitarization was begun in June 1871.[39]

Still, Hungarian pressure on the army issue did not wane. The next demands were for the introduction of the Hungarian language of command in all units of the common army recruited within the boundaries of the kingdom, regardless of ethnic composition—a step that the Hungarians, a minority within the overall population, considered vital to retain control over the various nationalities.[40] The military issue which Francis Joseph had hoped to settle for good in 1868 remained alive and became "the greatest liability of the Compromise" and the "Achilles heel of the dualistic system."[41]

The main weapon of the Hungarian extremists was parliamentary obstruction to hinder the passage of army bills, which, under the provisions of the Compromise, came up for discussion every ten years. Although Tisza, who dominated Hungarian politics from 1875 to 1890, though originally an opponent of the military settlement, had switched his position, he soon found himself hard pressed. The debate over the 1889 army bill was extremely bitter. The opposition, the Party of Independence, demanded the introduction of the Hungarian language of command, widely regarded as a preliminary step toward an ultimate division of the army. The governing Liberal party opposed these demands. Baron Géza Fejérváry, the minister of defense, warned that "one cannot maintain an army subject to notice of termination,"[42] while the aged Andrássy, now a member of the upper house, declared that "the question of a separate Hungarian army was discussed during the *Ausgleich* negotiations, and if we had believed that such an army was necessary for an independent Hungary we would have insisted on it." But, he continued, "we did not deem it desirable; in fact, we considered it dangerous both for Hungary and for the Monarchy."[43] In the end, the government prevailed, but only after obtaining further concessions, including a change in the title of the joint army from k.k. (*kaiserlich-königlich*) to k.u.k. (*kaiserlich und königlich*).[44]

Parliamentary obstruction was used again in 1898, when the joint war ministry asked for a modest increase in the annual recruit quota, and this time the confrontation, aggravated by rioting, lasted for eight years. In the end, the additional manpower was provided, and in turn the *honvédség* at long last gained its artillery, but not before, in April 1905, the emperor was on the verge of authorizing armed intervention in Hungary, the famous Operation "U."[45] A combination of personal and political considerations made the emperor hesitate to take this fatal step, and in the following year Hungarian troops restored order, while another round of concessions ended the parliamentary opposition.

The eight-year delay had weakened Austria-Hungary's military posture, and the Monarchy went to war in 1914 less well prepared than its resources warranted. Austria-Hungary's military budget was the lowest among the Great Powers, and its armies lacked trained reserves and firepower.[46] In the words of a German observer sympathetic to the Dual Monarchy, its military establishment was "adequate for a campaign against Serbia but inadequate for a major European war."[47] The major and unexpected positive development was that throughout over four years of bitter fighting, the army performed rather better than expected by friend and foe and, despite the dire predictions of the Habsburg loyalists, Hungarian units, joint-army as well as national-guard, performed with distinction.

Even the war could not extinguish the dream of an independent national Hungarian army, however, and the last Habsburg emperor, Charles I (Charles IV in Hungary), finally agreed to it in principle in 1917. Plans to implement his promise as soon as the war was over were under way before the end of 1917 and continued until September 1918.[48] In October 1918, finally, Charles released the military from their oath of allegiance, dissolving the empire into its various national and ethnic components, though he deceived himself in believing that this would not change the relationship between the crown and the soldiers.[49] Once again, symbols and words were used to substitute for hard reality. When early in November 1918 Hungary finally achieved its long-cherished objectives—national independence and its own army—it found that this meant not only the collapse of the Dual Monarchy, but also that of the ancient kingdom that army had been meant to preserve.

The military compromise of 1868, though repeatedly and perhaps radically modified, had managed to last for fifty years. For all their spiritual and traditional incompatibility, the joint army and the *honvédség* had developed a relationship that stood the test of a long and bloody war. And yet the struggle between the two probably had contributed to the defeat. Although the statement of an English historian that the "weakness of the Habsburg army in 1914 stemmed not from the disaffection of its soldiers but from the intransigence of politicians in Hungary"[50] is rather too simplistic, there is bitter truth in it. The struggle was one in which neither side could give in. The assertion made by General Heinrich Ritter von Pitreich, an Austrian, that "greater flexibility" would have softened the conflict is not convincing. He mentioned concessions on the "flag and insignia issue" and asked whether "the gallant Hungarians, who since the days of Maria Theresa had worn special uniforms, braids and tight pants, really would have changed if they had displayed the national emblem instead of the double eagle on their helmets."[51] The main issue, however, was the language question, and this could not be solved. The adoption of universal military service in 1867–68 required that the masses, ten different nationalities in the Monarchy, accept the essential legitimacy of their government, and to achieve this a compromise between Austria and Hungary, in both cases represented by governments elected on a restricted franchise at best, was inadequate. To retain their dominant status within their own kingdom, the Hungarians needed the Hungarian language of command; to grant this would have meant the division of the army, something no Habsburg loyalist could concede. Thus, the settlement of the military issue was doomed from the start.

Notes

* Portions of this essay appeared under the title "Toward a National Hungarian Army: The Military Compromise of 1868 and Its Consequences" in the December 1972 issue of the *Slavic Review* and are used here with permission.

1. Andrássy to Francis Joseph, July 17, 1868, Kriegsarchiv, Vienna (hereafter KA), Militärkanzlei seiner Majestät (MKSM), Sonderreihe F 29 (a) 3.
2. Walter Wagner, *Geschichte des k.k. Kriegsministeriums II, 1866–1888* (Vienna, 1971), p. 48.
3. Béla K. Király, *Hungary in the Late Eighteenth Century* (New York, 1969), pp. 104–5.
4. On this as well as additional details with regard to n. 3 above, see Zoltán Kramár, "The Military Ethos of the Hungarian Nobility," in *War and Society in East Central Europe*, ed. Béla K. Király and Gunther E. Rothenberg, vol. 1 (New York, 1979), pp. 69–72.
5. "Maria Theresa's Political Testament," in *The Habsburg and Hohenzollern Dynasties in the Seventeenth and Eighteenth Centuries*, ed. C. A. Macartney (New York, 1970), pp. 130–31.

6. Kramár, "Military Ethos," p. 71.
7. Gunther E. Rothenberg, *Napoleon's Great Adversaries: The Archduke Charles and the Austrian Army, 1792–1814* (London and Bloomington, 1982), p. 15.
8. Ibid., p. 71; Oskar Criste, *Erzherzog Carl von Österreich*, 3 vols. (Vienna-Leipzig, 1912), 2: 34.
9. King to Castlereagh, Vienna, June 2, 1812, Public Record Office, FO 7/99.
10. George Barany, "The Hungarian Diet of 1839–40 and the Fate of Széchényi's Middle Course," *Slavic Review* 22 (1963): 297–98.
11. Gunther E. Rothenberg, *The Army of Francis Joseph* (West Lafayette, 1976), pp. 18–19.
12. Ibid., pp. 25, 28–29.
13. Ibid., pp. 46–47.
14. Ivan Zolger, *Der staatsrechtliche Ausgleich zwischen Österreich und Ungarn* (Leipzig, 1911), pp. 5–13, 111–13.
15. Antonio Schmidt-Brentano, *Die Armee in Österreich: Militär, Staat und Gesellschaft 1848–1867* (Boppard a. Rhine, 1975), p. 101.
16. Haus-, Hof- und Staatsarchiv, Vienna, Ministerräte of November 12 and December 22–23, 1866, MRZ 108, 118.
17. Albrecht, *Wie soll Österreichs Heer organisiert sein* (Vienna, 1868), pp. 17–22.
18. Imperial order, December 28, 1866, KA, KSM 1867 82–1/1–2. For Andrássy's reaction, Eduard v. Wertheimer, *Graf Julius Andrássy*, 3 vols. (Stuttgart, 1910–13), 1: 250.
19. KA, MKSM 1867 82–5/1; Schmidt-Brentano, *Die Armee*, pp. 84–85; Wagner, *Geschichte*, p. 41.
20. Wagner, *Geschichte*, pp. 20–21; Zolger, *Der staatsrechtliche Ausgleich*, pp. 34–39; Julius Mikolczy, *Ungarn in der Habsburger Monarchie* (Vienna-Munich, 1959), pp. 135–36.
21. Wagner, *Geschichte*, pp. 21–22.
22. The order, actually a circular to all commanding generals, further declared that troops should be isolated from subversive influences by strict discipline and surveillance. KA, Kriegsministerium Präsidial (KM Präs.), 1867 44–46; cf. Edmund v. Glaise-Horstenau, *Franz Josephs Weggefahrte: Das Leben des Generalstabschef Grafen Beck* (Zurich-Vienna, 1930), pp. 144–45.
23. Albrecht, *Österreichs Heer*, pp. 19–20.
24. Walter Rogge, *Österreich von Vilagos bis zur Gegenwart*, 3 vols. (Leipzig-Vienna, 1873), 3: 148–50.
25. KA, MKSM 1867 82–5/1.
26. Rothenberg, *Army of Francis Joseph*, pp. 78–79.
27. "Gegen die Zweiteilung der Armee," November 27, 1867, KA, MKSM Sep. Fasz. 76/16 ad 36, Nachlass Beck Rzikowsky A 2, no. 143, and MKSM 1868 82–3/20.
28. Wertheimer, *Graf Julius Andrássy*, 1: 393. For a discussion of Andrássy's subsequent shift in the following year see Gunther E. Rothenberg, *The Military Border in Croatia, 1740–1881* (Chicago, 1966), pp. 168–73.

29. KA, MKSM Sep. Fasz. 76/36 and Nachlass Beck Rzikowsky A 2, no. 144.
30. Albrecht to John, December 1867, KA, Nachlass John, B 138–22.
31. Protocols and position papers, KA, KM Präs. 29–1/1–8; Kuhn's final report of March 27, 1868, ibid., 3/1.
32. KA, MKSM Sonderreihe F 29 (a) 2–5 e; cf. Wagner, *Geschichte*, pp. 48–49.
33. KA, MKSM Sonderreihe F 29 (a) 3.
34. Kuhn to Francis Joseph, telegram, ibid., 6; cf. Heinrich v. Srbik, *Aus Österreichs Vergangenheit* (Salzburg, 1959), p. 184.
35. Wertheimer, *Graf Julius Andrássy*, 1: 361–63.
36. For the military opposition see Wertheimer, *Graf Julius Andrássy*, 1: 347–49, 355.
37. The view of a Habsburg loyalist of liberal views, Joseph Redlich, *Emperor Francis Joseph of Austria* (New York, 1929), pp. 252–53.
38. KA, MKSM 1868, 82–3/14, in Wagner, *Geschichte*, pp. 50–51.
39. For detailed discussion, see Gunther E. Rothenberg, "The Struggle over the Dissolution of the Croatian Military Border," *Slavic Review* 23 (1964): 63–78. On the dissolution of the remaining border districts, see Anton Freiherr v. Mollinary, *Sechsundvierzig Jahre im österreichisch-ungarischen Heere, 1833–1879*, 2 vols. (Zurich, 1905), 2: 203–12, 215–51, 272–78.
40. Theodor v. Sosnosky, *Die Politik im Habsburgerreiche*, 2 vols. (Berlin, 1912), 2: 167–71, and, from the Hungarian point of view, Péter Hanák, "Hungary in the Austro-Hungarian Monarchy: Preponderance or Dependency?" *Austrian History Yearbook* 3, pt. 1 (1967): 296–97, and Gábor G. Kemény, *Iratok a nemzetiségi kérdés történetéhez Magyarországon a dualizmus korában*, 4 vols. (Budapest, 1952–66), 4: 295, 301, 305–6.
41. Kemény, *Iratok*, 4: 298; Miskolczy, *Ungarn*, p. 162.
42. Rothenberg, *Army of Francis Joseph*, pp. 119–20.
43. *Die Einheit der österreichisch-ungarischen Armee: Rede des Grafen Julius Andrássy gehalten im Ausschuss des ungarischen Magnatenhauses am 5. April 1889* (Vienna, 1889), pp. 18–19.
44. William A. Jenks, *Austria under the Iron Ring, 1879–1893* (Charlottesville, 1965), pp. 245–46.
45. For a full discussion, see Kurt Peball and Gunther E. Rothenberg, "Der Fall 'U': Die geplante Besetzung Ungarns durch die k.u.k. Armee im Herbst 1905," *Schriften des Heeresgeschichtlichen Museums in Wien* 4 (1969): 85–126.
46. A. J. P. Taylor, *The Habsburg Monarchy 1809–1918* (New York, 1965), p. 299.
47. Oskar Regele, *Feldmarschall Conrad: Auftrag und Erfüllung, 1906 bis 1918* (Vienna-Munich, 1956), pp. 161–64.
48. Ibid., pp. 439–41; KA, MKSM 1918, 38–2/1, 2; cf. Alexander Spitzmüller, *Der letzte österreichisch-ungarische Ausgleich und der Zusammenbruch der Monarchie* (Berlin, 1929), pp. 79–83.
49. Rothenberg, *Army of Francis Joseph*, pp. 215–17.
50. Norman Stone, "Army and Society in the Habsburg Monarchy, 1900–1914," *Past and Present*, no. 33 (1966), p. 103.

51. Anton Pitreich, *Der österreichisch-ungarische Bundesgenosse im Sperrfeuer* (Klagenfurt, 1930), p. 67.

The Founding of the *Honvédség* and the Hungarian Ministry of Defense, 1867–70

Zoltán Szász

In 1904, almost forty years after the Compromise (*Ausgleich*), the Joint Council of Ministers of the Austro-Hungarian Monarchy was once again discussing military issues when Emperor and King Francis Joseph recalled the suspicion he had felt at the idea and then at the actual formation of the Hungarian *honvédség*. He went on to say that time had proved his fears unfounded. Indeed, mutual distrust between the court, the high command, and Hungarian public opinion had defined the circumstances under which the *honvédség* was founded in 1868, and although the court's fears were never justified they were quite understandable.

The problem behind the 1867 Compromise between Austria and Hungary was how to cut the Habsburg Monarchy in two while leaving it in one piece. The Hungarian politicians at the Compromise talks, led by Ferenc Deák and Gyula Andrássy, saw from the start that it was vital to the interests of both parties for the imperial army to remain united and indivisible. The moderate opposition to the Compromise led by Kálmán Tisza and his associates talked a great deal about the objective of creating a separate Hungarian army, but to their closer acquaintances they would admit they were only doing so in order to have something to concede during the course of the bargaining. At one of the preparatory meetings (on May 7, 1866), Deák declared that he did not believe Hungary should attempt to obtain new rights in the military field; not since 1715 had there been a separate Hungarian army, and the task was to regain for the country the right to a say in the concerns of the joint army.

The leading Hungarian politicians' basic idea that there would be no contradiction between the autonomy of Austria and Hungary, i.e., political dualism, and the existence of a joint army was too new and bare a concept for all to accept. It was declared an impossibility by all who opposed the Compromise, including Hungarians, for dualism was bound to lead to a division of the army and thus to an erosion of the Monarchy's position as a great power. That was precisely what the general staff feared and not far from what those seeking full independence for Hungary dreamed of. But Francis Joseph was persuaded by the imperative necessity for reform of the empire and by the promises of the Hungarian negotiators to accept that dualism and a joint army were compatible, and he forced the high command to accept it too. Nevertheless, the military problem was still far from settled.

The Hungarian side was inclined to agree to dualism only if it meant the introduction or, as they put it, the "restoration" of constitutionalism, which they also considered the main precondition for modernizing the country and guaranteeing that dualism was maintained. Therefore they planned a series of measures which would, while maintaining the army's theoretical unity, serve to end the omnipotence of the high command, for the general staff was the main, consistent potential opponent of parliamentarism and also of Hungary's separate statehood.

The Hungarian liberals accepted that the leadership, command, and internal administration of the army were prerogatives of the monarch. The army would be held together by its united administration and common ruler. Once they were in a state of readiness, the armed forces would be at the ruler's disposal, but their recruitment, replacement, supply, and quartering "would both parliamentarily and administratively be the right of the nation," declared Deák, who went on to outline the need for further guarantees: Parliament should decide on the system of defense in order to prevent the high command from devising a system under which an overly large number of reserves could be mobilized at any moment, which would render Parliament's right to vote soldiers illusory. The Hungarians made no concessions on the rights of Parliament. On December 20, 1866, Deák told Friedrich Beust, "There are rights no constitutional nation will ever willingly abdicate." He compared them to a weapon kept in the family home: it might never be used, but one would never feel safe without it. The whole argument followed from dualism.

It was not the Compromise itself, but the task of making the Compromise acceptable to Hungary that obliged the liberals to raise a further demand: that a small separate Hungarian defense force be established. The memory of the battles of the *honvéd* (national defense) forces in 1848–49 was so vivid in the minds even of those who were in favor of the Compromise that it could not realistically be omitted from any policy, even though, as I have mentioned, a united army was the precondition for the Compromise. The *honvédség,* a separate Hungarian armed force, was seen by the nation as the symbol of its national sovereignty. Moreover, the restoration of the legal position of 1848, mentioned so often at the time of the Compromise, was inconceivable without the revival of the *honvédség*.

For tactical reasons, the Hungarian liberal politicians managed for quite a while to skirt the topic of establishing a separate Hungarian military force. This was partly because Vienna turned a deaf ear to it and partly because they themselves still lacked a well-defined concept. At the preparatory meetings the term "Hungarian army" was taken to mean only the Hungarian regiments in the joint army, and they pondered the question of whether, under the label of joint military expenditure, Hungary should undertake to maintain them. Eventually Deák, Andrássy, and József Eötvös found it impossible to divide the "joint defense fund" into Hungarian and Austrian parts. Unity was dictated by economic considerations as well, since proportionally Hungary provided far more soldiers than it would have been able to support out of its contributions to the joint expenses. The Compromise contained only a faint reference to a Hungarian military force. Article 11 declared that the unity of command and internal administration of the whole army, and thus of the Hungarian army as an integral part of that army, were the ruler's prerogative. Francis Joseph consented to the establishment of a Hungarian Ministry of Defense, with the proviso that it be headed by Andrássy, the Hungarian prime minister. On the previous day, the joint defense minister, Franz von John, has sent a circular instructing the military commands to ignore orders from the Hungarian ministry; on the day of Andrássy's appointment, Archduke Albrecht, commander-in-chief of the Monarchy's military forces, issued an order stating that all endeavors to separate the regiments on a nationality basis should be decisively thwarted. Thus the Hungarian Ministry of Defense was established, but it remained unclear how far its authority extended, what kinds of matters it could decide upon, and, most important, whether it would have command of any forces. Even the ministry's official publication admitted to uncertainty in evaluating the first phase of its work: "One may well conclude that it was established solely to obey the letter of the laws of 1848, which provide for the existence of a Ministry of Defense, that it lacked any due sphere of authority and thus any real reason for existence."

In 1867 the ministry's scope of activity corresponded to the military tasks undertaken by the Regency Council: the customary preparations for recruiting and the administration of civil and material affairs in connection with the military (e.g., the damages incurred in 1848–49 and 1866). The ministry's few officials (there were only four of them) were transferred to it from the Regency Council.

However, the Ministry of Defense developed and changed markedly between 1867 and 1869. Before the end of 1867, leading positions were taken by a colonel of the 1848 *honvéd* army and a *honvéd* major who had twice been sentenced to death. Work was done on a draft defense law to apply to the whole Monarchy. An 1848 *honvéd* general took part in the planning for the establishment of a Hungarian *honvédség*. The ministry administered an assistance scheme for 1848–49 *honvéd* soldiers, domestically a major issue, for which the funds had been provided by the ruling couple in the politically well-calculated gesture of handing over the hundred thousand gold pieces presented to them as a coronation present. In its first two years, however, it remained from the political point of view little more than an advisory body used by Prime Minister Andrássy to provide expert support for Hungarian military demands. Its significance cannot be compared with that of the parliamentary opposition, which constantly talked of dividing the army, or of the quite widespread movement of *honvéd* associations that demanded an independent army for Hungary. These two were the real forces that impelled the government to devise a detailed military policy and take firmer steps against the court.

Andrássy, as premier and defense minister, tried to win over the ruler and the military leaders step by step to the idea of establishing some kind of Hungarian military force. He often improvised in the various negotiations, maneuvering between the position of Vienna and that of the Hungarian opposition. Eventually the new *honvédség* was likewise the result of improvisation. After the defeat at Königgrätz, the Austrian defense minister had drawn up a plan for military reform which combined universal conscription with the introduction of a Prussian-type system of popular levy (*Landsturm*)—a second-line force that would embrace the entire adult male population, complement the standing army in time of war, and maintain internal security in the provinces. The Hungarian government would agree to that plan only if the secondary force at least, even if it existed more on paper than in real life, was subordinated to the Hungarian Ministry of Defense and termed a "national guard." The request was modest enough to break down the opposition (or rather the united resistance) of the general staff. The Hungarian proposal at the end of 1867 was for skeleton peacetime standing units amounting to a permanent armed force averaging five thousand men. Those permanently "on leave" would do annual military training lasting alternately for one week and three weeks. The initial training of the *honvéd* members would be given by the joint army, and the language of command would be German. The military did not want to concede so much, and at the meeting of the delegation in March 1868 they expressed opposition to the formation of the *honvédség* by recalling the split in the officers' corps in 1848 ("confusion in the interpretation of obligation"). Any insult to the memory of 1848 raised general uproar. Andrássy quarreled with the defense minister's side, and even the most peaceable followers of Deák became incensed, placing the whole army reform in danger. Eventually Andrássy and Beust managed to win over Francis Joseph, and, to use the contemporary expression, "military reaction" was defeated.

Supported by the otherwise suspicious but in this case flexible emperor, the Hungarian government managed to persuade the Austrian government and the joint defense minister to agree to the formation of the *honvédség*, with Hungarian as the working language, at the disposal of the Hungarian Ministry of Defense, the establishment of the standing units, and the enlistment of a proportion of new army recruits into the ranks of the *honvédség*. Later the Hungarian Council of Ministers allowed officers who had served in the *honvéd* army of 1848 to be admitted into the officers' corps that was being formed. To ensure parity, a *Landwehr* was set up in Austria. The price for this concession was that the sovereign, who was worried about the unity of the army as a whole, entrusted the military leadership of the *honvédség* to a *honvéd* commander-in-chief he himself appointed, i.e., kept ultimate command in his own hands.

In the summer of 1868 the National Assembly passed the laws on the joint army and the *honvédség* by a large majority. By the end of the year they had also been passed by the Austrian legislature and ratified by the monarch.

On the basis of the military laws of 1868, the structure of the Ministry of Defense had largely taken shape by 1869, and its staff had increased to 61. A major of the Imperial Engineers, Béla Ghyczy, was appointed to head the military departments, while Károly Kerkápoly, a member of Parliament of good repute, became the undersecretary and two important posts as ministerial councillors were also filled by strong-willed civilian politicians.

The ranks of the *honvédség* were filled from the excess of recruits for the joint army. Lots were drawn to decide which recruits would go into the joint army and which into the *honvédség*. Service in the latter was for two years (as opposed to three in the joint army). This was followed by a compulsory ten years in the reserves, while soldiers of the joint army who had served their time were also kept in the *honvéd* reserves for another two years. It was calculated that by 1878 the number in the *honvédség* would reach 350,000. Initially 48,900 recruits from five age groups were called up and given their training by 300 freshly trained *honvéd* officers at the end of 1869.

The country was divided into six *honvéd* districts, half of which, in the typical dualist manner, were headed by *honvéd* officers of 1848. Eighty-two battalion districts were set up, each of which included the same number of infantry battalions and 32 cavalry squadrons. In fact, the *honvédség* contained few regulars. From 9,370 in 1869 and 10,888 in 1871, the number dropped, only approaching 10,000 during the training weeks.

Thus, the *honvédség* was formed, but only as a second-class military force. The commander-in-chief was appointed not by the government, but by the monarch, who ultimately controlled the issue of commissions for officers too. The formation of artillery was forbidden, which rendered the *honvédség* incapable of conducting independent military operations from the outset. Nor did it have the manpower to do so: a battalion would contain a mere twenty-one to twenty-six men, sometimes even insufficient to mount a proper guard. Military bands were not allowed until the millennium celebrations of 1896, in part because it was feared that the band would outnumber the soldiers in any march it was leading.

Although the formation of the *honvédség* was to a great extent forced on the government as a means of alleviating public opposition to the Compromise, it transformed itself, within the limits set by the dualist system, into a national institution. The same compromise between nationalism and dualism was to be found in the *honvédség*'s Austrian counterpart, the *Landwehr,* and in the *honvédség* set up in Croatia. Without Parliament's consent, the *honvédség* could not be posted outside the country; the banner, language, and to some extent uniform were Hungarian (in Croatia, of course, Croatian), and each *honvéd* swore an oath on the laws of the land. The troops were likely to be stationed near their place of birth (or abode), and those belonging to ethnic minorities were kept together, officered to some degree by those of their own nationality. Moreover, the formation of the Hungarian Ministry of Defense made it possible in several important areas of administration to preclude interference injurious to sovereignty by a foreign body—a ministry in Vienna.

The Hungarian public initially viewed the *honvédség* with aversion, and it was maligned by the opposition, but time changed that, and it became a favorite child of dualism, for which no expense was spared: in 1870 the Hungarian Ministry of Defense's budget reached 8.6 million forints. The nationalistic public tried to use the *honvédség* to bolster patriotism and even demanded that it be made more Hungarian still. While it was occasionally used as an instrument of repression against popular movements, its limited numbers ill suited it to this task. Nonetheless, it remained for almost two decades, between the Compromise and the formation of the gendarmerie, the only armed force of a national character at the government's disposal, and thus by its very existence it contributed to the stabilization of dualism.

Thus the issue of the *honvédség* was a national one that engaged the attention of public political opinion. That attention tended to obscure the fact that the formation of the *honvédség* had less significance in the consolidation of the Hungarian government's position and authority over the country and in the limitation of the top military leaders than did the elimination in 1871 of the inimical phenomenon of the southern Military Frontier.

Gyula Andrássy and the Founding of the *Honvédség*

János Décsy

The disastrous defeat in the Austro-Prussian War of 1866 dramatized both the bankruptcy of Habsburg neo-absolutism and the organizational, operational, and material backwardness of the imperial army. A compromise with Hungary had been virtually complete before the war. Magenta and Solferino stressed the need for and Königgrätz made mandatory a recognition of Hungarian national aspirations and a reorganization and modernization of the imperial army.[1] The Monarchy was saved from political debacle by the *Ausgleich* with the Hungarians of 1867, which restructured the empire on the basis of constitutional dualism.[2] On February 17, 1867, Count Gyula Andrássy, the chief lieutenant of Ferenc Deák,[3] a central figure in the shaping of the settlement, was appointed by Emperor Francis Joseph as Hungary's first dualist prime minister and minister of defense.[4]

Andrássy was apparently the right man at the right time for the right job. He was unquestionably one of the outstanding statesmen of his time. A broad knowledge of Europe and the problems of European politics, including the internal problems of the multinational Austro-Hungarian Empire, breadth of view, resourcefulness, and excellent judgment of men and situations were the distinguishing features of his statesmanship. Andrássy was an honorable man of boundless energy and courage and remarkable political talents. His ability to combine prudence with promptitude and forethought with firmness were yet other marks of the statesmanship to which he largely owed his success.[5]

The most vital and immediate matter demanding Andrássy's attention was the military question. The prime minister understood that if the Monarchy (Hungary's bastion against hostile neighbors) was to attain internal consolidation and recover its Great Power status, a comprehensive reform of the army was indispensable.[6] He also believed, however, that this reform had to reflect Hungarian national aspirations in the establishment of a national defense force or *honvédség*.[7] Without this, he knew, his task of making the Compromise acceptable in Hungary would be difficult if not impossible.

After the defeat of 1866, the leading military circles, recognizing the gravity of the situation, deemed it imperative to transform the Monarchy's army from an old-fashioned, ineffective, and strictly dynastic establishment into a modern mass-based force. Franz von John,[8] the minister of war, in a December 26, 1866, memorandum to the emperor, voiced the idea of strengthening and reorganizing the army and urged the speedy implementation of a reform plan he attached.[9] The plan was based on the modern principle of universal conscription and aimed at preserving a unitary army, suggesting only the introduction of a Prussian-type second-line force (*Landsturm*) that would include males aged 18 to 45 who were not part of the army but would supplement the armed forces in time of war. For Hungary it proposed only a second-line role.[10] This was, from the Hungarian national point of view, quite unacceptable. For the Hungarians a separate army (the *honvédség*) was a symbol of their national sovereignty. John's plan, which necessarily excluded the "Hungarian state idea,"[11] was contrary to the demands of the Hungarian liberal politicians involved in the Compromise negotiations.

Two days later Francis Joseph approved the plan and made universal conscription the law of the empire.[12] Supported by Deák,[13] Andrássy sharply protested this "flagrant violation of the nation's rights" and demanded that any future army reform employ constitutional means.[14] As a consequence of this unexpected violent reaction, the emperor rescinded his order on February 17, 1867, but stressed that "the security of the monarchy requires increasing the fighting strength of the army depleted by the last campaign (1866) and the drastic reorganization of the existing system of defense."[15] In any case, the question of army reform and Hungarian aspirations for a separate army was bound to be part of the Compromise negotiations.[16]

Andrássy and Deák realized that Vienna would never agree to the idea of separate armies, accepted the past interpretation of the Pragmatic Sanction of 1722–23, and agreed to the notion of a joint army, but at the price of substantial concessions. The opposition, on the other hand, under Kálmán Tisza's[17] leadership, argued that the above law provided only for common defense and not for a common army. In order to speed progress in the political negotiations, both proponents and opponents agreed to bypass the army issue for the time being. Andrássy was fully resolved to get Hungary's fair share in military affairs. To appreciate the magnitude of his difficulties in this respect, one must understand the tremendous opposition he had to face from the powerful anti-Hungarian conservative forces around the court in Vienna and from a well-organized angry opposition at home.

The resolution of the military issue was not only a Hungarian, but also an imperial concern. The conservative military and court circles dominated by Archduke Albrecht formed a solid front against any military separatism. In his capacity as inspector general of the army,[18] Albrecht rejected the very thought of an independent Hungarian army and fought it at every level and by every means at his disposal.[19] He even took his case to the Austrian public in several pamphlets denouncing "political machinations . . . and the glorification of traitors."[20] The humiliating experiences of 1848–49 had convinced him that the salvation of the Monarchy lay in the unity of the army and its loyalty to the dynasty.[21]

What made matters worse was that Albrecht's conduct had aroused the Left-Center as well as the Radical Left opposition parties in the Hungarian parliament. They mounted one bitter attack after another against the Andrássy government for its failure to bring about the establishment of a separate national army and blocked the introduction of legislation on the new conscription system.[22] Thus a crisis situation was created that endangered the stability of the new dualist system. To aggravate things further, the *honvéd* associations inflamed national sentiment in favor of an independent national army by widespread agitation.[23] Andrássy was conscious of the general state of tension prevailing in Hungary and realistic enough to appreciate its dangers.

Even after the conclusion of the Compromise, Vienna's official position remained based on John's reform plan of December 1866. Its conception of a unitary army was diametrically opposed to the idea of a Hungarian national army; this the Viennese government was not yet ready to concede. Andrássy, of course, realized that John's plan was just as unacceptable as the demands of the Hungarian parliamentary opposition. His difficulties were compounded by the intentionally ambiguous language of Compromise Law XII, Article 11.[24] From its text one could deduce that the Hungarian army would constitute an integral part of the joint army. Among other things, this too was fully exploited both by the Hungarian parliamentary opposition and by the official Viennese circles. Meanwhile, besides the Albrecht-led conservative obstructionists, the Austro-German Centralists, at odds with the military leadership over the size of the army, also took a stand against the Hungarians' military ambitions.[25] Thus Andrássy's government came under crossfire: it was pressed by an outraged opposition[26] and a volatile public opinion at home, on the one hand, and hindered by Austrian officialdom, on the other. The military crisis thrust on Andrássy a role he could not have relished. Yet, characteristically, he welcomed this complex challenge and was prepared to extricate himself from the difficulties with his usual impressive ingenuity.[27]

In view of the division of opinion within and disagreement between the halves of the Monarchy, it is clear that the successful solution of the irritating military question could be effected only through a compromise. For the time being, however, neither side had shown any inclination toward concessions. At this stage, the opposing sides had not yet developed any concrete conception of a solution to the problem. Thus, as Tibor Papp has put it, "a period of time was needed during which the contending parties could shape their own plans, and through exchange of ideas become acquainted with each other's intentions and views in order to be able to reach an agreement."[28] During the conflict-ridden exploratory period, Andrássy emerged as a very influential figure, and his proposals eventually helped to turn the tide. He succeeded because he could speak from strength and had all the aggressiveness, self-confidence, and flexibility that the Austrian leaders and members of the court party lacked. He was always lucid and explicit and was able to present his views with unshakable conviction, all of which helped him to convince the monarch of the feasibility of the policy he was suggesting.[29]

The deadlock was broken by the emperor himself, who, in November 1867, ordered the establishment of a council of generals to develop a comprehensive army reform plan and draft an appropriate army bill.[30] Rothenberg rightly observes: "It was a sign of the changed times that he instructed the council on the one hand to observe the new constitutional framework, but on the other to guard zealously the unity of the army and preserve the old traditions."[31] In response to the emperor's directives, Minister of War John commissioned one of his confidants, Colonel G. Grivčić, to confer with Andrássy at Pest about the pending army bill and to mediate his differences with the Hungarian premier.[32] In the meantime, Andrássy and his defense councillor Richárd Gelich completed a detailed proposal for resolving the crisis. It is beyond any doubt that this initiative was prompted by the pressure of the opposition parties and the *honvéd* associations. Almost simultaneously, Colonel Beck, the head of the emperor's military chancery and one of his confidants, drew up a memorandum in support of a unitary army;[33] Francis Joseph transmitted this memorandum to Andrássy. Beck argued that Hungary could not manage alone and that a separate Hungarian army would become the center of agitation and social as well as ethnic unrest and serve as a green light for similar demands from other nationalities within the Monarchy.[34] The emperor then ordered Beck to enter into direct negotiations with Andrássy. During the negotiations, Beck and the Hungarian statesman came to understand each other's views and positions. Beck was impressed and moved closer to Andrássy's viewpoint. Andrássy had a persuasive tongue and a good sense of timing; he knew when to restrain himself and when to push forward. He knew how to win over the men he needed to attain his aims: Deák, Emperor Francis Joseph, József Eötvös, the parliamentary leaders and the delegations, and now Beck.[35]

Through Beck, Vienna became better acquainted with the premier's aspirations and was reassured that Andrássy was guided equally by Hungarian and imperial considerations. The emperor perceived similar merit in Andrássy's motives.[36] Consequently, he generally leaned toward or accepted the views of the prime minister in the military controversy. Beck understood that, considering the temper of the Hungarian parliamentary opposition and the country as a whole, Andrássy could ill afford to give up his demands for further concessions. Andrássy knew what he wanted and understood the art of the possible. His sense of proportion enabled him to understand that a statesman can only rarely achieve everything he sets out to. Therefore, in charting his course of action, he refused to rely on theories, for he knew that circumstances usually made their practical application impossible. The best program in any contingency was, as he himself succinctly put it, "to avoid stupidities."[37] His considerable intuition and experience enabled him to discern those factors that would limit his freedom of choice and action.[38]

These qualities permitted Andrássy to demonstrate his flexibility and his ability to improvise in his impasse-breaking plan. This plan provided for a common imperial-royal (k.k.) army under the emperor's control, with German as the language of command, and a separate Hungarian defense force (*honvédség*). The latter would be under its own ministry of defense, which would also represent the monarch in the parliamentary sessions that dealt with army-related issues. Beck accepted this proposal but suggested that in order to preserve parity, a similar force (*Landwehr*) shoudl be established in Austria.[39] Andrássy had no objection, and an agreement was reached. John, who held firmly to his position on a unitary army, resigned in protest and was replaced, on January 18, 1868, by General Baron Franz von Kuhn.[40] On January 22 the council of generals, under Kuhn's leadership, began its deliberations on the new army bill.[41]

The emperor approved the agreement at the end of March 1868, provided that the commander-in-chief of the *honvédség* be appointed by him.[42] This Andrássy conceded. Archduke Albrecht and the council of generals expressed serious misgivings about this new development,[43] but in the end they submitted to the wishes of the monarch. On March 23, they reported their acceptance of the new agreement based on Andrássy's proposals.[44]

The *honvédség*, established as a second-line force without artillery,[45] fell far short of Hungarian aspirations, but Andrássy, always a realist, accepted it in order to avoid endangering Hungary's newly gained position within the Monarchy. Then, with careful planning and single-mindedness, the premier pushed the necessary legislation through Parliament in July and August of 1868.[46] By the end of November the Austrian legislature had also enacted into the law the army bill.[47] On December 5, 1869, the Austrian and Hungarian delegations sanctioned and the monarch signed it.[48] Additional legislative acts in early 1870 provided for its implementation. On the same day, Emperor Francis Joseph issued a cautiously edited and phrased order of the day: "A new element, the *Landwehr* (*honvédség*), today joins the army as a valuable augmentation of the common defense. . . . [The new organizations] serve the same purpose as the army—being formed from similar elements, in fact partly from the army itself. . . . I expect that all officers . . . and in particular the generalcy, will do their utmost to further the bonds between all components of My Army."[49] The authoritative tone of the order silenced, for the time being at least, the military opposition to the new arrangement.

Under the provisions of Army Act XLI of 1868, the *honvédség* was established at the end of 1869 with eighty-two infantry battalions and thirty-two cavalry squadrons.[50] In 1872 and 1873, with the dissolution of the Military Frontier,[51] first two and then a further eight infantry battalions were added. In 1871, four additional cavalry squadrons were set up.[52] As specified by the statutes cited, all male citizens between 20 and 36 years of age were liable for twelve years of military service. Service time in the *honvédség* included two years on active duty and ten years in the reserve. The enlisted ranks in the *honvédség* were filled from the excess annual recruit intake of the joint army.[53] In peacetime both the *Landwehr* and the *honvédség* existed only as cadre formations.[54] Those on the active list could be called up in time of need in any season of the year; reservists could be called only for the annual two-week training period and the biannual fall maneuvers.[55]

Even though the monarch appointed the commander-in-chief of the *honvédség*, it was under the direct control of the minister of national defense, a portfolio held until 1872 by the current prime minister.[56] The Ministry of Defense itself, comprising two departments with a staff of forty-two, was established immediately after the Compromise of 1867. Its main task was to prepare defense bill proposals and deal with the organizational problems and principles of the *honvédség* being established. After the enactment of Army Act XLI, it was reorganized into six departments with a staff of eighty-two. The *honvédség* headquarters under the command of Lieutenant General Archduke Joseph directed and supervised training and discipline. Administratively, the *honvédség* itself was divided into six (1869) and then seven (1871) military districts under territorial commands. These were further divided into battalion districts.[57]

The *honvédség* had been set up as a second-line force, but, as a result of Andrássy's immediate and appropriate measures and generous funding by Parliament, its build-up proceeded rapidly. In 1870 the Hungarian military budget grew to 8.6 million forints. As a result, by 1873 the *honvédség* numbered 2,868 officers and 158,000 men[58] organized in ninety-two infantry battalions and forty cavalry squadrons.[59] As early as 1870 *honvéd* units participated in brigade formations in army maneuvers. Their preparedness was recognized by Archduke Albrecht and favorably commented on by foreign observers.[60] The officers' corps of the *honvédség* was a faithful reflection of the new dualist arrangement, equally balanced between former *honvéd* officers of the revolutionary army of 1848–49 and transfers from the imperial army. In organization, equipment, training, and uniform the *honvédség* resembled the common army, but its oath was to the Hungarian king and the national constitution. Furthermore, the language of command, distinctive insignia, and flags (except for the Croatian-Slavonian units)[61] were Hungarian. Thus the *honvédség* represented a partial fulfillment of Hungarian national aspirations.

Andrássy's remarks during the parliamentary debates over the army bill reveal that he regarded the *honvédség* as only the first step toward a fully equipped and totally independent national army.[62] They also implied the continuation of the struggle for the ultimate realization of Hungarian goals. Indeed, military problems, especially those of providing the *honvédség* with artillery and the matter of the German language of command in the Hungarian units of the common army, occasioned heated disputes[63] at the turn of the century. Andrássy was an ardent Hungarian nationalist but not a chauvinist. Alarmed by the growing militancy of Hungarian nationalism, he devoted one of his last speeches in the upper house to a denunciation of the perils of "national chauvinism,"[64] which he felt would compromise Hungary's vital national interests.

It was only after 1906 that the *honvédség* in all essential respects assumed the character of a national army. In retrospect, all the angry denunciations, misgivings, and fears were unwarranted, for the *hon-*

védség stood loyally by the common army and cooperated with it in a true spirit of comradeship and the Hungarian national troops fought with great distinction on all fronts[65] to the very end.

Notes

1. For details see János Décsy, *Prime Minister Gyula Andrássy's Influence on Habsburg Foreign Policy during the Franco-German War of 1870–1871* (Boulder, Colo., 1979), pp. 9–10. Cf. József Zachár, "Az Osztrák-Magyar Monarchia 1868-as véderőtörvényének néhány osztrák vonatkozása," *Hadtörténelmi Közlemények* 24 (1977): 166–67.
2. See Décsy, *Andrássy*, pp. 11–17. From the very beginning, Andrássy supported the principle of liberal government for both Austria and Hungary. "Hungary can be free, the whole empire can be strong only if both according to their own forms are equally free and constitutional," he emphasized in a telling speech on September 27, 1865. Cf. Béla Lederer, ed., *Gróf Andrássy Gyula beszédei*, 2 vols. (Budapest, 1891), 1: 306.
3. Deák's most recent biography in English is Béla K. Király, *Francis Deák* (Boston, 1975).
4. On the circumstances of Andrássy's appointment and the composition of his government, see Décsy, *Andrássy*, pp. 17, 126, n. 75.
5. Ibid., pp. 17–18. Cf. Lord Augustus Loftus, *Diplomatic Reminiscences*, 2 vols. (London, 1894), 1: 359; Lytton to Granville, Vienna, November 23, 1871, Public Record Office MSS, Foreign Office, Austria, 7/791.
6. See Lederer, *Gróf Andrássy Gyula beszédei*, 1: 204.
7. Ibid.
8. Baron Franz von John (1815–76), professional soldier; major general 1861; lieutenant general 1866; field marshal 1873; chief of staff 1866–69 and 1874–76; acting minister of war 1866–67; common minister of war December 24, 1867–January 18, 1868.
9. *Wiener Zeitung*, December 31, 1866.
10. Tibor Papp, "A magyar honvédség megalakulása a kiegyezés utan, 1868–1890," *Hadtörténelmi Közlemények* 14 (1967): 311.
11. Péter Hanák, "Hungary in the Austro-Hungarian Monarchy: Preponderance or Dependency?" in *Austrian History Yearbook*, vol. 3, pt. 1 (1967), p. 296.
12. See his decree of December 28, 1866, Vienna, Kriegsarchiv (hereafter KA), Akten der Militärkanzlei (hereafter AMK), separate fascicle 82-1/1-2. Cf. *Wiener Zeitung*, December 31, 1866.
13. See Manó Kónyi, *Deák Ferenc beszédei*, 2d ed. (Budapest, 1903), vol. 4, pp. 182–83.
14. See, for instance, Ede Wertheimer, *Gróf Andrássy Gyula élete és kora*, 3 vols. (Budapest, 1910–13), 1: 311–12.
15. For the repeal of the imperial decree, see KA, AMK, 1867, separate fascicle 82-1/1-2. Cf. Lederer, *Gróf Andrássy Gyula beszédei*, 1: 207.

16. See especially Gunther Rothenberg, "The Habsburg Army," in *Austrian History Yearbook*, vol. 3, pt. 1 (1967), p. 75.
17. Kálmán Tisza (1830–1902): head of the Left Center party, which developed from the Radical Resolution party of 1861, then leader of the Liberal party, which was established through the fusion of the Left-Center party with the Deák party; speaker of the lower house of the Hungarian parliament 1861; minister of the interior 1875; prime minister October 1875–1890.
18. After the introduction of the Army Laws of 1868, Albrecht was appointed inspector general of the army (March 24, 1869), a position which was especially created for him. For details see Gunther Rothenberg, *The Army of Francis Joseph* (West Lafayette, 1976), p. 79.
19. Cf. Gunther Rothenberg, "Toward a National Hungarian Army: The Military Compromise of 1868 and Its Consequences," *Slavic Review* 31 (1972): 807–8.
20. See Albrecht's anonymous pamphlet *Wie soll Österreichs Heer organisiert sein* (Vienna, 1868).
21. See KA, Kriegsministerium Präsidial (hereafter KMP), 1867, 44–46.
22. See Lederer, *Gróf Andrássy Gyula beszédei*, 1: 334–38. Cf. Rothenberg, "Toward a National Hungarian Army," p. 808.
23. For details, see Wertheimer, *Andrássy*, 1: 297 ff. Cf. Zachár, "Az Osztrák-Magyar Monarchia," p. 167.
24. "In accordance with the constitutional prerogatives of the sovereign, all matters relating to the unified command, control, and internal organization of the entire army, and also of the Hungarian army as an integral part of the entire army, are recognized as being reserved for the disposition of His Majesty." Cf. *Corpus Juris Hungarici, 1836–1868 évi törvénycikkek* (Budapest, 1896), p. 335.
25. See especially Zachár, "Az Osztrák-Magyar Monarchia." Cf. *Neue Freie Presse*, January 16, 1868.
26. Cf. Lederer, *Gróf Andrássy Gyula beszédei*, 1: 334–38.
27. See Décsy, *Andrássy*, pp. 22 and 128, n. 119.
28. Cf. Papp, "A magyar honvédség," pp. 313–14.
29. For details, see Décsy, *Andrássy*, pp. 7, 17. See also Alexander Novotny, "Aussenminister Gyula Graf Andrássy der Altere," in *Gesalter der Geschichte Österreichs*, ed. Hugo Hantsch (Innsbruck, 1962), pp. 457–71.
30. See KA, AMK, 1867, 82–5/1.
31. Cf. Rothenberg, *The Army of Francis Joseph*, p. 76.
32. For details, see Wertheimer, *Andrássy*, 1: 410.
33. Baron (later Count) Friedrich von Beck-Rzikowsky (1830–1920), professional soldier since 1846: as a lieutenant colonel, head of the emperor's military chancery since 1867; field marshal, chief of staff, 1876–81.
34. Colonel Beck's memorandum, Vienna, November 27, 1867, KA, AMK, 82–3/20, resp. separate fascicle 29a. Cf. Wertheimer, *Andrássy*, 1: 408.
35. For Beck's opinion, see Nachlass Beck, KA, AMK, A 2, 143 and 144. See also Wertheimer, *Andrássy* 1: 410.

36. Werther to Bismarck, Vienna, July 22, 1868, Deutsches Hauptarchiv des Auswärtigen Amts (hereafter DHAA), I.A.A. 1 (Österreich) 56 Acta betr. Schriftwechsel mit der Gesandschaft in Wien, sowie mit anderen Kgl. Missionen und fremden Kabinetten über die innere Zustände und Verhältnisse Österreichs, II (hereafter Austria), File 56, No. A 2493.
37. Cited by Sándor Okolicsányi, "Adalékok gróf Andrássy Gyula jellemrajzához," *Budapesti Szemle* 62 (1890): 119.
38. This contention is well demonstrated by Andrássy's speech in the Hungarian Delegation in 1882. See *A magyar delegáció naplója*, vol. 4, April 23, 1882.
39. See Nachlass Beck, KA, A 2, 143, and Nachlass Heller, Biographie des Erzherzog Albrecht, B/679, no. 1.
40. Baron Franz von Kuhn (1817–96), professional soldier: major general 1864; lieutenant general 1866; field marshal 1873; joint minister of war January 18, 1868–June 4, 1874.
41. Wertheimer, *Andrássy*, 1: 415 ff.
42. Papp, "A magyar honvédség," p. 314. On December 5, 1868, the emperor appointed Archduke Joseph commander-in-chief of the *honvédség* (see KA, AMK, 82–3/17).
43. For details, see Rothenberg, *The Army of Francis Joseph*, pp. 76–77.
44. Kuhn to Francis Joseph, Vienna, March 17, 1868, KA, AMK, 29–3/1.
45. On the urging of Kuhn, the emperor refused to concede this demand. See Kuhn to Francis Joseph, telegram, KA, AMK, separate fascicle F 29/a 6.
46. For details, see Wertheimer, *Andrássy*, 1: 427–28. Cf. Papp, "A magyar honvédség," p. 317.
47. *Neue Freie Presse*, November 15, 1868.
48. *Wiener Zeitung*, December 8, 1868.
49. Cf. KA, AMK, 82–3/14.
50. István Báti Berkó, *A magyarság a régi hadseregben* (Budapest: Hadtörténelmi Levéltár, 1926), pp. 54–55.
51. For details, see Wertheimer, *Andrássy*, 1: 476–501. The best and most recent monograph on the Military Frontier is Gunther Rothenberg, *The Military Border in Croatia, 1740–1881* (Chicago, 1976).
52. Berkó, *A magyarság a régi hadseregben*, pp. 57–58.
53. Recruits called up were apportioned by lot. For details, see Papp, "A magyar honvédség," pp. 326–27. Cf. Rothenberg, "Toward a National Hungarian Army," p. 811.
54. Berkó, *A magyarság a régi hadseregben*, pp. 54–55, nn. 1 and 2.
55. Papp, "A magyar honvédség," p. 322.
56. In 1872 Béla Szende was appointed to that post with Major General Baron Géza Fejérváry acting as military secretary. Cf. Rothenberg, "Toward a National Hungarian Army," p. 812.
57. For details, see Papp, "A magyar honvédség," pp. 318–19.
58. Cf. Rothenberg, *The Army of Francis Joseph*, p. 85.
59. On this, see Berkó, *A magyarság a régi hadseregben*, pp. 54–58.
60. Cf. Papp, "A magyar honvédség," p. 321, and *Hadtörténelmi Közle-*

mények 14 (1967): 694. See also the report of the Prussian consul general at Pest: Wäcker-Gotter to Bismarck, Pest, November 22, 1869, DHAA, Austria, File 58, I, no. A 405.
61. Rothenberg, "Toward a National Hungarian Army," p. 813.
62. For details, see Lederer, *Gróf Andrássy Gyula beszédei*, 1: 367. Cf. Werther to Thile, Pest, July 15, 1868, DHAA, Austria, File 56, II, no. A 2429.
63. See Hanák, "Hungary in the Austro-Hungarian Monarchy," pp. 296–97.
64. For the details of the speech, see Wertheimer, *Andrássy*, 3: 406–10.
65. Cf. Rothenberg, "The Habsburg Army," p. 83.

Book Two:
Sources

Józef Pawlikowski:
Can the Poles Attain Their Independence?

Edited by Emanuel Halicz

Introduction

Emanuel Halicz

Can the Poles Attain Their Independence?[1] was published both in Poland and abroad in seven editions between 1831 and 1843.[2] For many years its author was unknown, but it was widely held that only an outstanding military man, one who was well versed in the problems of politics and war, could have written it. At first, the work was attributed to Karol Kniaziewicz;[3] later, Józef Sułkowski was mentioned along with Kniaziewicz as one of those "who most clearly understood the Polish situation in 1794."[4] It was not until well over one hundred years after the first edition appeared that Wacław Tokarz established that the booklet had in fact been written by Tadeusz Kościuszko's secretary, Józef Pawlikowski, under Kościuszko's personal supervision.[5] Tokarz based his conclusions on the records of the Society of Polish Republicans housed at the Czartoryski Museum, but he did not make clear which materials he had consulted.[6] In studying Tokarz's findings, I have decided that he analyzed the letters of Alojzy Orchowski, a member of the Society of Polish Republicans. These letters, which constitute a personal account of life among the Polish émigrés in Paris, had been sent from Paris to Ignacy Pułaski in Warsaw and from Mainz to a certain Lachowiecki in Brody. Orchowski wrote, among other things, that "Kościuszko's compliance consigns all to Pawlikowski,"[7] that Pawlikowski "who writes in Tadeusz's name, betakes himself to him always,"[8] and that "the work [*Can the Poles* . . .] had been drawn up by both Kościuszko and Pawlikowski."[9] He also confirmed that Kościuszko was the *spiritus movens* of the discourse. "Tadeusz, who earlier had no inclination to make revolution, embraces it completely now and has decided to support it invariably; the work, which was published at his expense in Paris and in which all of the ideas are his own, testifies to this." He wrote further that "Tadeusz does not wish to involve himself in letter writing, but Pawlikowski corresponds in his name."[10] Orchowski added that Kościuszko's "ideas concerning a revolution in Poland are the product of his misguided imagination."

The people who surround him have convinced him that every Pole will take up arms. 'Sir,' they said to him, 'it is you who can save the Fatherland. Everyone expects you and calls for you in the belief that nothing can happen without you.' A person as obliging as Tadeusz, who already has amour-propre and feels the urge to lead, was inclined to credit these statements, and this is the basis of all his revolutionary dreams. Those who surround him have their own interests at heart, believing that when the plans for a revolution are revealed in Poland, they will find it easier to argue that the Poles must send them money. As soon as they receive this money, the plans for revolution will be dropped. Tadeusz Kościuszko is not involved in this ignominious plot in any way, but his poor head cannot see through their intentions.[11]

Orchowski himself took a decidedly negative attitude toward the idea of an uprising. He opposed Kościuszko's demand for powers of dictatorship or lifetime command, arguing that such a demand was "wicked" and that it was "ignorance to reveal the most intimate designs through a public letter."[12] We know that at that time there was a temporary break between Kościuszko and Orchowski. Orchowski charged that Kościuszko had revealed the secret of the conspiracy, even accused him of perjury, and sent back Kościuszko's oath (sworn when Kościuszko had joined the Society of Polish Republicans in 1799), demanding the return of his own.[13]

In a letter written many years after the events of 1833 to Mikołaj Rahoza, the speaker of the noble assembly of the guberniya of Lithuania-Vitebsk, Orchowski explained the circumstances surrounding the origin of the booklet:

> France was threated on all sides. A universal sorrow overwhelmed it. But in the month of September 1799, General Brune beat an English army and captured a Muscovite corps supporting it together with its commander, General Hermann, on the peninsula of Helder in Holland. This great victory gave the republicans heart, and shortly thereafter an even greater victory raised spirits still higher. In the month of October [September 25, explains the editor of Orchowski's correspondence] General Massena beat the Austrians and the Muscovites badly near Zurich, and came close to capturing Suvorov and his entire corps in the mountains of Switzerland. After these victories, I witnessed the greatest exultation in Paris; we Poles were again elated.
>
> Not long thereafter, however, Bonaparte, who had fled from Egypt, arrived. He overthrew the Directory, which had been favorably inclined toward us, and dashed all of our hopes regarding Poland when he entered into a political alliance with the Emperor Paul, to whom he returned all of the Russian prisoners of war neatly dressed and bearing French arms, and initiated very close relations with the Prussians through Sieyès.
>
> It was at that time that Kościuszko, Dąbrowski, and Kniaziewicz, all of

whom were staying in Paris, began deliberations about how to rescue Poland. The work *Can the Poles . . .* , ostensibly published in Perekop, issued from these conferences. We all offered our thoughts to him. General Fiszer had gathered the observations common to the generals and wrote about military affairs. Józef Pawlikowski busied himself with its publication in Paris. I called upon our sworn company to send any countryman who sought me to Frankfurt am Main. Ignacy Hułlawski, a very prudent young man, came all the way to the aforementioned city, where I gave him a realistic picture of political matters. Hułlawski took the booklets back to Poland where they were read eagerly, even though the unlikelihood of action was recognized by most. The movement within the Society eased.

Note. In all honesty, I should say that the booklet, which was printed after I withdrew from the project, was filled with ideas forced upon it by J. Pawlikowski, who was opposed to my opinions. I put the matter to Tadeusz Kościuszko in a lively manner, thereby provoking a brief quarrel between us. But the honored gentleman soon forgot my sharp remarks.[14]

So much for Orchowski. I have devoted so much space to his pronouncements because he is the chief (though not the only) source that provides an explanation of the circumstances that produced the work. Its inspirer was thus the leader of the Insurrection of 1794, Tadeusz Kościuszko. In an atmosphere of protest and dissatisfaction, exacerbated by the decline of faith in Napoleonic France, Kościuszko conceived the doctrine of the Polish national liberation movements and developed his ideas on guerrilla warfare. He had almost certainly been weighing these ideas ever since he arrived in France in 1798, having spent almost two years in the United States. He found that the situation in Paris was by no means simple, for the struggle between rival Polish political groups had become particularly intense after the disenchantments of 1797 and 1798. On the one hand there was the Agency (Agencja), composed of political moderates who sought to restore Polish statehood through a war against the partitioning powers—a war in which the Poles would have French military aid. On the other hand there was the Deputation (Deputacja), a group of people with republican convictions who wanted to restore the state through an armed uprising that would erupt as French armies neared the Polish frontiers. The dissension among the Polish émigrés was deepened by other factors: the tragic epic of the Polish legions, formations created to fight for the freedom of Poland but instead transformed into tools of French policy, fighting only indirectly on their own behalf in Italy; the relation of Bonaparte to the Polish question, which he ignored in the Treaty of Campo Formio; and finally the French generals' behavior toward the legions during the campaigns of 1798 (e.g., at Mantua).

In this situation, the position taken by Tadeusz Kościuszko, the highest national authority, was of extreme importance. All the Polish groups competed for his attention. Although he at first leaned toward the Agency, as attested by his close ties with its leadership (e.g., with Barss), he soon found that its program did not suit him and instead drew close to people with republican opinions. After 18 Brumaire Kościuszko's distaste for France and for the person of the first consul intensified. He surrounded himself with radicals and clung to the French republican movement. He saw Bonaparte as a usurper and a plunderer and became skeptical about Poland's regaining its independence at France's side. He still felt a moral responsibility for the legions, and, moreover, he lent his authority to initiatives to expand the Polish formations and to establish a new Danubian legion under the command of Kniaziewicz. But he did not trust France or Napoleon, and he did not believe that the path chosen by the legions was the most appropriate one or that it hastened the day of Poland's liberation. The evidence for these views includes his final break with the Agency and his joining the Society of Polish Republicans in August 1799;[15] his pronouncements; and his oft-noted postscript on the margin of the oath taken when he joined the Society: "Irrespective of foreign powers we shall seek strength from within, encourage and expand this spirit, and in the shortest possible time make preparations for a general uprising." He also mentioned "free peasants" and "obedience to the blind collective sovereignty."[16]

The instructions he issued to Orchowski were aimed at the immediate start of preparations for the insurrection in Poland, and at "the organization of the people in the Ostrołęka forest in the Kurpie region . . . in order to transform the Society [of Polish Republicans] into a military organization."[17] Orchowski also reported to Poland that "Tadeusz decided definitely to make revolution in Poland. . . . All of his thoughts and desires are engaged in making our country reject the idea of rescue from without and instead seek salvation in our own strength, courage, and suffering. That is his demand, and he is ready and eager to risk himself and everything else for the salvation of the fatherland."[18]

If Kościuszko was the initiator and creator of the concept of the work, then what role did Józef Pawlikowski play?[19] In my opinion, Pawlikowski, as Kościuszko's personal secretary, set forth and expanded upon Kościuszko's ideas, editing the work and taking care of its actual publication. I do not exclude the possibility that Pawlikowski may have made use of the opinions of military men in Kościuszko's entourage. Thus, although the idea of the work was not Pawlikowski's own, he elaborated upon it, gave it its final shape, and edited it, and thus, from the technical point of view, everything points toward Pawlikowski's authorship. The fact that Pawlikowski played an important part in the elaboration of the work was known to his contemporaries. Orchowski was aware of it, as was Barss, who wrote in a letter (October 4, 1799) to Józef Wyvicki: "The well-known philosopher and, today, the amanuensis of Kościuszko, Pawlikowski, is working with Kościuszko on a project. . . . Ultimately none of the Poles known to me here is as self-opinionated in that funny system as is our Pawlikowski, whose opinions are much appreciated by the Chief [Kościuszko], because of his amour-propre."[20]

Who, then, was Pawlikowski? Interest in him dates back to 1905, that is, to the appearance of Tokarz's above-mentioned work. Until that time, he had been known as a participant in the Insurrection of 1794, as the author of a polemic with F. Anthing,[21] and as the author of the articles "Sprostowanie pism względem Kościuszki"[22] [Clarification of works concerning Kościuszko] and "O przygotowaniach do insurekcji kościuszkowskiej"[23] [Preparations for Kościuszko's insurrection], fragments of which were published by L. Siemieński. A. Skałkowski and W. Tokarz pointed out Pawlikowski's remarkable role in the Kościuszko insurrection. Skałkowski must be credited with obtaining Bonneau's highly interesting report to Talleyrand (February 27, 1800), written in connection with the appearance of *Can the Poles*. . . . In this report Bonneau characterizes the author, that is, Pawlikowski, and says that "for a long time, this frenzied demagogue and rabid revolutionary, this intimate and servile creature of Kościuszko, has been constantly at his side; at this time he enjoys his full confidence."[24] Władysław Smoleński and Marian Kukiel also added some details to Pawlikowski's biography, including the fact that on August 22, 1795, he signed the charter establishing the Deputation in Paris.[25]

Szymon Askenazy tried to undermine the positive opinion of Pawlikowski as a prominent revolutionary and activist who enjoyed Kościuszko's high regard.[26] In his book *Napoleon a Polska* he unceremoniously rejected the favorable opinions of Pawlikowski held by Ignacy Prądzyński and Roman Załuski,[27] both of whom were active in the struggle for independence and knew Pawlikowski personally because during the years of the Kingdom of Poland they had served jail sentences with him in the former Carmelite monastery in Warsaw. Askenazy preferred the opinion of Count Stanisław Zamoyski, who probably did not know Pawlikowski personally, and, as a man of decidedly conservative outlook, he disapproved of Pawlikowski, seeing in him only a common swindler, a small and limited man, at best a firebrand and debaucher. To be sure, Askenazy could not dispute the thesis of Pawlikowski's authorship of *Can the Poles*. . . . But, with unprecedented wile, he attributed to Kościuszko "a few golden truths and a few bronze lessons straight from his great heart, characterized by the visible mark of his abiding faith and simple wisdom,"[28] while at the same time implying that Pawlikowski had abused the authority of his chief, because "abstract presuppositions were plunged deep into the flood of supposed immediate application, and fantastic, positively preposterous deductions were aimed toward the conclusion that revolt was an absolute necessity."[29] In his polemic with Askenazy, B. Limanowski correctly claimed that since "it was difficult to condemn Kościuszko, Pawlikowski was made to suffer for the sin of revolution."[30] Askenazy disregarded the criticisms leveled by Limanowski and M. Handelsmann,[31] and in his work on W. Łukasiński, he adjusted the material to his preconceptions and presented Pawlikowski in an even more negative light.[32]

Within the last decade our knowledge of Pawlikowski has increased considerably.[33] The works of E. Rostworowski and B. Leśnodorski are of particular merit.[34] Both of these outstanding historians joined the discussion about Pawlikowski in the interwar period, the same discussion in which Limanowski and Handelsmann had crossed swords with Askenazy. Thanks to them our knowledge of the period and of the person of our prominent Polish Jacobin was deepened.[35] They demonstrated the groundlessness and tendentiousness of Askenazy's opinions, while disclosing new aspects of Pawlikowski's activities. For example, he penned such tracts as *Myśli polityczne dla Polski* [Political thoughts for Poland] and *O poddanych polskich* [On Polish peasants], published in Warsaw in 1789; *O prawach kryminalnych* [On criminal law], published in Warsaw in 1818; and many political memorials.[36] The polemic between Rostworowski and Askenazy is especially valuable, for it reveals that many ideas that Askenazy attributed to Kościuszko are really Pawlikowski's. For example, in 1789 Pawlikowski wrote: "Many have said . . . that first we must educate them [the peasants] so that they will be capable of accepting their rights . . . but even the most unenlightened man should not suffer injustice."[37] At the same time it became clear that notions that Askenazy had criticized and attributed to Pawlikowski actually derived from Kościuszko, for example, the idea of "guerrilla warfare in the forests."[38]

The studies by Rostworowski and Leśnodorski signified the full rehabilitation of Pawlikowski, who had undergone an extensive evolution, renouncing his monarchistic past and becoming one of the most prominent Jacobins during the time of the Kościuszko insurrection. After the downfall of the Commonwealth, and while he lived in exile in Paris, he became one of the founders of the Deputation and later Kościuszko's closest collaborator. During the period of the Kingdom of Poland he was active in the movement for Polish national independence and was jailed by tsarist authorities in connection with the discovery of a patriotic organization in the Kingdom.[39]

The booklet *Can the Poles* . . . first appeared in mid-1800. Although it was intended to bring about a complete change in the program for attaining Polish statehood, its immediate results were insignificant.[40] Few émigrés were inclined to believe that an uprising was about to erupt or that a new field of operations would soon unfold. Moreover, the attempt to disseminate the booklet in the legions failed, in part because Kniaziewicz, endorsing the opinion of his staff, opposed its propagation. He sent a copy to Barss through Kossecki, one of his officers, and Barss persuaded his friend Bonneau to lodge a formal complaint with Talleyrand.[41] In a letter of February 27, 1800, to Talleyrand,[42] Bonneau condemned the work as inimical to the peace that France so strongly desired. He also advanced the idea of addressing a letter to the commanders of the legions demanding that they cut all ties with the conspiracy; this initiative was significant because many of the officers were seeking to resign in order to return to Poland.

Bonneau explained that *Can the Poles* . . . had been published not in Perekop on Don but in Paris, in the printing works of Baudouin, and that the work had without doubt issued from the pen of Pawlikowski, an extreme revolutionary and demagogue who had won the confidence of Kościuszko. Kościuszko's money had paid for transporting three hundred copies of the booklet through Frankfurt am Main to Poland.[43] As a result of Bonneau's letter, Pawlikowski was placed under police surveillance, the publication was confiscated, and the government issued a confidential warning to Kościuszko.[44] Some copies had been taken to Poland, where the booklet was read eagerly, but here, perhaps even more than in exile, readers acknowledged that an uprising was highly unlikely. Not even the governments of the partitioning powers were apprehensive: indeed, the Prussians recommended translating the booklet into German and publishing it.[45] I was unable to ascertain if in fact it was published, but if it was, it was probably primarily for military reasons.

Analysis of the Contents

Can the Poles . . . is an attempt to answer the question posed in its title. Basing his discussion on both native and foreign experiences, the author concludes that a nation striving for independence must trust its own strength, and "if it does not maintain its existence by its own efforts, but through foreign assistance or favor, one can boldly predict that it will attain neither happiness, nor virtue, nor glory." Freedom is won only through the emancipation of the peasants, Pawlikowski continued, because only then can they be drawn into the struggle. "Some have opined that we should enlighten the people before we give them freedom. I am of the opposite view: in order to enlighten the people we must free them." After the emancipation, the 450,000 troops of the partitioning powers (in the author's opinion this was the largest number they could muster against Poland) could be opposed by a Polish army of over one million men, an army aware of its goal, inspired by the energy of freedom, and armed with scythes because "there is no weapon that can resist the scythe and there is no army in Europe which cannot be beaten by means of it."

The author recommended a protracted war that would break out simultaneously in various enemy-occupied regions, a war conducted aggressively by means of guerrilla warfare during which the basic problems of organization and leadership would be resolved. The commander-in-chief was to be Kościuszko, who would hold dictatorial powers as he had in 1794. A congress, set up at his side on the American model, would occupy itself with legislative matters and would constitute a specific authority limiting the powers of the dictator.[46]

There are conclusions and general observations in the work based on the wars of liberation of Switzerland in the Middle Ages, the Dutch wars in the sixteenth century, and especially the revolutionary wars of the United States and France at the end of the eighteenth century. Polish experiences are also cited, including such distant experiences as Stefan Czarniecki's guerrilla warfare, the warfare of the time of the Confederation of Bar, which was still fresh in the mind, and the many experiences that belonged to the Insurrection of 1794. The work often draws upon the experiences and lessons of outstanding military commanders and theorists,[47] but its basic arguments proceed from the experiences of the Polish struggle for liberation. It is precisely to these experiences, as well as to those of the American struggle for liberation, that the author refers most often. There is nothing surprising in this; it was from this material that the author was able to draw the most lessons, thanks to Tadeusz Kościuszko.[48]

In weighing the reasons for the decline of the Polish Commonwealth, the work maintains that responsibility lay chiefly with the Polish magnates, who, guided by their own private interests, "persuade[d] the nation [in]to believing in its vileness and incompetence," weakened the spirits of their fellow countrymen, sought assistance at foreign courts and, like the nobility that was dependent on them, "were incapable of being anything other than tyrants over the peasantry." "The downfall of the Poles did not result from their country's situation or from the impossibility of opposing the enemy, but from a lack of determination and energy." In addition, in the case of the Insurrection of 1794, the downfall stemmed from "Kościuszko's misfortune," which "checked the impetus of the revolution and stopped the uprising in other provinces." The work holds it "a shame . . . that with the downfall of a single man, the life seemed to go out of them and they only awaited their end." The Insurrection of 1794, based on sound principles, ended unsuccessfully. "Nonetheless . . . this wonderful revolution brought respect for the Poles throughout Europe and revealed their spirit striving for virtue and freedom," and "the peasant realized that he could be free, obtain justice, and be counted as the equal of all." This war had serious international significance. It gave succour to a struggling France. But France, objectively interested in the existence of an independent Poland, did not come to its aid. Nor did France's posture toward Poland change after the collapse of the Polish state. And that is why the fine feats of the Poles in the legions and their courage were not used to free their fatherland from foreign domination. "If the 10,000 Poles who perished in the two Italian campaigns had instead fallen in defense of the freedom of their countrymen, how many others would they have saved, how much courage would they have imparted to their countrymen, and how many foes would they have extirpated? These valiant men died in a foreign land while their brothers suffered in bondage!"

In the situation that developed as a result of the disillusionment with Napoleonic France, Pawlikowski continued, only reliance on one's own strength could produce results in the struggle for independence. Enthusiasm for virtue and liberty and steady thinking are the indispensable premises of action. He proclaimed that a unified nation burning with the desire for war under conditions in which the commander will "hearten the people with liberty," a nation bold and firm in its endeavor, can obtain independence. Pawlikowski admitted that the enemy was two and one-half times more numerous than the Poles, but observed that historical experience teaches that even in less favorable conditions victory is possible in a war for independence.

According to Pawlikowski, the Polish nation was able to field an army 1 million strong, or almost three times the size of the forces available to the partitioning powers. In a guerrilla war conducted on one's own territory, a nation armed with scythes could more than equal the better-equipped armies of the partitioners: "The Poles have everything necessary for war, and can get along without foreign products and without foreign assistance."

Analyzing the strengths of Poland and of the partitioning powers, the author concluded that the military strength of the revolution would increase as time went on. He reasoned that the oppressed Russian peasant and the Cossack were natural allies of the revolution, that certain Prussian provinces would gladly toss off the Prussian yoke, and that both Prussian and Austrian Silesia would recognize the advantages of joining Poland. The allies of Poland were those peoples linguistically closest to them and oppressed by the Austrian monarchy. He also saw the Hungarians as allies, since like the Poles they desired an independent existence. By preaching the slogan of liberty everywhere, Pawlikowski argued, the Poles would increase the number of their allies. France ranked first among these—France which had for many years struggled against a coalition of European states, chief among which were the three partitioning powers. Finally, republicans throughout Europe were the allies of the Polish struggle. But in order to succeed it would be necessary first to give the people freedom and equal rights. The soldier would thus be made into a free citizen; he would then have an important role to perform not only as a warrior fighting for independence but also as a citizen championing democratic ideas. He must serve the nation and the revolution; "he must be a citizen, and not a blind tool or merely a self-interested being."

That, Pawlikowski explained, was the road to the creation of unbeatable regiments in a national army. "You have everything necessary to be victorious; only be brave enough to succeed"; that was the fine, optimistic chord struck by the work. The tasks placed before the nation were not easy ones, and in the concrete situation of 1800, they were unrealizable. Not enough time had passed since the Third Partition; there had been too many disappointments, and many people were reluctant to act. Polish society, like any other, was not monolithic; it had been torn apart and was divided among various orientations. Class differences played a fundamental role. Even thirty years later, during the November Uprising, neither the government nor the Noble Diet could bring itself to carry out a radical change by making the peasants into citizens. It was known that a part of the Polish landed class had cooperated with the partitioning powers immediately after the Third Partition. Moreover, there was disunity among the Poles in emigration, where a singularly hard-fought struggle between moderates and radicals had been joined.

As members of the Polish Democratic Society later pointed out, the peasant program of *Can the Poles . . .* was too general, and the program did not explain how to persuade the masses to rise up. "Let us not summon the people with the bare words of freedom, equality, and fraternity, but let us give them the means to carry out the rights to which they are entitled as well as the duties; let us really make them independent and free of their former oppressors. Let us return their property."⁴⁹ We must remember, however, that Polish democracy had not fully elaborated its program and that it did so only a quarter of a century later, after the series of disillusionments stemming primarily from the failure of the Insurrection of 1830–1831.

As a result, the estimates regarding the mobilization of the nation's strength were overly optimistic. The notion of waging war on three fronts against each of the three partitioning powers was unrealistic, and the estimates regarding the populations of Poland and of the partitioning powers were highly inaccurate. They had been taken from a dated work by A. Büsching.[50] According to T. Korzon,[51] the Polish Commonwealth comprised 11 million people before the First Partition, 7 million after it, and in 1791, as a result of population growth, 8.8 million people. In 1791 Prussia had 5.5 million people, Austria about 20 million, and European Russia contained 26.6 million in 1796. Meanwhile, in *Can the Poles* . . . the Commonwealth was said to contain a population of 16 million, Austria only 17 million, Prussia 3.6 million, and all of Russia 20 million, of which over 16 million were in European Russia. The population of Poland had clearly been inflated, while the estimates for the partitioning powers have been lowered markedly. This calculation was all the more misleading because the trained and well-equipped armies of the partitioning powers were evaluated on the same basis as the untrained Polish army was. The faith in guerrilla war as a higher form of warfare capable of bringing the Polish side victory without outside assistance, and without the Polish army's being transformed into a regular army during operations, was exaggerated.

The question of weapons—the "myth" of the scythe—was another problem. This "myth" persisted until the January Insurrection (1863), and if it was not that dangerous when the work was first published, it later acted as a brake, delaying the collection of weapons and even introducing elements of dangerous improvisation. Certainly the scythe was an imperfect weapon. Its potential was limited, but in the circumstances of the time, that is, at the end of the eighteenth century, much could be accomplished with it. The experiences of 1794 demonstrate this clearly. Its possibilities were relatively great then because the technical standards of firearms were incredibly low. Flintlock rifles, even the newest model of 1777, had a short range and were difficult to use. Their operation was dependent on atmospheric conditions, and accuracy was limited.[52] It is no accident that Suvorov valued the bayonet and hand-to-hand combat so highly and, conversely, that he put so little stock in the firearms of that period. But military techniques evolved quickly, especially after the mid-nineteenth century, and the persistence of the "myth" of the scythe was probably due chiefly to the difficult situation in which the Polish national uprisings found themselves, that is, with almost no chance of being provided with modern weapons.[53]

The Meaning of the Work for the Development of Polish Military Thought

It is not difficult to understand why *Can the Poles* . . . , almost forgotten during the Napoleonic period, was published twice during the November Uprising and repeatedly after its failure.[54] The Polish Democratic Society distributed it together with its manifesto, and in time it became something of a dogma, the catechism of the Polish revolutionary movement. Already in 1830 Bianco di Saint Jorioz accepted many of the theses of Kościuszko's work, especially the optimistic calculation of the possibilities of arming and fielding armies of guerrillas, the idea that a guerrilla war is the only possible form of warfare in an uprising, and that one condition of success was that a connection be established between the uprising for the ideas of freedom and unity and the peasant's struggle for land. He introduced these notions into his noted treatise,[55] which was the basis for Giuseppe Mazzini's famous discourse *Della guerra d'insurrezione conveniente all'Italia*, published in Marseilles in 1833.

Italian theorists deepened and expanded the fundamental principles of guerrilla war, basing themselves on, among other things, the historical experiences of the Spanish nation in its war of liberation against Napoleonic France. They outlined a plan for a national uprising that would differ from earlier struggles in Italy. This uprising would erupt through the initiative of the Italians themselves, not as a result of some foreign stimulus. It would be led by a temporary dictator, whose authority would pass to a legislative assembly after the liberation; this was to be the only source of authority in the state. Beginning as a guerrilla war, the uprising would cover the entire country, and the entire nation would participate. Once events began to take a favorable turn, a regular army would be formed and used to finish the work begun by the guerrilla forces.[56]

Appreciating the role played by the social element, Mazzini outlined a broad program of democratic reforms, but the socioeconomic demands of the peasantry and of the unpropertied classes were not taken into account sufficiently.[57] How many similarities there are between what the Italian theorists outlined and the propositions presented thirty years earlier in *Can the Poles*. . . !

The Poles joined the European discussion of the principles of guerrilla warfare which Italian revolutionaries were primarily responsible for initiating at the beginning of the 1830s. The basic precepts of a guerrilla war—confidence in one's own strength and the notion that a war of independence can be undertaken with the means already available within the country—attracted those who refused to accept the loss of their own independent state. The Poles minimized the difficulties in which they found themselves after the failure of the November Uprising—without any Polish armed forces, any free territory, or even a hinterland and administration—by exaggerating the mass-mobilizing potential of a guerrilla war that was linked to a proclamation that gave the peasants land in return for their joining the struggle. Inspired with the spirit of struggle, these millions of peasants—armed with scythes, stones, and sticks and only insignificantly with firearms—were to constitute a sufficient counterpoise to the half-million-strong armies of the partitioning powers, which were equipped with rifles and artillery.

W. Chrzanowski initiated the discussion in Polish circles:

> It is an incontrovertible truth that a guerrilla war can be conducted to great advantage in mountainous terrain, but it does not necessarily follow that such a war cannot be prosecuted where there are no mountains. Such a war can have a place anywhere in one's country, as long as the inhabitants have the courage to defend themselves, do not give in to insult and plunder, and above all, refuse to accept the yoke. In areas covered with forests or broken up by bogs, dikes, ravines, and ditches, such a war is carried out by infantry units in exactly the same manner as in mountainous regions; in open, flat areas, it must be conducted according to the same precepts with mounted units, the only differences being those dictated by the use of mounted troops.[58]

Although Chrzanowski concluded that a guerrilla war could be conducted with great success, he admitted that "the enemy can be destroyed and forced to leave the country by means of a guerrilla war only when his army has inadequate numbers to occupy the country. But such cases are rare, and guerrilla warfare can succeed only when it is connected with a war fought by regular armies, and conducted on the flanks and in the rear of the enemy."[59]

By arguing in this manner, Chrzanowski facilitated the task that faced his antagonist Wincenty Nieszokoć. Nieszokoć had no faith in the efficacy of guerrilla warfare, contending that it could not be the basis for a system of national defense and that it brought few advantages. Accordingly, Nieszokoć promulgated the idea that corps of regular army units should be organized from the very beginning of the uprising. Polemicizing with Chrzanowski, he wrote:

> Seeing things in this way, one cannot agree with General Chrzanowski.

> Experience has convinced us that there is little advantage to be gained from guerrilla warfare. It only multiplies defeats and the useless spilling of blood, and does not decide anything about the fate of the entire campaign. It squanders manpower uselessly on the flanks and at the rear of the enemy army, manpower which could, if collected at the front of the army, contribute to the winning of the battle at the decisive point. By assailing a strong enemy army at its sides and in its rear one can inflict pain, but such blows are never fatal. It was rightly stated that "les affaires ne se décident pas à la queue mais à la tête."

Nieszokoć concluded: "Having such conclusive examples [the campaign of 1809 against Napoleon and the Spanish wars of the Napoleonic period], there is no need to base the system of national defense on the creation of guerrilla units, but rather on the organization of regular units on the mode accepted by European peoples."[60]

Ludwik Mierosławski came closest to this point of view. He wrote in 1845 "I do not understand guerrilla warfare, . . . as a sovereign system, as the fundamental means of insurrection in Poland. I hate it. But that does not mean that classical organization, strategy, and tactics should not make effective use of it in many instances. Understood in this sense, guerrilla warfare is one of the most valuable weapons in the hands of an intelligent government and an able commander."[61]

The center of the Polish Democratic Society, which comprised the progressive Polish émigrés in France, assigned a substantial role to guerrilla activities in a modern, popular war. Although they duly appreciated the role of regular and semiregular units, they saw guerrilla warfare as valuable in facilitating the beginning of battle with the invaders, in weakening the physical and moral potential of the enemy, and finally in contributing to the victorious conclusion of the war. The participants in this great discussion of the national armed forces also recognized that the mass uprising that would initiate the national war must pass through a guerrilla phase. Its task would be to prepare conditions for the further development of the war, to lead to the creation of a regular army, and to shield its concentration. If there was no agreement in the matter of tactics, the members of the Society at least shared the conviction that the granting of land and equal rights to the peasant masses would constitute the foundation of the national army.[62]

The discussion that began in the 1830s was joined ten years later by the three outstanding theoreticians of national uprisings: K. B. Stolzman, H. Kamieński, and J. Bem. The first of them, an officer in the army of the Duchy of Warsaw and later in that of the Kingdom of Poland, a participant in the November Uprising, and an active member of the

Young Poland movement, expressed his opinion in *Partyzantka, czyli wojna dla ludów powstających najwłaściwsza* [Guerrilla warfare, or the most advisable war for peoples in revolt].[63] For the general section of this work, Stolzman drew many opinions from Mazzini's *Della guerra d'insurrezione conveniente all'Italia* and *Manuale pratico del Rivoluzionario Italiano desunto dal trattato sulla guerra d'insurrezione per bande*.[64] There are also many new ideas, however, especially in the sections treating the organization of the armed forces, tactics, and the use of weapons. But the basic concept, reliance on one's own strength and the belief that one can muster 4 million armed men (what optimism!), is similar to Kościuszko's. According to Stolzman, universality, an aggressive spirit, and gallantry were the three main attributes that should characterize an uprising. But these weapons were inadequate for a struggle against the three oppressors of Poland. Guerrilla warfare was the decisive weapon, the same weapon that had brought victory over the Turks to the Albanians under Skanderbeg, to the Serbs under Karageorge and Miloš, and later to the Greeks. The same weapon had also enabled the Netherlands to prevail over Philip, America over England, and Russia, the Germans, and Spain over the genius and power of Napoleon. In reciting Mazzini's list of past victories gained through the skillful conduct of guerrilla wars, however, Stolzman omitted the role of outside elements and thus made little of the military might of the partitioning powers. He also forgot that in the case of Russia and Spain guerrilla warfare had been an auxiliary factor; regular armies played the chief role in the victory over Napoleon.

Stolzman saw the possibility of launching a national uprising by means of a guerrilla war in which the entire nation would take part, armed with all kinds of weapons: "pikes, pitchforks, scythes, axes and clubs are the tools with which people can be most easily supplied in the first moments of an uprising, and the wounds made by them will be no less terrible or less deadly."[65] He does not forget about such weapons as rifles and artillery, however, and devotes considerable space to the tactics appropriate when using them. Stolzman gives a clear picture of the first stage of a guerrilla war, which depends on quick maneuvers, forced marches, surprise, and the avoidance of unevenly matched battles. When the author begins to treat the tactics used in the later stages of the war, however, the image of the struggle becomes more vague. He realizes that guerrilla units operating in various parts of the country can initiate the struggle, but that their impact will prove inadequate to attain final victory. Consequently, Stolzman posits a second stage of war in which these "molecular" units are increased in size to form fast-moving partisan battalions grouped into five army corps, the basis of the armed forces of the uprising. These five corps are subsequently called upon to deliver the decisive blow to the invaders.

Although there are many accurate observations in this plan Stolzman sketches, there is also considerable naiveté, and what is worse, Stolzman does not take the objective situation into account. He views Polish society as a monolith and ignores both the role of class differences and their impact on any war of national liberation. He overlooks the role of the partitioning powers, who not only disposed of massive military might but also, with greater or lesser success, tried to take advantage of class contradictions in times of crisis, especially in Polish villages, in order to thwart plans for an uprising.[66]

Henryk Kamieński, the noted political activist and social writer, took up the matter of guerrilla warfare at the same time as Stolzman, eventually producing three works on the subject: *O prawdach żywotnych narodu polskiego* [The vital truths of the Polish nation], *Katechizm demokratyczny* [The democratic catechism], and *Wojna ludowa* [People's war].[67] The first of these appeared in 1844; the second, a summary of the first, appeared a year later; and the third was written in 1863 and published in 1866. Kamieński differs from Stolzman in that he propounds a more developed system of national warfare and attaches specific importance to solving the peasant question. In Kamieński's view, the prerequisite for success in the struggle for national liberation is the close tie between the revolutionary character of the armed uprising and the consistent struggle to eliminate serfdom and enfranchise the Polish peasant. For him, social revolution is not a subordinate means of insurrection but the most important means. Only social revolution can return the strength inherent in the people to the nation; without the enfranchisement of the peasant there can be no uprising. For Kamieński, the solution of the peasant problem and the guerrilla war were a unity that he called an uprising, aimed at attaining independence. "The popular war is the highest expression of a national uprising and the only way on earth to use all of the national strength without exception to defend our native land."[68]

Kamieński also pays more attention than Stolzman does to the revolutionary way in which the war must be conducted. He stresses the need to inculcate the insurrectionaries with an awareness of the goals for which they are fighting. "Inspiring our peasants with the popular war," he proclaims, "is more important militarily than obtaining in some miraculous manner several hundred thousand weapons, artillery, etc."[69] Kamieński's sober attitude toward the outbreak of the uprising is characteristic. In his opinion, the war should not result from a conspiracy or because of an attack on some enemy target. Rather, it should occur in connection with the highest revolutionary stage of the masses, the peasant masses in particular. This will determine the uprising's strength and dynamism.

Kamieński devotes much space to the method of conducting the war. He divides the whole of the uprising into four periods. In the first two, guerrilla units fight, gradually joining to form larger units as they liberate specific areas. In the next two stages these units unite to form armies. It is impossible to suppose, he contended, that enemies could be defeated without concentrating the forces of the uprising, without facing one army against another. In his opinion, a decision should be sought in pitched battles, as was the case during the French Revolution in 1793.

The connection between social and military matters was also perceived by General J. Bem, the hero of Poland and Hungary. "In our present situation," he wrote in his *O powstaniu narodowym w Polsce* [On a national uprising in Poland], "one can count only on a national uprising, only on a guerrilla war, because when the hour of the uprising arrives we will be unable to field either a large or an organized national army."[70] But the nature of a guerrilla war does not preclude the existence of regular army units; indeed, the war should eventually produce just such units in the form of mobile columns, and the main weight of the struggle should rest upon them. Although Bem, like Stolzman, would have equipped the national army with firearms, he realized that at least during the first stage of the uprising this would be impossible and therefore proclaimed: "One should beat the enemy with whatever is at hand," and "for a valiant man a rock, a stick, a knife, an ax, or a scythe is sufficient to overcome an adversary."[71]

The Polish theoreticians of guerrilla war created a system appropriate to a captive country. A guerrilla war (as opposed to guerrilla warfare, which has a limited, auxiliary function) was to begin with the activities of guerrilla units that, with time, would develop into regular units capable of finishing the work that had been begun. Such wars are characterized by a profound sensitivity to social problems and the conviction that the idea of national liberation is integrally connected to the enfranchisement of the peasants and the granting of equal rights to all citizens. Polish concepts of guerrilla war, although making use of foreign models, were closely connected with the needs of the country and with native conditions. Polish theorists modified their opinions on the basis of practical experiences. The theory of guerrilla warfare was basic to all the Polish uprisings in the nineteenth century, especially the January Uprising, which proved the validity of many of the teachings of Stolzman, Kamieński, and Bem. The struggles the Poles fought during the nineteenth century enriched their knowledge of the methods of conducting a war of liberation, especially of such matters as basing guerrilla warfare on local manpower, imparting a planned character to the struggle, and tying guerrilla actions to the operations of regular units.[72]

This practical knowledge interested Prussian, Russian, and other military circles.[73] The Poles' struggle was highly appreciated by Col. Franz L. von Erlach, an officer of the Swiss General Staff. "The present Polish war," he wrote in 1863, "has great meaning for the thinking Swiss soldier who has examined it closely, not only from the position of the state, but, above all, as a universal, popular war—as guerrilla warfare. As a universal, popular war, it is a model difficult to surpass from the point of view of domestic enthusiasm, sacrifice, generosity, unheard-of perseverance, and absolute courage. Furthermore, it is an example of the constant, powerful, and virtuous cooperation of the popular authorities, who maintain themselves despite the enemy's armed preponderance over the units of the uprising. . . . The nature of Polish guerrilla warfare," he concluded, "can serve as an excellent example that can be applied very effectively in many parts of Switzerland."[74]

The Poles' experiences with guerrilla warfare in the nineteenth century lost none of their importance in the twentieth century. During the difficult days of the Nazi occupation, Polish guerrilla fighters returned to them.[75] The French resistance movement, seeking materials to instruct the *maquis,* made use of Kamieński's *Wojna ludowa,* and the brochure *L'insurrection est un art* is really only a condensed version of Kamieński's work. Furthermore, the Poles' achievements also interested Nazi authorities: in 1940 the research section of the German general staff prepared a special document about the January Uprising based on Polish and foreign literature. Entitled "Die polnische Methoden bei der Vorbereitung und Durchführung des Aufstandes gegen die Russen in Jahr 1863," the pamphlet sought to take advantage of Polish experiences in order to overcome the resistance movement in Poland.[76]

It is clear that Polish ideas on guerrilla warfare, modified and constantly enriched by practical lessons from the continuing struggle for national liberation, especially in the period from the 1840s through the 1860s, were immensely instructive. One can only be impressed by the wealth of solutions advanced and the accuracy of many of the uncommon approaches taken in the attempt to resolve the complicated problems of guerrilla war. Many of these theoreticians had different points of departure, and the methods used in solving some of the most basic problems were sometimes different. But they all shared a common foundation and a common aim. Basic to all their programs were the principles set forth in *Can the Poles Attain Their Independence?*: belief in one's own strength, trust in the people, and the conviction that a popular war is the essential or, as some wrote, the only means of attaining independence.[77] These were important lessons that furthered the development of the Polish historical process; they were the foundation of the uprisings of 1846, 1848, and 1863. These conflicts contributed to the crumbling of the old feudal system, to the development of national consciousness among the broad masses of the people; in short, they paved the way for modern Polish society. Nevertheless, we must recognize that when confronted with reality, these ideas and practices proved deceptive, and the struggle for national independence ended unsuccessfully in the nineteenth century. Why so? A broad analysis lies outside the scope of this discussion, but is important to note certain conclusions. I overlook the fact that there existed, as is usually the case, a rather essential divergence between theory and practice. Nevertheless, even had the Poles succeeded in organizing a mighty, universal, and therefore popular guerrilla movement, which Kamieński, among others, had exhorted them to do, they would not have been able to form a regular army in the course of the struggle against the partitioning powers without help from the outside. But none of the Western powers was willing to aid Poland militarily. The natural ally of a fighting Poland, Europe's popular-revolutionary forces, was weak. Therefore, despite the greatest heroism and sacrifice, there was no chance that the Polish struggle would end in victory.[78]

The struggle for national liberation undertaken by the Polish nation in the nineteenth century contributed, to be sure, to the process of national maturation. It also forced the partitioning powers to regulate certain problems more effectively (a step they took chiefly to weaken support for national uprisings) and thus caused them to make certain concessions to the Poles. But the struggle failed to achieve the primary goal which had motivated its participants, the independence of Poland. Nevertheless, the Polish national uprisings had an enormous significance for the life of the nation and its future development, and its lessons and experiences were invaluable.

Editions of the Work

The first edition of *Can the Poles Attain Their Independence?*, ostensibly published in Perekop on Don with the *in fine* date of June 1800, was printed in Paris in the printing works of Baudouin. These copies were never sold but instead were distributed secretly; the majority of them were confiscated by the French police. At the present time there is not a single copy of this edition in Poland, Paris, or Moscow. In detailed inquiries in the main libraries and even in the archives we found only the photocopy of the title page of this edition, which was included in a collection of sources and documents of selected Polish progressive thinkers published in Moscow in 1956.[79]

The second and third editions of the work, entitled *Dzieło Jenerała Kniaziewicza. Czy Polacy mogą się wybić na niepodległość* [The work of General Kniaziewicz. Can the Poles attain their independence], appeared in Warsaw in 1831 as the second revised edition and were prepared for publication by Jan Nepomucen Leszczyński, who held master's degrees in both law and administration and was an official of the State Commission on Revenue and the Treasury. He also supplied the work with a preface dated December 26, 1830. The second edition contains xii + 67 pages in octavo; the third, printed virtually without any change in the contents, xii + 71 pages in octavo. The third edition was also the basis for the next edition, which appeared under the title *Czy Polacy mogą się wybić niepodległość? Dzieło Jenerala Kniaziewicza. Na początku XIX wieku pisane. Wydanie nowe poprawne* [Can the Poles attain their independence? The work of General Kniaziewicz. Written at the beginning of the nineteenth century. New revised edition]. Ostensibly published in liberated Warsaw in 1831, it contains 39 pages plus one unnumbered page. In reality, it was printed in Lwów around 1834 at the Ossolineum by order of its director, Konstanty Leliwa-Słotwiński. It was, of course, printed secretly, and in order to fool the Austrian police Warsaw was given as the place of publication. The book was prepared for publication by Kazimierz Thomain. The finished edition of 500 copies was sent to the Wild printing works for distribution, and the remainder returned by him was hidden in a church cupola.[80] The entire stock was burned along with other illegal publications before a search of the Ossolineum. Today this edition is quite rare. This was the last edition published in Poland in the nineteenth century. A reprint of *Can the Poles Attain Their Independence?* appeared in 1839 in *Przegląd Dziejów Polskich,* 3, edited by the noted members of the Polish Democratic Society J. N. Janowski and W. Heltman. The editors suggested in a footnote that the work may have been written by Kniaziewicz or Sułkowski, and they certified that it contained many accurate observations and much sound reasoning, all of it set forth in a straightforward, clear, and popular manner. They had decided to place "the historical monument . . . in our collection . . . because of the benefits that could be expected from its dissemination." They also stated that the younger generation, which they represented, had been entrusted with the mission of more completely developing the ideas contained within the work, especially those that pertained to the mobilization of the peasant masses, and they further contended that the words liberty, equality, and fraternity no longer were enough, that the peasants should be really made free, self-dependent, and independent of their former oppressors. Their freedom should be returned to them.

It is not difficult to recognize the principles promulgated by the Polish Democratic Society in these statements. A new fifth edition of the work appeared in the printshop of F. A. Saurin at Poitiers in 1839, in twelvemo, containing iv + 68 pages, plus 4 unnumbered pages. It was furnished with an introduction explaining the goal of the work and arguing the need to expand upon the fundamental problem of the work, that is, the peasant question. The same introduction was included in the next two editions, the sixth and seventh, which appeared in Paris in 1843. Printed at the works of Bourgogne and Martinet, these editions were in sixmo, containing 102 pages. All of these editions appeared on the initiative of the Polish Democratic Society.

The work was reprinted in the collection *Pisma Tadeusza Kościuszki* [The works of Tadeusz Kościuszko], edited by Henryk Mościcki (Warsaw, 1947), pages 168—212. Though I do not know which edition this printing was based on, it contains a number of obvious errors and lapses. The work also appeared in the Russian language in a collection of documents entitled *Izbrannye proizvedeniia progresivnykh polskikh myslitetel,* edited by I. S. Miller and I. S. Narskii. The basis for their translation was the text of Henryk Mościcki, and the authors made essential corrections in a few places, in accordance with the intentions of the author of the discourse. Fragments of *Can the Poles* . . . also appeared in two recently published collections of the documents.[81]

Because nineteenth-century copies of the work today are very rare and the 1947 edition is far from perfect, I decided in 1967 to produce a new edition of the work. It was this edition which constituted the basis for the Japanese edition of Akiyoshi Nakayama, published in Tokyo in 1972, as well as the present English edition.

I undertook this work for two reasons: the work is valuable as a fundamental document in the development of the theory of guerrilla warfare in the nineteenth and twentieth centuries, and Tadeusz Kościuszko, its spiritual father, played a momentous role in the histories of both the American and the Polish nations. The appearance of the work in the English language coincides with the 165th anniversary of Kościuszko's death.

Relevance of the Work Today

In placing the work *Can the Poles Attain Their Independence?* in the hands of readers I feel obliged to explain why I consider the English edition of this work relevant today.

First of all, I consider the work a classic of military history unsurpassed in its treatment of the theory and practice of guerrilla, national, and popular wars. Constituting the foundation of Polish ideas on guerrilla war and national liberation, the work assumed a special meaning during the Second World War, and its lessons were put into practice in countries other than Poland. The principles of an unconventional war promulgated by the authors of *Can the Poles Attain Their Independence?* have not lost their importance, as we can see when we compare the contents of the work with actual wars of liberation, especially those fought by Third World countries since the Second World War, and when we compare its program with the theories of warfare developed in those countries.

Second, this work, which was written in the atmosphere of the Enlightenment, the French Revolution, and the American War of Independence, introduced the idea of the modern nation, the principles of "tout citoyen doit être soldat, tout soldat citoyen" (Dubois Crancé) and "la levée en masse." In the area of tactics and strategy it enriched the concepts born during the French Revolution, especially Carnot's thesis that "la guerre actuelle n'a aucun rapport avec les guerres communes." The work is also of interest as a practical application of the lessons of the French and American revolutionary wars.

Finally, the work increases our knowledge of Tadeusz Kościuszko, a national hero in both Poland and the United States.

The problems of guerrilla war, overlooked until recent years, are now of central interest to many military historians. It is hoped that the English-language version of this fundamental work may prove useful to them.

Notes

1. A fictional place of publication, Perekop on Don, was given in the first edition, with the date *in fine* of June 1800.
2. It was reprinted twice in Warsaw in 1831, in Lwów in 1834, in exile twice in 1839, and twice again in 1843. Henryk Mościcki erroneously puts the number of editions at five.
3. The title of the second, third, and fourth editions is *Dzieło Jenerała Kniaziewicza. Czy Polacy mogą się wybić na niepodległość?* [The work of General Kniaziewicz. Can the Poles attain their independence?] in K. Estreicher, *Bibliografia polska XIX stulecia* (Cracow, 1874), II, 391; L. Finkel, *Bibliografia historii polskiej*, vol. 1 (Warsaw, 1955), item 9713, p. 516, and item 28008, p. 1399; and even in J. Gąsiorowski, *Bibliografia druków dotyczących powstania styczniowego 1863–1865* (Warsaw, 1923). Kniaziewicz is mentioned as the author in all these works. Why authorship was attributed to him is unknown. It is possible that it

may be connected with the fact that Kniaziewicz, one of the first men active in the legions, asked to be dismissed and had left France by mid-1801. It was not known for many years that Kniaziewicz did not support the idea of an uprising in Poland and came out strongly against disseminating *Can the Poles* . . . in his legion. See S. Askenazy, *Napoleon a Polska* (Warsaw-Cracow, 1919), III, 139–140, 144–145, 213. Following the lead of Jan Nepomucen Leszczyński, the publisher of the second and third editions of the work, the conviction became widespread that it had been published in Wrocław. This information was given in *Przegląd Dziejów Polskich* and later by K. Estreicher and L. Finkel. Today we know that the work was published neither in Perekop on Don nor in Wrocław. It was published in Paris at the printshop of Baudouin, the only shop with Polish type.

4. A textual footnote in *Czy Polacy mogą się wybić na niepodległość?* which appeared in *Przegląd Dziejów Polskich* (Poitiers, 1839), III, 3.

5. W. Tokarz, *Ostatnie lata Hugona Kołłątaja (1794–1812)* (Cracow, 1905), I, 95n.

6. Czartoryski Museum, Cracow, manuscript 3929, Akta i listy Związku Republikańskiego 1798–1800, pp. 223–231, and manuscript 3930, Akta i listy Związku Republikańskiego 1799–1814, pp. 445–458, 447, 448, 453. This letter was bound incorrectly, and the order of pages given here corresponds to the proper order.

7. Czartoryski Museum, manuscript 3930, Akta i listy Związku Republikańskiego 1799–1814, f. 558.

8. Czartoryski Museum, manuscript 3929, Akta i listy Związku Republikańskiego 1798–1800, f. 229, report by Orchowski.

9. Czartoryski Museum, manuscript 3930, f. 557, letter of Orchowski to I. Pułaski, or to Lachowiecki in Brody, written at Mainz, October 27, 1800.

10. Czartoryski Museum, manuscript 3229, f. 226.

11. Czartoryski Museum, manuscript 3929, f. 324.

12. Czartoryski Museum, manuscript 3939, f. 557.

13. See Askenazy, *Napoleon a Polska*, III, 214.

14. "Listy Alojzego Orchowskiego do Mikołaja Rahozy z 1833," in *Sprawozdania Zarządu Muzeum Narodowego Polskiego w Rapperswilu za rok 1907* (Paris, 1908), pp. 70–71.

15. Askenazy, *Napoleon a Polska*, III, 138–139; see also E. Halicz, *Geneza Księstwa Warszawskiego* (Warsaw, 1962), pp. 132–133; and M. Handelsmann, *Rozwój narodowości nowoczesnej na Zachodzie Europejskim* (Warsaw, 1924), p. 185.

16. Askenazy, *Napoleon a Polska*, III, 207.

17. Ibid., pp. 207–208.

18. Ibid., p. 208.

19. Józef Pawlikowski, family coat-of-arms—*Cholewa*, born near Piotrków in 1770. Graduated from the Academy of Cracow (the present-day Jagiellonian University) as a burgher and later worked as an attorney. On Ingelström's list, he figured as "one of those damned Warsaw lawyers." See E. Rostworowski,

"Myśli polityczne Józefa Pawlikowskiego," in *Legendy i fakty XVIII w.* (Warsaw, 1963), p. 226; and Tadeusz Pawlikowski and Sławomir Jaros, "Kiedy i gdzie urodził się Jakobin Józef Pawlikowski," in *Kwartalnik Historyczny*, 1970, no. 1, pp. 95–96.

20. *Archiwum Wybickiego*, collected and edited by A. Skałkowski (Gdańsk, 1948), I, 442–443; and E. Rostworowski, "Jakobin Józef Pawlikowski anonimowym autorem słynnych pism politycznych," in *Kwartalnik Historyczny*, 1956, no. 2, p. 78.

21. In reply to the work of F. Anthing, *Les campagnes de feldmarechal Suworow Rymninsky* (Gotha and London, 1799), Pawlikowski wrote his *Réponse aux assertions de l'auteur des campagnes de Suworow, au sujet de celle, que ce général fit en Pologne dans l'année 1794* (Paris, 1800).

22. See *Weteran Poznański*, 1825, nos. 1–4.

23. See *Przegląd Polski*, 1876, no. 1.

24. A. Skałkowski, *O kokardę legionów* (Lwów, 1912), pp. 136–37; and W. Tokarz, *Ostatnie lata Hugona Kołłątaja*.

25. W. Smoleński, *Emigracja polska w latach 1795–7* (Warsaw, 1911), p. 4; M. Kukiel, *Próby powstańcze po III rozbiorze 1795–7* (Cracow, 1912), pp. 92, 342; and Rostworowski, *Jakobin Józef Pawlikowski*, p. 74.

26. Askenazy, *Napoleon a Polska*, III, 209.

27. See *Pamiętniki generała I. Prądzyńskiego*, 2nd ed. (Cracow, 1909), I, 168–169, and *Przegląd Polski*, 1866, I, 68. See also Rostworowski, *Legendy i fakty*, pp. 262–263.

28. Askenazy, *Napoleon a Polska*, III, 210.

29. Ibid., p. 121.

30. B. Limanowski, *Historia demokracji polskiej w dobie porozbiorowej*, p. I (Cracow, 1922), p. 83.

31. M. Handelsmann referred to Askenazy's characterization of Pawlikowski as unjust. *Rozwój narodowości nowoczesnej* (Warsaw, 1924), p. 188.

32. S. Askenazy, *Walerian Łukasiński* (Warsaw, 1928), II, 82, 378, 323.

33. See Rostworowski, *Jakobin Józef Pawlikowski*.

34. Rostworowski, *Jakobin Józef Pawlikowski*, and *Myśli polityczne Józefa Pawlikowskiego*; B. Leśnodorski, *Polscy jakobini* (Warsaw, 1960).

35. Rostworowski, *Legendy i fakty*, pp. 196, 211.

36. Leśnodorski, *Polscy jakobini*, p. 238. During my research on the origin of the Duchy of Warsaw, I came across a very interesting memorial by Pawlikowski written in Paris on August 29, 1807, and addressed to Napoleon (Archives des Affaires Étrangères, vol. Pologne 1807 et 1808). In this memorial, written after the treaty of Tilsit, Pawlikowski expressed his opinion that Russia would strive for revenge and could count on the support of the German states and Prussia in her struggle. The reconstruction of Poland, the real ally of France, was thus in France's interest. Pawlikowski also demonstrated that Russia should be partitioned for the good of Europe. This could be realized through war, or by supporting the pretensions of various dynasties with regard to Russia, or by inciting the various nations under the tsarist yoke to a war of liberation.

37. *Myśli polityczne dla Polski* (Warsaw, 1789), pp. 41–45, on the basis of Rostworowski, *Jakobin Józef Pawlikowski*, p. 76.
38. Rostworowski, *Jakobin Józef Pawlikowski*, p. 76; see also Czartoryski Museum, manuscript 3929, pp. 228–229.
39. Pawlikowski died in the Carmelite jail in 1829. He had been jailed in 1826 in connection with the discovery of a patriotic organization in the Kingdom of Poland.
40. A. Skałkowski, *Z dziejów insurekcji 1794 r.* (Warsaw, 1926), p. 29.
41. Askenazy, *Napoleon a Polska*, III, 213.
42. Skałkowski, *O kokardę legionów*, pp. 136–138.
43. Ibid.
44. Ibid.
45. According to Schultz, writing at Frankfurt on March 2, 1801, on the basis of *Listy znakomitych Polaków wyjaśniające historię Legionów* (Cracow, 1831), p. 112; see also Skałkowski, *O kokarde legionów*, p. 138.
46. See Tokarz, *Ostatnie lata Hugona Kołłataja*, I, 94–95.
47. The author often refers to the following authorities: Lloyd, Folard, Suvorov, and Turenne.
48. Kościuszko referred to his American experiences as early as 1792. See *Tadeusz Kościuszko. Dwie relacje o kampanii polsko-rosyjskiej 1792 roku* (Warsaw, 1964), pp. 81–82. See also J. Skowronek, "The Model of Revolution in East Central European Political Thought during the Napoleonic Era" in *Acta Poloniae Historica* 41 (1980).
49. *Przegląd Dziejów*, 1839, III, 23, the final footnote to *Can the Poles . . .* , and the introduction to the same work, sixth edition (Paris, 1843), p. 5.
50. A. Büsching, *Geografia Królestwa Polskiego i W. Ks. Litewskiego*, Polish trans. (Leipzig, 1758).
51. T. Korzon, *Wewnętrzne dzieje Polski za Stanisława Augusta*, 2d ed. (Warsaw, 1897), I, 62, 160–162.
52. P. Wilniewczyc, *Broń strzelecka* (Łódź-Warsaw, 1955), pp. 37–38, 53.
53. Skałkowski, *Z dziejów insurekcji*, p. 29; E. Halicz, "Problematyka wojskowa powstania styczniowego," in *IX Powszechny Zjazd Historyków Polskich. Powstanie styczniowe 1863* (Warsaw, 1963), p. 128n; and E. Halicz, *Partisan Warfare in 19th-Century Poland: The Development of a Concept* (Odense, 1975), pp. 44–46.
54. It was printed and distributed by the Polish Democratic Society.
55. Carlo Bianco Conte di Saint Jorioz, *Della guerra nazionale d'insurrezione per bande aplicata all'Italia*, II (Marseilles, 1830). M. Kukiel wrote of this matter in his review of Piero Piero, *Carlo Bianco conte di Saint Jorioz e lo suo trattato sulla guerra partigiana* (Turin, 1958), in *Teki Historyczne* 9 (1958), and in "Zagadnienia wojskowe powstania styczniowego," in *Teki Historyczne*, 1962–1963, XII, 97.
56. Piero Pieri, *Storia militare del Risorgimento* (Turin, 1962), pp. 107n, 129n.
57. Giorgio Candeloro, *Storia dell'Italia moderna, dalla restaurazione alla rivoluzione nazionale* (Milan, 1958), Russian trans. (Moscow, 1961), pp. 259–270.

58. W. Chrzanowski, *O wojnie partyzanckiej* (Paris, 1835), pp. 4–5.
59. Ibid., p. 5. The Polish Democratic Society adopted a critical attitude toward this work. See *Demokrata Polski*, 1840, II, 38–40.
60. W. Nieszokoć, *O systemie wojny partyzanckij wzniesionym wśród emigracji* (Paris, 1835), pp. 9, 10–11, 13.
61. L. Mierosławski, *Rozbiór krytyczny kampanii 1831 roku i wywnioskowanie z niej prawidła do wojny narodowej* (Paris, 1845), pp. 54–55; see also L. Mierosławski, *Instrukcja powstańcza* (Warsaw, 1958).
62. See *Towarzystwo Demokratyczne Polskie o sile zbrojnej narodowej*, ed. M. Anusiewicz, intro. E. Kozłowski (Warsaw, 1960).
63. The first edition of Stolzman's work appeared in 1844 in Paris and Leipzig, the second not until 1959, in Warsaw.
64. See E. Halicz, "O partyzantce Stolzmana," *Wojskowy Przegląd Historyczny*, 1960, no. 3, pp. 403–405.
65. K. B. Stolzman, *Partyzantka, czyli wojna dla ludów powstających najwłaściwsza*, ed. M. Anusiewicz, intro. E. Kozłowski (Warsaw, 1959), p. 20.
66. L. Mierosławski critically analyzed Stolzman's work. See *Demokrata Polski*, February 1, 1845, February 8, 1845, February 15, 1845. See also M. Żychowski, *Ludwik Mierosławski* (Warsaw, 1963), p. 185n.
67. H. Kamieński [Filaret Prawdoski], *O prawdach żywotnych narodu polskiego* (Brussels, 1844), *Katechizm demokratyczny, czyli opowiadanie słowa ludowego* (Paris, 1845), and [X.Y.Z.], *Wojna ludowa* (Bendlikon, 1866) written in 1863. The first two of Kamieński's works were reviewed in *Demokrata Polski* on the following dates: March 29, 1844, April 6, 1844, April 20, 1844, May 2, 1844, and March 15, 1845.
68. Kamieński, *Wojna ludowa*, p. 14.
69. Ibid., p. 21.
70. J. Bem, *O powstaniu narodowym w Polsce*, ed. E. Kozłowski (Warsaw, 1956), p. 72.
71. Ibid., p. 107.
72. E. Halicz, "La guerre de partisans en Pologne au XIX siècle," in *Etudes polonaises d'histoire militaire* (Warsaw, 1965), pp. 75–84.
73. S. Gesket, *Voennye deistviia v Tsarstve Polskom v 1863 g.* (St. Petersburg, 1894); J. Verdy du Vernois, *Im Hauptquartier der russischen Armee in Polen 1863–1865, Persönliche Errinnerungen* (Berlin, 1905).
74. F. L. von Erlach, *Die Kriegsführung der Polen im Jahr 1863* (Darmstadt-Leipzig, 1866), Polish ed., *Partyzantka w Polsce 1863* (Warsaw, 1919), 2nd ed. (Warsaw, 1960), p. 150.
75. See *Gwardzista*, no. 1, May 25, 1942, and no. 2(38), January 25, 1944; and *Trybuna Wolności*, no. 21, December 1, 1942, and no. 25, February 1, 1943.
76. The National Archives. National Archives and Records Services General Records Microfilms at Alexandria, Virginia. 32 Records of the Reich Leader at the SS and Chief of the German Police, part 1, vol. 175, serial II, roll number III. The full text of the document appeared in E. Halicz, "Doświadczenia powstania styczniowego w ujęciu naczelnych władz hitlerowskich," *Wojskowy Przegląd Historyczny*, 1965, no. 3, pp. 356–368.

77. Skałkowski, *Z dziejów insurekcji*, p. 234.
78. Halicz, *Partisan Warfare*, pp. 20–21; and E. Halicz, *Polish National Liberation Struggles and the Genesis of the Modern Nation* (Odense, 1982), pp. 95–96.
79. *Izbrannye proizvedeniia progresivnykh polskikh myslitelei*, ed. I. S. Miller and I. S. Narskii (Moscow, 1956), I, 539–584. A facsimile of the title page is on p. 554.
80. W. T. Wisłocki, *Tajne druki Zakładu Ossolińskich. W stuleciu procesu o zdradę stanu* (Lwów, 1935), pp. 30–32.
81. *Wybór tekstów źródłowych z historii Polski w latach 1784–1864*, ed. S. Kieniewicz, T. Mencel, and W. Rostocki (Warsaw, 1956), and in *Nurty lewicowe w dobie powstań narodowych 1794–1849*, ed. E. Halicz et al. (Warsaw-Wrocław-Cracow, 1961), pp. 125–129.

Can the Poles Attain Their Independence?
Józef Pawlikowski

Author's Preface

Poland has been erased from the ranks of the European powers. Is this terrible fate or sentence to be eternal? Or is it a passing calamity, like an extraordinary flood or mad torrent that destroys all but does not swallow it up and, subsiding, leaves what remains scarred by great losses? How can we solve this political problem? What a great advantage the Poles would have if they could foresee their future exactly. If justice were to pass sentence on countries, we could beseech her as follows: consider a nation that did not invade other nations, but wished only to preserve itself, a nation that did not seek gains by deceit from others, but sought only to better the lot of its countrymen, and, in whose defense, during the most recent struggle, Europe's outstanding representative of citizenly virtue fell on the field of battle. Should not such a nation not merely exist and be counted among the powers but be highly respected? But alas! Justice is merely a phantom among nations! The bandits' iron defines all with bitter rage, overcoming all, taking its plunder, appointing authorities, while millions are forced to submit to the yoke of rakish scoundrels. . . . O Pole! You have seen that complaints against this injustice from all parts of Europe are in vain: convince yourself that if you desire happiness, virtue, and glory for yourself and your descendants you must use every means with which nature endowed the soul of man in order to maintain what is right. As I turn my thoughts to attaining freedom, I place, as it were, a burnt offering on the altar of the Fatherland by showing my compatriots the faults that impeded them in earlier struggles. I do this so that they can rise to the point that they will inspire respect for themselves and affirm their own happiness. I seek to do justice to the attributes that can lead them to power.

The Faults of the Poles Which Keep Them from Political Independence

A nation seeking independence must have absolute trust in its own strength. If it lacks such trust, if it does not maintain its existence by its own efforts but through foreign assistance or favor, one can boldly predict that it will attain neither happiness, nor virtue, nor glory. Look to history. Is there any country whose memory we respect that achieved a high degree of glory through foreign patronage? On the contrary, we can observe the sorry results of such patronage. Passing over other examples, let us merely recall how the Romans esteemed the Greeks, from whom they learned wise laws. However, when the Romans began to interfere in the government of the Greeks, they ended by imposing their yoke on them. When the Poles trusted in their own strength, their victorious arms stretched from Vienna to Moscow. By underestimating themselves and constantly relying on foreign help, they declined into insignificance and suffered the imposition of a foreign yoke. Our low opinion of ourselves arose when Polish noblemen no longer sought the good of their country but the support of haughty, powerful families. During the *interregna* each of the parties, seeking to give their fellow countrymen a ruler, betook themselves to foreign courts to secure money and armed assistance. They wanted to bestow this money and protection on others, thereby increasing the number of their own supporters. The more of them a family had, the more certain it was of winning a matter before the tribunals, or of passing laws useful to it in the Diet, and, in this manner, of acquiring enormous estates, the likes of which cannot be found in any other European country. The weak were forced to seek the protection of the mighty in order that their property not be taken away from them in the courts. Neighboring kings, seeking intrigue in Poland, betook themselves to the magnates and gave them money; the latter instructed their base clients or scattered small sums among them, in order to create the tumult that was necessary for the monarch who paid them.[1]* That is why the Polish noblemen, and especially the mighty ones, were unaccustomed to making sacrifices for the Fatherland in public matters and sought only to derive greater wealth from the disorder. It was in the interests of the magnates to persuade the nation to believe in its vileness and incompetence, to convince it that it could do nothing on its own without the help of one of the neighboring powers. And thus did the magnates, bartering the blood of their nation at the footstools of the thrones, lord over the people. It was in the interests of the magnates to weaken the spirit of their fellow countrymen and belittle their good qualities; otherwise the people might feel their strength and throw off such shameful patronage, eradicating the magnates' influence and authority in the process.

    A nation, laboring on its own with no fear of anything whatsoever and not carried away by anything, seeks through wise laws to instill virtue in its citizens, to ensure their happiness in order that the general strength might have a more solid foundation. In such a nation the law restrains the passions of all equally, which is why its citizens can be neither oppressors nor extortioners. Let us recall the kind of opinion the Poles had of themselves, as unfit for industry, crafts, and science, and, worst of

---

* There are two sets of footnotes: notes 1–22 are the author's (Pawlikowski's), notes 101–165 are the editor's (Halicz's).

all, as unable even to defend themselves. That opinion, which exists to this day, maintains us Poles in our misfortune. Can it be that a nation of 16 million, once flourishing, second to no other nation in Europe in vigor and courage, with the most abundant land in the known world, cannot be free if it so desires? Wouldn't anyone who knows the government and fate of countries ponder this question? The Swiss[101] and the Dutch[102] maintained their independence in rugged mountains and marshes with population ten times smaller than ours but with an equally mighty foe: can it be that we, with more numerous supplies, with all of the treasures of nature, are to be sentenced to shameful bondage? Superstitions and vices are much more harmful than war. They have almost caused peasants to die of hunger in the midst of the greatest fertility; they have left Poles capable of understanding all of the sciences immersed in ignorance; they have left a land that abounds in horses, iron, and military stores without any means of defense, not even such means as are available to savages.[2] All was stained with transgression, and license was unbridled. The nobility was incapable of being anything other than tyrants over the peasantry. Not only does the heart bleed at the memory of these cruelties, but the imagination recoils before their variety. Poles! You have discovered many of your faults, and you know how to change your ways. Accept this truth as well: you cannot really be free unless you gain independence through your own efforts. A nation that owes no one anything other than the friendship it offers to those who are worthy of respect; a nation that makes alliances only as it sees fit to serve its own happiness; a nation whose will is unrestricted by anything, which rationally chooses what good sense dictates rather than what would endear it to a stronger power—the character of such a nation is filled with everything that is munificent and grand, all that invigorates and maintains valor, and with these qualities the nation raises itself to prosperity, virtue, and great glory. But if it can do nothing without permission, if it must submit each remedy to passion and to the interests of those who created it, its soul will grovel and the ideas that could raise it to great and creative acts will not take flight. Such a nation will remain abject, vile, and servile. I would have a law in Poland demanding the exile or death of any man who would rely on even the most friendly power in matters affecting Poland's government. The Dutch, the Swiss, and the Americans would never have become esteemed nations had they not fought their way to freedom with their own energies.

It must be confessed that the Poles cannot suffer a yoke, that they are enthusiastic about virtue and freedom. But while they are eager to embark on bold deeds, they are inconstant in their effort and weaken in the face of adversity. It is not enough to desire law and justice; fortitude is necessary to maintain them. But I see that the reason the Poles lacked fortitude in times of adversity was that they reflected too little on human fates and actions. Misfortune can sometimes be regarded as the head of Cadmus;[106] after it was cut off, new armies came forth. With time and under certain circumstances things that no human mind foresaw can occur. The very desire to resist oppression caused the conspiracy of the first three Swiss.[107] These good villagers did not lay plans for insurrection—their intellects were too limited—but their bold indignation at oppression heartened others and later made their Fatherland free and flourishing, a nation that for several centuries was recognized as the home of virtue. The American revolutionaries did not have even a quarter of their nation behind the revolt (as attested by Franklin),[108] but through their determination they won the public over to their cause. Revolutions are not planned like military campaigns. The elements of a revolution make nature herself tremble; everything is dislodged from its normal course, passions move like a wind that does not subside until it is cleansed by lightning and has driven away everything in its path. When an opinion reappears, it does not at first exhibit the strength it attains over time. Passing over the historical views of religion, let us consider the recent example of freedom in France. The kings of Europe gathered together to swallow up that nation and its laws. The French, without officers[3] because their best commanders had emigrated, and also without military plans, were so inspired by the rightness of their cause that they not only pushed the enemy out of France but later achieved such splendid power that they could themselves establish and overthrow thrones. Human thought clings to truth, the heart delights in justice, and when enthusiasm seizes the soul it imbues it with a peculiar resilience and quickness that dispassionate observation cannot perceive.

It can be said that heaven allowed mankind to comfort itself with the recognition that neither tyranny nor deception will ever be able to negate the means the people employ to maintain their laws and convictions. The art of war depends on chance, so much so that its rules are brought to nothing by the random events we commonly call luck. If military science were as infallible in its laws as mathematical calculations are, the Dutch would never have been able to resist the Spaniards, the Swiss the Austrians, the Americans the English. New approaches, new weapons, new kinds of armies render obsolete all the maneuvers to which soldiers have become accustomed. The best cavalry in Europe, that of the Prussians, was frightened of and could not resist Polish spears. The nation that has a just cause and that shows determination in its undertakings will bring them to a successful conclusion. The downfall of the Poles resulted not from their country's situation nor from the impossibility of resisting the enemy, but from a lack of determination and energy. No one will dispute the obvious truth that if the Ukraine were to rise up like Great Poland the Muscovite armies would be forced either to retreat or to split up. It would be easy for us to free ourselves from them if they were weakened in this way.[109] What would happen if Galicia were to rise . . .[110]

Kościuszko's misfortune[111] checked the impetus of the revolution and stopped the uprising in other provinces. I respect the attachment to this great man, and the deluge of tears shed over his defeat moves me. Perhaps this is the most beautiful, the most tender homage to virtue which we have in today's world—the moral feeling of the nation, and its respect for Kościuszko. But it is a shame that with the downfall of a single man, the life seemed to go out of his countrymen, who henceforth awaited only their end.[4] It was rightly observed that praise should be withheld from the living because otherwise their virtue can be undermined. Wherever you find yourself, Kościuszko, if a Pole boasts to you of your virtue, let it encourage you to uphold its integrity and to be wary of human weakness. You will remain a credit to humanity, the glory of the age and the pride of your countrymen, if you maintain this most beautiful of titles as splendidly as you did while you held office, and take it to the grave.

I do not speak here of Kościuszko's military talents, but if all of the Poles, or at least half of them, had his passion for delivering his whole nation from oppression, his love of freedom for all of the people, his willingness to die rather than to fail to reach his goal or give way on any of his just demands, I ask you, would they not have obtained their independence? But just as those people who remain constant in their justice and virtue will enjoy happy developments which they did not foresee, so, on the contrary, those who do not have this deep feeling of the moment will quickly give in to despair and throw away the banner of humanity. Seeking their own abject personal safety, they trick themselves out of their own happiness. What would have happened if the Poles had prevailed through the winter during the last uprising (which they could have managed)? At that time the Prussian king had asked France for peace, and, as he himself admitted before the Diet of the Reich at Ratisbona, he left the Coalition against France because of the Polish revolution. France would not have made peace with Frederick William[113] without forcing him both to remove his armies from Poland and to give weapons and other military supplies to the Poles.[114] The Prussian monarch would have had to accept all of these conditions because his country was exposed to all manner of adversity both from the French and from the Poles, and most of all, his throne was in danger.

Let us recall that during that winter the French had their most splendid victories, conquering the Dutch and drawing near to the Prussian possessions. I shall not repeat other obvious considerations, but everyone knows that it was in the French interest to support the Poles because they were the only other nation in Europe which took up arms to fight to uphold the rights of the people. And what an advantage for France to ward off Moscow and to place a foe on the other side of Austria. Are we to believe that no other powers would have come forth to support a country that was a threat to the court at St. Petersburg? Our own Polish incompetence lost it all; whom can we blame for our foreign yoke?

The Poles also suffer the fault of blind imitation, as a result of which things are little considered or thought out. Because we have a matter in common with France, we insist on having exactly the same stocks, the same army, and the same passions; it seems to us that without these things we cannot attain our goal. But we should stop to consider that our country is different; it is in a different situation, has a profusion of different things, a different national character, and needs a different defense and a different kind of war. Let us not imitate others thoughtlessly. Let us rather seek our own methods; when we find them, let us know how to use them, and we will no doubt obtain successful results.

Does the Polish Nation Have the Means to Rise Up, and What Are They?

Those who lack the courage to undertake bold and virtuous enterprises erect insurmountable difficulties for themselves whenever they contemplate action, and if encouraging examples are held up to them, they point to factors that favored those particular cases and see insurmountable difficulties for themselves. They say that the Swiss were protected by the mountains, the Dutch by the marshes, the Americans by the ocean, and the French by fortresses. Let us examine their vain reasoning and faulty comparisons. We have seen recently just how much the Swiss were aided by their mountains against the aggression of the French. They had their own arsenals and trained officers. Yet, when they obtained their freedom four centuries ago, they were untrained and unarmed, and even so they were victorious over those who have now defeated them. Likewise, who could have expected that the fellow countrymen of William Tell,[115] who then numbered not more than one million, would have been able to resist the enormous might of the Austrians? Energy, self-esteem, and enthusiasm for justice triumphed over all. Holland, which is today wealthy and numbers some 1 million inhabitants, had no more than half of its present population and was the poorest of countries when it began to grapple with the mightiest European power of its day. As a Spanish colony, it was not prepared for war, nor was it protected by any topographical features: it had only the valor of its countrymen to defend it. At the beginning of its revolution, America did not have even 2 million people; they were divided in their opinions, poor in supplies, and without any way, means, or plan of making war. But they devised various kinds of weapons, courageously stripped the enemy of his, and strove for independence. After a few years' struggle, foreign reinforcements were found.[5] The ocean, rather than helping the Americans, in fact made them weaker vis-à-vis England. The latter, possessing the mightiest of fleets, easily interfered with the purchase of arms, ammunition, and all the other necessities the Americans lacked and sought in Europe and elsewhere. Could and did the fortresses defend France? When the king of Prussia found himself on the plains of Champagne with 60,000 Prussians, was it a fortress that held him back, or was it a mass of French citizens? And, moreover, did not some fortresses surrender? There are no fortresses between Champagne and Paris, and the French army was not numerous, but the mass of assembled citizens surrounded the Prussians and forced them to withdraw from France.[6] When the enemy had conquered Toulon[119] and was joined by the revolt of Lyon and Bordeaux, and when the Vendée raised the banners of the republic's enemies, what prevented the enemy from reaching Paris if not the valor of the republicans? We know that there are no fortresses between Toulon and the Vendée. Lacking weapons and ammunition, the French gathered them from whoever possessed them and handed them over to the fighters; in the meantime, all of the craftsmen working in iron were employed to produce more. They had no gunpowder, so they dug up the cellars to make saltpeter. They lacked iron, so they tore out bars and gratings and melted them down to make cannonballs. The officers had emigrated, so they promoted the more able soldiers and made them officers. The power of freedom was their strength, providing everything they lacked and giving them victory.

But lest we dwell too much on foreign examples, let us reflect on the Poles themselves. A decade before 1794, who could have predicted that our 18,000-man army, with an internal enemy and its own government against it, would be able to make war on three powers, fight valiantly, and cover itself with glory? If someone had promised to move a mountain from one place to another, he would have been believed more readily than one who foretold this. Nonetheless, it happened. And even if, because of our mistakes, the aims of the nation were not crowned with success, this wonderful revolution gained respect for the Poles throughout Europe and revealed that their spirit was striving for virtue and freedom. The triumph of humanity had begun. The peasant realized that he had been reborn when he learned that he could be free, obtain justice, and be counted as the equal of all others. Our enemies brutally shed our blood, but they (not to mention the rest of Europe) never respected our nation more than after the last uprising. Righteousness and its defenders have such an impact on the human understanding that not even violent oppressors can deny them respect.[7]

We ourselves have learned through experience that neither numbers nor experienced soldiers can guarantee victory; rather, zeal for virtue and freedom, as well as determination, are what lead to victory. Can it be said that the defense of Warsaw,[120] which is considered a military miracle, was accomplished by sheer numbers or by trained soldiers when we know that there were only 16,000 Poles, including the scythemen,[8] to face more than 40,000 of the enemy? After two months of encircling and storming it, the same Frederick William who had taken the strong fortress of Mainz by siege could not take Warsaw, which had no fort and stood on level ground, open on all sides. The Poles, had they not weakened in their efforts, could have held out. But I should not disclose all of the resources which became evident at that time and which we knew how to use, for the Poles are now unflinchingly determined to obtain freedom by making revolution (if it will be in the interests of all its citizens) and scoring a victory over their enemies.

Only cold hearts and narrow minds can reckon that our means are small. We had fewer supplies in 1794 than in 1792—one-third as large an army, and one-third as large a country—but can the military feats and national glory of 1794 be compared to the feats and fame of 1792? Those who were active in the revolution of 1794 know that those who were unwilling to make a sacrifice claimed that an uprising was impossible, that the nation was slothful and lacking in courage. Such people saw bravery and wisdom only in the enemy and ended their argument with the claim that independence should have been considered during the time of the Diet . . . And thus, he who is not a friend of humanity and who does not wish to serve the cause of freedom and his countrymen's welfare will try to frighten others with the figments of his imagination, not seeking to overcome the obstacles and achieve real success. Let us now examine our means.

Before the First Partition Poland had 16 million inhabitants, and before the Second Partition, some 8.5 million. These estimates were made by Büshing before 1775, and the population has since increased.[121] Before the partitions, Austria had some 17 million people, Prussia not quite 3.5 million, and Muscovy not more than 20 million, four-fifths of whom must be counted as living in European Russia and one-fifth in Asia. We should always conceive of Poland within its original borders,[122] and virtuous countrymen should never cease to view the partitions as illegitimate, ever confident that the greedy wolves (as Mirabeau[123] called the kings who divided Poland) will not hold the prey in their jaws much longer. During the revolution of 1794 the Poles in the areas under Prussian rule since the First Partition gave a noble demonstration to their attachment to the Fatherland had not cooled. Are we to understand that in the imperial [i.e., Austrian] and Muscovite portions there are no Polish hearts, no splendid souls who love freedom and the happiness of their brothers? Comparing the Polish population with that of our enemies before the First Partition, we arrive at a ratio of about one to not quite two and one-half; whoever wishes to compare them after the partitions has an easy task.

Now let us consider France at the beginning of the Revolution and the revolutionary wars. The ratio of her population to that of her enemies can be estimated at no more than one to five,[9] and if we take France at the time of the Vendée revolt and the disorders in Lyon and Toulon, then we can consider the ratio as one to ten. The ratio for the Americans during their revolution was one to eight, and for the Swiss and the Dutch, one to twenty. Seeing these proportions, we notice that our enemies are not nearly so numerous as we had feared; other countries faced far larger odds. Our difficult position at the start of the uprising should certainly be taken into consideration, but the longer the uprising continues, the greater will be the strength of the revolutionary forces and the less that of the enemy. We have observed a similar pattern in France. Would not the oppressed peasant in Russia revolt if only he had the chance? Are we to believe that the downtrodden Cossack would not like to regain his liberty? Let us add that Little Russia [i.e., the Ukraine] is the most densely populated of Moscow's lands, containing some 4 million inhabitants. If this area were to undergo revolution, what would the position of the St. Petersburg court be then? Smolensk and Kiev are old Polish domains. Every day the Prussian becomes more enlightened and realizes that he is not merely a beast of the royal treasury. Certain abused provinces would gladly throw off their yoke. Both Austrian and Prussian Silesia would profit by joining with Poland. The imperial [i.e., Habsburg] lands, drawn close to Poland by language and old ties, would not hasten to fight against the Poles, and, once they saw freedom arising right next to themselves, might we not have reason to hope that they too would desire it? Do not the Hungarians wish to be independent?[10]

Let us consider our defense. At the beginning of the revolution the Poles should not seek to form army columns but instead should try to ruin and destroy the enemy. Given time and propitious circumstances, armies will arise. Our country is flat, open, and, indeed, easy to enter. But as J. J. Rousseau[128] said so aptly, "The Poles should not stop the enemy from entering their lands, they should endeavor to prevent him from leaving." This aim can be achieved by means of a small war [la petite guerre], that is, by tearing the enemy apart and not permitting him food. The Parthians,[129] whose country was similar to ours, beat the most renowned tacticians in the world, the Romans, with this kind of fighting. Lloyd[130] wrote incidentally of Poland, saying much cavalry was needed for its defense in order to hamper the enemy and create diversion. There is no nation in Europe more capable of mounting light cavalry than the Poles. Each of them can ride a horse (which people in other states should learn to do) and, armed with a lance or a saber, they will be of great use in attaining our goal.

For the infantry we have the best weapon of all, the scythe. It is Kościuszko's opinion that as long as the soldier maintains his courage, there is no weapon that can resist the scythe and there is no army in Europe that cannot be beaten by means of it. All of the battles won by the French, those in which they took the seemingly most impervious of positions and the enemy cannon, were won by the bayonet. They used little gunfire, if any at all; the bayonet was the victorious weapon. The scythe is far more useful, being longer and therefore putting the enemy within easier reach. The bayonet merely impales; the scythe impales and cuts at the same time. The bayonet is especially useful against infantry. It requires a particularly good army to resist cavalry using the bayonet, and then the bayonet is merely a defensive weapon. The scythe not only stops cavalry, but with it cavalry can be attacked and beaten. The bayonet can be used against only one man at a time; a strong soldier with a scythe can wound three or four at once. Many of today's military writers argue the uselessness of firearms in battle and urge a return to the pike, a weapon used by the ancients.[11] We know how many futile shots cannon must fire before they have any effect. Aiming them, particularly during an engagement, is difficult, and the smallest shortcoming renders the shot useless. The longer a cannon is fired the more it heats up, and the less it can be used. Cannon cannot fire on all sides, and the direction of cannonfire cannot be changed quickly enough to hit those pressing in from the front, the sides, and the rear. A shot fired into the distance is not at all useful because it cannot be aimed. Artillery only scares people, making an impact on the imagination. Finally, a change in the air pressure, rain, a headwind, fog, nightfall, and bad aim can all make a shot ineffective. Thus far, all battles have been won by the bayonet or the saber, not by firearms. Let us consider an example of our own. Before the engagement at Racławice, 400 peasants armed with scythes were brought forward during the night; the battle began in the morning. Standing before them, Kościuszko said, "This is for your freedom; follow me!" Despite the grapeshot, they immediately hurled themselves forward and fell on the battery, taking the cannon. Not a single bayonet remained; some of the Muscovites were cut down and some of them were taken prisoner. Let others use the scythe as bravely (which may happen), let them speak to the people in their own words, and the scythe will be victorious over all.[12]

I want the generals and the officers to speak to the people and to the soldiers, and to encourage them. Roman commanders never began a battle without first explaining to those who were to fight the reasons for the war and the justness of their cause. It is necessary to inspire courage and enthusiasm in the troops, but how can this be accomplished without addressing them? The human soul is not a physical machine; it cannot be moved by the push of a hand, only by moral means. I would like all of the generals and commanders to speak to those whom they will lead into battle. "Behold the enemy, who pulled down your Fatherland and wanted to appropriate it. Behold those who are against the freedom of your fathers, your brothers, and your own freedom. They have brought their soldiers to ensure that there will be no equality among us. They have come to ensure that we will not live as brothers but that one will keep the other in bondage, neglect, and contempt. We want you to be free. They want you to remain subjects of their kings, deprived of the fruits of your labor and without the right to establish your own laws. They want you to be dependent on their will and subject to their cruelty and whims. Their kings want to make recruits out of you and send you to rob faraway lands. You were born Poles on this land, the heritage of your fathers; your forefathers' graves and ashes are here. The enemy tramples on them with contempt while holding you, their descendants, in servitude. The enemy helped themselves to your homes, raped your mothers, wives, and sisters; they impaled Polish children on their bayonets. Follow me now; I will lead you in your inexperience. Let us thrash the enemy until he meets his death or lays his arms before us, the victors."

These and other reasons will inspire zeal, but what can the enemy say to his troops? Iniquity abounds in evasions, but it cannot find a way to stir the heart.[13] The cruel Suvorov[132] always spoke to his soldiers, and not having right on his side, constantly knocked it into their heads that they were the best army in Europe. He recalled certain victories and claimed they had achieved more under his command than under other generals. The more a man is convinced of his own valor, the braver he becomes, and, conversely, when one is scorned, the less sure of oneself one is. Some Polish generals placed no value on the scythemen; how, then, were these men expected to venture forth to perform brave deeds? Instead of instilling confidence in their weapon, they undercut it. Shallow minds think that unless a man is dressed in national uniform, he cannot fight or will do so with little enthusiasm. Neither quality of cloth nor type of weapons makes a good soldier; courage and the will to win are the decisive factors. I would not wish to employ in the defense of freedom any general who did not cherish it. I do not rely on loyalty, for that virtue is common even to slaves and flunkies. For the Polish general, the regular soldier should be not merely an instrument in the art of war but a citizen who treats the property of others inviolably, just as he treats his own. Everyone should be courageous, disciplined, just, and reliable because of their recognition that arms are taken up for the happiness of all, not for that of any individual. It is necessary for the commander to inspire the people with freedom, but how can he speak of it if he does not cherish freedom in his own heart? How will his efforts turn out? And, having heard someone utter a single word against the ideal of freedom, how can I feel he could ensure my safety?[14]

I think that anyone who knows how to bend everything to the cause he fights for has real military talent. I see in Kościuszko a genius; his are the qualities essential in a defender of the people's rights. The Poles had neither army nor weapons. He created a new national force, the scythemen. The inventiveness of the human mind is unlimited when it is inspired by enthusiasm; who knows what other remedies we will find? The enemy called the scythe a terrible weapon.[15] The Americans had no cannons, and, unable to forge them, they joined together pieces of iron and struck the enemy with that. They had no bullets for their guns, so they removed the lead from windows and cast bullets with it. Zeal can accomplish anything, and determination is the key to victory. Lloyd writes that freedom is the strongest inducement to courage among those who fight. With it the Spartans worked miracles, the Romans became the masters of the world, and the Swiss became heroes in the fourteenth century. If we can infuse the souls of our people with a zeal for freedom, not only will they never be conquered, but victory must be theirs. He who begins a revolution without a commitment to freedom and equality will only spill the blood of his countrymen in vain and achieve nothing. And, besides, why begin the fight without striving for the happiness of the whole nation? The more fervently the French strove for freedom, the more fearsome they became. If the Poles accepted this spirit, they would acquire a strength possessed by no other European nation, and how much they could achieve then! What other people striving for independence had such good fortune as we possess? Others did not know if they could fight a regular army. Our peasants have had some experience, having already come under fire, and in those provinces that did not revolt the people know that their brothers fought and took artillery with scythes. The spirit of freedom has already spread among the people of Poland. If someone does not realize the zeal required at first, he will find it with time if only he has firmness of spirit and a determination to infuse others with it. I witnessed how the peasants of Cracow resisted going into Kościuszko's camp. Even after the Battle of Racławice they used many devices to get out of it, but when they realized that all this was being done to win their freedom, they stood their ground. It would have been easy for them to seek shelter in Galicia (only the Vistula River, which was easy to cross, separated us from it), but none of them ran off. Their feelings were later visible throughout the villages, as were their thoughts with regard to exterminating the enemy!

Let us now reflect on military ways and means.

Consider an army that is several tens of thousands or even one hundred thousand strong. If it were to make camp, it would occupy at most three square miles of Polish land. What could it do to the revolutionaries who scurry about everywhere in small groups? A great army needs supplies and will be unable to collect them if the insurgents hamper them everywhere and hide the food. When the army divides up into smaller units to deal with the insurgents and to obtain supplies, the insurgents will come together and fall upon the smaller units. By this means they will be able to subdue and destroy the enemy and emerge victorious. In a guerrilla war, the population has it much easier than the enemy. The citizens know every crossing and all of the paths of which the enemy is ignorant. They can gather together, approach the enemy, attack him by surprise, and then take cover quickly. If the situation demands that the insurgents hide in the forest from the enemy's overwhelming strength, what use are his firearms and artillery? The methods used by the people cannot be employed by enemy soldiers.[16] Soldiers must march together in ranks; individually they are weak and almost defenseless. The Poles can make their way through thick brush and marshes with guns and scythes, but the enemy needs good roads for its artillery, as well as a secure place to put its soldiers. Finally, the Poles can stage night attacks with great skill, and the enemy's artillery and rifles are almost useless against such an attack. Conversely, the scythe does the most harm then. At night the enemy cannot muster his ranks, nor can he move in order; he remains confused. Even if the Poles do not fight, but merely alarm the enemy day and night, the enemy soldiers will grow fatigued, a condition that facilitates the spread of disease and a weakening of their morale. Is there anything that could be more irregular than the Confederation of Bar?[138] Yet, the Muscovites admit how damaging that war was for them. They compare the Confederation to a hydra[17] whose head always grew back, and it is obvious that for several years Muscovite power was unable to choke it. If it had not been for the mistakes of the confederates, the war would have ended differently. Only the nobility was involved in the Confederation of Bar, and it was divided, almost half supporting the king. Burghers and peasants were indifferent to both sides. Can one doubt the results had the entire nation moved as one? Let us consider another example from the Polish revolution of 1794. While the king of Prussia besieged Warsaw with 40,000 soldiers, the people of Great Poland rose up at the rear of his army and forced him to retreat. There were no more than 6,000 revolutionaries in Great Poland at the beginning. There may have been an equal number of Prussians in the garrisons of the region, but the king was unable to maintain the siege because the Prussian regiments were cut off from their country and exposed to hunger. The corps sent out under the command of General Dąbrowski contained no more than 3,000 men. Good leadership qualities were essential merely to muster and lead these troops, but even a talent greater than that of Turenne[139] or Caesar could not have saved this handful of soldiers when they were confronted with such a large army. But the Prussians, occupied with the uprising and alarmed by the insurgents that were appearing throughout the country, had to look after themselves and send their army wherever a few armed Poles appeared. Fatigued and distracted, the Prussians could not inflict injury on General Dąbrowski's corps, and, indeed, he had a considerable advantage over them. We know how much depends on good spies in wartime: knowledge of the enemy's strength and location is essential for those who must plan the attack against him. By appearing constantly and in varying numbers, the Poles left their enemy uncertain and fatigued, and the enemy, always afraid of meeting his opponent, had to stop and enquire about the terrain with each new step. Especially at night, the insurgents can surround the confused enemy, attack him, and win. Knowledge of the terrain is so necessary to whoever makes war that Gustavus Adolphus,[140] the leading hero of his age, said that without it even the most talented commanders will not be able to achieve anything.[18] An army, particularly a foreign one, can never take advantage of the terrain to the extent that those who were born and live in the area can. The French armies were victorious over all of Europe, but they could not overwhelm the Vendée. The republicans never suffered as many casualties against a foreign army as they did in this province. Although the struggle pitted Frenchman against Frenchman, the brave people of the Vendée knew every corner of their land. They were able to approach and surround the republican army and inflict great damage on it. As soon as they acceded to their conditions, they made peace. After that the people of the Vendée could no longer make war, because they were unable to unite again.

Some believe that it is difficult to withstand attack without fortresses, but I maintain that fortresses are not as useful to us as forests and field fortifications are. Fortresses must be supplied with a certain amount of food if they are to endure. Finding his opponent within a fortress, the enemy orders a part of his army to lay siege to it and sooner or later takes both the fort and the people inside it.[19] But when armed inhabitants are dispersed throughout the forests and the enemy checkmates them in one place, they can simply move to another; when he attacks their front, they attack his rear. In this kind of war not even mountains would help us much. In the mountains one needs cannon and guns to keep the enemy out. Once the enemy controls the mountains, he will block the passes, thereby starving and subduing the inhabitants. In our flatlands, when the Poles are driven from one place, they simply move to another. There is no spot in our country where the enemy will be totally safe. In some places there are forests that are several miles, even tens of miles across; an enormous army would be required to encircle even one of them. Others could not be surrounded at all, and if the entire country were in revolt, the enemy would not be able to besiege a forest because he would be under attack from all sides.

We know how important communications are between armies. When the whole nation rises and we establish a sizable light cavalry that can move about the enemy, we will cut his lines of communication, thereby weakening him immensely and isolating each of his corps. Without a firm footing, the enemy will lose his strength and become easier to defeat. It is virtually impossible to cut the people's lines of communication, especially in our flatlands. The people are well aware of the most secret paths and can give one another signs through which they orient themselves and coordinate their movements.

I have already said that the Poles should make every effort to prevent food from reaching the enemy, for without it even the best army must weaken, become ill, and waste away, finally either leaving the country or surrendering. In our country, our old self-indulgence and, so to speak, our fortuitous national instinct caused us to keep stocks of food. In many areas it is the custom to store the grain by burying it in pits. I wish that this practice would be adopted everywhere. Let the people dig pits in the nearby forests and light fires to dry them out. The pits should be lined with straw before the grain is poured in and covered with earth. The grain will not spoil, and in this way we will have stocks everywhere.

The enemy will not find the pits, as long as the populace do not wish them to, and this is the attitude the people will adopt if they are given their freedom. What other benefit derives from this practice? Moving from one place to another, the Poles will not have to carry grain with them, whereas the enemy will be forced to maintain storehouses wherever he turns.

Because of the beneficence of nature we have wood and earth everywhere. With these materials we can construct batteries, and, in particular, redoubts with bomb shelters [a l'épreuve des bombes] which will be just as strong as fortresses of stone or brick. The casemates will be constructed for the storage of food and other items, the collection of which will be dictated by need. The Americans made effective use of such redoubts. Five hundred to one thousand people could be protected in such a place, which would be encircled by a deep moat so that the enemy cannot escalade the walls.[141] He will instead be forced to dig trenches[142] or lay siege as to a fortress.

Poles! These are your mountains, these are your fortresses of which you can erect thousands. This type of fortification surpasses fortresses in excellence, and its construction will be described to you. We have iron, we have grain, and we have wood; let us merely have bravery, daring, and determination and we will obtain our independence. It is impossible that a country as vast as Poland, containing 16 million inhabitants, could be conquered if its inhabitants defend themselves vigorously and wish to be free of their servitude. History provides no such example. Even the tiny states of the Swiss and the Dutch won their freedom when the people wanted it. There have been cases in which rather sizable nations have been conquered by a handful of soldiers, but in those cases army fought against army, machine against machine, and the citizens were completely indifferent. When one or two million people are willing to fight, however, they will defeat a regular army. Let us calculate the strengths of the Poles and their enemies.

I will consider Muscovy, the emperor [i.e., the Habsburg Holy Roman Emperor], and the Prussian king and reason as if all their energies are concentrated on the war against us. We know that Moscow reckons its army at 400,000, Austria at 300,000, and Prussia at 200,000. The Muscovite army is composed of various nations such as the Bashkirs, Kalmyks, and so on, whose weaknesses we already know. These estimates include both land and sea forces. But wherever the Poles go, as long as they proclaim freedom—an idea that is more powerful than an army of one hundred thousand—their ideas will triumph. Moscow will not be able to rely on the Cossacks because they always long for their freedom. In past wars the court at St. Petersburg never sent more than

100,000 men out of Russia. This autocratic government, worse than any the devil could devise in its ability to perpetuate human misery, needs to keep many troops at home to maintain order. The vast Russian realm, which comprises some 3 million German square miles [a Prussian mile equals 7,32 meters, or over 4½ English miles], constantly preoccupies the army! If we do not include the Polish provinces of Muscovy, the rest of the country can be called weak and empty, with the exception of Livonia. When the Polish revolution begins, particularly if we demonstrate our ideas of freedom, equality, brotherly unity, discipline, reliability, and honesty to the peoples of Muscovy, the court at St. Petersburg will be forced to double its army in order to prevent an uprising by its own inhabitants. It seems to me that Moscow would put no more than 130,000 men in the field against the Poles, but let me assume a figure of 200,000. Austria, before it became debt-ridden and depopulated—while England was still paying for its auxiliaries—never put more than 150,000 men in the field against the French (the rest were those of the German Empire and of the Coalition). Since Austria is now harried by ill-fortune, its supplies exhausted and its treasury without English money, it could not send even this number into the field again. Austria's lands are extensive, and during the Polish revolution Hungary and Silesia will demand the emperor's particular attention. Despite this, let us presume that Austria will send 150,000 troops to Poland. The Prussian king never employed more than 60,000 men in any war, even when he was supported by England; let us imagine, however, that he will send 100,000 men against us.

No power, regardless of the size of its army, can commit its entire army in any war. To put an army in the field and support it costs almost twice as much as the pay of the soldiers alone. In addition to maintaining a country in subjection, a monarchical government must realize that in the event of a defeat it must have the reserves to reinforce its army. Yet it takes longer to collect recruits in those countries than it does to raise the people in Poland. It takes half a year for a soldier to be transferred from one border of Muscovy to another; in Prussia, which stretches from the Rhine to the Polish frontier, and in Austria, which reaches from the Adriatic Sea to Bielsko, several months are needed for such a transfer. After a proclamation is issued by the government of a free country, the citizen immediately takes up arms and fights. In monarchical states the recruit is taken by force and is sometimes led away in chains. He will not soon become accustomed to being a soldier or soon be fit for battle. We have yet another advantage, namely, that there are Poles in the armies of all three of the surrounding powers. Since these men often surrendered to the French, not wanting to fight, we have good reason to expect a similar pattern: the Ukrainians in Muscovite service will force their way across to their brothers as soon as the Ukraine revolts, the Cracovians will struggle across from the imperial service, and the people of Great Poland will escape from that of the Prussians. One-third of the Prussian army consists of foreigners who seek only the opportunity to escape, and we will make it easy for them to do so.

From the estimates of our opponents' strengths which I have given, it appears they will be able to field some 450,000 men against us. Although I am convinced that the enemy forces will never achieve this total, I prefer to consider the maximum figures in order to convince my fellow countrymen that regardless of the efforts of the powers that divide us, they should never be allowed to intimidate us. Counting 16 million people in Poland, and figuring four out of every five to be a woman or a child and only one out of five to be capable of fighting, we arrive at a figure of 3.2 million. Is there a foe that such a mass would be incapable of defeating? But suppose that only half went to war; we would still have 1.6 million. If one-third went to war, that would mean a figure of 1,066,666. Our country comprises 15,000 German square miles (30,000 French square miles). It contains 1,060 inhabitants per German square mile, 210 of whom are fit for fighting. Calculating 450,000 men for the enemy, that is not even thirty men per German square mile. After this calculation, who can doubt our victory? During the revolution of 1794, in the Battle of Racławice for example,.there was one Pole for every four Muscovites. During the siege of Warsaw, the ratio was one against three. In both cases we were victorious. Cannot we expect even greater advantages if we are more numerous than our opponents?

If the Poles decided to rise up in one thousand places (and the more the better), the enemy would have to separate into one thousand groups. Although we should strive to rally as many participants as possible, suppose that at first the uprising was not numerically strong. The enemy, not knowing our strength, would have to guard himself everywhere and divide into groups. The longer the uprising lasted, the more people would participate in it. Although the Poles are brave by nature, there is no need to become discouraged if they do not show themselves to be heroes in the beginning. The Americans ran away from the English, but when they realized that each shot did not kill or even harm them very much, they were emboldened to prevail over their tyrants. When the Prussian king was on the plains of Champagne, a few thousand Frenchmen ran away from a few hundred Prussians, but these same Frenchmen armed wih sabers later took a battery with several tiers at Mons.[143] At Arcole[144] the soldiers refused to cross a bridge, and neither Augereau,[145] who crossed with a standard, nor Bonaparte, who wanted to lead them across, could compel them to do so. If this incident had disheartened the French, they might have been beaten, but undaunted by adversity Napoleon marched to the gates of Vienna with these very soldiers. The same scythemen who ran away at Chelm[146] attacked cannons at Warsaw and became the terror of the enemy. Anything can be accomplished through rewards and punishments. The words of Peter I after losing his first battle with the Swedes[147] are memorable: "I am beaten," he said, "but I will learn to fight later." All nations begin in this way. They learn the art of making war by waging war. Jourdan and Hoche[148] were simple soldiers who knew nothing of geometry, and yet they beat the best German tacticians. Although many French generals are strangers to the military order, for example, Brune and Moreau,[149] they prevail over the enemies of their Fatherland nonetheless. Fighting depends on bravery and on the approach one takes. When an army is brave, new and unexpected approaches can be taken, making victory more certain. It is certain that the longer the Poles fight the better they will become at laying traps. The Poles are second to none in Europe in terms of courage. I mention this not because I wish to brag about the good qualities of my fellow countrymen, but because there were times in Italy when the valor of the Polish legions exceeded that of the brave French. Pleasant feelings are aroused in every Pole upon hearing of the fine deeds of his compatriots, but how sad it is that this valor is not used to wrench the Fatherland away from foreign domination. If the 10,000 Poles who perished in the two Italian campaigns[150] had instead fallen in defense of the freedom of their countrymen, how many others would they have saved, how much courage would they have imparted to their countrymen, and how many foes would they have extirpated? These valiant men died in a foreign land while their brothers suffered in bondage! I was told that when the shadow of death fell upon Rymkiewicz[151] he wept because he was not dying in his Fatherland. . . . Those were the tears of real virtue! If heaven has afforded you, his comrades, any talents, you would use them most worthily if you lead those of your comrades with less experience to victory! If it is your fate to die in battle, you will fall amidst the grief of your countrymen. Our land will provide a grave for you, the same land that nursed you in your youth. And if prosperity crowns your efforts, the most agreeable laurels are those received from the hands of the Fatherland—the glory that comes from helping your fellow countrymen. Some may hold back out of concern that the enraged enemy will burn our land, but one must recognize that in doing so he would only increase the rancor against himself. The enemy burns a country when he cannot stay in it; otherwise, he sends his army to loot it completely. But is there no way to prevent this crime? In 1794, when the Prussians began to persecute the Poles, leading trembling women to the gallows and placing the noose around their necks, the National Council issued a proclamation and gave orders that if the enemy did not stop his cruelty, they would reciprocate, an eye for an eye, with captured Prussians.[152] From that moment on, humaneness entered their hearts. . . . We know how cruelly the Coalition at first treated French prisoners, but as soon as the Coalition itself began to lose it was forced to discontinue its inhuman treatment and use less harsh measures. When the threat of capture hangs over his head, every officer and even every soldier has an interest in behaving decently toward the opponent into whose hands he may well fall. Even the most couragous man, or one who seeks death, is not safe from being taken prisoner, and the experience can be most unpleasant.

Our country has no workshops or handicrafts; the enemy cannot destroy the earth, for he cannot burn it or take away its fertility. With freedom and wise laws our country will flourish. But are we always to use our lands as a theater of war? The borders of Muscovy are open, as are those of northern Prussia and Austrian Silesia. The Poles should turn inward, proclaim freedom for those who inhabit their lands, and behave humanely. Let every act be a moral one and we will win the hearts of the population, who will prove helpful to us many times over. The enemy will accumulate more opponents while receiving fewer supplies. He will either have to leave Poland or lessen the number of troops stationed there in order to guard his own country. Even though the Prussians held the areas of Cracow and Sandomierz beyond the Vistula, when the insurgents of Great Poland threatened Silesia (they were already near its border), the Prussians suddenly abandoned those areas in order to protect Silesia, whose handicrafts would have suffered extraordinarily and whose inhabitants always resent the Prussian yoke. In his memoirs Dumouriez[153] recalls that he wanted to move the war from Poland to Muscovy during the Confederation of Bar. How easy this would be! The borders of both Muscovy and Prussia are so extensive that it is impossible for their armies to be everywhere and guard everything, and neither of these powers has any fortresses near us. With regard to fortresses, military thinkers already had doubts as to their usefulness in the time of Montecuccoli. War nowadays has shown that in the face of a large army fortresses cannot much impede a country's subjugation. A fortress and its garrison, according to Dumas,[154] does not even protect its environs beyond a distance of two miles. A fortress may have some uses for a regular army, but the Poles need not concern themselves with besieging or taking fortresses. Rather, they should enter a country and promulgate freedom. Without the support of the local populace a fortress will starve and must surrender. For a lightly equipped army like that of the Poles, fortresses do not pose an obstacle; this kind of army simply goes around it. All peoples will accept freedom joyously, because it is an aspect of their hearts and the key to their happiness. Let us not dwell on foreign examples. Everywhere those who promised to bring freedom were awaited with yearning. But when the army's insubordination and debauchery got out of hand, the people were forced, sadly, to take up arms to rid themselves of oppression. Let every Polish advance be moral and free of the dissolution of other armies. Let us conduct ourselves humanely, let discipline prevail, and other nations will look upon us with respect and unite with us, placing their strength in the service of a quicker victory.

Poles! Do not wait for circumstances; do not expect help from a foreign war, or peace. You have great strengths; use them against your enemies and you will prevail. Every moment is favorable for freedom and justice, and brave men can create new circumstances. The Swiss, the Dutch, and the Americans did not depend on their tyrants' being at war with another power, nor did they look to see who would assist them. Their feelings encouraged them to resist tyranny. They fought long and later received foreign aid. England and France, desiring to weaken Spain, finally gave help to the Dutch.[155] After three years of the American war, France and Spain, wishing to humble England, concluded treaties with the Americans.[156] If we persist in our endeavors, there will be European powers who wish to make alliances with us. Are we to understand that all of the governments and nations of Europe are friendly toward Muscovy, Prussia, and Austria, or even that these three powers will always maintain their conspiracy against us? The Coalition conspired to partition France. That republic did not know that it could field a million men, and the kings, who were beaten, began to argue among themselves and broke off their alliance. Not only did they fail to receive the plunder they had coveted, but they were shamefully defeated. Let us add that the horizon of freedom has spread throughout Europe, and we can count almost 40 million republicans.

Poles! You should regard yourselves as fortunate that heaven has given you gifts (which it has denied to others), with which you can become a free, esteemed, and flourishing nation without foreign assistance. Be brave enough to use them and persevere in your determination, and you will succeed. The Swiss attained their independence on barren rocks almost devoid of food. If you are insensitive to your shame and to the injustice done to the nation and to the rights of humanity, you will continue to bear your yoke and even like it, and with aggrieved soul I will say to you, with despair and contempt: "Gens ad servitutem nata."[157]

Some may think it impossible to prepare a secret revolution, to gather the people while deceiving the vigilance of the kings. Even if our tyrants had as many troops as all of Europe possesses, they could not prevent an uprising. Even if they posted a soldier in every house, they would be unable to post them in every forest. Even if, through carelessness, twenty out of every thirty of our men were jailed, a welcome result would follow if the ten who remain could accomplish their tasks. We must count on luck, and we shall be lucky. Before the revolution erupted in Warsaw, some who were involved in its preparation were frightened by the arrest of Węgierski[158] and fled into hiding. But there were others who did not wish to flee despite the danger. They promised themselves that no matter how many of them should be arrested, they would continue to work. Indeed, more were taken to prison, but those who remained continued to work and their undaunted will conquered everything; we saw how successful they were.

I have demonstrated that it is necessary to select numerous places and rise up in all of them on a certain day; the enemy will be unable to subdue us. The more insurrectionists appear, the fewer will perish. The people will rally around the voice of freedom and equality, if only they are proclaimed openly enough and effusively, from the heart, without cleverness. Order and obedience are needed, as well as suitable policies from the provisional government. The organization of the government is ready. I would wish to continue the revolution of 1794 with certain improvements. The general confidence in Kościuszko's virtue is fortunate. We saw how much dissension this confidence prevented in the past, how much pride it quenched, and how it overcame the differences among various parties. It seemed that people tried to compete in emulating Kościuszko's virtue. The Romans, so jealous of their own freedom, turned to a dictatorship during extraordinary outbursts of passion among the people, during wars, and in other times of danger. This remedy saved them. In our case, I wish dictatorship to be continued until our enemies are chased from our frontiers. But I should not wish this office to be a permanent one. In the event of the dictator's death, let control of the army pass to the government. If the nation should later need a dictator and find a suitable man, then let him reinstitute the office. I would like improvements in the organization of the National Council; in particular, the persons and activities of the legislators should be separated from those of the executors. The legislative body could be given the name "Congress." All officeholders should be nominated anew, and Congress should remain at headquarters.

Although the rules of freedom and equality admit all to office equally, I would like candidates for magistracies to be drawn from the old estate,[159] in order to ensure both the closer union of all citizens and complete trust in the revolution.

I do not, however, advise that we begin injudiciously or frivolously. It is necessary first to control the greater parts of the provinces and to make sure there are appropriate men there to lead the people—clear thinkers, well-known men of character. Among the Poles the most difficult thing is to keep a secret and to ensure that everyone really has the national interest at heart. People assume various characters and wear various masks in order to secure an office or wealth, and only later is it discovered that they are our enemies. There is need of a way to ascertain which of them are to be confided in. There are certain men who, although they believe in freedom and justice, cannot keep a secret. Their chattering can compromise and harm us more seriously than open hostility. Certain necessities—a proper organization, discipline, stores, supplies of food, and quick communication so that everyone knows what to do in various instances—can be attained only through a general enthusiasm for the common good, along with the firm conviction that nothing can be done without equal freedom for all and without the order and virtue appropriate to republicans. It is important to let the Poles know what is required of them if the nation is to be free and independent. It is not enough to bestir others; each must have a heroic soul in order to act humanely.

The Moral Condition of the Poles

In some cases it is fear and ignorance, in other cases it is egoism and the desire to obstruct good intentions—both kinds of behavior can discourage many other citizens, as has been the case in other countries during popular uprisings. But such people can be answered even on the basis of the Polish revolution of 1794. The people were free and armed; did they descend into wickedness? Hatred and jealousy awaken when oppression and persecution persist, but when someone opens his heart benevolently, the bile of anger has no power over him. In France at the beginning of the revolution the people were calm. In the villages perhaps a few offenses had been committed against those who had resisted the tide of freedom. Crimes took place in Paris, but these were the acts of profligate urban mobs. But how different the French character is from the Polish character! It is obvious from French history what kinds of murders and crimes were committed during periods of national disorder. It is quite the opposite with the Poles. Even during civil wars, their animosity ended on the battlefield; relatives were not persecuted, opponents were not sought out, nor were they tormented by punishments inflicted on their wives and small children. But black is the calumny of whoever attributes the offenses of the French to freedom. Why were these offenses not visible during the revolutions of the Swiss, the Dutch, or the Americans? There were other reasons for the behavior of the French, the most important being their impetuous character. During the Catholic-Huguenot wars, all manner of atrocities were committed. And what could be more horrible than the St. Bartholomew's Day massacre?[160] Was freedom the cause of this? In other countries fanaticism was the cause of the most cruel misfortunes. But in the history of Poland there is not a trace of that specter. The revolution is not meant to give free rein to license; it should aim to realize order, to draw all actions within the bounds of the law, to accustom everyone to obeying the authority conferred by the nation, and to recognize the preservation of all property as a sacred element of society. Everyone will enjoy freedom and equality, but no crimes will be allowed. No one's passions should oppress anyone else, and the government should pursue the welfare of all during the revolution. No one should hold office whose measures are dishonest, whose life does not exhibit a respect for either property or his fellow citizens, or who has not been faithful to his duties to the Fatherland. The official with a clean soul is the most esteemed magistrate. The citizen approaches him with a combination of respect and confidence; he leaves him with judgments that ensure sweet tranquillity. Justice, not vengeance, should be the nemesis of crime, and it should serve as the refuge of the innocent. Those who pay less attention to the security of the innocent in order to punish criminals make a terrible error. This cruel maxim did more harm to and created more enemies for the revolution than all of the armies of the kings. Justice, during a revolution or in other times, should give equal sentences and provide the greatest security for innocence. There are more innocent people in a country than criminals; the latter are punished to ensure the tranquillity of the former. Despotism reigns where innocence trembles in jeopardy. In the army, the men should be imbued with obedience, discipline, and respect for individuals and the property of citizens. The soldier must be a citizen, not a blind tool or a merely self-interested being. He who oversteps his authority, evades the law of the nation, or stoops to injury and plunder is a brigand and a scoundrel. The revolution is meant to correct faults, to stamp out crime, and to inspire mutual welfare and virtue in the hearts of all. It is fortunate that the will to do good still lives in the souls of the Poles, whose nation can be called one of the moral nations of Europe. While vigilant police and endless numbers of guards cannot stay crime in other countries, the Poles are repelled from this aberration by their own feelings. It is almost a wonder, but one at which the heart rejoices, that one can stay in safety in the large forests of Poland without any security arrangements' having to be made, while the people live in squalor almost everywhere! To be sure, license has thrust itself among us, introduced through the contempt of the last king, but this unfortunate vice will be rooted out. The Polish nation is the most hospitable in Europe, and this fact shows its kind heart. While in other countries people speak of nothing but business, the Poles speak, even in public, of generosity, which is a reflection of their handsome inclination toward pure justice and a sign of great character.

It must be admitted that the Polish nation has offered the greatest public sacrifices, with the exception of the English, and the fairer sex has never shown as much attachment to a fatherland as Polish women do. Because of the circumstances in which we find ourselves, where virtue must be concealed in order to escape persecution, I will not mention certain names. However, the vengeance of the kings cannot reach your ashes, O worthy Madame Zamoyska![161] Although a stranger to your person and to your gifts, I bear you my great esteem, and someday when the voice of the nation immortalizes your memory, a fellow countryman proud of your virtue will place flowers of gratitude upon your grave.

Polish women, you who are favored with virtue and tenderness, turn them now toward your Fatherland. Think; like yourselves, everything you love, all of the objects of your hearts are stained by servitude and contempt. The tyrants look upon you as members of a conquered nation who should grovel before them . . . Young Polish women! Your mothers bore Poles, free people; you are to produce, to breastfeed and take care of the subjects of kings who knavishly tore your nation apart. Instead of instilling virtue in the hearts of your children, you must accustom them to blind obedience in order that, with time, they will become the dumb slaves of the royal palaces. Men who are so insensitive to the shackles they wear that they leave them to their children—are such men worthy to be called fathers? Are those who bow to contempt, and wish to associate you with it, worthy of your love? O sensitive, virtuous Polish women! Show them that no one has the right to your hearts until he covers himself with glory through service to the Fatherland and to freedom, and until he celebrates peace following victory in church.

Some have opined that we should enlighten the people before we give them freedom. I am of the opposite view, that in order to enlighten the people we must first free them. Do we know of any nation that was unable to read but was free? Freedom is not something that is learned but a moral necessity of the soul that affects happiness in the same way that clean air affects the health. Legislation requires broad knowledge, and until now only a small part of each nation has devoted itself to this pursuit. Is the petty nobility in Poland more enlightened than the peasantry? All the same it lives in freedom. Are we to understand that the French people were enlightened? How could this be, since no one was engaged in their instruction[162] before the revolution, and since half of France speaks a language as different from French as Samogitian is from Polish? In many places throughout the cantons many hold office who cannot read or write, to this day. I think that the Polish peasant has more good sense than the French peasant, and would never fight for the same superstitions that the peasants of the Vendée fought for. Those people were persuaded that if they took up arms for fanaticism and were killed, they would rise from the dead after three days. Enlightenment is acquired when everyone recognizes its need and usefulness. The English began to enlighten themselves with freedom. Frenchmen were not interested in public affairs[20] before the revolution. When they earned the right to participate in the legislative process, they began to learn and to reflect on the interests of the nation.

Jean Jacques Rousseau demonstrated the rights of the people, the eloquent Mirabeau urged the French to recover them, and yet how many of them are still misled! In Poland the flame was accepted when it had barely been kindled, which demonstrates the open-mindedness of our fellow countrymen. Every sensible Pole will laugh at the political superstitions of kingship and nobility. Everyone knows that they have no privileged reason. Whence comes their right to rule the nation without its will? If it were not for the blindness of the monarchical armies who kill everyone at the order of who pays them,[21] who would not be ashamed to be ruled by the senseless beings who are the kings of Europe? The Poles have convinced themselves of these truths and are splendidly throwing off the political charlatanism that has discredited justice, shamed reason, and oppressed humanity. Let them show courage and determination in their undertaking and irreproachable virtue in their actions, and they will become one of the most venerable of nations.

The State of Poland's Riches

It would be difficult to find a Pole whose soul was so vile that he would shrink from devoting a part of his fortune to liberating his Fatherland. I would not bother to show such a base mentality the profits that accrue from such sacrifices; I would merely confront him with examples of those who served foreign courts by betraying the Fatherland. In addition to the well-deserved curses of their fellow countrymen, what did they gain from these monarchs? They must tremble humbly before their governors-general. Had they served their nation they would have enjoyed the respect of their compatriots and even of their enemies; instead, they became a spectacle of contempt for those at whose feet they groveled, bringing ruin upon their Fatherland. Whenever nations were famed for their riches, in past centuries as now, it is clear they always obtained them with the help of freedom. Carthage, Florence, Venice, Holland, and England—how did they achieve their renowned prosperity? A man cannot be sure how to use his industry, the creative force behind all riches, if he is unsure of freedom. What can reassure him more strongly than the knowledge that nothing can be done without his will and that what he creates cannot be taken away from him? Frederick II wanted to establish trading companies on the model of those of the free countries, but he saw no benefits arising from them. In France, even before freedom emerged from its infancy, its blessings could already be felt. Trade had suffered from the wars, but it increased greatly. Today every Frenchman can see the daily improvement in the villages. Before the revolution the yield of the land under cultivation was calculated as one to two and one-half; today it is more than one to three. The Poles have everything they need for war. They can get along without foreign products and without foreign assistance; indeed, they can live comfortably without any foreign trade at all. Our country abounds in grain, wool, iron, and so on. We can also have money in abundance, because currency can consist not only of gold and silver, but of any kind of metal and even of paper; it is essential only that the people place their trust in it. In England, Europe's wealthiest country, the amount of silver money in circulation is not even one-sixth the amount of paper money in circulation. Paper will have credit if the government proves its reliability and holds to its promises. English paper money maintains its credit in Europe through the sale of handicrafts; ours will maintain itself through the sale of grain and timber, which are an even sounder backing.[22] No other country has as many funds to safeguard the credit of paper money as Poland has. Our country possesses immense national riches and has no debt. England owes 10,000 French livres. France, at the beginning of the war, was 4,000 livres in debt. French treasury notes[163] had credit throughout Europe despite this debt, and would have maintained credit had the French adhered to the compass of reliability. But when, disdaining their promises, they began to print an excess of paper money, its value had to fall. We can produce whatever kind of money we wish, and it will always be met with confidence. The Americans redeemed their paper currency after their war. We shall exchange ours for precious metals as well, in peacetime. The Dutch will offer us a loan. Others will bring in silver and gold in payment for our grain, wood, and so on. Manufacturers will flock to a fertile country that is protected by wise laws.

Sacrifices have to be made during the revolution; we must be content with little now if we truly desire freedom. But later, a million advantages will accrue to us. Sacrifices for the revolution can be likened to outlays spent to rehabilitate a neglected estate with fertile land. We have the most pleasant country. There are many navigable rivers, and those other rivers that are choked by obstacles can be made useful. By digging canals according to the latest methods, we can open new communications between provinces throughout our country. The free Dutch erected dikes against the sea. The Swiss made fertile fields among the cliffs. In twenty years American doubled its population (which, according to Smith[164] occurs in other countries only once every 500 years). What great things we will achieve with such a blessed land!

Conclusion

Poles! I have shown you the way to independence. I do not seek to awaken in you a noble despair (you have already given proof of it), but I encourage you to certain victory. Throw yourselves with courage against your enemies. You have everything necessary for victory; only be brave enough to succeed. If all of you fight bravely, the enemy, though he be more numerous than he is at present, will be unable to defeat you. If you do not break the yoke now, do not blame heaven, for you alone will be authors of your ignominy. There is a measure of justice in this for those who are content to rot in servitude and who look with indifference on downtrodden justice and oppressed humanity. . . . But who among the Poles can embrace a life poisoned by vileness? Would you not rather join with those who, after being wounded, after enduring the tortures of the royal jails, are ready to spill their last drop of blood for the liberation of the Fatherland? How noble those endeavors that aim at the glory that comes from trampling the hydra of tyranny and restoring the altars of sacred freedom. My heart trembles with joy at this thought. And how pleasant it is to gaze upon the victorious free people in whose heart the flame of virtue burns! Whoever can be counted a member of that nation is fortunate; how his respect lifts the soul . . . What a delight for the conscience, even during persecutions, to recall that I applied myself toward breaking the shackles of my fellow countrymen and returning the sweet freedoms of nature to them! Montesquieu said that every man is capable of doing good to another man, but that he who contributes to the happiness of the whole nation is akin to a god.[165]

Notes

1. From the papers taken from the Muscovite legation during the revolution of 1794 it was clear that even the king did not demur from accepting a pension from the court at St. Petersburg.

2. In Poland, no one ever stopped to think what reserves were available, how to increase them, or how to use them. Whenever a confederation[103] was formed, backing was always secured, that is, one of the courts gave money and some supplies, the rest being raised by both sides through contributions. If the endeavor failed, the court of patronage was also to obtain an amnesty that would cover all. By means of it, the weak returned home in indigence and the magnates with money from the court and sometimes a *starostwo* [a local administrative post]. This old, deeply rooted addiction survives to the present day. The Polish nobleman does not ask about ways to deliver his Fatherland, nor does he seek them; he examines the backing and deduces[104] which of the powers is behind it. I think that the meet and the poor have much virtuous attachment to their country and make honest sacrifices of their lives and fortunes. Unaccustomed to political trickery, they do not ask about foreign alliances, but instead ask how to carry out their duties and how to liberate themselves. But some corrupt men take no step until the court at St. Petersburg, Berlin, or Vienna first casts a favorable eye on it, or unless French millions are forthcoming. O great Czarniecki![105] You did not travel about foreign courts and countries begging for help; the misfortune of your countrymen warmed your brave soul, and you brought enthusiasm to them. Your attachment to your Fatherland gave you authority, and you freed the land of the enemy deluge. O virtuous Kościuszko! You did not ask the powers when you hastened, alone, to rescue your compatriots from the shackles of captivity. You found treasures and stores, valor and arms that others scorned. It was your own fate, your misfortune, which stopped your great work, but your genius will yet support the oppressed Fatherland, and Poles will have the sweet joy of covering the wounds you received in the defense of freedom with laurel wreaths and thanks. It is necessary that those Poles seeking backing realize that without a heart, a head, and a soul, the back is worthless, and the least important part of the body.

3. Poles err in assuming that the French in general are enlightened, that each of them is fit to be an officer and possesses the knowledge to become one. The lack of this knowledge shows itself in the army, and French generals attest to the fact that Polish officers are better than their own. We can point out our own faults, but let us also know how to respect and do justice to our best qualities. The distribution of various types among the French is the same as that prevailing in other peoples.

4. How it shames the Poles (because it seems that they did not fight in the

cause of freedom, but in the interests of a single person) that after the disaster at Maciejowice it appeared as though they had lost the will to act. If the Romans had despaired after their defeat at Cannae,[112] Rome would have fallen under the yoke of the Carthaginians. But their valorous spirit transcended all of their misfortunes. Instead of blaming the leaders who lost the battle, the senate sent messengers to those returning from the battle, thanking them for returning to their fatherland and for refusing to despair of its integrity. The land upon which the Carthaginian camp stood was put up for sale. Through their great character, the Romans, without learning, prevailed over their enemies and worked a wonder: one city ruled over the whole world. Poles! Know how to be munificent and brave in misfortune and you will triumph over your tyrants!

5. The American revolution began in 1775. The alliance with France was concluded three years later, in 1778. French reinforcements were sent to the American states after the victory over Bourguignon [Bourgoyne], when that general was forced to lay down arms along with 12,000 other Englishmen.[116] At that time the Americans were almost certain of their independence.

6. In reading the *Monitor*[117] of those days one can see that such a large number of Frenchmen were swarming to Champagne that the generals wrote to the Convention[118] asking it to hold them back. The Prussian king had to capitulate, and the French inadvertently did him a favor by allowing him to retreat. Freedom alone was the cause of the enthusiasm that caused so many people to assemble. In all of French history there is not another trace of people's gathering with such enthusiasm after having been invaded by an enemy.

7. One can read this everywhere, even in the campaigns of Suvorov.

8. I do not base this figure on conjecture but on reports. The Narew Line (to Grodno) and the army around Warsaw totaled about 28,000 men, of which 16,000 defended the capital city, while 12,000 stretched along the River Narew.

9. I did not take into consideration the populations that England, Spain, and Portugal controlled outside of Europe. If we were to include the colonies of the enemies of France, such as the population of the Asian part of Muscovy, and us, then we would have to estimate the ratio as 1 to 15. To be sure, the English, Portuguese, and Spanish colonies and India did not fight against the French, but their stores and treasures did aid France's enemies.

10. The electricity of freedom always spreads quickly to neighboring countries, who are in the best position to see its great consequences. At the beginning of the French Revolution no one thought about a Cisalpine Republic,[124] a Roman Republic,[125] or about the changes in Switzerland[126] and Holland.[127] Our enemies resist the establishment of freedom in Poland with all possible means because its beautiful example might spark an assault on their own thrones.

11. Folard[131] shows that the ancient pike and similar weapons were more useful than the rifle. Lloyd, one of the most reliable of military writers, is of the same opinion, and advises that at least one rank of spears be placed among the ranks of the infantry. Some demonstrate the uselessness of the rifle by pointing out that only three of every one hundred shots fired hit their mark. Firearms can be used at a distance, but as soon as the opposing sides become entangled the shooting must stop.

12. If someone tells me that the enemy beat the scythemen, I answer that the enemy also beat the valiant French with their cannon, rifles, and bayonets. War is most often decided by chance and must be comprised of both propitiousness and misfortunes. Moreover, it consists of human actions, and mistakes must occur. What matters is to demonstrate the value of the weapon that brought victory; for the French it was the bayonet, for us it could have been and may yet be the scythe.

13. Lloyd has listed the three strongest factors that inspire courage in soldiers: freedom, religion, and plunder. The first is the most praiseworthy, and for it people have accomplished the miracles wrought by heroism. Three hundred Spartans held back the large Persian army at Thermopylae,[133] eight hundred Swiss stopped thirty thousand Frenchmen. Religion, or rather fanaticism, induces fervor. The man who understands that he has to render service to God, or rather that God requires his weapons, throws himself fiercely into danger. But between the courage of freedom and the courage of religion there is this difference. The first elevates the soul, filling the heart with the sweetest of feelings, giving intensity and power to all the strengths and qualities of the mind. Fanaticism, to be sure, imparts strength to the soul, but it fills one with blindness and impedes thought, and that is why it can never equal the heroism of freedom. Man feels freedom is the heritage of nature, a pleasant and natural property; its aim and struggle is virtue. Because fanaticism is a fancy of the imagination, its arousal of the soul is a trick. The fanatic does not seek to win, but to kill his opponent, and as a result he often takes risks. But even fanaticism bears the seeds of independence and freedom. Man wants to believe in what he wants to believe in; only reason can change him. No religious war can be raised against Poland, because no one was ever persecuted for his beliefs in Poland. In this respect government should copy heaven and spread a fertile mist for all religions equally. There were times when people killed themselves over the various gods that they had created for themselves, but today Europe recognizes that God does not need blood to be spilled on his behalf by creatures who are incapable of comprehending his essence; he sends them only blessings. No power can make religious war against Poland, although Moscow did make a fuss over matters of conscience.[134] Finally, the clergy of all the religions in Poland are too enlightened by the injustices, deceit, and violence of kings to fall into their trap. The third kind of inspiration, plunder, is very harmful. The soldier who goes beyond the bounds of discipline becomes accustomed to crime and loses his valor either because he squanders his loot on debauchery, which destroys his courage from within, or because he avoids battle in order to hide his loot from the enemy. The Poles and their army should always demonstrate the highest morality. Montecuccoli,[135] unaware of these great ways of inspiring enthusiasm, or perhaps unable to employ them under the yoke of his monarch, turned to drink and similar remedies (see vol. II, p. 134). I will not stop to demonstrate their futility because anyone can perceive them.

14. I consider political ideas to be like the religious ideas that men fought for during the wars between the Protestants and the Catholics. Could a Catholic,

serving in a Protestant army, induce vengeance against the Catholics? I would not wish to take anyone who was not sincerely attached to the idea of freedom. In the French armies the rules of freedom were at first driven home through the constant speeches of the officers. Generals mentioned it in every address. None of the French generals from the old government made a name for himself during the revolution, although many of them were educated. The famous French generals managed their feats with the help of freedom, although they were almost uneducated. I respect education, but it is nature that provides the attributes that make a general. Charlemagne could not write, yet he conquered Europe. In his work on the Prussian monarchy,[136] Mirabeau tells of the secretary of the Prince of Brunswick,[137] who gave the prince all of his plans yet never served in any army. Because some of our generals were attached to kings, they were opposed to everything created by the revolution. Instead of instilling confidence in the scythe, instead of encouraging the people, they were contemptuous of the weapon and of the people as well. The unbroken silence of the generals undermined the people's certainty. Because they never affirmed freedom, never even mentioned it, those who fought under them believed it was an empty promise. The frigidity with which freedom was proclaimed could be seen even among the civil magistrates, without whom we could not have and will not be able to make a showing against the enemy. I remember what a peasant told me when I explained the aim of the revolution. If so, he said, "I won't eat, I'll give the food to the soldier, and go fight myself." I also have to cite what one Lithuanian peasant told one of the republican generals: "Show us," he said, "that perfect freedom, and we will not send every fifth man as a recruit, but we'll all go and fight." Such people cannot be beaten.

15. "L'usage de cette arme terrible était de l'invention de Kościuszko." *Campagnes de Suworow,* II, 154.

16. The advantages of our struggle do not derive from falling all at once upon numerous enemies and thereby perishing imprudently. We must save ourselves and not lose people in vain, for used prudently, they can hurt the enemy. Let the people try their best to hide the stores that would otherwise feed the enemy, hide them anywhere they can. Then, at a chosen moment they should attack him *en masse,* especially at night. Our victory depends chiefly on this, that we endure long and always be numerous.

17. "C'était la tête de l'hydre que ces Polonais, ils se reproduisaient par-tout." *Campagnes de Suworow,* I, 60.

18. "Car sans le secours des ceux qui en sont et qui en connaissent les détours et les endroits, qui peuvent servir à la ruse et à l'artifice, disait le grand Gustave, le plus grand capitaine du monde n'exécuteroit jamais rien de fort éclatant." J. Folard, *Histoire de Polybe,* pref., I, 38.

19. In Italy the inhabitants locked themselves up in fortified cities and, if they had no means of escape, were always captured.

20. Before the revolution in France there was no more than one newspaper. In 1797 in Paris alone, that is, not including the Departments, there were one hundred fifty. Every day 40,000 copies were sent to the provinces.

21. In a free nation the estate of the soldier who offers his life in defense of his countrymen is an honorable one. But how vile is he who goes out blindly to do wrong, to kill. If such a man has the order from his monarch, he will be ready to trample all the laws of nature in order to serve him. The monarch, determined that his will be law and his whims authority, always wants his people to be as docile as cattle, which calmly place their necks under the butcher's hand! . . . The soldier of a monarch views his master's order as higher than justice. He respects it as the highest form of wisdom and if it contradicts his simple way of thinking, he is ready to extirpate the holiest of feelings in order to fulfill it. What can be more vile?

22. By imposing only modest taxes and without drawing on many private fortunes, we can make a revolution in Poland. *Huge national estates* will produce enough supplies to make war and to reward the defenders of the fatherland. Above all, the good will and economy of the Polish army guarantee propitious results for the treasury. Being a republican, the Polish soldier did not seek grandiosity like the captive of a monarch; he accepted any attire as suitable. *He sought only honor in virtuous deeds and valor.* We have witnessed certain monetary offers; if a sudden need presented itself, no one would murmur if we were forced to suffer.

101. The author is referring to the Swiss struggle for liberation against the Habsburgs, which began at the end of the thirteenth century. It was not until 1648, in the Peace of Westphalia, that Switzerland obtained its independence.

102. Reference is to the Dutch struggle for liberation from Spain during the sixteenth century. The Dutch won independence in the Peace of Westphalia in 1648.

103. In certain editions, as for example in Mościcki's, the word "conference" was used instead of "confederation."

104. The editor of the Polish text explains the use of the archaic word "rafinuje" rendered here by "deduces."

105. Stefan Czarniecki (1599–1665), Field Hetman of the Crown and Palatine of Rus', became famous for his use of guerrilla warfare during "The Deluge" (the Swedish invasion of Poland in the mid-seventeenth century).

106. The hero of an ancient Greek legend.

107. At the beginning of the fourteenth century three Swiss citizens, Walter Fürst, Werner Stauffacher, and Arnold Melchthal, created a union whose aim was the liberation of Switzerland from Habsburg rule.

108. Benjamin Franklin (1706–1790), statesman, scientist, prominent in the American nation's struggle for independence.

109. In 1794.

110. No mention was made of this in any plan.

111. The author is referring to the defeat at Maciejowice (October 10, 1794) and to Kościuszko's capture by the Russians.

112. In 216 B.C.

113. Frederick William II (1744–1797), king of Prussia.

114. The latest studies have fully confirmed the thesis that sees the Kościuszko

Uprising as a factor that weighed heavily on the course of the war on the Rhine. The insurrection tied down considerable Prussian strength, allowing the French to conduct a victorious offensive. The success of the French armies at Courtrai and Tourçoing, and later at Fleurus (June 26, 1794), decided the fate of the campaign and allowed the French to occupy Holland.

115. Legendary Swiss hero of the fourteenth century.

116. At Saratoga on October 17, 1777. Tadeusz Kościuszko's splendid fortification of the city was to a large degree responsible for the victory.

117. *Moniteur Universel,* from 1789 the official journal of the French.

118. The National Convention in France, 1792–1795 (from the overthrow of the monarchy to the establishment of the Directory).

119. Spring 1793.

120. Summer 1794.

121. Anton Büsching, German geographer and author of *Geografia Królestwa Polskiego i W. Ks. Litewskiego,* a Polish translation of which appeared in Leipzig in 1758. His estimates refer, of course, to the population in the middle of the eighteenth century.

122. That is, before 1772.

123. Honoré-Gabriele Count Mirabeau (1749–1791), prominent French politician during the first phase of the French Revolution, delegate to the Estates General in 1789, chairman of the National Convention. He was a supporter of constitutional monarchy.

124. Established in Italy in 1796.

125. Established in 1798.

126. The author refers to the establishment of the Republic of Helvetia in 1798.

127. Reference is to the establishment of the Batavian Republic in 1795.

128. Jean-Jacques Rousseau (1712–1778), prominent philosopher and political writer, author of *The Social Contract* and *Considerations on the Government of Poland.*

129. The Parthian-Scythian tribes in northeast Iran victoriously resisted the attacks of the Romans, especially under Trajan.

130. Henry Lloyd (Humphrey Evans), Englishman, the creator of strategy as a science. During his lifetime (1729–1783) he entered Prussian service, later served the Austrians, French, and Russians. His chief work, *History of the War between the Empress of Germany and Her Allies,* appeared in 1779. His works were translated into German and French, and Bülow and Jomini, among others, made use of them. Lloyd formulated the concept of the operational line as the fundamental principle of military operations. He attached much significance to geographical conditions as well as to demographic and psychological matters and expressed the conviction that democratic republics are capable of manifesting extraordinary powers of resistance.

131. Jean-Charles Folard, French military writer (1669–1752), author of the well-known commentaries on the historical works of the Greek historian Polybius that appeared in Paris between 1727 and 1730.

132. Aleksandr Suvorov (1729–1800), outstanding Russian commander.

133. In 480 B.C.
134. The author is referring to the Russian intervention in Poland in 1764 on the pretext of the defense of Orthodoxy.
135. Raymond Montecuccoli (1609–1681), renowned commander and military writer, author of *Mémoires sur la guerre*.
136. The title of the work was *De la monarchie prusienne sous Frédéric le Grand* (London, 1788).
137. Prince Karl Wilhelm Ferdinand of Brunswick (1739–1806), field marshal in Prussian service.
138. During the years 1768–1772.
139. Henri Turenne (1611–1675), illustrious French commander.
140. Gustavus Adolphus II (1594–1632), king of Sweden, one of the greatest of European commanders in the seventeenth century.
141. To scale the walls by means of ladders.
142. Siege works, in other words.
143. In 1792.
144. Napoleon defeated the Austrians at Arcole on November 17, 1796.
145. Pierre-François Augereau (1757–1816), French general during the French Revolution and the Napoleonic wars.
146. June 8, 1794.
147. Peter I (1672–1725), tsar of Russia, after the Battle of Narva in 1700.
148. Jean-Baptise Jourdan (1762–1833), French marshal; Lazare Hoche (1768–1797), French general and prominent republican.
149. Guillaume Brune (1763–1815), French marshal; Jean-Victor Moreau (1763–1813), French general known for his republican convictions.
150. 1797–1800.
151. Franciszek Rymkiewicz (1756–1799), general, one of the leaders of the Polish legions in Italy. He died in the Battle of Verona on April 5, 1799.
152. See "Deklaracja na obwieszczenie rządu pruskiego względem insurekcji Wielkopolan" by the Rada Najwyższa Narodowa (The Supreme National Council), session 129, September 29, 1794. The council recommended that this reply be "proclaimed and communicated to the commander-in-chief with the request that he issue orders to the military in accordance with it." *Akta powstania Kościuszko*, ed. S. Askenazy and W. Dzwonkowski, (Cracow, 1918), II, 206–208, 442.
153. Charles Dumouriez (1739–1823), French general, took an active part in the Confederation of Bar during the years 1768–1770. His memoirs were published in Polish in Poznań in 1872.
154. Alexandre Dumas (1762–1806), French general.
155. From 1587 to 1609.
156. In 1778.
157. "A people born to be slaves."
158. Jan Klemens Węgierski, member of the conspiracy preparing the Kościuszko Uprising. Arrested by the Russian police in Warsaw on March 2, 1794, before the outbreak of the uprising.

159. The nobility.
160. The author is referring to the massacre of the Huguenots on St. Bartholomew's Night, August 24, 1572. It is estimated that over 20,000 Huguenots were murdered in Paris and throughout France.
161. Konstancja *née* Czartoryski Zamoyska, the widow of Chancellor Andrzej Zamoyski. Died in Vienna in 1797.
162. That is, education.
163. Paper currency was introduced during the French Revolution.
164. Adam Smith (1723–1790), the creator of classical English economics and author of *An Inquiry into the Nature and Causes of the Wealth of Nations*.
165. Charles Montesquieu, *Lettres persannes*, I, number 89. Montesquieu (1689–1755), outstanding French political author. He was an ardent proponent of the separation of state powers into legislative, executive, and judicial branches.

Appendixes

Appendix 1

John Bull in the Kingdom of Poland: The Estate of Janów in the Period of Peasant Emancipation, 1861–64

[1846: Tsarist ukase prohibited *rugi* (clearances) of peasants from holdings over 3 morgs,[1] and obliged landowners to record tenancies in the district Land Register (Libella prestacyjna).]
(1) 1853: The Estate of Janów, in the district of Minsk Mazowiecki, was bought by JOHN BULL Esq., British Citizen, on mortgage. The price for 77½ *włóki* or 2325 *morgs* (Polish acres) was 320,000 florins,[2] or 4150 fl/włóka. At that time, the estate ("rustic land" + demesne) comprised:
— 21 włóki held in perpetuity by 29 tenant-leaseholders, each paying rent @ 210 fl/włóka. These were registered tenancies predating the ukaz of 1846.
— 10 włóki held by serf-cottagers, who owed corvée labor but lived in dwellings owned by the estate.
— 46½ włóki of "dominial land" (demesne) in absolute property.
— a tavern, with distilling rights (propinacja) earning 1000 fl. p.a.
1859: John Bull sold Janów for 360,000 florins, but re-leased it from the purchasers for 24,000 fl. p.a., staying on as manager-lessee. (His mortgage account stood at 230,000 fl.)
[1861: *Ukase* of 16 May, introduced by Marquis Wielopolski, converted corvée labor into money rents (okup pańszczyzny); it did not apply to holdings under 3 morgs or to previous tenancies.]
(2) *Reorganization of the Janów estate* (1861): Cost c. 11,000 fl.
— the 10 włóki of serf land were converted into tenancies on the same basis as other leaseholders, paying rent @ 210 fl/włóka.

— the ex-serfs were given enlarged plots, free building materials to construct new houses for themselves, and 6 months free of rent.
— 22 laborers were hired on verbal contracts of 1 year and 3 months' notice, to replace the lost serf labor and to work 2 days per week. Total wage bill, 2288 days p.a. = 3422 fl.
— housing was provided for the laborers: 6 cottages vacated by the serfs, 5 new cottages built, + enclosures + 2 acres each.
— education for village children: 2 schoolrooms were built, a school mistress employed to give free lessons.
— the tavern was closed down, to discourage intoxication.

[1864: *Ukase* of 2/18 March 1864 abolished rent, giving all peasants full property of their land. Landowners were indemnified for lost land and rents by a sum calculated on the basis of annual income less expenses over $16\frac{2}{3}$ years. The state recovered its expenditure on the indemnity scheme through new land taxes levied on all owners.]

(3) *Second Reorganization of Janów estate* (1864)
— all the leaseholders and laborers were given possession of their land (with rights to pasture and firewood) even though the laborers had no permanent contracts and had only been installed three years previously with no rights.
— Indemnity paid to the estate:
 — for rents of leaseholders:
  21 vlochs: $\frac{4}{5}$ annual rent of 4410 fl. × $16\frac{2}{3}$ =
   58,833 florins
  10 vlochs: $\frac{2}{3}$ annual rent of 2100 fl. × $16\frac{2}{3}$ =
   22,400 fl.
 — for laborers' rents:
  244 acres: $\frac{4}{5}$ annual rent of 352 fl. × $16\frac{2}{3}$ =
   4,693 fl. 10 g.
   TOTAL 85,926 fl. 10 g.
— The Estate was left with $46\frac{1}{2}$ włóki of land (62 percent of the original) having also lost pasture and firewood assets, labor income, and tavern.

(4) *Claim for compensation*
6 May 1864 John Bull to Col. E. Stanton, British Consul-General at Warsaw "I must, therefore, Colonel, most respectfully request you to lay my case before the Russian Gov-

ernment and make good my claims for restraining them to indemnify me the amount of my losses.

I am etc.,   John Bull."

Losses allegedly sustained:	fl.	(See attached table)
I from leaseholders' land	77,150	
II from laborers	80,147	
TOTAL	157,147	= 23,644 rubles
(corrected totals)	146,091	= 22,135 rubles
		£3,459 approx.

Bull claimed this represented ⅔ of his property.[3]

8 June 1864, Col. Stanton to Lord Napier (H.M. Ambassador at St. Petersburg) "I can't guarantee Mr Bull's figures," [but there does appear to have been] "an injustice to a certain class of proprietor, trusting in the good faith of the government," [and endeavoring] "to improve the condition of the peasants and the agricultural resources of the country."

Public Record Office (London) FO 65/665/pp. 180 ff.

Notes

1. Land measures (New Polish system, 1818–49):
włóka (vloch) = 30 *morgs* = 90 *sznurz* = 9000 sq. *pret* = 15.3 *dziesięcinas* = 506,250 sq. *łokci* (yards) = 16.796 hectares = 41.5 (British) acres
1 morg (Polish acre) = 0.5596 he = 1.4 British acre

2. Polish money (1834–1914):
1 *złoty* (= florin) = 30 *groszy*
10 złotych = 1.5 (Russian) rubles
1 *grosz* = ½ (Russian) kopieyek.
N.B. 1864 £1 sterling = c. 6.25 rubles.

3. Despite his shaky mathematics, Bull's calculations were not far from the mark. The indemnity actually received in 1864—51,575 florins—can be calculated to be only 35.3% of his estimated net loss (146,091 fl.) or 35.8% of the 1859 land value (144,000 florins).

Appendix 2

Arrest of a Young Scottish Adventurer at Częstochowa, 1864: The Prospect of Siberia

(Envelope)
to Mrs. John Macdonald, Dalelia,[1] Moidart,[2] Scotland.
(postal markings—via Hamburg, 21/3МОРАИ/PORAJ,[3] KATTO-WITZ 22/3.
LONDON 25 Mar 64.)

(Letter)

My dear Mother,

I will not enter into the history of my adventures, suffice it to say I have been arrested by the Russians for not having a passport. I have written to the British Consul at Warsaw but as yet have received no answer. I have been 4 weeks under arrest. My father must get Mr Hope Scott or Mr Robertson to write to the British Consul at Warsaw and my liberation will be the surer and sooner. If the Consul does not interfere on my behalf, the Russians may send me to *Siberia,* or at least will keep me here for perhaps a year. Suppose I am sent to Siberia you must not despair for in a few years I will be taken back. My occupation will be according to my choice. They give me a gun and I can hunt bears, wolves. The life of the Siberian hunter is in constant danger. But you know I am the son of a Scottish hunter, and there is no fears of me. The worse of it is, I cannot speak Polish. I am without clothes and money. Give my best respects to all. My love to father, Ronald, Henry and all the family. I am, dear Mother, yr afft son,

                                        Alistair Macdonald

P.S. If you write, do not mention *politics*. I have not received a word from Scotland since I left. I have had plenty of adventures but ? was brought all safe, Thank God. If there is a war between Russia and Great

Britain you will be sure to write to the Consul with haste for all the prisoners will be sent to the Russian fortresses. I am at present in Tchentstachow.[4] If you write to me it is better to address the letter to the British Consul, and tell him in case he has not received my letter that I was in Tchentsochow on 17 March. I may be moved at any time. Tell the Consul that the military brigade here is that commanded by Kolowanski. If I am removed he will know where I am. My dear Mother, farewell.[5]

Public Record Office, London PRO-FO 65/665/22

Notes

1. A hamlet on Loch Shiell in the Western Highlands.
2. A district in Western Argyll.
3. Poraj—10 miles S of Częstochowa, in 1864 the last Russian station before the German frontier. The letter was sent from Częstochowa to Katowice in Silesia, and thence to Hamburg and London.
4. An Anglicized form of the German name for Częstochowa-Tschentsochau.
5. Macdonald's fate is not mentioned in the consular correspondence for 1864, but it was the Russian practice to hand over foreign prisoners and pay their passage home as a demonstration of the tsar's liberality. See the similar case of H. F. Apel, a British subject fighting with the Polish insurgents, and captured near Terespol on 1 Sept. 1863. PRO-FO 65/640/26.

Appendix 3

Appeal of Generals György Klapka and Mór Perczel to the Hungarian Legionnaires, Genoa, May 20, 1859

"*Soldati.*

"Non dimenticate che voi siete ungheresi.

"L'Austria si è impadronita del vostro paese e lo detiene come un proprio possesso. I migliori dei vostri eroi sono stati impiccati. L'Austria vuol distruggere la vostra nazione. Ora che il pericolo è prossimo l'Austria attende che voi combattiate per essa e che per essa voi versiate il vostro sangue.

"Ciò non può essere.

"L'imperatore d'Austria non vuole più essere re d'Ungheria e se qualcheduno vi dice che egli lo vuole essere non gli credete! L'imperatore diffonde nel mondo la voce menzognera che è per le armi che si è impadronito del nostro paese ed egli vuole che l'Ungheria divenga tedesca.

"La bandiera nera e gialla è quella di tutti i vostri nemici più accaniti: per voi è la bandiera del tradimento.

"Voi non potete restare sotto questi colori.

"La bandiera ungherese sventola sui campi di coloro che l'Austria qualifica del titolo di nemici.

"Voi non potete restare sotto questi colori.

"La bandiera ungherese sventola sui campi di coloro che l'Austria qualifica del titolo di nemici.

"L'Ungheria coraggiosa che è rimasta fedele alla patria, deve unirsi all'esercito del potente imperatore dei francesi o a quello del magnanimo re della Sardegna.

"Colui che non ama il suo paese non sarà mai un eroe.

"La causa italiana è la stessa che la nostra.

"Se il governo austriaco è rovesciato in Italia, noi pure potremmo distruggerlo in Ungheria e noi pure saremo così liberi come lo furono i nostri padri.

"Da voi dipende l'avvenire della Patria.

"Voi componete la migliore parte dell'esercito austriaco, riunitevi alla bandiera ungherese.

"L'alba comincia a nascere sul nostro paese.

"Noi, vostri capi in questa ultima guerra gloriosa, noi siamo pronti ad accogliervi di gran cuore. Da voi dipende la prosperità del nostro paese.

"Per ordine superiore, tutti gli ufficiali e i sottufficiali potranno venire col loro grado. Di più tutti coloro che avranno titoli da far valere, saranno ricompensati e promossi nel futuro esercito a un grado superiore.

"Voi riceverete il manifesto del Comitato patriottico per la libertà, incaricato della direzione degli affari fino a quando la novella Ungheria, liberata dalle catene possa, avendo i suoi antichi diritti, governarsi da se stessa.

"Ecco il nostro motto: 'soldati, quando incontrerete una parte dell'esercito francese o dell'esercito italiano, non esitate punto ad unirvi ad esso: poi, appena lo potete riunitevi all'esercito ungherese, liberatore della Patria.'"

"Che il Signore benedica la Patria oppressa! Che Dio protegga l'Ungheria!

"Genova, 20 maggio 1859.

"Generale GEORGES KLAPKA
"Generale MAURIZIO PERSCKZEL."

Contributors

Bender, Ryszard—Professor, Catholic University of Lublin.

Bobango, Gerald—Director, Romanian-American Heritage Center, Jackson, Mississipi

Căzănişteanu, Constantin—Professor of History, Colonel, Center for Military History and Theory, Bucharest.

Ceauşcu, Ilie—Major General, Professor of Military History, Center for Military History and Theory, Bucharest.

Constantiniu, Florin—Doctor of History, Nicolae Iorga Institute of History, Bucharest.

Damianov, Simeon—Professor, Doctor, Institute of Balkan Studies, Bulgarian Academy of Sciences, Sofia.

Davies, Norman—Professor of History, Chairman, Department of History, School of Slavonic and East European Studies, University of London.

Deák, István—Professor of History, Columbia University, New York.

Djordjević, Dimitrije—Professor of History, University of California, Santa Barbara.

Dudek, Lesław—Professor, Council of Military Higher Education, Military History Institute, Warsaw.

Fischer-Galati, Stephen—Distinguished University Professor, University of Colorado, Boulder.

Florescu, Radu R.—Professor of History, Boston College.

Frank, Tibor—Assistant Professor of History, Eötvös Loránd University, Budapest.

Gabriel, Mordecai L.—Acting Vice-President of Academic Affairs, Brooklyn College.

Halicz, Emanuel—Professor of History, Slavic Institute, Copenhagen University.

Ionescu, Mihail E.—Captain, Center for Military History and Theory, Bucharest.

CONTRIBUTORS

Jelavich, Barbara—Professor of History, University of Indiana, Bloomington.

Kabdebo, Thomas—Librarian, Lecturer in Military Studies, University of Manchester, England.

Kieniewicz, Stefan—Professor, Committee on Historical Science, Polish Academy of Sciences, Warsaw.

Király, Béla K.—Professor Emeritus, Director, Brooklyn College Program on Society in Change.

Kofos, Evangelos—Ph.D., Historian, Special Counselor Greek Ministry for Foreign Affairs, Athens.

Kozłowski, Eligiusz—Associate Professor, Teachers College, Kielce

Lukács, Lajos—Doctoral Candidate, Eötvös Loránd University, Budapest.

Mańkowski, Zygmunt—Dean of Institute of History, Maria Curie-Sklodowska University, Lublin.

Mencel, Tadeusz—Professor, Maria Curie-Sklodowska University, Lublin.

Michalopoulos, Dimitris—Office of the President of the Hellenic Republic, Athens.

Moritsch, Andreas—Ph.D., University Dozent, Institute on East and Southeastern European Research, University of Vienna.

Ratajczyk, Leonard—Colonel, Professor of History, Military History Institute, Warsaw.

Rothenberg, Gunther E.—Professor of Military History, Purdue University.

Santarcangeli, Paolo—Associate Professor of History, University of Turin.

Somogyi, Éva—Ph.D., Institute of History, Budapest.

Stanley, John D.—Ph.D., Historian, Toronto.

Svolopoulos, Constantin—Professor of History, University of Thessaloniki.

Szász, Zoltán—Ph.D., Historical Institute of the Hungarian Academy of Sciences, Budapest.

Talpeş, Ioan—Ph.D., Captain, Center for Military History and Theory, Bucharest.

Zacek, Joseph F.—Professor of History, State University of New York at Albany.

Zdrada, Jerzy—Associate Professor, Polish Academy of Sciences, Cracow.

Živojinović, Dragan R.—Professor of History, Faculty of Philosophy, University of Belgrade.

BROOKLYN COLLEGE STUDIES ON SOCIETY IN CHANGE
Distributed by Columbia University Press (except No. 5)
Editor-in-Chief: Béla K. Király

No. 1
Tolerance and Movements of Religious Dissent in Eastern Europe.
Edited by B. K. Király, 1975. Second Printing, 1977.

No. 2
The Habsburg Empire in World War I. Edited by R. A. Kann, B. K. Király, P. S. Fichtner, 1976. Second Printing, 1978.

No. 3
The Mutual Effects of the Islamic and Judeo-Christian Worlds: The East European Pattern. Edited by A. Ascher, T. Halasi-Kun, B. K. Király, 1979.

No. 4
Before Watergate: Problems of Corruption in American Society. Edited by A. S. Eisenstadt, A. Hoogenboom, H. L. Trefousse, 1978.

No. 5
East Central European Perceptions of Early America. Edited by B. K. Király and G. Barany. Lisse, The Netherlands: Peter de Ridder Press, 1977. Distributed by Humanities Press, Atlantic Highlands, NJ.

No. 6
The Hungarian Revolution of 1956 in Retrospect. Edited by B. K. Király and P. Jónás, 1978. Second Printing, 1980.

No. 7
Brooklyn U.S.A.: Fourth Largest City in America. Edited by R. S. Miller, 1979.

No. 8
János Decsy. *Prime Minister Gyula Andrássy's Influence on Habsburg Foreign Policy during the Franco-German War of 1870–1871,* 1979.

No. 9
Robert F. Horowitz. *The Great Impeacher: A Political Biography of James M. Ashley,* 1979.

* * *

Nos. 10–19
Subseries: War and Society in East Central Europe (see Nos. 30–40 also)

BROOKLYN COLLEGE STUDIES ON SOCIETY IN CHANGE

No. 10 — Vol. I
Special Topics and Generalizations on the Eighteenth and Nineteenth Centuries. Edited by B. K. Király and G. E. Rothenberg, 1979.

No. 11 — Vol. II
East Central European Society and War in the Pre-Revolutionary Eighteenth Century. Edited by G. E. Rothenberg, B. K. Király, and P. Sugar, 1982.

No. 12 — Vol. III
From Hunyadi to Rákóczi: War and Society in Late Medieval and Early Modern Hungary. Edited by J. M. Bak and B. K. Király, 1982.

No. 13 — Vol. IV
East Central European Society and War in the Era of Revolutions, 1775–1856. Edited by B. K. Király, 1984.

No. 14 — Vol. V
Essays on World War I: Origins and Prisoners of War. Edited by P. Pastor and S. R. Williamson, Jr., 1982.

No. 15 — Vol. VI
Essays on World War I: Total War and Peacemaking, A Case Study on Trianon. Edited by B. K. Király, P. Pastor, and I. Sanders, 1982.

No. 16 — Vol. VII
Thomas M. Barker. *Army, Aristocracy, Monarchy: Essays on War, Society, and Government in Austria, 1618–1780,* 1982.

No. 17 — Vol. VIII
The First Serbian Uprising, 1804–1813. Edited by Wayne S. Vucinich, 1983.

No. 18 — Vol. IX
Kálmán Janics. *Czechoslovak Policy and the Hungarian Minority, 1945–1948,* 1982.

No. 19 — Vol. X
At the Brink of War and Peace: The Tito–Stalin Split in Historic Perspective. Edited by Wayne S. Vucinich, 1983.

* * *

No. 20
Inflation Through the Ages: Economic, Social, Psychological, and Historical Aspects. Edited by N. Schmukler and E. Marcus, 1982.

No. 21
Germany and America: Essays on Problems of International Relations and Immigration. Edited by H. L. Trefousse, 1980.

BROOKLYN COLLEGE STUDIES ON SOCIETY IN CHANGE

No. 22
Murray M. Horowitz. *Brooklyn College: The First Half Century*, 1982.

No. 23
Jason Berger. *A New Deal for the World: Eleanor Roosevelt and American Foreign Policy*, 1981.

No. 24
The Legacy of Jewish Migration: 1881 and Its Impact. Edited by D. Berger, 1982.

No. 25
Pierre Oberling. *The Road to Bellapais: Cypriot Exodus to Northern Cyprus*, 1982.

No. 26
New Hungarian Peasants: An East Central European Experiment with Collectivization. Edited by Marida Hollós and Béla Maday, 1983.

No. 27
Germans in America: Aspects of German-American Relations in the 19th Century. Edited by E. Allen McCormick, 1983.

No. 28
Linda and Marsha Frey. *A Question of Empire: Leopold I and the War of the Spanish Succession, 1701–1705*, 1983.

No. 29
Szczepan K. Zimmer. *The Beginning of Cyrillic Printing—Cracow, 1491. From the Orthodox Past in Poland.* Edited by Ludwik Krzyzanowski and Irene Nagurski, 1982.

No. 29a
Thomas R. Osborne. *A Grand Ecole for the Grands Corps: The Recruitment and Training of the French Administrative Elite in the 19th Century*, 1983.

* * *

Nos. 30–40
Subseries: War and Society in East Central Europe (continued; see Nos. 10–19 also)

No. 30 — Vol. XI
The First War Between Socialist States: The Hungarian Revolution of 1956 and Its Impact. Edited by Béla K. Király, Barbara Lotze, and Nándor Dreisziger, forthcoming.

BROOKLYN COLLEGE STUDIES ON SOCIETY IN CHANGE

No. 31 — Vol. XII
István I. Mocsy. *Effects of World War I: The Uprooted: Hungarian Refugees and Their Impact on Hungarian Domestic Politics: 1918–1921,* 1983.

No. 32 — Vol. XIII
The Effects of World War I: The Class War after the Great War: The Rise of Communist Parties in East Central Europe, 1918–1921. Edited by Ivo Banac, 1983.

No. 33 — Vol. XIV
The Crucial Decade: East Central European Society and National Defense: 1859–1870. Edited by Béla K. Király, forthcoming.

No. 34 — Vol. XV
The Political Dimensions of War in Romanian History. Edited by Ilie Ceausescu, 1983.

No. 35 — Vol. XVI
György Péteri. *The Effects of World War I: War Communism in Hungary,* 1984.